principles of
MICROECONOMICS

JAMES D. MILLER
Smith College

McGraw-Hill
Irwin

Boston   Burr Ridge, IL   Dubuque, IA   New York   San Francisco   St. Louis
Bangkok   Bogotá   Caracas   Kuala Lumpur   Lisbon   London   Madrid   Mexico City
Milan   Montreal   New Delhi   Santiago   Seoul   Singapore   Sydney   Taipei   Toronto

PRINCIPLES OF MICROECONOMICS

Published by McGraw-Hill/Irwin, a business unit of The McGraw-Hill Companies, Inc., 1221 Avenue of the Americas, New York, NY, 10020. Copyright © 2009 by The McGraw-Hill Companies, Inc. All rights reserved. No part of this publication may be reproduced or distributed in any form or by any means, or stored in a database or retrieval system, without the prior written consent of The McGraw-Hill Companies, Inc., including, but not limited to, in any network or other electronic storage or transmission, or broadcast for distance learning.

Some ancillaries, including electronic and print components, may not be available to customers outside the United States.

This book is printed on acid-free paper.

1 2 3 4 5 6 7 8 9 0 WCK/WCK 0 9 8

ISBN   978-0-07-340283-3
MHID   0-07-340283-4

Editorial director: *Brent Gordon*
Executive editor: *Douglas Reiner*
Developmental editor: *Karen Fisher*
Senior marketing manager: *Melissa Larmon*
Lead project manager: *Pat Frederickson*
Lead production supervisor: *Michael R. McCormick*
Designer: *Kami Carter*
Photo research coordinator: *Lori Kramer*
Photo researcher: *Ira C. Roberts*
Lead media project manager: *Cathy L. Tepper*
Cover design: *Kami Carter*
Interior design: *Kami Carter*
Typeface: *10/12 Utopia*
Compositor: *Aptara, Inc.*
Printer: *Quebecor World Versailles Inc.*

Library of Congress Cataloging-in-Publication Data

Miller, James D. (James Daniel)
    Principles of microeconomics / James D. Miller.
        p. cm.
    Includes index.
    ISBN-13: 978-0-07-340283-3 (alk. paper)
    ISBN-10: 0-07-340283-4 (alk. paper)
    1. Microeconomics. I. Title.
    HB172.5.M475 2009
    338.5—dc22

                                                    2007048719

www.mhhe.com

TO MY FAMILY, STUDENTS, AND TEACHERS.

—James D. Miller

James D. Miller is Associate Professor of Economics at Smith College. He has a Ph.D. in Economics from the University of Chicago, where his dissertation advisors included Gary Becker and Judge Richard Posner. He has a J.D. from Stanford Law School, where he was on the Law Review. He also authored the popular *Game Theory at Work* (2003). In addition, he has written several academic articles on topics such as litigation, state lotteries, and the economics of Greek mythology. He has also written well over one hundred journal articles presenting economic issues to a general audience.

Scores of microeconomics textbooks have been written, many by world-famous economists. So what, you might ask, makes this one special?

IT'S INTERESTING—Microeconomics should fascinate. It's a sin against our profession that microeconomics textbooks usually bore students. I wrote this book to read more like a nonfiction book than a traditionally stodgy textbook. To capture the minds of students, I've stuffed this book full of engaging and sometimes irreverent examples about topics like Viagra, space travel, immortality, illegal immigration, dating, Dr. Seuss, and Greek mythology. My hope is that students will find this textbook so engaging that some will even read the chapters that aren't assigned.

IT HAS FICTIONAL STORIES—Unlike other Principles texts on the market, I use many original, fictional stories to explain and complement the material. These stories do not displace analysis of traditional microeconomic theory; rather, they stimulate student interest in the theory and provide a nonmathematical, intuitive introduction to numerous concepts. Many reviewers wrote that these stories were the best part of the book.

IT'S NOT BIASED AGAINST MARKETS—No economist would assume that business people always seek to do what is best for society. Yet most microeconomic texts do implicitly assume that politicians always put the common good ahead of their own self-interests. In contrast, I use public choice theory to present a realistic view of politicians.

All microeconomics textbooks, including mine, stress market failures. Few texts, however, also stress government failures. Students are thereby left with the impression that governments are far more effective at improving markets than any objective analysis would indicate. This book does point out how omniscient, altruistic politicians could theoretically correct many market failures; it also explains why self-interested politicians often won't correct these failures in ways that economists would wish.

IT EMPHASIZES INNOVATION—Innovation is perhaps the single most powerful force in our economy today. It's also an inherently interesting topic, yet most microeconomic approaches ignore or, at best, briefly cover innovation. I consider innovation extensively in the text, addressing it in over one-half of the chapters.

This approach to microeconomics is markedly different from many others currently in use; love it or hate it, my method diverges from the status quo in some fundamental ways. My hope is that students and instructors alike will be engaged and inspired by this text.

James D. Miller

Focus on
STUGENT ENGAGEMENT

Principles of Microeconomics effectively engages students inside and outside the classroom.

Intuition—From desert lands to the supernatural, *Principles of Microeconomics* takes students on a journey of economic intuition, making concepts clear through fictional situations.

Innovation—A majority of the chapters feature a focus on technological innovation, one of the main driving factors in our contemporary economy. Examples including iPods® and open-source software resonate with students of the digital age.

"TEACH A PARROT THE TERMS *SUPPLY* AND *DEMAND*, AND YOU'VE GOT AN ECONOMIST."

—Thomas Carlyle (19ᵗʰ century intellectual)

CHAPTER 2

A FICTIONAL DESERT TALE[1]

Geologists found a substance buried under the sands of Arrakis. Arrakis was located in deep desert, far from any water. It was so dry and desolate that ordinarily no human would ever live there. But world markets placed a fantastically high value on the substance. So the government, which owned the lands of Arrakis, sent in 10,000 miners.

The miners, of course, needed water. At tremendous cost the government shipped in bottled water by trucks. These trucks had to cross 200 miles of desert and frequently broke down in fierce sandstorms. The government calculated that water for each miner would cost around $5,000 each month, an exceedingly high

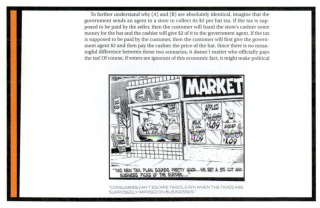

To further understand why (A) and (B) are absolutely identical, imagine that the government sends an agent to a store to collect its $2 per hat tax. If the tax is supposed to be paid by the seller, then the customer will hand the store's cashier some money for the hat and the cashier will give $2 of it to the government agent. If the tax is supposed to be paid by the customer, then the customer will first give the government agent $2 and then pay the cashier the price of the hat. Since there is no meaningful difference between these two scenarios, it doesn't matter who officially pays the tax! Of course, if voters are ignorant of this economic fact, it might make political

"CONSUMERS CAN'T ESCAPE TAXES, EVEN WHEN THE TAXES ARE SUPPOSEDLY IMPOSED ON BUSINESSES."

Humor—Each chapter incorporates cartoons, anecdotes, or quips that help bring levity to complex subject matter and facilitate perspective.

Cutting-edge Design—Bold graphics and engaging design elements appeal to students and reinforce the real-world ties of even the fictional stories.

Focus on
ECONOMIC CONCEPTS

Principles of Microeconomics presents a clear, complete approach to teaching Microeconomics. The text covers all sides of the economic picture today, including those gritty questions students want to know that other texts conveniently gloss over. Presented in a cogent, accessible manner, *Principles of Microeconomics* covers such relevant issues as:

- **Property Rights**—The book devotes an entire chapter to the concepts and controversies surrounding property rights both domestically and abroad. Students find this chapter especially salient as they begin to eke out their own place in the world.

- **National and International Examples**—Microeconomics encompasses more than just domestic issues. This book incorporates an international lens when dealing with the concepts it presents, helping students to make connections between the theory of the discipline and the reality of the world today.

- **Fallibility of Government**—Most texts (and indeed, courses) paint the government as an economic hero, when the real world is not quite so black-and-white. This text shows students that while markets can be imperfect, so can governments. Instead of confusing students, this approach actually clarifies learning, as students are then able to reconcile economic theory with their own experiences in a slightly messy world.

- **Costs and Elasticities**—Traditionally a dry chapter, the book presents costs and elasticities in a fresh, entertaining way that will capture students' attention while teaching them the underlying economic theory.

Focus on PEDAGOGY

Principles of Microeconomics employs only those pedagogical elements that instructors have said actually facilitate learning, avoiding clutter and keeping the text streamlined and accessible. Some of the most effective tools include:

- **CLASS DISCUSSION**—Most chapters feature thought-provoking topics and extensive end-of-chapter questions that encompass a variety of discussion topics, perfect for classroom dialogue. The study questions in Chapter 1, for example, can be covered in the first class as an introduction to the course. (These particular questions are designed to be answered by intelligent people who don't know any economics.)

- **RHETORICAL QUESTIONS**—The text poses several questions that prompt the students to consider what they would do in a certain situation, applying the economic concepts to their everyday lives. This approach encourages students to reevaluate the world that they often take for granted.

- **SHORT INTRO SECTION**—While most texts dwell on introductory material, *Principles of Microeconomics* combines the first two introductory chapters into one, opting to eliminate a great deal of needless textbook exposition in favor of using examples that students identify with immediately.

- **INTUITIVE ORGANIZATION**—The chapters can be covered in order up to Chapter 13. Chapters 14–17 can be covered in any order the instructor deems most relevant for the time period in which the class occurs (as current events change weekly, so do topics of interest). Additionally, for condensed courses, Chapters 11–13 can be skipped with no loss of continuity.

Focus on RESOURCES

Principles of Microeconomics includes a full complement of ancillary materials geared toward helping instructors teach effectively and students learn successfully.

STUDY GUIDE—Written by James Couch of the University of Northern Alabama, the Study Guide consists of short chapter reviews to jog student memory, multiple-choice quizzes as self-checks, short-answer questions, and potential exam essay questions for students to consider.

INSTRUCTOR'S MANUAL—Authored by Donald Bumpass of Sam Houston State University, the Instructor's Manual provides an invaluable resource to teachers of all levels. The manual includes chapter overviews and outlines to help instructors prepare lectures, short quizzes to administer in class as quick achievement-checks, priceless pearls of wisdom concerning common areas of student difficulty, and suggestions for bridging student learning gaps.

POWERPOINT PRESENTATIONS—Compiled by Nisha Aroskar of Baton Rouge Community College, the PowerPoint Presentations for this text are broken out by chapter, and are tied closely to the text's examples and exhibits, providing a near-seamless integration with the book. Animated graphs and tables facilitate student understanding, "drawing" the illustrations line-by-line on the screen.

COMPUTERIZED TEST BANK (EZ TEST)—The Computerized Test Bank, assembled by Ratha Ramoo of Diablo Valley College and Timothy Terrell of Wofford College, features a wide variety of multiple-choice, short-answer, and essay questions for instructors to compile custom exams. Available in an online interface, the EZ Test creation tool saves instructors time and energy while maintaining the high standards they expect in their classes.

ONLINE LEARNING CENTER—The Online Learning Center provides a repository for all the resources listed above, as well as for comprehensive chapter quizzes and other materials that enhance the learning experience. Please visit **www.mhhe.com/economics/miller1e** for more information.

Acknowledgments

The many reviewers of this textbook generously drew on their teaching experiences to help me craft this text. Many of the best parts of this book came from their suggestions, and some of the potentially worst parts were kept off these pages because of their criticisms.

Ali Akarca
University of Illinois, Chicago

Michael Applegate
Oklahoma State University

Chris Azevedo
*Central Missouri
State University*

Sudeshna C. Bandyopadhyay
West Virginia University

Scott Beaulier
Mercer University

Bruce Benson
Florida State University

Derek Berry
Calhoun Community College

Don Boudreaux
George Mason University

Lyle Bowlin
Southeastern University

Greg Brock
Georgia Southern University

Donald Bumpass
Sam Houston State University

Gregory Bush
*Suffolk County Community
College, Selden*

Joseph Calhoun
Florida State University

Shawn Carter
Jacksonville State University

Anosha Chaudhuri
San Francisco State University

Morris Coats
Nicholls State University

Mike Cohick
Collin County Community College

Jim Couch
University of North Alabama

Jim Cox
*Georgia Perimeter College,
Lawrenceville*

James Dorn
Towson University

Harry Ellis
University of North Texas

Molly Espey
Clemson University

Paul Engelmann
University of Central Missouri

Diego Escobari
Texas A&M University

Antonina Espiritu
Hawaii Pacific University

John Flanders
Central Methodist University

Fred Foldvary
Santa Clara University

Peter Frank
Wingate University

Indranil K. Ghosh
Winston-Salem State University

Lynn Gillette
Spalding University

Stephan Gohmann
University of Louisville

Richard Gosselin
Houston Community College

John Grether
Northwood University

Jim Hartley
Mount Holyoke College

Stephan Haworth
University of Louisville

David Henderson
*Naval Postgraduate School and
Hoover Institution*

Joseph Horton
University of Central Arkansas

David Kalist
Shippensburg University

Brian Kench
University of Tampa

Mark Killingsworth
*Rutgers University,
New Brunswick*

Frederic Kolb
University of Wisconsin, Eau Claire

Robert Krol
California State University, Northridge

David Kueutzer
James Madison University

Larry Landrum
Virginia Western Community College

Gary Lape
Liberty University

Robert Lawson
Capital University

Rodolfo Ledesma
Marian College

Tom Lehman
Indiana Wesleyan University

Andrew Light
Liberty University

Munir Mahmud
Pennsylvania State University, Hazelton

Yuri Maltsev
Carthage College

John Marcia
Coastal Carolina University

Michael A. McPherson
University of North Texas

Betsy Murphy
Missouri Valley College

Inder Nijhawan
Fayetteville State University

Kelly Noonan
Rider University

Laudo Ogura
Grand Valley State University

James Payne
Calhoun Community College

William Phillips
University of Southern Maine

Jennifer Platania
Elon University

Ivan Pongracic, Jr.
Hillsdale College

Ratha Ramoo
Diablo Valley College

Dan Rickman
Oklahoma State University

Terry Riddle
Central Virginia Community College

Paul Rubin
Emory University

Joseph Salerno
Pace University

Eric Schansberg
Indiana University Southeast

Ken Schoolland
Hawaii Pacific University

Anirban Sengupta
Texas A&M University

William Seyfried
Winthrop University

Barry Simpson
University of South Alabama

Timothy Terrell
Wofford College

Marie Truesdell
Marian College

Jogindar Uppal
University of Albany

Donald Vandergrift
The College of New Jersey

Khandker Wahhab
University of Wisconsin

Michael Welker
Franciscan University of Steubenville

William Wendt
University of North Carolina at Pembroke

Christopher Westley
Jacksonville State University

Kevin Young
Diablo Valley College

Michael Youngblood
Rock Valley College

Additionally, I'm extremely grateful for the help from the following people:

My wife, Debbie Miller
Michael Ash
Ardith Spence

Lewis Davis
Matt Morey

Tom Akiva
Randall Bartlett

All the McGraw-Hill people who have touched this project since its inception: Paul Shensa, Doug Hughes, Douglas Reiner, Heila Hubbard, Robin Pille, Kimberly Hooker, Karen Fisher, Brent Gordon, Kami Carter, Pat Frederickson, Lori Kramer, Ira Roberts, and Margaret Haywood.

All the outstanding individuals who contributed their time and energy to completing the ancillaries for the text: Nisha Aroskar, Baton Rouge Community College; James Couch, University of Northern Alabama; Lynn Gillette, Spalding University; Ratha Ramoo, Diablo Valley College; and Timothy Terrell, Wofford College.

All my former economics professors.

Finally and especially, all my past and present students.

BRIEF CONTENTS

CONTENTS

CHAPTER 3
SUPPLY AND DEMAND INTERTWINED   46

CHAPTER 4
ELASTICITIES   74

CHAPTER 5
POLICY ANALYSIS WITH SUPPLY AND DEMAND 104

CHAPTER 6
WEALTH CREATION AND DESTRUCTION   134

CHAPTER 7
TRADE   166

CHAPTER 14

CHALLENGE TO MARKET EFFECTIVENESS 4: INADEQUATE PROPERTY RIGHTS 340

PART FOUR
ECONOMICS IS EVERYWHERE

CHAPTER 17
ECONOMICS IS EVERYWHERE   402

part one

INTRODUCTION

1

"PRACTICAL MEN, WHO BELIEVE THEMSELVES TO BE QUITE EXEMPT FROM ANY INTELLECTUAL INFLUENCES, ARE USUALLY THE SLAVES OF SOME DEFUNCT ECONOMIST."

—John Maynard Keynes

The philosophy of business, the language of policymakers, the reason for the developed world's riches. We live in the age of economics. Economic tools have such power and utility that to understand our world, or to at least prosper commercially, we must understand economics.

WHAT IS ECONOMICS?

If this is your first economics course, you probably think that economics is the study of business. The domain of economics, however, is much larger. In this textbook, for example, in addition to learning about business, we will study dating, sports, politics, addiction, Neanderthals, the environment, organ transplants, space travel, Greek mythology, the military draft, college financial aid, and the cost and benefits of firing Santa Claus. Economics has so much to say about the human condition that economics is actually **the study of human behavior**.

True, other social science disciplines such as psychology, sociology, anthropology, and women's studies also study human behavior. Economics, therefore, should be viewed as a competing field to these subjects. One way economics differs from these competing fields is that economics tends to use more math and statistics. Economics can also be distinguished from competing disciplines through three assumptions the field usually employs:

1. People are self-interested.
2. People are rational.
3. People have unlimited desires but limited resources.

We will now consider each of these three key assumptions of economics.

WHAT IS MICROECONOMICS?

ASSUMPTION 1: PEOPLE ARE SELF-INTERESTED

Self-interested people maximize their own welfare, however they define it. If you care only about money and are self-interested, then you devote your life to acquiring riches. If you live for your children and are self-interested, then you do whatever it takes to help your offspring. A self-interested person, therefore, is not necessarily greedy, because one's self-interest might encompass many desires besides acquiring personal riches.

Economists usually assume that people care mostly for themselves and their family. We know that this assumption isn't 100 percent correct, but it seems to economists that most human behavior is motivated by self-interest. Consider, for example, the last candy bar you bought. Which of the following factors motivated your purchase?

a. The candy bar's taste.
b. The candy bar's price.
c. The wages of the workers who made the candy bar.
d. The effect the candy bar's production had on the environment.

Most of you, I suspect, made a self-interested candy choice and so took into account only factors (a) and (b). But, you might claim, candy bar purchases are matters of minor importance. On the really big issues, you might argue, you do take into account what is best for the common good. Most people, however, have the greatest impact on society through the large number of small decisions they make. But even on big issues, the great majority of humans have a self-interested outlook.

A TEST OF YOUR SELF-INTERESTEDNESS[1]

Pretend that two bad things happened today:

1. You hear on the news that an earthquake killed 200,000 people in a far away land.
2. While cooking you accidentally cut off your pinky finger.

At night your mom calls and asks how your day went. You tell her it was a horrible day. She asks why. What do you tell her? Most people would tell their mom about their lost pinky finger. Most people are so self-interested that they care more about their pinky finger than the lives of 200,000 fellow human beings.

SELF-INTERESTEDNESS IS USUALLY NOT A BAD THING

Is it a bad thing that most humans are self-interested? No! Much of this textbook will show that self-interested people often take actions that are in the best interests of society. That is, the action that will best serve your personal interests will often be the action that best serves the interests of everyone else.

Sometimes, however, self-interestedness does motivate individuals to take actions that harm society as a whole. Self-interested business owners, for example, often pollute too much. Imagine that an economist sees a factory dumping toxic waste into a river. The economist would not say to herself, "Someone needs to talk to the factory owner to convince him to be a better person and care more about the environment." Rather, the economist would assume that the factory owner is polluting because the personal benefits to him of polluting exceed the personal costs to him of polluting. Polluting, therefore, is currently in this factory owner's self-interest. So if she wanted to get the factory owner to stop polluting, the economist would try to change the factory owner's incentives so that it will no longer be in the owner's self-interest to pollute. Chapter 13 of this text considers various means of altering peoples' incentives to pollute.

ASSUMPTION 2: PEOPLE ARE RATIONAL

Other social science fields believe that humans are compelled to make decisions by stuff like peer pressure, advertising, "the man," class consciousness, and the type of potty training they received. Economists, however, believe people usually act rationally.

Rational people consider all the significant consequences of their actions and make decisions that further their self-interests. For example, when deciding whether to buy a car, a rational person would take into account not only the car's price and appearance, but also the car's gas mileage, reliability, and safety.

Rational people can make mistakes. For example, a rational person might buy a candy bar he ends up not liking. But as a rational person, he would learn from this mistake and avoid buying this type of candy in the future.

What's rational for one person is not always rational for another. Spending $3,000 on a television may be rational for me but crazy for you if you have a much better use for the money.

RATIONAL PEOPLE RESPOND TO INCENTIVES

Rational people respond to incentives. (And indeed if I had to distill all of economic wisdom into one sentence, that sentence would read, "People respond to incentives.") If, for example, the price of gas increased, rational people would drive less. If the wages received by economics majors increased, more students would study economics. If the government increased the punishment for theft, fewer people would steal. Or, if new information came out saying that there are health benefits to eating chocolate, then rational people would respond by eating more chocolate.

As this textbook will show extensively, citizens' rationality often creates problems for government policymakers. When politicians push people to do one thing, they often create incentives for rational people to do another.

Indirect Effects   When the price of Pepsi rises, the direct effect is that fewer people drink Pepsi. But an indirect effect is that more people drink Coke. You must understand indirect effects to evaluate government policies intelligently. Here are a few examples:

- **Policy**—To increase fairness, students with learning disabilities are given extra time to take the SATs.
- **Indirect effect**—Some rich students find doctors willing to say they have learning disabilities.[2]

- **Policy**—To make sure that poor people receive emergency treatment, the U.S. government forces emergency rooms to offer free care to poor patients.
- **Indirect effect**—Hospitals in poor areas close their emergency rooms because of the high cost of giving free treatment to the poor.

- **Policy**—To reduce its population, China forbids many women to have a child if they have already given birth.
- **Indirect effect**—Chinese couples who have not yet had a child take fertility drugs to increase their chances of having twins.[3]

- **Policy**—A nation increases its border security to reduce illegal immigration.
- **Indirect effect**—Many illegal immigrants work seasonally. They illegally cross the border to work for a few months, return to their country of birth for a few more months, and repeat the cycle by going back over the border to work. But with increased border security, these illegal immigrants now fear that they won't be able to return to work if they go home. As a result, the extra security causes the illegal immigrants to stay permanently in the country where they work.

- **Policy**—To reduce fires, the government makes it illegal for fire alarms to have off switches.
- **Indirect effect**—Fraternities frequently have smoke-filled parties. The fraternities would prefer to turn off their fire alarms before each party begins and then turn them on again when a party concludes. But since fire alarms don't have off switches, the fraternities tape plastic bags over each fire alarm. These plastic bags take a while to put in place. Consequently, the fraternities often don't bother removing the plastic bags.

- **Policy**—To help its families, the U.S. Navy gives extra benefits to married sailors.
- **Indirect effect**—Sailors go through sham marriages to receive these additional benefits.[4]

- **Policy**—To prevent discrimination against the elderly, the government makes it very difficult for companies to fire elderly employees.
- **Indirect effect**—Companies become afraid to hire elderly employees. They fear that, if they hire an elderly employee who turns out to be incompetent, they won't be able to fire him.

- **Policy**—To ensure that the poor have access to banks, the government makes it very difficult for banks to close branches in communities where mostly poor people live.
- **Indirect effect**—Banks avoid opening branches in poor areas because, even if such a branch continually loses money, they will have difficulty closing it.

- **Policy**—To give bad kids a second chance, the government imposes light punishments on juvenile criminals.
- **Indirect effect**—Gangs often use kids to commit murders because they know that, if caught, the kids won't be severely punished.

- **Policy**—To reduce the cost of medical care, governments force pharmaceutical companies to sell their lifesaving drugs at low prices.
- **Indirect effect**—Knowing that they will be forced to sell future products at low prices, pharmaceutical companies spend much less money researching new lifesaving drugs.

- **Policy**—To help parents, the government of Australia gives $3,000 to each newborn baby. The policy went into effect on July 1, 2004. Children born before this date don't receive the $3,000.
- **Indirect effect**—Many mothers who would have normally given birth shortly before July 1, 2004, extended their pregnancies by, for example, having a cesarean section surgery later than they otherwise would. Economists estimated that "over 1,000 births were 'moved' so as to ensure that their parents were eligible for the Baby Bonus, with about one quarter being moved by more than two weeks."[5]

- **Policy**—For reasons of fairness, a college gives more financial aid to a student the less wealth the student has.
- **Indirect effect**—High school students figure out that, if they get jobs and save their earnings, they will receive less college financial aid. As a result, fewer college-bound high school students avoid getting jobs or saving money they earned from jobs.

> "No very deep knowledge of economics is usually needed for grasping the immediate effects of a measure; but the task of economics is to foretell the remoter effects, and so to allow us to avoid such acts as attempt to remedy a present ill by sowing the seeds of a much greater ill for the future." —Ludwig von Mises

ASSUMPTION 3: PEOPLE HAVE UNLIMITED DESIRES BUT LIMITED RESOURCES

Compared to 99 percent of all the humans who have ever lived, this textbook's author and most of you readers are fantastically rich. Most of us live in warm residences that have indoor plumbing. Most of us can afford international travel and food grown around the world. We drive around in fast horseless carriages and receive significantly better health care than medieval kings did. We even have entertainment shows continually beamed into our homes. **Yet we want more!**

We want bigger houses, better food, flying cars, longer lives, cheaper plane fares, and more compelling television programs. Unfortunately, we can't have everything we want. The world has finite resources. Technology, fortunately, continually allows us to get more from our limited resources. But even with today's technology, we can't satisfy all of our desires. Much of economics concerns how people can best use their limited resources to partially satisfy their unlimited desires.

If we had infinite resources or modest desires we could afford everything we wanted. But since we have unlimited desires and limited resources, we always face trade-offs.

TRADE-OFFS

Scarcity forces many trade-offs on individuals and societies. Here are just a few examples:

- **Time at work / time with family**—The time you spend at work is time you don't spend with your spouse and children. But if you spend too much time with your family, your career will suffer and you won't be able to provide your family with all the material goods you would like to.

- **Party time / grades**—The more time you spend in college having fun, the less time you have to study and earn good grades. But if you spend too much time studying, you won't make as many college friends.

- **Cancer research / AIDS research**—The world has limited resources to spend on medical research. Therefore every dollar spent finding cancer cures is one dollar that wasn't spend on AIDS research.

- **Clean environment / money to poor**—It costs money to provide animal habitats, reduce factory pollution, or to clean litter off the streets. Any money spent cleaning the environment is money that could have been given to the poor.

- **Money spent on one good / money spent on another**—Whenever you spend $1 on one good, you lose the chance to spend this dollar on another.

Economics can't determine what trade-offs individuals and societies should make. Economics does, however, excel at pointing out the trade-offs that scarcity forces on us. One tool economics uses to illuminate trade-offs is the *production possibility frontier*.

PRODUCTION POSSIBILITY FRONTIERS

To keep everything simple, imagine that some hypothetical country produces only computers and televisions. If this country uses all of its factories and every worker labors as hard as he can, then the country is capable of producing 5 million televisions and 10 million computers.

Recall that producing 5 million televisions and 10 million computers requires the country to use all its productive resources. (Productive resources include things such as workers, raw materials, factories and transport vehicles.) Thus, if the nation wanted more than 5 million televisions it would have to shift workers and factory space away from making computers and toward making televisions.

Whenever a country is using all of its productive resources to make goods, the country is on its production possibility frontier. Figure 1.1 shows the production possibility frontier for our hypothetical country.

The production possibility frontier is a line, not a point. This is because a country can choose to use its productive resources in many ways. In Figure 1.1, for example,

FIGURE **1.1**

PRODUCTION
POSSIBILITY
FRONTIER

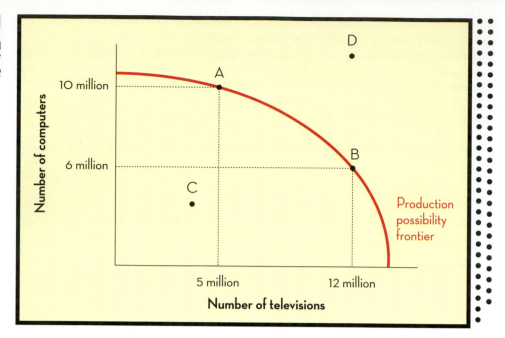

the country could be at point A and make 5 million televisions and 10 million computers, or be at point B and make 12 million televisions and 6 million computers.

Production possibility frontiers show the trade-offs a country must make if it is already using all its productive resources but wants to make more of one good. For example, if our hypothetical country desires to move from point A to point B, it gets an additional 7 million televisions but gives up 4 million computers. The 4 million computers the country would sacrifice, therefore, would be the cost of moving from point A to point B.

Point C in Figure 1.1 is inside the production possibility frontier. At point C the country is not using all of its resources. Whenever a country is inside its production possibility frontier, it is capable of producing more of everything. Or, a country inside its production possibility frontier can make more of one good without making less of another. In contrast, whenever a country is on its production possibility frontier, it can only make more of one good by making less of another. While a country is capable of being at any point on or inside its production possibility frontier, the country wastes resources if it is inside its frontier.

Point D is beyond the production possibility frontier. The country is not capable of being at point D. In general, societies cannot go past their production possibility frontier.

Imagine that if you worked as hard as possible, in one semester you could take (and pass) any five courses. Consequently, any combination of five courses your college offers would be on your personal production possibility frontier. If you took less than five courses, you would be inside your production possibility frontier. And if you took six or more courses, you would be beyond your production possibility frontier.

OPPORTUNITY COSTS

Production possibility frontiers are one tool economists use to show trade-offs. The concept of opportunity costs is another.

Normally, you think of the cost of a candy bar as how much money you must pay to buy the candy. Opportunity costs, however, provide an alternative measure of costs. Pretend that a candy bar costs $2 while a banana costs $1. The $2 you spent on a candy bar could have been used to purchase two bananas. The opportunity cost of a candy bar, therefore, is two bananas.

Opportunity cost is opportunity lost. The opportunity cost of a good represents what you could have bought had you not purchased the good. So in our example, the opportunity cost of a banana is one-half of a candy bar. If, however, a banana costs 10 times as much as a candy bar, then the opportunity cost of a banana would be 10 candy bars.

Let's now complicate the situation by assuming that

a. A candy bar costs $2.

b. A banana costs $1.

c. An apple costs 50 cents.

What now is the opportunity cost of a candy bar? Instead of buying the candy bar you could have bought (1) two bananas, (2) four apples, or (3) one banana and two apples. The opportunity cost of the candy bar is now whichever of these three alternatives you would have most enjoyed having. In general, the opportunity cost of purchasing a good is the most valuable bundle of goods (to you) that could have been purchased had you not bought the original good.

The Opportunity Cost of a Date

What is the opportunity cost of going on a date with Pat tonight? Imagine if you go out with Pat, you two will share a $20 pizza that you will pay for. If you didn't go out with Pat, you would have shared a $20 pizza with Chase, and Chase would have bought the pizza. The opportunity cost of your date with Pat, therefore, is the $20 cost of the meal and the lost enjoyment you would have received had you eaten with Chase.

Now imagine that if you dined with Chase, you would have paid for the pizza. The opportunity cost of your date with Pat now doesn't include the cost of the pizza since you would have spent $20 on pizza even if you didn't go on a date with Pat.

Opportunity Cost and Time

Let's apply opportunity costs to time. Imagine that it will take you two hours to read this chapter. If you hadn't read this chapter, the best use of your time would have been to read 10 pages of Shakespeare. So the opportunity cost of your reading this chapter is the forgone pleasure and knowledge you would have acquired reading those 10 pages of Shakespeare.

Imagine you can work at one (and only one) of two jobs. The first pays $10 an hour and the second $15 an hour. Economists using opportunity cost would say that the first job really cost you $5 per hour since a cost of working the first job is that you lose the opportunity of making that extra $5 per hour.

INCREASING WEALTH

Every dollar a society spends on one good is one less dollar it has to spend on another. We simply can't escape trade-offs. But we can increase the total number of goods we have to trade off. This textbook will devote significant space to considering ways society can become richer and thereby have more of everything. We will now briefly consider three such wealth-enhancing measures: specialization, innovation, and markets.

Method 1 of Increasing Wealth: Specialization

Imagine you get in a car accident and end up in a hospital emergency room. The doctor who will soon operate on you comes by to introduce herself. She explains that she works as a doctor only one day a

Opportunity cost—the value of the next best alternative that must be given up in order to engage in any economic activity.

Opportunity cost = Best opportunity lost

week. The other days she alternates working as a lawyer, farmer, construction worker, musician, bus station bathroom cleaner, and microeconomics textbook writer. You should be very scared. Your doctor devotes only one-seventh of her working hours to medicine. This means she probably hasn't had the time to master this or any other profession.

Specializing allows people to become very good at just one task. Society is far better off, for example, if people wishing to become doctors spend their time learning medicine and don't worry about how to farm, practice law, or construct skyscrapers.

Specialization allows workers to develop very high levels of skill at their chosen profession. And when many workers have high skill levels, a society is able to produce many valuable goods and services.

Method 2 of Increasing Wealth: Innovation

Innovation gives us another means of expanding our production possibility frontier. Innovation consists of finding improved ways to provide goods and services. One innovation, for example, might increase the survival rate of heart surgery while another reduces the cost of manufacturing electronic goods. Most of the wealth of rich countries is due to the innovations that have taken place over the past 200 years.

As Figure 1.2 shows, innovation shifts out a society's production possibility frontier. When a nation's production possibility frontier moves out, the country can produce more of everything. Anything that increases a nation's overall wealth shifts out its production possibility frontier.

Method 3 of Increasing Wealth: Markets

In markets individuals and businesses voluntarily exchange money, goods, services, and labor. This textbook extensively explores markets. We will see that while markets aren't perfect, they on average do a wonderful job of creating wealth. Markets excel at wealth creation because they often provide incentives for self-interested individuals to take socially beneficial actions.

FIGURE **1.2**

THE EFFECT OF INNOVATION ON A COUNTRY'S PRODUCTION POSSIBILITY FRONTIER

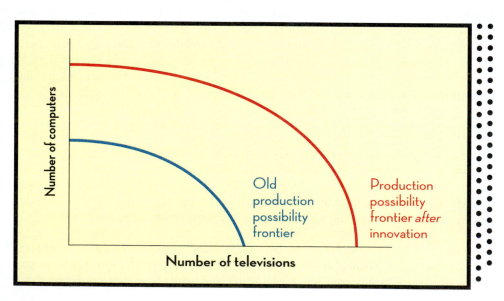

Old production possibility frontier

Production possibility frontier *after* innovation

North and South Korea provide an example of the value of markets. At the end of World War II, Korea was divided into two parts: North Korea and South Korea. North Korea was initially much richer than South Korea. North Korea outlawed markets and pursued a socialist path to economic development. South Korea, in contrast, tried to use markets to grow richer. The following picture illuminates which country did better:

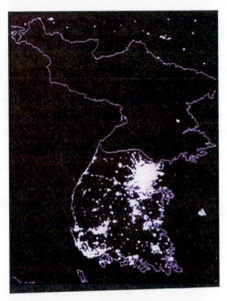

NORTH KOREA IS THE COUNTRY ON THE TOP, AND SOUTH KOREA IS THE NATION DEPICTED ON THE BOTTOM.

The satellite photo above shows both Koreas at night. Socialism has kept North Korea in the dark as it lacks the capacity to generate much electricity. Markets, however, have lit up South Korea, making it a fairly wealthy nation.

THE DIFFERENCE BETWEEN MICROECONOMICS AND MACROECONOMICS

Economics is basically divided into two subfields: microeconomics and macroeconomics. Microeconomics is the study of individuals and businesses. Macroeconomics focuses on the performance of entire economies and looks at issues such as unemployment, inflation, and monetary policy. Knowledge of both subfields is helpful to people in many different types of jobs.

JOBS FOR UNDERGRADUATE ECONOMICS MAJORS

Majoring in economics helps develop both verbal and quantitative skills and so is good preparation for many careers. As economics teaches much about business, majoring in economics is an excellent plan for students who want to work for (or even start) a business. Economics majors, however, also often accept jobs working for the government or not-for-profit organizations. Many undergraduate economics majors go on to various graduate school programs in fields such as law, public policy, and sometimes even economics.

The average starting yearly salary for U.S. economics majors in early 2007 was $51,631.70.[6] There is a huge variance, however, in the salaries of newly minted economics majors. Economics majors who take jobs in investment banking and management consulting earn the highest salaries while those who work for the government or nonprofit organizations usually receive starting yearly salaries well below $51,631.

ORGANIZATION OF THE TEXTBOOK

The first section of this textbook (this chapter) provides a brief introduction to economics and economic reasoning. Section two shows markets in all their glory. In section two you will learn why markets have created enormous wealth for rich countries. Section three considers some market failures and shows how governments could potentially improve the workings of markets. Section three, however, also illuminates government failures. This section shows that societies must often choose between imperfect markets and imperfect governments. Section four provides an economic analysis of many, mostly noncommercial, topics.

EXTRA READING

Some of you are no doubt so excited to learn microeconomics this semester that merely taking your microeconomics class and reading this textbook won't be enough. Here are some reading suggestions for you enthusiastic microeconomics consumers:

Books

- *The Invisible Heart* by Russell Roberts—A fictional romance story that incorporates economic reasoning and explains the benefits of free markets.
- *Naked Economics* by Charles Wheelan—Wonderfully written book presenting selected economics topics to a general audience.
- *The Economics of Life* by Gary S. Becker and Guity Nashat Becker—Collection of very short essays applying economics to everything.
- *The Shackled Continent* by Robert Guest—Explains why Africa is so poor; recommended for "do-gooders" who want to fight world poverty.
- *Basic Economics* by Thomas Sowell—Comprehensive but mostly nontechnical overview of micro- and macroeconomics; the book on this list most likely to help you with your micro- and macroeconomics exams.
- *Free to Choose* by Milton Friedman and Rose Friedman—Very readable and highly influential book arguing for reduced government control over the economy.

Periodicals   *The Wall Street Journal* and the *Financial Times* are the leading business newspapers. *The Economist, Forbes, Fortune,* and *BusinessWeek* are the top business magazines. All six of these publications frequently employ microeconomic reasoning. Students hoping for a career in business should read at least one of these publications regularly. Such reading will greatly prepare you for business job interviews and could help you determine which area of business to specialize in.

Blogs   Many economists keep blogs. As the names and Internet addresses of these blogs continually change, I won't list any here. Reading economics blogs is one of the best ways of connecting economics with current events.

QUESTIONS YOU SHOULD BE ABLE TO ANSWER AFTER READING THIS CHAPTER

Each chapter of this textbook has a list of questions you should be able to answer after reading the chapter. The answers to each question can be found on the listed page. You can use these questions as a quick study guide to make sure you're familiar with the concepts raised in the chapter.

1   What is the definition of economics? (page 2)
2   Are self-interested people necessarily greedy? (page 3)
3   Is self-interestedness necessarily a bad thing? (page 4)
4   What do rational people do? (page 4)
5   Do rational people ever make mistakes? (page 4)
6   Do all rational people act alike? (page 5)
7   What are some examples of indirect effects? (pages 5–6)
8   Why do we all face trade-offs? (page 7)
9   What is a production possibility frontier? (page 7)
10 What does it mean if a point is on the production possibility frontier? (page 7)
11 What does it mean if a point is inside the production possibility frontier? (page 8)
12 What does it mean if a point is outside the production possibility frontier? (page 8)
13 What are opportunity costs? (page 9)
14 How does specialization increase the wealth of society? (page 10)
15 How does innovation increase the wealth of society? (page 10)
16 What are markets? (page 10)

STUDY PROBLEMS

Each chapter in this textbook concludes with study questions. Although reading the textbook will help you with the questions, the answers usually cannot be found directly in the text. Your instructor might want to give you these questions as graded assignments. As a result, after this chapter, I will not be providing you with answers to the study questions. But since you're probably new to economic analysis, this chapter generously provides you with some answers. But beware! The answer to at least one question is incorrect.

I'M GOING TO LIE TO YOU!

Students, I believe, have far too much trust in textbooks. You often assume that everything in a textbook is right just because it's printed in a textbook. Such a trusting assumption reduces students' critical reasoning abilities. I certainly don't want you to trust everything written in my textbook. I'm therefore going to deliberately lie to you in the next few pages. The lie(s) is (are) revealed at the end of this chapter.

But, you might ask, "Given that the author is an admitted liar, how can I trust anything in this textbook?" Dear reader, I don't want your trust. I want your attention. Learning economics does not consist of memorizing true facts. It involves learning to think logically about human behavior. This textbook will present many theories. But I will not be saying "Here is the theory. I'm such an incredibly wise, smart, and handsome economist that you should trust my assertion that this theory is true." Rather, I will present logical reasons why I believe the theory is correct. Using your own brain you should verify or disprove the logic of my arguments.

STUDY QUESTIONS AND (MOSTLY TRUTHFUL) ANSWERS

Please try to solve each question before actually reading the question's answer.

1 **Why might it be cheaper to hire someone else to shovel your driveway than to do it yourself?**

It might be cheaper because of the opportunity cost of your time. Imagine that you can make $20 an hour working and it takes you two hours to shovel your driveway. The opportunity cost of shoveling your own driveway is $40. If you could hire someone to shovel your driveway for $30, then it would be cheaper to hire this person than to do your driveway yourself.

2 **Why do babysitters of equal skill make far more money in the United States than in India?**

Hourly wages are much higher in the United States than in India. Consequently, the opportunity costs of spending a few hours babysitting are also higher in the United States. Therefore, American parents must pay more than Indian parents to induce someone to watch their children.

3 **What are the opportunity costs of attending college?**

You must pay for tuition, housing, food, and (most important) textbooks so these are all obviously opportunity costs of college. But you also pay for college in time. If the time you spend attending college prevents you from working at a job that would have paid $30,000 a year, then this $30,000 is part of the yearly opportunity cost of college.

4 **You pay a $500 nonrefundable fee to join a gym. Should this fee motivate you to use the gym more?**

No. Once you have paid the $500, you can't (by definition) get back this nonrefundable fee. As a result, not using the gym doesn't cost you $500. Consequently, you should ignore the fact that you have paid this $500 when deciding how much to use the gym. This nonrefundable fee will be lost to you regardless of your gym usage. In contrast, however, imagine you promised your boyfriend/girlfriend that you would get in better shape. You also promised that you would give him/her $500 if you don't go regularly to the gym. This $500 should motivate you to use the gym more because you will lose it if, and only if, you don't work out regularly at your gym.

5 **How could we ever have too little pollution?**

Society faces pollution trade-offs. Society must pay some cost to reduce pollution. Pollution reduction could, for example, raise the price of products or even destroy whole industries. Consequently, we would have too little pollution if we have paid too high a price to eliminate some pollutants.

Imagine that radical environmentalists take over the United States and outlaw all pollution. Unfortunately, goods such as cars, lights, computers, and farm equipment all create pollution and so can no longer be used. As a result, the U.S. economy crashes and millions of Americans die of starvation. Under this scenario the United States would have far too little pollution.

6 **If doctors became better at curing lung cancer what would happen to the number of people who smoke cigarettes?**

The major cost of smoking is that it increases your chances of getting lung cancer. If doctors were better able to cure lung cancer, then the cost of smoking would decrease, which might cause more people to smoke. It's even possible (although not certain) that if doctors became better at curing lung cancer, so many more people would smoke that the total number of people who died from lung cancer would actually go up.

7 **You trade your car for another car that is equal in every way except that this new car gets more miles per gallon of gas. Will you now use more or less gas?**

For every mile you drive you will now use less gas. The cost of driving, however, has gone down so you will now drive more miles. We can't tell, therefore, whether you will use more or less gasoline.

8 **Imagine that starting next year, professors' salaries become determined entirely by student evaluations. Professors with the highest ratings will earn around $140,000 a year, while those with the lowest scores will receive about $30,000 a year. What will happen to teaching quality?**

Under this new salary scheme professors will have tremendous incentives to please students. It's not obvious, however, whether by pleasing students professors would do a better or worse job of teaching. Perhaps the best way to please students would be to assign little work and give all students As. In this case, teaching quality would plummet. But maybe at some colleges students have the highest opinion of professors who teach them the most. At these institutions basing salaries on evaluations would motivate professors to become better teachers.

Research indicates that a professor's appearance has a tremendous effect on his or her student evaluations.[7] Apparently, just as college students want to watch movies starring attractive actors, they prefer being lectured to by nice-looking professors. So, basing instructors' salaries on student evaluations would cause professors to dress better, spend more time at the gym, and consider getting plastic surgery.

If these two people were professors at your school would they get good student evaluations?

9 **Pretend that surgeons only got paid if their patients survived.[8] Provide an example of how this could harm patients.**

Imagine that a brain surgeon could perform one of two procedures. Under the first procedure the patient will live but suffer devastating brain damage. Under the second procedure the patient has a 70 percent chance of survival, but if he lives he will suffer no permanent harm. Most patients would prefer the second procedure. But if the doctor gets paid only if her patient lives, she would prefer to perform the first operation.

10 **Movie theaters in the United States charge different prices based on the customers' age, student status, and when the movie is shown. But U.S. theaters usually charge the same price for all movies regardless of the movie's quality or popularity. Why is this?**

If theaters charged higher prices for some movies, everyone would think these higher-priced movies were better. As a result, no one would pay to see the lower-priced movies.

11 **Why should you vote?**

You probably shouldn't. The chance of just your one vote making a difference is so extraordinarily small as to be effectively zero. Thus, if you don't enjoy voting for its own sake you probably shouldn't bother to vote. But, you might ask, "if no one votes, won't democracy collapse?" Although this is true, many people do vote and will continue to vote even if you don't. If some magic wizard told you that if you don't vote, then no one else will vote then you should indeed vote. But if you are not so advised by a wizard you shouldn't fret that your not voting will have any negative effect on democracy.

12 **A proposed law will increase the wealth of 100 people by $1 million each. It will also reduce the wealth of 100 million people by $2 each. Would a self-interested politician vote for this law?**

Yes. The 100 million voters won't care much about the $2. They probably will never bother learning about the law. And even if they do find out about the law, the loss of a mere $2 won't cause them to vote against the politician or make a campaign contribution to his political opponents. In contrast, the 100 lucky people will certainly learn of their $1 million gain. They will give campaign contributions to the politicians who helped them get the funds.

13 True or false: You shouldn't litter because you are worse off living in a world in which everyone litters than one in which no one litters.

False. Your littering is not going to cause other people to litter. People will decide whether to litter based on what is in their own self-interest, not based on what you do. As a result, even if you prefer to live in a world in which no one litters to a world in which everyone litters you might still prefer to litter.

For example, imagine your city has 1 million people. Assume that 200,000 of them, besides you, litter. If you litter then 200,001 people will litter, while if you don't, then 200,000 people will litter. It will make almost no difference to you whether you live in a city with 200,000 or 200,001 litterers. So if it's slightly easier to throw something on a street than in a garbage container, then a self-interested person will likely litter.

Don't infer from the question, however, that economists don't care about the environment. Rather, economists realize that self-interested individuals sometimes find it in their interests to pollute. Designing proper environmental policies, therefore, often requires changing individual incentives so that rational people find it in their self-interest to take environmental care.

14 Should you take advantage of the following rebate offer?

We're sending some money your way!

$1 CASH BACK

OFFICIAL REBATE MAIL-IN REDEMPTION FORM

Please complete the following information:
Name _____
Address_____
City _____ State _____ Zip _____

Please mail this card along with the original UPC code and a copy of the receipt to the address on the back. Please allow 6-8 weeks to receive your rebate check.

You should only use the rebate if the opportunity cost of your time is sufficiently low. Assume that you must use a 41 cent stamp to send in the rebate, meaning you would net 59 cents from using it. Let's also assume that it would take you six minutes to fill out the rebate form, find your receipt and UPC code, fill out the envelope and place the envelope in your mailbox. So the rebate allows you to trade six minutes of your time for 59 cents. If the opportunity cost of your time is higher than this you should ignore the rebate, and if it is lower you should send it in. (Note that if you get paid $6 for every hour you choose to work you earn 60 cents for every six minutes you work; therefore, you should not use the rebate because the opportunity cost of six minutes of your time is greater than 59 cents.)

THE LIES IN CHAPTER 1'S STUDY QUESTION ANSWERS

The answers to all questions but 3 and 10 were (to the best of my knowledge) accurate.

3   What are the opportunity costs of attending college?

Original Answer: You must pay for tuition, housing, food, and (most important) textbooks, so these are all obviously opportunity costs of college. But you also pay for college in time. If because you attend college you don't have the time to work at a job that would have paid $30,000 a year, then this $30,000 is part of the yearly opportunity cost of college.

The Lie: The full cost of housing and food are not part of the opportunity cost of attending college. If you didn't attend college you would still need to have shelter and food. The opportunity cost of college, therefore, just includes the extra housing and dining expenses you incur because you attend college.

10   Movie theaters in the United States often charge different prices based on the customers' age, student status, and when the movie is shown. But U.S. theaters usually charge the same price for all movies regardless of the movie's quality or popularity. Why is this?

Original Answer: If theaters charged higher prices for some movies everyone would think these higher-priced movies were better. As a result, no one would pay to see the lower-priced movies.

The Lie: This answer is silly. Firms often charge more for some products than others and yet customers still buy the less expensive products. Indeed, all else being equal, customers always *prefer* low prices and are more likely to buy a good the lower its price. So, what do *you* think the answer to question 10 is?

part two

THE MAGIC OF THE MARKETPLACE

19

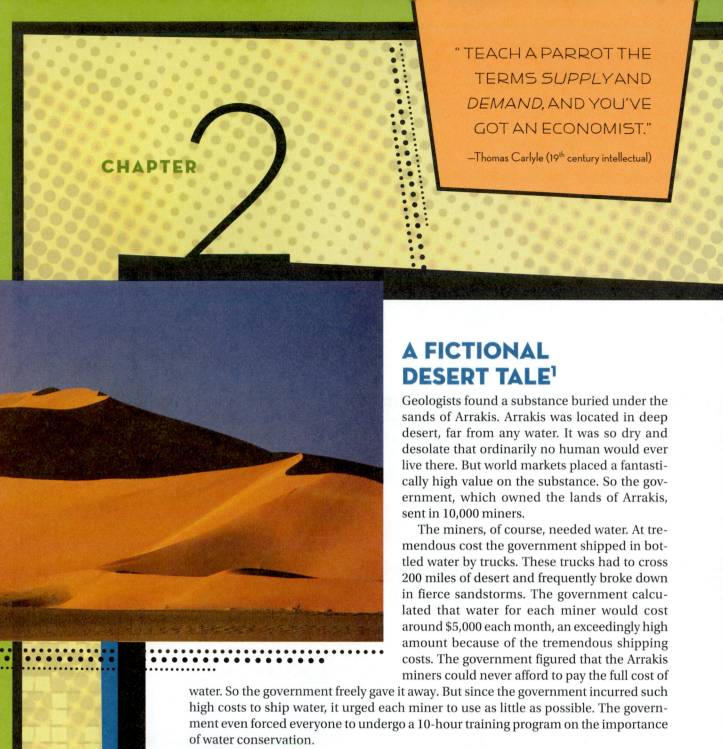

> "TEACH A PARROT THE TERMS *SUPPLY* AND *DEMAND*, AND YOU'VE GOT AN ECONOMIST."
>
> —Thomas Carlyle (19th century intellectual)

A FICTIONAL DESERT TALE[1]

Geologists found a substance buried under the sands of Arrakis. Arrakis was located in deep desert, far from any water. It was so dry and desolate that ordinarily no human would ever live there. But world markets placed a fantastically high value on the substance. So the government, which owned the lands of Arrakis, sent in 10,000 miners.

The miners, of course, needed water. At tremendous cost the government shipped in bottled water by trucks. These trucks had to cross 200 miles of desert and frequently broke down in fierce sandstorms. The government calculated that water for each miner would cost around $5,000 each month, an exceedingly high amount because of the tremendous shipping costs. The government figured that the Arrakis miners could never afford to pay the full cost of water. So the government freely gave it away. But since the government incurred such high costs to ship water, it urged each miner to use as little as possible. The government even forced everyone to undergo a 10-hour training program on the importance of water conservation.

But the miners didn't conserve. They took long showers. They kept water-hungry pets and plants. A few miners used water to grow outdoor gardens. And in one building, some miners actually built an indoor pool.

This water wastage forced the government to ship in higher quantities of water than it initially intended. As its shipping costs soared, the government again urged the miners to be good altruistic citizens and save water. But alas! The miners still kept wasting water. The miners paid nothing for water. So the miners maximized their self-interest

INTRODUCING SUPPLY AND DEMAND

by acting as if water were truly free. As a result, the average miner consumed around $20,000 worth of water each month.

AN ECONOMICS MAJOR TO THE RESCUE

An undergraduate economics major interning for Arrakis's top administrator formulated a bold plan to reduce water consumption. Until now, the government promoted conservation by encouraging the miners to behave altruistically. But the intern believed the government was mistaken in trying to combat the miners' self-interested nature. What the government needed to do was to change the miners' incentives so it would actually be in their self-interest to conserve. The intern proposed charging each miner the full cost of all the water he consumed. The price of water was set at the cost to the government of shipping it in.

The government also gave the miners a pay increase large enough to cover the cost of buying a reasonable quantity of water. So each miner was given a $5,000 per month pay raise. If a miner spent more than this on water, he had to pay the excess out of the rest of his salary. But if a miner spent less than $5,000 a month on water, he could keep the difference.

The intern's plan was implemented and immediately reduced water consumption. Now that they had to pay a substantial price for water, the miners took much shorter showers. They used waterless toilets. They didn't even consider using water for gardening or filling pools. Some exchanged their water-hungry indoor plants for cacti that needed little moisture to survive. Many miners sent their pets to live with relatives residing outside of Arrakis. Some miners even found a way of substituting sand for water. They bathed in a machine that flung warm sand at their bodies. Although uncomfortable, these sand showers were cheap and hygienically effective. In short, raising the price of water greatly decreased the quantity of water consumed by the miners.

NEW SOURCES OF WATER

Several months after the government started charging for water, a group of 50 miners explored the nearby desert and found a small underground reserve of water only 30 miles from Arrakis. These miners sold this water, at great profit, to others in Arrakis.

When the government gave the miners water for free, nobody had any incentive to find new sources. But now that the price of water was high, self-interested miners sought out new supplies.

After learning of the high price of water in Arrakis, many companies started shipping water across the desert to the miners. These companies used trucks better able to withstand desert conditions than the government's transport vehicles.

These companies created a market for water. In this market, water was bought and sold. The companies initially tried to sell their water at the high price set by the government. But at this price miners used little water. To sell more of their water, the companies had to lower prices. The market price of water fell until the amount of water sold equaled the amount of water brought into Arrakis. The government eventually realized that the water merchants could bring in water at a lower cost than it could. So the government stopped shipping water and instead relied on the market to supply its miners.

The water suppliers competed with each other. These suppliers kept finding cheaper ways of transporting in more and more water. A few firms, for example, figured out how to use solar power to inexpensively extract large amounts of moisture from the air around Arrakis. As a result, the price of water steadily fell. In the long run, each miner spent only $2,000 on water per month.

EXTRA INCOME CHANGES THE MINERS' BEHAVIOR

The government surprisingly allowed the miners to keep the full $5,000 a month water pay raise. As a result, after paying $2,000 for his water, the average miner had an extra $3,000 in salary each month. Many miners used this money to buy additional safety equipment and take extra trips home to see their families. Interestingly, however, this extra $3,000 contributed to the miners using more water. The miners detested their sand showers. But immediately after the government started charging for water, the miners felt they couldn't afford the luxury of real showers. After the price of water started to fall, however, water showers became cheaper. And more important, with an extra $3,000 a month in salary, the miners felt they were too rich to endure the highly unpleasant sand showers.

CONCLUSION TO THE FICTIONAL DESERT TALE

When water was free, miners used huge quantities of it and no one but the government supplied water to Arrakis. But when the price of water was high, miners greatly cut back on their water usage and people started selling water to the miners. This story shows that raising the price of a good such as water has two effects:

1. It causes people to use less of the good.
2. It causes people to sell more of the good.

Economists refer to effect (1) as the Law of Demand and effect (2) as the Law of Supply. The rest of this chapter and all of the next consider demand and supply.

DEMAND

I want a 100″ plasma TV, monthly exotic vacations, every DVD ever made, a Lexus, nightly gourmet dinners, maid service, and a mansion. Tragically, I lack the funds needed to make all these purchases. Because I can't get everything I want, I face *trade-offs*.

Since I have a limited amount of money, the more cash I spend on one good, the less I have to spend on others. Let's say that an apple and an orange each cost a quarter. Every time I spend a quarter buying an apple, I lose the opportunity to use that quarter to purchase an orange. So the opportunity cost of an apple is one orange. If an apple's price increases to $.50, then the opportunity cost of an apple would rise to two oranges. As a good's price increases, what you have to give up to acquire it also increases. Consequently, as the apples' price increases, consumers' willingness to purchase them decreases. This leads us to the Law of Demand:

> **Law of Demand: Consumers buy less of a good as its price increases and more of a good as its price decreases.**

Let's consider the demand for apples each month in a hypothetical town:

Quantity demanded—the amount of a good consumers want to purchase at a specified price over a specified time period. Quantity demanded is simply a number of goods, such as 18,000 apples.

Demand—the entire relationship between price and quantity demanded over a given time period. Demand is never just a single number.

Demand curve—a graph of demand.

Price of Apples	Quantity Demanded (of Apples)
$.05	30,000
.10	24,000
.15	18,000
.20	12,000
.25	6,000

TABLE **2.1**

Monthly Demand for Apples

According to this table, if the price of apples is $.05, then consumers will purchase 30,000 apples. I made up the numbers in the above table. But the table is consistent with the Law of Demand since the quantity demanded of apples always goes down as the price of apples goes up. *Quantity demanded* is simply economists' fancy name for the amount of a good consumers want to buy at a specified price. In contrast, *demand* refers to the entire relationship between prices and quantities demanded at these given prices.

In our example, if the price of apples increases from $.05 to $.10, the quantity demanded of apples would decrease from 30,000 to 24,000. But changing the price of apples *does not* change the demand for apples. When we say demand for apples, we are referring to all of Table 2.1. Consequently, moving from one row on the table to another does not, by definition, change demand. Let's now look at the demand for apples each month in graph form.

FIGURE **2.1**

A DEMAND CURVE
FOR APPLES

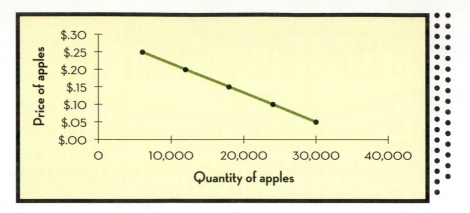

Figure 2.1 shows a demand curve. When you change the price of a good, you move along that good's demand curve. A demand curve such as Figure 2.1 thus shows how much consumers will buy at every price. All demand curves have a negative slope. This is because as price increases quantity demanded decreases. Consequently, on demand curves there is a negative relationship between what's on the X-axis (quantity) and what's on the Y-axis (price).

MARKET DEMAND

Figure 2.1 shows the demand for an entire town and therefore represents what economists call *market demand*, or the demand of an entire market. Market demand derives from individual demand curves. So, if 1,000 people had individual demand curves as in Figure 2.2, then the market demand would be Figure 2.3 where market demand is 1,000 times individual demand. (To see the difference between these two graphs, look at the units on the X-axes.)

To derive Figure 2.3, I unrealistically assumed that all 1,000 consumers have exactly the same individual demands. Table 2.2 derives a market demand for a market with three different people.

To calculate the market demand, we sum up the individual quantities demanded at each price. Of course, most markets have far more than three consumers. Large market demand curves come from the preferences of millions of consumers.

FIGURE **2.2**

INDIVIDUAL'S
DEMAND CURVE

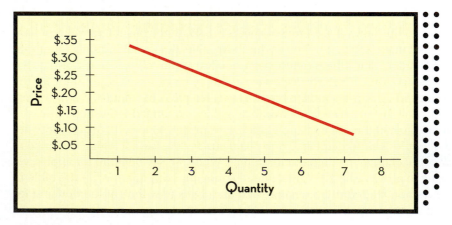

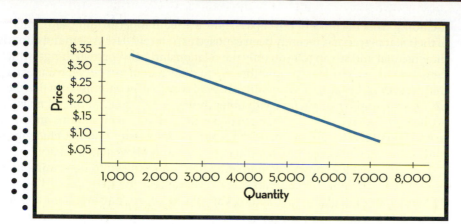

FIGURE **2.3**

MARKET DEMAND
CURVE

Price of Apples	Bill's Demand	Jane's Demand	Sophia's Demand	Market Demand
$.05	20	10	5	20 + 10 + 5 = 35
.10	16	8	4	16 + 8 + 4 = 28
.15	12	4	3	12 + 4 + 3 = 19
.25	8	1	1	8 + 1 + 1 = 10
.30	5	0	0	5 + 0 + 0 = 5

TABLE **2.2**

Market Demand for
Three People

25

MOVING ALONG A DEMAND CURVE VERSUS MOVING TO A NEW DEMAND CURVE

Figure 2.4 shows the demand for souvenir Boston Red Sox caps. Using Figure 2.4, please determine what happens to the quantity demanded for these caps if the Red Sox win the World Series.

Sorry, but that was a trick question for which you don't have enough information to answer. The quantity demanded for Red Sox caps is affected by many things,

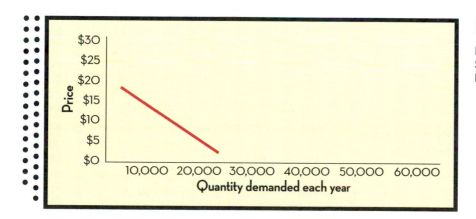

FIGURE **2.4**

DEMAND FOR
SOUVENIR BOSTON
RED SOX CAPS

including what the price of the caps is, how the team is performing, and whether any of their star players has recently been exposed as a steroid user. A demand curve is two-dimensional and so can tell you only the relationship between two things, which for a demand curve are price and quantity. So to draw a demand curve, we must assume that everything but price and quantity are held constant. Economists call this the *ceteris paribus* assumption, Latin for "with other things being equal." (Professionals, such as economists, often use Latin phrases to make their jobs seem mysterious and important to outsiders.) If you want to violate the *ceteris paribus* assumption by changing something other than price or quantity, you need an entirely new demand curve.

Figure 2.5, which shows two demand curves, allows you to determine how winning the World Series affects cap sales. Assume that the Red Sox had been losing 80 percent of their games and selling caps for $15 each, putting them at point 1 on Figure 2.5. If they lower the price of caps to $10 but our *ceteris paribus* assumption holds and nothing else changes, we move to point 2. If, however, the Red Sox win the World Series, we need to move to an entirely new relationship between price and quantity. Point 3 shows where cap sales are if the Red Sox win the World Series and charge $15 per cap.

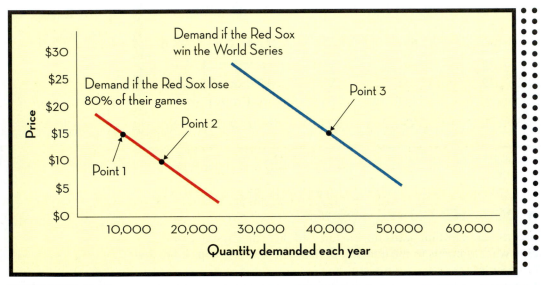

FIGURE **2.5**

EFFECT OF WINNING THE WORLD SERIES ON SALES OF CAPS

Change in quantity demanded— occurs when a change in the price of the good causes you to move along a demand curve.

Change in demand— occurs when a change in something other than the price of the good causes you to move to another demand curve.

As you would expect, the Red Sox sell more caps at every price when they win the World Series. Winning the World Series, therefore, increases demand, shifting the demand curve to the right. So, if the Red Sox want to sell more caps, they can take advantage of the Law of Demand by lowering the price of caps, or they can charge the same price but win the World Series.

In short, when you change the price of a good, you move along the demand curve for that good and get a new quantity demanded, that is, the amount of the good consumers buy, such as 37,000 caps. In contrast, when you change something other than the price of your good, you move to an entirely new demand curve, meaning that you get a different relationship between price and quantity demanded.

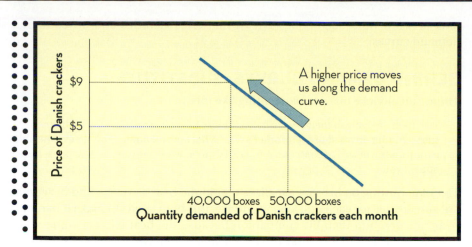

FIGURE **2.6**

THE DEMAND FOR
DANISH CRACKERS
IN AUGUST 2005

The Danish Boycott Figure 2.6 shows a hypothetical worldwide demand for Danish crackers in August 2005. When the price of crackers was $5 a box, the quantity demanded of crackers was 50,000 boxes. When this price increased to $9 a box, the quantity demanded fell to 40,000 boxes.

In September 2005 a Danish newspaper printed several cartoons of the Islamic prophet Muhammad. Many Muslims considered this a great offense against their faith. Some people were so angry over the cartoons they rioted and burned Danish flags. Because of the cartoon, many Muslims boycotted Danish products. Using Figure 2.6, please determine what happened to the quantity demanded for Danish crackers after this boycott.

Ha! That was another trick question. The demand curve in Figure 2.6 assumes *ceteris paribus* that nothing but price changes. If we change something other than price, we need an entirely new demand curve. The boycott, therefore, did not cause a movement along the demand curve. Rather it moved the entire demand curve. The boycott reduced the amount of Danish goods purchased throughout the world. So, as shown in Figure 2.7, the boycott moved the entire demand curve to the left. Let's now

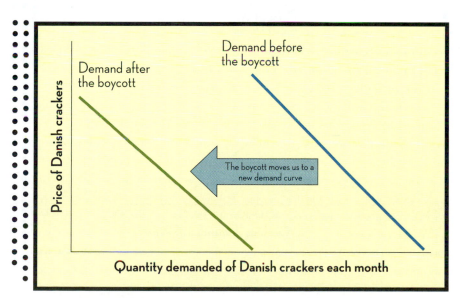

FIGURE **2.7**

BOYCOTT'S EFFECT
ON DEMAND FOR
DANISH CRACKERS

look at a few other factors besides World Series victories and boycotts that shift demand curves.

BEHIND DEMAND CURVES: SUBSTITUTES

There's an old joke that goes something like this:

> Two men are lying in their tents when a hungry bear approaches. One of the men starts putting on his shoes. The other says, "What are you doing? You'll never be able to outrun the bear! The first man replies, "I don't have to outrun the bear. I just have to outrun you."

The man putting on his shoes realizes that in the bear's eyes he and his companion are **substitutes** for each other. So to survive, this man needs to make it harder for the bear to catch him than his companion because the bear will consume whichever camper is easier—that is, less costly—to catch. When two goods are substitutes, the cheaper it is to consume one good, the less you will consume of another.

Goods such as Coke and Pepsi, books and television, toothpaste and cavity fillings, train tickets and airline tickets, and laser printers and ink-jet printers are also substitutes. Substitutes fulfill a similar need for a consumer, so if the price of a good goes up, consumers will switch to buying more of their good's now relatively cheaper substitute. **Two goods are defined as substitutes when an increase in the price of one causes an increase in demand for the other.**

Figure 2.8 shows hypothetically what happens to the demand for Pepsi when the price of Coke goes from $.50 to $1. An increase in the price of Coke causes the demand curve for Pepsi to increase and therefore shift right so that, at every price of Pepsi, consumers want more Pepsi. For example, assume that the price of Pepsi is $.73. The quantity demanded of Pepsi is 10,000 if the price of Coke is $.50, but 25,000 if the price of Coke is $1. Consequently, raising the price of Coke increases the quantity demanded of Pepsi, even if the price of Pepsi remains unchanged.

Of course, the universe doesn't dictate that Coke and Pepsi be substitutes. Some of you, for example, might love Pepsi but hate Coke. For you, then, Pepsi and Coke

FIGURE **2.8**

EFFECT OF PRICE INCREASE FOR ONE GOOD ON DEMAND FOR ITS SUBSTITUTE

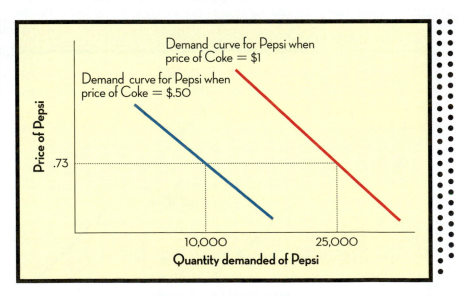

CHAPTER 2 • Introducing Supply and Demand

aren't substitutes because you would never drink Coke, so the price of Coke is completely irrelevant to how much Pepsi you consume. But I strongly suspect that the similar tastes of Pepsi and Coke make them substitutes for most consumers, and therefore, from the point of view of the worldwide market of colas, Pepsi and Coke are indeed substitutes.

Accepting that Coke and Pepsi are substitutes, an increase in the price of Coke increases and so shifts right the demand for Pepsi as in Figure 2.8. Consequently, when we draw a demand curve for Pepsi we are implicitly assuming, *ceteris paribus*, that the price of Coke remains constant along Pepsi's entire demand curve. So if you just change the price of Pepsi you move along the demand curve of Pepsi to a new quantity demanded. But if you change anything else that affects the demand for Pepsi (including the price of substitutes such as Coke) you need to move to a new demand curve even if the price of Pepsi remains unchanged.

Substitutes—two goods (such as Coke and Pepsi) are **substitutes** if an increase in the price of one good increases the demand for the other.

Substitutes and Animal Protection

Many older men suffer from impotence and desperately seek help. For reasons falling more under the scope of psychology than economics, some of these men believe that eating certain wild animal parts can cure impotence. Animal lovers, therefore, should rejoice at the creation of the anti-impotence drug Viagra, which is a more effective and cheaper substitute for wild animal-based remedies. As the editors of *New Scientist Magazine* wrote in 2002:

> The success of the anti-impotence drug Viagra has drastically reduced the demand for wild animal body parts used in traditional cures for impotence, a new analysis shows. Researchers in Canada and Australia have shown that since the drug was introduced in 1998, worldwide trade in parts of some species has fallen by more than 70 percent.
>
> The reason for Viagra's popularity is clear, says Frank von Hippel of the University of Alaska: 'Viagra is cheaper than many animal products and its action is pronounced, immediate and effective.'
>
> ... Antler sales fell by 72 per cent from $700,000 in 1997 to $200,000 in 1998. The number of seal [parts] being traded fell from around 40,000 in 1996 to 20,000 in 1998. The decline in the trade of harp seal [parts] has also been documented by Canada's Department of Fisheries and Oceans, who reported the price per organ had dropped from $100 to $15 by 1999.[2]

Environmentalists should praise the oil industry as well as Viagra. Whales used to be hunted for their naturally produced oil, which was used in lamps. Fortunately for the whales, however, the petroleum industry discovered that it was cheaper to extract oil from the ground than to take it from whales.[3]

Chickens, too, might someday benefit from substitutes. Indeed the great British leader Winston Churchill once claimed that rather than killing whole chickens to get their meat someday we might grow chicken breasts or wings in suitable (nonliving) mediums.

Animal rights groups should fund research into ways of growing animal meat artificially.[4] These groups don't want

When the French queen Marie Antoinette was told that the peasants had no bread to eat, she was reported to have said "let them eat cake."* The queen correctly believed that cake and bread were substitutes. Unfortunately, the price of cake was too high for peasants to substitute it for bread.

---

*Actually, there is no historical evidence that she ever said this.

people to kill animals. People kill animals because they enjoy eating real animal meat. But, if artificial animal meat existed it would be a substitute for real animal meat. As a substitute it would reduce the demand for real meat and therefore reduce the number of animals that humans kill.

Used Textbooks

How does the market for used textbooks affect the demand for new textbooks? Used and new textbooks are obviously substitutes. So you would think that the existence of used textbooks would reduce the demand for new ones. But the story is a bit more complicated.

Pretend you're shopping for textbooks with your sociology major friend. One of his sociology professors assigned a $150 textbook for a required course on capitalist exploitation. Let's assume that this book just came out and so no used copies are available. Your friend doesn't want to enable greedy textbook authors. He therefore refuses to pay $150 for the book. He figures that he can always borrow a friend's copy or use the copy on reserve in the library.

You point out to your friend, however, that because of the used book market he won't really be paying $150 for the text. After the semester is over he could sell the book for $70. The real price he pays, therefore, will be $150 − $70 = $80. After checking your math on a calculator, your friend buys the new book. In this instance the existence of the used textbook market increased the demand for a new textbook.

When a textbook first comes out and no used copies are available, the possibility of resale increases demand. But after a textbook has been out for a while, students mostly buy used texts. Overall, however, it's not clear if the used book market increases or decreases the demand for new textbooks.

BEHIND DEMAND CURVES: COMPLEMENTS

A man feeding bread to pigeons sees a bear approaching. As the pigeons fly away in fear, the man throws all his bread at the bear, hoping that the bear will substitute eating the bread for eating him. Alas, the bear grabs the man while thinking: "I was going to leave this guy alone, but then he threw the bread at me and, well, I've always wanted to try a sandwich."

Substitute goods compete with each other. Complements, by contrast, go together. Buying a good's complement increases the likelihood that a consumer will purchase the original good. Our bear considers bread and humans to be complements, so when offered free bread he decides to increase his consumption of human. Other examples of complements include: golf clubs and golf balls; cars and gasoline; hotdogs and hotdog buns; cigarettes and chemotherapy; laser pointers and cats*; and hamburgers and ketchup.

The Demand for Ketchup

Formally, **two goods are complements if an increase in the price of one good causes a decrease in the demand of the other.** For example, hamburgers and ketchup are complements. If the price of hamburgers increased but the price of ketchup didn't change, consumers would buy less ketchup. An increase in the price of a good's complement shifts the good's entire demand curve to the left since consumers will now buy less of the original good at every price of the original good.

---

*If you don't understand why these two items are complements, try them together.

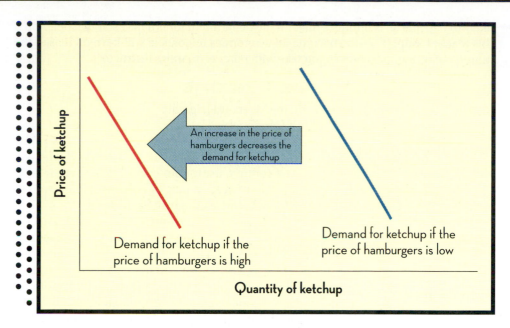

FIGURE **2.9**

EFFECT OF PRICE
INCREASE FOR
ONE GOOD ON
DEMAND FOR ITS
COMPLEMENT

Figure content:
- Price of ketchup (y-axis)
- Quantity of ketchup (x-axis)
- An increase in the price of hamburgers decreases the demand for ketchup
- Demand for ketchup if the price of hamburgers is high
- Demand for ketchup if the price of hamburgers is low

COMPLEMENTS AND SUBSTITUTES

The city of Mystic, Connecticut, has both an aquarium and seaport museum. The aquarium has a wide variety of fish life and the seaport museum depicts a 19th century seaport. The visitors to these facilities are mostly families with young children. Since both facilities are sea-based kid-oriented attractions you might think they are substitutes.

A family living near Mystic will likely go to only one facility in a given day, so the lower the price of one attraction, the less likely the family will be to go to the other. So for families living near Mystic, the aquarium and seaport are substitutes.

But families living far from Mystic must travel many hours and spend the night in a Mystic hotel if they wish to visit the aquarium or seaport. These families are more likely to incur the necessary travel expenses if they plan to visit both the aquarium and seaport. If the price of the aquarium were to rise, fewer families would visit the aquarium. But if they knew the high aquarium price would prevent them from attending the aquarium, many families would not incur the travel and hotel expense needed to visit the seaport. So for families living far from Mystic, the aquarium and seaport are complements.

Similarly, several cities, such as Aspen, Colorado, have many ski slopes. For those living in one of these cities, the different slopes are substitutes. But people who must travel a long distance will be attracted to the city because it has a diversity of slopes. So for these visitors from far away, the different slopes are complements.

Analogously, imagine your college hires a new economics instructor who is a fantastic teacher—better than anyone else in the department. Will this star teacher increase or decrease enrollments in the economics classes taught by other faculty? Let's say you will take 10 classes to complete the major and all courses have unlimited enrollment. If you are already an economics major, then economics instructors are substitutes to you. If you take three of these classes with the fantastic new teacher, you will take fewer classes with the rest of the economics faculty. But if you are considering becoming an economics major, then the professors are complements to each other. You are more

Complements—Two goods (such as cars and gas) are **complements** if an increase in the price of one good decreases the demand for the other.

likely to become an economics major if the department hires a new star teacher. And if this teacher induces you to become an economics major, she will have increased the number of economics courses you take with other economics instructors.

BEHIND DEMAND CURVES: INCOME

"The rich are different from you and me." F. Scott Fitzgerald
"Yes, they have more money." Ernest Hemingway

Many of you no doubt dream of becoming one of the business tycoons who will shape humanity's destiny over the 21st century, using your economic power for good to better the human condition. But admit it: at least part of the reason you want to succeed at business is so you can get rich, because money buys nice stuff.

The rich can afford goods beyond the means of financially struggling college students, meaning that the rich have different demand curves than most of you do. When your career success brings you riches, you will alter your consumption patterns, probably spending more on luxury automobiles, charitable contributions, opera tickets, fine foods, and exotic vacations. All of these products constitute "normal" goods. Economists label a good as normal if consumers buy more of it as their income increases. Not all goods, however, are favored by the rich.

> As consumers get richer, they buy more **normal** goods but fewer **inferior** goods.

Student poverty probably forces some of my readers to regularly subsist on "cup-noodly" foods that they will happily abandon once they achieve financial success. Economists label a good as "inferior" if consumers buy less of it as their income increases. Other examples of inferior goods include pre-owned cars and tiny apartments.

Figure 2.10 shows two demand curves for the inferior good *pleather*, synthetic leather made out of plastic.

FIGURE **2.10**

DEMAND CURVES
FOR PLEATHER

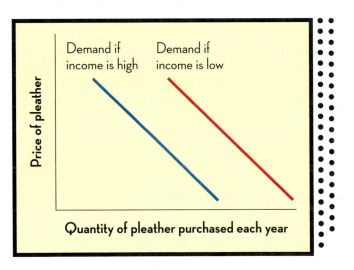

We know the good in Figure 2.10 is inferior because when the consumer's income increases, the good's demand curve shifts to the left and the consumer buys less of the good at every price.

Glasses: Normal and Inferior   Eyeglasses in rich countries such as the United States are becoming inferior goods. This occurs as more of the rich and middle class of these nations get laser eye surgery.

But in poor nations reading glasses are a normal good. In countries where many people make less than $2 a day, glasses are a luxury item and so a sign of wealth. This example shows that whether a good is normal or inferior isn't fixed but rather determined by economic circumstances.

Car Alarms: Normal or Inferior?

Are car alarms normal or inferior? To have a car you must have some money. Furthermore, rich people have nicer cars and so suffer a greater monetary loss when their automobiles are stolen. These two facts support car alarms being normal goods.

But affluent people park their cars in garages and usually live and work in relatively safe neighborhoods. In contrast, the poor often reside in dangerous neighborhoods and often don't have garages. As a result, poor car owners generally face a greater risk of vehicle theft. So perhaps car alarms are inferior goods. To actually find the answer we would have to survey which income groups are most likely to buy car alarms.

Is a Degree in Economics Inferior?

At my college, many students from poor countries major in economics. When I ask them why they chose economics, they often say that their parents would never allow them to major in something less practical, such as art history. Because these students often come from poorer families than their American counterparts, they look on college primarily as a way to improve their future economic welfare.

For many, economics is a fascinating field intrinsically worthy of study. But college students find many majors interesting. Some majors, including economics, are not only interesting but also useful. If students from poor backgrounds are more likely than wealthier students to study practical fields, then these fields, such as economics, are inferior goods. Of course, in the microeconomics context, inferior doesn't mean bad; it means favored by the relatively less affluent.

BEHIND DEMAND CURVES: EXPECTATIONS AND THE OSBORNE EFFECT

The popular Internet blogger Instapundit.com posted this plea for help:

> TECH-ADVICE BLEG*: I'm thinking of buying a flat-panel TV for the bedroom... But my main sense is that this is a purchase where waiting a few months is probably likely to lead to big improvements on the price-performance curve. Or are we past that phase now? Any advice?[5]

What if you intend to buy a flat-panel TV but think that you might get a much better deal in the near future? Obviously, you should consider waiting before making a purchase. Consequently, expected future improvements in product quality decrease current demand.

In the 1980s computer pioneer Adam Osborne announced that his firm would soon be developing a far superior computer. Unfortunately for Mr. Osborne, this announcement discouraged consumers from buying his existing computers. As a result, his company went bankrupt before it had time to sell these superior computers. The "Osborne Effect" is now a nightmare scenario that marketing executives present to hubristic corporate presidents to dissuade them from bragging publicly about not-yet-developed superproducts.

---

* *Bleg* means "to use one's blog to beg for assistance."

TORN JEANS

Torn clothes should be an inferior good. Yet many affluent people wear ripped clothing. Doctor and social critic Theodore Dalrymple finds this troubling:

"At the nurses' station in the hospital ward where I work hangs a pinup of British soccer star David Beckham, perhaps the world's most famous sports figure. His annual income is in the region of $25 million.

The picture has him wearing a white T-shirt and a pair of designer jeans, carefully torn at the left knee, with a loose thread hanging down. This hint at rags is a fashion, or affectation, that I find offensive. It is an insult to all those who must wear clothes with holes in them for lack of better ones: of whom, sadly, there are still many millions in the world.

When I think back to the heroic efforts I have witnessed of poor Africans to make themselves clean, smart, and tidy for special occasions—efforts that filled me with admiration—I feel a visceral anger at this frivolous assumption of false poverty by people who have never had to wear rags in their lives. Once, only Marie Antoinette played at being a shepherdess; now, it is a mass phenomenon.

Do the people who affect torn clothes really want to be taken for poor? A vocation for actual poverty is actually quite uncommon. Do they imagine instead that they are expressing solidarity with the poor by wearing pants with holes? At the very least, the assumption of torn clothes suggests an inchoate idea, or complex of ideas, about poverty and the poor.

It implies a residual guilt at not being impoverished, at being rich enough to afford clothes without holes. Yet why should anyone feel guilt about being rich, unless his wealth were ill-gotten? Today, though, as a result of cultural indoctrination, many people, particularly the young, believe that all wealth is fundamentally ill-gotten.

On this view, one can only accumulate wealth at someone else's expense. Therefore, if you wear untorn clothes, you in effect are condemning someone else to wear rags, for one man's wealth is another man's poverty. Best, then, to side (symbolically at least) with the wretched of the earth by wearing rags. Of course, jeans with pre-torn holes are often pricier than jeans without. No doubt, laborers toil somewhere in the Third World to produce these carefully ripped garments. It is an irony that a taste for symbolic poverty provides employment to people who might have to wear real rags.

But the idea behind the affectation—that economies are zero-sum games, that my wealth is your poverty, and vice versa—has done incalculable harm, far greater than any slight economic benefit that it might have brought to the tearers of jeans. One could say, in fact, that a high proportion of the twentieth century's catastrophes resulted from this fundamentally stupid notion.

Gestures are important, of course; those of solidarity and compassion may bring relief, even without material benefit. But cheap, thoughtless, or condescending gestures may enrage. Rich people do poor people no favor by wearing rags, even by famous designers."[6]

Theodore Dalrymple, "Torn Jeans," *City Journal*, Autumn 2004. Reprinted by permission.

BEHIND DEMAND CURVES: FEAR OF SHORTAGES

In 1973 the most popular nighttime television program in the United States was the *Tonight Show* starring Johnny Carson. One December night Carson told a joke claiming that U.S. stores were running out of toilet paper. Many viewers didn't realize that Carson was kidding. The next day the demand for toilet paper skyrocketed as people across the nation rushed out to buy this vital product.

BEHIND DEMAND CURVES: EVERYTHING ELSE

Far more variables than complements, substitutes, income, expectations, and fear of shortages affect demand curves. Tastes, advertising, and even the prevailing fashion influence what we buy. For example, a Pepsi advertising campaign should shift out the demand curve for Pepsi (causing consumers to buy more of it at every price) whereas a new fashion trend dictating shorter skirt lengths should similarly shift out the demand curve for gym memberships.

Always remember (because it's an easy question to ask on tests) that when you change the price of your good, you move along the demand curve, changing quantity demanded; but when you change anything else that influences how much of a good consumers purchase (including the price of other goods), you move to an entirely new demand curve.

SUPPLY

Supply is the mirror image of demand. Demand curves let us know how much consumers **buy** at various prices. Supply curves tell us how much firms **produce** at various prices. A firm is any organization that produces goods or services.

When you walk into a store, you don't get to pick prices. What might surprise you, however, is that firms, too, often don't set prices. The price of wheat, for example, is determined by the market. (We will see how in the next chapter.) A wheat farmer chooses how much wheat to grow. But once he has grown his wheat, the market, not the farmer, determines the price. If, for example, the price of wheat were $3.50 a bushel and a farmer wanted to sell his wheat for $3.51 a bushel, no one would buy it. This farmer, therefore, is forced to sell his wheat at $3.50 a bushel.

Some firms can set prices. The PepsiCo firm, for example, determines the price of Pepsi. But many firms don't have pricing power and must accept prices as given by the market. **Markets in which individual buyers and sellers can't set prices are called competitive markets.** These markets usually exist where there are many buyers and sellers. The rest of this chapter focuses on competitive markets.

SUPPLY CURVES IN COMPETITIVE MARKETS

Imagine that you're a farmer with two nearly identical plots of land. On the first you grow corn and on the second wheat. What should you do if the price of corn drastically increases? To maximize your farming profits, you should grow corn on both plots of land. Indeed, if the price of corn keeps rising, you should consider buying even more farmland on which to grow corn.

A firm's primary motive is profit. Profit is how much a firm sells its products for minus how much it costs the firm to make its products. The higher the price of a good, the more profitable its production will be. This leads us to the Law of Supply.

> **Law of Supply: Firms produce less of a good as its price falls and more of a good as its price increases.**

Competitive markets—Markets in which individual buyers and sellers can't set prices.

Quantity supplied—The amount of a good suppliers want to produce at a given price over a specified time period. Quantity supplied is a single number, such as 15,000 apples.

Supply—The entire relationship between price and quantity supplied over a specified time period. Never just a single number.

Supply curve—A graph of supply.

Supply curves show the relationship between quantity supplied and price. Quantity supplied is the amount of a good firms want to produce at a given price over some specified time period. A change in the price of a good moves you along the supply curve. A change in anything besides price that influences supply moves you to a completely new supply curve. Unlike demand curves, supply curves have a positive slope because by the Law of Supply, higher prices induce firms to produce more. There always is, therefore, a positive relationship between quantity supplied and price.

THE SUPPLY OF APPLES

Table 2.3 shows the relationship between individual firms' supply and market supply. The market supply is the sum at every price of each individual firm's supply.

TABLE 2.3

Individual Firms' Supply versus Market Supply (All Numbers in Thousands of Apples per Week)

Price of Apples	Firm A's Supply	Firm B's Supply	Firm C's Supply	Market Supply
$.05	0	0	0	0 + 0 + 0 = 0
.10	0	5	0	0 + 5 + 0 = 5
.15	1	8	0	1 + 8 + 0 = 9
.25	3	10	5	3 + 10 + 5 = 18
.30	5	20	30	5 + 20 + 30 = 55

In Figure 2.11, which shows the supply of apples for a different market, if the price of apples is $.25 then quantity supplied is 15,000 apples. If the price of apples increases to $.50 then quantity supplied increases to 50,000 apples. Figure 2.11 is consistent with the Law of Supply because quantity supplied increases as price increases, or equivalently, the slope of the supply curve is positive. Please use Figure 2.11 to determine what happens to quantity supplied if the weather improves.

Ha! Ha! That was yet another trick question. Supply curves show the relationship between quantity supplied and price. A change in the price of a good moves you along the supply curve, and a change in anything else that influences supply moves you to a completely new supply curve. Figure 2.12 shows what happens to supply if the weather changes.

FIGURE 2.11

SUPPLY INCREASES AS PRICE INCREASES

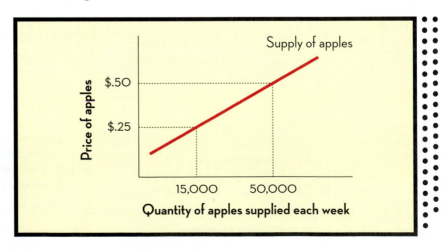

CHAPTER 2 • Introducing Supply and Demand

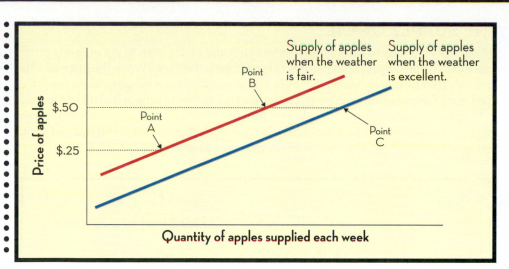

FIGURE **2.12**

EFFECT OF
WEATHER CHANGE
ON SUPPLY

As Figure 2.12 shows, if the weather is fair and the price of apples is $.25, we will be at point A. If the weather stays the same and the price of apples rises to $.50, we move to point B on the same demand curve.

By the *ceteris paribus* assumption, everything on a single supply curve, except price and quantity supplied, stays constant. If, therefore, something other then price or quantity changes, we need to move to another supply curve. Consequently, if the price stays at $.50 but the weather improves, we move to point C, which is on a new supply curve. Excellent weather reduces the cost of growing apples. Therefore, better weather increases the amount of apples produced at every price of apples.

A COMMON MISTAKE

Students sometimes disbelieve the Law of Supply. They **incorrectly** think that quantity supplied increases if price goes down. Their **false** reasoning often goes like this:

> "If the price of apples falls, more people will buy apples and so the quantity supplied of apples will increase."

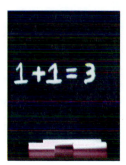

This is **wrong** because it confuses quantity supplied and sales. Quantity supplied is the amount of goods firms want to produce at a given price. If the price of apples were a $1 million an apple, producers would want to produce an enormous amount of apples. True, consumers wouldn't buy any of these $1 million apples. Consumers' desires, however, are by definition irrelevant to supply curves. The quantity supplied of apples tells us how many apples firms would produce at a given price if, hypothetically, they could sell all the apples they wanted at that given price. Clearly, the higher the price of apples, the more apples farmers would want to grow.

It is true that in the real world more apples would be sold if the price of apples were $.25 each rather than $1 million each. But, also in the real world, farmers would want to grow more apples if they could sell them for $1 million each rather than for only $.25 an apple. Consequently, the quantity supplied of apples must be higher at the price of $1 million than $.25.

Another mistake students often make is to think that firms always want to sell as many goods as possible to consumers. But, as we will see in Chapter 8, the costs to firms of producing a good often increases as the firm produces more of that good. Therefore, firms usually lose money if they produce too much of a good.

THE SUPPLY OF OIL

Oil deposits are located throughout the world. Some oil is cheap to get at, while other deposits of oil are extremely expensive to extract from the earth. When the price of oil is low, only the cheaply accessible deposits will be pumped from the ground. As the price of oil rises, more deposits will be extracted, and the quantity supplied of oil will go up.

Imagine there are four oil-producing firms in a certain country. Each firm owns one oil well. Table 2.4 shows how much it costs each firm to extract oil from its well, and how many barrels of oil each well is capable of producing.

TABLE 2.4

Cost of Oil Extraction and Production Capabilities for Four Firms

Firms' Name	Cost of Extraction per Barrel	Quantity Supplied of Oil Each Day if the Firm Operates
Firm 1	$ 10	50,000 barrels
Firm 2	50	40,000 barrels
Firm 3	80	10,000 barrels
Firm 4	120	200,000 barrels

A firm will produce oil if the price of oil is greater than the cost of extracting oil. Imagine, for example, that the price of oil was $60 a barrel. Firms 1 and 2 would produce oil while Firms 3 and 4 would not. At a price of $60 a barrel, therefore, 50,000 + 40,000 = 90,000 barrels of oil a day would be produced. Table 2.5 shows the supply of oil.

Price of Oil	Firms that Produce Oil	Total Quantity Supplied of Oil Each Day
Less than $10	None	0
Between $10 and $50	Firm 1	50,000 barrels
Between $50 and $80	Firms 1 and 2	50,000 + 40,000 = 90,000 barrels
Between $80 and $120	Firms 1, 2, and 3	50,000 + 40,000 + 10,000 = 100,000 barrels
More than $120	All firms	50,000 + 40,000 + 10,000 + 200,000 = 300,000 barrels

TABLE 2.5

Oil Supplied When Price Is $60 per Barrel

TAR SANDS

The world consumed about 28 billion barrels of oil in 2003. Yet the Canadian province of Alberta has over 1.6 trillion barrels of oil in tar sand.[7] So, why isn't Alberta the world's leading oil producer? Because at current prices, it's too expensive to extract oil from most types of tar sand. Similarly, there is a tremendous amount of oil too far under the ocean floor to extract profitably at today's prices. But if the price of oil drastically increased, or if changes in deep-water drilling technology reduced drilling costs sufficiently, or if the cost of extracting oil from tar sand fell sufficiently, oil from these other sources would be pumped into the world economy.

BEHIND SUPPLY CURVES: EXPECTATIONS

Table 2.4 assumed that the price of oil was always going to stay constant. Imagine, however, that the price of oil is $55 a barrel today but everyone expects it to increase to $70 a barrel in a month. Firms 1 and 2 can produce oil at a cost below $55 a barrel. But if these firms expect the price of oil to rise soon, they might hold back production or extract the oil now but not sell it on the market until the price of oil increases.

By the *ceteris paribus* assumption, expectations about future prices are held constant on a supply curve. If, therefore, the price of oil today doesn't change but people suddenly expect the price of oil to rise in the near future, then we will move to a new supply curve. Generally, if firms expect prices to rise, they will withhold their goods from the market to await the better price.

BEHIND SUPPLY CURVES: INPUT PRICES

Anything that raises costs reduces supply. Inputs are what firms use to make goods. The inputs used to make cars, for example, include steel and rubber. Raising the price of these inputs makes it less attractive for firms to make cars and so decreases the number of cars firms make at every price.

Paying workers' salaries represents the biggest cost to most businesses. The most important input for most firms, therefore, is labor. So an increase in the price of labor reduces supply.

Wage Increases   Let's consider the effect on supply of a $1 increase in wages paid to apple pickers who used to make $5.15 an hour. Assume that an apple-growing firm initially employs 10,000 pickers who each work 2,000 hours a year. If the firm employs the same number of workers after the wage increase, then this firm will have to spend an extra $20 million a year. This firm, however, will probably respond to an increase in wages by reducing its output and so employ fewer workers. If, for example, the firm didn't want to spend any more money on salaries after the wage increase, it would have to fire 1,627 workers. Using fewer workers would decrease this firm's supply. Figure 2.13 shows how a higher wage can decrease supply.

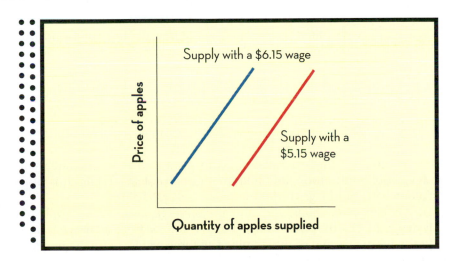

FIGURE **2.13**

INCREASE IN WAGES DECREASES SUPPLY

BEHIND SUPPLY CURVES: INNOVATION

Innovators create a new product or improve existing ones. Innovation has greatly reduced the cost of producing many goods. When innovation reduces cost, it shifts supply curves to the right. Figure 2.14 shows the possible rightward shift in supply caused by producers in the market acquiring better drilling technology. After the rightward shift in supply, firms would produce more oil at every price.

FIGURE 2.14

EFFECT OF BETTER DRILLING TECHNOLOGY ON SUPPLY

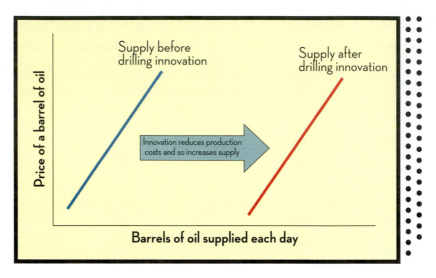

BEHIND SUPPLY CURVES: JOINT PRODUCTION

On an episode of the television show *The Simpsons*,[8] Lisa tells Homer, her father, that she is a vegetarian. Shocked, Homer asks if this means that she will never eat bacon, ham, or pork chops ever again.

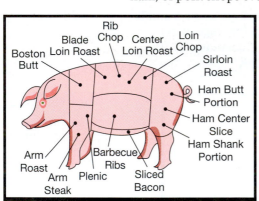

Lisa: "Dad! Those all come from the same animal!"

Homer "[chuckles] Yeah, right Lisa. A wounderful magical animal."

Lisa is, of course, right as bacon, ham, and pork chops all come from different parts of a pig. A critical question *The Simpsons* left unanswered is "What is the relationship between the supply of these three pig meats?" Imagine the price of ham goes up while the price of bacon falls. Pig farmers would want to produce more ham and less bacon. Unfortunately, since ham and bacon come from different parts of a pig, if you want more of one, you must accept more of the other.

Ham, bacon, and pork chops are examples of jointly produced goods. Two or more goods are jointly produced if the process that produces one of the goods necessarily produces the others. Other examples of jointly produced goods include steak and cow hides; wool and mutton; and helium and natural gas. (Helium is often extracted along with natural gas from certain kinds of gas fields.)

Because bacon, pork chops, and ham are jointly produced, the supply of each is highly dependent on the price of the other goods. If the price of one goes up, farmers will raise more pigs and so the supply of all three will increase. If, therefore, the price of bacon increased, the supply of both ham and pork chops would increase.

BEHIND SUPPLY CURVES: EVERYTHING ELSE

Supply curves are mostly affected by production costs, but many factors influence such costs. For example, better roads would reduce delivery costs, increasing the supply of many goods. In contrast, a widespread flu virus would reduce worker effectiveness and so decrease many products' supply.

SUMMARY OF SOME EFFECTS ON SUPPLY, DEMAND, QUANTITY SUPPLIED, AND QUANTITY DEMANDED

Price of the good—A change in the price of a good affects the quantity supplied and quantity demanded of that good but does not change the supply or demand of that good. (If you don't understand this last sentence go back to the beginning of the chapter.)

Factors affecting demand:

Price of substitutes—An increase in the price of a good's substitute will increase demand for the good.

Price of complements—An increase in the price of a good's complement will decrease demand for the good.

Consumers' income—A rise in income increases the demand for normal goods and decreases the demand for inferior goods.

Consumers' expectations—If consumers expect a product's quality to increase in the near future, they will have a lower demand for the product today. Similarly, if consumers expect a good's price to decrease in the future they will also have a lower current demand for the good.

Fear of shortages—If consumers expect that there will soon be a shortage of a product, they will have a higher demand for the product today.

Factors affecting supply:

Cost—An increase in production cost will decrease supply.

Firms' expectations—If firms expect the price of a good such as oil to increase in the future, then current supply will decrease.

Input prices—An increase in the cost of an input used to make a good decreases the supply of that good.

Innovation—Innovation that lowers the cost of a good increases supply.

Price of a jointly produced good—If X and Y are jointly produced, then an increase in the price of Y increases the supply of X.

so what?

Why, you might rationally wonder, have we spent so much time studying supply and demand curves? Well, as the next chapter will show, supply and demand curves determine price, and prices have tremendous influence over human behavior.

QUESTIONS YOU SHOULD BE ABLE TO ANSWER AFTER READING THIS CHAPTER

1   What is the Law of Demand? (page 23)

2   What is the difference between a change in demand and a change in quantity demanded? (page 23)

3   What is the sign (+ or −) of the slope of the demand curve and why does the demand curve have this sign? (page 24)

4   What is a market demand? (page 24)

5   When do you move along a demand curve and when do you move to an entirely new demand curve? (page 25)

6   What does *ceteris paribus* mean? (page 25)

7   How does a boycott affect demand? (page 26)

8   Why does a boycott move the entire demand curve rather then move us to a different point on the same demand curve? (page 27)

9   What are substitutes and how does a change in the price of a good's substitute affect the demand for the original good? (page 28)

10   How does the existence of the used textbook market influence the demand for new textbooks? (page 29)

11   What are complements and how does a change in the price of a good's complement affect the demand for the original good? (page 30)

12   What are inferior goods and how does a change in income affect the demand for an inferior good? (page 32)

13   What are normal goods and how does a change in income affect the demand for a normal good? (page 32)

14   How can expectations affect demand? (page 33)

15   How can fear of shortages affect demand? (page 34)

16   What is the Law of Supply? (page 35)

17   What are competitive markets? (page 35)

18   What is the difference between a change in supply and a change in quantity supplied? (pages 35–36)

19   What is the sign of the slope of the supply curve and why does the supply curve have this sign? (page 36)

20 How do costs affect supply? (page 38)

21 How do expectations affect supply? (page 38)

22 How do input prices affect supply? (pages 38–39)

23 How can innovation affect supply? (page 40)

24 If X and Y are jointly produced goods, then how does an increase in the price of X affect the supply of Y? (pages 40–41)

STUDY PROBLEMS

1 In the "Fictional Desert Tale" that started this chapter, separately identify all the goods that are (a) complements for water, (b) substitutes for water, (c) inferior goods, or (d) normal goods.

2 For each of the following determine if, for the good in bold print, there is an increase or decrease in demand.

A. A new fashion trend dictates the wearing of **kilts.**

B. The price of **apples** increases.

C. The price of Pepsi, a substitute for **Coke,** increases.

D. The price of **dog food** increases.

E. The cost of manufacturing **cars** decreases.

F. The price of food used to feed **dogs** increases.

G. A fall in income forces prospective **yacht** owners to cut back on luxuries.

H. Growers of **oranges** unexpectedly receive extremely favorable weather.

I. An increase in crime worries prospective new owners of **cats** and dogs.

J. An outbreak of infectious diseases increases the number of people who buy **soap.**

3 For each of the following determine if, for the good in bold print, there is an increase or decrease in supply.

A. The price of steel, a material used to make **automobiles,** increases.

B. The price of **steel** increases.

C. Growers of **oranges** unexpectedly receive extremely favorable weather.

D. A new medical report indicates that drinking **orange juice** is extremely healthy.

4 Assume that in some market there are 100 Type A people, 200 Type B people, 300 Type C people, and 500 type D people. Graph the demand for this market.

Price	Type A's Demand	Type B's Demand	Type C's Demand	Type D's Demand
$1	10	5	5	1
$2	8	3	2	0
$3	5	2	1	0
$4	4	1	0	0
$5	2	0	0	0
$6	1	0	0	0

5 On the same diagram draw two demand curves for candy. On the first demand curve assume that the price of dental work is low; on the second assume that it is high.

6 Determine in the following diagram if G and H are complements or substitutes.

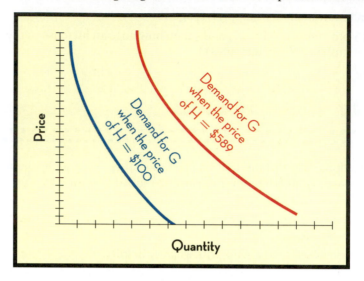

7 Determine in the following diagram if good H is a normal or inferior good.

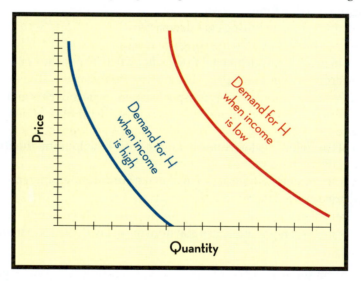

8 Why do publishers keep coming out with new editions of textbooks?

9 Imagine that for some crazy reason the Law of Demand doesn't apply to a certain good. As the price of this good goes up, would consumers spend more or less money on this good?

10 Assume there are six firms in a market. Each firm will produce either 0 units or 10 units. The following chart shows the minimum price at which each firm will produce 10 units of output.

Firm	Minimum Price
A	$30
B	$50
C	$52
D	$52
E	$60
F	$65

Graph the market supply curve.

11 Assume that W, X, and Y are types of buffalo meat. You use the same part of the buffalo to make meats W and X. Meat Y, however, is taken from a different part of the buffalo than are meats W and X. On the same diagram, draw three supply curves for W. On supply curve 1, the prices of X and Y are both low. On supply curve 2, the price of X is low and the price of Y is high. On supply curve 3, the price of X is high and the price of Y is low.

12 Assume that the price of a bottle of Pepsi is $.50. If the price of a bottle of Coke is also $.50, consumers will buy 60,000 bottles of Pepsi. But if the price of Coke, for some crazy reason, went up to $1 million per bottle, then consumers would purchase 80,000 Pepsis. How many Pepsi bottles do you think consumers would purchase if the price of Coke went to $1 billion per bottle?

13 Why do bars often give away peanuts for free but charge for water? Relate your answer to complements and substitutes.[9]

14 Are tattoo parlors and tattoo removal services complements or substitutes?

15 Speculate as to whether children are normal or inferior "goods." If your professor assigned you a research paper to determine whether children really are normal or inferior, what kinds of data would you look it?

CHAPTER

3

"IT IS NOT FROM THE BENEVOLENCE OF THE BUTCHER, THE BREWER, OR THE BAKER THAT WE EXPECT OUR DINNER, BUT FROM THEIR REGARD TO THEIR OWN INTEREST."

—Adam Smith

HOW SUPPLY AND DEMAND DETERMINE PRICES

Mikhail Gorbachev was the last dictator of the former Soviet Union. He once asked then British Prime Minister Margaret Thatcher how she saw to it that her fellow citizens got fed.[1] It's easy to understand how a socialist dictatorship tries to feed its people. First, the government determines how much food is needed. Then it simply orders farmers to grow the required amount of food.

In a market economy such as Great Britain, however, no one is forced to grow food. Farmers in a market economy are paid money to farm. The more money you offer them, the more they will grow. Thus, if we don't give farmers enough money, there will be a food shortage and many will go hungry; but if we give farmers too much cash, we will have a rotting surplus of food. The absolute key in a market economy is to give the farmers exactly enough money to create neither shortages nor surpluses.

So who in a market economy determines how much farmers get paid? Is it government officials who perform feats of mathematical wizardry to establish these optimal payments? No! In market economies the interaction of supply and demand sets just the right prices. These prices ensure that farmers produce the right amount of food to cause neither shortage nor surplus.*

WHEN SUPPLY AND DEMAND INTERSECT

Let's start our consideration of the interplay between supply and demand by looking at a market for apples. Figure 3.1 shows both the supply and demand curves for apples. Clearly, something special happens at the intersection point—price $.45. At the

---

*Unfortunately, most rich countries depart significantly from market-based farming policies. See Chapter 5 for more details.

SUPPLY AND DEMAND INTERTWINED

LEARNING OBJECTIVES

AFTER READING THIS CHAPTER, YOU SHOULD BE ABLE TO:

- Understand the concept of market equilibrium.
- Analyze how supply and demand determine market equilibrium.
- Explain how markets react to shortages and surpluses.
- Determine market equilibrium when supply and demand shift.
- Define the Invisible Hand.
- Describe why water costs less than diamonds.

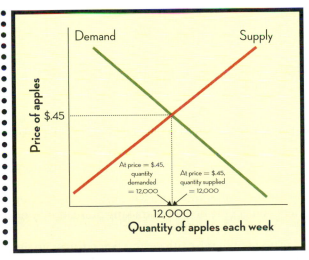

FIGURE **3.1**

SUPPLY AND DEMAND INTERSECT

price of $.45, the number of apples that consumers want to buy (quantity demanded) equals the number of apples that firms want to produce (quantity supplied). In this example $.45 is the only price at which quantity supplied equals quantity demanded. To understand the importance of this supply and demand intersection price, let's consider what happens at other prices.

WHEN QUANTITY SUPPLIED IS GREATER THAN QUANTITY DEMANDED

As Figure 3.2 shows, if the price of apples was $.70, then quantity supplied would be 14,600, whereas quantity demanded would be only 10,000. Consequently, at this price firms would produce more apples than consumers would want to buy, resulting in a surplus of apples. **Whenever quantity supplied is greater than quantity demanded, a surplus occurs.** Now, if you were a farmer and couldn't sell all your apples, what would you do? Rather than let them rot, you should sell more by lowering prices.

FIGURE 3.2

SUPPLY GREATER THAN DEMAND

At a price of $.70, Quantity supplied > Quantity demanded, causing a surplus.

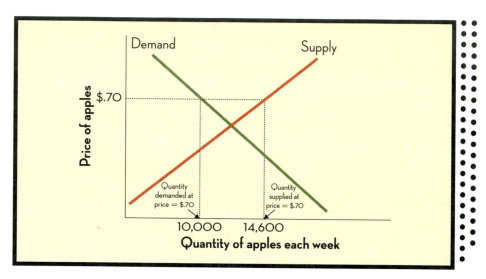

Surpluses put downward pressure on prices. Fortunately, however, when prices fall, the Law of Demand causes consumers to buy more and the Law of Supply causes firms to produce less. Consequently, markets correct surpluses by lowering prices, thereby increasing quantity demanded and decreasing quantity supplied.

WHEN QUANTITY SUPPLIED IS LESS THAN QUANTITY DEMANDED

As Figure 3.3 shows, if the price of apples was $.25, then quantity supplied would be 9,000, whereas quantity demanded would be 15,000, creating a shortage. **Whenever quantity supplied is less than quantity demanded, a shortage results.**

Imagine that you run a grocery store and sell apples for $.25 each, but at this price you keep running out of apples. Obviously, you should raise prices. If you have a shortage, slightly raising prices won't reduce sales, since you were previously turning away customers, and by raising prices you get the benefit of making more money on each sale.

So, whenever a shortage occurs, firms should raise prices. But when prices go up, the Law of Demand causes consumers to buy fewer goods while the Law of Supply causes firms to produce more. Shortages, therefore, like surpluses, are corrected by markets.

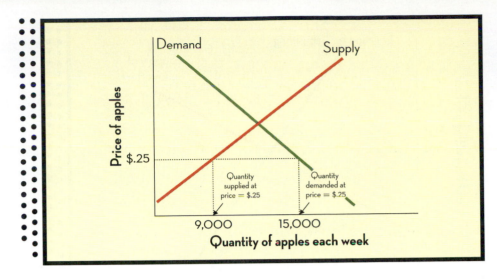

FIGURE **3.3**

SUPPLY AND DEMAND CURVES DEMONSTRATING A SHORTAGE

At a price of $.25, Quantity supplied < Quantity demanded, causing a shortage.

QUANTITY SUPPLIED EQUALS QUANTITY DEMANDED

In this example, when the price of apples is $.45, quantity supplied equals quantity demanded and the market doesn't put any pressure on the price. So in Figure 3.1, $.45 is the only stable market price of apples. If, therefore, the price of apples is $.45, then the price will stay at $.45 so long as the supply and demand curves for apples don't shift. In contrast, if the price of apples is anything other than $.45, then the market will cause the price of apples to move toward $.45. Let's now consider supply and demand in the context of babysitting.

THE BABYSITTING MARKET

Figure 3.4 shows the supply and demand for babysitters on Friday nights in a hypothetical city. Notice that at $9 per hour, quantity supplied equals quantity demanded at 1,000 sitters. Nine dollars per hour, therefore, is the stable market price.

WHEN THE PRICE OF SITTERS IS $10/HOUR

What would happen if the prevailing babysitting price was $10 an hour? The more babysitters get paid, the more people will want to become babysitters. Consequently, if 1,000 individuals wanted to become babysitters at $9 an hour, more than 1,000 will want to babysit at $10 per hour. But the higher the price of babysitters, the fewer parents will hire them. So, if 1,000 families wanted to hire babysitters at $9 per hour, fewer than 1,000 will employ them at $10 per hour. Therefore, at $10 per hour a surplus of babysitters will exist since not all babysitters will be hired.

Now imagine the prevailing wage of babysitters is $10 per hour and you are one of the babysitters who wasn't hired. How could you convince a nice family to buy your services? You win their business by undercutting the competition. If others charge $10 per hour, you should offer to work for only $9 per hour. As long as the prevailing wage of babysitters is over $9 per hour, a surplus of babysitters exists, so some should offer to work for lower wages, pushing down the prevailing babysitting wage. When babysitters get $9 per hour, however, all babysitters will find employment, and no babysitter has an incentive to lower her wages.

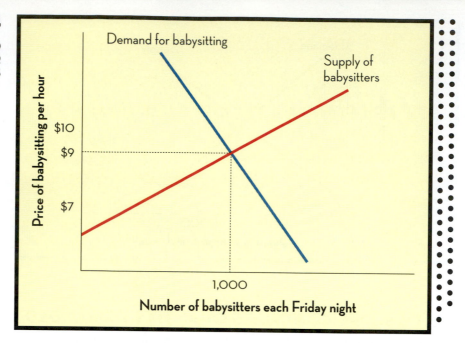

FIGURE **3.4**

SUPPLY AND DEMAND FOR BABYSITTERS

Demand for babysitting

Supply of babysitters

Price of babysitting per hour

$10

$9

$7

1,000

Number of babysitters each Friday night

WHEN THE PRICE OF SITTERS IS $7/HOUR

What would happen if the prevailing wage of babysitters were only $7 per hour? At this wage the quantity supplied of babysitters is less than the quantity demanded of babysitters, so a shortage exists. Because of the shortage, some parents who want to hire a babysitter won't be able to find one. Now, imagine you're a parent who is unable to hire a babysitter at the prevailing $7 per hour wage. What should you do? You should outbid other parents and pay more than $7 per hour. This, of course, will put upward pressure on wages. As long as babysitters earn less than $9 per hour, some parents will be motivated to pay more than the prevailing wage, thereby putting upward pressure on prices. At the price of $9 per hour, however, no parent has any incentive to pay more than $9 because everyone who wants to hire a babysitter at $9 per hour can get one. Consequently, in our example $9 per hour is the stable market price.

GIVING THANKS

"I went to Wegman's less than 24 hours before Thanksgiving and purchased a turkey, yams, cranberries, a pumpkin pie, wine, cranberry cheese, fresh bread, peanut butter and some more wine. Not a single item was in short supply let alone in shortage. I give thanks for capitalism."[2] —Alex Tabarrok, Economist

EQUILIBRIUM

When a market reaches stability, economists say the market is in equilibrium. Markets achieve equilibrium at the intersection of the supply and demand curves where quantity supplied equals quantity demanded.

SUMMARY OF WHY PRICE ADJUSTS UNTIL QUANTITY SUPPLIED EQUALS QUANTITY DEMANDED

- When quantity supplied is greater than quantity demanded, a surplus exists, putting downward pressure on prices and thereby reducing quantity supplied and increasing quantity demanded.

- When quantity supplied is less than quantity demanded, a shortage exists, putting upward pressure on prices and thereby increasing quantity supplied and decreasing quantity demanded.
- When quantity supplied equals quantity demanded, the market is at equilibrium.

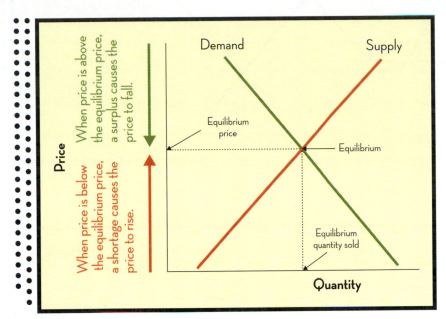

FIGURE 3.5

SUPPLY AND DEMAND REACH EQUILIBRIUM

Warning: many instructors ask exam questions requiring understanding of this diagram.

EQUILIBRIA

When quantity supplied equals quantity demanded, the market is at equilibrium. Supply and demand equilibria have two key characteristics:

1. A market at equilibrium will stay at equilibrium unless disturbed by outside forces that shift the supply or demand curves.
2. A market not at equilibrium will move toward equilibrium.

MOVING TOWARD EQUILIBRIUM

When you change a supply or demand curve, you destroy the old equilibrium and create a new one. The market will move from the old to the new equilibrium. Figure 3.6 shows the new equilibrium that results when supply increases. In this new equilibrium, the price is lower and the quantity is higher. Figure 3.7 shows what happens to the equilibrium price and quantity when you: (1) increase supply, (2) decrease supply, (3) increase demand, and (4) decrease demand.

When a supply or demand curve shifts, it will take some positive amount of time for a market to reach its new equilibrium. For example, in the market in Figure 3.8 it takes five days for the market to reach its new equilibrium resting point. During this five-day interval, the market slowly moves from its old equilibrium to its new one.

It doesn't always take five days for markets to reach new equilibria. In some markets achieving a new equilibrium takes only seconds whereas in others it takes years. And often, before a market reaches its new equilibrium, its supply or demand curve

AN ECONOMICS HAIKU

shortage raises price
surplus causes price to fall
equilibrium

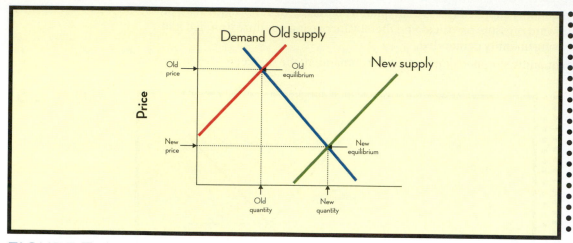

FIGURE **3.6**

NEW EQUILIBRIUM WHEN SUPPLY INCREASES

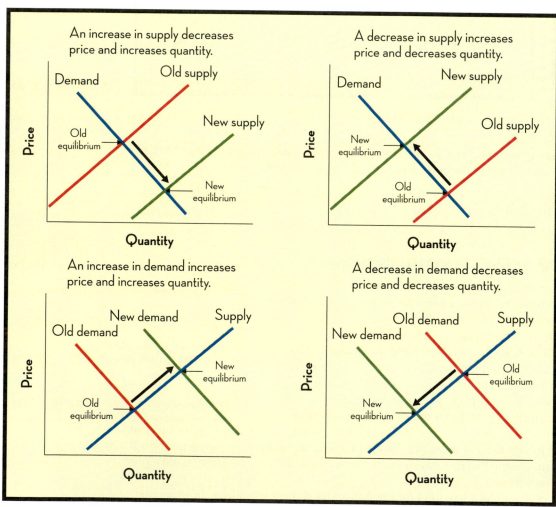

FIGURE **3.7**

EFFECTS ON EQUILIBRIUM OF SUPPLY AND DEMAND INCREASES AND DECREASES

shifts again causing the market to move toward yet another equilibrium. To help you understand the critical concept of equilibria, let's consider three physical examples.

FIGURE **3.8**

NEW EQUILIBRIUM
AFTER FIVE DAYS

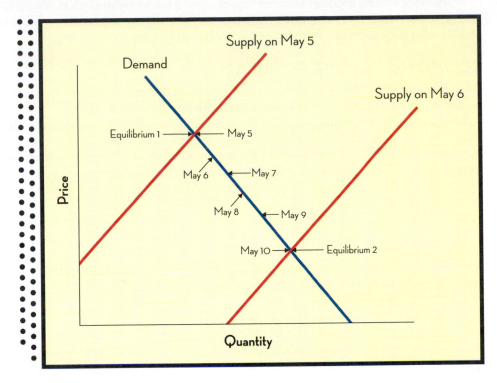

Equilibrium Example 1: A Rock on a Mountain
Equilibria are resting points. A rock at the top or bottom of a mountain, therefore, is at equilibrium. In contrast, a rock falling down a mountain is not at equilibrium since its position is changing.

Right now there is probably a rock somewhere in the world rolling down a mountain. Similarly, markets exist that currently have shortages or surpluses. As with the falling rock, however, the shortages or surpluses can't exist in stable environments and will soon self-correct. The self-corrections don't happen instantly, though.

Equilibria can be disturbed by outside forces. A powerful rainstorm could knock down the rock at the top of a mountain. Likewise, technological changes can alter the supply curve of a good that was previously in equilibrium. Given the ever-changing nature of the universe, markets are more often in disequilibrium than in a state of long-term stability.

Equilibrium Example 2: A Cork in Water
Drop a cork in water and it will first bob up and down. Eventually, however, the cork will stop moving and come to an equilibrium resting point. Any movement in the water, though, will cause the cork to move again.

We can think of the cork as a market for some good and the surrounding water as the rest of the economy. If the economy remains completely still the market will eventually reach a stable, unmoving equilibrium. But the economy, like most bodies of water, often gets disturbed. As a result markets, like our cork, are usually in motion.

Equilibrium Example 3: Ripples in the Water
For our final equilibrium example, consider a body of water as being like a market for some good. If nothing disturbs the water it will eventually settle into a stable, flat, unmoving equilibrium. But throw some rocks in the water and the equilibrium is disturbed. The ripples caused by each rock spread out and interact with each other, creating highly

53

complex patterns. Eventually, the ripples caused by any one rock die out. But if the water is continuously hit by rocks, it will always be in motion.

Wars, labor strikes, unusual weather, changing tastes, and technological discoveries are all like falling rocks that disturb markets. And the effects of these disturbances overlap with each other in surprising and ever-changing ways.

ECONOMISTS LOVE EQUILIBRIA

Since markets are rarely at equilibrium you might think that economists rarely pay attention to equilibria. But actually economists lavish attention on them.

Imagine you're an anthropologist studying a primitive tribe. The tribal land is divided into two areas, labeled *equilibrium* and *nonequilibrium*. The tribe allows you to watch them in the equilibrium lands. In the nonequilibrium lands, however, the tribe forces you to wear a blindfold. In studying the tribe you will likely devote most of your time to the equilibrium lands, not because these lands are more important, but rather because they are easier to examine.

Economists have excellent tools (such as supply and demand diagrams) that identify equilibria. In contrast, we have a much harder time figuring out what happens while markets are moving from one equilibrium to the next. As a result, much of economic analysis consists of studying equilibria. And economics instructors, you should especially note, frequently test students on equilibria.

MARKETS IN TIMES OF CRISES

We now shift from studying equilibria to looking at how markets perform in times of crises. We start with a story.[3]

A FICTIONAL SMUGGLER'S TALE

You're a ship's captain in 16th century Europe. You own a merchant ship that transports luxury goods such as silk from London to the city of Antwerp. But you just found out that the Spanish Empire intends to conquer Antwerp. The Spaniards will soon blockade the city to prevent any food from getting in, hoping that starvation will force the city to surrender.

Before Spain can implement the blockade, Antwerp will want to stockpile as much food as possible. The people of Antwerp, therefore, will now place a relatively higher value on food than luxuries. You consequently decide that on your next voyage to Antwerp you will ship in food.

After arriving in Antwerp with food, you are treated as a hero. Everyone knows you are a shipper of luxury items. They figure that you switched to shipping food to help the city withstand the coming Spanish onslaught. Although you're grateful for the praise, you really don't care who wins the war. The only reason you decided to transport food rather than luxuries was to increase your profits.

Shortly after you return to London, Spain blockades Antwerp, trying to sink any ship headed to its harbor. You are, however, an excellent seaman. You would give yourself a 90 percent chance of being able to avoid the blockade. But being no hero, you shrink from facing even a 10 percent chance of death. So you decide to ship goods to a safer city.

But then you run into another ship's captain who just got back from running the Spanish blockade. The blockade, he says, has drastically raised the price of food in Antwerp. You can now make a huge profit shipping food to the city. Well, your greed overcomes your fear and you again set sail for Antwerp with a cargo of food.

When you arrive in Antwerp, you sell your food for much gold and are again treated as a hero. This time, however, you believe that you might actually be heroic. After all, you just defied the mighty Spanish Empire to deliver food to hungry, besieged people. True, you did it for gold. But you still did it.

You make it safely back to London and intend again to transport food to Antwerp. But then you learn that the government of Antwerp has forbidden merchants from selling food above normal prices. The city government feels it's unjust for merchants to profit from the misery of Antwerp.

You quickly decide to ship goods to a safer city. You feel bad for the people of Antwerp, but your crew agreed to risk their lives only in return for large bonuses. When the price of food in Antwerp was high, you could pay these bonuses and still make a significant profit yourself. If you sailed to Antwerp today, though, you would still have to pay the crew their danger bonuses but would receive only low prewar prices for the food. So if you foolishly transported food to Antwerp now, you would not only put your life at risk, but also lose money.

Conclusion to the Fictional Smuggling Tale

The above fictional tale is based on real events. During the 16th century, the Spanish Empire, in its quest to reconquer the city of Antwerp, besieged the city, trying to keep out all food. The siege did raise the price of food, causing merchants to smuggle food into the city. This smuggled food initially gave Antwerp the ability to hold out against Spain.

The government of Antwerp, however, decided that it was unfair to allow the merchants to profit from the siege, so it prevented supply and demand from operating and set a below-market price for food. The result was a drop in the price of food, which curtailed the smuggling and so reduced the quantity of food supplied, forcing the people of Antwerp to surrender to avoid starvation.

This smuggling story shows that markets, when allowed to operate, can lessen misery during times of trouble. To better understand supply and demand, let's examine three other markets struck by disaster.

PESTS DESTROY THE WHEAT CROP

Imagine that in some country people eat just wheat and fish. But then pests destroy the wheat crop. As a result, everyone must subsist solely on fish. The destruction of the wheat crop will cause some to starve. Fortunately, though, the forces of supply and demand will reduce the amount of starvation by increasing the fish catch.

Fish and wheat are substitutes. The destruction of the wheat crop, therefore, increases the demand for fish. As Figure 3.9 shows, an increase in the demand for fish increases the price of fish. Since the price of fish is higher, fishermen will catch more fish. And because of this additional food, fewer people will starve.

Imagine you are a poor subsistence fisherman in this country. You work about 50 hours each week and catch just enough fish to feed your family. Since the pests destroyed only the wheat crop, they did you no harm. You could, therefore, catch enough food for your family by still working 50 hours a week. But after the elimination of the wheat crop, you notice that the price of fish has increased considerably. As a result, you realize that if you work harder and catch more food than your family needs, you could make a lot of extra money. After the annihilation of the wheat crop, you put in 80 hours a week. Consequently, you catch enough food to feed your family and several extra people.

MARKETS TO THE RESCUE

This pest example shows how markets often work to benefit society. After the wheat crop's destruction, this country desperately needed more fish. So the country needed some way of convincing fishermen to work harder. Markets, fortunately, provided this

FIGURE **3.9**

INCREASE IN
DEMAND CAUSES
INCREASE IN PRICE

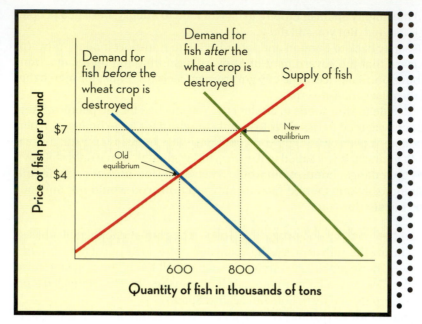

convincing through raising the price of fish. As Figure 3.9 shows, before the wheat crop was destroyed, the price of fish was $4 a pound and 600,000 tons of fish were caught. The annihilation of the wheat crop increased the demand for fish, thereby pushing up the price of fish to $7 a pound. And at this higher price, 800,000 tons of fish were caught.

Interestingly, no one had to tell fishermen to work more hours. All that was necessary was for fishermen to be self-interested. Self-interested fishermen follow the Law of Supply and produce more output as the price they receive increases.

WAR IN THE MIDDLE EAST REDUCES SUPPLY OF OIL

Let's now assume that a war in the Middle East greatly reduces the supply of oil. Billions of people use oil. Because of the war, less oil is available. As a result, people have to be convinced somehow to use less oil. Fortunately, markets do a fantastic job of getting people to use less of a good that has become scarcer. As Figure 3.10 shows, a reduction in the supply of oil raises oil's price. This higher price, by the Law of Demand, causes people to use less oil.

FIGURE **3.10**

DECREASE IN
SUPPLY CAUSES
INCREASE IN PRICE

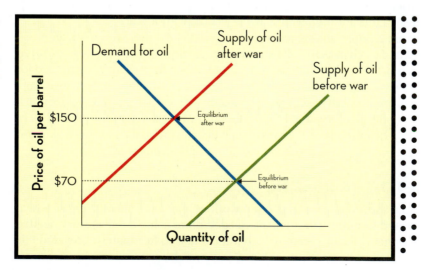

ALTERNATIVES TO THE MARKET

Let's imagine that the price of oil was not allowed to change after the war. The world, of course, would still need to use less oil because less oil was being produced. How then could our demand for oil be reduced if the price of oil didn't change? Here are a few possibilities, all of them inferior to the market's solution of raising the price of oil:

Method 1 of Reducing Oil Use: Propaganda Campaign
World governments could launch a massive propaganda campaign urging us all to use less oil. Everyone could be constantly told that, for the sake of the common good, we must reduce our oil consumption. Of course, given that most people are self-interested, this campaign will likely fail.

The advantage of using the market to reduce oil consumption is that the market works through self-interest. When the price of oil goes up, self-interest motivates people to follow the Law of Demand and use less oil.

Method 2 of Reducing Oil Use: Benevolent Government Officials Allocate Oil
Benevolent government officials could determine how much oil everyone should use. Since billions of people use oil, however, it would require a tremendous amount of information to figure out how much oil everyone needs. For example, imagine that these officials decide that people living in New Hampshire can heat their homes to only 61 degrees Fahrenheit in the winter. One family however, claims that for medical reasons it must heat its home to 70 degrees. The government officials would have to find out if this family is telling the truth or faking the medical condition to get an extra oil allocation. Similarly, the government officials might decide that everyone in Massachusetts can have enough gas to drive at most 200 miles a week. But what if one family claims that its wife and husband work at jobs that are 100 miles apart and so they must have more gas? Again, the government officials allocating oil would have to check out this family's claim.

The advantage of using the market to allocate oil is that the market allows for decentralized decision making. If the price of oil goes up everyone can individually decide how much oil to use. If you have a special need for oil, you can use more than your neighbor. No one has to check on you to make sure you really need the extra oil.

Because markets are interconnected, our benevolent government officials would have to make decisions about many goods other than oil. Plastics, for example, are made from oil, so an economy that must cut back on oil should also use fewer plastics. But other containers, like glass, indirectly use oil because oil is often used as the energy source in manufacturing. So, should an energy shortage cause consumers to switch from plastic to glass or the reverse, and how would this vary among individuals? Perhaps glass is best, except for the Friedman family who has a young child who likes to throw containers. Or maybe plastic is better except for the Johnson family, which has a tradition of pickling cucumbers in glass containers. To make the right decision, the government would need to know about the Friedman's and Johnson's container needs before deciding which type of containers to allocate to them. But of course, no government agency could ever gather such detailed information about people. In contrast, the market does know about each household's peculiarities and takes them into account in market demand curves.

Method 3 of Reducing Oil Use: Self-interested Government Officials Allocate Oil
Method 2 assumed that the government officials work for the common good. But government employees, like everyone else, are mostly

self-interested. If self-interested government officials controlled how much oil everyone could use, they would allocate the most oil to their friends and supporters.

Markets don't care about consumers' politics. When markets allocate gas, for example, the amount you get isn't influenced by your political beliefs. But now imagine that each town put a government official in charge of oil allocation. This official is likely to care about who his political supporters are. As a result, under Method 3, your political activities will likely influence how much oil you receive.

Method 4 of Reducing Oil Use: Do Nothing and Let the World Run Out of Oil
If the quantity supplied of oil was drastically reduced but people still used the same amount of oil then the world would quickly run out of the stuff. When oil is allocated by the market, however, we can never really run out. As the supply of oil decreases, the price of oil rises. This increase in price reduces the quantity of oil consumed. Markets, therefore, use increasing prices to successfully ration goods that become scarcer.

HURRICANE DAMAGE AFFECTS THE SUPPLY AND DEMAND FOR BOTTLED WATER

A hurricane strikes your town. It destroys the water utilities, meaning that when faucets are turned on, no water comes out. Consequently, the demand for bottled water goes up. Unfortunately, the hurricane also demolishes many stores that used to sell bottled water. Finally, the hurricane damages roads, making it harder for surviving stores to get new goods. As a result, the supply of bottled water decreases.

Unlike all our previous examples, therefore, in this situation *both* the supply and demand curves shift. Figure 3.11 shows a possible consequence of an increase in

FIGURE 3.11

DEMAND INCREASES, SUPPLY DECREASES

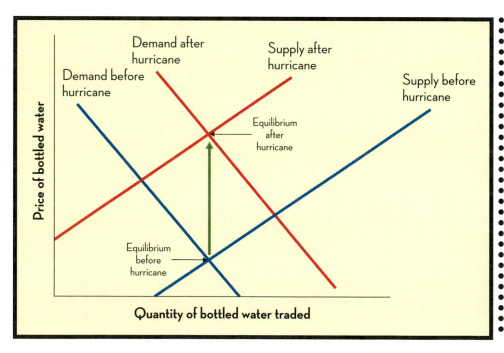

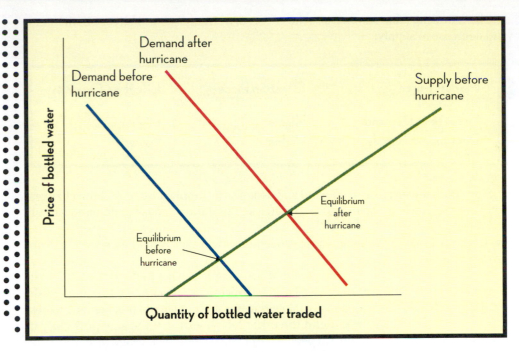

FIGURE **3.12**

PRICE INCREASES,
QUANTITY
INCREASES

(Figure 3.12 labels: Demand after hurricane; Demand before hurricane; Supply before hurricane; Price of bottled water; Equilibrium after hurricane; Equilibrium before hurricane; Quantity of bottled water traded)

demand and a decrease in supply. In Figure 3.11 the price of bottled water increases while the quantity of bottled water traded doesn't change.

Figure 3.12 shows what happens if we increase only the demand for bottled water. As you can see, just increasing demand increases both price and quantity. Figure 3.13 shows what happens if we decrease only supply. Just decreasing supply increases price and decreases quantity.

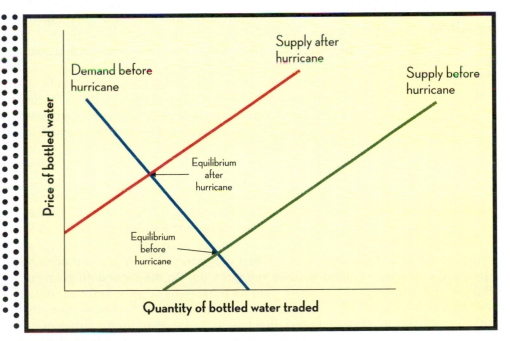

FIGURE **3.13**

PRICE INCREASES,
QUANTITY
DECREASES

(Figure 3.13 labels: Supply after hurricane; Supply before hurricane; Demand before hurricane; Price of bottled water; Equilibrium after hurricane; Equilibrium before hurricane; Quantity of bottled water traded)

The following table summarizes the effects of a simultaneous increase in demand and decrease in supply:

Market Force	Effect on Price	Effect on Quantity
Increase in Demand	Higher	Higher
Decrease in Supply	Higher	Lower

Since both the increase in demand and decrease in supply raise price, both changes acting together will cause the price to increase. But if the increase in demand causes an increase in quantity traded while the decrease in supply causes a decrease in quantity traded, should both changes acting together cancel each other out, resulting in no change to quantity traded?

Imagine that two people push a table to the left. What happens? The table obviously moves left. If they both push right, the table moves right. But what if one person pushes right and the other left, does the table stay put? Only if the two people are of equal strength. If I were pushing to the right and a football lineman were pushing to the left, the table would move very decisively left. In other words, two forces moving in opposite directions don't necessarily cancel each other out.

Returning to our supply and demand problem, recall that the increase in demand causes an increase in quantity traded, while the decrease in supply causes a decrease in quantity traded. So, what happens to quantity traded? The answer is that we don't know unless we first determine the relative strength of the two opposing forces. Figure 3.11 showed an example where both forces were equal and quantity traded didn't change.

Figure 3.14 shows an example where the demand change is more powerful and so quantity traded increases. Figure 3.15 presents an example where the supply effect dominates and so quantity traded decreases. We don't have enough information to know what *actually* happens to quantity traded since the outcomes in Figures 3.11, 3.14, and 3.15 are all possible.

So, to answer your big question: If my professor asks me to solve a problem where both supply and demand change, what do I do? You isolate both the supply and demand effects for changes in price and changes in quantity sold. You do this by drawing two supply and demand diagrams. On the first diagram you shift just the demand curve and note what happens to price and quantity. On the second diagram you shift just the supply curve and again note what happens to price and quantity. If both effects move in one direction (as they do for price in this bottled water example), then things move overall in that direction. If the forces of supply and demand move you in opposite directions (as they do for quantity in our bottled water

WAL-MART'S RESPONSE TO HURRICANES

"[During hurricanes] Wal-Mart knows that people eat more things like Pop-Tarts—easy-to-store, nonperishable items—and that their stores also sell a lot of kids' games that don't require electricity and can substitute for TV. It also knows that when hurricanes are coming, people tend to drink more beer. So the minute Wal-Mart's meteorologists tell headquarters a hurricane is bearing down on Florida, its supply chain automatically adjusts to a hurricane mix in the Florida stores—more beer early, more Pop-Tarts later."

Source: Thomas L. Friedman, *The World Is Flat* (New York: Farrar, Straus and Giroux, 2005), p. 136.

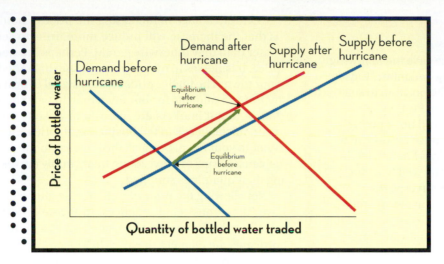

FIGURE **3.14**

PRICE INCREASES,
QUANTITY
INCREASES

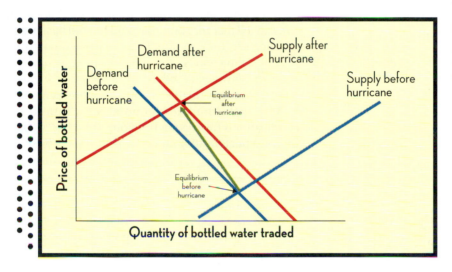

FIGURE **3.15**

PRICE INCREASES,
QUANTITY
DECREASES

example), then write on your exam that you can't be sure what happens without having more information about the relative magnitude of the supply and demand changes.

In general, if only supply or only demand change, then the effects on both quantity and price are predictable. When both curves shift, however, only one of the effects, either on price or on quantity, can be determined while the other is ambiguous.

PRICE GOUGING

In this example the market pushed up the price of bottled water. But sometimes the government stops markets from operating. Sometimes government officials believe that it's immoral for people to pay more for goods in a disaster. These officials feel that when firms raise prices in a disaster they are "price gouging" and should be stopped. But price gouging often benefits society.

One advantage of increasing the price of bottled water is that the increase will induce more firms to sell bottled water than they otherwise would. Perhaps at a new, higher price, businesses in other areas will ship in bottled water to your town. The higher price sends a signal to firms that water is more valuable in your town than in neighboring ones. Notice that if markets are allowed to operate, no government official needs to tell businesses to bring more bottled water to your town, because the increase in the price of water causes firms to move along their supply curves, increasing their quantities supplied.

Not allowing the price of water to rise after a disaster can have "disastrous" consequences. In Figure 3.16 below, the price of water before the hurricane was $1 a bottle. After the hurricane, the market price rises to $7 a bottle. At $7 a bottle, more bottled water is sold after than before the hurricane. But if the government didn't allow the price to rise above $1 a bottle, then zero bottles of water would be sold after the hurricane. We can tell that zero bottles would be sold because the price of $1 intersects the new supply curve when quantity is zero. The cost of selling goods after a hurricane may have gone up. If, therefore, firms can't sell their products for a higher price after a hurricane, they might decide to temporarily shut down.

You might think it's immoral for a firm to stop selling goods after a hurricane, but consider what is going on from the perspective of a store's employees. These employees

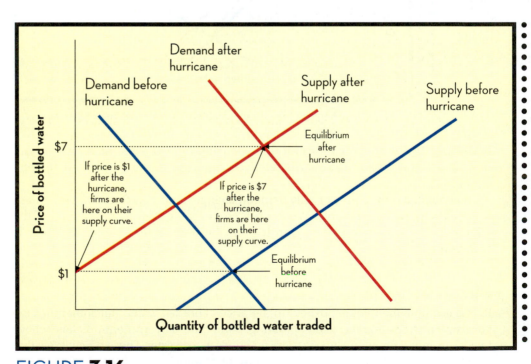

FIGURE **3.16**

THE MARKET FOR BOTTLED WATER

will likely live nearby and want to take care of their families and homes after the disaster. So the firm's owner might feel his social obligation is to let his employees stay home. Of course, if the firm can make an extremely large amount of money after a hurricane, the owner might beg his employees to come to work and perhaps offer them a large bonus.

Another advantage of allowing the price of bottled water to increase after a disaster is that it will cause consumers to use water more carefully. If the price of water stays at $1 a bottle, someone might buy 30 bottles and fill a bathtub. This will leave less water for other people to drink. If the price of water rises to $7 a bottle after a hurricane, however, far fewer people will use water for baths.

Price Gouging after Hurricane Katrina[4]
In 2005 Mississippi was devastated by hurricane Katrina. John Shepperson, who lived in Kentucky, realized that many people in Mississippi would be without power. To make some money, he bought 19 power generators in Kentucky. Shepperson then rented a U-Haul and drove 600 miles to Mississippi. He offered to sell his generators for "twice what he paid for them." Shepperson had many eager buyers.

The state of Mississippi, alas, makes it a crime to price gouge. Consequently, after a natural disaster it's illegal in Mississippi to sell goods at higher than normal prices. The police arrested Shepperson. His generators were confiscated and he was sent to jail for four days.

This price-gouging law is designed to protect Mississippians from greedy suppliers. But Shepperson would never have bought and shipped the generators 600 miles if he couldn't have charged high prices for them. The consequence of the price-gouging law, therefore, is to prevent self-interested people from selling goods in Mississippi after a natural disaster.

CONCLUSION TO MARKETS IN TIMES OF CRISES

This section examined how markets respond to crop destruction, wars, and hurricanes. In each case we showed how markets create incentives for consumers and firms to take beneficial actions that reduce the damage done by the disaster. And these beneficial actions are taken even when consumers and firms are guided by self-interest rather than altruism.

THE INVISIBLE HAND

Kids don't care about nutrition, but parents can still get their children to eat yucky vegetables. Parents often bribe their kids, for example, by giving them money, extra television time, or later bed times if the children eat foods such as broccoli, spinach, and carrots. A child who was concerned about nutrition would eat his vegetables. A child who wanted his parents' bribes would also eat his vegetables. So, parental bribes can cause kids to make the same eating choices as they would if they cared about nutrition. In an analogous manner, markets can induce selfish individuals to act as if they cared about the needs of society.

The great 18th century economist Adam Smith noted that the markets function as if guided by an *invisible hand* that causes people to act as if they were

> "Every individual endeavours to employ his capital so that its produce may be of the greatest value. . . . And he is in this led by an invisible hand to promote an end which was no part of his intention. By pursuing his own interest he frequently promotes that of the society more effectually than he really intends to promote it." —Adam Smith

altruistic. If consumers suddenly want more corn, the market causes farmers to grow more corn. Why? Not because farmers are necessarily concerned with the welfare of consumers, but rather because the increase in demand causes an increase in price, which in turn makes it more profitable for farmers to grow corn. Consequently, the invisible hand of the marketplace guides farmers to do what consumers need.

Similarly, markets respond to an energy shortage by raising the price of gas, resulting in consumers driving fewer miles. In response to an energy shortage, altruistic consumers will drive less because they care about their society and want to conserve gas. But a shortage also causes selfish consumers to drive less because it raises the price of gasoline. The invisible hand of the market thus causes the selfish to act as if they care about the needs of society.

It would certainly be nice to live in a society in which everyone cared about everyone else and took actions only for the betterment of all. Absent large-scale genetic engineering, however, most humans are likely to put their own self-interest ahead of the needs of their community. The genius of markets is that they cause selfish people to act as if they were altruistic. Restated, markets make it profitable to act as if you care about others.

Let's consider another example of market-induced altruism. Imagine that in a few years breakthroughs in genetic medicine mean that with great effort molecular biologists are able to cure many types of cancer. Altruistic college students who put the needs of society above their own desires might therefore decide to switch from studying economics to studying molecular biology. The increased demand for molecular biologists will cause their wages to rise. Consequently, selfish college students pushed by Adam Smith's invisible hand might also decide to switch from an economics to a molecular biology major. Either way, students will act as if they prioritize the needs of their society. As a result the number of molecular biologists will increase and more people will be cured of cancer.

BABYSITTER CERTIFICATION

Adam Smith's invisible hand is so powerful that it guides 12-year-old girls to learn how to care for choking toddlers. Many 12-year-old girls have the opportunity to take babysitting classes. These classes provide instruction on how to care for young children. Graduates of these classes usually receive a certificate. Parents often pay more money for babysitters who have such a certificate.

Notice that the government doesn't have to force 12-year-old girls to take babysitting classes. An altruistic 12-year-old babysitter would take a babysitting class so she could better care for kids. A self-interested 12-year-old babysitter would take a babysitting class so she could earn more money. And I imagine many babysitters take the classes for both altruistic and monetary reasons. Of course, if a choking toddler is saved by a babysitter who learned the rescue technique in a babysitting class, then no one would really care what her motives for taking the class were.

TWO MORE APPLICATIONS OF SUPPLY AND DEMAND
WHY DIAMONDS COST MORE THAN WATER

Diamonds might be forever but water is life. Go only a day without water and thirst blots out all other feelings. Go two days and the pain from dehydration overwhelms you. Go five days and you die.

But try trading an entire glass of water for a tiny diamond. Why do markets place higher value on unneeded diamonds than on precious water? Because water is in much greater supply than diamonds. If water were as rare as diamonds, its price would be far greater. But because the earth has literally oceans of water, the market price of water is very low. Figure 3.17 shows possible demand curves for both water and diamonds. From these two demand curves you should see that at every given price consumers want more water than diamonds. Figure 3.18 shows the effects when supply curves for both water and diamonds are added to our graph.

Because the supply of water is so much greater than the supply of diamonds, the equilibrium price of water is lower. This diamond/water example yields two lessons. First, market price is determined not only by a good's demand but also by its supply. Second, a good's price is influenced by its marginal value to consumers.

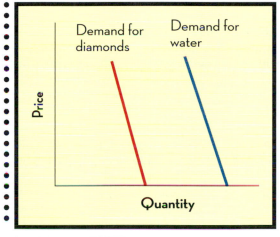

FIGURE 3.17
DEMAND CURVES FOR DIAMONDS AND WATER

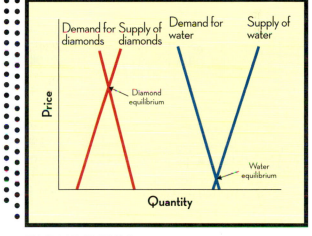

FIGURE 3.18
SUPPLY AND DEMAND CURVES FOR DIAMONDS AND WATER

MARGINAL VALUE

The marginal value of a good is how much value you received from the last unit of the good you consumed. So, if you eat 10 slices of pizza the marginal value of pizza to you is the most you would have paid for the 10th slice.

Economists assume that people usually receive less marginal value from a good the more they have of it. All this means is that as you have more of a good, you tend to "get sick of it" and get less and less pleasure from consuming each additional unit.

Imagine that the following chart illustrates the marginal value you get from water:

Unit Number	Marginal Value for the Last Unit of Water
1	Very, very high
2	$50,000
3	4,000
4	3,000
5	1,000
6	200
7	100
8	10
9	1
10	.50
11	.20
12	.10

Interpreting the chart: The marginal value is the amount of additional benefit you get for an extra unit. So the first unit of water gives you enormous benefit. The second unit of water gives you $50,000 of benefit. Once you already have two units of water, however, you get only $4,000 of additional benefit from receiving one more water unit. Although not shown on the chart, if you drink enough water you could actually get a negative value from consuming another glass.

Pretend that you already have 11 units of water. How much are you willing to pay for a 12th? The first 11 units of water satisfied most of your water needs, so you don't receive much added benefit from getting yet another water unit. According to the chart, therefore, the 12th unit of water is worth only 10 cents to you, so this is the most you would pay for it. It's true that you have received tremendous value from the water you have already consumed, but in deciding whether to purchase a 12th unit of water, the benefit you received from the first 11 units is irrelevant; all that matters is the benefit you could get from the 12th.

There is so much water in the world that the market will reach equilibrium only if most everyone consumes huge amounts of water. In terms of our example, this essentially means that markets must convince large numbers of people to consume their 12th unit of water and so the market price of water must be at most 10 cents.

> If you get married you will spend a huge amount of time with your spouse. So be sure that the person you marry is not someone from whom you receive significantly diminishing marginal value the more time you spend together.

ENVIRONMENTAL PROTECTION AND HOUSING MARKETS

Let's conclude this chapter by using supply and demand to analyze the ripple effects of a government law restricting housing development. Governments often limit the rights of property owners. For example, to protect the environment and prevent urban sprawl, governments frequently forbid construction on certain parcels of privately owned land. If you own such land and build on it, you can go to prison.

Let's consider how antidevelopment laws affect housing markets. Imagine that some local government enacts an antidevelopment law prohibiting construction on 50 percent of all currently undeveloped land.

Step 1: The Market for Developable Land

Property developers often buy large tracts of land on which to build houses. But developers can build houses only on developable land—land on which you can build legally. So to understand how an antidevelopment law influences the housing market, we must first determine how it affects the market for developable land.

The supply curve of developable land represents the amount of such land owners will sell at every given price. Clearly, our antidevelopment law will reduce the supply of developable land and so move us to a new equilibrium. As Figure 3.19 shows, the decrease in supply caused by the antidevelopment law will raise the price and decrease the quantity traded of developable land.

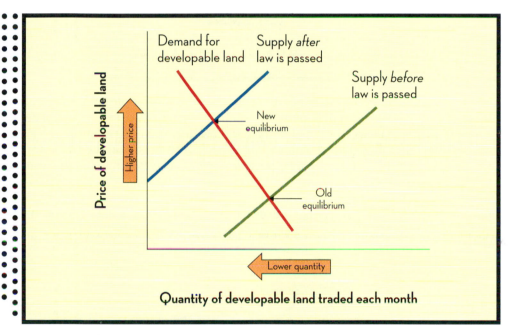

FIGURE **3.19**

MARKET FOR
DEVELOPABLE LAND

67

Step 2: The Market for Newly Built Housing

Next, let's consider how the increase in the price of developable land affects the market for newly built housing. Remember, anything that increases the cost to producers will decrease supply. Since the price of developable land represents a major cost to firms that build and then sell new housing, higher land prices will reduce the supply of newly built housing, shifting the supply curve left. Figure 3.20 shows that the decrease in supply caused by the higher price of developable land will raise the price and decrease the quantity of newly built homes.

Step 3: The Market for Previously Occupied Homes

You have two choices when you buy a home. You can either purchase a newly built home from a property developer or purchase a previously occupied home from a homeowner.

FIGURE **3.20**

MARKET FOR
NEWLY BUILT
HOMES

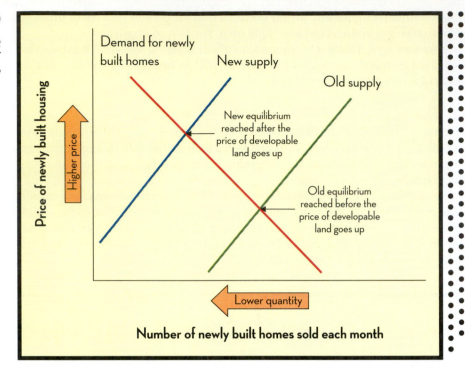

Market for newly built homes

Price of newly built housing

Higher price

Demand for newly built homes

New supply

Old supply

New equilibrium reached after the price of developable land goes up

Old equilibrium reached before the price of developable land goes up

Lower quantity

Number of newly built homes sold each month

Owners of previously occupied homes don't need to buy developable land since their houses are already situated on property. Consequently, an increase in the price of developable land won't affect the supply curve for previously occupied homes.

Newly built and previously occupied homes are substitutes, however, as buyers in the market for one usually consider purchasing the other. Recall that if the price of a good's substitute increases, the demand for the original good increases. Consequently, the increase in price of newly built homes that occurred in step 2 will increase the demand for previously occupied homes. As Figure 3.21 shows, the

FIGURE **3.21**

MARKET FOR
PREVIOUSLY BUILT
HOMES

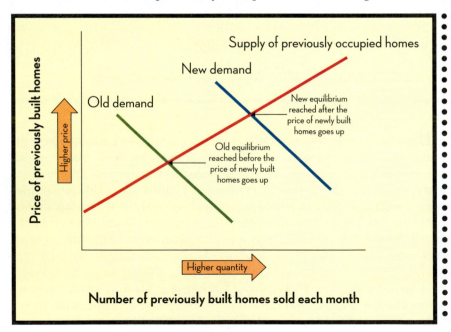

Market for previously built homes

Price of previously built homes

Higher price

Supply of previously occupied homes

New demand

Old demand

New equilibrium reached after the price of newly built homes goes up

Old equilibrium reached before the price of newly built homes goes up

Higher quantity

Number of previously built homes sold each month

increase in demand causes an increase in both price and quantity traded of previously built homes.

In sum, the antidevelopment law will move markets to new equilibria in which (1) the price of newly built homes increases, (2) the price of previously occupied homes increases, (3) the quantity of new homes built each month decreases, and (4) the quantity of previously occupied homes sold each month increases.

Housing Market Dynamics

It takes varying amounts of time for different markets to reach equilibrium, so let's trace out how our housing markets will respond over time to the antidevelopment law. Imagine that there are two types of land whose contingent values are given by the following table:

Type of Land	Price (per acre) before the Antidevelopment Law Is Proposed	After the Antidevelopment Proposal Is Enacted, Can You Legally Build on This Type of Land?	Price (per acre) after the Antidevelopment Law Is Enacted
Type A	$30,000	Yes	$50,000
Type B	30,000	No	10,000

As you can see from the table, the antidevelopment law will raise the price of Type A land to $50,000 (reflecting the decrease in supply) but lower the price of Type B land to $10,000 because developers now can't build on it. But when will these price changes occur?

Political Markets Imagine that a powerful state senator has just announced that he will propose an antidevelopment law and political observers expect his law to be enacted in one month. The price of Type A and Type B land will change immediately and not wait one month until the law actually passes. If, for example, people expect that Type A land will be worth $50,000 in one month, no one will sell Type A land today for $30,000. Sometimes market prices anticipate future events and don't wait until the expected event actually occurs.

An unethical senator could profit from proposing an antidevelopment law. For example, before announcing his proposal our senator could buy Type A land for $30,000 and then sell this land after his proposal passes into law. The senator could also profit by classifying land as Type A or Type B based on which landowners contributed to his campaign. The advantage of this last approach is that the senator wouldn't leave any direct evidence to his corruption. Rather, he could count on landowners figuring out, based on past experience, that the senator doesn't propose laws harmful to the interests of his campaign contributors.

Housing Markets Let's leave political markets and return to the market for housing. After the antidevelopment law has been proposed, the price of Type A land will rise. Home builders will immediately try to increase their prices because it will now cost them more to build a new house. But some of these builders will be locked into contracts under which they already promised customers houses at certain fixed prices. These contracts will have been signed before the building companies knew that the antidevelopment law would be proposed, so it will take awhile for builders to be able to raise their prices to all customers.

A jump in the price of newly built homes will immediately cause potential home-buyers to look more at previously occupied homes. Consequently, sellers of previously occupied homes will get lucky and see an immediate increase in demand and in the price of their homes.

Interestingly, even if the buyers and sellers of previously occupied homes don't know about the antidevelopment law, the price of previously occupied homes will still go up. Imagine that builders, but not individual home buyers and sellers, follow politics closely enough to know that an antidevelopment law has been proposed. The builders will raise the price of newly built homes, causing home buyers to look more at previously occupied houses. These home buyers won't know why the price of newly built homes has increased, but this ignorance won't stop them from understanding that higher prices of newly built homes means they should increase their demand for previously occupied homes. Similarly, sellers of previously occupied homes won't understand why more people are suddenly interested in buying their homes. But so what? These sellers will still realize that the greater demand for their homes means they can now get a higher sale price. Markets are often moved by information that is unknown to buyers and sellers, meaning that a market can be smarter than any of its participants.

Our housing market analysis is not quite over because the quantity traded of previously occupied homes will not immediately increase to its new supply-and-demand-determined equilibrium. For example, consider an elderly widow who is considering retiring to a warmer climate but who doesn't think she can quite afford to move. Three months after the antidevelopment law is passed, however, she realizes that her neighbors are getting relatively high prices for their homes and so she starts looking for a new place to live in Florida. Two months later she finds a new Florida home and puts her old house on the market. It therefore took five months for the increase in housing prices to cause this widow to try to sell her home. It's easy to draw supply and demand curves and label the equilibrium. But remember, markets often take a long time to reach this equilibrium.

QUESTIONS YOU SHOULD BE ABLE TO ANSWER AFTER READING THIS CHAPTER

1 Why is the market equilibrium the point of intersection between the supply and demand curves? (pages 47–49)

2 When does a surplus arise? (page 48)

3 How do markets react to surpluses? (page 48)

4 When does a shortage arise? (page 49)

5 How do markets react to shortages? (page 49)

6 What are two characteristics of supply and demand equilibria? (page 51)

7 Do markets move to new equilibria instantaneously? (page 51)

8 What are some examples of forces that can disturb market equilibria? (pages 53–54)

9 Are markets more often in equilibrium or nonequilibrium? (page 53)

10 Why does a higher price of food cause farmers to grow more food? (page 56)

11 Why does a higher price of oil cause consumers to use less oil? (page 56)

12 If two forces move in opposite directions do they always cancel each other out? (page 60)

13 If both supply and demand change, how do you determine what happens to price and quantity? (pages 60–61)

14 What is price gouging? (pages 61–62)

15 What are some of the benefits of having a high price of a good after a disaster? (page 63)

16 What is Adam Smith's "invisible hand"? (pages 63–64)

17 Why does water cost less than diamonds? (page 65)

18 How does marginal value relate to the price of water? (pages 65–66)

STUDY PROBLEMS

1 Essay question. Consider a country of 100 million people. Assume that a dangerous flu virus is predicted to strike this country in a month. Fortunately, people who take a vaccine will not get the flu. Unfortunately, only 40 million doses of the vaccine are available and it would take at least a year to make more doses. While anyone could potentially die from this flu, children and the elderly face the greatest chance of death if they catch this flu virus. All the flu vaccines are owned by a company. Normally, the company would sell the vaccines to the people willing to pay the most. The government, however, could force the company to give the government all doses of the vaccine. The government could then give the vaccine to those it deems in most need. Do you think that the government should take control of the vaccine?

2 The demand and supply of a good increase. What happens to price and quantity?

3 The demand and supply of a good decrease. Draw three separate supply and demand diagrams. On the first, price should increase; on the second, price should decrease; and on the third, price should stay the same.

4 Everyone would agree that economists are far less important to an economy than sanitation workers are, yet in market economies, economists usually earn more than sanitation workers do. Why in market economies do relatively less valuable economists receive higher wages than absolutely vital sanitation workers?

5 How does a market economy work through supply and demand to eliminate shortages or surpluses? Use a graph in your explanation.

6 Omega-S is a product made with steel. Omega-W is a product made with wood. Assume that a significant percentage of the steel produced in the world is used to make Omega-S. Also assume that Omega-S and Omega-W are substitutes for consumers. How will an increase in the price of wood influence the price of steel? Justify your answer using three supply and demand diagrams.

7 In his science fiction comedy *The Hitchhiker's Guide to the Galaxy,* Douglas Adams writes of a world destroyed by an overabundance of shoes:[5]

Many years ago [there] was a thriving, happy planet—people, cities, shops, a normal world. Except that on the high streets of these cities there were slightly more shoe shops than one might have thought necessary. And slowly, insidiously, the numbers of these shoe shops were increasing. It's a well-known economic phenomenon but tragic to see it in operation, for the more shoe shops there were, the more shoes they had to make and the worse and more unwearable they became. And the worse they were to wear, the more people had to buy to keep themselves shod, and the more the shops proliferated, until the whole economy of the place passed what I believe is termed the Shoe Event Horizon, and it became no longer economically possible to build anything other than shoe shops. Result—collapse, ruin and famine.*

Evaluate the economic plausibility of Adams's shoe scenario. True, his conclusion seems silly, but what are the economic flaws in his logic chain?

8 The following headline appeared in the U.K. paper the *Times Online:* "World 'Cannot Meet Oil Demand.'" What's wrong with this headline?[6]

9 All the gas stations in a state used to be self-service, meaning that drivers had to pump their own gas. The state, however, mandated that all gas stations become full-service, meaning that a gas station attendant must pump gas for customers. Assume that for the same price of gas, consumers would prefer full- to self-service. What will happen to the price and quantity traded of gas in this state?

10 Last year the price of grapes was lower than it is this year. Yet, last year consumers bought fewer grapes than they did this year. Does this violate the Law of Demand?

11 What's wrong with this picture? Relate your answer to a concept covered in this chapter.

*From *The Hitchhiker's Guide to the Galaxy,* by Douglas Adams, © 1979 by Douglas Adams. Used by permission of Harmony Books, a division of Random House, Inc.

"POLICY MAKERS WHO IGNORE ELASTICITIES ARE QUITE LIKELY TO MAKE BAD POLICY."

John Palmer, Economist[1]

CHAPTER 4

The Law of Demand forces a cruel trade-off on firms. Firms want high prices for their goods. But they also hope many consumers will buy their products. Alas, by the Law of Demand, higher prices mean fewer interested customers. The Law of Demand, however, is silent over exactly how many customers are lost when prices increase.

Imagine that Pepsi considers increasing its price by 20 percent. Pepsi knows that higher prices drive away some customers. But how many? If the 20 percent price increase caused only 1 percent fewer people to buy Pepsi, then the drink maker would want to increase prices. But if, however, the 20 percent price increase resulted in 90 percent fewer customers, then Pepsi certainly wouldn't want to raise prices, so Pepsi needs to learn how responsive its quantity demanded is to price changes.

Fortunately for Pepsi, economists have an elegant measure of the responsiveness of quantity demanded to changes in price: price elasticity of demand.

PRICE ELASTICITY OF DEMAND

$$\text{Price elasticity of demand} = \frac{\text{Percentage change in quantity demanded}}{\text{Percentage change in price}}$$

So if a 10 percent price increase causes a 30 percent fall in quantity demanded, then

price elasticity of demand $= \dfrac{-30\%}{10\%} = -3$, meaning that the percentage change in

ELASTICITIES

LEARNING OBJECTIVES

AFTER READING THIS CHAPTER, YOU SHOULD BE ABLE TO:

- Understand the concept of price elasticity of demand.
- Identify factors that influence the price elasticity of demand.
- Explain the relationship between price elasticity of demand and total revenue.
- Define income elasticity of demand and cross elasticity of demand.
- Understand the concept of price elasticity of supply.
- Identify factors that influence the price elasticity of supply.

quantity demanded is three times greater than the percentage change in price. If the price elasticity of demand was –6, then the percentage change in quantity demanded would be six times as much as the percentage change in price. Elasticity measures responsiveness. The more elastic demand is, the more responsive quantity demanded is to price changes. Before studying price elasticity of demand in greater detail, let's consider three nonprice examples of responsiveness.

1. **Tummy elasticity**—You want to lose weight and shrink your tummy, so you run one hour a day for a year. The running will cause you to lose weight, but how much? If your tummy is very responsive (or elastic) to exercise, then you might lose 15 pounds over the year. In contrast, if your tummy is relatively unresponsive (or inelastic) to exercise, you might lose only an ounce of mass this year.

2. **Dating elasticity**—You meet someone at a party you really want to date. How much good will flirting with him/her do? Perhaps the object of your desire would never date you. In this situation, he/she is completely unresponsive

$$\text{Elasticity} = \frac{\text{Percentage change in one variable}}{\text{Percentage change in another variable}}$$

(perfectly inelastic) to your flirting efforts. If, however, flirting will greatly increase the chance of him/her accepting a date with you, then he/she is highly responsive (or elastic) to your flirting.

3. **Grade elasticity**—Studying increases your grades, but by how much? For some types of exams, extensive studying improves performance only slightly. These exams are unresponsive (or inelastic) to studying. For other exams, you can greatly improve your grade even through modest studying. These exams are very responsive (or highly elastic) to studying.

CATEGORIZING ELASTICITY

Recall that the price elasticity of demand measures how responsive quantity demanded is to changes in price. Due to the Law of Demand, the price elasticity of demand is always negative. If the price of a good increases (meaning that the percentage change in price is positive), then quantity demanded must decrease (meaning that the percentage change in quantity demanded is negative). Similarly, a decrease in price causes an increase in quantity demanded. Restated, by the Law of Demand, percentage changes in price and percentage changes in quantity demanded always move in opposite directions.

Negative signs cause confusion when discussing whether elasticity is high or low, so because all price elasticities of demand are negative, **we will hereafter ignore negative signs when discussing price elasticities of demand.**

Elasticities fall into three categories:

1. If the price elasticity of demand is **greater than 1,** then demand is **elastic.** Quantity demanded changes by a greater percentage than price does.
2. If the price elasticity of demand is **less than 1,** then demand is **inelastic.** Quantity demanded changes by a smaller percentage than price does.
3. If the price elasticity of demand **equals 1,** then demand is **unit elastic.** Quantity demanded changes by the same percentage as price does. (Unit means one.)

For example:

A. If a 10 percent decrease in price causes a 40 percent increase in quantity demanded, then the price elasticity of demand is 4 and demand is labeled as elastic. Quantity demanded in this situation is very responsive to price changes.

B. If a 100 percent increase in price causes only a 20 percent decrease in quantity demanded, then the price elasticity of demand is .2 and demand is labeled as inelastic. Quantity demanded in this case is relatively unresponsive to price changes.

C. If a 15 percent increase in price causes a 15 percent decrease in quantity demanded, then quantity demanded changes by the same percentage as price does. The price elasticity of demand thus equals 1 and is labeled as unit elastic.

ELASTICITIES AND THE SHAPE OF DEMAND CURVES

Elasticities shape demand curves. The demand curve in Figure 4.1 is elastic. On this demand curve a relatively small percentage change in price causes a big percentage

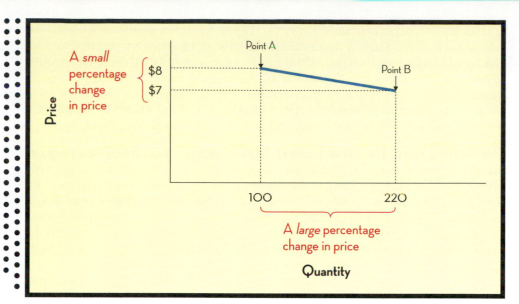

FIGURE **4.1**

A RELATIVELY ELASTIC DEMAND CURVE

The price elasticity of demand between Point A and Point B is high.

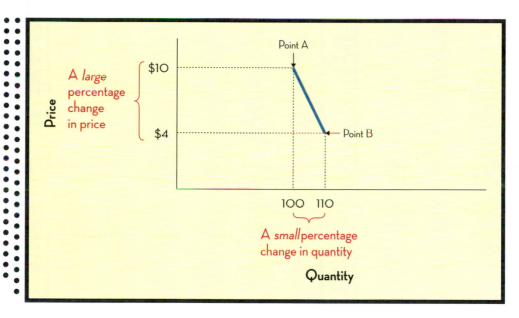

FIGURE **4.2**

A RELATIVELY INELASTIC DEMAND CURVE

The price elasticity of demand between Point A and Point B is low.

change in quantity demanded. As we move along the demand curve from Point A to Point B, the percentage change on the X-axis (quantity) is greater than the percentage change on the Y-axis (price).

The demand curve in Figure 4.2 is inelastic. On this demand curve, a large percentage change in price causes a relatively smaller percentage change in quantity. Restated, as we move along the demand curve, the percentage change on the X-axis (quantity) is smaller than the percentage change on the Y-axis (price).

Perfectly Inelastic Demand Curves Figure 4.3 shows a perfectly inelastic demand curve where quantity demanded is constant and so does not respond to price changes. In other words, no matter how much you change price in Figure 4.3, quantity demanded doesn't change. Mathematically, this results in the percentage change in quantity demanded being zero. Since zero divided by anything is zero, this results in the price elasticity of demand always being zero. The demand curve in Figure 4.3, however, violates the Law of Demand and so doesn't exist in the real world.

Perfectly Elastic Demand Curves The easiest way to understand a perfectly elastic demand curve is to consider one, such as Figure 4.4, which is *almost* perfectly elastic. If we increase the price in this figure by a mere one penny from $4 to $4.01, then quantity demanded plummets from 20 to 1. Quantity demanded, therefore, is extremely responsive to price changes. The closer the demand curve is to being flat, the closer it is to being perfectly elastic. The flatter a demand curve is, the smaller the price change is that you need to radically change quantity demanded. A perfectly elastic demand curve, such as in Figure 4.5, is completely flat.

Think of a ball as the quantity demanded of a good. Think of price as a mallet used to hit that ball. The more elastic the ball, the farther it moves when hit by the price

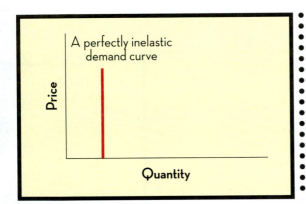

FIGURE **4.3**

A PERFECTLY INELASTIC DEMAND CURVE

FIGURE **4.4**

AN EXTREMELY ELASTIC DEMAND CURVE

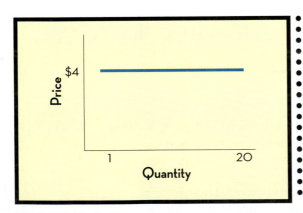

FIGURE **4.5**

A PERFECTLY ELASTIC DEMAND CURVE

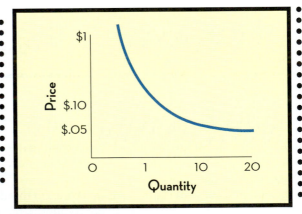

FIGURE **4.6**

DEMAND CURVE WITH ELASTICITY ALWAYS EQUAL TO 1

mallet. If the ball is perfectly inelastic, then it doesn't move at all when hit. If the ball is perfectly elastic then even the smallest tap will cause it to move an infinite amount.

Price Elasticity of Demand Equals 1

Figure 4.6 shows a demand curve with a price elasticity of demand always equal to one. (Don't worry about how we derived it.) Figure 4.6 also demonstrates that elasticity is not the same as slope, since the slope of the demand curve in Figure 4.6 is not constant although the elasticity is.

Elasticity Along a Straight-Line Demand Curve that Goes from Axis to Axis

Imagine that quantity demanded initially is one. Quantity demanded then increases to three. The *absolute* change in quantity demanded is only two units. The *percentage* change in quantity demanded, however, is huge. (See the appendix for how to calculate percentage changes in quantity and price.) Now assume that quantity demanded is 1,000. Assume again that quantity demanded increases by two. The percentage increase in quantity demanded is now very low. The same two-unit increase in quantity demanded causes a much bigger percentage change in quantity demanded when quantity demanded is low than when it is high. In general, for a given absolute change in quantity demanded, the percentage change in quantity demanded is higher the lower the initial quantity demanded. And indeed if you start with quantity demanded of zero, then any increase in quantity demanded causes an infinite percentage increase in quantity demanded.

As you recall, price elasticity of demand is defined as:

$$\text{Price elasticity of demand} = \frac{\text{Percentage change in quantity demanded}}{\text{Percentage change in price}}$$

Near the top of the demand curve in Figure 4.7, quantity demanded is very small. Consequently, when you move down a little on the demand curve, you get a very large percentage increase in quantity demanded.

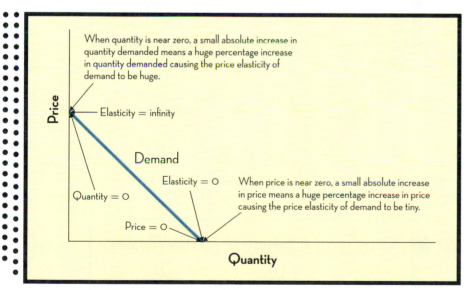

FIGURE 4.7

ELASTICITY ALONG A STRAIGHT-LINE DEMAND CURVE

Imagine that I start a Church of Microeconomics and on the first day of the church's existence I am the only member. On day two my wife joins. Membership in my church just doubled! So, in its second day of existence my church experienced faster growth (measured in percentage change in membership) than any of the world's major religions, surely a sign that my church is blessed. Well, actually, it's really easy to get high percentage changes when you start out with a low base.

So, at the top of the demand curve (where quantity demanded is almost zero), when you decrease price a little you get a huge percentage increase in quantity demanded, meaning that the price elasticity of demand is extremely high. Similarly, near the bottom of the demand curve (where the price is almost zero), when you increase price the percentage change in price is astronomically high, making the price elasticity of demand almost zero.

PRICE ELASTICITIES OF DEMAND AND TOTAL REVENUE

Imagine that you run a lemonade stand and want to bring in more total revenue. Should you increase or decrease price? Total revenue, which is simply how much money a firm takes in from customers, is defined as sales times price. (Sales is the same as quantity demanded when the market is at equilibrium. We assume in this chapter that the market is always at equilibrium.) If you sell 100 glasses of lemonade a day for $.25 a glass, your total revenue is $25 a day. The price elasticity of demand is vitally important to you and other firms because it tells you if lowering or increasing price boosts total revenue.

It's easy to understand how elasticities affect total revenue when you consider extreme, if unrealistic, cases. Assume that you can sell lemonade for either 10 or 20 cents a glass. Let's first say that the demand for lemonade is extremely elastic, meaning that you will have far, far more customers when you charge 10 cents.

Price	Sales	Total Revenue
$.10	50/day	$5/day
.20	2/day	.40/day

Lemonade Sales with Highly *Elastic* Demand

As the above example shows, when demand is highly elastic, you have greater total revenues at lower prices. Since demand is extremely elastic, when you raise the price of lemonade you lose a tremendous number of customers, so total revenue plummets. Similarly, when demand is extremely elastic and you lower price, you gain a huge number of customers and so your total revenue soars.

Now imagine that the demand for your lemonade is extremely inelastic, meaning that you lose very few customers when you raise price.

Price	Sales	Total Revenue
$.10	50/day	$5/day
.20	48/day	9.60/day

Lemonade Sales with Highly *Inelastic* Demand

With highly inelastic demand, when you increase price, you lose few customers and so your total revenue increases. Similarly, when you cut prices, you gain few customers and so cutting prices reduces your total revenue.

$$\text{Total revenue} = (\text{Price}) \times (\text{Sales})$$

By the Law of Demand, higher prices mean lower sales. Whenever demand is *elastic*, a percentage increase in price causes a correspondingly greater percentage decrease in sales, so raising prices when demand is elastic decreases total revenue. Similarly, with elastic demand a percentage decrease in price causes a proportionally greater percentage increase in sales, increasing total revenue.

The reverse holds for *inelastic* demand. Inelastic demand means that quantity demanded changes by a lower percentage than price does, so increasing price increases total revenue, whereas decreasing price causes a decrease in total revenue.

If demand is unit elastic, any percentage change in price is matched by an equal but opposite percentage decrease in sales. With unit elastic demand, therefore, total revenue stays the same when price changes.

Here's an easy way to remember the relationship between price and total revenue: When demand is elastic, price and total revenue "stretch apart" like the two ends of an elastic rubber band, meaning that if you pull price in one direction, total revenue moves in the other. (So if you increase price, total revenue decreases.) In contrast, when demand is inelastic, price and total revenue don't stretch apart. When you pull price in one direction, total revenue also moves in that direction.

The following table summarizes total revenue and price elasticity of demand:

Price Elasticity of Demand	Effect of a Price Increase	Effect of a Price Decrease
Elastic	Total revenue decreases	Total revenue increases
Unit elasticity	No change in total revenue	No change in total revenue
Inelastic	Total revenue increases	Total revenue decreases

Summary of Total Revenue and Price Elasticity of Demand

Graphing Total Revenue

We can show graphically how price changes affect total revenue, but first we need to establish how to illustrate total revenue on a graph. Imagine that a firm sells three goods at $2 apiece. Total revenue is simply $2 times three, or $6. If we put price on the Y-axis and sales on the X-axis, then total revenue is illustrated by the area contained in the six boxes in Figure 4.8.

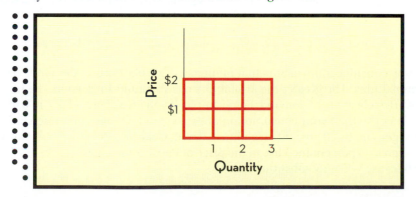

FIGURE **4.8**

TOTAL REVENUE GRAPH

If we know a good's price, we can use the good's demand curve to show its total revenue. Figures 4.9 and 4.10 graphically show the total revenue for a good that has an elastic demand curve. As you should see, the total revenue is bigger in Figure 4.10 where the price is lower. Figures 4.11 and 4.12 graphically show the total revenue for a good that has an inelastic demand. The total revenue is greater in Figure 4.11 where the price is higher.

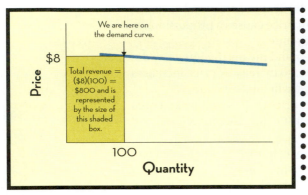

FIGURE **4.9**

TOTAL REVENUE AND A VERY ELASTIC DEMAND CURVE

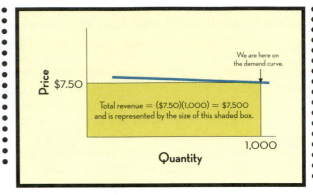

FIGURE **4.10**

TOTAL REVENUE AND A VERY ELASTIC DEMAND CURVE, LOWER PRICE

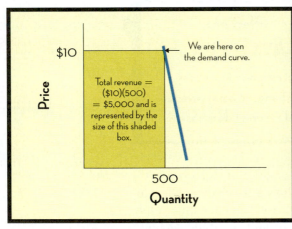

FIGURE **4.11**

TOTAL REVENUE AND A VERY INELASTIC DEMAND CURVE

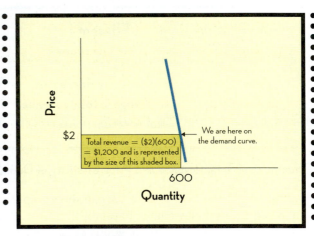

FIGURE **4.12**

TOTAL REVENUE AND A VERY INELASTIC DEMAND CURVE, LOWER PRICE

BEHIND PRICE ELASTICITY OF DEMAND: SUBSTITUTES

Let's now consider some factors that influence price elasticity of demand. We'll start with substitutes. The greater the availability of substitutes for a good, the higher the good's price elasticity of demand. For example, if you love cola and live in a town that has only Pepsi, then your consumption of Pepsi won't change very much if the price of Pepsi goes up by 20 percent. In contrast, if both Coke and Pepsi are available in your town, then a 20 percent increase in the price of Pepsi could cause you to drink far less Pepsi because you now substitute Coke.

Tuna Fish and Cat Food

Tuna Fish and Cat Food   The following table shows a hypothetical demand for cat food in a given town:

Price	Cat Food Sales/Month
$4	100,000
8	90,000

But then an article comes out in the town newspaper explaining that cats love tuna fish. Tuna fish and cat food, therefore, are substitutes. But tuna fish is more expensive than cat food. Let's assume that when cat food costs $4, no cat owner gives her feline tuna. But when the price of cat food is $8, then 20,000 owners decide to pay a little extra to give their cat the best. Consequently, the new demand for cat food is as follows:

Price	Cat Food Sales/Month
$4	100,000
8	70,000

Notice that tuna fish has increased the price elasticity of demand for cat food. When cat food producers raise prices, they lose some customers to tuna companies. Consequently, tuna makes the quantity demanded for cat food more responsive to increases in the price of cat food. Also, when cat food companies lower prices, they capture some customers who used to feed their pets tuna. As a result, tuna also makes the quantity demanded of cat food more responsive to decreases in the price of cat food. Substitutes therefore increase price elasticity of demand.

Chinese Restaurants

Chinese Restaurants   Let's see how the existence of substitutes affects two Chinese restaurant owners:

Sam—who owns the only Chinese restaurant in Deerfield.

Joseph—who owns one of the five Chinese restaurants in his town of Greenfield.

To keep everything simple, assume that people eat only at restaurants in their own town. If Sam cuts prices, he will draw in customers who normally don't eat at Chinese restaurants. If Joseph cuts prices, he will draw in these customers plus those who had previously eaten at one of the other Chinese restaurants in his town. The other four restaurants' existence proves to Joseph that many people in his town like Chinese food but are as yet unwilling to eat at his place. Thus, Joseph knows that if he cuts prices, he could draw in these Chinese food diners. Because there are close substitutes for Joseph's restaurant but not Sam's, Joseph has more reason than Sam does to believe that reducing prices will increase quantity demanded.

Similarly, Joseph will lose more customers by raising prices than Sam would. If Sam increases prices, he will lose only those customers who now stop eating restaurant Chinese food. If Joseph increases prices, he will lose not only these people but also those who decide to go to a different Chinese restaurant. Consequently, the existence of substitutes makes the price elasticity of demand for Joseph higher than for Sam.

In general, substitutes make the quantity demanded for goods more responsive to price changes because:

- Firms that lower prices take away customers from their products' substitutes.
- Substitute products draw customers away from firms that raise prices.

Again, we see that substitutes increase a good's price elasticity of demand.

Snowboarding   Imagine that you sell custom-made snowboards in a New Hampshire town. The nearest competing store is two hours away.

But then one day snowboarders discover the Internet. Recognizing the Internet's potential, you create your own online store. You now sell custom-made snowboards throughout the world. But, alas, the Internet doesn't just offer you a business upside. People who live near your store can now ignore you and buy custom-made snowboards from other online retailers. So, how has the Internet affected the price elasticity of demand for your snowboards? Take a look at Figure 4.13, below.

FIGURE **4.13**

THE DEMAND FOR
SNOWBOARDS

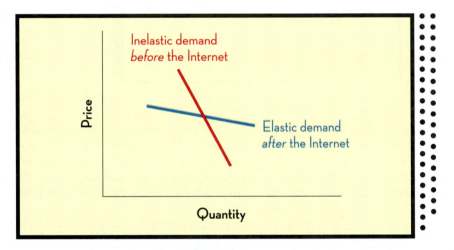

The Internet has made snowboards sold by other stores better substitutes for yours. Few customers would drive two hours just to save a couple of dollars. So before the Internet, you wouldn't lose any customers to competitors if you raised your prices a few dollars above what others charge. But on the Internet, the competition is always just a mouse click away. Consequently, if a comparable store offers slightly lower prices than you, your old customers may defect. Therefore, because of the Internet you lose more customers when you raise prices.

The Internet, however, also helps you attract customers when you lower prices. Imagine that your store is similar to one in Alaska. Before the Internet you would have been insane to lower your prices in the hope of winning away this store's customers. But the Internet puts you in direct competition with this store. So now if you lower prices you might acquire a few of this Alaskan store's clientele.

In sum: the Internet has increased the number of substitutes for your products. These additional substitutes mean you lose more customers when you raise prices and gain more customers when you lower prices. The Internet, therefore, has increased the price elasticity of demand for your snowboards.

Portable Phone Numbers   While you are shopping at the mall, a salesman tells you of his company's cell phone plan. You realize that this plan is better and cheaper than your current one. But all your friends and relatives already have your cell phone number. So you tell the salesman that although you like his plan, you don't want to go to the trouble of changing phone numbers.

This persistent salesman, however, says that you can keep your phone number if you switch to his plan. In 2003, he informs you, the U.S. Federal Communications Commission mandated that cell phone companies allow you to transfer your phone number when you change cell phone providers. Because you can keep your old number, you decide to switch to the new company.

Cell phone number portability increased the price elasticity of demand for cell phone plans. It did this by making different plans better substitutes for each other. Interestingly, most cell phone companies tried to use their political influence to stop mandatory phone number portability. Why do you think they attempted this?

BEHIND PRICE ELASTICITY OF DEMAND: BROAD PRODUCT DEFINITIONS

If the price of Pepsi goes up you can switch to Coke, but if the price of all drinks increases you can hardly go without liquids. Generally, the more broadly we define a product, the less elastic the product's demand is.

A narrowly defined product such as *Pepsi* has many substitutes, whereas a broadly defined good such as *drinks* has few. Analogously, there are closer substitutes for apples than for fruits or for Honda Accords than for automobiles. As we broaden the definition of a good, we reduce the number of substitutes available for that good and so reduce the good's price elasticity of demand.

BEHIND PRICE ELASTICITY OF DEMAND: NECESSITIES

Some goods, which consumers believe they *must* have, are called *necessities*. Imagine you spend $100 a week on both heart medication and restaurant meals. If the price of both doubles, you will likely keep buying the same quantity of heart medication but cut down on eating out. Generally, consumers are relatively less likely to shift away from buying necessities when the price of necessities increases. Necessities, therefore, usually have low price elasticities of demand.

Products that are necessities don't have very good substitutes. If, after all, a product had a good substitute then the product wouldn't be a necessity since you could take the substitute instead of the original product. Not having very good substitutes is another reason why necessities frequently have inelastic demands.

BEHIND PRICE ELASTICITY OF DEMAND: STRONG COMPLEMENTS

Two goods are strong complements if they almost always go together. In the developed world, most cats get vaccinated for rabies, making rabies vaccines and cats strong complements. So how does the fact that cat rabies vaccines have a strong complement affect the price elasticity of demand for rabies vaccines? The price of rabies vaccines makes up a small percentage of the price of cat ownership. Even if you were to double the price of these vaccines, you wouldn't change the demand for cats much, and so you would not significantly decrease the demand for rabies vaccines. Similarly, if the price of rabies vaccines fell to zero, not many more people would acquire cats, and so not many more rabies vaccines would be sold. The demand for cat rabies vaccines, therefore, is very price inelastic.

Most personal computers run on Microsoft's operating system. So, complementarily speaking, Microsoft's operating system is to personal computers as rabies vaccines are to cats. Since the price of Microsoft's operating system is a relatively small percentage of the price of a personal computer, the demand for this operating system is very price inelastic.

Companies sometimes deliberately create two products that are strong complements. Many computer printers require special ink cartridges. For example, imagine that Dell printers can use only Dell ink cartridges and Dell ink cartridges work only in Dell printers. Dell ink cartridges and printers, therefore, are strong complements. As a result of having a strong complement, the price elasticity of demand of Dell cartridges is low. If, for example, the price of Dell cartridges goes up, it would be very costly for you to switch to another firm's cartridges because switching cartridges would force you to buy another printer.

As of this writing the hottest electronic product is the iPod. The iPod is a portable music player. Imagine you bought a $200 iPod and then spent a thousand dollars on iPod accessories such as music files and wireless headphones. Let's assume that all of these complements work with the iPod but not with rival portable devices. These accessories are strong complements to iPods.

Suddenly, let's say, two very bad things happen to you. Your iPod breaks and the price of iPods doubles. Will you replace your old iPod with a new, more expensive one? Probably yes. Because you have so many iPod complements it would be very costly for you to switch to another portable music player. As a result of having many iPod complements, therefore, iPod's price elasticity of demand for you is low. And generally, as these examples have shown, having a strong complement reduces a good's price elasticity of demand.

SOME ACTUAL ELASTICITIES[2]

Good	Price Elasticity Demand
Liquor	.7
Christmas trees	.674
Food	.45
Electricity	.13
Jewelry	.41
Shoes	.73

BEHIND PRICE ELASTICITY OF DEMAND: TIME

If the price of heating oil drastically increases, in the short run you will save fuel by lowering your thermostat during the winter. In the long run you will save even more by installing insulation or perhaps even moving to a warmer climate. If the price of seafood decreases, in the short run you will buy more shrimp dinners. In the long run, however, you could master new seafood recipes, resulting in your buying even more shrimp. If the price of gas goes up, in the short run you might take fewer unnecessary trips. In the long run, however, you might purchase a more fuel-efficient car or buy a home closer to your workplace. We're more flexible in the long run than in the short term, so the price elasticity of demand is usually higher the more time consumers have to adjust to price changes.

Firms need to be wary of differing elasticities across time. If a firm increases its price and doesn't see much immediate drop in sales, this doesn't mean that the firm's customer base is safe. Its old customers might have only recently started searching for new substitutes.

BEHIND PRICE ELASTICITY OF DEMAND: SHARE OF INCOME SPENT ON A GOOD

If you spend 20 percent of your income on rent and your rent goes up, you are effectively much poorer than before and will likely have to cut back on everything, including the amount you spend on rent. In contrast, if you spend just 2 percent of your income on a good, then an increase in the price of that good won't have much effect on your overall wealth. Generally, the greater the percentage of your income you spend on a good, the more price elastic its demand is for you.

WHY ADDICTION FIRST INCREASES AND THEN DECREASES ELASTICITY

Goods such as cigarettes, alcohol, and heroin are addictive, meaning that once you get "hooked" on them, you suffer extreme displeasure if you don't continue to consume. You might think addictive goods have very inelastic demands. After all, if getting your next fix is all that matters, you will spend whatever you have to maintain your habit.

> "Drug misuse is not a disease, it is a decision, like the decision to move out in front of a moving car."—Philip K. Dick (author)[3]

But addiction cuts both ways and can make demand more inelastic *or* elastic. Most addictive goods are considered immoral, and this immorality makes it difficult for some to analyze rationally the behavior of addicts. So, let's invent some addictive good that has no moral taint: a pill that will help your allergies. Your doctor suggests you consider taking it, but gives you one warning: once you start using this pill your body will become dependent on it and you will have to take it for the rest of your life. How does this pill's addictiveness affect its elasticity?

When deciding whether to use this pill, you must now consider not only the cost of the pill today, but the money you will have to pay for it over your lifetime. The addictive nature of this pill has therefore made its price far more important to you. So before you start taking the pill, its addictive nature has made your demand more elastic. But after you become addicted, you will desperately need to keep taking the pill regardless of price, so your demand becomes very inelastic.

Some of you may have considered smoking. Although the main cost of smoking is to your health, the monetary costs of smoking are also far from trivial. If you start smoking today, you know there is a chance you will become addicted and be stuck with the monetary costs of smoking for the rest of your (shortened) life. The price of cigarettes, therefore, is more important to people contemplating smoking for the first time than the cost of pretzels is to potential first-time pretzel eaters. Consequently, although addiction might make the demand for cigarettes more inelastic for those who already smoke, addiction should increase the price elasticity of demand for tobacco for potential first-time smokers.

HOW ELASTICITY SUBVERTED A LUXURY TAX

In 1990 the U.S. government imposed an extra tax on several luxury goods, including yachts. But the demand for these luxury goods proved to be very elastic and the 10 percent tax on boats selling for over $100,000 caused a 70 percent drop in their sales, destroying around 25,000 jobs. Bowing to the power of elasticities, the government repealed the tax in 1993.

The U.S. government enacted the luxury sales tax because they thought it would be paid by the rich. But because the rich had a high price elasticity of demand for the taxed items, they avoided paying the tax by not buying yachts. The luxury tax ended up causing the most harm to the lower middle class workers who used to build the yachts.

AN ELASTICITY MYSTERY

You work part time at Freedom Gyms. Three months ago Freedom Gyms cut its monthly membership fee from $40 to $20 at both of its locations. You overhear Freedom Gyms' owner wondering why the price cut had such different effects on her two gyms. Feeling ambitious, you tell the owner that you will use your knowledge of microeconomics to explain the different customer responses to the price cut, if she gives you $1,000. The owner agrees.

First, you use elasticities to quantify mathematically how membership at both gyms changed in response to the price reductions. You find that the price elasticity of demand for the Freedom Gym you work at is 1.44, while the price elasticity of demand for the second location is .318. (See the appendix for the derivation of these elasticities.) So the price elasticity of demand is much higher for the first gym.

You remember from your microeconomics class that substitutes can have a large effect on price elasticities. The location you work at has a clear substitute as there is another almost identical gym less than a mile away that you in fact belonged to before you took your current job at Freedom Gyms. You can easily see why this other gym's existence combined with the $20/month price cut caused a significant increase in membership at the gym where you work. Customers previously at the other gym must have noticed Freedom Gyms' lower price and decided to switch memberships.

Unfortunately, you realize that the other Freedom Gym (which is located about 30 miles from yours) also has a nearby competitor, named Hayek-Workout, so you can't yet explain the radically differing elasticities. You remember, however, that your microeconomics professor claimed that economics was a science and you know that scientists often solve problems through investigation, so you decide to visit Hayek-Workout.

Shortly after arriving at Hayek-Workout, a salesman, thinking you're a prospective customer, offers you a day pass. You notice that Hayek-Workout has a swimming pool, something that Freedom Gyms lack. You also learn that Hayek-Workout has a popular aerobics instructor who looks like the actress Jessica Alba. Unusual for an aerobics teacher, she has somehow managed to attract many men to her workout classes. So it seems that the second Freedom Gym is not really a very good substitute for Hayek-Workout and this partially explains the lower price elasticity of demand for the second Freedom Gyms location.

As you are about to leave Hayek-Workout, the salesman starts talking to you about membership plans. Unlike all the other gyms in your city, it turns out that you must join Hayek-Workout for at least a year. (The other gyms in the city require you to join for only a month at a time.) Therefore, you now realize that the price elasticity of demand for Freedom Gyms' second location will probably be higher in the long run. This is because customers at Hayek-Workout who want to switch to Freedom Gyms because of the $20-per-month price cut won't make the switch until their Hayek-Workout membership expires.

After successfully explaining the differing elasticities to your boss, she gives you the promised $1,000 and, admiring your entrepreneurial spirit, a higher-paying job. You immediately decide to spend some of your bonus and higher salary purchasing laser eye surgery. Thinking again about microeconomics, you realize that being richer has affected your demand for the laser surgery.

SUMMARY OF WHAT AFFECTS PRICE ELASTICITIES OF DEMAND

- **Substitutes**—The better substitutes a good has, the higher is its price elasticity of demand.
- **Broad product definition**—The broader the definition of a product is, the lower is the good's price elasticity of demand.
- **Necessities**—Necessities have low price elasticities of demand.
- **Strong complements**—Having a strong complement reduces a good's price elasticity of demand.
- **Time**—The longer the time frame is, the higher is a good's price elasticity of demand.
- **Share of income**—Goods on which consumers spend a large percentage of their income have high price elasticities of demand.
- **Addiction**—If a consumer fears he could become addicted to a good, his price elasticity of demand will be high; if he is already addicted, it will be low.

INCOME ELASTICITY OF DEMAND

Elasticity measures responsiveness. The *price* elasticity of demand measures how quantity demanded responds to changes in price. In contrast, the *income* elasticity of demand measures how quantity demanded responds to changes in income.

The income elasticity of demand is formally defined as

$$\text{Income elasticity of demand} = \frac{\text{Percentage change in quantity demanded}}{\text{Percentage change in income}}$$

The income elasticity of demand is positive for normal goods and negative for inferior goods. As you recall from Chapter 2, the higher a consumer's income is, the *more normal* and the *fewer inferior* goods he purchases.

ECONOMIC DEVELOPMENT, THE ENVIRONMENT, AND INCOME ELASTICITIES

India and China have a combined population of over 2.3 billion people, and these countries' rapid economic growth promises to lift hundreds of millions of people out of poverty over the next 30 years. Many people fear that the world's environment will suffer as India's and China's economies grow.

Automobiles, air conditioning, and many other energy-guzzling goods have positive income elasticities of demand. Consequently, as these two nations prosper, humanity will almost certainly burn more energy, thereby increasing some forms

INDUSTRIAL CITY IN CHINA

of pollution. But environmentalists need not necessarily despair over India's and China's growth. Many environmental goods such as clean air, fresh drinking water, cute animals, forests, and wetlands also have positive income elasticities of demand, meaning that people also want more of these goods as they get richer. Consequently, as a nation gets richer, its citizens usually put more pressure on politicians to enact environmentally friendly laws.

CROSS ELASTICITY OF DEMAND

Cross elasticity of demand measures how the change in price of one good impacts the demand for another.

$$\text{Cross elasticity of demand} = \frac{\text{Percentage change in quantity demanded of good A}}{\text{Percentage change in the price of good B}}$$

If the price of Coke increased, then the quantity of Pepsi demanded, a substitute for Coke, would also increase. Therefore, the cross elasticity of demand for substitutes such as Coke and Pepsi is positive.

If the price of hotdogs increased, people would buy fewer hotdogs and consequently fewer hotdog buns, a complement of hotdogs. Therefore, the cross elasticity of demand for complements such as hotdogs and hotdog buns is negative.

FREE VERSUS SLAVE SUGAR

In the late 18th century, an English consumer could buy sugar grown in India or the Americas. At this time slave labor was used to grow American but not Indian sugar. Around 1791 some English consumers boycotted sugar made with slave labor.[4] How did this boycott affect the cross elasticity of demand between sugar made in India and sugar made in the Americas?

Ordinarily, sugar made in India and the Americas were substitutes, so their cross elasticity of demand was positive. This is because a decrease in the price of sugar from one area would normally cause consumers to buy less sugar from the other area.

Because of the boycott, some English consumers wouldn't buy American sugar regardless of prices. For these consumers, therefore, the cross elasticity of demand for the two sugars was zero because a change in the price of one type of sugar would have no effect on the quantity demanded for the other type of sugar. Taking the average for all British consumers, therefore, the boycott lowered the cross elasticity of demand between Indian and American sugar.

PRICE ELASTICITY OF SUPPLY

You own a college town music store that has to lower prices because of competition from illegal downloads. By the Law of Supply, lower prices mean you will offer less music, but how much less? You decide to fire two salespersons immediately and reduce your Sunday hours. In the long run, however, you realize that you will need to save rent by moving to a smaller space, and that will reduce sales even more.

Just as the price elasticity of demand quantifies how quantity demanded responds to price changes, the price elasticity of supply shows the responsiveness of quantity supplied to price changes. The higher the price elasticity of supply, the more quantity supplied increases when price increases.

$$\text{Price elasticity of supply} = \frac{\text{Percentage change in quantity supplied}}{\text{Percentage change in price}}$$

By the Law of Supply, an increase in price causes an increase in quantity supplied, whereas a price decrease causes a reduction in quantity supplied. Consequently, the Law of Supply makes the price elasticity of supply positive.

CATEGORIZING PRICE ELASTICITY OF SUPPLY

Price elasticities of supply are categorized analogously to price elasticities of demand.

1. **Elastic supply,** where quantity supplied **is very responsive** to price changes.
   If the percentage change in quantity supplied is greater than the percentage change in price, then the price elasticity of supply is **greater than one** and supply is considered elastic.
2. **Inelastic supply,** where quantity supplied **is relatively unresponsive** to price changes.
   If the percentage change in quantity supplied is less than the percentage change in price, then the price elasticity of supply **is less than one** and supply is labeled as inelastic.
3. **Unit elastic supply,** where quantity supplied changes **by the same percentage** as price does.
   If the price elasticity of supply **is equal to one,** then a change in price causes an equal percentage change in quantity supplied. Elasticities of one are labeled as **unit elastic.**

   Figure 4.14 shows an elastic supply curve, Figure 4.15 shows an inelastic curve, and Figure 4.16 shows a supply curve with unit elasticity.

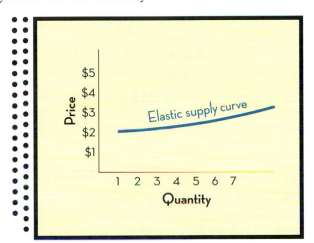

FIGURE **4.14**

ELASTIC SUPPLY CURVE

91

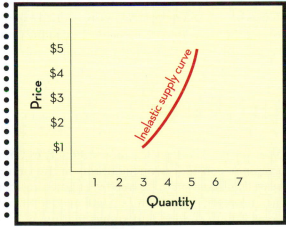

FIGURE **4.15**

INELASTIC SUPPLY CURVE

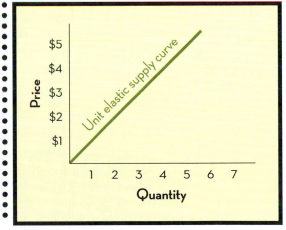

FIGURE **4.16**

UNIT ELASTIC SUPPLY CURVE

BEHIND PRICE ELASTICITY OF SUPPLY: COSTS

You're at a party when an extremely alluring person starts flirting with you. Do you take advantage of the opportunity? Well, it depends on the costs. Perhaps you're in a great relationship that you would have to end to date this attractive person, so you ignore the flirting. Or, maybe this attractive person lives 100 miles away, and so starting a relationship would involve too much travel time. Only if the costs are low enough will you pursue this new romantic opportunity.

When the price of a good increases, firms gain additional opportunities. For example, pretend that the price of steel sold in Minneapolis unexpectedly increases. Your firm doesn't currently make steel, but it could. Perhaps, however, to free up factory capacity to make steel, you would have to stop making aluminum. But you make a huge profit manufacturing aluminum, so the opportunity costs of making steel are too high. Or perhaps you can make steel cheaply in Buffalo, but the costs of shipping steel from Buffalo to Minneapolis are excessive. Only if the costs of making steel are relatively low will you start selling steel.

Generally, whether firms can produce a new product profitably depends on costs. The lower the costs of entering a market, the more firms will enter when market prices increases. These firms will produce additional goods and so increase quantity supplied. Consequently, low costs result in relatively high price elasticities of supply.

BEHIND PRICE ELASTICITY OF SUPPLY: CAPACITY

Whether a farm, factory, or restaurant, most companies need additional capacity when they increase production. Having such capacity readily and cheaply available, therefore, increases a firm's price elasticity of supply.

BEHIND PRICE ELASTICITY OF SUPPLY: GOVERNMENT PERMISSION

Many local governments require firms to get their permission before expanding. If such permission costs a lot to obtain, then the firm's price elasticity of supply will be low. In many poor countries, small business owners must spend years paying bribes and overcoming bureaucratic obstacles before receiving legal permission to expand their operations. These small businesses have a low price elasticity of supply and consequently can't greatly increase production to take advantage of higher prices for their products.

BEHIND PRICE ELASTICITY OF SUPPLY: SPECIALIZED INPUTS

Firms whose workers have highly specialized skills have the most difficulty expanding output in the short run. For example, consider two restaurants in the United States, both of which are doing very well and so want to expand by lengthening their operating hours. To stay open longer, however, each restaurant will need to hire an extra chef. The first restaurant serves American food and knows that many local chefs could successfully prepare all the items on its menu. The second restaurant, however, serves only dishes traditional to northern Uzbekistan and there are no other chefs in the country familiar with northern Uzbekistan cuisine. As a result, to expand operations, the second restaurant would have to hire an unqualified chef and then train him for two years before this extra chef could be trusted to work a shift on his own.

Although in the long run both restaurants might have the same price elasticity of supply, in the short run the Uzbekistani restaurant's elasticity of supply is much lower because it can't find additional qualified employees as easily.

BEHIND PRICE ELASTICITY OF SUPPLY: ABILITY TO FIRE WORKERS

Let's consider a steel-producing firm with a very elastic supply. The more workers this firm employs, the more steel it produces. When the price of steel goes down, the firm will fire many workers and so reduce its quantity supplied. Similarly, when the price of steel goes up, the firm will hire additional employees and produce much more steel.

Many businesses, however, can't fire their workers easily. Sometimes governments make it legally very challenging to fire people. And sometimes employees have sufficient organizational influence to prevent firings. For example, college professors who have what is known as *tenure* are almost impossible to terminate.

Let's now consider a steel firm that can't fire its workers. When the price of steel drops, the firm will not be able to save money by reducing the number of its employees. As a result, it won't reduce its quantity supplied as much as it would if it could fire workers. But also, when the price of steel rises, this firm won't hire many new workers. The firm will fear that, if it hires these workers, it will be stuck with them when the price of steel falls again. As a result, this firm won't greatly expand output when the price of steel increases. Consequently, not being able to fire workers reduces a firm's price elasticity of supply.

BEHIND PRICE ELASTICITY OF SUPPLY: TIME

As with consumers, firms can adjust better to new prices the longer the time frame. To take advantage of a price increase, for example, a firm might have to spend a year building a new factory or training new workers before it can increase output significantly. So, price elasticities of supply are often greater in the long run than in the short run.

Overtime   Imagine your firm pays workers $20 an hour and each worker labors for 40 hours a week. Suddenly, the price of the good your firm makes skyrockets. You want to produce more. Over the next few months you can hire extra workers. But this month, however, the only way you can produce more is if your existing employees work additional hours. Unfortunately, however, you will have to pay your employees overtime wages of $30 an hour if they work more than 40 hours a week. To avoid paying too much overtime, you might not significantly expand production.

Many types of workers receive overtime if they work excessive hours. The cost of this overtime reduces price elasticities of supply. Given enough time, however, firms can eliminate overtime by hiring more workers. Consequently, the shorter the time frame is, the more overtime contributes to price elasticities of supply being lower.

The table below demonstrates how time can affect the price elasticity of supply of wheat.

Time Frame	Effect of a Higher Price of Wheat on the Supply of Wheat
Immediately	No more wheat is supplied since farmers haven't yet had time to change anything.
Next harvest	A little more wheat is supplied since farmers have had enough time to hire more workers and buy more farming equipment.
Medium term	Somewhat more wheat is supplied as farmers have had time to buy new land on which to grow wheat and shift from growing other crops on their land to growing wheat.
Long term	A lot more wheat is supplied as new people have had time to enter the wheat farming business.
Very long term	Vastly more wheat is supplied. Seed companies realize that the higher price of wheat increased the demand among farmers for enhanced genetically modified wheat. The seed companies start researching a "super-wheat" that is faster growing and more pest resistant. After a decade or so, super-wheat is developed, tested, and finally made available to farmers.

How an Increase in the Price of Wheat Affects the Supply of Wheat Over Different Time Frames

BILLIONAIRES BANKRUPTED BY ELASTICITY

In the late 1970s, the Hunt brothers tried to corner the world's silver market. They used their own considerable fortune and borrowed money to buy huge amounts of silver and store the metal in vaults. The more silver they bought, the less silver was available for everyone else. As the brothers bought silver, the market price of silver increased, making the silver in their vaults ever more valuable. The brothers started buying silver at $10 an ounce and kept buying until silver's price hit $54 an ounce.

But the massive increase in silver's price drastically increased the quantity supplied of silver as households melted down coins, jewelry, and anything else containing silver to sell to the market. This increase in quantity supplied drove the price of silver back down to around $10, financially destroying the Hunt brothers.

The brothers' mistake was in not realizing that although silver had an inelastic supply in the short run, it had a very elastic long-run supply. In the short run, the Hunt brothers were able to drive up the price of silver. In the long run, however, the high price elasticity of supply meant that the increase in the metal's price greatly increased the quantity supplied of silver, thereby reducing silver's market price.

Figure 4.17 provides a graphical explanation of what happened. The Hunt brothers begin buying huge amounts of silver at Point 1. These purchases increased the demand

FIGURE **4.17**

SHORT-RUN VERSUS
LONG-RUN
ELASTICITY

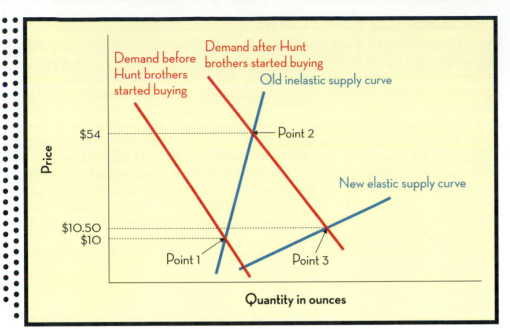

for silver, which moves us to Point 2. This shift in demand happened gradually, and while it was occurring, the Hunt brothers bought large amounts of silver at higher and higher prices.

Initially, households didn't think of their silverware as potential assets. So as the price of silver increased, most households didn't consider selling their silver to the market. The price elasticity of supply of silver coming from households, therefore, was almost zero. (Investors and businesses were willing to sell silver, so the price elasticity of supply of all types of silver was well above zero.)

When the price of silver became very high, businesses started advertising to households, urging them to bring in their silver to be melted down. Because of these advertisements, households' attitudes toward their silverware changed. By our *ceteris paribus* assumption, if we change anything about the supply of silver except the price of silver, then we need a new supply curve. Households' different attitudes toward their silver, therefore, created a new supply curve for silver. This new supply curve was much more elastic than the old one because on this curve, households were willing to sell their silver if the price became high enough. As a result of this new elastic supply we move to Point 3 in Figure 4.17, where the price of silver is just a little higher than $10. Since the Hunt brothers had been paying on average far more than $10 an ounce of silver, they went bankrupt when the new elastic supply curve happened.

CAN THE SUPPLY OF LAND BE ELASTIC?

You might think that land is the ultimate inelastic good and that, as the world's population continues to increase, humans will, on average, have to live on smaller and smaller plots of land. But although the size of the earth doesn't respond to price pressures, the area available for human habitation *is* very price sensitive.

High city land values cause urban developers to build upwards, creating new living areas in the sky. Also, the higher the price of land used for housing, the greater incentives farmers have to invest in expensive technologies that provide higher crop yields, allowing farmers to grow more on less land, thereby freeing up housing space.

THE ELASTICITY OF SLAVES

Slavery, unfortunately, is still practiced in several parts of the world including, as of this writing, the Sudan. Antislavery groups often pay around $100 a person to buy Sudanese slaves who are then immediately freed. Any economist critiquing this approach to fighting slavery would want to know about the price elasticity of supply of slaves.

The antislavery groups' purchases increase the demand and, therefore, the price of slaves. If the price elasticity of supply of slaves is very high, then this increase in price will cause slavers to capture many more Sudanese. So, for example, with an elastic supply, the purchase and freeing of 700 slaves might cause slavers to capture an additional 500 people, meaning that the net number of people who have been set free by the antislavery groups is only 200. In contrast, if the price elasticity of supply is very low, then the purchase and freeing of 700 slaves would cause slavers to capture "only" a small number of additional Sudanese.

Figure 4.18 graphically illustrates how the price elasticity of supply influences the effectiveness of the antislavery groups' purchases. This figure contrasts what happens under the extreme (and unrealistic) cases where the supply curve is perfectly inelastic or perfectly elastic.

In Figure 4.18, 1,000 slaves are traded before the antislavery groups interfere in the market. The antislavery groups then change the market equilibrium by purchasing 700 slaves. These purchases increase the demand for slaves. If, however, the supply of slaves is perfectly inelastic then the increase in demand has no effect on the quantity of slaves traded. Thus, 1,000 slaves will still be captured after the increase in demand. Since the antislavery groups will free "their" 700 slaves, this means that the antislavery groups' purchases and freeing of slaves reduces the number of people in slavery by 700.

In contrast, however, if the supply of slaves is perfectly elastic, then the antislavery groups' purchasing of 700 slaves will cause an additional 700 slaves to be captured. By assumption, the antislavery groups purchase 700 slaves regardless of the price of slaves.

FIGURE **4.18**

ANTISLAVERY GROUPS' PURCHASE OF 700 SLAVES

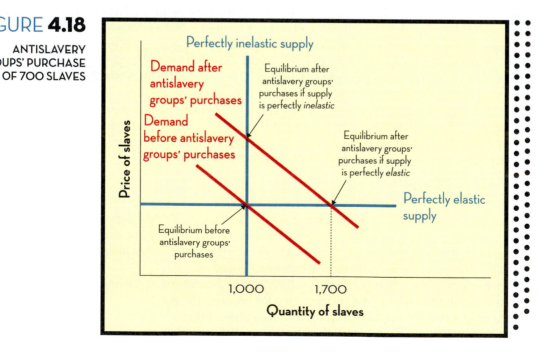

This causes the demand curve to shift out by 700 units at every price. Thus, if the price does not change, the quantity at the new equilibrium must be exactly 700 units higher than the quantity at the old equilibrium. Consequently, at the new equilibrium, 1,700 people will be captured by the slavers. After the antislavery groups' purchases and freeing of slaves, consequently, the total number of people in slavery will stay at 1,000.

Of course, the supply of slaves will not be perfectly inelastic or elastic. The less elastic the supply, the greater the humanitarian benefit created by the antislavery groups' purchases.

REVIEW OF IMPORTANT FORMULAS

$$\text{Price elasticity of demand} = \frac{\text{Percentage change in quantity demanded}}{\text{Percentage change in price}}$$

Price elasticities of demand are always negative, but we ignore the negative sign.

$$\text{Income elasticity of demand} = \frac{\text{Percentage change in quantity demanded}}{\text{Percentage change in income}}$$

Income elasticities of demand are positive for normal goods and negative for inferior goods.

$$\text{Cross elasticity of demand} = \frac{\text{Percentage change in quantity demanded of good A}}{\text{Percentage change in the price of good B}}$$

Cross elasticities of demand are positive for substitutes and negative for complements.

$$\text{Price elasticity of supply} = \frac{\text{Percentage change in quantity supplied}}{\text{Percentage change in price}}$$

Price elasticities of supply are always positive.

QUESTIONS YOU SHOULD BE ABLE TO ANSWER AFTER READING THIS CHAPTER:

1 What does the price elasticity of demand measure? (page 74)

2 What does it mean if demand is (a) elastic, (b) inelastic, or (c) unit elastic? (page 76)

3 What is the shape of a perfectly inelastic demand curve? (page 78)

4 What is the shape of a perfectly elastic demand curve? (page 78)

5 What is the shape of a demand curve with an elasticity of 1? (page 78)

6 How does the price elasticity of demand vary along a straight-line demand curve that goes from axis to axis? (page 79)

7 How does an increase in price affect total revenue when demand is (a) elastic, (b) inelastic, or (c) unit elastic? (page 81)

8 How does a decrease in price affect total revenue when demand is (a) elastic, (b) inelastic, or (c) unit elastic? (page 81)

9   How can you use a demand curve to graph total revenue? (page 82)

10 How do substitutes affect price elasticities of demand? (pages 82–85)

11 How does a broad definition of a product affect that product's price elasticity of demand? (page 85)

12 How does a good being a necessity affect that good's price elasticity of demand? (page 85)

13 How do strong complements affect price elasticities of demand? (pages 85–86)

14 How do long time frames affect price elasticities of demand? (page 86)

15 How does the percentage of income you spend on a good affect that good's price elasticity of demand? (page 87)

16 How does a good being addictive affect that good's price elasticity of demand? (page 88)

17 What does income elasticity of demand measure? (page 89)

18 When is the income elasticity of demand positive and when is it negative? (page 89)

19 What does the cross elasticity of demand measure? (page 90)

20 When is the cross elasticity of demand negative and when is it positive? (page 90)

21 What does the price elasticity of supply measure? (page 90)

22 What is the sign of the price elasticity of supply and why does it have this sign? (page 90)

23 What does it mean if supply is (a) elastic, (b) inelastic, or (c) unit elastic? (page 91)

24 How do costs influence price elasticities of supply? (page 92)

25 How does capacity influence price elasticity of supply? (page 92)

26 How do specialized inputs influence price elasticities of supply? (pages 92–93)

27 How does the ability to fire workers influence price elasticities of supply? (page 93)

28 How does a long time frame affect price elasticities of supply? (page 93)

STUDY PROBLEMS

1   If a 7 percent increase in price causes a 34 percent decrease in quantity demanded, what is the price elasticity of demand? Is demand elastic, inelastic, or unit elastic?

2   Graph the following: a perfectly inelastic demand curve, a perfectly elastic demand curve, a perfectly inelastic supply curve, and a perfectly elastic supply curve.

3   Assume that the demand for corn is very inelastic. Scientists develop a new fertilizer that doubles the yield of ordinary corn, and they generously give it away for free to all corn farmers. Will farmers be helped or hurt by this? Hint: consider total revenue.

4   Assume that the demand for milk is very inelastic. Would milk producers benefit if they all destroyed one-half of their milk before selling their milk to the market?

5   Assume that the facts in question 4 apply and you are a milk producer. If all other producers destroy one-half of their supply, are you better off destroying yours as well?

6 A 10 percent increase in the price of oranges causes a 9 percent decrease in the quantity demanded of tomatoes. What is the cross elasticity of demand between oranges and tomatoes? Are these two goods complements or substitutes?

7 If a 4 percent increase in income causes consumers to buy 3 percent more milk, what is the income elasticity of demand for milk? Is milk a normal or inferior good?

8 A cookie manufacturing company uses one milliliter of a special red dye to make each of its red cookies. This company buys its special red dye from the market at a price of five cents a milliliter, although this price would change if the demand for this special red dye changed. This cookie company is the major purchaser of this special red dye. Assume that the price elasticity of supply of special red dye is **extremely inelastic.** Would this inelasticity tend to make the price elasticity of supply of red cookies inelastic or elastic? (Hint: Draw an inelastic supply curve for special red dye and see what happens to the price of this dye if its demand increases. Now, if the price of red cookies went up, would the cookie company want to increase its output greatly?)

9 How much money would the government raise from imposing an extra 30 percent tax on red sports cars? Explain your answer in terms of elasticities.[5]

10 A genie gives you unlimited wealth. What happens to your various price elasticities of demand?

11 Assume that the demand for a good is perfectly elastic and that the supply and demand determined equilibrium price is $15. What happens to price if supply increases? What would happen to quantity sold if the government mandated a price of $17?

12 Think of any real-world business and assume that this business intends to increase its price. Explain what this business could do to make the demand for its product more inelastic.

APPENDIX: CALCULATING PRICE ELASTICITY OF DEMAND BETWEEN TWO POINTS

If somebody gives you the percentage change in quantity demanded and the percentage change in price, it's easy to calculate the price elasticity of demand. But we run into a problem when we actually try to calculate these percentage changes between two points on a demand curve. To understand this problem, let's compare the weight of the dog and cat in Figure 4.19.

There is a 10-pound difference in the animals' weight. But now let's express this difference in percentage terms. The dog weighs 100 percent more than the cat, and the cat weighs 50 percent as much as the dog. So, in comparing weights using percentages, which percentage is right: 50 percent or 100 percent? Neither is right or wrong; it just depends on your perspective.

Let's see how this perspective problem manifests in the calculation of the price elasticity of demand between the two points indicated in Figure 4.20. First, start at point (4,20) then move to point (8,10) and use our formula:

$$\text{Price elasticity of demand} = \frac{\text{Percentage change in quantity demanded}}{\text{Percentage change in price}}$$

Appendix: Calculating Price Elasticity of Demand between Two Points

FIGURE **4.19**

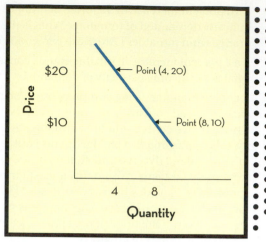

FIGURE **4.20**

CALCULATION OF PRICE ELASTICITY OF DEMAND

The quantity demanded goes from 4 to 8, so it doubles, increasing by 100 percent. Price goes from 20 to 10, so it is halved, decreasing by 50 percent. Consequently, our price elasticity of demand = 100%/50%, or 2. But if we start at point (8,10) and move to point (4,20) then the quantity demanded goes from 8 to 4 or gets cut in half, so it decreases by 50 percent, while price goes from 10 to 20, or increases by 100 percent. Consequently, price elasticity of demand is now 50%/100%, or .5. So is the price elasticity of demand 2 or .5 or something in between? Well, that depends on your perspective, but economists go with the in-between calculation.

THE AVERAGING METHOD OF CALCULATING PERCENTAGE CHANGES AND ELASTICITIES

Let's return to the 10-pound cat and 20-pound dog. Remember, we want to obtain a percentage measure that tells us the difference in the animals' weights. The absolute difference in the pets' weights is 10 pounds. But to turn this into a percentage, we must divide this 10-pound difference by some base. We could use the cat's weight as the base and so the percentage difference in the animals' weights would be

$$\frac{10 \text{ pounds}}{\text{Cat's weight}} = 1, \text{ or } 100\%$$

(To get a percentage from a simple number you multiply by 100 and attach the % sign.) We could alternatively use the dog's weight as the base and so the percentage difference in the animals' weights would be

$$\frac{10 \text{ pounds}}{\text{Dog's weight}} = .5, \text{ or } 50\%$$

ELASTICITIES AND CALCULUS

The reason we get two very different elasticity measures in Figure 4.20 is because the two points we used to calculate elasticity are very far apart from each other. Although I won't prove why, as you take points closer to each other, you usually get smaller differences in elasticity measures. If you were to use calculus (which we won't in this book) and consider the "limit" as the two points get so close they become one point, then you have only one elasticity measure.

Unfortunately, we have no reason to prefer one of these bases to the other. Economists solve this kind of problem by using averages. To use this averaging method, we divide the 10-pound difference in the animals' weights by the average of the animals' weights. Thus, by the averaging method the percentage difference in the pets' weights is

$$\frac{10 \text{ pounds}}{(\text{Dog's weight} + \text{Cat's weight})/2} = 66.7\%$$

When calculating the percentage change between two points on a demand curve economists analogously use as the base the average of the two points. So the percentage change in quantity demanded is $= \dfrac{(Q_1 - Q_0)}{(Q_1 + Q_0)/2}$ where Q_0 and Q_1 are the different quantities. Similarly, the percentage change in price is $\dfrac{(P_1 - P_0)}{(P_1 + P_0)/2}$ giving us the formula

$$\textbf{Price elasticity of demand} = \frac{\dfrac{(Q_1 - Q_0)}{(Q_1 + Q_0)/2}}{\dfrac{(P_1 - P_0)}{(P_1 + P_0)/2}}$$

So the price elasticity of demand between (4,20) and (8,10) in Figure 4.2 is

$$\frac{\dfrac{(4 - 8)}{(4 + 8)/2}}{\dfrac{(20 - 10)}{(20 + 10)/2}} = -1, \text{ or 1 since we are ignoring negative signs}$$

The previous calculation assumed we moved from (4,20) to (8,10). Let's now do the reverse and calculate the price elasticity of demand from (8,10) to (4,20). Our price elasticity of demand is now

$$\frac{\dfrac{(8 - 4)}{(8 + 4)/2}}{\dfrac{(10 - 20)}{(10 + 20)/2}} = -1, \text{ or 1 since we are ignoring negative signs}$$

This is exactly the same as we got before. The advantage of using the averaging method is that you always get the same elasticity measure regardless of what point you start at.

ELASTICITIES AND FREEDOM GYM

Let's calculate price elasticities of demand for the two Freedom Gyms. Recall that at both gyms the monthly membership fee was cut from $40 to $20. At the location where you work, assume that the price reduction increased membership from 1,014 to 2,880, but at the second location membership went up only from 1,600 to 1,980.

Using the averaging formula to compute percentage change, we find that the percentage change in price (at both locations) is $\dfrac{(20 - 40)}{(20 + 40)/2} = -66.7\%$. The percentage increase in membership for the location you work at is $\dfrac{(2{,}880 - 1{,}014)}{(2{,}880 + 1{,}014)/2} = 95.8\%$.

The percentage increase in membership at the second Freedom Gyms location is $\dfrac{(1{,}980 - 1{,}600)}{(1{,}980 + 1{,}600)/2} = 21.2\%$. Consequently the price elasticity of demand for the Freedom Gym location you work at is $\dfrac{95.8\%}{66.7\%} = 1.44$, while the price elasticity of demand for the second location is $\dfrac{21.2\%}{66.7\%} = .318$.

STUDY PROBLEM FOR APPENDIX

In the following diagram, find the price elasticity of demand between Point X and Point Y, and between Point X and Point Z.

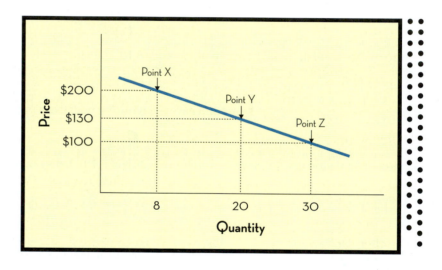

5

CHAPTER

WALTER WILLIAMS

Decent wages, affordable housing, fair prices for farmers: markets don't always deliver these outcomes, so politicians frequently fight the forces of supply and demand. But markets are powerful beasts—possible to predict but impossible to tame. When politicians attempt to force markets down particular paths, the markets usually bolt, causing unwanted but very predictable harm, with the magnitude of the harm determined by elasticities.

PRICE FLOORS

Governments sometimes use price floors to interfere in markets. A price floor is a minimum legal price. If the government sets a price floor of $12, for example, you can't legally charge less than $12, although you could charge more. Figure 5.1 shows the effect of a $12 price floor on a market in which the supply-and-demand-determined equilibrium price is $8.

Although the market in Figure 5.1 wants to push the price down to $8, market forces hit the price floor and get stuck at $12. At this price, firms want to sell 78 goods, but consumers buy only 40, creating a surplus of $78 - 40 = 38$. At the price of $12, firms will produce 78 goods, sell 40 goods, and have 38 goods remain unsold. Unfettered markets move to eliminate surpluses by lowering prices, but the price floor in Figure 5.1 prevents this from happening.

Price floors affect markets only when set above the supply-and-demand-determined equilibrium price. For example, a government prohibition on the price ever going below $2 is meaningless if the unfettered market doesn't want to set a price this low. So if a price floor of $2 were set in Figure 5.1, the free market price (where there is no price floor) of $8 would still prevail.

THE MINIMUM WAGE

Labor markets don't reward everyone equally. Lawyers billing their time at $300 an hour often have their groceries packed by bagboys making only $5.50 per hour. Politicians objecting to such disparities sometimes abolish low-paying jobs by

POLICY ANALYSIS WITH SUPPLY AND DEMAND

LEARNING OBJECTIVES

AFTER READING THIS CHAPTER, YOU SHOULD BE ABLE TO:

- Explain both the costs and benefits of a minimum wage.
- Describe the unintended consequences of rent control programs.
- Understand restrictions on the sale of human organs.
- Analyze the effects of government health care subsidies.
- Identify the impact of agricultural subsidies.

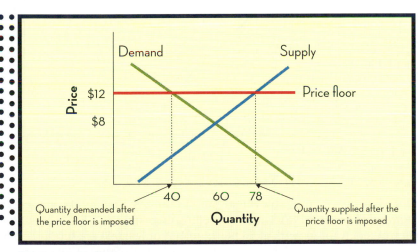

FIGURE 5.1

PRICE FLOOR ABOVE SUPPLY-AND-DEMAND-DETERMINED
EQUILIBRIUM PRICE

implementing a minimum wage. A minimum wage creates a price floor below which the wage cannot legally go.

In labor markets, firms are the *buyers,* not the sellers, because firms purchase labor. Firms thus determine labor market demand curves. In labor markets, workers supply labor to firms. Workers, therefore, determine labor market supply curves. Let's consider the effect of a minimum wage on the market for unskilled labor.

MINIMUM WAGE'S WINNERS AND LOSERS

As shown in Figure 5.2, before the government implemented a minimum wage, the forces of supply and demand set the wage at $4 an hour. At $4 an hour 13,000 workers had jobs. After the $6 minimum wage is imposed, firms can't legally pay less than $6 per hour. At $6 per hour, firms hire only 8,000 workers. So the minimum wage destroys $13,000 - 8,000 = 5,000$ jobs.

A minimum wage law, however, increases the wages of unskilled workers who have jobs after the law is implemented. A minimum wage, therefore, helps some workers while harming others.

A minimum wage harms all firms by forcing them to pay higher wages. Customers, too, are often hurt by a minimum wage law because the law usually causes firms to raise product prices.

FIGURE **5.2**

EFFECT OF MINIMUM WAGE ON MARKET FOR UNSKILLED LABOR

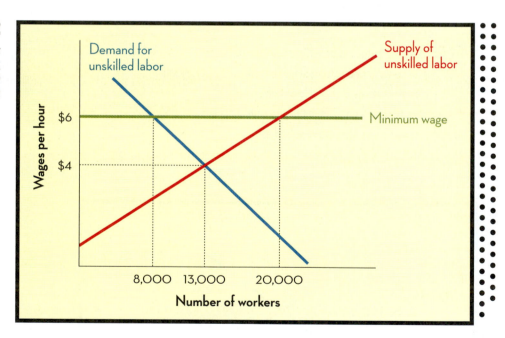

UNEMPLOYMENT AND THE MINIMUM WAGE

The minimum wage creates unemployment. An unemployed person is defined as someone who would like to find work at the prevailing wage but can't. Since in our example 20,000 workers want to work at $6 per hour but only 8,000 are hired, 12,000 people are unemployed because of the minimum wage. Not all of these 12,000 people, however, are significantly harmed by the minimum wage.

Some unemployed people in Figure 5.2 (a) don't want jobs at $4 an hour, (b) do want jobs at $6 an hour, but (c) aren't hired after the minimum wage is implemented. These people, therefore, are unemployed but are not deprived of a job because of the minimum wage. Many of these people, however, will have gone to the trouble of applying for a job they then didn't get.

The unemployed are surplus labor. Free markets correct surpluses by driving down prices. But since the government punishes those who violate minimum wage laws, minimum wages usually create persistent labor surpluses.

PERFECTLY INELASTIC DEMAND AND THE MINIMUM WAGE

Consider a firm that always needs to have exactly 500 workers regardless of costs. Sure, this firm would like to pay wages of only a penny per hour, but if necessary it will pay $20 an hour for its workers' labor. Figure 5.3 shows the relevant supply and demand curves. (Because this demand curve violates the Law of Demand it doesn't exist in the real world, but it is still useful to consider for teaching purposes.)

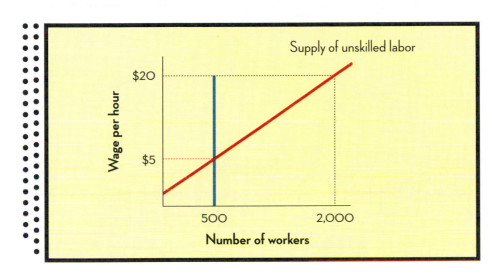

107

FIGURE **5.3**

SUPPLY AND DEMAND CURVES WHEN MINIMUM WAGE IS $20

The free market would have our firm pay $5 per hour. At this wage, the firm employs 500 workers. If a minimum wage of $20 per hour were enacted, however, the firm would still employ 500 workers. Because the firm's demand for labor is perfectly inelastic, by definition the firm doesn't employ fewer workers when the price it must pay for workers increases. When the demand for labor is perfectly inelastic, therefore, the minimum wage doesn't destroy jobs.

The $20 per hour minimum wage in Figure 5.3, however, might still cause some workers to get fired. At the market wage of $5 an hour, 500 workers want jobs and the firm hires all 500 of these workers. At the minimum wage of $20, though, 2,000 workers will want jobs but the firm employs only 500 of these. The firm will almost certainly not pick the same 500 workers it hired before the minimum wage was enacted.

For any given wage, a firm tries to hire the best workers it can. Perhaps at the market wage of $5 only unskilled high school dropouts wanted to work for the firm. At $20 per hour, however, many well-educated and highly skilled people might apply to the firm for a job. As a result of the minimum wage, therefore, the firm might have fired all 500 of its previous workers and hired 500 new, more highly skilled employees. So even if a minimum wage doesn't destroy jobs, it can still harm low-skilled workers. But a minimum wage often does destroy jobs. And the amount of jobs destroyed depends on firms' price elasticities of demand for unskilled labor.

ELASTIC DEMAND AND THE MINIMUM WAGE

If a firm has a very elastic demand for labor, the number of workers it wants to hire is highly price sensitive. Consequently, a minimum wage significantly reduces the number of workers a firm employs if the firm has an elastic demand for labor. Overall, the more elastic the demand for labor is, the more jobs a minimum wage destroys.

FIGURE 5.4

EFFECT OF ELASTICITY ON EMPLOYMENT

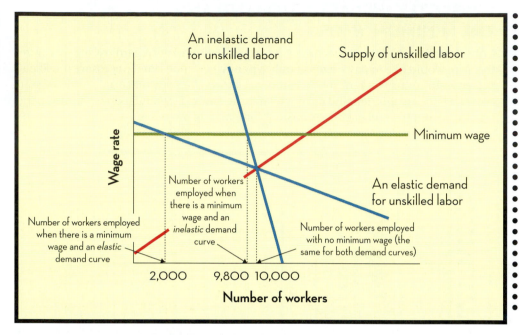

Figure 5.4 shows the dramatic effect elasticity can have on firms' employment. This figure presents two possible demand curves for labor and shows how the minimum wage eliminates far more jobs when firms' demand for labor is elastic.

FRENCH GROCERY BAG PACKERS

"American shoppers are used to having others bag their groceries. Large supermarkets in France, however, require customers to do their own bagging. France has a much higher unemployment rate than the United States, so it seems very inefficient for the French economy not to put some of its unemployed to work bagging groceries."[1]

France's minimum hourly wage is 8.27 euros, which, as of this writing is $10.92. About one-half of U.S. retail employees earn less than France's minimum wage.[2] So although it's profitable for U.S. stores to hire baggers, France's high minimum wage makes it unprofitable for French supermarkets to do the same.

ACORN'S MINIMUM WAGE FIGHT

The Association of Community Organizations for Reform Now (ACORN) is a U.S. political activist group that continually fights to raise the minimum wage. ACORN hires a large number of workers to conduct grassroots activism.

But ACORN wanted to pay its workers less than the minimum wage. ACORN has a limited amount of money. So the higher the

About 1.6 million U.S. workers have minimum wage jobs, 53 percent of whom are under 23. Over 30 percent of the minimum wage workers 23 and older are high school dropouts. Less than 5 percent of all minimum wage workers both work full time and are the only working members of their family.[3]

wages ACORN must pay, the fewer people the group can hire. And the fewer employees it has, the less politically effective ACORN will be. So ACORN argued that the minimum wage law imposed an unconstitutional limitation on its ability to conduct grassroots activism. A California court, however, ruled against ACORN and forced it to abide by the minimum wage law.[4]

ACORN also argued that if its workers were paid the minimum wage, they would have so much money that they could no longer empathize with poor people. And as a result, ACORN claimed, its workers would be less effective at political activism in underprivileged communities.

Interestingly, it's perfectly legal for ACORN to hire volunteer activists and pay them nothing. But minimum wage laws do prevent ACORN from paying their activists a few dollars an hour.

WORSE WORKING CONDITIONS

Even workers who benefit monetarily from minimum wages might still on average be made worse off by them. Businesses usually face a trade-off between working conditions and the wages they must pay. If Burger King offered you an $8.00-an-hour job this summer while McDonald's offered you one at $9 per hour, you might accept the lower-paying Burger King job if Burger King but not McDonald's kept its kitchens air conditioned.

Firms usually compete for employees across many dimensions, including by providing favorable working conditions. When a minimum wage creates a surplus of laborers, however, firms no longer need to compete for employees and so save money through reducing the quality of their working environment by, for example, cutting back on air conditioning, heating, and advancement opportunities.

EXPLAINING THE HARM CAUSED BY A MINIMUM WAGE

Many noneconomists feel minimum wages are an unquestioned good because they raise pay while harming only greedy corporations unwilling to provide decent salaries. If a friend of yours holds this view, ask her if she would like to be subject to a personal minimum wage of $30 per hour, meaning that no firm could pay her less than $30 an hour. Such a high minimum wage would prevent most college students from ever getting a job. Even if your friend hopes to make more than $30 per hour after she has worked a few years, being subject to such a high minimum wage would stop her from ever getting enough experience to be worth $30 an hour.

Now ask your friend to imagine that she is an unemployed yet ambitious inner city high school dropout hoping to make $10 per hour in a few years. She recognizes, however, that her current lack of skills means she isn't yet worth this much to most firms, so she would like to work briefly at $4 an hour until she gets enough experience to be able to acquire a $10 per hour job. In this situation, would your friend welcome a $6 per hour minimum wage?

In other words, minimum wages impose the greatest cost on those with the least skills. Imagine that you run a fast-food restaurant, and because of a minimum wage, you face a surplus of job applicants. Whom should you hire? Obviously, the most skilled. This, unfortunately, makes it impossible for workers with the lowest skills to find employment. Normally, those with the lowest skills can still be hired if they are willing to work for a little less than higher-skilled workers. Minimum wages, however, foreclose such a strategy and can prevent low-skilled workers from gaining enough experience to become highly skilled employees.

MINIMUM WAGES AND HIGHLY SKILLED WORKERS

Construction companies can hire either low or highly skilled workers. High- and low-skilled construction workers, therefore, are substitutes. High-skilled workers receive higher salaries but they also accomplish more for every hour they work. Assume that

Market wage of high-skilled workers = $15 an hour.

Market wage of low-skilled workers = $4 an hour.

What would be the effect of a $7/hour minimum wage? The minimum wage will cause some low-skilled workers to lose their jobs and some to keep their jobs but receive a higher wage.

The minimum wage will cause construction firms to hire fewer low-skilled workers. The minimum wage, therefore, will increase the demand for high-skilled workers. This increase in demand will increase the market wage of high-skilled workers. And since this new higher wage is still determined by the intersection of supply and demand, all high-skilled workers will get hired at this higher wage. In this example, therefore, the minimum wage helps all high-skilled workers.

Imagine that one highly skilled worker can accomplish exactly as much as three low-skilled workers can. So if low-skilled workers cost $4 an hour whereas high-skilled workers cost $15 an hour construction firms would never employ high-skilled workers because it would be cheaper for the firms to instead hire three low-skilled workers and pay them in total $12 an hour. But if the government imposes a $7 an hour minimum wage on all workers, construction firms would profit by firing all their low-skilled workers and replacing them with one-third as many high-skilled workers.

In the United States, labor unions are among the biggest political supporters of increasing the minimum wage. Unions members, however, are usually highly skilled workers who earn well above any proposed minimum wage. As the above analysis shows, though, unions are very rational to support high minimum wages for unskilled nonunion members.

THE MOBILITY OF MINIMUM-WAGE WORKERS

Many minimum-wage workers in the United States quickly find higher-paying jobs. One study determined that after only one year, 63 percent of minimum-wage workers found above-minimum wage jobs.[5]

MINIMUM WAGE: FACILITATOR OF RACISM?

Assume that some society is prejudiced against blacks. Because of this prejudice, black workers have had lower educational opportunities. As a result,

Market wage of nonblack workers = $10 an hour.

Market wage of black workers = $6 an hour.

A minimum wage of $7 would prevent many black workers from being employed. A $7/hour minimum wage would therefore increase the demand for those white workers who are substitutes for black workers. Because of the minimum wage, these white workers would get higher wages while all keeping their jobs. Racist white workers concerned about black workers "taking their jobs" should, in this example, strongly support a high minimum wage.

Let's now assume that Mexican and white construction workers in the United States have exactly the same abilities. But assume that the Mexican workers are willing to work for $10 an hour, while the white workers won't do construction work unless they are paid at least $18 an hour. Let's finally assume that a construction firm is owned by a racist who, all else being equal, would prefer to hire white rather than Mexican workers.*

---

*This is an arbitrary assumption. I have no reason to believe that any construction firm owners are racists.

Normally, construction firms would hire only the Mexican workers. A racist construction firm that paid $18 an hour to hire white workers could never compete against a less racist firm that paid $10 an hour to Mexicans. But now imagine that the U.S. government passes a law requiring that all construction workers be paid $22 an hour. Racist construction firms will now not suffer a penalty if they just hire white workers.

Generally, markets pit greed against bigotry. An employer who doesn't hire the best person for a job loses profits. But when a minimum wage law creates a surplus of labor, employers must turn away some otherwise qualified employees. If all potential employees have the same skill level, then employers don't suffer by choosing workers through criteria that are not profit-based. So as long as the government doesn't punish them for such behavior, racist employers don't suffer from engaging in racially discriminatory hiring practices when minimum wages create a surplus of labor.

The Davis-Bacon Act

In the 1930s many openly racist U.S. congressmen became concerned that black southerners were moving north and "stealing" construction jobs from white workers by offering to work for less. Denial of educational and training opportunities often meant that black workers had fewer skills than white workers and so could compete only by accepting lower salaries. Congress decided to protect white workers by enacting the Davis-Bacon Act, which mandated that the prevailing union wage be paid on all federally funded construction projects. This union wage was often well above what black workers had been getting. The law made many black workers legally unemployable. Davis-Bacon is still the law of the land in the United States.

While advocating that Davis-Bacon be passed. Congressman William Upshaw complained about a "superabundance or large aggregation of negro labor." A union leader who also supported Davis-Bacon said that "colored labor is being sought to demoralize wage rates."

BLACK MARKETS WITH MINIMUM WAGES

Whenever the government prohibits supply and demand from operating, it creates incentives for lawbreaking. For example, if the minimum wage is $6 per hour but a firm wants to hire me for $5 per hour and I'm willing to work at this wage, both the firm and I can profit from having me work illegally for $5 per hour.

ADMINISTRATIVE COSTS

To combat black markets, governments need to employ inspectors to ensure that firms pay no less than the minimum wage. The cost of these inspectors adds to the social cost of the minimum wage.

PRICE CEILINGS

Price ceilings are the opposite of price floors. When a government imposes a price ceiling, it forbids firms from selling products at a price above the price ceiling. Whereas price floors create surpluses, price ceilings create shortages.

Figure 5.5 shows the effect of a $6 price ceiling on a market with an equilibrium price of $8. The forces of supply and demand would like to push the price up to $8, but the price gets legally stuck at the $6 ceiling. At the $6 ceiling, firms want to sell 50 goods whereas consumers want to buy 71 goods. Consequently, firms will sell all 50 of the goods they produce, and 21 customers who want to buy the good will go without.

Price ceilings are meaningful only when imposed below the market price. For example, a price ceiling of $1,000 in Figure 5.5 would have no effect because the market does not want to push the price above $1,000.

FIGURE **5.5**

PRICE CEILING
CREATES SHORTAGE

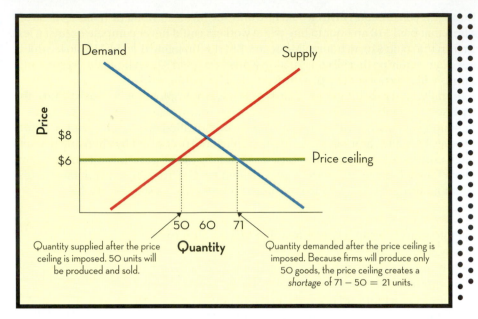

GUILLOTINES AND PRICE CEILINGS

In 1793 the government of revolutionary France became concerned about rising prices of necessities so it imposed the "Law of the Maximum." The government set price ceilings for many goods. Unfortunately, the market price of most goods was well above these price ceilings.

Farmers and merchants did everything they could to avoid complying with the law. To catch violators who sold goods for prices above the legal limit, the government set up a spy system. Those who were caught had their dwellings destroyed and (this being revolutionary France) were sometimes sent to the guillotine. Farmers who refused to sell their crops often had their crops confiscated by the government.

The confiscations, executions, property destruction, and price limitations greatly reduced farmers' and craftsmen's incentives to work and trade. The Law of the Maximum so decreased manufacturing and agricultural production that the French government abolished it in 1794.

PRICE CEILINGS DURING THE AMERICAN REVOLUTIONARY WAR[6]

Price ceilings almost destroyed George Washington's army. In 1777, during the American Revolutionary War, much of George Washington's army was in Pennsylvania. To reduce the cost of supplying this army, Pennsylvania's politicians imposed price ceilings on many of the goods the army needed. As a result, the quantity supplied of these goods plummeted, driving Washington's army to the brink of starvation. After the price ceilings were lifted in 1778, it was much easier for Washington to supply his troops.

RENT CONTROL

High land values in many communities make it difficult for residents to find affordable housing. Politicians often attempt to create affordable housing by enacting rent control, which is a price ceiling on rents. Rent control laws set a maximum price that landlords can charge tenants. Although these laws are designed to protect tenants

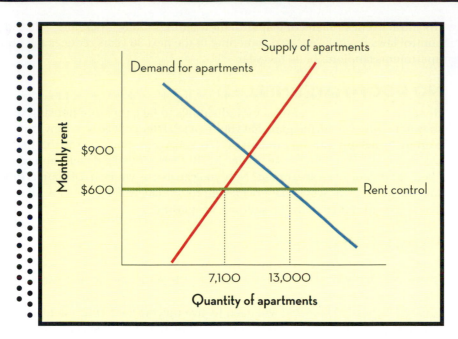

FIGURE **5.6**

SUPPLY AND
DEMAND FOR
APARTMENTS

against high prices, they, like minimum wage laws, create both winners and losers within the group they are supposed to help. Whereas the minimum wage creates a surplus of labor, rent control laws generate a shortage of apartments.

Figure 5.6 shows the supply and demand curves for apartments in a fictional city. For simplicity, assume that all apartments are exactly alike. Absent government interference, the market price for apartments is $900 per month. If the government imposes rent control, making it illegal for apartments to rent for more than $600 per month, then there will be a shortage of apartments equal to $13{,}000 - 7{,}100 = 5{,}900$.

Existing apartment holders can benefit from rent control because it lowers their rent. Landlords, obviously, are harmed by rent control as are potential tenants who can't find apartments because of rent control-induced shortages. Price elasticities of supply and demand determine the size of this shortage. Rent control decreases the price of apartments, so the greater the price elasticity of demand, the more apartments consumers will want to rent in response to this price decrease. Similarly, the greater the price elasticity of supply, the less willing landlords will be to rent apartments at rent control-reduced prices.

But how can rent control reduce the actual number of apartments? In the short run, rent control can't have much effect on quantity supplied. (So Figure 5.6 must not represent the short run.) In the medium term, however, rent control can reduce quantity supplied by causing landlords to not rent out space. For example, after an apartment goes vacant, the landlord might decide to turn the space into an extra office for herself rather than lease it out for reduced (rent-controlled) rent. In the long run, rent control causes landlords to build fewer apartments and so can drastically reduce quantity supplied.

Even the fear of rent control being imposed in the far future can reduce the quantity supplied of apartments. Erecting an apartment building is a very long-term investment in which you pay a lot of money up front in return for receiving tenants' rents over the building's lifetime. Anything that reduces the rents you expect to receive over the next 30 years will reduce

A study on rent control in New York City found that "tenants in low- and moderate-income areas receive little or no benefit from rent [control], while tenants in more affluent locations are effectively subsidized for a substantial portion of their rent."[7]

the attractiveness of erecting apartment buildings today. Therefore, a fear that rent control laws *might* be enacted sometime in the next 30 years reduces the number of apartments landlords build this year.

NO ROOMMATES NEEDED

Rent control creates incentives for individuals to take up more housing space than they otherwise would. Imagine that your first job after college is in New York City. The extremely high prices of apartments in New York mean you will probably need to have a roommate if you want to live in the city. But what if you get lucky and score a very cheap rent-controlled apartment? Now you can live by yourself. Of course, this means that the person who would have been your roommate will need to look for someplace else to live, thus increasing the shortage of apartments.

REDUCTIONS IN MOBILITY

Rent control reduces tenants' incentives to move. Pretend that you have a great rent-controlled apartment for which you pay $500 a month below market rates, but you are offered a good job in another city that pays an extra $400 per month in salary. Unfortunately, to take the job you will need to give up your rent-controlled apartment, so you turn down this attractive offer. Rent control, therefore, has just stopped you from accepting a job where you might have been more productively employed.

Rent control can also increase workers' commutes. If you get a job on the other side of your city, you might prefer to keep your rent-controlled apartment and drive an extra 30 minutes to work than to move closer to your new place of employment. By reducing mobility, therefore, rent control can increase traffic congestion and car exhaust pollution.

REDUCTIONS IN QUALITY, AGAIN

As discussed earlier, minimum wage laws create incentives for employers to spend less on their employees' working environment. Employers forced to spend more money on wages have incentives to cut back on other expenses that the government cannot regulate as easily. Rent control laws have a similar effect on the quality of apartment buildings. To understand this let's first consider a grading analogy.

Imagine that your college grades determine how much money you make after graduating:

College Grade Point Average	Starting Salary
A	$60,000/year
B	$40,000/year
C	$25,000/year

You obviously have a strong incentive to earn an A average. But now imagine that the government places a $20,000 price ceiling on your salary. Now, regardless of how much you study, you will never make more than $20,000 a year. Because of the ceiling, you have much less incentive to study and are far more likely than before to graduate with a C average.

Now imagine you are an apartment building owner. The quality of your building determines how much you receive in rents from tenants:

Quality of Your Apartment Building	Rent per Apartment Unit
Excellent	$2,000/month
Fair	$1,000/month
Poor	$700/month

You have a strong financial incentive to keep up the quality of your building. You will, for example, quickly fix broken windows and toilets. But now assume that, through rent control, the government imposes a $600/month price ceiling on the rent you can charge. Why should you now go to the effort and expense of maintaining your building if it doesn't enable you to charge higher rents?

Sometimes rent control makes it so unprofitable for landlords to maintain their buildings that they let them deteriorate and then abandon them. In fact, New York City, which has rent control, has more than four times as many abandoned housing units as homeless people.

Strip Clubs and Rent Control[8]

Rent control can subvert Adam Smith's invisible hand. Consider a hypothetical New York City landlord who owns a building with 10 units. The first unit is located on the ground floor. It is rented out to a business. The city places no restrictions on what the landlord can charge a business that rents this ground floor unit. The other nine units are residential apartments rented to families. The market value of these residential units is $2,000 a month each. But because of rent control the landlord can charge no more than $1,300 a month for his residential units.

Two businesses want to rent the ground floor unit: a bakery and a strip club. The strip club is willing to pay $400 a month more than the bakery. But most families don't want to live above a strip club. The strip club, let's say, will reduce the market value of each residential unit from $2,000 a month to $1,500 a month. In a free market (where there is no rent control) having a strip club would reduce the rents the landlord receives from each family by $500. Since the strip club is willing to pay only $400 a month more than the bakery, if the landlord could charge market rents, he would never allow the strip club to move into his building.

But then the landlord remembers that his nine residential units are rent controlled. The most he can charge a family is $1,300 a month, so it doesn't matter to the landlord if the market value of the units is $2,000 or $1,500. And because rent control creates a shortage of apartments, he will have no trouble renting out the nine residential units even if they are above a strip club. As a result, the landlord loses nothing if the strip club moves in. Rent control, consequently, has negated Adam Smith's invisible hand because the landlord doesn't personally suffer if he angers his customers. The landlord, therefore, calls the strip club's owner to offer him the building's ground floor unit.

But, alas, the strip club's owner tells the landlord that he overestimated how much his club could pay in rent. (Apparently graphic-rich Internet pornography has become such a good substitute for strip clubs that club revenues are down.) Now the bakery is willing to pay $300 more a month in rent than the strip club. But then the landlord remembers that under his city's rent control he can raise rents when a tenant moves out of an apartment. So the landlord will benefit if the strip club causes some families to vacate his building. Consequently, the landlord decides to still rent the ground floor unit to the strip club explicitly because it will anger his other tenants. For this landlord, therefore, rent control has actually reversed Adam Smith's invisible hand by rewarding him for driving away existing customers.

WOULD YOU LIKE TO LIVE ABOVE THIS?

ADMINISTRATIVE COSTS, AGAIN

Rent control, like minimum wage laws, imposes additional administrative burdens on the government. To combat landlords' incentives to spend little on maintenance, cities with rent control must continually monitor landlords to ensure they don't allow their buildings to fall into disrepair. Rent-controlled cities must also spend resources thwarting landlords' desires to accept under-the-table payments.

BLACK MARKETS, AGAIN

Similar to a minimum wage law, rent control creates black markets. If your apartment is worth $800 a month but you can legally rent it for only $600 per month, you will be bestowing a large benefit on whomever you rent to. This means you have an incentive to accept an under-the-table bribe. If you don't accept illegal bribes, you might rent the apartment to a friend, family member, or if you're a bigot, only to someone with the same skin color as you.

DISCRIMINATION, AGAIN

As with the minimum wage, rent control laws increase discrimination. Consider a greedy, racist landlord. In the absence of rent control laws, this landlord's greed will cut against his racism. To make the most money, he would need to rent his apartment to the tenant willing to pay the most, so if he rented only to those of certain ethnicities, he would likely lose money. Although markets don't eliminate racism, they often mitigate racism's effects by punishing those who put racial considerations ahead of profit.

In contrast, when rent control creates a shortage of apartments, a racist landlord loses nothing by renting only to those of his race. Rent control abolishes the penalty that free markets usually impose on racist landlords.

RESTRICTIONS ON HOUSING CONSTRUCTION

Many rent-controlled cities also enact restrictions on new property and housing developments. These construction restrictions reduce the supply for housing and thus raise apartments' market price. Combined with rent control, housing restrictions can drastically diminish the number of housing units available in a city.

Workers displaced by rent control and housing restrictions will bid up housing prices in other areas. The measures one town enacts to reduce rents and preserve open spaces result in increased construction, housing prices, and rents in neighboring towns.

POLITICS AND RENT CONTROL

Imagine you are a self-interested city politician. You are considering voting for a law that will help 80,000 people but harm 100,000 people. Do you vote for it? Probably not. But now imagine that the 100,000 people who will be harmed by the law don't live in your city. So supporting the law will win you favor among 80,000 people and anger only people who can't vote against you. Now you are likely to vote for the law.

Most of the people harmed by a city's rent control law are would-be tenants who can't find apartments. Many of these people will be forced to live outside the city. As a result, they won't be able to vote in the city's elections. They therefore won't be able to vote against the politicians who supported rent control. As a result, city politicians who support rent control are insulated from many of the people harmed by rent control. This insulation creates incentives for city politicians to support rent control laws.

THE DRAFT VERSUS VOLUNTARY ENLISTMENT

How should a nation man its armed forces: through draft or voluntary enlistment? Imagine that Figure 5.7 shows the supply curve of young citizens smart and healthy enough to be soldiers.

With a voluntary army, the government decides how many troops it wants. The supply curve then tells the government what salary it must pay to get its desired number of soldiers. According to Figure 5.7, if the armed forces want 2.5 million troops, they will have to pay wages of $30,000 per year; whereas if they desire 5 million troops, they must pay each soldier $60,000 a year. An armed forces that can draft citizens, however, can pay whatever it wants.

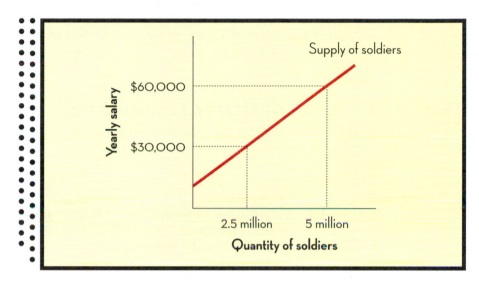

FIGURE 5.7

SUPPLY OF SOLDIERS

Figure 5.7 also shows the relative advantage of the wartime draft. In wartime, when you need many troops, if the supply of labor is inelastic, the armed forces will need to pay extremely high wages if it relies on voluntary enlistment. Of course, the draft imposes costs on those forced to serve. Draftees lose the opportunity cost of their time. The draft even harms soldiers who would have enlisted voluntarily since the draft reduces all soldiers' wages.

A draft, however, can greatly benefit citizens not subject to conscription. For example, during WWII the United States drafted over 10 million Americans. Had the United States not implemented this draft, it would have had to raise taxes to pay for higher military salaries. These higher salaries would have been needed, in the absence of a draft, to induce millions more Americans to volunteer for the military. A draft is effectively a forced transfer of wealth in which the government takes money from soldiers and gives it to civilian taxpayers.

Do Soldiers in Drafted Armies Receive Better Treatment?
Does a draft cause a military's leadership to care more or less about its troops? Some claim that in a democracy a draft will ensure that soldiers receive better treatment. This argument theorizes that if citizens know that their sons could be drafted, then they would never vote for leaders who would take unnecessary military risks. Many proponents for the draft believe that it increases the *political* incentives for the military to care for its troops.

Some people, however, believe that since, under a draft, the military does not have to compete for labor, the draft reduces incentives for the military to care for its troops. Organizations tend to not value greatly resources they can get for free, so a draft can sometimes cause militaries to mistreat their own troops. Imagine that you were the owner of a local McDonald's who, for some odd reason, had the power to force people to work for you. Your business could now tolerate horrible working conditions because dissatisfied employees couldn't quit or demand a compensating pay raise. Similarly, a military that can conscript workers need not be overly worried about its troops' job satisfaction.

One of this author's great-grandfathers immigrated to the United States to escape being drafted into the Russian army.

The Russian army, which pays draftees almost nothing and sometimes subjects conscripts to hazing bordering on torture, would have to reform quickly if it ever lost the power to draft. A military that must compete with private firms for workers has to create a satisfactory work environment or at least pay high salaries. Having an all volunteer military, therefore, increases the *economic* incentives for the military to care for its troops.

THE MARKET FOR HUMAN ORGANS[9]

Kidneys, hearts, and livers: not items you ever want to run out of. But in the United States, over 86,000 people can't get a transplant because of an organ shortage.[10] Free markets correct shortages by raising prices, but under U.S. law it's illegal to pay individuals or their families for donated organs.

If you cut my lawn, I can legally give you $20; if you give me a kidney, I'm forbidden from compensating you. Does this prohibition prevent the laws of supply and demand from operating on organs? No; it merely sets the price of precious organs at zero.

Figure 5.8 shows possible supply and demand curves for kidneys. But if the government imposes a price of zero, a shortage of organs manifests. And this shortage kills thousands people a year in the United States who die before they can get a needed kidney transplant. Some generous souls freely donate their organs after death. Since it's illegal to be paid for such donations, and since many of us prefer not to dwell on our organs' fate after our passing, all too few of us agree to become post-life organ donors. This creates huge economic waste.

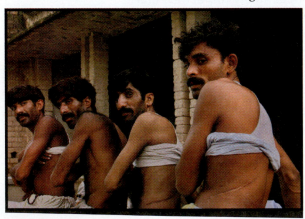

PAKISTANI VILLAGERS SHOW THEIR SCARS AFTER THEY EACH SOLD A KIDNEY TO PAY OFF DEBTS. IN SOME POOR PAKISTANI VILLAGES, 40 TO 50 PERCENT OF RESIDENTS HAVE SOLD A KIDNEY.[11]

Consider two hypothetical people, John and Bill, both staying in the same hospital. John will soon die if he doesn't get a kidney, and so he would gladly pay $50,000 for one to a donor or donor's family. Bill has just been in a motorcycle accident and will die in a few days. Bill, however, has fully functional kidneys that could be successfully transplanted into John. Although Bill doesn't have life insurance, he does have a dependent family, so Bill is very concerned about his family's financial welfare after he dies. Bill has never signed an organ donor card, so in a few days his kidneys will die with him. The same doctor treats both Bill and John and knows of their needs. John and Bill's family could be made immensely better off if their doctor could arrange for John to buy Bill's kidneys. Unfortunately, such transactions are forbidden by the government. Markets are resilient, however,

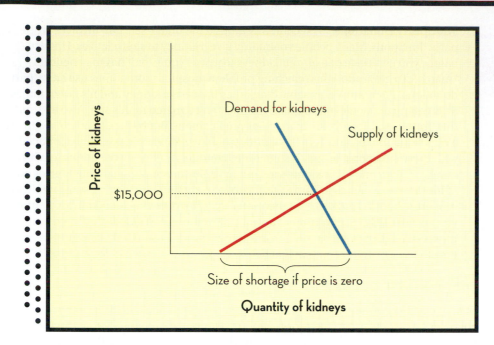

FIGURE **5.8**

SUPPLY AND
DEMAND CURVES
FOR KIDNEYS

Demand for kidneys

Supply of kidneys

$15,000

Size of shortage if price is zero

Quantity of kidneys

Price of kidneys

and often find ways of getting around government prohibitions. The invisible hand of the market often thwarts the heavy hand of government.

BLACK MARKETS, AGAIN

As with the minimum wage and rent control, government restrictions on organ sales create black markets. Imagine that you live in Pakistan and make $500 a year and know you will probably be okay if you sell one of your two kidneys since you only need one good kidney to lead a perfectly healthy life. (The operation to remove a kidney, however, does entail a small health risk.) If someone offers you $15,000, the equivalent of 30 years' salary, for one kidney, wouldn't you be tempted to accept the offer? Now imagine that you're a middle-class American who will die without a new kidney. Surely you would benefit by paying $60,000 to a Pakistani broker (who will keep $35,000 for himself and give $10,000 to the surgeon) to procure a kidney. If both the middle-class American and the Indian donor are made better off by the trade, why should anyone else object?

LEGAL MEANS AROUND ORGAN-SALE BAN

When governments restrict markets, clever people seeks ways around the restriction, and indeed two clever *legal* means have also been devised to get around the U.S. organ-sale ban and effectively compensate people for donating their organs to strangers.

1. **LifeSharers**   One way to get around the ban involves a program called LifeSharers. Participants agree to donate organs when they die and in return get preferential access to organs they might need while they are alive.

THE MARKET PRICE FOR KIDNEYS

Economists have estimated that if it were legal to buy and sell kidneys from living donors, the market price would be about $15,000.

2. **Multiparty Donations**   A second way around the organ-sale ban involves cross-party donations. Many people voluntarily give a kidney to sick relatives. Unfortunately, you can't give one of your kidneys to just anyone, for it has to genetically "match." To get around this matching problem, hospitals sometimes use cross-party donations. For example, imagine that James Jr. needs a kidney and his father James Sr. is willing to donate one, but his kidneys aren't a match for his son. Also assume that Tom Jr. and Tom Sr. are in a similar predicament. But by luck James Sr.'s kidney is a match for Tom Jr., and Tom Sr.'s kidney would work nicely inside James Jr. Faced with these situations, hospitals sometimes conduct multiparty donations in which James Sr. gives one of his kidneys to Tom Jr. while Tom Sr. simultaneously gives one of his kidneys to James Jr. Tom Sr. and James Sr. are therefore getting substantial non-monetary benefit (the saving of their sons' lives) for donating their kidneys to strangers. Because the U.S. government doesn't allow the sale of kidneys, affected parties must often resort to such cumbersome barter trades. Fortunately, economists have developed a computer system that helps people arrange such kidney trades.[12]

HEALTH CARE

Many governments pay for their citizens' health care with elasticities determining the cost. Let's examine the market for magnetic resonance imaging (MRI). Doctors use it to look inside the body. Imagine, for example, that you wake up with a horrible headache and fear you have a brain tumor. Your doctor explains that the headache is probably caused by your confessed binge drinking the previous night. But since your doctor can't *guarantee* that you don't have a brain tumor, you get him to give you an MRI. The MRI scans your brain and allows your doctor to see if anything unusual lurks inside your skull. Imagine that Figure 5.9 shows a hypothetical market for MRIs.

FIGURE **5.9**

HYPOTHETICAL
MARKET FOR MRIS

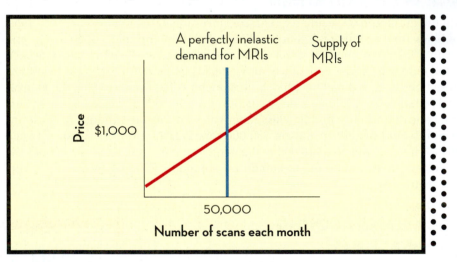

At the market equilibrium 50,000 MRIs are performed each month at a cost of $1,000 each. Consumers, therefore, spend $50 million a month on MRIs at market prices.

Now, however, imagine that the government decides to pay all consumers' MRI costs. Because the demand for MRIs in Figure 5.9 is perfectly inelastic, consumers will still want only 50,000 operations at a price of zero. Consequently, the cost to the government of paying for MRIs is $50 million a month.

Figure 5.9, however, incorporates the unrealistic assumption that consumers won't increase their quantity demanded for MRIs as the price of MRIs falls. Surely most of us would be more willing to get an MRI if the price were low. Figure 5.10 shows the market demand for MRIs when consumer demand is more elastic.

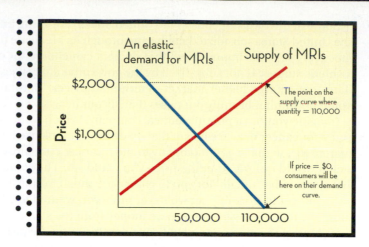

FIGURE **5.10**

DEMAND CURVE
WHEN DEMAND FOR
MRIS IS ELASTIC

Figure 5.9 shows that, if the government doesn't interfere in the market, consumers will still purchase 50,000 procedures at a price of $1,000 each. But since the demand curve in Figure 5.10 is price sensitive, consumers will want more MRIs if the price they pay falls to zero.

If the government now pays all health care costs and the price of health care goes to zero, quantity demanded of MRIs becomes 110,000. To avoid a shortage, the government would have to pay suppliers enough so that quantity supplied is 110,000. In Figure 5.10, quantity supplied is 110,000 at the price of $2,000.

So by offering "free" health care, the government will have to pay for 110,000 MRIs that cost $2,000 each for a total cost of $220 million a month. Recall that when the demand for health care was perfectly inelastic, the cost to the government of offering free MRIs was only $50 million a month.

A practical policy application of this analysis is that governments should be wary of paying for health care costs for services with very price-elastic demands. For example, consumers probably won't desire many additional heart operations as their price falls, but consumers undoubtedly would get more plastic surgery if it were free. The government, therefore, should be far more wary of offering free plastic surgery than free heart operations.

RATIONING

Figure 5.10 shows why many countries offering free health care ration services. Countries don't want to pay for health procedures consumers only "buy" because the cost of the procedure to the consumer is zero. So, many countries evaluate their citizens' health care needs before agreeing to provide the requested services. Furthermore, providing free health care to all can be extremely expensive, so governments such as Canada and the United Kingdom often attempt to limit costs by rationing needed care.

HEALTHY CANADIAN PETS AND GOOD-LOOKING AMERICANS

Canada has a shortage of MRI machines. In 1988, however, a Canadian hospital rented an MRI machine to a nearby veterinarian even while humans were waiting to be tested.[13] Canada strictly limits the prices hospitals can charge humans, but allows veterinarians to collect whatever the market will bear. Consequently, Canadian hospitals sometimes find it more profitable to rent their MRI machines to veterinarians than to use the machines to diagnose tumors in people.

Some of the best surgeons in the United States "are going into cosmetic surgery."[14] The United States subsidizes health care through its Medicare program. This program effectively sets maximum prices that doctors can charge for critical services. Since cosmetic surgery is not subsidized by the government, plastic surgeons in the United States can charge higher market-determined prices. Naturally, the best surgeons would now rather beautify our noses than fix our hearts.

Imagine you run a pharmaceutical company. Which would you prefer to discover: a cure for cancer or a face cream that made its user look like he or she was 18 again? I guarantee you that if your company found a cancer cure most of the world's governments would quickly limit the price you could set. They would undoubtedly argue that it would be "unfair" for you to charge too much for this life-saving drug. In contrast, you could probably set whatever price you wanted for the face cream, so your company might actually make more money from the skin treatment than the cancer cure. Most noneconomists would consider this outcome just and argue that people should pay lower prices for medical necessities than cosmetic luxuries. But when the government dictates lower prices for necessities than for luxuries, it guarantees that companies will have greater financial interest in developing the luxury goods.

PARKING METERS

Can't find parking? Blame low prices. Even on streets with meters, finding parking spaces can be challenging, because the number of spaces is often far below the quantity demanded. As with most shortages, the solution is to raise prices.

Higher prices won't increase the number of street parking spaces in the short run, but they will decrease the number of cars seeking these spaces. If parking meters were controlled by a private firm, price would increase when quantity supplied is less than quantity demanded, because doing so would increase profits. But cities that set parking meter prices often ignore market forces.

Figure 5.11 shows what could happen when a city always sets the same price for parking spaces. High demand creates a shortage; low demand creates a surplus.

What benefit, though, would be obtained by cities charging market prices for parking? After all, doing so wouldn't increase the number of parking spots. When there is a shortage of parking spaces, people often pay with time: they drive around the block waiting for someone to leave a space. In contrast, if the city were to raise the price of parking to eliminate the shortage, drivers would pay exclusively with cash.

THE DEADWEIGHT LOSS OF WAITING

The problem with time payments is that when you wait, no one gains. Consider the following example: Imagine that at the parking meter price of $2 per hour, the quantity demanded of spaces equals the quantity supplied and drivers willing to pay need not wait for a space. Further assume that at a price of $1 per hour, the average driver waits 15 minutes for a space. When drivers pay $2 per hour, the money all goes to the government so no waste is involved. True, the driver loses $2 per hour, but the city gains this $2 each hour, so on net no resources are lost. In contrast, if drivers must pay $1 per hour and wait 15 minutes, the 15-minute wait benefits nobody. Drivers lose time but the city doesn't, in any way, benefit from the loss. The lost time is an example of a deadweight loss: a loss one party suffers that does not benefit another party or, restated, a loss that reduces society's net wealth.

WHAT PRIVATE OWNERS OF PARKING METERS WOULD DO

A private owner of parking meters would never throw away money by setting a price so that there was a persistent shortage of spaces. By trying to make as much money

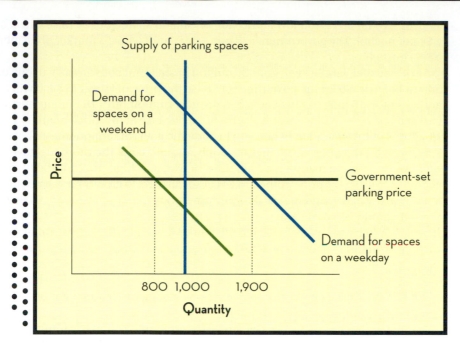

FIGURE **5.11**

CONSTANT PRICE
FOR PARKING
SPACES

as possible, this owner would conserve his customers' time and prevent deadweight losses.

A few cities have started using supply and demand to reduce parking problems by installing smart parking meters. These meters charge higher prices during times of the day when quantity demanded is the highest.

AGRICULTURAL SUBSIDIES

Politicians in rich countries love farmers and show their affection by showering them with billions in agricultural subsidies. In 2003 the European Union spent $121 billion supporting agriculture while the United States spent "only" $39 billion. For this sum, you could fly all the cows in these nations around the world and still have cash left over.[15]

Figure 5.12 shows hypothetical supply and demand curves for wheat. Absent government intervention, the market price of wheat is $3 a bushel. Imagine that the government

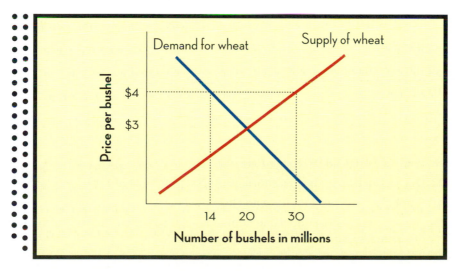

FIGURE **5.12**

HYPOTHETICAL
SUPPLY AND
DEMAND CURVES
FOR WHEAT

believes $3 a bushel is too low a price for wheat and so decides to raise wheat's price to $4 per bushel. The government will buy wheat until wheat's market price increases to $4 a bushel.

At $4 a bushel, farmers will grow 30 million bushels but consumers will buy only 14 million bushels. So for the government to raise the price of wheat to $4, it will have to buy 30 − 14 = 16 million bushels. When the government buys 16 million bushels, the market achieves equilibrium at the price of $4, because at this price quantity supplied equals quantity demanded (when you include the government purchases).

The greater the price elasticities of supply and demand, the more the government will have to spend to maintain a high price of wheat. A high price elasticity of supply means that raising the price from $3 to $4 causes farmers to grow far more wheat. A high price elasticity of demand means that consumers buy much less wheat at $4 than $3.

What should the government do now with the vast quantity of wheat it has purchased. Could it just sell the wheat to the market? Alas, no. If the government sold the wheat, this would shift out the supply curve and place downward pressure on prices. Even giving away the wheat to the poor would cause the poor to purchase less wheat, decreasing wheat's price. To maintain artificial agricultural prices, governments often purchase food and let it rot. Such practices wastes farmers' time and resources and unnecessarily burdens the environment.

Sometimes governments pay farmers *not* to grow crops, thereby shifting in the supply curve, raising the price of food. Although paying people not to work might seem inefficient, it's actually far more sensible than paying people to do unnecessary labor. Of course, a problem with paying people not to farm is that many will volunteer for the job. After all, wouldn't most college students accept government money in return for not growing wheat in their dorm rooms?

For millennia, humans struggled to get enough food to eat. Now, ironically, rich governments buy up unwanted surpluses of food and even bribe farmers to grow less while at the same time doctors in rich countries warn that *overeating* has become a major health problem.

FARM SUBSIDIES FOR THE RICH AND FAMOUS

The super-rich often benefit from farm subsidies. Basketball superstar Scottie Pippen, media billionaire Ted Turner, and super-banker David Rockefeller have each received over $100,000 in agricultural subsidies from the U.S. government.[16] The Queen of England has received over $1 million in agricultural subsidies from the European Union.

QUESTIONS YOU SHOULD BE ABLE TO ANSWER AFTER READING THIS CHAPTER:

1 What is a price floor? (page 104)

2 Does a price floor create a shortage or a surplus? (page 104)

3 When does a price floor have no effect on a market? (page 104)

4 How can you use a supply and demand diagram to determine how many jobs are destroyed by a minimum wage? (page 105)

5 Why might an unemployed person not be harmed significantly by a minimum wage? (page 106)

6 How can workers be helped by a minimum wage? (page 106)

7 How does price elasticity of demand affect the number of jobs destroyed by a minimum wage? (page 108)

8 How can you use a supply and demand diagram to determine how many people are made unemployed by a minimum wage? (page 108)

9 How does price elasticity of demand affect the number of people made unemployed by a minimum wage? (page 108)

10 How can workers who don't lose their jobs be harmed by a minimum wage? (page 109)

11 Why can the minimum wage and rent control promote racial discrimination? (pages 110–111 and 116)

12 What is a price ceiling? (page 111)

13 Does a price ceiling create a shortage or surplus? (page 111)

14 When does a price ceiling have no effect on a market? (page 111)

15 Why do the minimum wage and rent control create administrative costs for governments? (pages 111 and 116)

16 Why can the minimum wage law and rent control create black markets? (pages 111 and 116)

17 Why does rent control reduce incentives for landlords to care for their buildings? (page 114)

18 How can a draft harm soldiers who enlist voluntarily? (page 117)

19 How does the elasticity of demand for health care affect the cost to a government that provides free health care to all of its citizens? (pages 120–121)

20 Why does a shortage of parking spaces, caused by below-market parking meter rates, create a deadweight loss? (page 122)

21 How can you use a supply and demand diagram to determine the cost to the government of raising the price of wheat to a certain level? (pages 123–124)

22 How do the price elasticities of supply and demand affect the cost to the government of raising the price of an agricultural good? (page 124)

STUDY PROBLEMS

1 Essay question: The United States criminalizes drugs such as crack, cocaine, and heroin. Should the United States legalize the purchase and sale of these drugs? In your essay address how legalization would affect the price and quantity sold of these drugs. You might want to make use of the following facts in your essay:[17]

- Over 300,000 people are in jail in the United States on drug-related charges. The U.S. government spends about $33 billion a year fighting drugs.
- Americans spend about $64 billion a year on drugs. Much of this money goes to U.S. criminal gangs.
- Criminal gangs in other countries such as Columbia and Mexico earn large profits from selling drugs to the United States.

- In the U.S. alcohol kills around 100,000 a year while tobacco kills approximately 400,000 a year. Illegal drug use in the U.S. kills "only" about 20,000 per year.
- The U.S. government provides extensive welfare benefits to those unable to support themselves.
- Drug addicts on average make poor parents.
- Absenteeism and poor job performance resulting from alcoholic hangovers cost the U.S. economy an estimated $148 billion each year.
- People receive pleasure from consuming illegal drugs.
- Illegal drug use can create long-term health problems for users.
- Many U.S. politicians, including Bill Clinton, Barack Obama, and Al Gore have admitted using drugs. None of these politicians volunteered to serve the long prison terms that convicted drug offenders often face.[18]

2   Moral question: A minimum wage law limits the freedom of both workers and firms. Is this loss of freedom something that should be taken into account when considering the costs of a minimum wage law? Or, is it absurd to worry about a business owner losing the "freedom" to pay his workers low wages?

3   For the following two graphs, determine quantity supplied, quantity demanded, and the extent of any shortage or surplus.

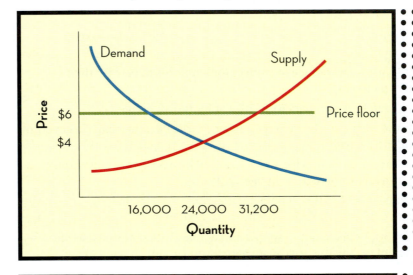

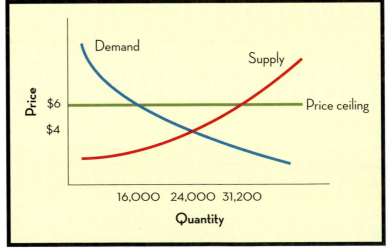

4 For the following diagram, determine (a) how many jobs the minimum wage destroys and (b) how many workers are made unemployed by the minimum wage.

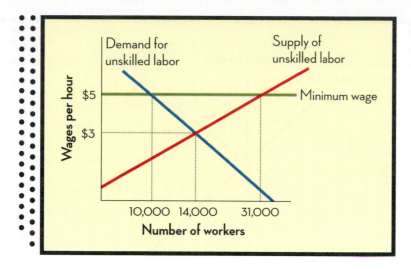

5 Why do city politicians have greater incentives than national politicians to support rent control laws?

6 In the following graph assume that the government imposes a price floor of $10 a unit and buys up the entire surplus. How much will the government spend purchasing the surplus?

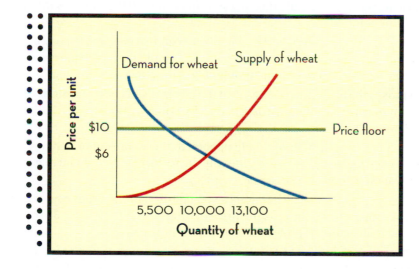

7 In question 6, would the government spend more or less if the price elasticity of demand was more elastic? Would the government spend more or less if the price elasticity of supply was more elastic?

8 In the following diagram, determine the shortage of apartments rent control causes in (a) the short run and (b) the long run.

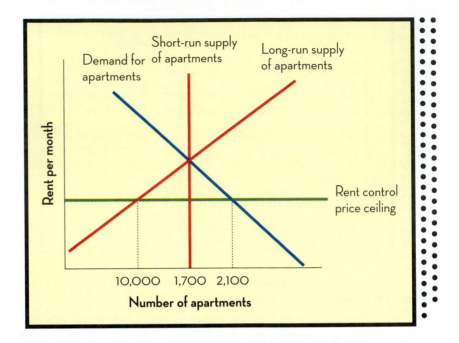

9 Cities often pass laws restricting the rents landlords can charge, but not laws restricting how much individual homeowners can sell their houses for. Why do you think this is?

10 Assume that the government pays part of the costs of some medical procedure. If the demand for this procedure suddenly increases, would the cost to the government increase more if the price elasticity of supply of this procedure was high or low?

11 Will more jobs be destroyed in a city if the city by itself enacts an $8-per-hour minimum wage law or if the country the city is in enacts an $8-per-hour minimum wage law?

12 Speculate on what you think would happen to the income of prostitutes if prostitution were legalized. Separately identify the factors that would increase and decrease their incomes.

13 A police captain claims he has done a great job at fighting drugs over the past year because during this time the price of drugs has increased by 30 percent. Has the police captain proved he is worthy of praise?

14 Americans spend about $64 billion on illegal drugs each year. Could the U.S. government stop illegal drug use in the United States if it just bought and then destroyed all $64 billion of these drugs every year? What does your answer say about the price elasticity of supply of illegal drugs?

15 In the following diagram, show the difference in the number of jobs destroyed when the supply for unskilled labor is elastic compared to when it is inelastic. Explain in words the cause of this difference.

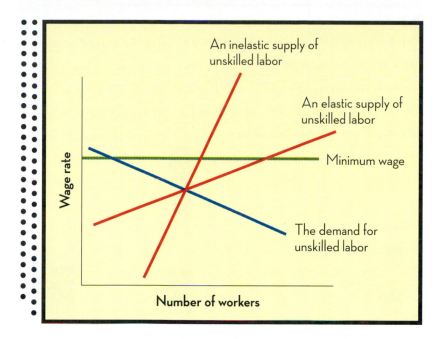

16 Sports gambling is illegal in Massachusetts. Bookies who accept bets sometimes go to jail. Assume small-time bettors, however, are never punished. Imagine you bet $20 with a bookie on a New England Patriots football game. There is a 50 percent chance that the Patriots will win this game. If the Patriots win, the bookie gives you $18. If the Patriots lose, you give the bookie your $20 bet. If gambling were legal and you bet $20 on the game, would you win more or less than $18 if the Patriots won?

17 If the U.S. legalized cocaine, would the total amount of money U.S. citizens spend on cocaine go up or down?

18 Assume that U.S. public high schools in some state have the same demand for English and math teachers. Because they have greater employment opportunities, however, the supply of math teachers is lower than the supply of English teachers. Assume, however, that by the rules of teachers unions, English and math teachers must be paid the same amount. Use supply and demand analysis to explore what is likely to happen in the market for English and math teachers.

19 Imagine that the New York Yankees baseball team sells tickets for $30 each. At this price, however, quantity supplied is less than quantity demanded. As a result, there is a financial incentive for ticket scalpers to buy up lots of Yankees tickets and resell them at a price above $30. What are the social costs and benefits of ticket scalping? Should ticket scalping be illegal?

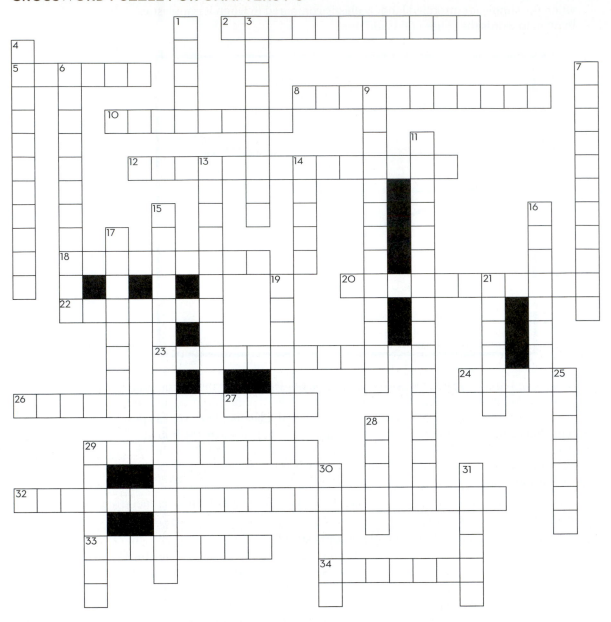

Across

2. Higher prices mean lower quantity demanded.
5. This type of elasticity can show inferiority.
8. Stability.
10. If you decrease supply and increase demand, price will_____.
12. With other things being equal.
18. Relatively unresponsive.
20. Reduces incentives for owners to maintain their buildings.
22. An increase in price will cause a decrease in total revenue if demand is _____.
23. Price times sales.
24. If a nation goes to war and the government wants to increase the number of troops it has, the government probably must either impose a draft or raise troops' _____.
26. If you increase supply and decrease demand, price will _____.
27. Any organization that produces goods or services.
29. Hot dogs are a _____ to hot dog buns.
32. These can create rotting mountains of food.
33. These types of goods have negative income elasticities of demand.
34. Demand is usually less elastic in the short run than the _____.

Down

1. A price _____ can cause a surplus.
3. Economist who illuminated the invisible hand.
4. Causes more unemployment the higher the elasticities.
6. A type of market with many buyers and sellers.
7. Higher prices cause greater production.
9. It pushes self-interested people to benefit society.
11. An increase in price gives us less of this.
13. Responsiveness.
14. Has a positive cross elasticity of demand to Coke.
15. An increase in price gives us more of this.
16. Markets correct this by raising price.
17. Sign of cross elasticity of demand for complements.
19. Firms are less responsive in this time frame.
21. _____ goods have positive income elasticities of demand.
25. Markets correct this by lowering price.

28. This type of elasticity distinguishes between complements and substitutes.
29. Can cause a shortage.
30. _____ and demand determine price.
31. Shows how much buyers want at every possible price.

"TO GET RICH IS GLORIOUS."

—Deng Xiaoping, former dictator of Communist China

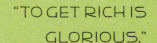

CHAPTER

6

In the 1,500 years before the early 19th century's industrial revolution, the average economic growth rate was approximately *zero*.[1] But since the Industrial Revolution, free market economies have created wealth at an astonishing pace. Indeed, a middle-class American is in most material respects better off than the wealthiest of Roman emperors. For unlike a Roman emperor, a middle-class American enjoys the riches of vaccines, antibiotics, automobiles, movies, newspapers, televisions, refrigerators, computers, telephones, the Internet, air-conditioning, electric lighting, candy, dental fillings, airplane travel, central heating, indoor plumbing, microeconomics textbooks, and food grown around the world. Furthermore, the free-market-driven economic growth engine shows no signs of slowing down; in 50 years it will likely provide consumer goods that would seem as advanced to us today as the Internet would have been to Julius Caesar.

But *why* do free markets excel at wealth creation? To answer the question, this chapter will first define wealth, then show why voluntary trades increase wealth, and then explain why the supply-and-demand-determined equilibrium squeezes the most wealth possible out of a market. And finally, this chapter will explore how markets facilitate that most important of all wealth-creating activities: innovation.

WHAT IS WEALTH?

I have a 20-pound computer monitor. If I gave you the monitor, it would still weigh 20 pounds. Weight is objective, so the monitor's weight is the same regardless of who owns it.

WEALTH CREATION AND DESTRUCTION

LEARNING OBJECTIVES

AFTER READING THIS CHAPTER, YOU SHOULD BE ABLE TO:

- Define the economic concept of wealth.
- Derive a consumer's surplus from a demand curve.
- Derive a producer's surplus from a supply curve.
- Understand why the supply-and-demand-determined equilibrium maximizes wealth.
- Recognize that taxes and subsidies can destroy wealth.
- Explain why innovation is critical to wealth creation.

Now imagine that the monitor is worthless to me because I have a better one. I keep this worthless monitor in a closet. So while I have the monitor, its value is zero. Assume, however, that if you had the monitor, you would use it. The value of the monitor to you, let's say, is $200. So if I gave you the monitor, its value increases from $0 to $200. The value of a good depends on who has it. Unlike weight, therefore, value is subjective.

A good is valued at the most its owner is willing to pay for it. So if you have the monitor and the most you would pay for your monitor is $200, then $200 is how much it is worth. A good, consequently, is *not* worth what its owner *actually paid for it*. For example, let's now assume that you bought the monitor for $170, but you would have been willing to pay up to $200 for it. You would rather have the monitor than $170, so the monitor is worth more than $170 to you.

Economists define an individual's wealth as the value of everything he owns. The total wealth of society is defined as the sum of each individual's wealth. Economists' definitions of value and wealth have a profound implication. If I give you the

REVIEW OF DEFINITIONS

Value of a good—the most its owner would pay for the good.

Individual's wealth—the value of all his possessions.

Total wealth of a society—the sum of each individual's wealth in whatever society one is looking at.

monitor (which is worthless to me), I lose nothing but you gain $200 in wealth. So my gift to you increases the total wealth of society by $200. Wealth, therefore, can be created not only when people produce new stuff, but also when they exchange existing goods!

SALES AND MONEY TRANSFERS

Imagine that rather than giving away my monitor, I sell it to you for $170. What now happens to the total wealth of society? I gain $170 from the sale since I traded a monitor that's worthless to me for $170. You gain $30 since you got something worth $200 in exchange for only $170. Thus, society's total wealth goes up by

$$\text{The increase in my wealth} + \text{The increase in your wealth}$$
$$= \$170 + \$30 = \$200$$

If I sold you the monitor for $199, I would gain $199 while you would gain $1, so society's total wealth would still go up by $200. In fact, at whatever price I sell you the monitor, society is always made $200 richer because you value the monitor for $200 more than I do. Generally, the price a good sells for has no effect on the total wealth of society, because this price represents a money transfer.

A money transfer is money paid from one person to another. Although money transfers affect individual wealth, they can't affect the total wealth of society. For example, pretend that the tallest student in your economics class gives $20 to the shortest. This $20 money transfer would make the tallest student poorer and the shortest student richer, but these changes in individual wealth would exactly cancel out and therefore not affect the total wealth of your class.

Money transfer—money paid from one person to another.

Money transfers have no effect on the wealth of society.

When you buy my monitor, two things happen:

1. The monitor goes from me to you.
2. A money transfer (in the amount of the monitor's price) goes from you to me.

Because of (1), the wealth of society increases by $200 since you value the monitor $200 more than I do. But (2) has no effect on society's wealth. Consequently, if the monitor is sold, the price at which it was sold does not affect society's total wealth. Generally, when one person sells a good to another, the wealth of society goes up by the additional amount that the buyer values the good over the seller.

WHY FREE TRADE PROMOTES WEALTH CREATION

If a seller sells a good to a buyer and no third party is hurt by the sale, then the sale must increase the wealth of society. The seller would have agreed to the sale only if

1. The value of the good to the seller < the good's sale price

The buyer would have agreed to the sale only if

2. The good's sale price < the value of the good to the buyer

Combining (1) and (2), we know that

3. The value of the good to the seller < the good's sale price < the value of the good to the buyer

Because of (3) we know that if a sale takes place, the seller must value the good less than the buyer does. The sale, therefore, increases the wealth of society since it moves a good to someone who places a higher value on it.

Let's consider two examples:

Example 1: Jane has a car she values at $5,000. Xavier would value the car at $6,000 if he owned it. Both parties are made better off if Xavier buys the car for between $5,000 and $6,000. If the parties are allowed to negotiate, they should be able to reach an agreement that makes them both better off. If Xavier buys the car for some amount X, he gains $6,000 − X. If Jane sells the car for X, she gains X − $5,000. Thus, the total wealth of society changes by

$$\text{The increase in Xavier's wealth} + \text{The increase in Jane's wealth}$$
$$= (\$6{,}000 - X) + (X - \$5{,}000) = \$1{,}000$$

Example 2: Jane has a car she values at $5,000. Xavier would value the car at $3,000 if he owned it. If Xavier bought the car, the wealth of society would go down since Xavier gets less value from the car than does Jane. But Jane and Xavier would never agree on a sale price. Jane would insist on getting more than $5,000 while Xavier would pay only less than $3,000. In general, when parties are free to trade (and their trades don't harm other people), they never make trades that reduce the wealth of society.

INCREASING WEALTH THROUGH PRODUCTION

Production, as well as trade, can increase wealth. Imagine that a buyer values a car at $20,000, and it costs an automobile manufacturer only $15,000 to make the car. If the car is made and then sold to the buyer, the wealth of society goes up by $5,000. The amount the buyer pays for the car is a money transfer and thus has no effect on the total wealth of society.

If no outside parties are harmed, voluntary trades between a buyer and manufacturer will increase the wealth of society because the manufacturer will only sell the good for more than it costs to make, and the buyer will only pay an amount less than what the good is worth to her. Consequently, if the buyer ends up with the good, the sale must have benefited both the buyer and manufacturer.

WALLY THE WEALTH CREATOR

Each day a typical free man or woman engages in many wealth-creating trades. Consider, for example, Wally. At 7:00 a.m. Wally's alarm clock wakes him up. Wally paid $20 for the alarm clock that was worth $50 to him, and the alarm clock costs only $15 to make. Wally then eats a bowl of cereal for breakfast that Wally bought for $1 but was worth $2 to Wally although the cereal costs only $.50 to make. Wally then receives $60 for giving a one-hour piano lesson. Wally would offer the lesson only if he valued an hour of his time at less than $60. Similarly, the person who received the lesson must have valued it at more than $60 or she would never have hired Wally.

The genius of free markets is that Wally engages in each of these trades only if they make him better off. Similarly, the person on the opposite end of each trade must also be made better off from her interaction with Wally or else she would not have agreed to the trade.

WEALTH CREATION AND GROWTH

Over the long run, the rate of growth of wealth creation is the most important force shaping a society. Consider two economies that start out with equal wealth but then grow at different rates. The first economy grows by 2 percent a year, meaning that each year the economy is 2 percent richer than the last. The second economy grows at 5 percent a year. After a mere 38 years the second economy will be *three times* richer than the first. Imagine what it would mean to a society to have three times the resources to devote to health care, housing, travel, food, science, culture, the military, and microeconomics textbooks. When evaluating the long-term consequences of any economic policy, a wise person's first question will always be, "How does it affect the growth rate of wealth creation?"

SEVEN WAYS GOVERNMENTS DESTROY WEALTH

So far we have seen how free transactions increase the total wealth of society. But governments often restrict, regulate, or tax such transactions, and this market interference often destroys wealth. In Part III of this textbook, we will examine how governments can assist markets in wealth creation. But we now consider seven ways by which governments destroy wealth.

1. RENT CONTROL

Imagine that using the third floor in my house for storage is worth $700 a month to me. In contrast, you would pay up to $1,200 a month to live there. If you rent this floor, society will be $500 ($1,200 − $700) a month richer. But now assume that because of rent control I can't charge more than $600 a month in rent. At this price I won't rent this floor and will instead use it as storage space. But because the trade between us doesn't take place, society loses the chance to create $500 a month in wealth.

2. MINIMUM WAGES

Assume that the opportunity cost of John's time is $4 an hour—meaning that this is the value of his time to him. Further assume that a company values John's time at $5 an hour. If John sells his time to the company, society will be $1 an hour richer. Since the wage at which John would sell his time would be a money transfer, it has no effect on the total wealth of society. But now imagine that a minimum wage law prevents anyone from working for below $5.50 an hour. The company will not want to hire John at this wage because it is above John's worth to them. The minimum wage law, therefore, prevents John from working for the company and will thus keep $1 of wealth from being created for every hour John would have been employed.

3. TAXES

Taxes, too, can destroy wealth. Imagine that you own a construction company. It would cost you $210,000 to build a new house for Sam. Sam would value this house at $240,000, so if you build the house for Sam, society is $30,000 richer. Since the price that Sam pays for the house is just a money transfer, it has no effect on the wealth of society. Being a rational businessperson, however, you wouldn't build the house unless Sam paid you at least $210,000. Like all self-interested individuals, you care about your own wealth, not the total wealth of society.

Let's now assume that if you build the house for Sam, he will have to pay $40,000 in taxes. Because of this tax, Sam will never pay you more than $200,000 for the house ($240,000 − $40,000) and at this price or lower, you won't agree to build the home. The house tax, therefore, has prevented society from being $30,000 richer while raising zero money for the government. If, in contrast, the house tax had been less than $30,000, then you and Sam would have been able to find a sale price that made you both better off.

4. SUBSIDIES

Subsidies, the mirror image of taxes, can also destroy wealth. Assume that your college freely gives students all the paper they want even though the paper costs the college five cents a page. Imagine that you have just typed into your computer a 50-page draft of your economics research paper titled, "On the Waste Caused by Subsidies." Further assume you would get a $1 benefit from printing out the draft. The benefit comes from being able to proofread the paper copy rather than having to read it on a computer screen. Since it costs you nothing to print this draft, you will do so. But the printing of your 50 pages costs your college $2.50. So printing out this draft destroys $1.50 of wealth (the printing gives you $1 of value but costs the college $2.50). Since, however, your college and not you suffers from the destroyed wealth, it's in your self-interest to print out the draft. Consequently, your college's subsidization of computer paper creates incentives for you to destroy wealth.

Printing the draft uses $2.50 of resources. If you had to pay $2.50 you would never have printed it. But because your college gives you zero-priced paper, you do print out the 50 pages and so waste paper.

U.S. Flood Insurance Flood insurance subsidies in the U.S. destroy significant amounts of wealth. The U.S. government sells cheap flood insurance to people who build homes near water. Imagine that you are considering building a $1 million second home on the coast. You want to build on the coast so your home will have an ocean view. Unfortunately, over the next 20 years there is an 80 percent chance that your home will be destroyed by flooding. Normally, you wouldn't build the home and risk an 80 percent chance of losing a $1 million investment. But the U.S. government will sell you very cheap flood insurance. If you buy the insurance and floods destroy your home, then the government pays for the complete rebuilding of your home. Because of the flood insurance, you will likely build the home. But since it's grossly inefficient to build expensive homes in flood zones, the insurance causes a misallocation of resources.

Some Americans take repeated advantage of flood insurance. They build in areas prone to flooding and then repeatedly use government money to rebuild their homes after they have been damaged by floods. One homeowner in Houston, for example, received government compensation for flood damage on 16 separate occasions. He received $807,000 in total payments even though his property was valued at only $114,480.[2]

Water Subsidies Growing alfalfa requires a lot of water. But California farmers not only grow alfalfa in the desert, they also grow the crop using water-wasting methods. Why do California farmers waste so much water? Because the government greatly subsidizes their water use. Many California farmers pay only 10 percent of the cost of the water they use.[3]

5. FORCED SHARING

Your kindergarten teacher, at some point, probably forced you to share your toys with another child. Perhaps mandatory sharing in kindergarten is beneficial for youngsters. But when governments force their adult citizens to share, the result can be famine.

Imagine that you're a productive farmer and for every hour you work you can produce $20 worth of food. But now assume that you live on an agricultural commune with 1,000 people. Under the commune's rules, all food is shared equally. If you grow 1,000 carrots, you get to keep only one and each member in the commune is given one of the carrots you produced.

So, for every extra hour you work you get an extra \$20/1,000, or two cents' worth of food. True, you get a share of everyone else's food as well, but you get this share regardless of whether you do any work.

Working for two cents an hour is a horrible deal for most anyone. Consequently, you will work as little as possible. This result might seem impossible; after all, if no one works on your commune, everyone will starve. Unfortunately, this is exactly what happened with communal agriculture in the Soviet Union and Communist China. In the 20th century, millions of people starved in these two countries because of forced-sharing agricultural rules.

Forced Sharing in Chinese Agriculture

This chapter opens with a quote from Deng Xiaoping saying, "To get rich is glorious." Here's the quote's historical context: Mao Zedong, the founder of Communist China, forced hundreds of millions of Chinese farmers into agricultural communes where they had to share all their food. Under Mao, Chinese communist ideology held that it was "wrong" for any one farmer to get richer simply because he was able to work harder. So the communists made successful farmers share their food with the less successful to the extent that nearly all farmers on a commune ended up with the same amount of food regardless of how hard they worked. The predictable result was that farmers worked few hours and grew little food. Chinese agriculture under Mao therefore created little wealth.

MAO

Mao Zedong was a ruthless dictator who killed political dissidents and enacted anti-market economic policies that plunged hundreds of millions of people into poverty. He thought poverty, for other people, was a good thing. At an important 1957 Communist summit in Moscow, Mao said: "People say that poverty is bad, but in fact poverty is good. The poorer people are, the more revolutionary they are. It is dreadful to imagine a time when everyone will be rich."[4] Mao himself, however, lived more luxuriously than an American billionaire.

Xiaogang's Revolution

In 1978, Chinese peasants in Xiaogang village were starving. Xiaogang village had some fertile farm land, so its people should have had plenty to eat. But Mao's agricultural policies eliminated the villagers' incentives to work, and as a result, they didn't produce enough food to feed themselves.

Xiaogang's farmers, fortunately, had an excellent intuitive grasp of microeconomics. The farmers secretly agreed to disobey the law and give every village family its own piece of land. Each family could keep everything it grew on its land. Xiaogang farmers, henceforth, had tremendous incentives to work hard to grow lots of food. The farmers' elimination of sharing was extremely successful:

> A rapid turnaround followed. The farmers of Xiaogang immediately became more productive. 'Now is different from the past,' one said. 'We work for ourselves.' Working their own plots of land, they could see a direct link between their effort and their rewards . . . The amount of land planted in rice nearly doubled in one year . . . As a farmer said, 'You can't be lazy when you work for your family and yourself.'[5]

Observing their success, other Chinese villages started copying Xiaogang. The Chinese government eventually realized that some farmers were disobeying Mao's agricultural laws. If Mao had then been alive (he died in 1976), he probably would have killed everyone in Xiaogang. But by the time that Xiaogang's disobedience had been officially found out, Deng Xiaoping was the leader of China.

XIAOGANG'S REVOLUTION

Deng Xiaoping wanted to increase China's agricultural production. In 1983, after learning how successful the Xiaogang's farmers were, Deng ordered the rest of China to copy Xiaogang. As a result, Chinese farmers now didn't have to share, and so they had significantly greater incentives to grow food. Because of Deng's reforms, hundreds of millions of Chinese escaped starvation-level poverty. For a formerly starving person, getting rich is indeed glorious.

Forced Sharing among Pilgrims   Like the Chinese under Mao, the American Pilgrims also suffered from forced sharing. When the pilgrims first landed at Plymouth Rock in 1620, they practiced "farming in common," in which all the food grown was divided according to need. So Pilgrims initially each received the same amount of food regardless of how hard they worked. The predictable result was that the Pilgrim farmers didn't work very hard and many almost starved during each of their first three winters in America. But in 1623, the Pilgrim's leader ended farming in common by giving each family a plot of land. A family could keep all of the food it grew on its own. And as a result, Pilgrims who previously claimed they were "too old or ill to work" eagerly farmed their own land.[6] The Pilgrims soon had so much food they traded some of it to natives for furs.

6. THEFT

Throughout much of human history, the strong have had the ability to take property from the weak. For example, in the Congo, if an armed soldier "asks" a farmer for his hoe, the farmer had better comply. Unfortunately, if the soldier values the hoe less than the farmer does, then this forced transfer reduces wealth.

Since in a free market a good is sold only if the buyer values the good more than the seller does, every sale increases wealth. Unfortunately when an armed member of the government (or a freelance criminal) steals, we can't assume that this thief places a higher value on the good than its rightful owner did. Unlike voluntary transactions, theft often reduces the total wealth of society.

7. EMINENT DOMAIN

Eminent domain is the power of a government to take private property. It can, theoretically, increase the wealth of society. Imagine that building a new airport will increase the wealth of a city by $2 billion. But to build the airport, 100 homes would have to be destroyed. Ideally, the city would buy all these homes from their owners. But if even one homeowner refused to sell, the airport couldn't be built. To guarantee that the airport gets built, therefore, the city could use eminent domain to take all 100 homes. Under the U.S. Constitution, local governments can expel private property holders if they pay the owners the prevailing market rate for their land and meet a few other legal requirements.[7] Unfortunately, politicians often abuse the power of eminent domain to help their supporters, and this abuse can destroy wealth.

Assume, for example, that Mega-Industries wants to build a factory on Janice Green's land. Rather than buying the land, however, Mega-Industries convinces the government to force Mrs. Green to sell her land at the prevailing market rate.

Why, you might ask, would a local government use eminent domain to allow a business to forcibly buy private land? The benevolent reason is that the government believes that the new owners of the property will help their community by, say, paying a significant amount of taxes. A malevolent reason is that the business has greater political power than the homeowner. Perhaps, for example, Mrs. Green

In the 2005 case of *Kelo v. City of New London,* the U.S. Supreme Court ruled that it was constitutional for a city to use eminent domain to force a property owner to sell his home to a firm. One of the five Supreme Court Justices who supported this decision was David Souter. Outraged at the decision, several people unsuccessfully tried to use eminent domain to forcibly take a farmhouse that Souter owned and turn it into a "Lost Liberty Hotel."[8]

values her land at $300,000 and would have been willing to sell her land for just a little bit more than this. But instead of paying this amount, Mega-Industries gives $20,000 in political contributions to local government officials who then force Mrs. Green to sell her land for a mere $200,000. If Mega-Industries values the land at $290,000, the seizure and transfer of the land lowers the total wealth of society because Mega-Industries values the land less than Mrs. Green does. But since Mega-Industries, like most everyone else, is concerned only with its wealth, not the wealth of society, it will still take Ms. Green's land even if the transaction makes society poorer.

Eminent domain is similar to theft. In both cases, property is taken without its owner's permission. Consequently, the new owner of the property doesn't necessarily place a higher value on the property than the old owner did.

SUPPLY, DEMAND, AND WEALTH

We are now going to study why the supply-and-demand-determined equilibrium maximizes wealth. The analysis will be somewhat complicated and so will require readers to pay close attention. Here is a brief summary of what we will establish:

■ The maximum amount consumers are willing to pay for goods determines the height of demand curves.

■ The difference between the most that consumers are willing to pay for a good and the price of a good is the net benefit that consumers receive from buying a good. This net benefit is called the *consumers' surplus.* The greater the consumers' surplus, the better off consumers are.

■ The cost of producing goods determines the height of supply curves.

■ The difference between the price of a good and the cost of producing a good is the net benefit that producers receive from selling a good. This net benefit is called the *producers' surplus.* The greater the producers' surplus, the better off producers are.

■ The sum of consumers' and producers' surplus is called the *total surplus.* The total surplus is the value that society gets from the production and consumption of a good.

■ The total surplus is maximized at the supply-and-demand-determined equilibrium. If, therefore, the government interferes in a market and moves society away from this supply-and-demand-determined equilibrium, then the government will make society poorer.*

DEMAND CURVES AND THE MAXIMUM AMOUNT CONSUMERS ARE WILLING TO PAY

Let's now use our old friends supply and demand to analyze wealth creation. We start by deriving the demand for hats. The following chart shows the maximum amount each consumer would pay for a hat. Assume that a consumer will buy either zero or one hat.

---

*We will see in Chapter 13 why this isn't necessarily true if a good creates "externalities."

Consumer	Most Consumer Is Willing to Pay
Abe	$7
Ben	6
Calvin	5
Debbie	4
Ed	3
Fran	2
Gene	1

We can use this chart to determine the demand for hats. Let's assume that if a consumer is indifferent between buying or not buying a hat, then she will buy a hat. This means, for example, that if the price of hats is $2, Fran will purchase a hat. Figure 6.1 shows the staircase-like demand for hats.

To read Figure 6.1, look at the price of hats on the Y-axis. We will start with a price of $10 and work our way down to the price of zero. At the price of $10 no one wants to buy a hat, so the quantity demanded is zero. The quantity demanded stays at zero as long as the price is above $7. But at $7 the quantity demanded jumps to one, because at this price Abe buys a hat. The quantity demanded of hats stays at one until the price reaches $6, at which point it jumps to two, because at $6 both Ben and Abe want a hat. Between a price of $6 and $5, the quantity demanded stays at two. But once we reach the price of $5, quantity demanded jumps to three. This process continues until the price of hats reaches $1, at which point quantity demanded reaches seven, its highest value.

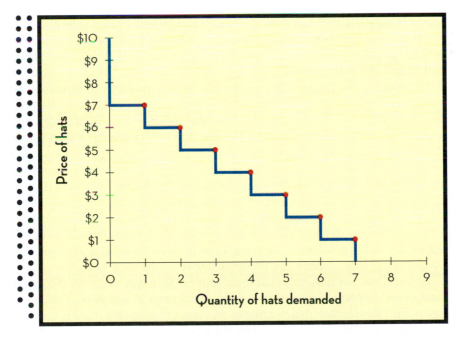

FIGURE **6.1**

DEMAND FOR HATS

CONSUMER'S SURPLUS

A *consumer's surplus* is the difference between the value the consumer places on a good and the amount the consumer actually paid for the good. So if you purchase a hat for $2 but value the hat at $7, then your consumer's surplus is $7 − $2 = $5. Recall that the value of a good to you is the most you would have been willing to pay for the good. So a consumer's surplus is also the difference between the most the consumer would have paid for a good and the amount the consumer actually paid for the good. We will now calculate the consumer's surplus for each buyer if the price of hats is $2.

Consumer's surplus = (the most you would have paid) − (what you actually paid)

Consumer	Most Willing to Pay	Consumer's Surplus if the Price of Hats Is $2
Abe	$7	$7 − $2 = $5
Ben	6	6 − 2 = 4
Calvin	5	5 − 2 = 3
Debbie	4	4 − 2 = 2
Ed	3	3 − 2 = 1
Fran	2	2 − 2 = 0
Gene	1	zero since no hat will be bought

Figure 6.2 graphically shows all the consumers' surpluses if the price of hats is $2. In a way, Abe will buy the first hat because he values it the most. The point on Figure 6.2 where price equals $7 and quantity equals 1 represents Abe's valuation of that first hat. It means that the first hat is worth $7 to a consumer (Abe). If the price of hats is only $2, then Abe gets a consumer's surplus that is equal to the difference between $7 and $2 multiplied by one hat.

Ben will buy the second hat since he has the second highest valuation of hats. His consumer's surplus is his valuation of $6 minus the price of $2 multiplied by one hat. To graphically show Ben's consumer's surplus we need an area of length $6 − $2 and width of one unit of output. Calvin, Debbie, and Ed's consumer's surplus is similarly shown in Figure 6.2. Fran gets no consumer's surplus since she pays exactly what the hat is worth to her. At a price of $2, Gene also doesn't receive any consumer's surplus since she won't buy a hat at this price. The total consumers' surplus in this example is the sum of Abe, Ben, Calvin, Debbie and Ed's individual consumer surpluses.

If you compare Figure 6.2 and 6.3, you see that the total consumers' surplus is the area between the demand curve and the price. This generally holds true. Figure 6.2 represents only a small number of consumers, so its demand curve looks "lumpy." If we had many more consumers, however, it would look more normal.

Figure 6.3 shows the total consumers' surplus for a typical demand curve. The total consumers' surplus is the area between the demand curve and price. The demand curve shows the value each consumer places on the good while the price is how much each consumer has to pay for the good. The difference is the total consumers' surplus.

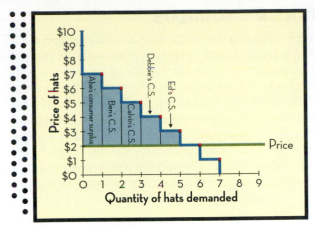

FIGURE 6.2

CONSUMERS' SURPLUSES WHEN HAT PRICE IS $2

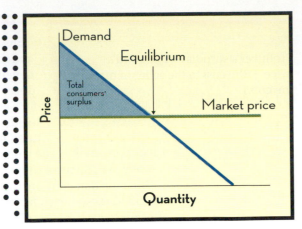

FIGURE 6.3

TOTAL CONSUMERS' SURPLUS FOR A TYPICAL
DEMAND CURVE

Figure 6.4 shows what happens to the total consumers' surplus when the price of a hypothetical good falls from $9 to $7. As you would expect, the total consumers' surplus increases, since consumers benefit from lower prices. But this increase can be broken up into two parts: the benefit to the old consumers who would have bought the good at $9, and the benefit to new consumers who buy the good at $7 but not $9. Analogously, Figure 6.5 shows the effect on total consumers' surplus when the price of a hypothetical good increases from $9 to $13.

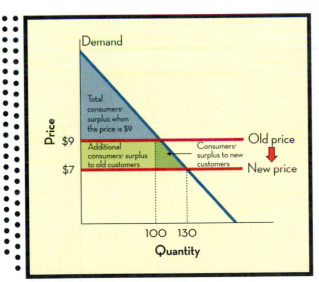

FIGURE 6.4

EFFECT OF $2 PRICE DECREASE ON TOTAL
CONSUMERS' SURPLUS

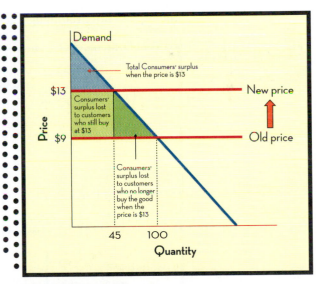

FIGURE 6.5

EFFECT OF $4 PRICE INCREASE ON TOTAL
CONSUMERS' SURPLUS

PRODUCER'S SURPLUS

> Producer's surplus = The good's price − the cost to the seller of making the good

Consumer's surplus is the net benefit a consumer gets from purchasing a good. Similarly, *producer's surplus* is the net benefit a producer receives from the sale of a good. The producer's surplus is defined as the amount that a seller receives for a good (the good's price) minus the cost to the seller of making the good. (Or, if the seller is a trader rather than a manufacturer, it's the good's price minus the value of the good to the seller.) Just as we used a demand curve to indicate graphically the total consumers' surplus, we can use a supply curve to show graphically the total producers' surplus.

Imagine that there are five hat factories. Assume that for some very strange and unspecified reason each factory can make either zero or one hat. The following shows the cost to each factory of making a hat.

Factory	Cost to Make a Hat
A	$1.00
B	1.50
C	2.00
D	3.00
E	3.50

Figure 6.6 shows the staircase-like supply curve for a market consisting of these five firms. The cost to a factory of making a hat is the lowest price that a factory would ever accept to make a hat. Assume that, if a firm is indifferent between producing and not producing a good, it will produce the good. To read Figure 6.6, let's

FIGURE 6.6

SUPPLY CURVE FOR FIVE FIRMS

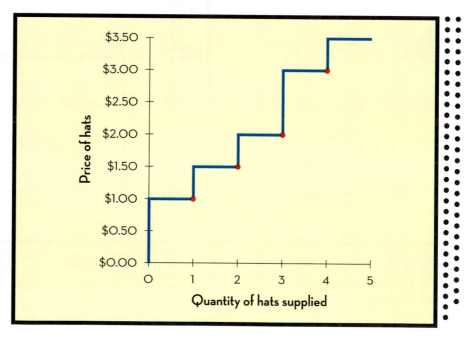

start at a price of zero and work our way up to a price of $3.50. At a price of 0, quantity supplied will also be zero. Quantity supplied will stay at zero until we hit the price of $1, where it will jump to 1 because at this price factory A will make a hat. Quantity supplied will stay at 1 until we reach the price of $1.50, at which point quantity supplied jumps to 2 because at a price of $2 both factory A and B make a hat. Quantity supplied continues to increase in this staircase-like manner until the price becomes $3.50, at which point quantity supplied reaches its maximum value of 5.

Let's calculate the producer's surpluses if the price of hats is $3.

Factory	Cost to Make a Hat	Producer's Surplus if the Price of Hats Is $3
A	$1.00	$3 − $1 = $2
B	1.50	3 − 1.50 = 1.50
C	2.00	3 − 2 = 1
D	3.00	3 − 3 = 0
E	3.50	zero since no hat will be made

Figure 6.7 graphically shows the producers' surpluses when the price of hats is $3. Since factory A can make its hat the cheapest, in a sense factory A will make the first hat. Its producer's surplus is the difference between the $3 price of hats and its $1 cost of making a hat multiplied by one hat. Factory B makes the second hat since its costs are the second lowest. Factory B's producer's surplus is the price of hats minus its $1.50 cost multiplied by one hat. Factory C's producer's surplus is calculated likewise.

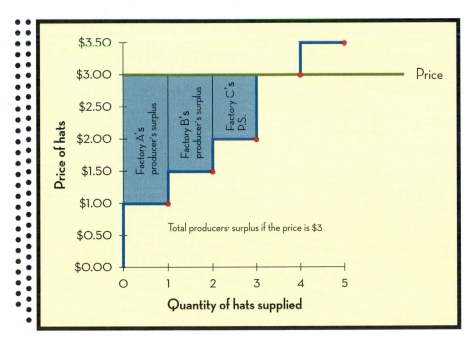

FIGURE **6.7**

PRODUCERS' SURPLUSES WHEN HAT PRICE IS $3

As you should see by comparing Figures 6.6 and 6.7, the total producers' surplus is the area between the supply curve and the price. Figure 6.6 has only five producers, so its supply curve looks lumpy. If we had many more sellers, however, it would look more normal.

Figure 6.8 shows the total producers' surplus for a normal supply curve. The total producers' surplus is the area between the supply curve and price. The supply curve shows how much it costs each firm to make a good, while the price is how much each firm sells its good for. This difference is the total producers' surplus.

FIGURE **6.8**

TOTAL PRODUCERS' SURPLUS FOR A NORMAL SUPPLY CURVE

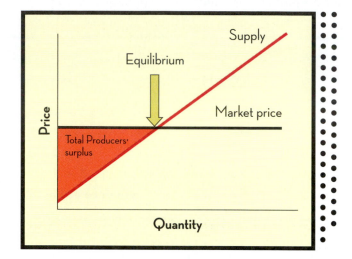

CONSUMERS' AND PRODUCERS' SURPLUS COMBINED

Total surplus is defined as the sum of the total consumers' surplus and total producers' surplus. Figure 6.9 shows the total surplus for a typical market. **Of all possible prices, the free-market equilibrium price maximizes the total surplus.** (This is

FIGURE **6.9**

TOTAL SURPLUS FOR A TYPICAL MARKET

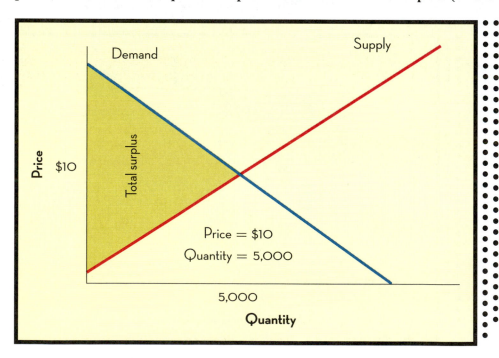

important!) Consequently, the market equilibrium price squeezes the most possible wealth out of a market. To prove this graphically we will show that the total surplus for the market in Figure 6.9 would be lowered if the government forced the price higher or lower than the free-market equilibrium price.

THE DEADWEIGHT LOSS OF A GOVERNMENT-DICTATED PRICE

Figure 6.10 contains the same supply and demand curves as Figure 6.9, but now the government sets the price above the market equilibrium price. As you can see from comparing Figure 6.9 to Figure 6.10, the total surplus is lower in Figure 6.10. It's lowered by the entire green area labeled *deadweight loss.* Moving from the market equilibrium price of $10 to the government-imposed price of $12 has two effects:

1. Consumers pay $2 more for every good they buy.
2. Consumers buy 1,000 fewer goods.

Effect (1) represents a money transfer from consumers to producers and so increases the total producers' surplus while reducing the total consumers' surplus. But since it's a money transfer, it has no effect on total wealth. In contrast, (2) represents a real loss of wealth to society. Recall that the demand curve represents the value of the good to consumers while the supply curve shows the cost to producers of making the good. As long as the demand curve is above the supply curve, wealth is created when additional goods are sold. For example, according to Figure 6.10, it costs producers $9 to make good number 4,800, whereas consumers' value this good at $10.55. So not making this good reduces society's wealth by $1.55. The loss in wealth is caused by consumers buying fewer goods than they would have at the market equilibrium price and is given by the green area labeled *deadweight loss* in Figure 6.10.

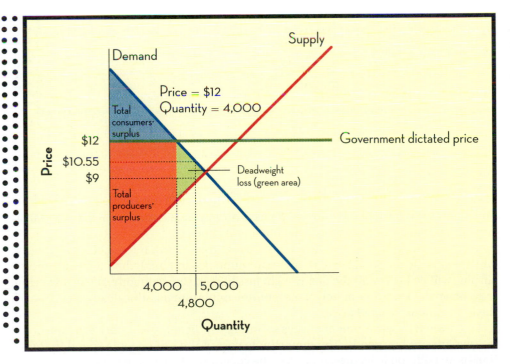

FIGURE **6.10**

GOVERNMENT-DICTATED PRICE ABOVE MARKET EQUILIBRIUM PRICE

A deadweight loss benefits no one—it represents a net loss of resources to society. Suppose you accidentally drop your watch and $100 in cash. The cash and watch are picked up by a stranger. This stranger keeps the cash but throws away the watch. Your loss of $100 is not a deadweight loss because although you suffered a real loss, the stranger receives a compensating gain. In contrast, the loss of your watch benefits no one and so represents a deadweight loss to society.

Figure 6.11 contains the same supply and demand curves as Figure 6.9, but now the government sets the price below the market equilibrium price, at $6. At the price of $6, quantity traded is only 3,000. As you can see from comparing Figure 6.11 to 6.9 the total surplus is lower in Figure 6.11. It's lower by the area labeled *deadweight loss*. As before, this deadweight loss arises because the quantity traded is wastefully too small.

We have shown that the supply-and-demand-determined equilibrium price produces more wealth than would a higher or lower price. Therefore, we have established that the market price creates more wealth than any other price.

FIGURE 6.11

GOVERNMENT-DICTATED PRICE BELOW MARKET EQUILIBRIUM PRICE

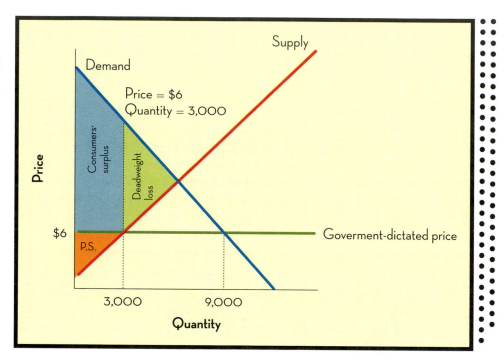

An Even Bigger Deadweight Loss

The deadweight loss shown in Figure 6.11 probably understates the actual deadweight loss of the government-dictated below-market price. At the price of $6, 9,000 consumers want to buy the good but only 3,000 goods will be produced, meaning that 6,000 consumers will not get the product. Without additional information, however, we have no way to determine which of the 9,000 consumers will be the lucky ones who obtain the product.

The consumers' surplus shown in Figure 6.11 assumes that the 3,000 consumers who most value the good get it. If this assumption doesn't hold, then the consumers' surplus will be lower and the deadweight loss higher. Consequently, the deadweight loss shown in Figure 6.11 merely represents the minimum possible deadweight loss of the government-dictated price.

Often when the government creates a shortage by dictating a low price, people wait in long lines to buy goods. The opportunity cost of the time people spend in these lines is an additional deadweight loss of the government-mandated price.

WHY THE SUPPLY-AND-DEMAND-DETERMINED EQUILIBRIUM PRICE MAXIMIZES WEALTH

Will the wealth of society be increased or decreased if good number X is produced? The demand curve above output number X in Figure 6.12 tells us the value that consumers would place on having this good. The supply curve above output number X tells us the cost to producers of making this good. So, society's wealth is increased by the production of good X if, and only if, the demand curve is above the supply curve at this level of output.

To maximize the wealth of society, therefore, goods must be produced if, and only if, the demand curve is above the supply curve. As Figures 6.12 and 6.13 show, this is exactly what happens in free markets. The free market, therefore, produces just the right amount of goods to squeeze the most possible wealth out of a market.

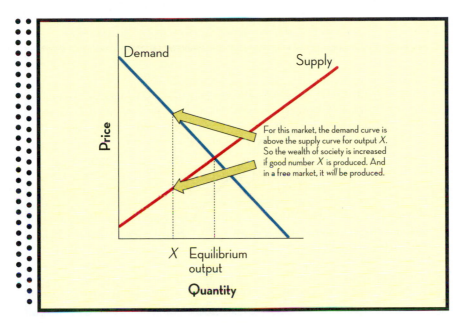

FIGURE 6.12

DEMAND AND SUPPLY CURVES WHEN PRODUCING A GOOD INCREASES SOCIETY'S WEALTH

For this market, the demand curve is above the supply curve for output X. So the wealth of society is increased if good number X is produced. And in a free market, it *will* be produced.

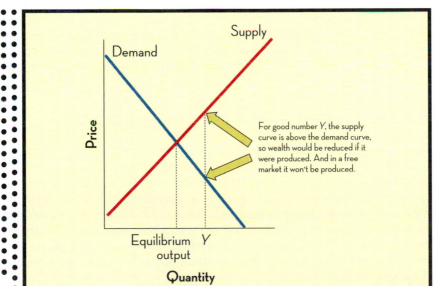

FIGURE 6.13

SUPPLY AND DEMAND CURVES WHEN PRODUCING A GOOD REDUCES SOCIETY'S WEALTH

For good number Y, the supply curve is above the demand curve, so wealth would be reduced if it were produced. And in a free market it won't be produced.

Supply, Demand, and Wealth

Why It's Bad to Produce Too Much   In Figure 6.13, society will be poorer if good number Y is produced. But how could overproduction reduce wealth? Producing a good requires resources. When you produce too much of a good, it means that the resources used to make the good could be better used elsewhere.

SUPPLY, DEMAND, AND TAXATION

All governments raise revenue through taxation. Let's use the tools of supply, demand, and total surplus to examine the effects of a sales tax. Figure 6.14 shows the total surplus in a market before a tax is imposed. In this market, the price is $10 and quantity traded is 5,000. Figure 6.15 shows the consequences of the government imposing a $2 tax per good on consumers. Under the tax, buyers pay $2 more than sellers receive.

FIGURE **6.14**

TOTAL SURPLUS
BEFORE TAX

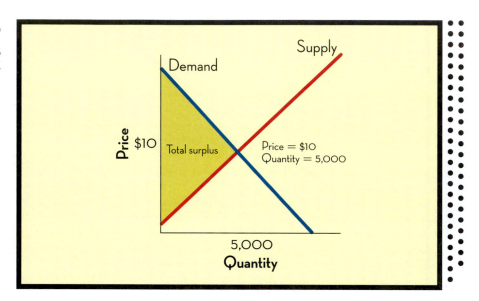

To find our posttax equilibrium, we need to find a level of output in which quantity supplied equals quantity demanded if the price to consumers is $2 higher than the price to sellers. In other words, we need a quantity traded at which the supply curve is $2 lower than the demand curve. In Figure 6.15, this quantity traded is 4,200.

The total consumers' surplus is given by the area between the price paid by consumers and the demand curve. Similarly, the total producers' surplus is shown by the area between the price producers receive and the supply curve. The tax revenue raised by the government is $2 multiplied by the quantity traded.

Notice from Figure 6.15 that the tax moves consumers up their demand curve and so reduces quantity demanded, while the tax also moves producers down their supply curve and so lowers quantity supplied. The tax discourages consumers from buying the good and discourages producers from selling the good. As a result, the tax reduces the quantity of the good traded. But, as we have already seen, the untaxed free market produces the optimal number of goods. Taxation, therefore, creates a deadweight loss by causing markets to underproduce products.

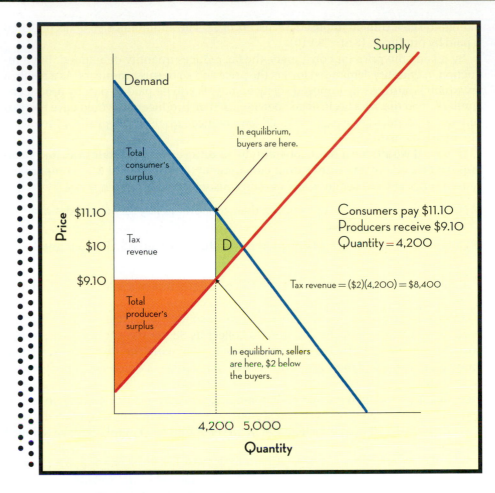

FIGURE **6.15**

SUPPLY AND
DEMAND CURVES
AFTER $2 TAX
IMPOSED

Demand

Supply

Total
consumer's
surplus

In equilibrium,
buyers are here.

Price

$11.10

$10

Tax
revenue

D

$9.10

Consumers pay $11.10
Producers receive $9.10
Quantity = 4,200

Tax revenue = ($2)(4,200) = $8,400

Total
producer's
surplus

In equilibrium, sellers
are here, $2 below
the buyers.

4,200   5,000

Quantity

153

THE DEADWEIGHT LOSS OF THE TAX

If you carefully compare Figure 6.14 to 6.15 you see that most, but not all, of the lost consumers' and producers' surplus from Figure 6.14 goes to the government in Figure 6.15. The lost consumers' and producers' surplus that is not recovered by the government is given by area D in Figure 6.15, which represents the deadweight loss of the tax.

In Figure 6.15, the government raised $8,400 from the tax. Because the tax created some deadweight loss, however, the harm to consumers plus the harm to producers from the tax is *greater than* $8,400.

The deadweight loss of the tax is caused by consumers no longer buying some goods that they value more than it costs producers to make. In Figure 6.15, as long as quantity is below 5,000, the supply curve is below the demand curve. And recall that whenever the supply curve is below the demand curve, the value of a good to some consumers is more than the cost to some producers of making the good. So because the tax prevents goods from being traded for which the demand curve is above the supply curve, it destroys wealth, thereby creating a deadweight loss.

WHO PAYS THE TAX?

The sales tax in Figure 6.15 harms consumers by causing them to pay more. But interestingly, the tax raised the price to consumers by only $1.10 ($11.10 − $10) even though the government imposed a sales tax of $2. The additional $.90 of tax per good is paid by producers ($10 − $9.10).

By raising the price for consumers, the tax reduces quantity demanded. But a reduction in quantity demanded lowers the price and so harms producers. As a result, a tax which is supposedly imposed solely on buyers will be paid in part by producers. Similarly, had the sales tax instead been imposed on producers, it would have harmed consumers. A sales tax on sellers would have reduced quantity supplied and so raised the price to consumers.

In fact, **it would have made absolutely no difference if the sales tax had been imposed on producers rather than consumers.*** To understand this, compare the consequences of a $2 per good sales tax on consumers and producers:

(A) If the tax is imposed on consumers, then **consumers pay $2 per good more than producers receive.**

(B) If the tax is imposed on producers, then **producers receive $2 less per good than consumers pay.**

But (A) and (B) are exactly the same! The consequences of a sales tax are identical whether the tax is imposed on buyers or on sellers.

To further understand why (A) and (B) are absolutely identical, imagine that the government sends an agent to a store to collect its $2 per hat tax. If the tax is supposed to be paid by the seller, then the customer will hand the store's cashier some money for the hat and the cashier will give $2 of it to the government agent. If the tax is supposed to be paid by the customer, then the customer will first give the government agent $2 and then pay the cashier the price of the hat. Since there is no meaningful difference between these two scenarios, it doesn't matter who officially pays the tax! Of course, if voters are ignorant of this economic fact, it might make political

"CONSUMERS CAN'T ESCAPE TAXES, EVEN WHEN THE TAXES ARE SUPPOSEDLY IMPOSED ON BUSINESSES."

---

*This assumes there are zero costs to collecting the tax. It may well be cheaper, for example, for the government to collect a sales tax from a few sellers than from many buyers.

sense for politicians to declare that their hat tax is paid by producers and not consumers.

SUPPLY, DEMAND, AND SUBSIDIES

Supply and demand analysis can also illustrate the deadweight loss caused by subsidies. Figure 6.16 shows the consequences of the government giving a $5 per good subsidy to consumers. As with a tax, a subsidy causes buyers and sellers to pay different prices.

In Figure 6.16 the equilibrium quantity traded is the point at which quantity supplied equals quantity demanded if the price to consumers is $5 lower than the price to sellers. Restated, at equilibrium the demand curve must be $5 below the supply curve. In Figure 6.16 the subsidy equilibrium manifests where quantity traded is 5,800, the price paid by buyers is $7.70, and the price received by producers is $12.70.

Had there been no subsidy, the total surplus would have been given by area **A + B + C.** You can see this by comparing Figure 6.16 to Figure 6.14.

With the subsidy, the total consumers' surplus is given by the area between the demand curve and the price paid by consumers, which is triangular area A + B + F. With the subsidy, the total producers' surplus is given by the area between the supply curve and the price received by producers, which is triangular area C + B + E.

Of course, the subsidy must be paid by the government. The amount the government pays is quantity sold times the $5 difference between the price received by

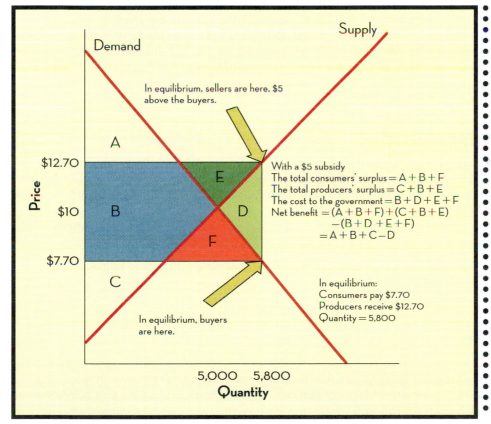

Supply

Demand

In equilibrium, sellers are here, $5 above the buyers.

A

$12.70

E

$10   B   D

F

$7.70

C

In equilibrium, buyers are here.

With a $5 subsidy
The total consumers' surplus = A + B + F
The total producers' surplus = C + B + E
The cost to the government = B + D + E + F
Net benefit = (A + B + F) + (C + B + E)
            − (B + D + E + F)
            = A + B + C − D

In equilibrium:
Consumers pay $7.70
Producers receive $12.70
Quantity = 5,800

5,000   5,800

Quantity

Price

FIGURE **6.16**

CONSEQUENCES OF A $5 PER GOOD GOVERNMENT SUBSIDY

the sellers and the price paid by the consumers. This is given by the rectangular area B + E + F + D.

The total wealth-creating benefit to society of this market is given by the benefit to consumers plus the benefit to producers minus the cost of the subsidy, which is (A + B + F) + (C + B + E) − (B + E + F + D) = **A + B + C − D.** Since the total surplus before the subsidy was imposed was A + B + C, the subsidy creates a deadweight loss represented by area D.

The subsidy creates a deadweight loss because it increases quantity to levels where the supply curve is above the demand curve. When the supply curve is above the demand curve, the cost to producers of making a good is greater than the benefit consumers receive from having the good. So because the subsidy results in goods being wastefully overproduced, it creates a deadweight loss.

INNOVATION

So far we have examined markets for existing goods in which producers have complete information about the cost and demand for their products. But economic growth is driven by innovation, which is the development of new products or the improvement of existing ones. An innovator can't know for certain what the demand for his innovation will be. Yet he must still spend development money in the hope that this demand will be high. Consider, for example, the very textbook that you are now reading.

I had to devote considerable time to writing this textbook without knowing if anyone would actually buy it. Furthermore, my publisher spent over $500,000 on this textbook before students bought even a single copy. If this book sells well, both my publisher and myself will profit; if it fails in the marketplace, we will both suffer a loss.

SUPER-VISION

Markets do an extraordinary job of promoting wealth-creating innovations. To understand this, pretend that in college you double major in economics and physics. After taking an advanced course in optical physics, you formulate an idea for making a highly innovative contact lens that would give its users "super-vision" enabling people to see 10 times better than an unaided person with perfectly healthy eyes. But you face three obstacles to developing your super-vision contact lenses:

1. Researching and developing the contact lenses would cost $2 billion.
2. You're not certain that even after spending the $2 billion you could get the contacts to work.
3. You have no idea how much people would actually pay for super-vision contact lenses.

I suspect few of this textbook's readers have the resources to spend $2 billion researching and developing a new product. But this wouldn't necessarily stop you from fulfilling your super-vision dream. You could perhaps find a firm that believed your idea had merit. This firm would provide you with funding and technical assistance in return for part of your future profits should your innovative lenses succeed commercially. Alas, it won't be easy for you to convince a firm to actually spend $2 billion on your super-vision scheme.

RATIONING FUNDS FOR INNOVATORS

Not all innovation should be funded. In *Gulliver's Travels*, author Jonathan Swift satirizes wasteful attempts at innovation. Swift wrote of a man who "had been eight years upon a project for extracting sunbeams out of cucumbers, which were to be put into vials hermetically sealed, and let out to warm the air in raw, inclement summers." A well-functioning market would never fund such a hopeless attempt at innovation.

Perhaps your super-vision contact lens concept is about as promising as the idea of extracting sunbeams from cucumbers. In a market economy, you will get resources to develop your innovation only by convincing people that it has a good chance of success. And with $2 billion at stake you can bet that potential backers would consult experts in optical physics before spending the resources needed to fund your innovation.

Many people have expensive ideas. No society could afford to fund every would-be innovator's research. Therefore, society needs some means of rationing resources so that only promising innovators receive research and development funding. Under the market system, money goes to the potential innovators who can best convince funders of their likely commercial success. Since these funders are spending their own money, they have tremendous incentives to fund only innovations that will produce products that appeal to consumers.

"The capitalist engine is first and last an engine of mass production which unavoidably means also production for the masses. . . . Electric lighting is no great boon to anyone who has money enough to buy a sufficient number of candles and to pay servants to attend them. It is the cheap cloth, the cheap cotton and rayon fabric, boots, motorcars and so on that are the typical achievements of capitalist production, and not as a rule improvements that would mean much to a rich man. Queen Elizabeth owned silk stockings. The capitalist achievement does not typically consist in providing more silk stockings for queens but in bringing them within the reach of factory girls in return for steadily decreasing amounts of effort."—Josheph Schumpeter (economist)[9]*

SILLY SCIENCE

Markets force practicality on innovators. Nazi Germany rejected Einstein's theory of relativity as "Jewish science." Under Stalin, the Soviets rejected Darwin's theory of evolution because it conflicted with their ideological theory of the Marxist advancement of man. And in these dictatorships, no innovator could dare reject the "scientific" proclamations of the all-powerful state.

In a free market economy, however, an innovator who substituted ideology for science would get little financial support. Markets care about consumer-applicable results, not political correctness.

IF AT FIRST YOU DON'T SUCCEED (YOU CAN) TRY, TRY AGAIN

In a centrally-planned economy, if the government rejected an innovator's idea, the innovator would have no other place to turn to get funding. But in a competitive market, an innovator rejected by one firm can always look to others. For example, Western Union Telegraph initially thought that the telephone had no future and refused to help finance its early development. Fortunately, others did foresee the benefits of the telephone and supported its commercial start.

In the 1950s music executives believed that rock and roll music was a passing fad and gave it almost no support.[10] Independent record companies that initially had little status or money, however, decided to bet on rock and roll and, of course, this bet paid off.

Microsoft initially didn't think very much of the Internet. But even though Microsoft was the leading software firm, its lack of support didn't kill the early Internet because others did believe in it.

BAD PREDICTIONS[11]

"Drill for oil? You mean drill into the ground to try and find oil? You're crazy."
—Drillers who Edwin L. Drake tried to enlist to his project to drill for oil in 1859

"Heavier-than-air flying machines are impossible."—Lord Kelvin, president, Royal Society, 1895

"The wireless music box has no imaginable commercial value. Who would pay for a message sent to nobody in particular?"—David Sarnoff's associates in response to his urgings for investment in the radio in the 1920s

"All a trick." "A Mere Mountebank." "Absolute swindler." "Doesn't know what he's about." "What's the good of it?" "What useful purpose will it serve?"—Members of Britain's Royal Society, 1926, after a demonstration of television

"There is not the slightest indication that nuclear energy will ever be obtainable. It would mean that the atom would have to be shattered at will."—Albert Einstein, 1932

"Space travel is bunk"—Sir Harold Spencer Jones, Astronomer Royal of Britain, 1957, two weeks before the launch of Sputnik

"There is no reason anyone would want a computer in their home."—Ken Olson, president, chairman and founder of Digital Equipment Corp., 1977

"The concept is interesting and well-formed, but in order to earn better than a 'C,' the idea must be feasible."—A Yale University management professor in response to soon-to-be Federal Express Corp. Founder Fred Smith's paper proposing reliable overnight delivery service

"640K ought to be enough for anybody."—Bill Gates, 1981

SMALL-SCALE INNOVATION

Marketplace innovation isn't limited to grand projects such as the invention of supervision, the telephone, the Internet, or rock and roll music. Much marketplace innovation involves small changes to existing products. This year, perhaps, air-conditioning units will become a little cheaper because of a better design, while refrigerators become slightly more reliable due to superior manufacturing techniques. By themselves, these minor innovations have a small effect on society. But taken together, the millions of small-scale innovations that take place each decade significantly improve the human condition.

Consider, for example, how much parents have benefited from diaper innovation. Babies will often flail their arms and legs while twisting their bodies to prevent their diapers from being changed. Most diapers made today have sticky tabs that make it easy to affix the diaper to the baby. Furthermore, today most diapers are made out of very inexpensive disposable material. But 40 years ago diapers were affixed with pins and were made out of relatively expensive nondisposable cloth. Here's a description of what diaper changers used to endure:

> Not all that long ago, diapers were made of cloth, and you had to pin them into place, and like as not you'd stick the baby or your own finger and then there'd be screaming and cussing like you wouldn't believe. And then when the diaper's all covered with feces or soaked with urine, you got to take it to the toilet and rinse it off and then load it all into the washing machine. Up to your elbows in piss and poop, that's what it was like to have a baby in the old days.[12]

The minor innovation of making disposable diapers with sticky tabs has greatly improved the welfare of parents.

Another benefit of innovation is that it continually creates differentiated products such as a new flavor of toothpaste, a different style of blouse, or a tool redesigned for use by the arthritic. New product variations compete in the marketplace. Those that fail to attract customers are discontinued and die. Those that win customers stay on store shelves until further transformed by innovation. This evolutionary-like aspect of markets is well illustrated by the excerpt from Russell Roberts' fictional story "The Invisible Heart." See "Innovation and Evolution."

INNOVATION AND EVOLUTION

An economist starts explaining small-scale marketplace innovation to an English teacher. The economist says:

"A paper straw works fine. But even for a product as trivial as a straw, it gets improved. You can have paper or plastic. You can have it in color or with stripes. You can pay a little bit more and get it with a bend built in. You can have it with a little spoon on the end. Or take floss. You can have floss with mint, without mint, unwaxed, with Grotex or fruit-flavored, in a clear dispenser or solid. No one sits still. People are constantly trying to find ways to make your life better. Every possible niche of consumer taste gets explored."

[The English teacher responds:] "I don't know. It seems trivial. Do we need more than one kind of straw or floss?"

[The economist responds:] "I can't answer that question any more than I can tell you if we need more than one kind of cell phone or one kind of cancer treatment or one kind of shirt or one kind of cereal. Trivial or sublime, you can no more stop the marketplace from filling every obscure niche of consumer desire than you can stop the rain forest from blossoming in every direction. Does a rain forest really need more than ten kinds of flowers? Does every square inch need to be alive with life? Can't some of it be left alone? In the rain forest, species compete for sunlight and moisture and nutrients. The same thing is going on in the marketplace. In the marketplace, the competition is over customers—the sunlight that catches the attention of the innovator. Profits are the reward for discovery . . ."

Excerpted from Russell Roberts, *The Invisible Heart* (Cambridge, MA: The MIT Press, 2001), p. 69. Reprinted with permission.

FEEDBACK AND INNOVATION

Innovators make mistakes. But markets continually send signals to innovators allowing them to correct their errors.

CONSUMERS HATED
THE NEW COKE.

In the mid-1980s, Coke was the leading soft drink in the nation, but Pepsi was quickly catching up. To maintain its lead, the Coca-Cola company decided to innovate by changing the taste of Coke. Consumers, however, hated this New Coke, and so Coca-Cola quickly went back to selling "classic" Coca-Cola. A key advantage of market economies is that bad innovations are quickly rejected and removed from the marketplace.

Let's contrast New Coke with Mao Zedong's agricultural policies. Both New Coke and Mao's agricultural innovations were hated by most people. Consumers in market economies were free to accept or reject New Coke. Since they rejected it, the Coca-Cola company had to go back to selling "classic" Coke. Citizens in Communist China, alas, were not free to reject Mao's agricultural innovations. So even though these innovations caused millions to starve, the Chinese people were stuck with them until Mao died.

RESISTANCE TO INNOVATION

Even successful innovations harm some people. In the science-fiction novel, *The Ultimate Hitchhiker's Guide to the Galaxy,* a race of "hyperintelligent pandimensional beings" design a computer called Deep Thought to answer the ultimate philosophical question.[13] Deep Thought is asked to determine the answer to "Life, the Universe, and Everything."

But on the day Deep Thought is activated, representatives of the Philosophers' Union burst into the computer's room demanding that it be turned off. Philosophers make their living speculating on the meaning of existence. If a machine actually found the ultimate answer to Life, The Universe, and Everything, these philosophers would be out of a job.

Deep Thought, however, tells the philosophers that it will take seven and a half million years for it to find the ultimate answer, so the philosophers' jobs are safe for quite a while. Often, however, new technology does pose an immediate risk to some workers' employment, and these endangered workers sometimes rage against the machine—literally.

LUDDITES

In 18th century England, innovators developed machines that made clothing manufacturing quicker and cheaper. But since these machines did the work formerly done by people, they caused many workers to lose their jobs. Attempting to preserve their livelihoods, in 1779 Ned Lud and his gang of workman destroyed some machines belonging to a sock maker. Since then, people who oppose new technology have been called *Luddites.*

People alive today are extremely fortunate that Luddites failed to stop technological progress in 1779. Deprived of new technology, the world would not have experienced the tremendous increase in wealth production that occurred since 1779.

But Luddites often act in their own self-interest. For example, a robot that gave brilliant economic lectures would endanger your professor's job and my own. We would both be quite rational in destroying such a new line of economic robots even if the robots did a far better job teaching students than we ever could.

Society as a whole, however, gains wealth from job-destroying technologies. Workers are an economy's most valuable resource. When you eliminate the need for workers to do some tasks, you ultimately free them up to do other jobs that grow the economy.

"It's no accident that capitalism has brought with it progress, not merely in production but also in knowledge. Egoism and competition are, alas, stronger forces than public spirit and sense of duty." —Albert Einstein

A BRIEF HISTORY OF ECONOMIC TIME

Modern humans first emerged about 100,000 years ago. For the next 99,800 years or so, nothing happened. Well, not quite nothing. There were wars, political intrigue, the invention of agriculture—but none of that stuff had much effect on the quality of people's lives. Almost everyone lived on the modern equivalent of $400 to $600 a year, just above the subsistence level. True, there were always tiny aristocracies who lived far better, but numerically they were quite insignificant.

Then—just a couple of hundred years ago, maybe 10 generations—people started getting richer. And richer and richer still. Per capita income, at least in the West, began to grow at the unprecedented rate of about three quarters of a percent per year. A couple of decades later, the same thing was happening around the world.

Then it got even better. By the 20th century, per capita real incomes, that is, incomes adjusted for inflation, were growing at 1.5% per year, on average, and for the past half century they've been growing at about 2.3%. If you're earning a modest middle-class income of $50,000 a year, and if you expect your children, 25 years from now, to occupy that same modest rung on the economic ladder, then with a 2.3% growth rate, they'll be earning the inflation-adjusted equivalent of $89,000 a year. Their children, another 25 years down the line, will earn $158,000 a year.

Rising income is only part of the story. One hundred years ago the average American workweek was over 60 hours; today it's under 35. One hundred years ago 6% of manufacturing workers took vacations; today it's over 90%. One hundred years ago the average housekeeper spent 12 hours a day on laundry, cooking, cleaning and sewing; today it's about three hours.

The moral is that increases in measured income—even the phenomenal increases of the past two centuries—grossly understate the real improvements in our economic condition. The average middle-class American might have a smaller measured income than the European monarchs of the Middle Ages, but I suspect that Tudor King Henry VIII would have traded half his kingdom for modern plumbing, a lifetime supply of antibiotics and access to the Internet.

The source of this wealth—the engine of prosperity—is technological progress. And the engine of technological progress is ideas—not just the ideas from engineering laboratories, but also ideas like new methods of crop rotation, or just-in-time inventory management. You can fly from New York to Tokyo partly because someone figured out how to build an airplane and partly because someone figured out how to insure it. I'm writing this on a personal computer instead of an electric typewriter partly because someone said, "Hey! I wonder if we can make computer chips out of silicon!"

Some good ideas even come from economists. Julian Simon came up with the idea of bribing airline passengers to give up their seats on overbooked flights—and gone were the days when you relied on the luck of the draw to make it to your daughter's wedding. Economists first suggested creating property rights in African elephants, a policy that has given villagers an incentive to harvest at a sustainable rate and drive the poachers away. The result? Villagers have prospered and the elephant population has soared.

Engineers figure out how to harness the power of technology; economists figure out how to harness the power of incentives. Our prosperity relies on both.

FREEDOM AND WEALTH CREATION

In the 20th century, many intelligent men feared freedom was doomed. They believed that an uncoordinated free economy run by the whims of the marketplace could never compete against centrally directed countries such as the Soviet Union. After all, the leaders of the Soviet Union were willing to do *anything* to grow their economy. They enslaved millions in Siberian work-prison camps. They forbid most of their population from "wasting" wealth on luxuries and instead used the saved wealth to build their economy and military. They directed students to go into the most socially useful fields. If, for example, a brilliant student wanted to study art history but the state deemed it more beneficial that she study engineering, then into engineering she went. How, many thought, could the unplanned, undirected, unsynchronized economies of the free world ever compete against the ruthless central coordination of the Soviet Union?

But free market economies produced vastly more wealth than the Soviet Union. The Soviet Union, in fact, fell so far behind in wealth creation that it was attempting to give up central planning to become a free market economy shortly before internal ethnic and political tensions caused its breakup.

It turns out that markets make magnificent coordinators. Indeed, if the central planners running the Soviet Union were perfectly informed, wholly honest, and totally competent, they would have directed their citizens to take mostly the same actions as these citizens would have undertaken voluntarily under a free market. But, of course, no central planner will ever be perfectly informed, wholly honest, or totally competent. Consequently, central planners can never match the wealth-creating abilities of a free economy.

QUESTIONS YOU SHOULD BE ABLE TO ANSWER AFTER READING THIS CHAPTER:

1 What was the approximate average growth rate in the 1,500 years before the early 19th century's Industrial Revolution? (page 134)

2 What is value? (page 135)

3 What is wealth? (page 135)

4 What is the total wealth of society? (page 135)

5 How can one person giving a good to another increase the total wealth of society? (pages 135–136)

6 How do money transfers affect individuals' wealth? (page 136)

7 How do money transfers affect the total wealth of society? (page 136)

8 How can production increase wealth? (page 137)

9 How can rent control destroy wealth? (page 138)

10 How can minimum wage laws destroy wealth? (page 138)

11 How can taxes destroy wealth? (page 138)

12 How can subsidies destroy wealth? (page 139)

13 How can forced sharing destroy wealth? (pages 139–140)

14 How can theft destroy wealth? (page 141)

15 How can eminent domain destroy wealth? (pages 141–142)

16 What is a consumer's surplus? (page 144)

17 How can you use a demand curve to find the total consumers' surplus? (page 145)

18 What is a producer's surplus? (page 146)

19 How can you use a supply curve to find the total producer's surplus? (pages 147–148)

20 What is total surplus? (page 148)

21 How can you graphically show that the free market equilibrium price maximizes total surplus? (pages 149–150)

22 How can you graphically show the deadweight loss caused by a sales tax and the revenue raised by this tax? (page 153)

23 Does it matter if a sales tax must be paid by buyers or sellers? (pages 153–154)

24 How can you graphically show the deadweight loss caused by a subsidy and the cost of such a subsidy to the government? (pages 155–156)

25 Why does the marketplace promote innovation? (pages 156–160)

26 What are Luddites? (page 160)

27 What is the ultimate answer to Life, the Universe, and Everything? (Just kidding!)

STUDY PROBLEMS

1 Tom paid $8,145 for his car. The most Tom would have paid for this car is $9,000. Tom sells this car to Judy for $10,245. The most that Judy would have paid for this car is $11,000. (A) By how much does this sale increase the wealth of society? (B) What was Tom's producer's surplus from the sale? (C) What was Judy's consumer's surplus from the sale?

2 Seller Sam values his car at $13,300. Buyer Bill values Sam's car at $14,500. But if Bill buys Sam's car, he will have to pay a tax of $T. For what values of T will it be impossible for both Bill and Sam to come to a mutually beneficial agreement for Sam to sell his car to Bill?

3 Imagine that the supply-and-demand-determined equilibrium price in a market is $23. Assume that the government imposes a price floor of $30. Use a supply and demand diagram to show the deadweight loss caused by the price floor. Show the change in total consumers' surplus and total producers' surplus caused by the price floor.

4 Imagine that the supply-and-demand-determined equilibrium price in a market is $14. Assume that the government imposes a price ceiling of $10. Using a supply and demand diagram show the loss in total surplus caused by the price ceiling. Show the change in total consumers' surplus and total producers' surplus caused by the price ceiling.

5 Draw a supply and demand curve for a good where the market price is $15. Now assume that the government imposes a $3 tax on buyers for every good they purchase. Graphically show the deadweight loss of the tax and the amount of money the government raises through the tax. Show the change in total consumers' surplus and total producers' surplus caused by the tax.

6 Draw a supply and demand curve for a good where the market price is $15. Now assume that the government gives a $3 per good subsidy to buyers for every good they purchase. Graphically show the deadweight loss of the subsidy and the cost of the subsidy to the government. Show the change in total consumers' surplus and total producers' surplus caused by the subsidy.

7 Imagine the government gives a $.50 subsidy to milk producers for every gallon of milk sold. How much better off would milk consumers be if they, rather than the producers, received this subsidy?

8 In medieval Europe monarchs thought that the wealth of their kingdoms was determined by the amount of gold and silver in these kingdoms. Explain why these monarchs were wrong.

9 The market price for a good is $120. The government dictates a price of $70. Draw a supply and demand diagram in which the dictated price increases total consumers' surplus. Draw another supply and demand diagram in which the dictated price decreases total consumers' surplus. Draw a third supply and demand diagram in which the dictated price increases total producers' surplus. Draw a fourth supply and demand diagram in which the dictated price decreases total producers' surplus. Actually, you should draw only three of the four above described diagrams since drawing one of them is impossible.

10 You are a peasant farmer who grows wheat on his lord's land. The harder you work, the more wheat you will grow. Over an average year, if you put in an average amount of effort, you will grow 1,000 bushels of wheat. Your lord, however, will take much of your wheat. There are three possible mechanisms your lord could use to tax you:

A. Your lord takes one-half of all the wheat you grow.

B. Your lord takes 500 bushels of your wheat regardless of how much wheat you grow.

C. You always get 500 bushels of wheat and your lord takes the rest.

Under which mechanism will you work the most? Under which mechanism will you work the least?

11 In Britain, the buyer of a home must pay a "stamp tax" of between 1 percent and 4 percent of the home's value. A British politician proposed that the stamp tax instead be paid by home sellers. He argued that switching the tax liability to sellers would lower home prices and so make it easier for young people to get their first home.[14] Evaluate this politician's proposal.

12 (Advanced) The wealth of society goes down when a minimum wage law destroys jobs. But the wealth of society goes up when technology destroys jobs. Explain.

13 (Advanced) Before any taxes or subsidies are imposed, 20,000 each of widgets and gizmos are sold every month. Politicians hate widget manufacturers and so impose a $2 tax on the sale of each widget. Politicians like gizmo manufacturers and so give gizmo manufacturers a $2 subsidy for each gizmo they sell.

Let X = The tax revenues received by the government − The subsidies paid by the government

All else being equal, will X be larger if widgets and gizmos are complements or substitutes?

7

NEANDERTHALS AND TRADE

Humankind may well owe its dominance of the earth to trade.[1] The Neanderthals, intelligent cousins of humans* originated around 300,000 years ago. But about 35,000 years ago, shortly after encountering humans, Neanderthals became extinct. There's no evidence that disease or war with humans caused their extinction, and DNA analysis shows that we probably didn't interbreed with Neanderthals and become one species.

Neanderthals existed for longer than humankind has so far. Until recently, the cause of Neanderthals' extinction mystified scientists. But now some *economists* think they may have finally figured it out. Archaeological evidence indicates that 35,000 years ago humans engaged in trade but Neanderthals didn't. And trade made humans more efficient wealth creators than Neanderthals. As humans captured and created more resources, our population grew—while theirs gradually shrank to extinction. We don't know for certain that trade was the reason humans out-competed Neanderthals. But because of the wealth-generating power of trade, it's an extremely plausible theory.

A MODEL OF PRIMITIVE PRODUCTION

The following simplified model explains how trade gave humans a key advantage over Neanderthals. Let's divide all wealth into two categories:

1. Meat.
2. Other stuff (including tools, clothing, and shelter).

Neanderthals and humans obtain meat by hunting animals. Besides catching meat, both species create other goods that aid their survival.

Let's assume that Neanderthals, like people today, have different natural abilities. And further imagine there are two types of Neanderthals: hunters and craftsmen.

---

*By "humans," I mean *homo sapiens*, which is what I, and presumably you are.

TRADE

The hunters are better at catching meat, and the craftsmen are better at making other stuff. Assume the following describes how much each type of Neanderthal could make in a day:

- If a hunter spends a day catching meat, he produces two units of meat.
- If a hunter spends a day making other stuff, he produces one unit of other stuff.
- If a craftsman spends a day catching meat, he produces one unit of meat.
- If a craftsman spends a day making other stuff, he produces two units of other stuff.

In short, a hunter is twice as good as a craftsman at catching meat, and a craftsman is twice as good as a hunter at making other stuff.

To survive, a Neanderthal needs both meat and other stuff. So all Neanderthals have to devote some days to catching meat and some days to making other stuff. Let's assume that to maximize his chance for survival, each week a hunter spends three days catching meat and four days making other stuff. Thus, each week a Neanderthal hunter gets six units of meat and four units of other stuff. Further assume that each week a Neanderthal craftsman spends four days catching meat and three days making other stuff, giving him four units of meat and six units of other stuff. The following table summarizes this information.

	Units of Meat	Units of Other Stuff
Neanderthal hunter	6	4
Neanderthal craftsman	4	6

Wealth Available Each Week

Human Production and Trade

Assume that humans are exactly the same as Neanderthals except that humans trade. Consequently, in a given day a human hunter can produce either two units of meat or one unit of other stuff. A human craftsman, in a given day, can produce either one unit of meat or two units of other stuff. Like Neanderthals, humans need both meat and other stuff to survive. But since humans trade, a human hunter could spend every day catching meat and trade for other stuff.

Assume that in human society, hunters only hunt and craftsmen only make other stuff. So if both hunters and craftsmen spend every day doing what they are best at, then every week hunters will catch 14 units of meat while craftsmen produce 14 units of other stuff. At the end of the week, hunters could trade seven units of meat to craftsman in return for seven units of other stuff. Therefore, every week human hunters and craftsmen would each have seven units of meat and seven units of other stuff, as summarized in the following table:

	Units of Meat	Units of Other Stuff
Human hunter	7	7
Human craftsman	7	7

Wealth Available Each Week

As you can see, trade allows humans to have more of everything than the nontrading Neanderthals. Over time, these greater resources would cause the human population to grow relative to Neanderthals. In evolution, if two species occupy the same ecological niche but one of these species does slightly worse, it will eventually become extinct. Consequently, if humans and Neanderthals were basically alike except that only humans engaged in trade, then Neanderthals would indeed go extinct.

WHY DIDN'T NEANDERTHALS TRADE?

We don't yet know why Neanderthals did not trade. Perhaps Neanderthals lacked the verbal abilities necessary to negotiate trade, or they didn't trust each other enough to trade, or maybe they lacked the social skills needed to organize trade. Or possibly, whereas humans of 35,000 years ago had a basic grasp of microeconomics, allowing them to see the enormous potential gains available to traders, Neanderthals' thinking processes were incompatible with microeconomic logic. And under this last theory, Neanderthals' punishment for failing ancient microeconomics was extinction!

A Prehistoric Conversation   Imagine a conversation that took place 35,000 years ago between a human hunter named Slayer of Mammoths and a human craftsman called Builder of Tools. This meeting occurred before humans learned to trade. Builder of Tools had just spent the day catching meat, and since he was a craftsman, he killed only one meat unit. Let's listen in:

> *Slayer:* "You, Builder of Tools, are a horrible hunter for had I, Slayer of Mammoths, spent the day hunting meat, I would have caught twice the amount that you have."

But Builder of Tools notices that the hunter had spent the entire day making only one tool.

> *Builder:* "But you, Slayer of Mammoths, are a terrible toolmaker for had I, Builder of Tools, spent the day making tools, I would have produced twice the amount you have."

At this moment, both Slayer of Mammoths and Builder of Tools realize their mistake.

> *Slayer:* "We are both stupid."
> *Builder:* "But today our stupidity ends. Never again shall another day pass in which we both do what we are bad at."
> *Slayer:* "I agree. You will build, I will hunt. At week's end we will trade meat for tools."
> *Builder:* "Yes, and through trade we will have more of everything!!!"

After a year, Slayer of Mammoths and Builder of Tools realize further benefits from specializing. Because they now both devote all their time to one task, they have each become better at this task than they were before they traded. Slayer of Mammoths, for example, now catches three units of meat each time he goes hunting. Soon other humans, recognizing the benefits these two have achieved from cooperating, begin trading as well.

Poor Neanderthals, however, don't ever discover the wealth-creating magic of trade. As a result every Neanderthal must do everything for himself, even the tasks he performs poorly. And because a Neanderthal must divide his time and do everything, he doesn't have the opportunity ever to really master one skill.

INTERNATIONAL TRADE

Let's now leave the prehistoric world and focus on present-day trade between two countries. For our first example, consider the United States and Italy.

ABSOLUTE ADVANTAGE

As with hunters and craftsman, the United States and Italy have different wealth-generating abilities. To keep everything simple, assume that goods are made only with labor. Further assume that it costs the United States 1 hour of labor to make a computer and 10 hours of labor to make a television. It takes Italy 20 hours of labor to make a computer but only 1 hour of labor to make a television. These hypothetical figures are summarized in the following table:

	A Computer	A Television
Cost to the United States	1 hour of work	10 hours of work
Cost to Italy	20 hours of work	1 hour of work

A nation has an **absolute advantage** in producing a good if it can make the good using fewer resources than its trading partners.

The United States has what economists call an *absolute advantage* in producing computers, while Italy has an absolute advantage in producing televisions. A nation has an absolute advantage in producing a good if it can make the good using fewer resources than its trading partners.

Let's keep everything simple and assume that without trade Americans work for 11 hours producing one computer and one television. Italians, meanwhile, work 21 hours also producing one computer and one television. Let's see how they both can become better off through trade.

The Outcome with Trade

Trade Scenario I The United States could make two computers in two hours and Italy could make two televisions in two hours. They could then trade one television for one computer. Both would have the same exact amount of goods they had without trading, but with far less work.

Trade Scenario II Or, if they both wanted to work the same number of hours as they did before, they could use trade to create additional wealth. Americans could work 11 hours producing 11 computers while the Italians could work 21 hours making 21 televisions. They could then trade, say, five televisions for five computers and each have more stuff, while putting in the same amount of work that they had without trade. The following tables summarize our discussion:

	Hours Worked	Number of Computers	Number of Televisions
America	11	1	1
Italy	21	1	1

Without Trade

	Hours Worked	Number of Computers	Number of Televisions
America	2	1	1
Italy	2	1	1

Trade Scenario I

	Hours Worked	Number of Computers	Number of Televisions
America	11	6	5
Italy	21	5	16

Trade Scenario II

Trade is economic magic. Through trade you can work less time and still produce the same amount of wealth or work the same amount of time and produce more wealth.

But, the careful reader might ask, does trade always increase wealth or did I just pick convenient examples? After all, in the last example Italy was much better at producing one good while its trading partner was vastly superior at making the other. What if, however, one country was better at making everything? Could the magic of trade still create wealth?

COMPARATIVE ADVANTAGE

The theory of comparative advantage proves that countries always benefit from trade, even if one country has an absolute advantage in the production of everything. To illuminate the theory of comparative advantage, let's invent a country called SlowLand, where it takes an enormous amount of time to make anything. Assume that in SlowLand workers require 2,000 hours to make a computer and 1,000 hours to manufacture a television. The following table compares U.S. and SlowLand costs for making these items:

	A Computer	A Television
Cost to the United States	1 hour of work	10 hours of work
Cost to SlowLand	2,000 hours of work	1,000 hours of work

Now, you might ask, could the United States ever benefit from trading with SlowLand since it appears that the United States is better at making everything than SlowLand is? The United States does have an absolute advantage over SlowLand in producing both computers and televisions.

But in terms of opportunity costs, SlowLand actually has an advantage in the production of televisions. Recall that the opportunity cost of something is what you have to give up to get it. In the United States, the opportunity cost of a television is 10 computers because it takes 10 hours to make a single television—10 hours that could have produced 10 computers. Therefore, to produce a television domestically, the United States must give up 10 computers. Analogously, the opportunity cost of a computer in the United States is 1/10 of a television. This just means that to make a computer, you must use 1/10 of the resources needed to build a television.

In SlowLand it takes twice as much work to build a computer as a television, so in SlowLand the opportunity cost of a computer is two televisions. Analogously, the opportunity cost of a television in SlowLand is 1/2 of a computer. The following table shows these opportunity costs:

	A Computer	A Television
Cost to the United States	1/10 of a television	10 computers
Cost to SlowLand	2 televisions	1/2 computer

A nation has a **comparative advantage** in producing a good when it can produce that good at a lower opportunity cost than its trading partners.

When measured in opportunity costs, we see it's cheaper for the United States to make computers, but it's cheaper for SlowLand to make televisions. The United States, therefore, has a comparative advantage in making computers, while SlowLand has a comparative advantage in making televisions. A nation has a comparative advantage in producing a good when it can produce that good at a lower opportunity cost than its trading partners.

The Outcome with Trade Imagine that before trade, the U.S. and SlowLand each build 10 computers and 10 televisions. So, Americans work 110 hours while SlowLanders work 30,000 hours. Now consider the following two trade scenarios.

Trade Scenario I Americans work 20 hours building 20 computers while SlowLanders work 20,000 hours building 20 televisions. America then trades 10 computers for 10 televisions. Both then have the same exact amount of goods they had without trading, but with much less work.

Trade Scenario II Or, if both nations want to work the same amount of hours as before trade, then the Americans could work for 110 hours building 110 computers. SlowLanders could work 30,000 hours building 30 televisions. The United States could then trade, say, 15 computers for 15 televisions.

	Hours Worked	Number of Computers	Number of Televisions
America	110	10	10
SlowLand	30,000	10	10

Without Trade

	Hours Worked	Number of Computers	Number of Televisions
America	20	10	10
SlowLand	20,000	10	10

After Trade Scenario I

	Hours Worked	Number of Computers	Number of Televisions
America	110	95	15
SlowLand	30,000	15	15

After Trade Scenario II

Even when one nation has an absolute advantage in the production of all goods, nations can still benefit by trading the goods for which they have a comparative advantage.

ROUNDABOUT PRODUCTION

Trade gives nations an indirect, or roundabout, means of production. Imagine, for example, that SlowLand is willing to give the United States a television every time the United States gives SlowLand a computer. The United States now has two means of producing televisions. First, it could spend 10 hours of its own labor making a television. Second, it could spend one hour of labor making a computer and trade this computer to SlowLand for a television. Obviously, the roundabout way of producing televisions is far cheaper for the United States.

Trade gives me a roundabout means of farming. I have never directly farmed, but I strongly suspect that if I really put my mind to it and worked extremely hard, I would make a horrible farmer. Fortunately, some people (you presumably) are willing (or at least forced by your professor) to pay money for my writings on microeconomics. I have found that this money can be exchanged for food. Since it's much easier for me to write than to directly farm, this roundabout method of farming through writing a microeconomics textbook is the cheapest means I have of obtaining food.

YOUR COMPARATIVE ADVANTAGE

This summer you apply for an internship with the genetically blessed actress Jessica Alba. Unfortunately, you realize that she is better at *everything* than you are. To keep things simple, pretend that the only two activities you or Jessica can do this summer are to clean and to act.

Jessica cleans twice as fast as you do. But she is 10,000 times better at acting than you, because Hollywood studios will pay her $10,000 an hour to star in a movie but will pay you only $1 an hour to play a movie extra. So how can you convince Jessica to hire you this summer?

Although Jessica has an absolute advantage over you in everything, you have a comparative advantage over her in cleaning. The opportunity cost to you of spending an hour cleaning is not spending that hour acting, meaning that for every hour you clean you lose the chance to make $1 acting. In contrast, every hour Jessica cleans is one less hour she can make $10,000 through acting. Therefore, the opportunity cost to Jessica of cleaning for an hour is $10,000.

So you tell Jessica that you will spend eight hours each day cleaning for her. (She has a huge house which takes a long time to clean.) Because she cleans twice as fast as you do, this saves Jessica four hours a day of cleaning time. But this four hours of saved time is worth $40,000 to Jessica because she can now use this time to act. So if she pays you, say, $100 a day (and as a bonus takes you along to a few parties), both you and she benefit.

EVERYONE HAS A COMPARATIVE ADVANTAGE

Every person and every nation must have a comparative advantage in something. Your comparative advantage is what you are comparatively best at, or alternatively what you are the least bad at. Even if you stink at everything, you must still be least bad at something. The theory of comparative advantage holds that you benefit from trade when you sell (export) goods for which you have a comparative advantage and buy (import) goods other people or nations have a comparative advantage in producing.

DAVID RICARDO
(1772–1823)

David Ricardo

David Ricardo formulated the theory of comparative advantage. In addition to writing on trade, Ricardo conducted important economic research on production costs, taxation, and monetary policy. He was also a leading advocate for the elimination of Britain's Corn Laws, which restricted the importation of grains.

WHERE DO COMPARATIVE ADVANTAGES COME FROM?

Some countries derive comparative advantages from extracting the natural resources on their lands. Soil and climate give a few nations a comparative advantage in agriculture. Having a significant number of citizens educated in certain skills, such as computer programming, confers comparative advantages. Extreme poverty gives a few unfortunate countries comparative advantages in goods that can be produced with cheap unskilled labor. Some of the many other factors that confer comparative advantage are discussed in the following paragraphs.

Freedom

Freedom can be the source of many comparative advantages. Only countries with freedom of expression, for example, will nowadays likely have a comparative advantage in the production of movies, books, or music.

English

English language skills give India a comparative advantage in providing phone-based technical support to Americans. India is a relatively poor country with many English speakers. Many computer firms train Indians to provide computer support to Americans. Interestingly, some of this training involves learning to speak English with an "American accent."

Education

Individuals as well as countries have comparative advantages. Many individual comparative advantages arise from natural born skills. But education and practice can reinforce these skills, enhancing innate comparative advantages.

The educational choices you make shape your comparative advantages. Perhaps you will study medicine and develop a comparative advantage as a healer. Or maybe you will learn about markets and acquire a comparative advantage in business. Education increases what economists call your *human capital*. Your human capital comprises your productive skills.

Think of people as machines. At birth these machines can't do anything. But as these machines age and become more educated, they can do useful tasks. Some machines can practice medicine while others can start a new business. The education that machines receive greatly influences the tasks they can perform. The set of useful tasks a human "machine" is capable of executing is that machine's human capital.

Work

Work, along with education, greatly affects people's human capital and thus shapes comparative advantages. Imagine you decide to become a lawyer. After law school you get a job with a large law firm. Just by chance, the firm directs you to work on a medical malpractice case defending a doctor accused of carelessly harming a patient. You work on the case under a senior member of the law firm. During the case you learn a bit about medical malpractice law. So when another malpractice suit arises you are again chosen to assist the senior attorney working on the case. After working on many such cases over seven years, you become a top legal expert on medical malpractice. You now have a very strong, and lucrative, comparative advantage in medical malpractice law.

Working at a job often increases your human capital in a way that makes you better at the job. (This just means that you become more skilled at your job the longer you work at it.) As you develop more job-related human capital, your comparative advantage at the job grows.

Genetics and Family Environment   Genetics and family environment can be just as important as education and work at determining individual comparative advantages. Children, for example, often develop powerful comparative advantages in a parent's profession. Consider, for example, the offspring of two musicians. Both of the parents were probably born with strong musical skills. There is a good chance that they will genetically pass along these innate skills to their children. These musicians, furthermore, will be far more likely than most parents to push their children to take music lessons. They will likely nurture any musical talent their children might have. Finally, if one of their children does become a musician, the parents will be able to use their professional contacts to help the offspring get a job.

Former Harvard President and well-regarded economist Larry Summers provides an interesting data point, indicating that comparative advantages can be inherited. Larry Summers' mother is an economist, his mother's brother is Nobel Prize-winning economist Kenneth Arrow, his father is an economist, and his father's brother is Nobel Prize-winning economist Paul Samuelson.

SUPPLY AND DEMAND

One of microeconomics' comparative advantages is using supply and demand curves to study society. Let's now apply this extremely useful comparative advantage to trade. Figure 7.1 shows the market for grain in the imaginary nation of RicardoLand. Let's initially assume that RicardoLand does not trade with the outside world. As you can see, the market price of grain is $10 a bushel and 650 bushels of grain are produced.

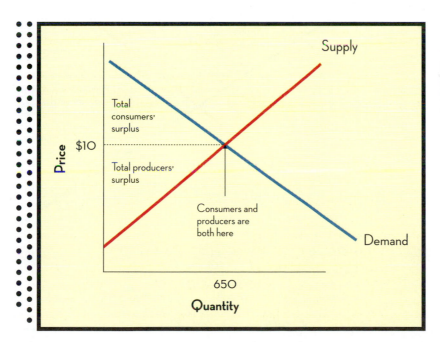

FIGURE **7.1**

THE MARKET FOR GRAIN IN RICARDOLAND BEFORE TRADE IS ALLOWED

Let's now assume that RicardoLand suddenly opens up to world trade, and the world price of grain is $11 a bushel. Further assume that RicardoLand is such a small country that it can't affect the world price for grain. RicardoLand's consumers, therefore, can buy as much grain as they want from the rest of the world without affecting the world price of grain. Similarly, RicardoLand's producers can sell as much grain as desired to the rest of the world without changing the world price of grain.

After RicardoLand opens itself to trade, its grain price will become equal to the world price of grain.

- If the price of grain in RicardoLand were below the world price, no producer would sell its grain in RicardoLand. This would cause the price of grain in RicardoLand to rise until it hit $11.

- If the price in RicardoLand were above the world price, then every producer in the world would sell its grain in RicardoLand. This tremendous influx of grain would lower the price of grain in RicardoLand until it hit the world price of $11.

EXPORTS

Figure 7.2 shows the domestic supply and demand curves for grain in RicardoLand when the world price of grain is $11. Unlike our normal supply and demand diagrams, in Figure 7.2 consumers and producers are at different points in equilibrium. Since the price of grain is $11, consumers are at the point on their demand curve where price is $11. Similarly, producers are at the point on their supply curve where price is $11.

FIGURE 7.2

EXPORTS

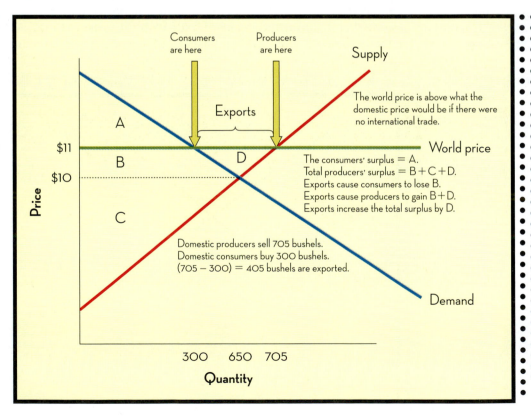

Consumers are here

Producers are here

Supply

Exports

The world price is above what the domestic price would be if there were no international trade.

$11 — World price

A

B

D

$10

The consumers' surplus = A.
Total producers' surplus = B + C + D.
Exports cause consumers to lose B.
Exports cause producers to gain B + D.
Exports increase the total surplus by D.

C

Price

Domestic producers sell 705 bushels.
Domestic consumers buy 300 bushels.
(705 − 300) = 405 bushels are exported.

Demand

300   650   705

Quantity

At the price of $11 the quantity supplied of grain in RicardoLand exceeds the quantity demanded of grain in RicardoLand. Without trade, this excess would cause the price to fall to $10. But because of trade, the price stays at $11 and the excess is exported to the rest of the world. Exports are goods that a nation produces at home but sells abroad to other countries.

If a nation exports a good, then it must produce more of this good than is domestically consumed. Consequently, for a nation to export, quantity supplied must exceed quantity demanded.

Exports harm domestic consumers by raising prices. But these high prices, of course, help domestic producers. As Figure 7.2 shows, the benefit of exports to producers exceeds the harm of exports to consumers. Exports, therefore, increase the total surplus and so raise the wealth of society.

IMPORTS

Figure 7.3 is exactly the same as Figure 7.2, but now the world price of grain is $5, below the no-trade RicardoLand domestic price. As before, trade will cause the price of grain in RicardoLand to become equal to the price of grain in the rest of the world.

In Figure 7.3 the price of grain is $5. As a result, consumers will be at the point on their demand curve where price equals $5, and firms will be at the point on their supply curve where price equals $5.

At a price of $5, quantity demanded of grain in RicardoLand will exceed the quantity supplied of domestically grown grain. The excess demand will result in imports of grain equal to the difference between quantity demanded and quantity

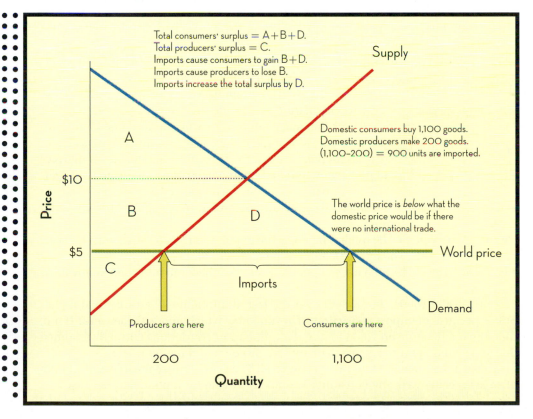

Total consumers' surplus = A+B+D.
Total producers' surplus = C.
Imports cause consumers to gain B+D.
Imports cause producers to lose B.
Imports increase the total surplus by D.

Supply

A

$10

B   D

Domestic consumers buy 1,100 goods.
Domestic producers make 200 goods.
(1,100–200) = 900 units are imported.

The world price is *below* what the
domestic price would be if there
were no international trade.

$5   World price

C

Imports

Demand

Producers are here   Consumers are here

200   1,100

Price

Quantity

FIGURE **7.3**   **177**

IMPORTS

supplied. Imports are goods that a nation consumes that are produced in other countries.

By lowering domestic prices, imports benefit consumers while harming producers. As Figure 7.3 shows, the benefit from imports to consumers exceeds the harm caused by imports to producers. Consequently, imports increase the total surplus, making society richer.

CONSUMERS VERSUS PRODUCERS

Figures 7.2 and 7.3 show that trade increases the wealth of a society. But trade creates losers as well as winners. Imports help consumers while harming producers; in contrast, exports benefit producers while harming consumers.

It's tempting to argue that governments should care more about consumers than firms because consumers are real people. But this argument is false since firms are owned and operated by real people. Many consumers, in fact, work for firms and, through the stock market, own parts of firms.

Nothing in economic theory says it's better to help producers over consumers or vice versa. Politicians, however, often talk about the need to protect consumers from exploitation by companies. So you would expect that politicians would generally support imports and oppose exports. But exactly the opposite is true. In most democracies, politicians usually consider exporting to be beneficial and importing to be detrimental. So why do politicians dislike imports?

Imagine that the United States currently prohibits the importation of sugar, and the world price of sugar is below the U.S. price of sugar. An economist gets elected to the U.S. Congress and proposes a bill that would allow the free importation of sugar. Sugar importation will help consumers while hurting producers. But trade theory proves that the benefits to consumers will be greater than the harm to producers, so sugar importation will make the United States wealthier.

Let's assume that 1,000 domestic sugar producers would lose $1 million a year each from the importation of sugar, for a total loss of $1 billion. Two hundred million American consumers of sugar, however, would each gain $7 a year from sugar importation for a total gain of $1.4 billion. So importation will increase the wealth of the United States by $400 million a year.

> American consumers pay an extra $1.9 billion a year because of restrictions on sugar imports.[2]

The 1,000 sugar producers will spend considerable resources opposing importation. They will hire lobbyists, throw parties for politicians, hire the relatives and former employees of politicians, and make campaign contributions to antisugar-importation politicians. So, if a politician votes against sugar importation, he gets the grateful support of 1,000 rich sugar producers.

But what about the 200 million people who benefit from sugar importation? Surely in a democracy the voices of 200 million people count for more than the desires of 1,000. Alas, most of the 200 million people won't ever become informed about sugar trade policy.

Many of the goods you bought over the last month almost certainly had higher prices because of import restrictions. Do you know which goods these were? If not, then the politicians who voted for the relevant import restrictions correctly assumed that you would not vote against them for forcing you to pay higher prices.

Even if a U.S. consumer knows that he saved $7 a year because the free importation of sugar was allowed, the consumer is unlikely to vote for a politician because of a mere $7. So a politician who votes for sugar importation gains little from consumers while making enemies of 1,000 rich domestic sugar producers. In a democracy such as the United States, the concentrated desires of 1,000 often do count for more than the diffuse interests of 200 million.

Politicians, therefore, often find it beneficial to restrict imports and so protect domestic producers from foreign competition. Tariffs are a common means of providing such protection.

TARIFFS

A tariff is a tax on imports. Figure 7.4 illustrates the effect of a $2 tariff on the market shown in Figure 7.3. This tariff simply increases the price that domestic consumers pay by $2.

By raising prices, tariffs hurt consumers while benefiting producers. In addition, tariffs raise money for the government. But as Figure 7.4 shows, the harm caused to consumers by a tariff is greater than the sum of the benefit to producers plus the money raised by the tariff. Tariffs, therefore, create a deadweight loss.

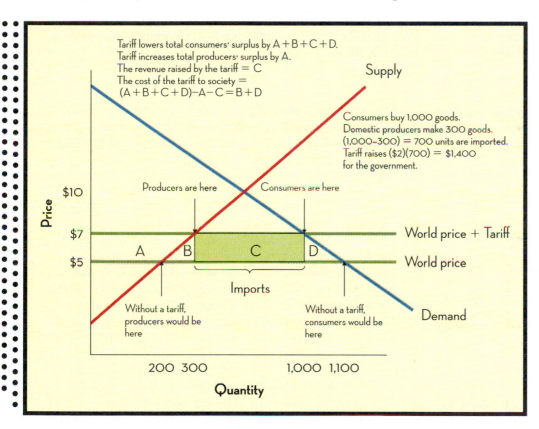

FIGURE **7.4**

IMPORTS WITH A TARIFF

179

The Deadweight Loss of Tariffs
Tariffs create a deadweight loss by causing consumers to buy goods from domestic producers that could be produced more cheaply abroad. Imagine it costs $30,000 for Inefficient-Auto to make a car. Inefficient-Auto is located in RicardoLand. This exact same car, however, is sold by Efficient-Auto for $25,000. Efficient-Auto, though, is located in another country. A large tariff could cause consumers in RicardoLand to buy only cars made in RicardoLand. Such

a tariff would destroy wealth. To understand why, let's compare what happens when a RicardoLand consumer buys a car made by Efficient-Auto to when he purchases one from Inefficient-Auto:

If there is no tariff and a RicardoLand consumer buys a car from Efficient-Auto for $25,000, then:

1. The consumer gives up $25,000. (Of course, Efficient-Auto would get $25,000 and have to pay the cost of producing the car. But let's ignore these effects and just consider the consequences to RicardoLand's consumers and firms.)

If there was a tariff that caused a RicardoLand consumer to buy a car from Inefficient-Auto for, say, $33,000 then:

2. Inefficient-Auto pays $30,000 to build the car.
3. The consumer gives up $33,000.
4. Inefficient-Auto gets $33,000.

Effects (3) and (4) are money transfers that cancel out and have no effect on the total wealth of RicardoLand. But (1) imposes less cost on RicardoLand than does (2). It is, after all, cheaper to pay another country $25,000 than to use $30,000 of your own country's resources. A tariff that causes a consumer to buy a car from Inefficient-Auto, therefore, destroys wealth in RicardoLand.

QUOTAS

Quotas are another means of protecting domestic producers by restricting imports. A quota places a limit on the number of goods that can be imported. Like tariffs, quotas help producers but harm consumers and create a deadweight loss. The primary difference between a tariff and quota is that the quota raises no money for the government.

Imagine that RicardoLand wants to limit the importation of foreign grain to 700 bushels. As Figure 7.4 shows, if the world price of grain is $5, then a $2 tariff would accomplish this. RicardoLand could also, however, simply impose a 700-bushel quota on the importation of foreign grain. With the quota, RicardoLand would give selected foreign firms the right to sell, collectively, 700 bushels of grain in RicardoLand. In this example, the only difference between the quota and tariff is that the government raises no money with the quota. Instead the revenue represented by area C in Figure 7.4 would go to foreign firms who, under the quota, get the right to sell grain in RicardoLand. These foreign firms benefit because the quota raises the price of grain in RicardoLand and so increases their revenues.

> Studies have estimated that if governments removed all trade restrictions and agricultural subsidies, the world would be between $254 billion to $2,080 billion a year richer.[3]

It might seem silly for a government ever to impose a quota instead of a tariff. But a quota is a means of reducing international political opposition to import restrictions. For example, imagine that RicardoLand is a military ally of SmithLand. The politicians in RicardoLand want to impose import restrictions on SmithLand, but if they impose a tariff then producers in SmithLand may complain to their government and this could threaten the military alliance. So instead RicardoLand imposes a quota on SmithLand's grain. Grain producers in SmithLand don't get upset because they now get the benefit of area C in Figure 7.4. So the quota allows RicardoLand to protect domestic grain producers without endangering the country's alliance.

FOUR ADDITIONAL BENEFITS OF TRADE

ADDITIONAL BENEFIT OF TRADE #1: SPECIALIZATION

Trade allows nations to develop expertise through specialization. Consider the following analogy. Imagine that your college's swimming and tennis teams stink. The coaches of these two teams get together and realize that every single one of their players is on both teams. The coaches decide to double the practice time for each team and to force each player to drop one sport. Players then concentrate fully on their chosen sport. As a result, the quality of both teams improves. Similarly, when trade allows someone to specialize in just one job, this person gains time to become extremely competent at her chosen profession.

Pottery and the Fall of Rome[4]

The fall of the Roman Empire in the 5th century AD shows what happens to specialization when trade collapses. Under the Roman Empire, merchants could sell goods throughout Western Europe. And this trade made it profitable for craftsmen to make many types of high-quality goods.

Assume, for example, you were considering becoming a master potter. To become such a potter, you would have to buy a pottery wheel and devote several years to studying under an established master potter. As a master potter you would be able to make five high-quality pots a day. And, indeed, to make a decent living, you would have to sell four or five such pots each day. But the people in your village don't need this many pots. If you were a citizen of the Roman Empire, however, you could sell your pots throughout Western Europe. Under the Empire, consequently, you could become a successful master potter.

But after the Empire's fall, it wasn't safe to travel long distances. Consequently, potters could only sell their products locally. Master potters, however, couldn't possibly sell enough pots to local residents to sustain themselves. As a result, after the fall of the Roman Empire, the quality and quantity of many products, including pottery, greatly decreased. Interestingly, some people today think we should emulate 5th century trading patterns and buy only locally made goods.

Buy Local?

An advertising campaign running in my area urges people to buy locally grown food. According to this campaign, you are a local hero if you buy from local farmers.

Imagine, however, what would happen if everyone bought only locally grown food. Pretend, for example, that all the land near where you live is relatively unsuitable for growing corn. Corn can be grown on nearby land, but doing so requires greater use of environmentally damaging pesticides. And even after using extra pesticides, farmers get less corn per acre of land than do farmers in other parts of the world. Normally, farmers in your area would not grow corn. But if people become convinced that they "should" buy locally grown foods then the demand for locally grown corn will increase. This will raise the price of locally grown corn and so induce some farmers to cut down a few local forests so they can plant corn. The desire to buy locally grown food, therefore, will harm the environment while increasing the price of food.

Economists always look for trade-offs. And one trade-off that comes from buying locally grown food is that you don't buy food grown far away. So for an economist the following two slogans are identical:

1. "Help Local Farmers. Buy Locally Grown Food."
2. "Help Keep Africans Poor. Don't Buy Their Agricultural Exports."

ADDITIONAL BENEFIT OF TRADE #2: INNOVATION

Trade increases innovation. Imported goods often contain new technologies. For example, in the 1980s Japanese cars sold in the United States had safety features that American-made vehicles lacked. To compete for American consumers, U.S. car companies had to innovate by improving their own safety technology.

Companies from technologically advanced countries often set up and run factories in poor nations. For these transplant factories to run effectively, the companies must train their local workforces in the latest wealth-producing technologies. These workers then have the skills to set up their own technologically sophisticated factories someday.

China's Lost Opportunity

China's 15th century trade policy may be the reason most Americans don't speak Chinese. In the 15th century, China was the world's most technologically sophisticated nation and had by far the world's most advanced ships. But China's leaders decided to wall off their country from the rest of the world and forbid Chinese ships from engaging in international trade. While Europeans eagerly copied Chinese technology, China did her best to limit outside influences. Consequently, China never developed the shipbuilding technology needed to cross the world's oceans. As a result, it was Western Europe, not China, that colonized the Americas.

ADDITIONAL BENEFIT OF TRADE #3: REDUCED CORRUPTION

Imagine that you play basketball for a team in an amateur league in Springfield. You love to win, and fortunately your team always does. The basketball referees in Springfield, who are extremely well-paid, are chosen by the mayor. The mayor's son is on your team. All the referees know that, to keep their jobs, they must ensure that the mayor's son's team never loses a game.

My big question for you is, "How hard do you work during practice?" My guess is that since you know you're always going to win, you don't put much effort into practice. So the corruption in Springfield reduces the quality of Springfield's basketball teams.

But now pretend that next season you start playing games outside of Springfield where the referees are honest. Knowing that you will be playing honest games will motivate your entire team to work harder during practice since basketball skills rather than political connections will decide the outcome of away games.

Here's how this basketball story relates to trade theory: Many countries have corrupt economies in which the politically powerful always win local economic competitions. Imagine you're the manager of a lightbulb manufacturing firm in some corrupt dictatorship where international trade is forbidden. Your company produces low-quality but high-priced lightbulbs. In a normal market economy, other firms would enter the lightbulb market to take away your customers by offering better products. But your company is owned by the dictator's favorite mistress. Anyone who tries to compete with your company gets thrown in jail. As a result, no one in your company bothers to work very hard because they don't fear economic competition.

Now, however, imagine that your country opens itself to international trade. Suddenly you have to compete with imported lightbulbs. The manufacturers of these lightbulbs live outside your country and so can't be threatened with jail. To beat the imports and attract customers, you have to work harder producing better, cheaper lightbulbs.

International trade forces companies to play against firms beyond the political influence of their country. So trade reduces the "home court" advantage available to local elites, thereby compelling them to compete for customers based on price and quality, not political influence.

ADDITIONAL BENEFIT OF TRADE #4: BRAIN GAIN

Imagine you're a mathematical super-genius living in a poor country. None of the jobs in your area require knowledge of mathematics so your talents go unused. But then an Internet café opens in your city. You spend some spare time learning computer programming, and because you're a mathematical super-genius, you quickly become a top programmer. You get a job with Microsoft as a software engineer. Your brain is now productively employed increasing the wealth of humanity.

Socrates, Plato, Isaac Newton, William Shakespeare, Thomas Edison, Albert Einstein, Adam Smith, and David Ricardo: had any of them been born a poor person in a poor country, they would have spent their lives doing low-skilled agricultural labor, and their intellects would likely have gone to waste. But brains are the most valuable assets of international corporations, and competition drives these firms to seek brainpower throughout the world. Through trade, corporations such as Microsoft can hire rich brains in poor nations. The brains can even stay in their home countries and use the Internet to collaborate with fellow employees located throughout the world.

SIX OBJECTIONS TO TRADE

Although economists mostly support free trade, many noneconomists believe that free trade worsens the human condition. Sadly for the academic economist, many of the most vocal opponents of free trade are college professors. Below is an analysis of six frequently made objections to free trade.

OBJECTION TO TRADE #1: TRADE HARMS WORKERS IN POOR COUNTRIES

You want to buy a pair of sneakers for $100. You find out, however, that the sneakers you most desire were made in a poor country by workers earning only $4 a day. Is it exploitation for you to purchase these sneakers? Does buying them contribute to global poverty?

> Question: Why would a worker take a job that pays only $4 a day?
>
> Answer: Because it's the best job she could get.

If you, and many people like you, don't buy products made by poor workers, then these workers aren't going to suddenly get high-paying employment opportunities. Rather, they will lose their low-paying jobs and replace them with even *lower-paying jobs.* Or, as a Mexican ambassador to the United States once said, "In a poor country like ours the alternative to low-paying jobs isn't high-paying jobs—it's no jobs at all.[5]

The counter-argument to this reasoning is that these workers shouldn't lose their jobs making sneakers, but rather these sneaker jobs should pay "decent" wages, and until the international capitalist trading system causes this to happen, moral people shouldn't buy products made by "underpaid" workers.

But to counter the counter-argument, I ask you to consider why workers in poor countries make so little money compared to employees in rich nations. The reason is that rich nations are

Nhep Chanda is a 17-year-old Cambodian girl who doesn't earn $4 a day making sneakers; she is "one of hundreds of Cambodians who toil all day, every day, picking through the dump for plastic bags, metal cans and bits of food. The stench clogs the nostrils, and parts of the dump are burning . . . Nhep Chanda averages 75 cents a day for her efforts. For her, the idea of being exploited in a garment factory—working only six days a week, inside instead of in the broiling sun, for up to $2 a day—is a dream."[6]

much better at creating wealth than poor countries are. Wages in North America, Japan, and Western Europe used to be extremely low by today's standards. But as countries in these regions became richer, their companies became better at wealth creation and much of this additional wealth went to workers. So, if you want workers in poor nations to make more money, you should support policies that make poor nations richer. And as this chapter has shown, trade increases the wealth of nations.

New York Times columnist Tom Friedman calls those in rich countries who oppose trade with poor nations "The Coalition to Keep Poor People Poor." Trade is the best means by which poor nations can grow richer. In the 20th century South Korea, Taiwan, Singapore, Ireland, and Hong Kong all went from extreme poverty to relative affluence through trading with richer nations. At the start of these nations' climbs to prosperity, the average wages in all these nations were extremely low.

The antitrade forces would create a poverty trap for the world's poor. They object to trade until workers in these poor nations make "decent" salaries. But without trade, poor nations won't ever become rich enough for their workers to receive such salaries.

Around 250 million children between the ages of 5 and 14 work in poor countries.[7] Some of these kids are employed making products that are exported to rich nations. Should countries such as the United States ban the importation of all goods made with child labor?

One hundred years ago it was common in the United States, even normal, for children to work. As the United States became richer, American parents could afford the luxury of not having their children work. Americans, however, shouldn't be surprised that poor nations—poorer than the United States was 100 years ago—employ child labor.

Poverty forces cruel choices on parents. Poor parents can send their children to work knowing that their kids might die in an industrial accident. Or these parents can keep their kids at home knowing that, deprived of their kid's income, they'll have less money for necessities such as food, shelter, insecticides, and health care. And spending less money on necessities could also result in a child's death. If we assume that most parents love their children, then we need to accept that, when poor parents send their kids to work, they have probably acted in the best interests of their children.

In 1992 Wal-Mart was found to be selling clothing made by Bangladeshi children.[9] Bangladesh is one of the world's poorest nations. The U.S. Congress threatened to cut off imports from Bangladesh if it didn't curtail child labor. To prevent this from happening, many Bangladeshi children were fired from their jobs. What happened to these fired children was very predictable to economists. Making clothing for Wal-Mart had been the best way for these children to survive. Now that the U.S. Congress had foreclosed this option, the children moved on to less pleasant means of subsistence. Many became prostitutes.

> Imagine that a Nike vice president proposed to his boss that Nike make cheap T-shirts in Ethiopia:
>
> " 'Look, boss, it would be tough to operate there, but a factory would be a godsend to one of the poorest countries in the world. And if we kept a tight eye on costs and paid 25 cents an hour, we might be able to make a go of it.' The boss would reply: 'You're crazy! We'd be boycotted on every campus in the country.' "[8]

OBJECTION TO TRADE #2: TRADE HARMS WORKERS IN RICH COUNTRIES

Imagine you're a U.S. factory worker earning $50,000 a year. You know that in India millions of hardworking people would love to get a factory job that paid even $5,000 a year. Shouldn't you do everything you possibly can to stop trade with India? After all, trade forces workers to compete, and how could you possibly compete against someone willing to work for one-tenth of your salary?

Actually, U.S. workers *can* successfully compete against workers in poor countries who make only a tiny fraction of their wages. Rich countries such as the United States, Japan, Canada, France, and Australia are rich because they are good at creating wealth. These nations all have the infrastructure, technology, skills, government, climate, and markets that allow their workers to be enormously productive. So the average worker in the United States produces vastly more wealth every hour he works than the average worker in India does. And if India were to become as effective at wealth production as the United States is, then Indian wages would likely become as high as U.S. wages.

But trade always creates losers as well as winners, so some workers in rich nations will be hurt by trade with poor countries. And someday your professor might lose his or her job because of trade.

Professors as "Trade Losers"

Consider a professor at your college who had been getting $15,000 to teach a one-semester introductory microeconomics class for 250 students. This year, however, your college is considering hiring a professor living in India to teach the class via the Internet.

The Indian professor would get only $5,000 for the course. Students watching the lecture would be able to both see and hear the professor. During the lecture they would be able to submit questions in real time through instant messaging. The professor could answer these questions during his talk.

Because $5,000 is a huge amount of money for a professor in India to receive for teaching a one-semester course, your school would be able to attract one of the best lecturers in India to teach the class. Furthermore, this professor would commit to having 20 hours a week of "office hours" during which students could ask questions by telephone, e-mail, or Internet instant message. The professor would even grade papers and problem sets submitted by e-mail. True, students wouldn't be able to meet personally with the professor. But in a class of 250, students usually can't get much professorial face time anyway. And keep in mind that if your college replaces enough of its professors with Indians, it will be able to cut tuition rates drastically. So my question for you is, "Should your college fire the local introductory microeconomics professor and replace him with a teacher living in India?"

OBJECTION TO TRADE #3: NATIONS NEED TRADE RESTRICTIONS TO PROTECT INFANT INDUSTRIES

Taiwanese manufacturers are very skilled at making computer memory chips. Imagine that a Brazilian company wants to start making memory chips. But without some experience, the Brazilian company won't be able to compete with Taiwanese manufacturers. So this Brazilian company asks its government to prohibit temporarily the importation of memory chips into Brazil. The Brazilian company will then be able to make and sell memory chips in Brazil for a few years and so gain profits and experience. After these few years have passed, the trade restrictions can be eliminated because the Brazilian company will then be strong enough to compete against the Taiwanese firms.

Businesses often claim that infant industries need temporary protection from foreign manufacturers. This temporary protection will supposedly give them time to grow. But although the infant industry argument for trade restrictions seems sensible, it's not economically justified.

A new business could borrow money to overcome startup difficulties. For example, let's assume that, after operating for three years, our Brazilian company could indeed succeed in the chip marketplace. Rather then needing a tariff, the company could borrow money for three years. During these three years, it would lose money but gain experience making memory chips. After these three years have passed, the company will start making profits and use these profits to pay back investors. Many companies, such as Amazon.com, have received substantial money from investors before they became profitable.

The Harm that Comes from Protecting Infant Industries
If a parent shields his child from every difficulty, then the child will never acquire the strength needed to be a responsible adult. Similarly, when governments protect infant industries from foreign competition, the industries can maintain inefficient practices and avoid reform. Firms that receive infant industry protection, therefore, never need "grow up."

Businesspeople also might start inefficient businesses just to get infant industry protection. For example, imagine that you are a politically well-connected businessperson. No one in your country currently makes refrigerators. You realize that you could never make refrigerators as well or as cheaply as foreign companies can. But you also realize that if you started to manufacture refrigerators, you could get the government to block all refrigerator imports to protect your infant refrigerator company. You therefore start producing expensive but poor quality refrigerators, knowing that any domestic consumer who wants a refrigerator will have to buy one of yours.

Since foreign competition would destroy your company, your business's profitability depends on pleasing politicians. You consequently don't bother "wasting" money trying to improve the quality of your refrigerators. Rather, you make generous contributions to many politicians. You furthermore "take hostages" by hiring many politicians' relatives. This way if politicians end your infant industry protection and so destroy your company, they will be effectively firing their own kin.

OBJECTION TO TRADE #4: NATIONS SHOULDN'T TRADE WITH POTENTIAL MILITARY ENEMIES

Trade makes nations richer. But sometimes one country wants another to be poorer. For example, assume that the United States fears a future military conflict with the hypothetical nation of EvilLand. If the United States engaged in trade with EvilLand, it and EvilLand would gain $100 million a year in wealth. Unfortunately, EvilLand would use this wealth to develop chemical, biological, and nuclear weapons, which it would give to anti-American terrorists. So perhaps the United States should forgo the economic benefits of trade with EvilLand. Sometimes countries are better off ignoring comparative advantages and not trading with military enemies.

Trade, however, might reduce EvilLand's desire to harm the United States. For example, imagine that if the United States and EvilLand engage in trade, the Hello Kitty Company will open up a factory in EvilLand that exports products to the United States. This factory will generate wealth for EvilLand's political elite. After the Hello Kitty factory is built, EvilLand might not want to destroy U.S. cities with weapons of mass destruction because such destruction would reduce U.S. purchases of Hello Kitty paraphernalia.

After World War II, the European Coal and Steel Community (the forerunner of the European Union) was created to reduce the chance of war between France and

Germany. The goal of the European Coal and Steel Community was to so intertwine the economies of France and Germany that a war between them would devastate both economies.

Trade may have prevented India and Pakistan from going to war in 2002.[10] India and Pakistan are longtime military adversaries who both have nuclear weapons. Indian and Pakistani politicians often publicly threaten each other. Both sides enjoy acting tough and pretending that they don't fear war. Unfortunately, tough talk can sometimes lead to military conflict.

In May of 2002, the threatening talk emanating from India and Pakistan was so inflammatory that the U.S. State Department issued a travel advisory saying, "We urge Americans citizens currently in India to depart the country." But by this date a large number of American companies were in India generating substantial wealth for the Indian economy. Many of these companies told India that if it kept threatening Pakistan they would leave. The companies weren't interested in the outcome of the Indian-Pakistani conflict, but they didn't wish to conduct business in a country that might shortly be involved in a nuclear war. As a result, India toned down her war rhetoric, and the chances of an India-Pakistani conflict were greatly reduced.

> "The great virtue of a free market is that it enables people who hate each other, or who are from vastly different religious or ethnic backgrounds, to cooperate economically. Government intervention can't do that. Politics exacerbates and magnifies differences." —Milton Friedman

OBJECTION TO TRADE #5: NATIONS CAN USE THE THREAT OF RETALIATORY TRADE RESTRICTIONS TO PROMOTE FREE TRADE

Imagine that South Korea refuses to allow U.S. companies to sell automobiles in Korea. Korea, however, does want to sell Korean-made cars in the United States. If the United States has a choice between (A) having no automobile trade with Korea and (B) having Korean cars sold in the United States but no U.S. cars sold in Korea, then the United States would be much better off with (B). This is because, as Figure 7.3 shows, when a nation imports goods, it becomes richer. The United States, however, would be even better off with option (C), where both Korean and U.S. firms sell cars in each others' countries.

But imagine that Korean automobile makers have a great deal of political power in their country. Imports of cars into Korea harm Korean automobile manufacturers. So let's assume that Korean car firms successfully pressure their government to block the importation of U.S. vehicles. To change this situation, the U.S. government could threaten to block the importation of Korean cars unless Korea accepts U.S. automobile imports. Since Korean car firms would suffer if they couldn't sell cars in the United States, they might get their government to accept such a deal. Threatening to reduce trade, therefore, can sometimes increase trade. Of course, if Korea doesn't accept the deal, then the United States becomes stuck in option (A).

U.S. Steel Tariffs
When George W. Bush first ran for president in 2000, he promised to protect U.S. steel manufacturers from foreign competition. After he was elected, he attempted to keep this campaign promise by imposing tariffs on foreign-made steel.

The European Union threatened to impose restrictions on goods imported from the United States in retaliation for the steel tariffs. To maximize the political cost to President Bush, the European Union planned to impose import restrictions on goods made in states that would likely be key battlegrounds in Bush's 2004 re-election bid. The U.S. dropped the steel tariffs in part because of the threatened retaliation but also because these tariffs were ruled to have violated international trade agreements.

Brazilian Models

The U.S. restricts the importation of Brazilian sugar. One commentator has come up with a novel way for Brazil to pressure the United States to drop these restrictions. He advises Brazil to "Stop letting any of your models come to the U.S. and pose in Victoria's Secret catalogs until the U.S. government agrees to let in Brazilian sugar."[11]

OK, this advice was probably meant as a joke. But it might actually work. U.S. restrictions on sugar importation help a very small number of people while hurting all Americans who consume sugar. Most Americans, however, don't know about sugar trade restrictions, so U.S. politicians who support sugar trade barriers suffer no political penalty. If Brazil really did protest U.S. trade policy by stopping its models from appearing in Victoria Secret catalogs, it would draw massive media attention to U.S. sugar policy. Such attention would make it a little more difficult for U.S. politicians to craft sugar trade restrictions that benefit the few at the expense of the many.

OBJECTION TO TRADE #6: THE SANTA CLAUS PROBLEM[12]

Each Christmas Santa Claus gives presents to hundreds of millions of children. Economists classify these presents as imports since they are all made by elves laboring in a North Pole sweatshop.

Consider how many jobs Santa Claus destroys. If it wasn't for Santa, millions of human workers could be employed making Christmas toys. But how could a human toy maker ever compete with Santa's elves who work so cheaply that Santa can actually afford to give away his products? So, although this may sound cruel, shouldn't we fire Santa Claus, thereby creating millions of jobs for human toy makers?

Well, actually, most economists adamantly oppose the firing of Santa Claus. Economists know that there are not a fixed number of jobs in the economy. True, Santa Claus's Christmas generosity does destroy millions of toy-making jobs. But this is a good thing! Workers who would have been employed making toys are now able to make other goods.

Candle Makers

Santa Claus hurts toy makers, but at least toy makers can take comfort knowing that Santa gives away goodies only one day a year. Candle makers, in contrast, suffer from competition from a rival who both gives away its product and operates every single day of the year. Candle makers' arch competitor is, of course, the sun!

A 19th-century economist satirically suggested that the government help candle makers by mandating the closing of all "windows, dormers, skylights, inside and outside shutters, curtains, casements, bull's-eyes, deadlights, and blinds."[13] And indeed if we blocked out the sun we would create far more jobs for makers of illumination devices.

But even though the sun destroys countless jobs, the economy still benefits from sunlight. By reducing the need for candle makers, sunlight frees up human labor that can be used to produce other products.

The Benefits of Job Destruction
Opponents of trade often claim that cheap imports destroy jobs. They are right, but this job destruction helps the economy by freeing up workers to do other wealth-creating tasks.

Destruction of agricultural jobs has been responsible for much of the economic growth the United States has experienced since 1850. As shown in the table below, from 1850 to 1990 the U.S. farm population shrank from 64 percent to 1.6 percent. Technology destroyed millions of farm jobs by increasing the amount of food each farmer grew. And because technology eliminated so many farm jobs, it pushed would-have-been farmers to take many other types of employment. Without job destruction in the agricultural sector, the United States today would have vastly fewer doctors, engineers, scientists, artists, teachers, and economists.

Year	Percentage of U.S. Population Living on Farms
1850	64%
1920	30%
1990	1.6%

Source: U.S. Census Bureau

An Honest Economist
In 2004 Greg Mankiw, the U.S. president's chief economic advisor, said that the U.S. economy benefits when foreign trade destroys U.S. jobs. Although almost every economist believes this to be true, Mankiw was widely condemned for his comments. The Speaker of the U.S. House of Representatives (the third-highest elected official in the U.S.) said that Mankiw's theory "fails a basic test of real economics." Actually, by speaking an uncomfortable economic truth, Mankiw failed a basic test of real *politics*.

Trade Also Creates Jobs
Trade both destroys and creates jobs. For example, many U.S. computer companies hire people in India to provide phone technical support to U.S. customers. Because of this outsourcing of jobs, there are fewer employment opportunities for Americans to offer computer support. U.S. companies hire Indians for such customer service jobs because the Indians work at lower wages than computer-savvy Americans do. This cost savings reduces the price of computers and so, by the Law of Demand, causes Americans to buy more computers. And because Americans purchase more computers, there are, for example, more jobs for computer salespeople at U.S. electronics stores and more employment opportunities at U.S. software companies such as Microsoft.

India, furthermore, is made richer because many Indians work for U.S. computer companies. Indians spend some of this wealth buying U.S. goods made by American workers.

TRADE: THE BASIS FOR CIVILIZATION[14]
This chapter began by discussing why trade might be responsible for mankind's dominance of the earth. We now conclude by showing why trade enables human civilization.

The centrality of trade to human civilization is perhaps best illuminated by the pencil. A pencil seems like a simple device. But no single human has the ability to make one.

To make a pencil, you need a lumberjack to cut down a tree. This lumberjack, however, will need a saw. The saw will be made of metal. The metal will have to be mined and refined. The rubber and graphite in the pencil also have to be found and refined. All the materials needed to make the pencil must be shipped to their assembly place. The means of shipment, whether a boat, train, or wagon, will also have to be produced. Furthermore, all the people doing these pencil-related tasks will have to be fed and housed. And those building homes and growing food will themselves need tools.

It takes the efforts of millions to create a simple pencil. By trading, these millions can produce the humble pencil. But without trade, where every individual would have to fend for himself, we would have none of the tools of civilization. Without trade, therefore, humans would be forced back to primitive Neanderthal-like existences.

QUESTIONS YOU SHOULD BE ABLE TO ANSWER AFTER READING THIS CHAPTER:

1 Why might trade have caused the extinction of the Neanderthals? (pages 166–168)

2 When does a nation have an absolute advantage in the production of a good? (pages 169–170)

3 When does a nation have a comparative advantage in the production of a good? (pages 171–172)

4 What is roundabout production? (page 173)

5 Why must every nation and every person have a comparative advantage in something? (page 173)

6 Who was David Ricardo? (page 174)

7 Where do comparative advantages come from? (pages 174–175)

8 How can you use supply and demand curves to show the benefits of trade? (pages 175–178)

9 What are exports? (pages 176–177)

10 What are imports? (pages 177–178)

11 Do domestic firms benefit from imports or exports? (page 178)

12 Why do politicians often oppose imports? (pages 178–179)

13 How can you use supply and demand curves to show the consequences of a tariff? (page 179)

14 Do governments raise more money through tariffs or quotas? (page 180)

15 What's the advantage of specialization? (page 181)

16 How can trade promote innovation? (page 182)

17 How can trade reduce corruption? (page 182)

18 How can trade cause human brains to be used more effectively? (page 183)

STUDY PROBLEMS

1   Refer to the table below. In which goods does France have an absolute advantage?
In which goods does Syria have an absolute advantage? Rewrite the table using
opportunity costs. In which goods does France have a comparative advantage? In
which goods does Syria have a comparative advantage?

	Coat	DVD Player
Cost to France	3 hours of work	8 hours of work
Cost to Syria	1 hour of work	2 hours of work

2   Refer to the table below. Assume initially that Spain makes three units of food
and three desks while India makes five units of food and four desks. (a) Show
how through trade both countries can have the same goods while working
fewer hours. (b) Show how through trade both countries can work the same
number of hours but have more goods.

	A Unit of Food	A Desk
Cost to Spain	1 hour of work	4 hours of work
Cost to India	5 hours of work	5 hours of work

3   Assume that initially RicardoLand does not trade with the outside world and the
price of grain in RicardoLand is $5 a bushel. Further assume that RicardoLand is
such a small country that it can't affect the world price for grain.

a.   Draw the relevant supply and demand curves. Now assume that Ricardo-
Land opens itself up to trade and the world price of grain is $9 a bushel.
Show the change in total consumers' surplus and total producers' surplus
resulting from trade.

b.   Repeat (a) but assume that the world price of grain is $2 a bushel.

c.   If the world price of grain is $2 a bushel, show the deadweight loss caused by
a $1.50–per–bushel tariff.

4 Evaluate the reasonableness of the following advice: "A human being should be able to change a diaper, plan an invasion, butcher a hog, conn a ship, design a building, write a sonnet, balance accounts, build a wall, set a bone, comfort the dying, take orders, give orders, cooperate, act alone, solve equations, analyze a new problem, pitch manure, program a computer, cook a tasty meal, fight efficiently, and die gallantly. Specialization is for insects."[15]

5 Evaluate the reasonableness of the following statement: "A patriotic American should buy only American-made goods. After all, when he buys American products his money goes to American companies and American workers. In contrast, when he buys goods made in another country, he helps foreigners at the expense of Americans."

6 If every human was born with the exact same abilities and resources, would there be any reason to trade?

7 The country that the United States trades with the most is Canada. Why do you think this is, and what does this tell you about international trade?

8 This chapter listed four additional benefits of trade. Make the argument that additional benefit #4 (Brain Gain) is really an example of additional benefit #1 (Specialization).

9 In the textbook I wrote, "If we assume that most parents love their children, then we need to accept that when poor parents send their kids to work they have probably acted in the best interests of their children." Does this argument hold for U.S. parents?

10 Moral Question: You are the president of an American company that is considering opening a factory in Bangladesh that will employ 30,000 poor workers. Assume that if you open the factory you could get as many qualified employees as you wish at wages of $4 a day. Assume that no negative or positive publicity will result from choosing any of these options. Assume that your company will make the same profits with options b–f. Please rank the following options from most morally preferable to least morally preferable and briefly justify your answer. There is no correct economic answer to this question.

a. Don't open the Bangladeshi factory.

b. Open the Bangladeshi factory and pay each worker $4 a day in wages.

c. Open the Bangladeshi factory, pay $9 a day in wages, but save money on factory safety measures thereby exposing each worker in the Bangladeshi factory to a 1 in 4,000 chance of being killed in the factory each year. The Bangladeshi workers will be aware of this risk. Ninety percent of your Bangladeshi workers would prefer this to option (b).

d. Open the Bangladeshi factory, pay $9 a day in wages, but save money by paying small bribes to Bangladeshi officials that will significantly reduce the amount of taxes you will have to pay the Bangladeshi government.

e. Open the Bangladeshi factory, pay $9 a day in wages, but save money by reducing the safety of the product you are manufacturing. Each year you will export 1million goods to the United States. Each American who buys the product will have a 1 in 100,000 chance of losing a finger. Your American consumers will not be aware of this risk.

f. Open the Bangladeshi factory, pay $9 a day in wages, but save money by not installing pollution-control equipment. Each year your factory will now contribute as much to global warming and ozone destruction as 20,000 large trucks driven 32,000 miles each.

> "THE BATTLE TO FEED ALL OF HUMANITY IS OVER. IN THE 1970S AND 1980S HUNDREDS OF MILLIONS OF PEOPLE WILL STARVE TO DEATH IN SPITE OF ANY CRASH PROGRAMS EMBARKED UPON NOW."
>
> —Paul Ehrlich, (Neo-Malthusian 1968)[1]

THE IMPORTANCE OF COSTS

If you dissect a firm to examine its heart, you'll find costs. When the world's population was only 1 billion, a famous economist convincingly argued that mass starvation was our species' future. But agricultural costs changed, and now food producers can feed 6.5 billion. Analyzing costs also shows why big-budget movies are superficial and why the economic development of China and India gives pharmaceutical companies greater incentives to research cancer cures. And transforming the cost of space travel might just allow you to visit the moon sometime during the next 30 years.

THE COST OF SPACE TRAVEL

Let's examine the cost of a hypothetical new fleet of one-man rocket ships. The first step in constructing these ships is creating a design detailing exactly how the ships will be built, specifying, for example, what kinds of material will be used and how the engine will be constructed. Formulating a practical design can take many years and significant sums of money. Assume that it costs $1 billion to design this ship.

Now imagine that after the design phase it costs $10 million to construct each individual ship. So, for example, to build 10 rocket ships a firm would first spend $1 billion on the design and then $10 million multiplied by 10 to construct the 10 ships, for a total cost of $1.1 billion. The ships are not reusable, so you need a new rocket ship each time you take someone into space. Let's introduce some economic terminology to categorize our costs:

Output—the number of goods produced. If 10 ships are built, output is 10.

Fixed costs—costs that are the same regardless of output. Fixed costs must be paid before even one unit of output is produced. Imagine, for example, that you own a restaurant that must pay $5,000 a year in property taxes. These property taxes must be paid regardless of how many customers you have. This $5,000, therefore, is a fixed cost. You have to pay your fixed costs even if you have zero

COSTS

customers. In our rocket ship example, the fixed cost equals $1 billion, since you must pay the same $1 billion in design cost regardless of whether you build zero, 1, 100, or 1 million rocket ships.

Variable costs—costs that vary with output. Variable costs are simply all the costs that are not fixed. If you own a restaurant, then the money you spend on food is one of your variable costs because the quantity of food you use varies with the number of people you serve. In the rocket ship example, variable costs are output multiplied by $10 million, so if output is 10, variable costs are $100 million.

Total costs—the sum of all the costs. Total costs = Fixed costs + Variable costs.

Marginal costs—the extra cost of making one more good. Since the additional cost of building another rocket ship is $10 million, the marginal cost of a rocket ship is always $10 million.

A SPACE ELEVATOR

The high marginal cost of space travel is why you will not be spending the next spring break on the moon. But your children might take a lunar spring break if humanity constructs a space elevator.

A space elevator would essentially be a 62,000-mile cable stretching from the earth's surface out into space. Because one end of the cable would be in high orbit, gravity would prevent it from falling back to earth. Once the cable was in place, space travelers would board an elevator-like device and ride up the cable.

The 62,000-mile cable would endure tremendous stress from supporting its own mass, so the primary challenge in building a space elevator lies in constructing the cable out of material strong enough not to break. Fortunately, scientists have determined that carbon nanotubes, which are over 100 times stronger than steel, could be used for the cable. Unfortunately, no one yet knows how to fashion miles-long strands of carbon nanotubes. But I suspect that within the next 20 years or so innovative humans will figure out how to make a 62,000-mile, carbon-nanotube space elevator.

But it won't be cheap. Let's assume that the cost of building and positioning a space elevator would be $50 billion. Consequently, $50 billion is the fixed cost of leaving earth on a space elevator. The advantage of the space elevator is that once it's in place, the marginal cost of space travel becomes very low.

Imagine that once the elevator was positioned, it would cost only $1,000 to put a person into space. So with the elevator, the marginal cost of going into space is $1,000. The output of the space elevator is the number of people who have traveled into orbit on the elevator. If 10 people each take a trip on the elevator, output is 10.

So, which is cheaper: the rocket ship or the space elevator? As illustrated by the following table, this depends on output.

	Fixed Costs	Variable Costs	Total Costs
Rocket ship	$1 billion	Output × $10 million	$1 billion + (Output × $10 million)
Space elevator	$50 billion	Output × $1,000	$50 billion + (Output × $1,000)

Comparing Costs of the Rocket Ship and Space Elevator

If, for example, you want to take just one journey to space, it's far cheaper to use the rocket ship. Since the space elevator has an enormous fixed cost, it's worth building only if you plan to use it many times and so can spread out its high fixed cost over numerous trips.

AVERAGE TOTAL COSTS

Average total costs provide another means of comparing the rocket ship and space elevator. Imagine you build two goods. You pay $10 in fixed costs. It then costs you $3 to build the first good and $5 to build the second good. You built two goods for $10 + $3 + $5 = $18. Your average total costs, therefore, are $18/2 = $9. In general:

$$\text{Average total costs} = \frac{\text{Total costs}}{\text{Output}}$$

Average total costs tell you how much the average unit of output costs. Since the total cost of building 10 rocket ships is $1.1 billion, the average total cost of building 10 rocket ships is $\frac{\$1.1 \text{ billion}}{10} = \$110$ million.

Let's break down average total costs into two components. Recall that

$$\text{Total costs} = \text{Fixed costs} + \text{Variable costs}$$

If we divide both sides of the above equation by output, we get:

$$\frac{\text{Total costs}}{\text{Output}} = \frac{\text{Fixed costs}}{\text{Output}} + \frac{\text{Variable costs}}{\text{Output}}$$

The term on the left side of the above equation is average total costs. The terms on the right also have special meaning for economists.

$$\frac{\text{Fixed costs}}{\text{Output}} = \text{Average fixed costs}$$

$$\frac{\text{Variable costs}}{\text{Output}} = \text{Average variable costs}.$$

So we ultimately get:

$$\text{Average total costs} = \text{Average fixed costs} + \text{Average variable costs}$$

In our rocket ship and space elevator examples, average variable costs will always be constant. Total variable costs for the rocket ship are $10 million multiplied by output. Average variable costs for the ship, therefore, are $\dfrac{[\$10 \text{ million} \times \text{Output}]}{\text{Output}} = \$10$ million.

Similarly for the space elevator, average variable costs are $\dfrac{[\$1{,}000 \times \text{Output}]}{\text{Output}} = \$1{,}000$.

Whenever marginal costs are constant, average variable costs will always be equal to marginal costs. (Later in this chapter we will examine situations where marginal costs are not constant.)

Average fixed costs *always* decrease as output increases.

Average fixed costs $= \dfrac{\text{Fixed costs}}{\text{Output}}$. Since fixed costs don't, by definition, change as output changes, then average fixed costs must go down when output goes up.

Let's compare the average total costs of using a rocket ship and space elevator for a few levels of output:

Output	Average Fixed Costs $= \dfrac{\$1 \text{ billion}}{\text{Output}}$	Average Variable Costs $= \dfrac{\text{Output} \times \$10 \text{ million}}{\text{Output}}$	Average Total Costs = Average Fixed Costs + Average Variable Costs
1	$1 billion	$10 million	$1.01 billion
10	100 million	10 million	110,000,000
1,000	1 million	10 million	11,000,000
4,900	.2 million	10 million	10,200,000
1,000,000	1,000	10 million	10,001,000
1 billion	1	10 million	10,000,001

Costs for a Rocket Ship

Output	Average Fixed Costs $= \dfrac{\$50 \text{ billion}}{\text{Output}}$	Average Variable Costs $= \dfrac{\text{Output} \times \$1{,}000}{\text{Output}}$	Average Total Costs = Average Fixed Costs + Average Variable Costs
1	$50 billion	$1,000	$50 billion + $1,000
10	5 billion	1,000	5 billion + $1,000
1,000	50 million	1,000	50,001,000
4,900	10.2 million	1,000	10,201,000
1,000,000	50,000	1,000	51,000
1 billion	50	1,000	1,050

Costs for a Space Elevator

As you can see from the above tables, the average total costs of the rocket ship and elevator are about the same at an output of 4,900. For levels of output more than this, it's on average cheaper to use the elevator. For outputs less than 4,900, it's cheaper to use the rocket ships.

The Break-Even Price for the Space Elevator

Imagine you were going to build a space elevator and use it just once. To break even you would have to charge your single passenger the entire $50 billion fixed costs plus the $1,000 marginal costs. No one could afford to pay this much to go into space.

But now imagine you intend to build the space elevator and sell 1 billion space trips. To break even you would have to charge each passenger his $1,000 marginal cost plus one one-billionth of the fixed costs. Thus, you would need to set a price of only $1,050 to break even. The lesson here is that if fixed costs are high, you need a high level of output so you can spread the fixed costs out over many customers.

Firms Break Even When Price Equals Average Total Costs

Let's determine in general how much a firm must charge each customer to break even. Firms, of course, would like to charge more than their break-even price, but this price represents the minimum a firm can charge without losing money.

Price tells a firm how much each customer pays. Average total costs tells a firm how much on average each customer costs. For a firm to break even, the amount it gets from each customer must equal the amount on average that each customer costs it. A firm breaks even, therefore, when price equals average total costs. Let's now examine the general shape of average total cost curves when marginal costs are constant.

The Shape of the Average Total Costs Curve When Marginal Costs Are Constant

Recall that:

Average total costs = Average fixed costs + Average variable costs

Remember that average fixed costs always go down as output increases. Further recall that average variable costs are equal to marginal costs when marginal costs are constant. So,

Average total costs = Dollar amount that goes down as output increases + Marginal costs

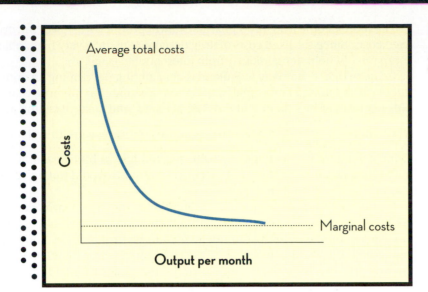

FIGURE **8.1**

AVERAGE TOTAL
COSTS CURVE

When marginal costs are constant, therefore, average total costs continually decrease as output increases. Average total costs, however, never become lower than marginal costs. Figure 8.1 shows a typical average total costs curve when marginal costs are constant.

Firms with constant marginal costs, consequently, benefit from having many customers to lower their average total costs. Firms that have very high fixed costs especially benefit from having many customers because this allows them to spread out their fixed costs over lots of customers.

THREE EXAMPLES OF HIGH FIXED-COSTS GOODS

Let's use our knowledge of costs to examine three high fixed-costs goods.

HIGH FIXED-COSTS GOOD #1: PHARMACEUTICALS

Pharmaceutical products such as drugs that lower blood pressure, fight infections, or attack cancer cells cost vast amounts to design. Pharmaceutical companies spend billions each year trying to find medicinally useful chemical compounds. Once a firm has discovered the formula for a useful compound, however, it's relatively cheap to make the actual pills. For example, imagine that it would cost $200 million to design a new cancer-fighting pill, but once the pill has been designed, it costs only $1 to make each copy of the pill. Therefore

Fixed costs = $200 million

Marginal costs = $1

If the pharmaceutical company intends to sell only one pill, its total costs would be $200,000,001 and this is how much it would have to charge to break even. In contrast, if it sold 10 million pills, its total costs would be $210 million and its average total costs would be $\frac{\$210 \text{ million}}{10 \text{ million}} = \$21$.

199

The more people who buy a pharmaceutical product, the lower the drug's average fixed costs. Since the fixed costs of drug design are usually very high, pharmaceutical companies benefit tremendously from international trade.

Imagine that a company in Finland is considering developing an anticancer drug. But because Finland has a small population, assume that no more than 1,000 of the pills would ever be sold in Finland. The average total costs of selling just 1,000 pills would be $\frac{\$200,001,000}{1,000} = \$200,001$. So if the company were to sell its drug only to Finns it would have to charge $200,001 per pill just to break even! Since few Finns have this much money, the pharmaceutical company would not design the drug if it knew it could sell it only to Finns.

In contrast, imagine that through international trade the pharmaceutical company could sell 10 million pills to people around the world. This would result in reducing the average total cost per pill to just $21. So if the firm believes, for example, that it could sell these 10 million pills for $30 each it would invest the $200 million to design and develop the drug. International trade, therefore, tremendously increases the number of pharmaceutical drugs produced.

The economic development of such poor nations as India and China spurs drug development. A pharmaceutical company will incur the huge fixed costs of drug development only if it predicts it will be able to sell its drugs to enough people to cover its fixed costs. As poor nations develop economically, they will buy more pharmaceuticals. So India's and China's recent rapid economic growth will increase the number of pharmaceutical drugs available to humanity.

AIDS vs. Malaria Treatment in Africa[2]

Imagine that a pharmaceutical company is considering developing a treatment for Disease-X. The company would have to spend $2 billion in fixed costs researching and developing the treatment. Once these fixed costs have been paid, however, it will cost only 10 cents in marginal costs to make each copy of the drug.

Let's further imagine that many poor Africans suffer from Disease-X. Selling the treatment to Africans would never generate $2 billion in revenue. So if only Africans have Disease-X, then it would never be profitable to pay the $2 billion in fixed research and development costs.

But now imagine that many rich Americans and Europeans also have Disease-X. A pharmaceutical company, therefore, could profitably sell the treatment to Americans and Europeans. And once the pharmaceutical company paid the fixed research and development costs of the treatment, it could afford to sell cheaply (or even give away) the drug to Africans.

AIDS and malaria both ravage poor Africans. But whereas AIDS also infects rich people, malaria is almost exclusively a poor person's disease. Consistent with the above analysis, pharmaceutical companies devote vastly more resources to fighting AIDS than malaria.

Thankfully, pharmaceutical companies have developed many effective treatments for AIDS. Because the marginal costs of producing many AIDS drugs are so low, pharmaceutical companies can afford to sell them cheaply to poor Africans. Impoverished African AIDS victims, therefore, are fortunate that their disease is shared by many rich people.

HIGH FIXED-COSTS GOOD #2: MOVIES

Films, like pharmaceuticals, rocket ships, and space elevators, can have high fixed costs. Imagine you're a movie producer who wants to make a $100 million special effects-loaded movie. You'll have to pay the $100 million fixed production cost regardless of whether thirty thousand or thirty million people see your film.

Just as pharmaceutical companies must sell their products throughout the world to recover their fixed costs, producers of expensive movies must also sell to a worldwide audience. But while Americans, Germans, Mexicans, and Japanese all have approximately the same pharmaceutical needs, people from different countries have radically different tastes in movies.

So, to make a high-cost but commercially successful movie, you must design your film to transcend cultural boundaries. And what do audiences the world over appreciate? Explosions, beautiful people, and slapstick humor. Subtle jokes, political commentary, and witty dialogue don't translate easily from one language and culture to another. If you want to spend $100 million on stars and special effects, you will need to attract an international audience. This means you must avoid intellectual sophistication and instead produce a superficial, common-denominator movie.

HIGH FIXED-COSTS GOOD #3: JET FIGHTERS

Imagine you're the United States Air Force general in charge of buying the next generation of fighter aircraft. Your job is to hire a defense contracting firm to design and then build 100 technologically advanced fighter jets. The firm tells you it will cost $5 billion to design the jet and then $30 million to build each aircraft. Therefore

Fixed costs = $5 billion

Marginal costs = $30 million

Total costs = 5 billion + (Output) × ($30 million) = $5 billion + 100($30 million) = $8 billion

Average total costs = $\frac{\$8 \text{ billion}}{100}$ = $80 million

Just to break even, the defense firm will have to charge you $80 million per jet. Eighty million is a lot of money, even for the U.S. armed forces, and so you ask the defense contractor if it could cut costs. The defense contractor says that normally it wouldn't be allowed to sell the advanced jet to foreign nations. But if you waived this rule, it could spread out its fixed cost over more output and therefore save the Air Force some money.

If the contractor were to make 200 jets, its total costs would be $5 billion + 200 ($30 million) = $11 billion, and its average total costs would be $\frac{\$11 \text{ billion}}{200}$ = $55 million.

So if the contractor is allowed to sell an additional 100 jets to foreign governments, its average total costs per jet would fall from $80 million to $55 million. Consequently, the contractor offers to greatly reduce its price to you if it can sell jets to foreign nations.

Unfortunately, the U.S. Air Force wants to build these new jets so it will have the most advanced fighter jets in the world. True, if the contractor is allowed to export, it would be permitted to sell jets only to friendly nations. But a friendly country today might turn into an enemy next year. And even friendly nations sometimes resell their arms to other governments.

So you face a dilemma. If you don't allow the defense contractor to sell jets to foreign governments, the U.S. Air Force will have to pay a very high price for the jets. But if you do allow foreign sales, then Air Force pilots might someday have to fight against these jets in combat. Economic analysis cannot solve your dilemma, but it *can* illuminate the relevant trade-offs.

A COST-BASED SCIENCE FICTION STORY

So far this chapter has assumed that marginal costs are constant. But we will now shift focus to look at firms with increasing marginal costs. We start with a fictional story:

In A.D. 2238 the Interstellar Agricultural Corporation colonized the planet Ixion. Interstellar Agricultural sent 1 million farmers to Ixion. Each of the 1 million farmers produced one food unit per day and were paid $1 per day.

Unfortunately, space pirates moved into the region of the galaxy near Ixion. By the rules of the Galactic Farmers' Union, any agricultural world threatened by space pirates had to be protected by a defense force of three space battleships. This defense force cost Interstellar Agricultural $10 million a day. Since Interstellar Agricultural paid Ixion farmers a total of $1 million a day, their total costs on Ixion were now $11 million per day.

Villich Granfortuma   Interstellar Agricultural was the sixth biggest company in the galaxy, so Ixion was a fairly unimportant operation to them. The company realized, however, that Ixion with its expensive pirate troubles would be the perfect training ground for the young Villich Granfortuma.

Villich was an inexperienced great-grandson of the company's founder. As Interstellar Agricultural was a family-run business, Villich was destined to play a huge leadership role in its million-world business empire.

Normally, Interstellar Agricultural tried to maximize its profit from each world. But profit maximization was deemed too complex a task for the young Villich. So, instead, Villich was told to minimize the average total costs of producing food on Ixion. (*Warning: Minimizing average total costs is normally a stupid business goal*. If you ever find yourself in charge of a planet, don't do it!)

AVERAGE TOTAL COSTS

Since Ixion produced 1 million food units per day at a total cost of $11 million, its average total costs were $11 million divided by output, or $\frac{\$11 \text{ million}}{1 \text{ million}} = \$11$.

Villich recalled that average total costs can be broken up into average fixed costs plus average variable costs. The $10 million defense costs would have to be spent regardless of how many food units Ixion sold. This $10 million is a fixed cost since it didn't vary with output. Ixion's average fixed costs therefore are $\frac{\$10 \text{ million}}{1 \text{ million}} = \$10$.

The more food Ixion produced, the more workers it needed. The wages that Interstellar Agricultural paid, consequently, varied with output and so were variable costs. Since it employed 1 million workers at $1 a day, its variable costs were $1 million per day. Its average variable costs were this $1 million divided by an output of 1 million units, or $1.

Interstellar's average costs are

Average fixed costs = $10 per day
Average variable costs = $1 per day
Average total costs per day = $10 + $1 = $11

More Farmers   Villich quickly figured out four simple ways to lower average total costs: (1) reduce expenditures on the defense force, (2) pay each farmer less, (3) force each farmer to do more work for the same pay, or (4) improve agricultural technology so that each farmer would grow more food even while putting in the same amount of work. Unfortunately, the Galactic Farmers' Union forbade the first three options, and it would have taken scientists too much time to implement the fourth measure.

Villich remembered that average fixed costs always go down as output increases. At the current level of output, average fixed costs were $10. Villich realized that if he could increase output by a factor of 100, then average fixed costs would go down by a factor of 100. Villich, therefore, decided to increase Ixion's workforce from 1 million to 100 million. If he succeeded in increasing output to 100 million units a day then average fixed costs would fall to only $\frac{\$10 \text{ million}}{100 \text{ million}} = 10$ cents.

New Average Fixed Costs

Unfortunately, the additional 99 million workers were far less productive than Villich had hoped. With 100 million farmers Ixion produced only 5 million food units rather than 100 million. Average fixed costs, therefore fell to only $\frac{\$10 \text{ million}}{5 \text{ million}} = \$2$ rather than 10 cents. Still, this was a significant improvement over the previous average fixed costs of $10.

New Average Variable Costs

Recall that wages were $1 per day. Since Interstellar Agricultural now employed 100 million workers, its variable costs were $100 million. If these workers, as Villich had hoped, produced 100 million units of food a day then average variable costs would have been $\frac{\$100 \text{ million}}{100 \text{ million}} = \$1$, the same as before. But because these 100 million farmers produced only 5 million food units, average variable costs actually were $\frac{\$100 \text{ million}}{5 \text{ million}} = \$20$. Average total costs are now $2 + $20 = $22, much higher than before. Villich, therefore, failed miserably at his assignment.

What Went Wrong?

When Ixion had 1 million farmers, each produced one food unit per day. Had this continued to happen when Ixion had 100 million farmers, Villich's plan would have worked brilliantly. But the 99 million new farmers were far less productive than the original 1 million workers. Instead of producing an extra 99 million food units, they grew only an extra 4 million.

After investigating, Villich found out that the original 1 million farmers had been using the best agricultural land on Ixion. When the new workers arrived they had to use less fertile soil. Many ended up farming mountains or desert terrain.

Villich thought that if he increased the number of workers he used by a factor of 100, his output would also go up 100 fold. Unfortunately for Villich, food on Ixion was grown with both labor and land. Villich, however, increased only the quantity of labor. As a result, when more farmers were sent to Ixion, each on average had less land to work with. Output per worker, therefore, plummeted.

Bring in the Econometrician!

Villich started thinking about how average total costs would vary as output varied. Average fixed costs continually decrease as output increases. So if he just looked at average fixed costs, he should choose as high an output as possible to minimize average total costs. But if output gets too high, average variable costs will start to rise. So if he just looked at average variable costs, he would want a very low level of output to minimize average total costs.

Villich, of course, needed to consider both average fixed costs and average variable costs. He realized that, without more information about Ixion's costs, he couldn't find the optimal level of output. Villich decided to bring in an econometrician, one who has power to use advanced statistics to estimate costs. After the econometrician did his work, Villich figured he would be able to determine the optimal number of farmers to employ.

Villich realized that the lesson he was supposed to learn on Ixion was humility. Villich had blindly assumed that he should increase output drastically. Success in business, however, always requires that you calculate costs carefully before determining output.

Conclusion to the Fictional Story

You have just finished reading a science fiction story about costs. In this story, land was a fixed input, meaning that the amount of land available didn't change even as the number of farmers increased. The main point of the story was to get you to think about what happens to average total costs when there is a fixed input and increasing marginal costs.

• •

INCREASING MARGINAL COSTS

Up until the last story, we have considered only examples where average total costs go down as output increases. But we will now see that the existence of a fixed input causes average total costs curves to first decrease but then increase as output goes up, resulting in a U-shaped total costs curve.

HOW FIXED INPUTS CAUSE THE AVERAGE TOTAL COSTS CURVE TO HAVE A "U" SHAPE

Fixed inputs cause average total costs curves to have a U shape because

1. A fixed input causes diminishing marginal returns.
2. Diminishing marginal returns cause increasing marginal costs.
3. Increasing marginal costs cause increasing average variable costs.
4. Increasing average variable costs cause the average total costs curve to have a U shape.

We will now discuss these four steps in detail.

Step 1: A Fixed Input Causes Diminishing Marginal Returns

Imagine you're a farmer who uses two inputs to grow wheat: land and labor. Assume that you have 100 acres of land, but you can't sell this land nor buy additional land. Land, therefore, is a fixed input for you, meaning that the amount of land you have is fixed. But assume that you can hire as many workers as you wish. Since you can vary the amount of workers used, labor is a variable input for you.

What would happen, however, if you kept hiring additional workers? Because you have a fixed amount of land, as you hire more workers, each one would have less land to cultivate. Furthermore, if you hired enough workers, they would start bumping into each other. The marginal benefit of new workers (the amount of extra food a new worker produces), therefore, goes down as you employ more and more laborers.

You receive what economists refer to as **diminishing marginal returns** from employing additional workers. Diminishing marginal returns to an input occurs when you receive lower and lower benefits from increasing the amount of the input used. The following table shows the benefits you would hypothetically receive from hiring different numbers of workers.

> **Diminishing marginal returns** to an input occurs when you receive lower and lower benefits from increasing the amount of the input used.

Number of Workers	Bushels of Wheat Produced Each Year	Marginal Benefit in Bushels of Last Worker Hired
1	900	900
2	1,790	1,790 − 900 = 890
3	2,500	2,500 − 1,790 = 710
4	3,100	3,100 − 2,500 = 600
5	3,400	3,400 − 3,100 = 300
6	3,500	3,500 − 3,400 = 100
7	3,510	3,510 − 3,500 = 10
8	3,511	3,511 − 3,510 = 1

According to the table above, workers are subject to diminishing marginal returns because the marginal benefit of workers decreases as the number of workers employed increases.

Diminishing marginal returns affect many human endeavors. For example:

- The first hour you study for an economics exam will likely be extremely effective in raising your test score. But after studying for, say, seven or eight hours you start covering the same material over and over again and so additional study hours become less fruitful. After studying for seven or eight hours, you still learn a bit more about economics for each additional hour you study, but the marginal benefit of studying another hour is much lower than it was when you first started studying.

- Most people receive significant health benefits from exercising a few hours a week. As you continue to increase your exercise time, however, the health benefits you obtain per hour go down. And indeed, too much exercise can damage your health. So, if you exercise too much, you incur negative marginal benefits from exercising for another hour.

Step 2: Diminishing Marginal Returns Cause Increasing Marginal Costs

When production is subject to diminishing marginal returns, marginal costs must increase as output increases. For example, assume that you need one worker to get an output of 1, three workers to get an output of 2, and seven workers to achieve an output of 3. Each additional increase in output requires more and more workers and so costs more and more to achieve.

Step 3: Increasing Marginal Costs Cause Increasing Average Variable Costs

Imagine that, one by one, a number of people enter a room, and each one is taller than the one before. The average height of the people in the room must continually increase. Marginal height is the height of the next person to enter the room. If the marginal height keeps going up, then the average height of the room must also be increasing.

Or, imagine that you take one exam per week in your economics class. You keep improving in the class, and the grade you get on each week's exam is higher than what

FIGURE **8.2**

U-SHAPED AVERAGE
TOTAL COSTS
CURVE

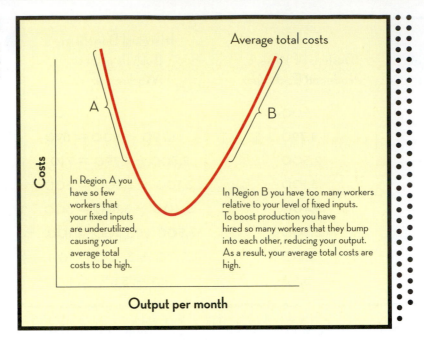

In Region A you have so few workers that your fixed inputs are underutilized, causing your average total costs to be high.

In Region B you have too many workers relative to your level of fixed inputs. To boost production you have hired so many workers that they bump into each other, reducing your output. As a result, your average total costs are high.

you earned the week before. This must mean that your overall exam average for the class is also increasing. Your marginal grade is the grade you will get on the next exam. If your marginal grade keeps increasing, then your average grade must also keep increasing.

Marginal costs tell you how much it costs to produce your next unit of output. Average variable costs are the average of all the previous marginal costs. If marginal costs are increasing, then the cost of each new good is higher than the last, so average variable costs must be increasing as well.

Step 4: Increasing Average Variable Costs Cause the Average Total Costs Curve to Have a U Shape

You spend $10 million building a factory. But, inexplicably, you hire only one worker. This worker can't come close to utilizing the entire factory. As a result, he produces only a small number of goods each month. Because of your $10 million fixed costs, however, your average total costs are huge. But then you hire a few more employees and increase production. As a result, your $10 million fixed costs get spread out over more output and so your average total costs fall.

But as you keep hiring additional workers, you run into diminishing marginal returns to labor. You eventually have too many workers and they keep bumping into each other, becoming less and less productive. Consequently your average variable costs increase. At some point as you increase output, the increase in your average variable costs becomes greater than the decrease in your average fixed costs, and as a result your average total costs increase. Your factory, therefore, faces a U-shaped average total costs curve, as shown in Figure 8.2, because as you increase output, average total costs first go down but then go up.

Recall that when marginal costs are constant, the average total costs curve decreases as output increases (See Figure 8.1). Firms with constant marginal costs have lower average total costs the more goods they sell. In contrast, when firms face increasing marginal costs, their average total costs curve is U-shaped.

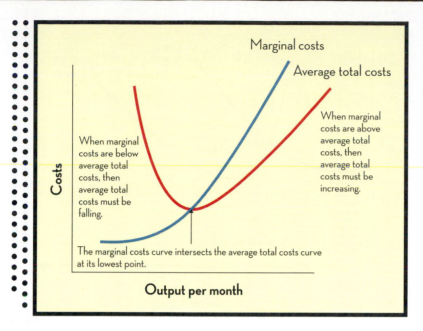

FIGURE **8.3**

INCREASING
MARGINAL COSTS
AND THE MARGINAL
COSTS CURVE

Marginal costs

Average total costs

When marginal
costs are below
average total
costs, then
average total
costs must be
falling.

When marginal
costs are above
average total
costs, then
average total
costs must be
increasing.

The marginal costs curve intersects the average total costs curve
at its lowest point.

THE MARGINAL COSTS CURVE GOES THROUGH THE LOW POINT ON THE U-SHAPED AVERAGE TOTAL COSTS CURVE

As Figure 8.3 shows, when marginal costs are increasing, the marginal costs curve always goes through the low point on the average total costs curve. The next chapter will make use of this fact.

Imagine that the average height of people in your economics class is 1.7 meters. Suddenly a new person enters your class. If this new person's height is above 1.7 meters, then the average height of people in your class will increase. But if this new person is shorter than 1.7 meters, then the average height of people in the room will decrease.

Marginal cost gives the cost of making the next good. Therefore, if marginal costs are greater than average total costs, then the next good costs more than what it costs on average to make all the previous goods. So if marginal costs are greater than average total costs, then average total costs must increase. The reverse also holds. Consequently the marginal and average total costs curves must satisfy the following two criteria:

1. If marginal costs > average total costs, then average total costs are increasing.
2. If marginal costs < average total costs, then average total costs are decreasing.

Figure 8.3 is consistent with both criteria.

In Figure 8.4 the marginal costs curve intersects the average total costs curve at a point to the left of the low point on the average total costs curve. Between the intersection point and the low point on the average total costs curve, marginal costs are above average total costs. Consequently by criterion (1) average total costs must be *increasing.* But in between these two points in Figure 8.4, average total costs are *decreasing.* Therefore, Figure 8.4 shows a **mathematically impossible** relationship between marginal costs and average total costs. Consequently, the marginal costs curve and average total costs curve shown in this diagram can't both be real.

FIGURE **8.4**

A **MATHEMATICALLY
IMPOSSIBLE**
RELATIONSHIP
BETWEEN
MARGINAL COSTS
AND AVERAGE
TOTAL COSTS

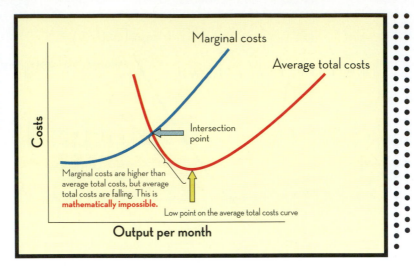

In Figure 8.5 the marginal costs curve intersects the average total costs curve at a point to the right of the low point on the average total costs curve. Between the low point on the average total costs curve and the intersection point, marginal costs are below average total costs. Consequently according to criterion (2), average total costs must be *decreasing*. But in between these two points in Figure 8.5, average total costs are *increasing*. Therefore, Figure 8.5 also shows a **mathematically impossible** relationship between marginal costs and average total costs.

FIGURE **8.5**

ANOTHER
**MATHEMATICALLY
IMPOSSIBLE**
RELATIONSHIP
BETWEEN
MARGINAL COSTS
AND AVERAGE
TOTAL COSTS

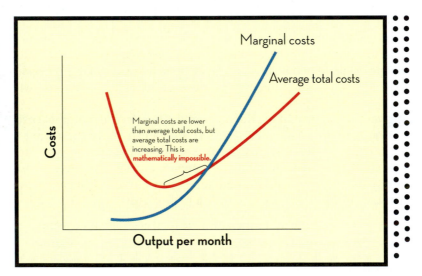

Figures 8.4 and 8.5 show that it's mathematically impossible for the marginal costs curve to intersect the average total costs curve at a point to the left or right of the low point on the average total costs curve. Consequently, they establish that if marginal costs are increasing, then they must go through the low point on the average total costs curve. (If marginal costs are not increasing, then marginal costs will always be below average total costs and so the marginal costs curve and average total costs curve will never intersect.)

DIMINISHING MARGINAL RETURNS AND STARVATION

Thomas Malthus was an economic "prophet of doom." He famously predicted that the human population would increase at a faster rate than the food supply, making starvation almost inevitable.

Malthus believed that mass starvation was the likely stable equilibrium for a nation. If most people in a country have enough food to eat, then the population will grow because many children will be born but few of these children will die from malnutrition. But when a population increases, the amount of farmland per person must go down. As a result, each person will produce less and less food. (When Malthus was alive, most humans were food producers.) Consequently, at some point a country with an increasing population will be unable to feed itself and will suffer from mass starvation.

Malthus was worried about diminishing marginal returns to agriculture because land was a fixed input. He believed that as we increased the number of farmers, the extra food each additional farmer grew would decrease. Eventually, new farmers would not produce enough food to feed themselves and so would starve.

Let's use a U-shaped cost curve to illuminate Malthus's prediction. Imagine that Figure 8.6 shows the costs of producing food in some country. Further imagine that this country currently produces 10,000 units of food per year. As the country's population increases, however, it will need more food. But producing extra food will raise the average total costs of growing food. If the population increases enough, the average total costs of producing food will be so high that the country won't have enough resources to feed everyone.

THOMAS MALTHUS
(1766–1834)

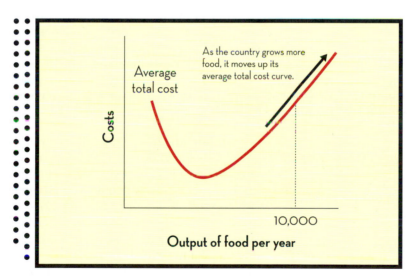

FIGURE **8.6**   209

COSTS OF
PRODUCING FOOD
IN SOME COUNTRY

Malthus Was Wrong   Malthus's prediction proved wonderfully wrong. The world has over six times as many people now as when Malthus made his starvation prediction, and yet humans produce more food per person today than they did when Malthus was alive. What happened?

Had an extra five billion people been magically dumped into the world of Malthus's time, most of them would have starved. These additional people would have greatly increased the average total costs of growing food and so made it economically unfeasible

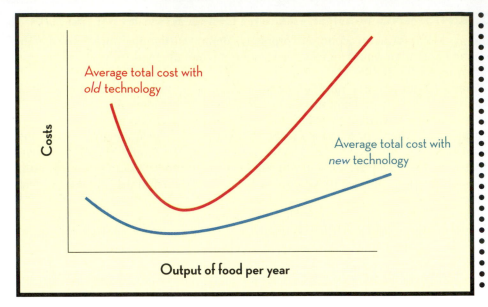

FIGURE 8.7

TECHNOLOGY CUTS COSTS OF FOOD PRODUCTION

Average total cost with *old* technology

Average total cost with *new* technology

Costs

Output of food per year

to feed everyone. But technology saved billions from starvation by moving humanity, in the long run, to a new average total costs curve.

Economists often break the future up into the short run and the long run. In the short run, we don't have time to change technology. But over the long run we can. Since Malthus's doomsday prediction, innovation has changed the costs of agriculture. People have developed crops that grow faster and are more resistant to disease and pests. Innovators have developed better fertilizers and pesticides that have multiplied crop yields. The gains from agricultural innovation have more than outweighed the harm of diminishing marginal returns. Agricultural innovations have greatly reduced the cost of growing food and so allowed humanity to feed more people with fewer resources. Figure 8.7 shows one possible way technology can change the average total costs of food production.

Agricultural scientist Norman Borlaug has done more than anyone else to defeat Malthus's doomsday prediction. He bred high-yield dwarf wheat that is pest-resistant and produces two to three times more edible food than other types of wheat.[3] He then worked with poor countries such as India and Mexico, teaching them how to use dwarf wheat. By preventing mass starvation, Borlaug has likely saved more lives than anyone else in human history.

Neo-Malthusians This chapter opened with a 1968 quote from Stanford University professor Paul Ehrlich: "The battle to feed all of humanity is over. In the 1970s and 1980s hundreds of millions of people will starve to death in spite of any crash programs embarked upon now." Professor Ehrlich would have been proved right if agricultural innovation stopped in 1968. But Ehrlich, like Malthus, underestimated agricultural innovation.

Many Neo-Malthusians today predict disaster because of humanity's population and economic growth. As we get richer and more numerous, humans consume more resources such as oil, coal, fish, and trees. Neo-Malthusians predict we will soon run out of these vital resources and face catastrophe. But optimists believe that markets will protect us from disaster.

The earth has a fixed amount of many inputs, including land and oil. So if the human population increases and *nothing else changes,* we will have fewer of these inputs per person and much of human economic activity will become subject to diminishing marginal returns. But innovation can effectively multiply the existing supply of a "fixed" input. More fuel-efficient cars, for example, effectively raise the earth's oil supply. So the future welfare of humanity will be decided by a race between innovation and fixed resources. If innovation wins, we will produce more wealth per person even as the size of the human population grows. If innovation stagnates, however, then human population growth will strain the earth's fixed resources, causing a reduction in humanity's per capita wealth.

Adam Smith's invisible hand, fortunately, will push innovators to overcome problems caused by fixed inputs. If, for example, we start to run out of oil, the price of oil will rise. But alternative energy sources are substitutes for oil. A rising price of oil, therefore, will increase the demand for alternative energy sources and so reward innovators who find these new types of energy. Generally, whenever a resource becomes scarce, its price increases. This increase in price causes (a) consumers to use less of the resource, (b) producers to find more of the resource, and (c) innovators to find substitutes for the resource.

MORE LONG-RUN ANALYSIS

In the short run, we are stuck on one average total costs curve. We have already seen how in the long run innovation allows us to move to a new average total costs curve. This section explains how in the long run firms can also move to a new average total costs curve by changing a fixed input.

Economists assume that in the short run, firms can't change fixed inputs but in the long run, they can. For example, if workers are a variable input but factories are a fixed input, then in the short run you can change only the number of workers you employ; in the long run you can change both the quantity of workers and the number of factories you have.

Students often ask exactly how long the long run is. Economists don't have a precise answer but rather say that the length of the long run is different for different firms. In all situations, however, the long run is the time a firm needs to vary all its inputs.

The long run is the planning period. In the long run, for example, you can plan how many factories to build. Once you have built your planned number of factories, you are back in the short run.

This long-run/short-run distinction does not apply to the goods presented in the first part of this chapter, where marginal costs were constant. Because we (implicitly) assumed that these goods didn't have any fixed inputs, there is nothing these firms couldn't do in the short run that they could do in the long run.

The key difference between the long and short runs is that over the long run you can vary everything, whereas in the short run some things cannot change. Over both the long run and short run, you make the best of your situation, but you always do better in the long run since over this time frame you have more choices. Let's look at how some life decisions differ in the long and short run:

Life Decisions Made In the Short and Long Run

- In the short run, you struggle to find someone to date. In the long run, you improve your body in the gym and your mind in economics classes and get anyone you want to date you. [In the short run, you can't improve your mind and body; in the long run, you can.]

- In the short run, you do the best you can with your $25,000-a-year income. In the long run, you go back to school to improve your market worth and then get a higher-paying job. [In the short run, you can't change your career; in the long run, you can.]

Overlapping Short-Run Average Total Costs Curves Imagine that a firm produces goods with the variable input of workers and the fixed input of factories. In the short run the firm can't change the number of factories it has. Figure 8.8 shows two average total costs curves for this firm. One shows average total costs when the firm has one factory and the other shows these costs when the firm has two factories. Because we are now distinguishing between the long and short run, we will label these curves short-run average total costs curves since along each curve the fixed input doesn't change.

FIGURE **8.8**

TWO AVERAGE
TOTAL COSTS
CURVES

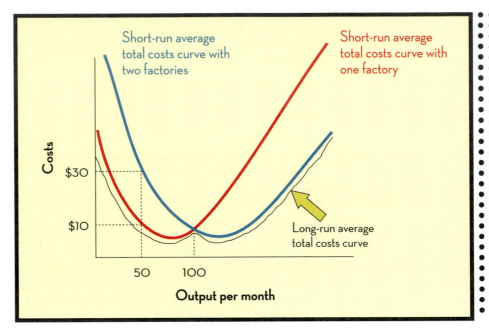

For levels of output below 100 per month, average total costs are lower if the firm has only one factory. For example, if output is 50 per month, it costs $10 per good if the firm uses one factory but $30 per good if it uses two factories. For low levels of output, it's wasteful to have too many factories because the firm can't efficiently use them or spread out the fixed costs over sufficient output. For output above 100 per month, average total costs are lower with two factories due to diminishing marginal returns. In the short run the firm is stuck with either one or two factories. In the long run, however, it can switch by building or selling a factory.

In the long run, for any given level of output, the firm will choose its fixed input to minimize its average total costs. So, for example, if the firm intends to produce 50 goods per month, it would have only one factory, but if it wanted output to be 104 goods per month, it would choose to have two factories. Consequently, a firm's long-run average total costs curve consists of the low points on its short-run average total costs curves. For any given level of output, the long-run average total costs are the lowest short-run average total costs for that level of output.

The following table calculates the long-run average total costs for a different firm that can choose to build one, two, or three factories in the long run. For any given level of output, the long-run average total costs will always be the lowest short-run average total costs.

Output per Day	Short-Run Average Total Costs with One Factory	Short-Run Average Total Costs with Two Factories	Short-Run Average Total Costs with Three Factories	Long-Run Average Total Costs
1	$103	$200	$300	$103
2	100	150	250	100
3	99	130	200	99
4	108	110	170	108
5	112	99	140	99
6	120	110	130	110
7	140	120	115	115
8	180	150	101	101
9	200	180	110	110
10	500	200	114	114

Imagine that this firm initially has one factory and has been producing four goods per day. Suddenly, the price for this firm's goods significantly increases and the firm starts making eight goods per day. In the short run it will be stuck with one factory and so its average total costs will be $180. In the long run, however, the firm will build two more factories to lower its average total costs. If it still produces eight goods a day then the firm's average total costs will become $101, but the lower cost of production caused by the addition of two factories might result in the firm producing more than eight goods per day in the long run.

Smooth Long-Run Average Total Costs Curves Figure 8.9 on page 214 shows a long-run average total costs curve when there are a large number of possible factories. The large number of factories causes the long-run average total costs curve to look smooth. In Figure 8.9 the long-run average total costs are constant for all levels of output, but this is not always so.

ECONOMIES AND DISECONOMIES OF SCALE

- When long-run average total costs are **constant,** then these costs are said to exhibit **constant returns to scale.** As shown in Figure 8.9.
- When long-run average total costs **decrease** as output increases, then costs are said to exhibit **economies of scale.** As shown in Figure 8.10.
- When long-run average total costs **increase** as output increases, then costs are said to exhibit **diseconomies of scale.** As shown in Figure 8.11.

Economies and diseconomies of scale also tell us what happens to output in the long run if we increase all inputs by the same percentage. For example, imagine that in the long run all inputs increase by 10 percent. If output increases by exactly 10 percent, then we have constant returns to scale; if output goes up by more than 10 percent,

FIGURE **8.9**

CONSTANT
RETURNS TO SCALE

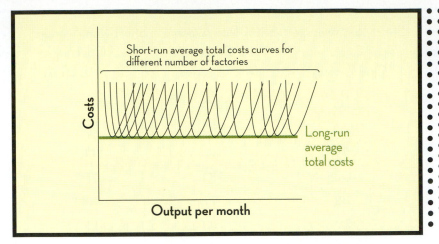

FIGURE **8.10**

ECONOMIES OF
SCALE

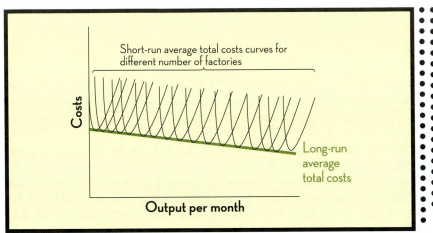

FIGURE **8.11**

DISECONOMIES OF
SCALE

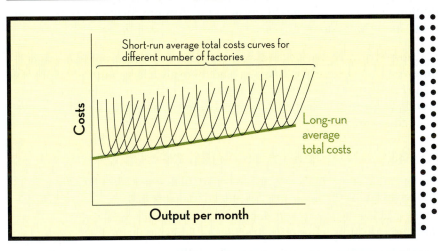

then we have economies of scale; and if output rises by less than 10 percent, then we have diseconomies of scale.

Figure 8.12 shows a U-shaped long-run average total costs curve that exhibits both economies and diseconomies of scale.

Consider a firm that decides to double in size in the long run by doubling the amount of all its fixed and variable inputs. So, if the firm had 100 workers employed in

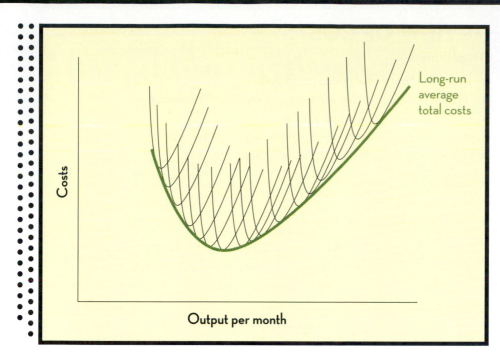

FIGURE **8.12**

BOTH ECONOMIES
AND DISECONOMIES
OF SCALE

Long-run
average
total costs

Costs

Output per month

one factory, after the doubling it would have 200 workers employed in two factories. What do you think will happen to this firm's long-run average total costs?

If the new factory and workers were exactly the same as the old, you would expect long-run average total costs to remain unchanged and so the firm would exhibit constant returns to scale. After all, if the first factory was producing goods at an average total cost of, say, $18, and the second factory is identical to the first and the quality and price of workers hasn't changed, then you would expect the second factory also to produce goods at an average total cost of $18. A firm that grows by replicating all of its inputs exactly, therefore, should have constant returns to scale.

But now imagine that the firm had previously spent millions developing a software program that ran some of the machines in its first factory. After building the second factory the firm could freely copy this software package. Building an additional factory, therefore, would cause the fixed costs of this software package to be spread out over more output and so the firm's average total costs would go down. Costs that don't increase, even in the long run as output expands, can cause the long-run average total costs to exhibit economies of scale.

But what if, in doubling its size, the firm has to hire inferior quality workers even when adjusting for the lower wages paid to these new employees? Inferior labor would cause this firm's long-run average total costs to increase after it doubled output. Diseconomies of scale can arise when a firm must use inferior inputs when expanding.

Government regulations can also cause diseconomies of scale as many regulations apply only to large firms. For example, in the late 1940s my grandfather owned a movie theater with 510 seats. A new fire regulation came into effect, forcing each theater with over 500 seats to construct a water tower. To avoid building the costly water tower, my grandfather removed a few seats from his theater. The fire regulation created tremendous diseconomies of scale for theater owners who had seating capacities of around 500. My grandfather responded to these diseconomies by lowering output and so saving himself from much higher long-run average total costs.

REVIEW OF COSTS

Definitions

- Output—Number of goods produced.
- Fixed costs—Costs that are the same regardless of output.
- Variable costs—Costs that vary with output.
- Marginal costs—Extra cost of increasing output by one.
- Total costs = Fixed costs + Variable costs.
- Average fixed costs $= \dfrac{\text{Fixed costs}}{\text{Output}}$
- Average variable costs $= \dfrac{\text{Variable costs}}{\text{Output}}$
- Average total costs $= \dfrac{\text{Total cost}}{\text{Output}} = \dfrac{\text{Fixed costs}}{\text{Output}} + \dfrac{\text{Variable costs}}{\text{Output}}$
- Variable inputs—Inputs that can be changed in both the short and long run.
- Fixed inputs—Inputs that can be changed in the long run but not the short run.

Important cost facts

- Average fixed costs always decrease as output increases.
- Average total costs are a firm's break-even price.
- You really have to learn all this stuff to do well on your next microeconomics exam.

If marginal costs are constant, then:

- Average total costs always decrease as output increases.
- Average variable costs equal marginal costs.

If marginal costs increase as output increases, then:

- The firm likely has a fixed input.
- Average variable costs increase as output increases.
- Short run average total costs curves have a U shape.
- The marginal cost curve goes through the low point on the average total costs curve.

Short run versus the long run

- In the short run, firms can't innovate or change fixed inputs; in the long run, they can.
- In the short run, firms are stuck on one short-run average total costs curve.
- In the long run, firms can move to another short-run average total costs curve through innovation or through changing fixed inputs.
- The long-run average total costs curve consists of the low points on all the short-run average total costs curves.

QUESTIONS YOU SHOULD BE ABLE TO ANSWER
AFTER READING THIS CHAPTER:

1 Why is international trade important to pharmaceutical companies? (pages 199–200)

2 Why do poor African AIDS victims "benefit" when their disease is shared by rich people? (page 200)

3 Why are large-budget movies usually superficial? (pages 200–201)

4 What is the advantage to the U.S. military of allowing advanced fighter jets to be exported? (page 201)

5 Why can fixed inputs cause diminishing marginal returns? (pages 204–205)

6 Why do diminishing marginal returns cause increasing marginal costs? (page 205)

7 Why do increasing marginal costs cause increasing average variable costs? (pages 205–206)

8 Why do increasing average variable costs cause the average total costs curve to have a U shape? (page 206)

9 Why does the marginal costs curve go through the low point on the average total costs curve when marginal costs are increasing? (pages 207–208)

10 Why did Thomas Malthus predict mass starvation? (page 209)

11 Why was Malthus wrong? (pages 209–210)

12 What are constant returns to scale, economies of scale, and diseconomies of scale? (pages 213–214)

13 Why do we expect to sometimes observe economies of scale? (pages 214–215)

14 Why do we expect to sometimes observe diseconomies of scale? (pages 214–215)

STUDY PROBLEMS

1 For some products, such as music distributed over the Internet, marginal costs are zero. Do these products exhibit (a) constant returns to scale, (b) increasing returns to scale, or (c) decreasing returns to scale?

2 Can average variable costs ever be higher than average total costs?

3 What happens to the difference between average total costs and average variable costs as output increases?

4 The average total cost of producing 1,000 goods is $18. What is the total cost of producing 1,000 goods?

5 Can long-run average total costs ever be greater than short-run average total costs?

6 If marginal costs are always increasing, can average total costs ever be decreasing?

7 If average fixed costs are always decreasing, can average total costs ever be increasing?

8 On the same diagram, draw four short-run average total costs curves for a firm that faces increasing marginal costs. Now use the short-run average total costs curves to find the firm's long-run average total costs curve.

9 In the following table, fill in the blanks with numbers that are consistent with the other numbers in the table. Assume that in the long run the firm can have only one, two, three, or four factories. There may be multiple correct answers for some blanks; in such instances just write one possible answer.

Output per Day	Short-Run Average Total Costs if the Firm Has One Factory	Short-Run Average Total Costs if the Firm Has Two Factories	Short-Run Average Total Costs if the Firm Has Three Factories	Short-Run Average Total Costs if the Firm Has Four Factories	Long-Run Average Total Costs
1	$100	$200	$300	$390	____
2	____	180	250	380	$90
3	105	170	220	____	105
4	120	140	190	300	____
5	____	130	170	250	130
6	____	135	____	____	135
7	____	____	160	____	160
8	400	170	166	169	____
9	____	____	____	168	168
10	500	300	200	166	____
11	____	____	____	____	

10 A pharmaceutical company makes the hypothetical AIDS drug Zxyran. The marginal cost of making a Zxyran pill is always $1. The pharmaceutical company sells these AIDS pills for $50 each. The pharmaceutical company has sold millions of Zxyran pills. Yet the pharmaceutical company has lost money off of Zxyran. How can this be?

11 "A tourist in New York's Greenwich Village had his portrait sketched by a sidewalk artist, who charged him $100. 'That's expensive,' the tourist said. 'But it's a great sketch, so I'll pay it. But, really, it took you just five minutes.' 'Twenty years and five minutes,' the artist replied."[4] What does the artist mean? Your answer should use some of the cost terminology presented in this chapter.

12 Moral question: Do pharmaceutical companies have a moral duty to develop treatments for diseases that afflict only poor people?

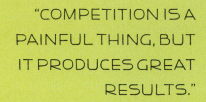

"COMPETITION IS A PAINFUL THING, BUT IT PRODUCES GREAT RESULTS."

—Forbes[1]

MARKET STRUCTURE

Each of the next three chapters examines a different market structure. Market structure affects how firms compete. The next chapter explores monopolistic markets that have limited competition. The chapter after that considers oligopolistic markets that contain a small number of firms that both compete and cooperate with each other. This chapter examines perfectly competitive markets where competition among firms is *total*.

This chapter explains how vigorous competition influences firms. We will see that Adam Smith's invisible hand works extremely well in perfectly competitive markets. We will also conclude that intense competition causes firms to earn zero profit in the long run. To intuitively understand this surprising zero-profit outcome, let's examine an unusual auction.

AUCTIONING MONEY[2]

How much should a $20 bill sell for? To find out, I auctioned one off to my students. I started the bidding at one penny and asked how many would be willing to pay this price for my currency. Almost everyone raised their hands. I then slowly raised the bid amount, and as long as I asked for less than $20, nearly everyone offered to pay what I asked. The bidding continued until the price reached $20. I then inquired whether any student was willing to pay more than $20, but none were. (Too bad; it would have been an easy way for someone to get an A.) When the bidding stopped, I collected $20 from the winning student and handed her the $20 bill.

After the auction I chastised my students for throwing away money. I had been willing to sell a $20 dollar bill for a mere penny, yet my students' greed cost them this profitable opportunity. Because they kept competing against each other, the bid price

PERFECT COMPETITION

LEARNING OBJECTIVES

AFTER READING THIS CHAPTER, YOU SHOULD BE ABLE TO:

- Explain the assumptions of perfect competition.
- Calculate a firm's profit graphically.
- Distinguish between economic and accounting profit.
- Understand a firm's incentive to innovate in perfect competition.

went up to the point where the winner took no profit from me. Although this $20 auction doesn't replicate all the conditions of perfect competition, it does illuminate its profit-destroying effects.

THE SEVEN ASSUMPTIONS OF PERFECT COMPETITION

Economists have assembled a set of assumptions under which firms have no choice but to compete fiercely, and we label markets as perfectly competitive if they satisfy these seven assumptions:

1. There are many buyers and sellers.
2. Firms can enter and exit the market freely in the long run.
3. Everyone has perfect information about the product sold.
4. All firms make exactly the same product.
5. All firms face exactly the same costs.
6. Average total costs do not continually decrease.
7. All buyers and sellers are *price takers,* meaning that no one buyer or seller can affect the price of the good sold.

Let's examine why firms vigorously compete when these seven assumptions hold.

1. THERE ARE MANY BUYERS AND SELLERS

What would have happened in my $20-bill auction if there had been only one student in class? She would have bid one penny and never raised her bid, thereby earning herself a $19.99 profit.

If there were only two students in my auction and they were smart and cooperative, they might still have taken my $20 for only a penny if they had colluded rather than outbid each other. As the class size increased, however, it would have become more and more difficult for the students to cooperate.

If all but one student in my auction had agreed to bid only one penny and split the profits among themselves, then the student left out of the agreement could bid two cents and possibly make herself a $19.98 profit. Of course, the remaining students would probably not allow this deviator to make a $19.98 profit, so they would have raised their bids, likely causing the deviator to raise hers, thus creating a bidding spiral resulting in the students again collectively making no profits.

Competition hurts competitors, so competitors benefit from agreeing to limit competition. But such collusion becomes very unlikely in crowded markets.

2. FIRMS CAN ENTER AND EXIT THE MARKET FREELY IN THE LONG RUN

Pretend that all the students in my auction did collude by deciding to bid no more than a penny. I could defeat this plan by going out into the hall and bringing in other students to my auction. After all, if a $20 bill was being auctioned and the current price was only a penny, wouldn't you want to participate in the bidding?

Imagine what would occur if all gas stations in a city decided to double prices—not because of any change in demand or costs but because of collusion. Running a gas station would suddenly become far more profitable and so new firms would enter the market, thereby increasing supply and lowering price.

Free entry inhibits collusion. If the current market participants try to earn profits through collusion, outside firms will wish to enter the market to appropriate some of these profits by offering a more favorable price.

Perfect competition exists only in markets with no collusion. Long-term collusion is almost impossible in a market with free entry. Such collusion would require not only that all firms in the market come to an agreement, but also that all firms capable of entering the market agree to the collusive arrangement.

3. EVERYONE HAS PERFECT INFORMATION ABOUT THE PRODUCT SOLD

What if, before my auction, I put the $20 bill in an envelope and just told my students that the envelope contained some amount of currency? The final sale price might have been far from $20. Buyers and sellers lacking complete information may compete less vigorously because they don't know the value of the good being sold.

Imagine that you have a serious medical condition you treat successfully by taking one company's $20 pill each day. Another company starts selling an $18 pill for the same ailment, but you're not sure of this new medicine's quality. Even if this new pill is exactly the same as the old one, if you have imperfect information about the pills' relative qualities, you might continue to take your old, more expensive, medicine. Knowing this, new companies capable of making your needed medicine might not enter the market. They rightly fear that customers won't buy their pills even if their medicines are lower priced but of identical quality to pills already on the market.

Imperfect information can limit competition by creating confusion among customers. So in perfect competition, the market structure with maximum competition, everyone has perfect information.

4. ALL FIRMS MAKE EXACTLY THE SAME PRODUCT

Firms making exactly the same product compete the most vigorously. Coke and Pepsi compete with each other more than Coke and Tropicana Orange Juice do because Coke is more like Pepsi than orange juice. Of course, if Pepsi and Coke used the same formula, these two colas would compete even more. Two products compete when consumers who buy one of them are less likely to buy the other, meaning that the products are *substitutes* for each other. The better substitutes two products are, the more they compete. And when are two products the strongest possible substitutes? When they are exactly the same product.

5. ALL FIRMS FACE EXACTLY THE SAME COSTS

Imagine that your firm is considering entering a new market. But you realize that it would cost you far more to produce goods in this market than it costs existing firms. As a result, you don't enter and hence don't compete with the existing firms in the market. In contrast, under perfect competition, we assume that all firms face exactly the same costs. Consequently, fear of having higher costs doesn't deter new firms from competing with existing firms. Furthermore, if all firms face the same costs, then no one firm can produce goods at such a low cost that other firms can't compete with it.

6. AVERAGE TOTAL COSTS DO NOT CONTINUALLY DECREASE

If average total costs are continually decreasing, then once a single firm captures most of the market it will be nearly impossible for other firms to challenge it. This dominant firm will, because of continually decreasing average total costs, have the lowest costs. Consequently, when average total costs are continually decreasing in a market, usually just one firm will be in this market, not many firms. We will assume that under perfect competition, firms face increasing marginal costs causing short-run average total costs to have a U shape.

7. ALL BUYERS AND SELLERS ARE *PRICE TAKERS,* MEANING THAT NO ONE BUYER OR SELLER CAN AFFECT THE PRICE OF A GOOD SOLD

When you buy candy, you increase the demand for candy. This minuscule increase in demand, however, doesn't really affect the price of candy. In contrast, if the U.S. Army placed an order for a billion candy bars for its troops, the demand for candy would probably change enough to affect price. Economists assume that in perfect competition all buyers and sellers are too small ever to have any meaningful effect on price. This doesn't mean that price won't change if thousands of small buyers acquire more products, but rather that the influence of an individual buyer is too negligible to meaningfully affect price.

Assumption 7 enhances competition by eliminating a reason for firms not to compete. A firm would be reluctant to sell more products if such sales would decrease price. By assuming that individual sellers can't affect price, therefore, we eliminate a

FIGURE **9.1**

DEMAND CURVE OF
A FIRM FACING
PERFECT
COMPETITION

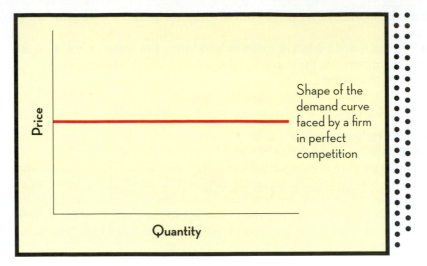

Shape of the demand curve faced by a firm in perfect competition

reason for sellers to restrict output. We will also see the importance of assumption 7 in the next two chapters, where its nonapplicability has significant consequences.

A *price taker,* by definition, receives the same price for goods regardless of how much it produces. Consequently, assumption 7 causes the demand curve facing a firm in perfect competition to be perfectly horizontal, as shown in Figure 9.1.

The entire market demand curve for a perfectly competitive industry, however, will not be horizontal. Rather, any one firm makes up so small a percentage of the overall market that it has a trivial effect on market prices.

PERFECT COMPETITION AS AN APPROXIMATION

No market perfectly fulfills the seven assumptions of perfect competition. After all, firms never sell *exactly* the same product or face *exactly* the same costs, and who on planet Earth has ever had perfect information about anything?

Similarly, there are no perfect spheres in the universe. A sphere is a mathematical construct that nature approximates but never actually produces. Still, since so many real objects on earth come close to being spheres, it's reasonable to use the theoretical idea of a sphere as a model for many objects.

Imagine you want to develop a model to predict the moon's orbit. Through gravity, the moon's orbit is affected by the sun and the Earth. But the moon's orbit is also gravitationally influenced by all the planets in our solar system, all the stars in our galaxy, and indeed all the stars and planets in all the other galaxies of the universe. Trillions upon trillions of heavenly bodies, therefore, affect the orbit of the moon. You could, consequently, never account for everything that gravitationally affects the moon. But to develop a useful model of the moon's orbit, you don't have to. Well over 99 percent of the moon's orbit is determined by the gravitational influence of just the sun and Earth. So in studying the moon's orbit, you could reasonably assume that just our sun and the Earth gravitationally interact with the moon. This assumption is, technically, false. But this assumption is scientifically useful if it allows you to better understand the moon's orbit.

The universe is too complex for humans to understand in its entirety. The job of scientists is to break through this complexity by developing simplified models that approximate reality. Economist-scientists have done this with perfect competition. Economists know that the assumptions of perfect competition are never perfectly satisfied outside of a textbook. But these assumptions are a reasonable approximation of many real-life economic situations. Firms in numerous industries act similarly to how textbook models of perfect competition predict they should act.

Nobel Prize winning economist Vernon Smith has studied how much markets can deviate from economists' assumptions of perfect competition and yet still function as perfectly competitive markets do. Smith has created many simulations of markets and seen how the participants act. For example, he might ask some of his students to be sellers and others buyers, and then let them trade an imaginary good. Smith has found that markets with as few as four buyers and four sellers produce outcomes similar to what happens in perfectly competitive markets. Smith's experiments have also shown that markets reach a perfectly competitive equilibrium even if buyers and sellers lack significant amounts of information.[3] Smith's work shows that the model of perfect competition has vast applicability to the real world.

FIRMS' BEHAVIOR IN PERFECTLY COMPETITIVE MARKETS

Let's examine the behavior of C-Farm, an unimaginatively named corn-growing firm in a perfectly competitive market. We'll first determine how C-Farm uses marginal costs to set output.

PRICE AND MARGINAL COST

Would you pay $8 to get $10? Of course! Would you pay $11 to get $10? No way! Imagine that C-Farm is considering growing one more bushel of corn. Assume that

- Marginal cost = $8.
- Price = $10.

225

Recall that marginal cost is the cost of producing one more unit of output. If C-Farm grows another bushel, therefore, it must pay its $8 marginal cost. But it can then sell this bushel for the $10 market price. So, C-Farm should grow this bushel. Let's now assume that

- Marginal cost = $11.
- Price = $10.

If C-Farm now grows another bushel it must pay its $11 marginal cost but will receive only $10 in extra revenue. In this instance, C-Farm should not grow another bushel.

Whenever price is greater than marginal cost, C-Farm should produce another bushel. Price gives the benefit of producing another good. Marginal cost tells you the harm of producing this additional good. So if price is greater than marginal cost, a firm in perfect competition should make at least one more good.

Imagine again that the price of corn is $10 while C-Farm's marginal cost is only $8. C-Farm therefore produces another bushel. How does this additional production affect price and marginal cost? By assumption 7, price stays the same regardless of output. But we have also assumed that the marginal cost of firms in perfect competition increases as output increases. C-Farm's marginal cost therefore goes up when its output increases.

If producing one more bushel causes the marginal cost to become greater than $10, then C-Farm should stop increasing output. In contrast, if after producing this additional bushel the

When price > marginal cost, a firm in perfect competition increases its profit by producing more.

When price is < marginal cost, a firm in perfect competition increases its profits by producing less.

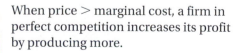

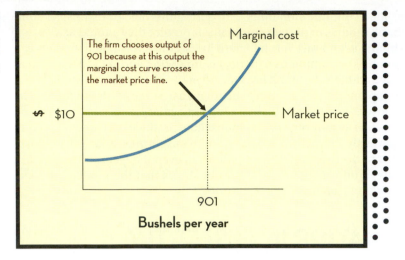

FIGURE **9.2**

OUTPUT WHERE
MARGINAL COST
INTERSECTS PRICE

The firm chooses output of 901 because at this output the marginal cost curve crosses the market price line.

Marginal cost

$ $10 — Market price

901

Bushels per year

marginal cost is still less than $10, then C-Farm should continue to increase production. Of course, this increase in production will further increase C-Farm's marginal cost. C-Farm should keep producing corn so long as its marginal cost is less than the price of corn.

C-Farm maximizes profit when it produces just enough corn so that marginal cost equals price. If, for example, marginal cost is just a little bit below price, then C-Farm can make slightly more profit by producing slightly more output. To squeeze every last cent of profit out of its business, C-Farm therefore should keep growing corn until price exactly equals marginal cost. As in Figure 9.2, a firm maximizes profit by setting output at the point where marginal cost intersects price.

SHORT-RUN PROFIT IN PERFECT COMPETITION

To further study C-Farm's behavior we must determine its profit graphically. If the price of corn is $10, then C-Farm gets $10 for every bushel it sells. If the average total cost of growing corn is $7, then it costs C-Farm on average $7 to make each bushel. Consequently, C-Farm makes on average $10 − $7 = $3 from each bushel. If C-Farm sells 1,000 bushels and makes on average $3 of profit from each bushel, then its total profit is (1,000)($3) = $3,000. This example shows that in general

> Profit = Average profit per good sold × Output, or
> Profit = (Price − Average total cost) × Output

Figure 9.3 gives C-Farm's profit if output is 1,000. The profit rectangle in Figure 9.3 has a height of $3 and a width of 1,000 bushels. Its area is height times width, or $3,000. The $3 height represents the difference between the price of corn and C-Farm's average total cost of growing corn. The $3 height, therefore, represents C-Farm's average profit per bushel sold. The 1,000 bushels width of the profit rectangle represents the total number of bushels sold.

In Figure 9.3 *we assumed* that output is 1,000. But if we add the marginal cost curve to our diagram, we can *determine* C-Farm's output because C-Farm will set output such that price equals marginal cost. Recall from Chapter 8 that the marginal cost curve goes through the low point on the average total costs curve.

Figure 9.4 gives other possible cost curves for C-Farm. We know that in Figure 9.4, C-Farm will produce 2,000 bushels because at this output, price equals marginal cost.

> In perfect competition a firm maximizes profit by setting output such that price equals marginal cost.

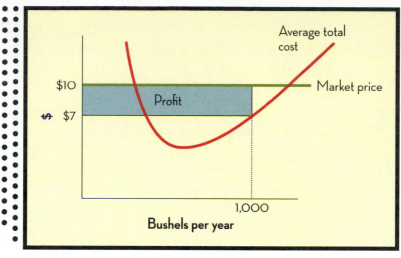

FIGURE **9.3**

PROFIT AT OUTPUT = 1,000 BUSHELS

If output = 1,000, total profit is ($10 − $7)(1,000) = $3,000 per year.

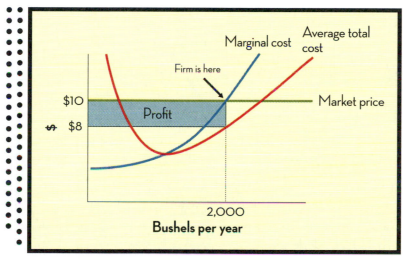

FIGURE **9.4**

PROFIT AT OUTPUT = 2,000 BUSHELS

Profit = ($10 − $8)(2,000) = $4,000 per year.

Figure 9.5 gives an example in which C-Farm produces 600 bushels and makes zero profit. If it produces 600 bushels, it will get $10 a bushel in revenue but pay on average $10 a bushel in costs. By producing 600 bushels, C-Farm breaks even. Notice that at any level of output other than 600 bushels, C-Farm's average total cost curve would be above the market price and C-Farm would lose money. In Figure 9.5, therefore, the best C-Farm can do is break even.

Figure 9.6 provides an example in which C-Farm loses money. In Figure 9.6 price equals marginal cost at the output of 500. C-Farm, therefore, maximizes its profit at the output of 500. But at an output of 500, it costs C-Farm on average $12 to make each bushel while C-Farm must sell each bushel for only $10. C-Farm, therefore, loses $2 for each good sold.

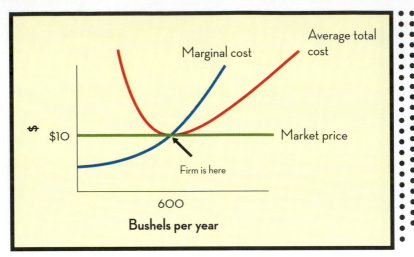

FIGURE **9.5**

BREAK EVEN AT OUTPUT = 600 BUSHELS

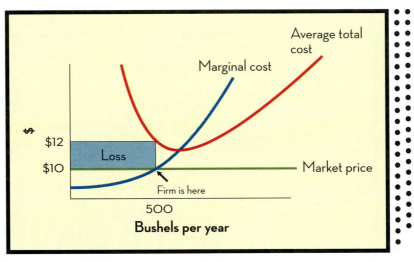

FIGURE **9.6**

LOSS AT OUTPUT = 500 BUSHELS

Total profit = ($10 − $12)(500) = −$1,000. C-Farm would lose even more than $1,000 if it chose another level of output.

You might wonder why C-Farm doesn't simply shut down rather than suffer a loss. This is because in the short run, a firm can sometimes lose less money by producing goods than by shutting down production.

FIRMS IGNORE SUNK COSTS WHEN DECIDING WHETHER TO SHUT DOWN

A firm will not necessarily shut down if it's losing money. For example, imagine you own a restaurant in a shopping mall. You must pay $10,000 a month in rent to the mall. This $10,000 is a fixed cost since you have to pay it regardless of how many customers you serve. If you operate you must also pay $20,000 a month in food and labor costs. This $20,000 is a variable cost because the amount of food and labor you need varies with the number of customers you serve. Let's finally assume that if you operate you will bring in $25,000 a month in revenue. Your profit per month, therefore, is

$$\text{Total revenue} - \text{Fixed costs} - \text{Variable costs, or}$$

$$\$25{,}000 - \$10{,}000 - \$20{,}000 = -\$5{,}000$$

So if you operate, you lose $5,000 a month. In contrast, if you shut down you lose your $25,000 in revenue and no longer have to pay your $20,000 in variable costs. But let's assume that you signed a contract forcing you to pay the $10,000 in rent for the next year even if you stop serving customers. If you shut down, therefore, your profit is −$10,000 per month. Consequently, you are better off operating at a loss than shutting down. A firm with fixed costs will lose money if it shuts down, because in the short run a firm must pay its fixed costs regardless of whether or not it operates. In the short run, fixed costs are also sunk costs.

A sunk cost is a cost that has already been paid or a cost that must be paid regardless of what you do. In the short run, fixed costs are sunk costs because we assume that you must always pay your fixed costs. In our restaurant example, your fixed costs of rent for the next year are sunk costs. Sunk costs are costs you can't get back even if you shut down.

Rational people ignore sunk costs when making decisions. Below is a ghost story illuminating the perils of letting sunk costs influence choices.

The Ghost of Sunk Costs

Thomas and Hector sought Blackbeard the Pirate's treasure. Just before he died, Blackbeard threw his treasure in a deep well where it sank down through the sand at the well's bottom. The men found the well and spent their days trying to unearth the treasure. After two long years of searching, they saw what looked like a chest.

The sight of the chest filled Thomas with greed, making him as cutthroat as Blackbeard himself. To avoid having to share the treasure, Thomas stabbed Hector to death. But on examining the "chest," Thomas saw that it was just an oddly colored stone. Consumed with guilt over having killed his friend for a rock, Thomas wanted to abandon his treasure hunt.

But then a strange fog moved towards Thomas. The fog congealed into the shape of a bearded man holding a sword. "I am the ghost of Blackbeard!" the fog bellowed. "By killing your partner, you have proven yourself worthy of pirate booty. So keep digging!" Thomas acquiesced.

After five more years of fruitless searching, Thomas considered quitting. But then the ghost reappeared to remind Thomas that he had already devoted seven years to treasure hunting. If he stopped now, the ghost said, those seven years will have been wasted. Persuaded by the ghost's logic, Thomas continued digging.

When four more years had passed, Thomas hired a mining engineer to examine his well. The engineer said that since the well was extremely deep, Thomas had at best a 5 percent chance of ever uncovering the treasure. On hearing this, Thomas resolved to quit. But then the ghost reappeared and urged Thomas to keep digging. The ghost reminded Thomas that he had now devoted 11 years of his life to treasure hunting. These 11 years, the ghost said, were too much of an investment to throw away. "True," said the ghost, "your chance of finding the treasure is small. But you're now digging primarily to justify all the time you have spent on your hunt." Thomas accepted the ghost's logic and continued his treasure quest.

As the years passed, Thomas kept digging. Every time he was about to give up, the ghost reminded him of how much time he had already put into the treasure hunt. And of course the longer Thomas dug, the more of his life would be wasted if he didn't find the treasure. As time went by, Thomas felt that the cost to him of giving up continually increased. So Thomas kept digging and digging and digging.

Finally, after digging for 50 years Thomas was exhausted and drained of life. As Thomas lay down to die, the ghost materialized and mockingly said: "You fool! I'm the ghost of Hector, not Blackbeard! You took my life with a knife, so I took yours with faulty logic!"

Analysis of the Ghost Story
At various points in the story, Thomas decided to keep digging because he had already spent so much time digging. But if he stopped digging, he wouldn't regain his lost time. The time he had already spent digging was a sunk cost. Therefore, when deciding whether to continue digging Thomas should rationally have ignored all the time he had already spent digging. Below are some other examples of how rational people should treat sunk costs.

- You spend 10 hours drafting a paper on whether real estate agents work in almost perfectly competitive markets. You estimate it will take an additional 20 hours to finish the paper and it will receive a B-. But if you started over and wrote a paper on innovation in perfectly competitive markets, it would take you 19 hours to finish and the paper would get a B+. True, starting over would mean that the 10 hours you already put into your real estate paper would be wasted, but these 10 hours are a sunk cost you can never get back. Rationally, you should forget about these 10 hours and compose the second paper.

- For pleasure you read 450 pages of a 500-page novel but then realize you don't enjoy the book. The time you spent reading the first 450 pages is a sunk cost you should ignore when deciding whether to finish the book. If you wouldn't receive pleasure from reading the final 50 pages, you should stop reading the novel.

- You're a military officer trying to capture a hill. So far 20 of your men have died trying to take the hill. You estimate that capturing the hill will require 40 more of your soldiers to die and the hill isn't worth 40 lives. But you think to yourself, "If I give up now, 20 men will have died for nothing." These 20 deaths, however, are a sunk cost that shouldn't influence whether you continue the battle.

- (Ignore this bullet point if you haven't taken calculus.) Find the value of X that minimizes: $X^2 - 2X + C$ where C is some constant. The answer is $X = 1$. You get this answer for all values of C. C is irrelevant to the answer since the value of X has no effect on C. In a sense, you must "pay" C regardless of what value of X you choose, so C is a sunk cost that you should ignore when solving the minimization problem.

The conclusion you should draw from all of this is that firms should ignore sunk costs when deciding whether to shut down. Since, to keep things simple, we assume in the short run that all fixed costs are sunk costs, this means that in the short run, firms should ignore their fixed costs when deciding whether to shut down.

COSTS CURVES AND THE SHUT-DOWN DECISION

Imagine that a firm is considering whether to operate or shut down in the short run. The advantage of shutting down is that the firm no longer has to pay any variable costs. The disadvantage of shutting down is that the firm no longer receives any revenue. A firm should shut down, therefore, if its variable costs are always greater than its total revenue.

If a firm operates, it can choose whatever level of output it wants. A firm should shut down only if it is better off shutting down than operating at any possible level of output. Pretend that the following table shows a firm's total revenue and variable costs for three levels of output.

Output	Total Revenue	Variable Costs
100	$1,000	$1,050
200	2,000	1,900
300	3,000	3,050

The firm is better off shutting down than producing 100 goods. By producing 100 goods, the firm gets $1,000 in revenue but pays $1,050 in variable costs. Producing 100 goods, therefore, lowers the firm's profit $50 below what it would be if it shut down. For similar reasons, the firm is better off shutting down than producing 300 goods. But, if the firm produces 200 goods, its total revenue will exceed its variable costs. The firm, therefore, does better if it produces 200 goods than if it shuts down. If fixed costs are above $100, however, the firm will still lose money producing 200 goods. Because the firm is capable of producing levels of output other than 100, 200, or 300, we don't know if this firm will produce 200 units of output. But we do know that the firm won't shut down because there exists a level of output at which the firm is better off operating than shutting down. The lesson here is that a firm should shut down only if, *for all levels of output,*

$$\text{Variable costs} > \text{Total revenue}$$

If we divide the above inequality by output, we find that a firm should shut down only if, *for all levels of output,*

$$\text{Average variable costs} > \text{Price}$$

Figure 9.7 shows at which prices a hypothetical firm will operate and shut down in the short run.

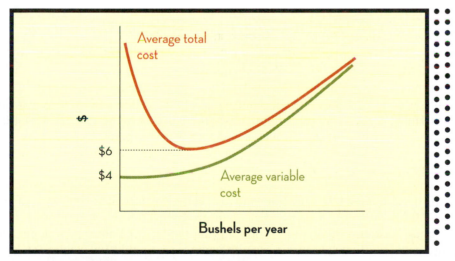

FIGURE 9.7

OPERATING VERSUS SHUTTING DOWN IN SHORT RUN

If the price is greater than $6, the firm operates at a profit.
If the price is $6, the firm operates and makes zero profit. If the price is between $6 and $4, the firm operates at a loss. If the price is below $4, the firm shuts down in the short run.

SHUTTING DOWN VERSUS EXITING THE MARKET

Economists distinguish between a firm shutting down and exiting its industry. A firm shuts down when it produces zero output but still must pay fixed costs. A firm exits the industry when it produces zero output and has no fixed costs. Economists assume that in the short run, firms have the option of operating or shutting down. In the short run, we assume, firms cannot exit the industry, because in the short run, firms must pay their fixed costs. In the long run, we assume that firms can either operate *or* exit the industry. In the long run, a firm would never choose to shut down because it would always be better off exiting the industry.

The following table summarizes the differences between shutting down and exiting the industry:

Shutting Down	Exiting the Industry
Occurs only in the short run.	Occurs only in the long run.
Firms pay no variable costs.	Firms pay no costs.
Firms receive no revenue.	Firms receive no revenue.
Firms must still pay their fixed costs.	

Imagine again that you own a mall restaurant that has a year-long lease. Under the lease, you must pay $10,000 a month even if you stop serving customers. After the year lease has expired, however, you can get out of your lease and completely free yourself of all fixed costs. Only after a year, therefore, can you exit the restaurant industry.

PROFITS AND OPPORTUNITY COSTS

A firm's profits determine in the long run whether it will exit or enter an industry. To further study firms' behavior, we need a better understanding of profits.

Imagine that you just inherited some land that two companies want to buy. C-Farm is willing to pay you $100,000 for the land, while a housing developer is willing to pay $109,000 for it. What is your profit if you sell the land to C-Farm? You might be tempted to answer $100,000. After all, you got the land for free so if you sell it for $100,000, you are $100,000 richer. But by the way economists calculate profit, if you sell the land to C-Farm you lose $9,000.

One opportunity cost of selling your land to C-Farm is that you can't sell it to the housing developer. So by selling your land to C-Farm, you lose $109,000 while gaining only $100,000. When economists calculate profits, we always take into account opportunity costs. Consequently, if you sold your land to the housing developer, you would make only $9,000 in profits even though you get paid $109,000 for the land. This is because an opportunity cost of selling the land to the housing developer is that you can no longer sell the land to C-Farm.

What if both C-Farm and the housing developer offer to pay you $109,000 for the land? If you sell the land to either, you make zero profit. This is because, for example, if you sell the land to C-Farm for $109,000, you lose the chance to sell the land to the developer for $109,000. What this zero profit really means is that you have not benefited from selling the land to C-Farm. Or, if C-Farm's offer didn't exist, you would be no worse off.

Now imagine that C-Farm offers to pay you $1 more than the developer for the land. If you sell to C-Farm, you have made a $1 profit. This $1 profit represents how much better off you have been made by selling your land to C-Farm as opposed to taking advantage of your next best opportunity.

Economic versus Accounting Profit   Accountants define profit differently than economists do. Accountants don't consider opportunity costs when determining profits. For example, imagine that Microsoft billionaire Bill Gates gets a job mowing lawns for $10 an hour. Gates must spend $1 an hour on gas for his mower. An accountant would say that Gates makes a profit of $9 an hour mowing lawns. An economist, however, would argue that the opportunity cost of Bill Gates's time is thousands of dollars an hour. To an economist, consequently, Bill Gates loses a huge amount of money if he spends his time mowing lawns.

Consider another example. Assume that you own and operate a restaurant. Your total revenue is $200,000 a year. You have $120,000 in expenses from rent, food, and salaries. If you stopped operating the restaurant, you could get a job making $75,000 a year. An economist would say you are making a profit of $5,000 a year ($200,000 − $120,000 − $75,000). An accountant, however, would not consider the $75,000 opportunity cost of your time and so conclude that you were making an $80,000 a year profit.

Whenever this book uses the term *profit,* it refers to economic and not accounting profit. But be warned, the media use accountants' definition of profits. So if you read in the paper that some company made a $100 million profit, it means accounting profit and does not take into account the full opportunity cost of the company's assets.

IN THE LONG RUN A FIRM WILL EXIT IF PROFITS ARE NEGATIVE

If a firm is operating at a loss, then in the long run it should exit the industry. If a firm leaves the industry, then it has zero revenue and zero costs so it obviously has a profit of zero. Earning zero profit, however, is better than suffering a loss. Consequently, firms earning negative profits will, in the long run, exit their industries.

If a firm earns a negative profit in the long run, then its assets can be better used somewhere else. The firm would consequently be better off exiting its industry and using its assets where they will generate greater profit.

"Capitalism without failure is like religion without sin. Bankruptcies and losses concentrate the mind on prudent behavior." —Allan H. Meltzer (economist).[4]

IN THE LONG RUN FIRMS WILL ENTER IF PROFITS ARE POSITIVE

Economists assume that in the long run, any firm can enter a perfectly competitive industry. And if a firm can make a positive profit in such an industry, it will enter. Imagine you make $60,000 a year working as a manager at Target. If you took a job at Wal-Mart, you would make $65,000 a year. An opportunity cost of working at Wal-Mart is that you lose the opportunity of making $60,000 at Target. Consequently, if you work at Wal-Mart, you will make only a $5,000 profit. (Of course, you will take home a $65,000-a-year paycheck.) But your ability to make a $5,000 profit at Wal-Mart means you could make more working at Wal-Mart than at your current job.

Similarly, if a firm can make a positive profit moving to a new industry then it could earn greater money in this new industry than in its old one. Consequently, the firm should move to this new industry.

IN THE LONG RUN PROFITS ARE ZERO

We now come to the big long-run conclusion: In the long run, firms in perfect competition make zero profit. Firms losing money will leave their market. Such exiting will decrease supply and raise price, thereby increasing profits for firms in the market. If firms in a market are making a positive profit, then other firms will enter, thereby increasing supply and decreasing price, thus reducing profits. Only when firms make zero profit will a perfectly competitive market be at long-run equilibrium, because at zero profit there will be no entry or exit.

To sum up, in the long run firms make zero profit in perfect competition because

- Positive profit causes entry, which increases supply, thereby lowering price and reducing profit.
- Negative profit causes exit, which lowers supply, thereby increasing price and increasing profit.
- At zero profit, price is at an equilibrium because firms neither enter nor exit the market.

Moving to a Long-Run Competitive Equilibrium   Imagine there are 1 million corn-growing firms exactly like the one in Figure 9.8. Each earns zero profit. The market demand is given by Figure 9.9. Since all firms earn zero profit, this market is in

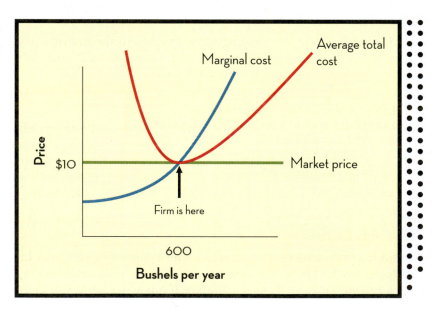

FIGURE 9.8

REPRESENTATIVE CORN-GROWING FIRM

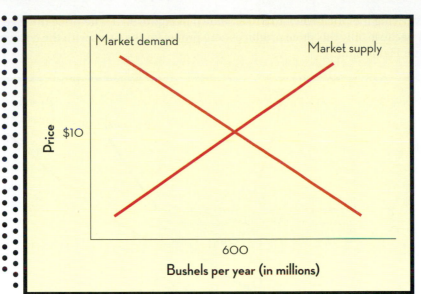

FIGURE **9.9**

MARKET
EQUILIBRIUM

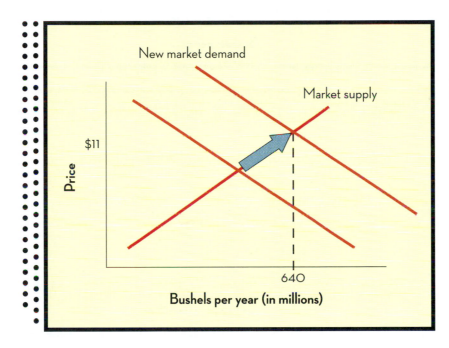

FIGURE **9.10**

INCREASED MARKET
DEMAND,
INCREASED PRICE
OF CORN

235

equilibrium. Suddenly, however, the market demand increases because, say, the price of butter, a complement of corn, decreases. This causes an increase in the price of corn to $11 as shown in Figure 9.10.

This increase in price causes each of the 1 million corn-growing firms to increase production but also causes these 1 million firms to temporarily earn a positive profit as shown in Figure 9.11. Firms now face higher average total cost because they are no longer at the low point on their average total cost curve. But the positive profits that the firms earn causes new firms to enter the market, which increases supply, eventually driving the price down to $10 as shown in Figure 9.12. The price must go back to $10 because only this price produces zero profits for the firms with the cost curves shown in Figure 9.8.

FIGURE **9.11**

INCREASED PRICE, INCREASED PRODUCTION

The price increase causes the firm to move along its marginal cost curve and increase output from 600 to 640.

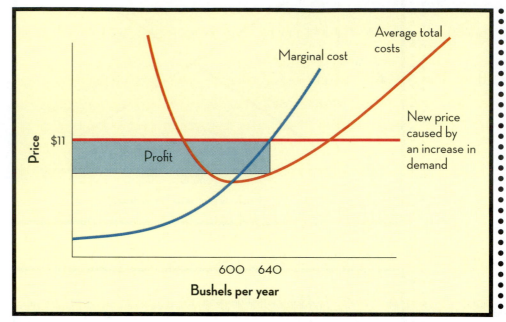

FIGURE **9.12**

INCREASED SUPPLY, DECREASED PRICE

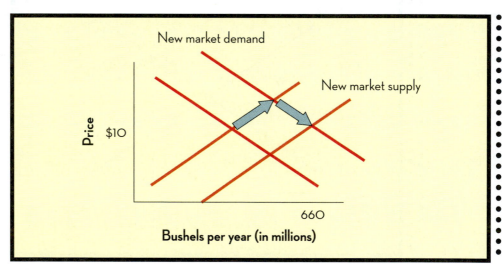

Many students initially find it strange that firms would stay in a market in which they make zero profit. But this is because these students are thinking in terms of accounting profits. A firm could make an accounting profit of $100 million a year (enough to pay its owners substantial dividends) but still earn zero economic profits if this firm could still earn $100 million a year if it left its current market and moved to another.

To summarize, in perfect competition in the long run:

- All firms produce at the low point on their average total cost curve.
- Price equals marginal cost for all firms.

Figure 9.13 illustrates this situation.

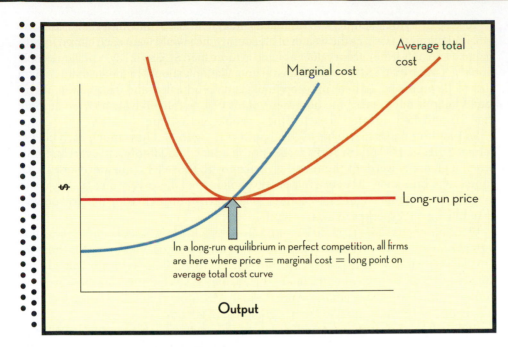

FIGURE **9.13**

LONG-RUN
EQUILIBRIUM
IN PERFECT
COMPETITION

Average total
cost

Marginal cost

$

Long-run price

In a long-run equilibrium in perfect competition, all firms
are here where price = marginal cost = long point on
average total cost curve

Output

THE SOCIAL BENEFITS OF PERFECT COMPETITION

In the long run in perfect competition, firms are at the low point on their average total cost curve. This means that under perfect competition in the long run, society gets goods at the lowest possible cost.

MARKETS PRODUCE THE OPTIMAL NUMBER OF GOODS WHEN PRICE EQUALS MARGINAL COST

Consider an economy where a government official, whom we will call Vladimir, tells businesses what to produce. We have seen before in discussing supply and demand that if the government sets the wrong prices for goods, the government could cause wasteful shortages or surpluses. Now, however, assume that Vladimir doesn't mind a little capitalism and just decides how much of a good gets produced. He then lets the market set prices so there will never be a shortage or surplus. Vladimir, for example, picks the number of gizmos made and then lets supply and demand decide prices. Therefore, if he declares that many gizmos will be produced, the market price will be low and many people will get gizmos; however, if Vladimir dictates that only a small number of gizmos will be made, the market price will be high and few will get gizmos.

How should Vladimir determine gizmo production? If Vladimir truly cared about his people's welfare, he would balance the social costs and benefits of producing each gizmo. Each person who owns a gizmo in Vladimir's country benefits some, but his country will incur some costs each time a gizmo is produced. To maximize the wealth of his country, Vladimir should produce gizmos as long as the benefit people receive from gizmos exceeds the costs of making them. The cost of making another gizmo, however, is simply that gizmo's marginal cost.

237

To keep everything simple, let's say that the marginal cost of making a gizmo is always $15. If Vladimir maximizes the wealth of his country, he should want each citizen to get a gizmo if and only if the citizen values a gizmo at more than $15. So if, say, 1 million people would get more than a $15 benefit from a gizmo, Vladimir should mandate that 1 million gizmos be produced. To determine optimal gizmo production and distribution, therefore, Vladimir must determine how many of his people value having a gizmo at more than $15 and then see to it that each of these people gets a gizmo.

So Vladimir needs to use his magical powers to figure out how much each citizen values a gizmo. If Vladimir lacks magic powers, he could simply ask everyone how much a gizmo is worth to them and give gizmos to those who answer over $15. Of course, if people know they get a free gizmo (which, trust me, is very nice) if they claim to value them at more than $15, Vladimir might have more luck using magical powers than relying on responses to his question.

Vladimir needs some method to truthfully determine how many people value gizmos at more than $15. What if, instead of giving away gizmos, Vladimir sells them for $15 each? Obviously, if the price of a gizmo equals $15 Vladimir's citizens will buy gizmos if and only if they value them at greater than $15. Vladimir can then produce enough gizmos to satisfy demand at price equals $15. More generally, Vladimir should set the price of gizmos equal to the marginal cost of gizmos.

But wait! In perfect competition, price automatically equals marginal cost. Thus, rather than deciding how many gizmos to produce, Vladimir simply needs to ensure that the market for gizmos is perfectly competitive. Restated, in perfect competition, markets function exactly as Vladimir would if he had magical powers and desired to maximize the wealth of his society.

ADAM SMITH'S INVISIBLE HAND WORKS PERFECTLY WHEN PRICE EQUALS MARGINAL COST

Setting marginal cost equal to price causes selfish people to act as if they were altruistic. Imagine that you value a gizmo at $G. You know, however, that it costs society something to make a gizmo, this something being the marginal cost of making an extra gizmo. If you are altruistic and concerned about maximizing the wealth of society, you will buy a gizmo only if the marginal cost of making it is below $G. Of course, being a selfish person you will actually buy a gizmo if the price is below $G. To summarize:

1. If you're altruistic you will buy a gizmo if **the marginal cost of making a gizmo** < **$G.**

2. If you're selfish you will buy a gizmo if **the price of a gizmo** < **$G.**

So to get the selfish person to act altruistically, we should set the marginal cost of making a gizmo equal to the price of a gizmo. Doing this will make conditions (1) and (2) identical. Perfect competition, however, automatically sets price equal to marginal cost. So under perfect competition, Adam Smith's invisible hand works to ensure that selfish people buy goods if and only if the purchase would increase the wealth of society.

LIMITED INNOVATION IN PERFECT COMPETITION

Perfect competition is not without costs, however, as firms in intensively competitive markets have limited incentives to innovate. Imagine you have the only Thai restaurant in town and are considering adding a new dish. The dish will clearly challenge your customers' palates as it represents tastes they have never encountered. Of course, you're not sure if your customers will welcome this challenge. Should you go to the trouble of changing your menu and teaching your chefs how to make the new dish? If you are indeed the only Thai restaurant in town, you probably should. If it doesn't work, you can quickly drop the item from your menu. If it does, you will increase your customers' satisfaction level and thus boost your profits.

Now imagine that you face the same decision but there are many Thai restaurants in your area that compete intensely. In this case you probably should not introduce this new dish. If it doesn't work, you will lose a small amount of money. If it does work then you will probably just break even as others will quickly copy you.

In intensively competitive markets, firms know any successful innovation will be quickly copied, thus reducing the benefits of the innovation. If you come up with a way of making your product cheaper in the short term, you will make positive profits. But in an intensively competitive market, other firms will quickly copy you and eventually your profit will be driven down to zero. Indeed, regardless of the innovations you develop in a perfectly competitive market, your long-term profit will always be forced down to zero by competition and imitation. In contrast, if competition is limited you can permanently keep positive profits derived from successful innovations.

Perfect competition maximizes the amount of wealth squeezed out of an existing market with unchanging goods. But perfect competition is not the best environment for promoting innovation needed to improve existing goods. In the next two chapters, we will consider market structures that are better at promoting innovation but worse at squeezing wealth out of static markets.

Once innovation occurs, however, perfect competition is the ideal market structure to promote the *spread* of already discovered innovations. If a few firms in a perfectly competitive market lower their costs through innovation, then other firms will be forced to follow or be driven out of the market. Firms making zero profit are on the very edge of leaving a market. So if a firm in perfect competition falls just a little bit behind its rivals in adopting cost-reducing technology, it will be quickly compelled to exit its industry.

For example, intense competition has obligated dairy farmers to continually improve their productivity. As one farmer describes it:

> "A fellow was all but forced to milk twice as many cows in the same length of time, once milking machines came along . . . just to stay in business. Had to trade in the horses for a tractor. Automatic cleaning and feeding are now a must too, not that they don't make life easier. But as soon as farmers had time and power to get more done, they had to go right ahead and do more just to pay for all the labor-saving devices."[5]

To summarize:

- There is little incentive to innovate in perfectly competitive markets.
- But once an innovation has been somehow created, it will quickly spread throughout all firms in a perfectly competitive market.

THE INTERNET AND PERFECT COMPETITION

What does it mean for two firms to compete? Do bookstores in Buffalo and Boston compete even when they sell the same products? Two bookstores compete to the degree that one loses sales when the other cuts prices.

Imagine two neighboring bookstores in a mall. If a customer found a book that she liked in one store, it would be easy for her to check the price in the other store. If one of these stores had consistently higher prices, therefore, it would generate little business. Now imagine instead that these two bookstores are on opposite ends of a large mall. It would be much more of a hassle for customers to compare prices. A store now could afford to maintain higher prices because its customers (a) might not realize its prices were higher, and (b) might not be willing to walk to the other store just to save a few cents. The closer the stores, the more likely they are to compete, because price will have a greater influence on sales.

On the Internet, however, all stores are next to each other. Internet retailers face more competition than their bricks-and-mortar cousins do. If there were, say, 10,000 bricks-and-mortar widget retailers spread across the United States, but only 20 online sellers of widgets, the Internet retailers might actually face more competition. Two stores in the real world compete only if a customer is willing to shop at either of them. Consequently, in the real world two bookstores should consider themselves rivals only if they are within, say, 15 miles of each other. In contrast, any connected person can visit any virtual retail store regardless of where the store is located physically. The actual number of competitors an Internet retailer faces will thus usually be much higher than the number faced by real-world stores. Consequently, the Internet has brought the world's economy closer to perfect competition and so lowered the profits of many businesses.

> "Halima Khatuun is an illiterate woman in a Bangladeshi village. She sells eggs to a dealer who comes by at regular intervals. She used to be compelled to sell at the price he proposed, because she did not have access to other buyers. But once, when he came and offered 12 taka for four eggs, she kept him waiting while she used the mobile phone to find out the market price in another village. Because the price there was 14 taka, she was able to go back and get 13 from the dealer."[6]

QUESTIONS YOU SHOULD BE ABLE TO ANSWER AFTER READING THIS CHAPTER:

1 What are the seven assumptions of perfect competition? (page 221)

2 How do firms in perfect competition set output? (pages 225–226)

3 How do you graphically determine profits using the price and average total cost curve? (page 227)

4 How do you graphically use the price and average total cost curves to determine if a firm is (a) making a positive profit, (b) operating at a loss, and (c) making zero profit? (pages 227–228)

5 What are sunk costs? (pages 228–230)

6 Why should rational people ignore sunk costs when making decisions? (pages 228–230)

7 When will a firm in perfect competition shut down? (pages 230–231)

8 How can you graphically show when in the short run (a) a firm will operate at a profit, (b) a firm will operate at zero profit, (c) a firm will operate at a loss, and (d) a firm will shut down? (page 231)

9 What's the difference between shutting down and exiting a market? (page 232)

10 When will a firm in perfect competition enter or exit its industry? (pages 233–234)

11 What's the difference between how economists and accountants calculate profit? (page 233)

12 Why do firms in perfect competition in the long run make zero profit? (page 234)

13 What is the social benefit of firms in the long run being on the low point of their average total cost curves? (page 237)

14 Why will a society produce the optimal number of goods if price equals marginal cost? (pages 237–238)

15 Why does Adam Smith's invisible hand work perfectly if price equals marginal cost? (page 238)

16 Why is there limited innovation in perfect competition? (pages 238–239)

17 Why has the Internet moved the economy closer to perfect competition? (pages 239–240)

STUDY PROBLEMS

1 A firm in perfect competition produces 1,000 goods. The total cost of producing these goods is $180,000. The price of each good is $200. In the short run is the firm making a profit? What will happen to the price of this good in the long run?

2 There are 20,000 firms in a perfectly competitive market that until today was in a long-run equilibrium. The price of the good in this market had been $50 and each firm used to make 27 goods. Today, however, a sudden decrease in demand caused the price of the good to decrease to $40. Assume that, after the price change, price is still higher than average variable costs for some levels of output.

    A.   In the short run, will firms in this market make a profit or loss?

    B.   In the short run, will firms in this market produce more or fewer than 27 goods?

    C.   In the short run, will the average total cost of making the good increase or decrease?

    D.   In the long run, will firms enter or exit this market?

    E.   What will happen to the supply curve in the long run?

    F.   How will this change in supply curve affect the market price in the long run?

    G.   In the long run, how many goods will each firm in this market produce?

    H.   In the long run, will the average total cost of making the good increase or decrease compared to what it was before the price of the good fell?

3 Assume that for firms with cost curves like those in Figure 9.13, the average total cost of producing all levels of good suddenly falls. (Before this decrease in costs, the market was in a long-run equilibrium.) Describe what happens in the short run and long run to firms in this market. In the long run does this fall in costs benefit firms? In the long run does this fall in costs benefit consumers?

4 A firm can make either watches or clocks, but not both. It is currently making an economic profit of $93,000 a year making watches. If it stopped making watches and started making clocks, it would make an economic profit of $120,000 a year. Therefore, this firm should exit the watch market so it can enter the clock market. But in the chapter we learned that a firm should leave a market only if it is making a loss. Something about this question is therefore contradictory. What is it?

5 You have already spent $60 million making a movie. It will cost you another $X million to finish the film. You somehow know that the movie will take in exactly $70 million in revenue. For what values of X should you finish the movie?

6 You find out that your boyfriend/girlfriend cheated on you. You tell your boyfriend/girlfriend that you're terminating the relationship. But he/she is an economics major and so explains that you're being irrational because the harm you have suffered from knowing that you have been cheated on is a sunk cost. And since you should ignore sunk costs when making decisions you should not dump your boyfriend/girlfriend over something that happened in the past and therefore can't be changed. Is your boyfriend/girlfriend correct?

7 Argue that assumption 7 (page 221) follows from the other six perfect competition assumptions.

8 The following shows *incorrect* cost curves for a firm in perfect competition in the long run. Find everything wrong with the diagram.

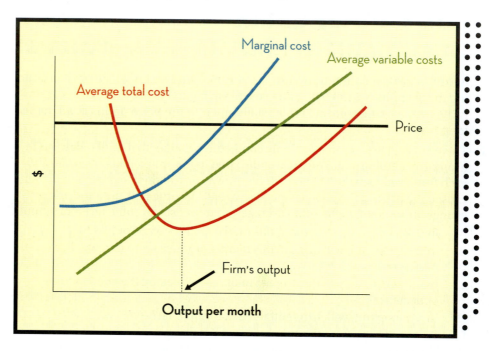

9 Should firms always seek to minimize their average total costs?

part three

IMPERFECT MARKETS/ IMPERFECT GOVERNMENTS

The last section of the textbook was titled "The Magic of the Marketplace" because it showed how markets improve the human condition. Until now, this textbook has said mostly positive things about markets. But sometimes markets don't work perfectly. Sometimes Adam Smith's invisible hand doesn't guide self-interested individuals to act in the best interests of society. This section considers several challenges to market effectiveness. Unless overcome, each challenge degrades the performance of markets.

Sometimes, but not always, markets themselves have the strength and creativity to overcome these challenges. Through government regulation, politicians who are altruistic and omniscient could, theoretically, surmount all market challenges. But governments as well as markets have imperfections. And when imperfect governments try to correct market failures they often worsen the situation. Yet sometimes unfettered markets perform so poorly that even semi-incompetent governments can improve market outcomes.

When studying each challenge to market effectiveness keep in mind the following questions:

1 How does each market challenge prevent Adam Smith's invisible hand from operating?

2 How and to what extent could consumers and firms overcome the challenge?

3 How, theoretically, could politicians who are altruistic and omniscient overcome the market challenge?

4 If given the power to regulate the market, would imperfect, self-interested politicians improve or worsen the outcome?

MONOPOLYSKI

You own one of eight ski resorts in the town of Nives. Competition among resorts keeps the price you charge skiers down, causing you to earn zero profit. Fortunately, an almost completed nearby airport will soon increase the number of ski tourists visiting Nives. Unfortunately, anticipating this increase in market demand, two new resorts are scheduled to open in the next few years.

Competition is great for everyone but competitors. When firms fight over customers, the customers get lower prices but the firms end up with lower profits.

In your quest for riches, you scheme to banish competition, thereby becoming a monopolist. First, you raise some money and acquire four of the other resorts, combining them into your own. Alas, the owners of the three remaining independent resorts refuse to sell. So you get creative to take them down:

- You convince the Nives town government to seize another resort's property to build an elementary school. Acting as a mere private citizen, you would never have been able to force a resort's owner to sell. But by working through the government, you can use the power of eminent domain to legally confiscate this resort's land.

- Over the last decade, 20 skiers in your state have had tragic accidents. As a result, your state hired ski safety inspectors and empowered them to close dangerous facilities. You find a lawyer who's an expert on ski safety regulations. And when your lawyer determines that another resort doesn't fully comply with state safety regulations, you feel it's your civic duty to report this resort to the state. After this resort is shut down, its owners decide to sell out to you.

CHALLENGE TO MARKET EFFECTIVENESS 1: MONOPOLIES

LEARNING OBJECTIVES

AFTER READING THIS CHAPTER, YOU SHOULD BE ABLE TO:

- Define *monopoly*.
- Understand why monopolists create deadweight losses.
- Explain monopolists' incentives to innovate.
- Recognize barriers to market entry.

- All the resorts in Nives employ union labor. You mention to the unions that if you were a monopolist you could afford to pay higher wages. Not being fools, the unions ask you to start paying these higher wages right away. After you give your union employees higher salaries, the unions go on strike against the last independent resort. This resort's owner decides to leave the ski business to build luxury houses on its hills. Now you're a monopolist! But wait, you forgot about the two new resorts that will be opening soon.

- You have always been a strong supporter of the environment. Consequently, you're terrified that the two new ski resorts will negatively impact local ecosystems. These new resorts will bring extra traffic, cause more pollution, and require the construction of additional roads. You start an environmental group called "Earth Yes, Profits No!" that fights against new business construction on any of Nives' pristine hills. Fortunately, the town government sides with the environmentalists and refuses to give the two proposed new resorts permits to build and operate.

Your scheming succeeds as you now control all your town's skiing facilities. You fittingly name your resort MonopolySki.

WHAT IS A MONOPOLY?

A pure monopoly is a firm without any competition. But pure monopolies don't exist. You, for example, don't have an absolute monopoly on skiing. Skiers wishing to avoid your high prices could travel to another ski resort. Furthermore, you must still compete for customers with other entertainment establishments such as movie theaters and ice-skating rinks.

There are no clear tests for determining whether a firm has a monopoly. All firms, even those traditionally considered monopolists, face competition. For example, the sole provider of electricity to a town still faces competition from candles, gas-powered generators, and energy-saving appliances.

Economists believe that the fewer substitutes there are for a firm's product, the more monopolistic the firm is. So, eliminating all competing resorts in Nives does gain you considerable monopoly power.

MONOPOLISTS' LONG-RUN PROFITS

In the long run in perfect competition, firms can freely enter any market. Such freedom of entry causes firms to make zero profits in the long run.

A monopolist, however, can earn long-term positive profits if it keeps other firms from entering its market. Stopping entry into a profit-earning market is like stopping water from flowing downhill. Water always seeks its lowest level and, if unhindered, will flow from high to low elevations. Similarly, firms always seek high profits. If not obstructed, firms will flow from markets offering zero or negative profits to those earning positive profits. A monopolist needs entry barriers to stop firms from entering its market and destroying its profits. Anything that prevents entry or makes entry relatively expensive is called a *barrier to entry*. No monopoly can earn long-run profits without a barrier to entry.

MonopolySki relied on the local government to prevent other resorts from opening up in its town. Governments frequently provide barriers to entry for monopolists.

SIX BARRIERS TO ENTRY
1. THE GOVERNMENT

Government is often a monopolist's best friend. Government-built entry barriers work extremely effectively at guarding monopolists' markets because a businessperson who would climb over such a barrier risks imprisonment.

Licenses   In the United States you can't become a doctor or a lawyer without a license. In many U.S. states you can't work as a plumber, cab driver, hair stylist, or K-12 school teacher without also receiving a government-granted license. Indeed, entry into over 20 percent of U.S. jobs is restricted by licenses.[2] By limiting entry, licenses allow members of protected professions to earn monopoly profits.

Licensing Can Kill[3]   Many U.S. states require electricians to obtain licenses. To get a license an electrician must prove he has a high level of skill. Faulty electrical work can kill homeowners. Using licensing to raise the quality of professional electricians, therefore, might seem like a worthy goal. One study, however, found that state licensing of electricians actually increased the death rate from accidental electrocutions. Licensing increased the price of electricians. By the Law of Demand, this increase in price caused fewer homeowners to hire electricians. Consequently, some homeowners didn't repair faulty electrical work while others attempted to make electrical repairs themselves. Both of these methods of doing without electricians increased accidental deaths.

Barriers to Becoming a Lawyer Want to make $90,000 a year? Become a lawyer. After working for just six months in private practice, the average American lawyer earns $90,000 a year.[4] But of course it's not that easy.

If anyone could become a lawyer, then many would. Such a huge influx into the legal profession would increase the supply of lawyers, thereby lowering lawyers' wages. Lawyers protect their income by using their political muscle to keep up high barriers of entry into the legal profession.

To become a lawyer, you must graduate from college, complete three years of law school, and then pass a state bar exam. Only after passing a bar exam will the state grant you a license to practice law.

Most practicing lawyers specialize, meaning that they devote their careers to something specific such as real estate law or criminal defense. Law schools, however, offer only a few courses in each specialty. Consequently, most of the material taught in law school will be of no practical use to students once they graduate. Furthermore, since every prospective lawyer in a state takes the same bar exam, this exam can at best only cover a small amount of material from each legal specialty. So most of the material on which a prospective lawyer is tested will have nothing to do with the type of law she may practice.

Many U.S. states require hair stylists to get a license before they can cut hair. To obtain a license, hair stylists usually have to complete a state-mandated training program. The next time you get a haircut, ask your stylist about any training programs she took and inquire whether they have helped her become a better stylist.

The lower the supply of lawyers, the higher their price is. Practicing lawyers, consequently, use their political influence to ensure that those wishing to become lawyers must travel a long and expensive path before the government will permit them to compete for customers.

Barriers to Becoming a Teacher Public school teachers, like lawyers, also benefit from licensing. Consider a Nobel Prize-winning scientist who teaches at a top university. Undergraduates enthusiastically attend her lectures. But our scientist decides that she wants to teach high school students. This scientist, who could get a job at any university in the world, would be barred from teaching at many U.S. public high schools.

To become a teacher in most U.S. states, you must take certain educational courses and then pass certification tests. Without certification our Nobel Prize winner couldn't teach high school in many areas. There is no evidence that certification requirements produce better teachers, yet most teachers' organizations enthusiastically back certification requirements.

Teachers' organizations argue that certification requirements ensure that only highly qualified individuals become teachers. Interestingly, however, these organizations also support laws making it almost impossible to fire poorly performing teachers.

Certification requirements create barriers to entry into the teaching profession. Some economists tend to believe that teachers support such barriers because they raise teachers' salaries. This doesn't mean that teachers are bad people, but rather that they are normal, self-interested individuals. Teachers behave just like lawyers

247

and doctors by getting the government to raise wages by limiting entry into their profession.

Outlawing Competition

Sometimes the government simply outlaws competition to a monopolist. For example, it's illegal for anyone to compete with the U.S. Post Office by delivering certain types of mail. Throughout history, rulers have sold and bestowed official monopolies. For such a monopoly to have any value, however, the government must make it illegal for any businessperson to compete with the monopolist.

One unusual, state-protected monopoly is the Indian government's monopoly on weather forecasting.[5] In India it's a crime for anyone other than the Indian Meteorological Department to forecast monsoons. The Indian government claims that the monopoly is needed to prevent confusion. I suspect, however, that the forecasting bureaucrats don't want to be embarrassed by superior competing weather predictors. So rather than working harder to ensure that their forecasts are the best, the Indian Meteorological Department has taken what appears to be the much easier step of banning competing forecasts.

State Religions

Governments often create religious monopolies. In a free marketplace of faith, religions compete for followers. But when the government outlaws competition against the state-approved religion, clergymen don't have to fear losing their flock to another faith. Clergymen, therefore, don't have to work as hard to keep their followers when the state grants them a monopoly.

Imagine that the king of some nation forces all of his subjects to practice faith X. Which of the following do you think is the most plausible reason for this religious monopoly?

1. The king is so certain of the divine truth of faith X that he doesn't want any of his citizens to endanger their souls by practicing another faith.
2. The king receives significant political support from the leaders of faith X, but the king is so uncertain of faith X's appeal he dares not allow his people to choose another faith.
3. The king receives significant political support from the leaders of faith X, but the king fears that if faith X were forced to compete with other religions, then its leaders would be forced to curtail their unpopular support of the king.

2. UNIONS

When a profession can't get the government to grant it monopoly power through licenses, it often uses unions to increase its wages. Unions are organizations of workers. Unions typically seek to forbid anyone who is not in the union from working at a given type of job.

Unions engage in collective bargaining with employers. For example, imagine that workers in some factory make $15 an hour. The union demands that workers be paid $20 per hour. If the employer refuses, the union's members will go on strike, thereby withholding their labor. A successful strike forces the factory to shut down.

The factory's owners may seek to operate during the strike by hiring nonunion replacement workers. Many unions will attempt to intimidate or shame those replacements into not working at the factory. The union's members may form a picket line around the factory and yell at the replacements as they come to work, perhaps calling them "scabs."

Sometimes firms break unions by successfully hiring replacement workers. In other instances, a strike inflicts so much pain on a firm that it gives in to the union's demands. In still other cases, the strike causes the firm to go bankrupt or relocate to an area without strong unions.

3. CONTROL OF A VITAL RESOURCE

Some firms maintain a monopoly by controlling a vital resource. For example, MonopolySki achieved monopoly by controlling all the developable slopes in Nives. OPEC, an oil-producing countries' organization, achieves significant monopoly power by controlling much of the world's supply of oil. Similarly, the South African firm DeBeers maintains a near monopoly on diamonds by controlling most of the world's diamond mines.

In 1960, 40 percent of American workers belonged to unions. In 2005 this figure had dropped to 12.5 percent. In 2005 only 7.8 percent of private sector workers belonged to unions while 36.5 percent of government workers were union members.[6]

Silk For awhile, ancient China kept a monopoly on silk by executing anyone caught exporting silk-making technology.[7] Unfortunately for China, around A.D. 400, silk-producing caterpillars were smuggled to India in the headdress of a Chinese princess traveling to marry her Indian prince. According to legend, the princess was motivated by a desire to have silk fabrics in her new homeland.[8]

Alum[9] Wool was one of the most important industries of 15th century Western Europe. Wool makers used the chemical alum to help dye their products. Before 1460 the only source of quality alum was in the Ottoman Empire. The Ottoman Empire, therefore, earned monopoly profits from the sale of alum to Western Europe. These profits helped finance the Muslim Ottomans in their many military clashes with Christian Western Europe.

In 1460, however, a large deposit of alum was discovered near Rome. The Pope took control of this deposit. He tried to establish an alum monopoly by declaring that any Christian caught using Ottoman alum would be excommunicated. Excommunicated Christians were banned from the Church, and according to Catholic doctrine, risked burning in hell. The Pope tried to establish an alum monopoly to earn high profits for his church and to deny alum profits to the Ottomans. For the Pope's plan to succeed, though, Christian wool makers would have to buy the Pope's alum even when the price of Ottoman alum was lower. Unfortunately for the Pope, however, Christian wool makers continued buying Ottoman alum. The threat of eternal damnation, therefore, was not sufficient to win the Pope a resource monopoly.

4. INCOMPATIBILITY

Software Incompatibility-based barriers to entry are a prime source of Microsoft's riches. Imagine that you own a personal computer running on Microsoft's operating system. You also have 100 video games for your computer. Suddenly, Google comes out with a superior operating system. Unfortunately, none of your video games will run on Google's operating system. So if you abandon Microsoft's operating system, you will also have to abandon all your games. The incompatibility of old software with a non-Microsoft operating system provides a barrier to entry into the operating system market.

Now imagine you're a freelance journalist who writes articles from home and then e-mails them to magazines. You have been writing your articles in Microsoft Word, the

249

most popular word processing program in the English-speaking world. Because Microsoft Word is so popular, you know that all the magazines you write for will be able to open and edit your Microsoft Word documents.

Recently, however, you found a superior word processing program called MacroWord. Unfortunately, MacroWord is incompatible with Microsoft Word. So, if you sent in a MacroWord file to a magazine, they wouldn't be able to open it unless they had the MacroWord program. Magazines, however, don't bother buying MacroWord because they know that all their writers use Microsoft Word. Everyone uses Microsoft Word because it is the most popular program, not necessarily because it is the best. If documents produced in other word processing programs were compatible with Microsoft Word, then you could risk using another program, but incompatibility provides Microsoft Word with a powerful barrier to entry into the word processing market.

Individuals continually share computer files. So you would only want to buy MacroWord if you knew that many other people had MacroWord and could read MacroWord documents. MacroWord, therefore, faces a popularity trap: No one will buy it because it's not popular, but it will not be popular until many people buy it.

For many types of computer software, individuals want to use the same software as their friends and associates so they can easily share information. Popularity provides a powerful entry barrier for this type of software because few users would want to switch to a new (and thereby not yet popular) program.

Sports Leagues
Pretend that after college you and a few very rich friends decide to create your own baseball team. First you attempt to get Major League Baseball (MLB) to accept your team into their league, but they refuse. You decide to build your team anyway. Unfortunately, even though you put together a team of world-class athletes, you have no one to play against. In a sense your team is incompatible with other teams because MLB won't let you play against their teams. The only way, therefore, you could compete economically against MLB is to create at least 10 teams that could play against each other. Since it's much harder to create 10 teams than 1, incompatibility provides a strong barrier to entry, protecting all professional sports leagues.

5. ECONOMIES OF SCALE

Economies of scale can also protect monopolies from competition. Consider an industry that has the continually decreasing average total costs shown in Figure 10.1. Assume that a monopolist currently dominates this market. If a new firm were to enter this industry, it would initially have much lower sales than the monopolist. Because in this industry average total costs decrease as output decreases, the new firm's costs would be extremely high compared to the monopolist's costs.

In a market with economies of scale, once one firm attracts most of the customers it will, by definition, have very low average total costs compared to other firms. Consequently, in industries with significant economies of scale, it's difficult for a new firm to challenge a monopoly. Monopolies based on economies of scale are called *natural monopolies.*

Utility companies that sell water or electricity are often natural monopolies. Water and electric companies must build, respectively, a network of water pipes and electrical lines to every home in a town. These networks represent enormous fixed/sunk costs. Once the networks have been built, the marginal costs of providing water and power are constant. As we saw in Chapter 8, high fixed costs combined with constant marginal

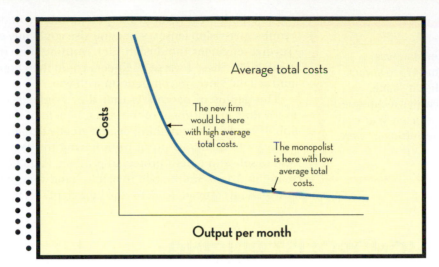

FIGURE **10.1**

CONTINUALLY
DECREASING
AVERAGE TOTAL
COSTS

costs create continually decreasing average total costs, thereby causing an industry to have economies of scale.

The telephone industry used to be a monopoly protected by economies of scale. But cellular technology has dug a hole through the landline phone industries' protective entry barrier. Analogous to water and electric utilities, landline telephone companies need to build a network of phone lines to each home. The huge sunk costs of building such a phone network used to protect telephone companies from competition. But cellular technology has allowed wireless phone carriers to connect with customers without building expensive landline networks themselves.

6. INTELLECTUAL PROPERTY

You own the physical property of MonopolySki. This means that you have the legal right to charge a fee to anyone who wants to use MonopolySki's slopes. One can own intellectual as well as physical property. If you own intellectual property, you also have the legal right to demand payment from all who would use your property. The two most common forms of intellectual property are copyrights and patents.

Copyrights   Writers automatically receive copyrights on their creations. No one but the copyright's holder can legally sell the copyright-protected work. Copyrights, therefore, grant writers monopolies on their books. Of course, just as this book competes with other introductory microeconomics texts, copyright-protected authors must still compete with other writers.

Without copyrights, few textbooks would ever get published. For example, assume that the marginal cost of making another copy of this textbook is $20. Absent copyrights, competition would drive the price of this textbook down to $20. If, for example, the price were $30, someone could make a positive profit copying the book for $20 and then selling it for $30. Such copying would push the price to $20. Without copyright protection, no publisher would have ever paid the considerable fixed costs needed to produce this textbook.

Patents   Patents are like copyrights for inventions. If, for example, you developed the super-vision contact lenses discussed in Chapter 6, you would hopefully get a patent on the lenses. This patent would give you the exclusive right, for around 20 years, to sell the lenses. Without the patent, once you developed your super-vision lenses, someone else could buy a pair and reverse-engineer the design, determining how the lenses were built. These reverse engineers could then manufacture and sell the lenses in competition with you.

The genius of patents is that they confer a benefit on innovators proportional to the social benefit of their innovation. If you invent something people greatly demand, you will receive a tremendous profit from having the exclusive legal right to sell your patent-protected product. Patents, therefore, create an Adam-Smith-style invisible hand that pushes self-interested inventors to work for the benefit of society.

MONOPOLIST PRICING

So far in this chapter we have learned that monopolies can earn long-term positive profits if they erect protective barriers to entry. Now we will consider how monopolies set prices to maximize these profits.

Monopolists, unlike firms in perfect competition, set their own prices. But don't think that a monopolist can sell as much as it wants for whatever price it wants. The Law of Demand constrains even a monopolist's price-setting powers. A monopolist can choose price, but once the price has been set, the demand curve determines how much consumers buy. If a monopolist wants to increase sales, it must, by the Law of Demand, lower price.

A monopolist that lowers its price to attract new customers gives a discount to its old customers. For example, assume that MonopolySki charges a very high price and consequently attracts only hardcore skiers. You decide, however, that you want to attract casual skiers, but unfortunately realize that if you set a price low enough to draw in casual skiers, you will also have to charge this low price to your hardcore customers.

Consider another simple example:

Customer	Most Willing to Pay for the Monopolist's Product
Jim	$50
Debbie	30

If the monopolist wants to sell to only Jim, it will charge him $50. (Jim won't pay more than $50 and the monopolist would be throwing away money if it sold to Jim for less than $50.) But now imagine that the monopolist wants to sell to both Jim and Debbie. Since Debbie will pay at most $30, if the monopolist wants to sell to her, it must lower its price from $50 to $30. But after it lowers the price, Jim will pay $30 as well. Consequently, to sell to Debbie, the monopolist must give Jim a $20 discount.

A firm in perfect competition doesn't have to give discounts to old customers to attract new customers. In perfect competition all firms are price takers and face the same prices regardless of how much they sell. So if a firm in perfect competition had been selling a single good for $50 and expands output to two, it could sell this second good for $50 as well. In contrast, a monopolist's output does influence the market price. So when a monopolist expands output, it must charge lower prices to all customers.

MARGINAL REVENUE AND MONOPOLIST PRICING

Marginal revenue is the increase in total revenue a firm receives by selling one more good. For a firm in perfect competition, marginal revenue always equals price. Assume, for example, that the price of a good in a perfectly competitive market is $50. If a perfectly competitive firm sells another good, its total revenue increases by $50. This is because firms in perfect competition are, by assumption, price takers. So no matter how many goods a firm in perfect competition sells, the price will always remain the same. Monopolists, by contrast, are not price takers. Consequently, price does not equal marginal revenue for monopolists.

> Marginal revenue is the increase in total revenue a firm receives by selling one more good.

For a firm in perfect competition:　　Marginal revenue = Price
For a monopolist:　　Marginal revenue ≠ Price

Consider again the monopolist who can sell to only Jim and Debbie. If it sells one good, its marginal revenue is $50. But when it sells the second good, it gets $30 from Debbie but must also give Jim a $20 discount. Consequently, the marginal revenue the monopolist receives from selling its second good is only $10. Another way to calculate the marginal revenue from selling the second good is to note that if the monopolist sells one good it will get a total revenue of $50, but if it sells two goods it will charge $30 for each of them and receive a total revenue of $60. Thus the marginal revenue from selling the second good is $60 − $50 = $10.

The following table calculates the marginal revenue for a monopolist that has eight potential customers.

Customer	Most Willing to Pay	Total Revenue	Marginal Revenue of Selling to This Customer
A	$100	$100	$100
B	90	90(2) = 180	180 − 100 or 90 − 10(1) = 80
C	80	80(3) = 240	240 − 180 or 80 − 10(2) = 60
D	70	70(4) = 280	280 − 240 or 70 − 10(3) = 40
E	60	60(5) = 300	300 − 280 or 60 − 10(4) = 20
F	50	50(6) = 300	300 − 300 or 50 − 10(5) = 0
G	40	40(7) = 280	280 − 300 or 40 − 10(6) = −20
H	1	1(8) = 8	8 − 280 or 1 − 39(7) = −272

If the monopolist were to sell only one good, it would obviously sell to the customer willing to pay the most and thus sell to person A for $100. Similarly, if the monopolist were to sell to five people, it would choose to sell to A, B, C, D, and E and charge $60— the highest price that will attract five customers.

The marginal revenue of selling another good equals the good's price minus the sum of the discounts that must be given to old customers. For example, if the monopolist goes from selling five to six goods, it will have to lower its price from $60 to $50. Consequently, the marginal revenue the monopolist receives from selling its sixth good is the $50 the monopolist receives from its sixth customer minus the $10 discount it must give to each of the old five customers. Therefore, the monopolist receives zero marginal revenue from selling its sixth good, meaning that the monopolist receives exactly as much revenue from selling five as six goods.

PROFIT IS MAXIMIZED WHEN MARGINAL REVENUE = MARGINAL COST

A monopolist, similar to a firm in perfect competition, will keep producing more goods as long as its marginal revenue is greater than its marginal cost. Marginal revenue is what you get if you sell another good. Marginal cost is what you pay if you sell an additional good. Consequently:

If Marginal revenue > Marginal cost, the firm increases its profit by producing more.

If Marginal revenue < Marginal cost, the firm increases its profit by producing less.

THE MATH BEHIND MARGINAL REVENUE = MARGINAL COST

(Skip this if you don't know calculus.)

For those of you who know calculus, it is easy to show why all firms set price so that marginal revenue equals marginal cost. A firm's goal is to maximize profit, meaning the firm wants to maximize:

Total revenue − Total cost

The calculus first order conditions for maximization require that you set the derivative of profit equal to zero. Consequently, a necessary condition for a firm to maximize profit is that the derivative of total revenue minus the derivative of total cost equals zero.

Marginal revenue tells you how total revenue changes as output changes. Marginal revenue, therefore, is the derivative of total revenue with respect to output. Marginal cost tells you how total cost changes as output changes, so marginal cost is the derivative of total cost with respect to output. Consequently, the first order profit maximization condition for all firms is:

Marginal revenue − Marginal cost = 0, or Marginal revenue = Marginal cost

A monopolist, therefore, will set output so that marginal revenue equals marginal cost. At any other output the monopolist would benefit from increasing or decreasing its output.

Figure 10.2 shows a demand curve, marginal cost curve, and marginal revenue curve for a monopolist.* The monopolist will set output so that marginal revenue

---

*Don't worry about how the marginal revenue curve is graphically derived from the demand curve.

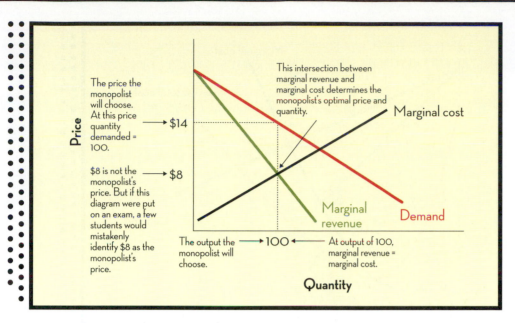

The price the monopolist will choose. At this price quantity demanded = 100.

$8 is not the monopolist's price. But if this diagram were put on an exam, a few students would mistakenly identify $8 as the monopolist's price.

$14

$8

This intersection between marginal revenue and marginal cost determines the monopolist's optimal price and quantity.

Marginal cost

Marginal revenue

Demand

The output the monopolist will choose.

100

At output of 100, marginal revenue = marginal cost.

Price

Quantity

equals marginal cost. In Figure 10.2 this profit-maximizing level of output is 100. The monopolist will then use the demand curve to determine what price it must charge if it sells 100 goods. In Figure 10.2 this price is $14.

THE SOCIAL COST OF MONOPOLIES
MONOPOLISTS DON'T PRODUCE AT THE LOWEST POSSIBLE AVERAGE TOTAL COST

Recall that in the long run in perfect competition, firms are driven to produce at the low point on their average total cost curves, as shown in Figure 10.3. Thus, in the long run, society gets goods produced at the lowest possible cost in perfect competition. Nothing, however, pushes monopolies toward the low point on their average total cost curves. Figure 10.4 shows a hypothetical monopolist's average total costs.

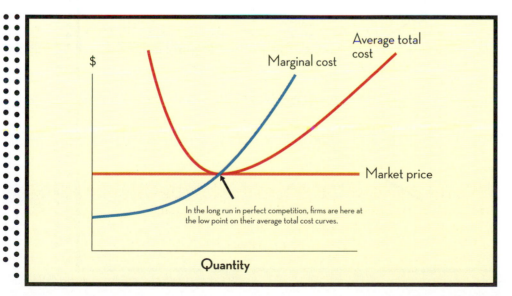

FIGURE **10.3**

LOW POINT ON AVERAGE TOTAL COST CURVES

$

Average total cost

Marginal cost

Market price

In the long run in perfect competition, firms are here at the low point on their average total cost curves.

Quantity

255

FIGURE **10.4**

A MONOPOLIST'S
AVERAGE TOTAL
COST

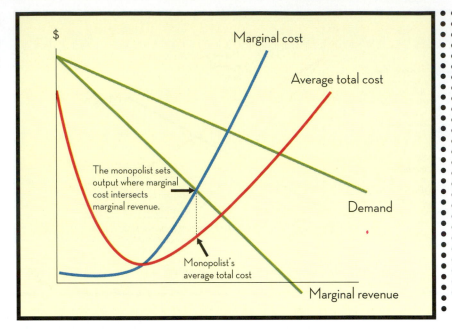

DEADWEIGHT LOSS OF THE MONOPOLIST

The primary social cost of monopolists is that they usually produce output below the level that maximizes the wealth of society. Monopolies often underproduce because of the discount they must give to old customers to attract new ones.

In Figure 10.5 the monopolist will produce output of 100 because this is the level of output at which marginal revenue equals marginal cost. But the socially optimal level of output—the level that maximizes the wealth of society—in Figure 10.5 is 150.

FIGURE **10.5**

SOCIALLY OPTIMAL
LEVEL OF OUTPUT

The monopolist will
produce output of 100.
The socially optimal
level of output is 150.

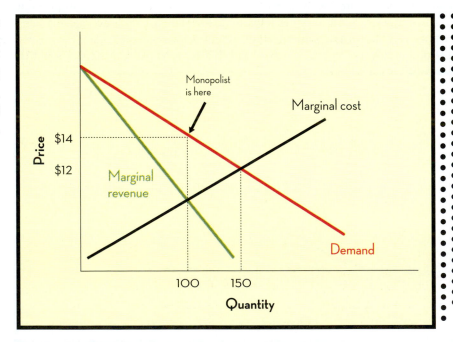

The demand curve shows the benefit of producing a good, while the marginal cost curve gives the cost of producing a good. As long as demand is above marginal cost, society is wealthier if another good is produced. Society's wealth, therefore, is maximized if production takes place at the point at which marginal cost equals demand, which in Figure 10.5 is 150. (Review Chapter 6 if you don't understand this paragraph.)

The monopolist will produce until: Marginal cost = Marginal revenue

The wealth maximizing level of
output is where: Marginal cost = Demand

In Figure 10.5 the monopolist charges $14 and gets 100 customers. To attract another 50 customers, the monopolist would have to lower its price to $12. The monopolist would make a profit selling to customers 101–150 at a price of $12. But to attract these extra 50 customers, the monopolist would have to give a $2 discount to each of its original 100 customers. This discount is a money transfer. Recall from Chapter 6 that money transfers have no effect on the wealth of society. But the monopolist, who cares about its own wealth, not the wealth of society, wants to avoid making this money transfer and so will not sell to customers 101–150.

Imagine that the following will happen if the monopolist decreases its price:

A. **The monopolist gives $200 to consumers.** (One hundred old customers will each get a $2 discount, reducing the monopolist's total revenue by $200. This discount decreases the monopolist's profit by $200 but increases the total consumers' surplus by $200.)

B. **The monopolist creates, say, $80 of extra wealth and keeps, say, one-half of it.** (Lowering the price to $12 will cause additional people to buy the good. These people will value the good at an amount greater than the marginal cost of producing the good. Consequently, selling additional goods creates wealth.)

Based on (A) and (B), the monopolist won't decrease price because doing so reduces its profit by $160 ($200 − $40). But the price decrease would increase the wealth of society.

Fact (A) represents a money transfer that has no effect on the wealth of society. But Fact (B) causes the wealth of society to increase by $80. Society's wealth, therefore, would increase if the monopolist lowered its price from $14 to $12. But to prevent the money transfer in (A) from occurring, the monopolist is willing to prevent the wealth creation in (B) from ever taking place.

Basically, the monopolist is given a choice between having most of a small pie or having half of a large pie, and the monopolist chooses the former. The monopolist gets more pie with the first option but society, obviously, has more pie with the second. Consequently, by serving its own self-interests the monopolist does not act in the best interest of society. This doesn't mean that the monopolist is evil. Rather, it, like most everyone else, is self-interested. But unfortunately Adam Smith's invisible hand breaks down here and doesn't cause our self-interested monopolist to set prices that maximize the wealth of society.

Graphically Showing the Monopolist's Deadweight Loss

Figure 10.6 shows the total consumers' and producer's surplus if the monopolist, hypothetically, produced the socially optimal level of output of 150. Recall that under perfect competition this socially optimal level of output is produced. Figure 10.7 shows the consumers' and producer's surplus for the 100 units of output that the monopolist will actually choose.

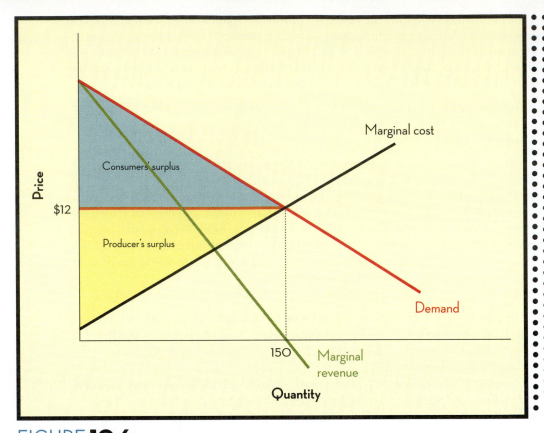

FIGURE **10.6**

CONSUMERS' AND PRODUCER'S SURPLUS AT 150 UNITS OF OUTPUT

This diagram shows the producer's and consumers' surplus if the monopolist produces 150 units. The monopolist, however, will not produce this much output.

The consumers' surplus at output 100 is lower than it is at output 150 for two reasons:

1. The consumers who buy the good at both levels of output pay a higher price if the monopolist sells only 100 goods.
2. If the monopolist sells only 100 goods, then the consumers who would have bought goods 101–150 don't receive any consumers' surplus.

Although it might not be apparent from the diagram, the producer's surplus is higher in Figure 10.7 than Figure 10.6. When the monopolist reduces output from 150 to 100, it gains producer's surplus because it can charge more for the first 100 goods. It loses producer's surplus, however, because it no longer sells goods 101 to 150. The benefit to the monopolist from the price increase, however, more than compensates for the loss the monopolist incurs from not selling the additional goods.

Selling only 100 goods creates a deadweight loss. If you compare the surpluses in Figures 10.6 and 10.7, you see that much of the lost consumers' surplus in Figure 10.6 goes to the monopolist. But some of it becomes part of the deadweight loss. The deadweight loss occurs because, if the monopolist is selling only 100 goods, it is not producing output for which the demand curve is above the marginal cost curve.

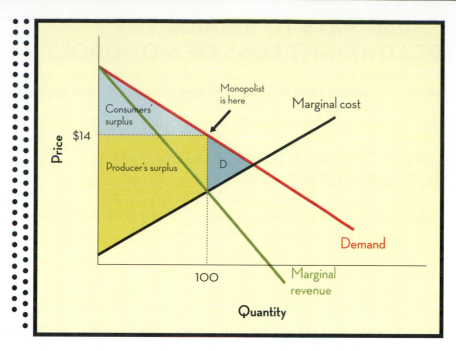

FIGURE **10.7**

CONSUMERS' AND
PRODUCER'S
SURPLUS AT 100
UNITS OF OUTPUT

D = Deadweight loss
of the monopolist

Figure 10.8 illuminates why the monopolist causes a deadweight loss. As Figure 10.8 shows, the marginal cost of producing the 120th good is $11. But a consumer would value the good at $13. Thus, the value of the 120th good to consumers is greater than the extra cost of making this good. Consequently, the wealth of society would be higher if the 120th good were produced. So why doesn't the monopolist produce this good?

As Figure 10.7 showed, the monopolist maximizes its profit by charging $14. At a price of $14, consumers don't want to buy the 120th good because they value this good at only $13. So the monopolist could sell the 120th good only by lowering its price from $14 to $13. But since the monopolist maximizes its profit charging $14, it won't do this.

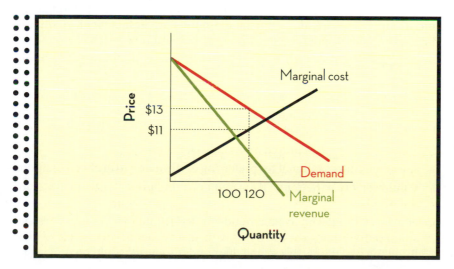

FIGURE **10.8**

MONOPOLIST
CAUSES A
DEADWEIGHT LOSS

Consumers value the
120th good at $13. It
would cost the
monopolist an extra $11
to produce the 120th
good.

THREE WAYS TO REDUCE THE DEADWEIGHT LOSS OF MONOPOLY

A monopolist will tend to create a deadweight loss by producing less than the wealth-maximizing level of output. We now consider three ways by which this deadweight loss might be reduced: competition, price discrimination, and antitrust laws.

1. HOW COMPETITION REDUCES THE HARM OF MONOPOLY

The best cure for the deadweight loss of monopoly is competition. As the following examples show, profit-seeking businesspeople will continually attempt to break through entry barriers protecting profitable monopolistic markets:

- The U.S. Post Office's monopoly has been eroded by faxes, e-mail, and overnight delivery companies such as Federal Express.
- Microsoft's near-monopoly on operating systems is being challenged by the open source operating system Linux. (We will discuss Linux further in Chapter 14.)
- Cable television's monopoly in many cities has been ended by satellite television. And even if you will always stick with cable, you benefit from the existence of satellite television. This is because competition from satellite providers has forced cable firms to improve service while lowering price.
- DeBeers' near-monopoly on diamonds has been damaged by the creation of artificial diamonds. Although man-made diamonds don't yet substitute for earth-diamonds in jewelry, artificial diamonds have replaced their more expensive earth-made look-alikes in industrial applications.

Competition lowers prices and expands output, thereby reducing deadweight losses.

. . . .

A DIAMOND ASIDE

Manufactured diamonds and earth-created diamonds can be distinguished only by microscope. To a chemist, artificial diamonds are in fact "real" diamonds because they have the molecular carbon structure of diamonds. Yet the price of artificial diamonds is much lower than the price of earth-made diamonds. The market for diamonds confuses me and here are five questions I have about it:

1. Why are consumers willing to pay so much more for earth-created diamonds than for artificial diamonds?
2. Is the high price of earth-created diamonds just the result of extremely effective advertising by the diamond monopoly DeBeers?
3. Are consumers irrational for preferring earth-made to artificial diamonds?
4. Would society be better off if consumers didn't prefer earth-made to artificial diamonds?
5. For those of you who like diamond jewelry, would you have more respect for a suitor if the suitor gave you a ring with an artificial or earth-created diamond? By giving you the earth-created diamond the suitor would be proving his/her

generosity. But by giving you an artificial diamond would the suitor be proving his/her intelligence?

If you think that earth-created diamonds have some inherent romantic essence lacking in artificial diamonds, please do an Internet search on "conflict diamonds."

* *

Potential Competition   Even the mere threat of competition can induce a monopolist to expand output, thereby reducing deadweight loss. For example, imagine that MonopolySki is considering charging a very high price and serving only hardcore skiers. This would leave a large market opening for a resort to serve casual skiers. MonopolySki, therefore, might want to attract casual skiers just to prevent another resort from doing so, especially since after attracting casual skiers the new resort could then expand to serve hardcore skiers.

Analogously, consider a dog named Tova who lives in a fenced-in yard. Tova is extremely well-fed. In fact, Tova is given so much food that much of it lies in her yard uneaten. Seeing this uneaten food going to waste, other dogs desperately try to get into Tova's yard by digging under the fence. Even if she isn't hungry, therefore, Tova might be wise to eat all of the food in her yard so that the food doesn't draw other animals into her domain.

Whenever a monopolist creates deadweight loss, it necessarily does not sell to customers who could be profitably served. A monopolist that creates deadweight loss, therefore, is essentially leaving uneaten food in its yard that other firms would like to consume. The more such customers go unserved, the more tempting it is for firms to try to scale the barriers to entry to compete with the monopolist. To prevent entry, consequently, a monopolist facing potential competition might set a lower price and sell to more customers than it would in the absence of potential competition.

2. HOW PRICE DISCRIMINATION REDUCES THE HARM OF MONOPOLIES

Remember that a monopolist causes a deadweight loss because it produces too little output. It produces too little output because it must give a discount to old customers to sell to new customers. Price discrimination, however, provides monopolists with a profitable escape from their discounting dilemma.

Price discrimination occurs when a firm charges separate customers different prices. So, for example, because airlines frequently price discriminate, you could pay $400 for an airline seat while the person sitting next you might have paid only $150. With price discrimination, a firm can charge its old customers high prices but still attract new customers by selling to them at low prices.

Normally, most people think discrimination is evil. But for economists, price discrimination is beneficial because it increases the wealth of society. For example, consider a monopolist facing two potential customers.

Customer	Most Willing to Pay
Tom	$1,000
Kelly	6

Assume further that the marginal cost of making each good is only $1. If the monopolist couldn't price discriminate, it would never sell to Kelly, because to sell to Kelly it would have to charge Tom only $6. Not selling the good to Kelly creates a deadweight loss because Kelly values the good at $6 although the good costs only $1 to make. So preventing Kelly from having the good prevents $5 of wealth from being created. But if the monopolist could price discriminate, it could sell to Tom for $1,000 and Kelly for $6, thereby eliminating the deadweight loss that arises from not serving Kelly. If a monopolist *perfectly* price discriminates, then it completely eliminates the deadweight loss caused by its being a monopoly.

Perfect Price Discrimination   Under perfect price discrimination, the monopolist charges every customer the maximum that customer is willing to pay. So if a monopolist had the following four potential customers and the marginal cost of making each good was less than $70, then it would charge $100 to person A, $90 to person B, $80 to person C, and $70 to person D.

Customer	Most Willing to Pay
A	$100
B	90
C	80
D	70

Under perfect price discrimination, the total consumers' surplus becomes zero since each consumer pays exactly what the good is worth to him. Because the monopolist gets the entire surplus from the transaction, the monopolist makes this surplus as large as possible and so maximizes the wealth of society. The monopolist maximizes this surplus by selling to all consumers who value the good more than the marginal cost of making the good.

Perfect price discrimination is easy: just ask each customer, "What is the most you would pay for my product?" You then charge each customer his answered amount. OK, I was just kidding. Customers would never play along with such a game as they would tell you that the good is worth little to them even if it wasn't.

Imperfect Price Discrimination   Perfect price discrimination is nearly impossible to achieve. Monopolists, however, can imperfectly price discriminate by separating customers into groups and then charging separate groups different amounts.

For example, hardcore skiers are probably willing to pay MonopolySki more than casual skiers. Furthermore, hardcore skiers will likely be the only ones who want to ski more than six hours a day. So MonopolySki could sell two types of passes, one that allows customers to ski for up to six hours a day and another that allows skiing 24 hours a day. The 24-hour pass would naturally cost more.

When a monopolist can only imperfectly price discriminate, it mitigates, but doesn't eliminate, the deadweight loss caused by monopoly. For example, imagine that the following people are potential movie theater customers.

Customer	Most Willing to Pay	Student?
A	$10	No
B	10	No
C	10	No
D	10	No
E	10	No
F	10	No
G	6	No
H	6	Yes
I	6	Yes

Assume that the marginal cost of having another person in a movie theater is zero. If this monopolist theater couldn't price discriminate, it would charge $10 a ticket and sell to only customers A, B, C, D, E, and F. But since the marginal cost of allowing another person to sit in the theater is zero, not selling tickets to G, H, and I creates a deadweight loss. If the monopolist could perfectly price discriminate, it would sell to all nine customers for the most each was willing to pay, but such perfect price discrimination is likely impossible.

What the monopolist could do, however, is sell tickets for $10 but give a $4 discount to those with student IDs. If the monopolist is confident that students are willing to pay less for its movies, then this type of price discrimination would increase the monopolist's profits. Of course, such price discrimination in this example will still create a deadweight loss since Customer G is not a student but still values the movie at only $6.

My local theater price discriminates by charging students a lower price than other customers. I have gotten this lower price, however, by asking for a student ticket and then showing my college faculty ID, which is almost identical to student ID cards. Have I acted immorally?

The Challenge of Price Discrimination
To profitably price discriminate for and against different groups, a monopolist must overcome three challenges:

1. It must roughly determine the value each group places on the monopolist's product.
2. It must figure out how to sell to separate groups at different prices.
3. It must prevent customers who paid a low price from reselling the good to those customers who paid a high price.

Let's examine how monopolists attempt to overcome these challenges in different industries.

Further Examples of Price Discrimination *Al Gore's Mom and Her Dog*
During his unsuccessful 2000 United States presidential campaign, Al Gore told a great price discrimination story. The story, alas, turned out to be fiction, but it was economically plausible. Gore claimed that his mom and her dog took the exact same arthritis medication but that his mom paid a much higher price.[11]

Imagine that you own a pharmaceutical company that has a patent on arthritis medication that could help both dogs and humans. The marginal cost of making each pill is only $1. Human arthritis sufferers will pay up to $10 a pill, whereas dog owners will only pay up to $3 a pill. If you can't price discriminate, you would probably just sell to humans for $10 a pill. But if you can discriminate, you will sell a $10 pill to humans and a $3 pill to dogs.

Of course, under your price discrimination scheme, some enterprising individual would adopt many arthritic dogs. He would then take each dog to several veterinarians, accumulating a huge number of dog arthritis prescriptions. Finally, he would buy many of the "dog" arthritis pills for $3 each and resell them to humans for a bit less than $10 a pill. To prevent this resale, the pharmaceutical company could coat its "dog" pills with something that tastes horrible to humans but is inoffensive to dogs.

RAPHAEL'S *THE SCHOOL OF ATHENS*

Price Discrimination by Raphael[12] The Italian Renaissance artist Raphael (1483–1520) engaged in price discrimination. As an artist fortunate enough to be famous in his own time, he charged high prices for his paintings. To maximize his income, however, Raphael wanted to sell art to members of the middle class. He faced the traditional monopolist dilemma, though. If Raphael charged a high price, he could sell only to the rich. But if he charged a moderate enough price to attract middle-class customers, he wouldn't get huge amounts of money from the rich.

To overcome his dilemma, Raphael had a less famous artist make copies of his work. He sold these copies for a much lower price than his original artwork. As a consequence, the rich paid big bucks for the originals and the middle class paid more moderate prices for the copies. Through price discrimination, therefore, Raphael found it profitable to increase his output well beyond what he would have done if he had to charge all customers the same price.

Financial Aid Colleges often price discriminate with tuition. At many expensive colleges only about one-half of the students pay the full cost of tuition; the rest get some financial aid. When colleges, through financial aid programs, charge different students separate prices, they price discriminate.

Colleges give most of their financial aid to relatively less affluent students. Colleges claim that they help their poorest students because it's the fair thing to do. Economists, however, become suspicious whenever an organization claims to be acting fairly. Instead, many believe that organizations usually act in their own self-interest and label whatever actions coincide with this self-interest as "fair." So let's consider why colleges find it in their self-interest to give the most financial aid to relatively poor students.

Colleges compete for students and selectively deploy financial aid to lure desirable students. Whenever a college gives financial aid to a group of students, it lowers the price paid by these students and so, by the Law of Demand, increases the number of students in this group who will attend the college. The poorer a student is, the more weight he will likely give financing when deciding what college to attend. So because poorer students have a greater price elasticity of demand than richer students do, offering the same amount of financial aid to the same size group of poor and rich students will cause more of the poor students to attend.

For example, assume that both Richie Rich and Oliver Twist have been accepted to Adam Smith University and the university desperately wants both of these highly-intelligent boys to attend. Richie Rich is extremely rich while Oliver Twist is desperately poor. Richie Rich may or may not end up going to Adam Smith University, but his decision will not be affected by his financial aid package. In contrast, Oliver Twist is far more likely to attend the university if he is given a substantial amount of financial aid. The university, therefore, should give none of its limited financial aid to Richie Rich but give Oliver Twist a generous aid package.

The college is not giving more money to Oliver than Richie because it wants to help the poor. Rather the college is giving its limited financial aid to the student with the greatest price elasticity of demand, and the poorer a student is, the greater is his price elasticity of demand for college.

Colleges can price discriminate far more easily than businesses. If a bookstore tried setting higher prices for lawyers than for economists, the economists would simply buy the books for the lawyers. When a college offers one student a substantial amount of financial aid, however, the student can't give her aid package to someone else. Furthermore, colleges require students to submit financial information such as their parents' tax returns, allowing the schools to determine whom they can charge the most. Since businesses rarely have access to their customers' tax forms, firms must devise alternate means of determining which customers should receive discounts.

Self-Selection, Price Discrimination, and Greek Mythology[13]   Many businesses price discriminate through customer self-selection. Before we analyze this, let's consider a story from Greek mythology that uses self-selection:

Odysseus was one of many suitors for Helen, the most beautiful mortal woman in the world. To avoid conflict, the suitors of Helen agreed that she would pick her husband, and they would all support her choice and protect the rights of the man she chose. Helen did not choose Odysseus, but Odysseus had still sworn an oath to protect her.

After she got married, the Trojans kidnapped Helen from Greece. Helen's husband demanded that the men who had sworn an oath to protect his rights join him in a war against Troy. Odysseus did not want to keep his oath, however, for he was now happily married, had an infant son, and had been told by an oracle that if he fought, he would not return home for 20 years.

When the Greeks came for him, Odysseus tried to dodge the draft by acting insane: he plowed his fields randomly. Since an insane Odysseus would be useless to their cause, almost all of the Greeks were ready to abandon Odysseus to his strange farming practices. But one Greek, Palamedes, suspected that Odysseus was faking. Palamedes, however, still needed to prove that Odysseus was sane, so he took Odysseus' infant son and put him in front of the plow. Had Odysseus continued to plow, he would have killed his son. If Odysseus really had been insane, he would not have noticed or cared about his son's position and would therefore have killed him. Since Odysseus was rational, however, he stopped plowing and thus revealed his sanity.

Palamedes had made it very costly for Odysseus to continue to act insane. By increasing the cost to Odysseus of lying, Palamedes was able to change Odysseus' behavior, forcing him to reveal his previous dishonesty and join the Greek military expedition to Troy. Although the Greeks did conquer the Trojans, unfortunately the oracle was right and it was 20 years before Odysseus returned to his wife and son.

To summarize the economically important parts of this myth: there were two types of Odysseus, sane and crazy. By placing the baby in front of the plow, Palamedes ensured that a sane Odysseus and a crazy Odysseus would take different visible actions. Palamedes used a *self-selection* mechanism to get Odysseus to voluntarily reveal his type.

Self-Selection of Customers

Businesses often use self-selection to induce different groups of customers to take different visible actions. By inducing customers to voluntarily self-select into separate groups, businesses can enhance their profits through price discrimination.

Coupons Coupons are a brilliant means of getting customers to self-select into two groups: (1) price-sensitive customers and (2) price-insensitive customers. Superficially, coupons seem silly. In return for slowing down the checkout line and turning in some pieces of paper, you get a discount. Coupons, however, effectively separate customers and give discounts to the price sensitive.

Coupons allow customers to trade time for money. To use a coupon you must usually go to the effort of finding, clipping, and holding a small piece of paper. Coupons therefore appeal most to those who place a low monetary value on their time. Coupon users are consequently the customers most likely to shop around to find the best prices and so are exactly the type of people companies most like to give discounts to. In contrast, shoppers who don't use coupons are probably not as price conscious, and companies can safely charge these people more, confident that their high prices won't cost them too much in sales.

Let's now consider a coupon-centered reimagining of the Odysseus myth. Odysseus went to his local supermarket and demanded price reductions. Odysseus pretended to be a discount shopper. He told the supermarket that if it didn't offer him a discount, he would go on a long, epic journey to find one that did. The supermarket's manager believed Odysseus and so started offering him a 15 percent discount on all items to keep Odysseus from traveling to another store. Assistant Manager Palamedes, however, sensed that Odysseus was lying. Palamedes believed that Odysseus was an extremely busy man who would never take the time to travel to a far away supermarket just to save 15 percent on his groceries. But how could Palamedes, a mere assistant manager, convince the supermarket that Odysseus was lying?

Palamedes told the manager to hold off on the discount but instead place 15 percent off coupons in Odysseus' local paper. Palamedes knew it would take Odysseus considerable time to find and cut out these coupons. Odysseus now had a choice. If he really were the type that would travel to a distant supermarket to save 15 percent, then he would surely take the time to clip coupons. But since Odysseus was the type that was extremely busy, he would not go to the trouble of cutting the coupons to save a mere 15 percent. When presented with the coupon plan the busy Odysseus was forced to reveal his true type and so had to pay full price.

Airlines Airlines rely upon self-selection to price discriminate. It's usually much cheaper to fly if you stay over a weekend. But business travelers generally don't want to spend weekends away from home. Therefore, by giving discounts to those who do stay over a weekend, airlines effectively charge business customers more than other travelers. Business travelers usually have more fixed schedules than other airline customers; consequently they are, on average, less price sensitive. So airlines increase their profits by charging business travelers more than other flyers.

Ideally, the airlines would like to verify independently whether a passenger is flying for business or pleasure and charge the ones traveling for business more, but, of course, if they attempted this, business travelers would hide their true purpose. The airlines therefore have to rely upon self-selection and assume that most travelers staying over a weekend are not flying for business.

THEY PROBABLY PAID VERY DIFFERENT PRICES FOR THEIR SEATS.

Price Discrimination through Impatience Book publishers get buyers to self-select based on impatience. Books frequently come out in paperback about one year after they are first published in hardcover. Paperback books cost significantly less than hardcovers. Only a tiny bit of the difference comes from the extra cost of producing hardcovers. Publishers assume that customers who are most eager to buy a book are the ones willing to pay the most. Publishers make impatient customers, who are less price sensitive, buy expensive hardcover books and allow patient readers to acquire relatively inexpensive paperback copies.

Hollywood also uses impatience to price discriminate through self-selection. Movies usually first come out in theaters, then become available for video rental and pay-per-view-TV. Next they are shown on premium cable channels, and finally the movies are broadcast on free network TV. Customers who most want to see a movie, and are presumably willing to pay the most, see the film when it first comes out in the theater. More patient and more price-sensitive customers wait longer and pay less.

3. HOW ANTITRUST LAWS REDUCE THE HARM OF MONOPOLIES

So far we have considered how competition and price discrimination can reduce the deadweight loss of monopolies. The third method by which the loss can be reduced is antitrust law.

Antitrust laws regulate, restrict, and punish monopolies. They even prescribe prison terms for businesspeople attempting to create monopolies. Unlike competition and price discrimination, antitrust laws rely on the government, not the market, to reduce the harm of monopolies. We will consider antitrust laws more extensively in Chapter 11.

MONOPOLIES' INCENTIVE TO INNOVATE

In the last chapter we saw that firms in perfect competition have limited incentives to innovate because their innovations will be quickly copied. The opposite holds true for monopolies. When a monopoly innovates, it keeps most of the gains from its innovation because there is no one else in the market to copy its innovation.

Imagine that some innovation would save refrigerator manufacturers a total of $100 million. Assume that the innovation is not patentable. If there were just one monopoly refrigerator manufacturer, it would spend up to $100 million to develop this innovation. In contrast, if there were 100 refrigerator makers of equal size, then no one manufacturer would spend more than $1 million developing this innovation. So if the innovation costs $80 million, it would be created only if the market was monopolistic. When a monopolist innovates, there are no other firms in the market to share in the benefits. And because it doesn't have to share, monopolies get great monetary rewards from innovation. But is money everything?

INNOVATION, MONOPOLIES, AND LAZINESS: A MORE COMPLEX VIEW OF THE FIRM

So far this textbook has assumed that firms always seek to maximize their profits. Let's now take a more complex view of firms. Firms are run by people. These people have many objectives. Yes, they usually want their firms to make money. But they also don't want to work very hard. And they most definitely don't want to get fired.

Imagine that if the employees of some firm work extremely hard for one year, they will develop an innovation that significantly improves the quality of their firm's products. First let's assume that this firm is in a competitive market. The innovation will boost the firm's profits. But if this firm doesn't innovate, its competitors might. And in competitive markets, firms that fall behind often lose their customers and must fire their employees.

Now imagine that our firm is a profitable monopolist. The innovation will bring the monopolist higher profits. But if the monopolist doesn't innovate, it will still keep its old customers. Lack of innovation, therefore, won't cause the firm to fire its workers. The monopolist's employees, consequently, don't have the same personal incentives to work extremely hard developing the innovation as they would if their firm were in a competitive market.

Consider a studying analogy involving two students each with a 70 percent grade point average. Both attend a college where they lose all financial aid if their average goes below 70 percent. One student, Oliver Twist, is on financial aid and will have to drop out if his grade point average falls below 70 percent. The other student, Richie Rich, doesn't receive financial aid. Richie Rich probably won't work as hard as Oliver Twist because he has less to lose if his grade point average falls. Similarly, employees working for a monopoly protected by strong barriers to entry know that even if they are lazy their firm won't be kicked out of its market.

QUESTIONS YOU SHOULD BE ABLE TO ANSWER AFTER READING THIS CHAPTER:

1   When is a firm considered to have a monopoly? (page 246)

2   What are barriers to entry? (page 246)

3   Why are government-created barriers to entry so strong? (page 246)

4   Why do lawyers and teachers support strong professional licensing requirements? (page 247)

5   What effect does a religious monopoly have on clergy members' incentives to work hard? (page 248)

6   How can unions increase the salaries of their members? (pages 248–249)

7   What is the main weapon unions use against firms? (pages 248–249)

8   What are some examples of how control of a vital resource leads to monopoly? (page 249)

9   How can software incompatibility provide a barrier to entry? (page 249)

10 What is the popularity trap? (pages 249–250)

STUDY PROBLEMS

1 In Figure 10.9, graphically label (a) the price the monopolist will charge, (b) the amount the monopolist will sell, (c) the monopolist's total revenue, (d) the total consumers' surplus, (e) the total producers' surplus, and (f) the deadweight loss caused by the monopolist.

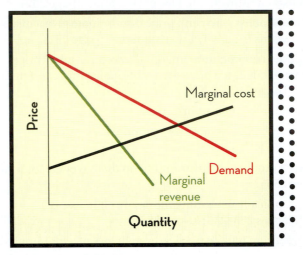

FIGURE **10.9**

2 Assume that all the players in some American sports league are U.S. citizens. Who would be more in favor of allowing players from all over the world to play in the league: the team owners or the players' union?

3 Imagine that the exact same AIDS drug is sold for $.50 a pill in Africa but $10 a pill in the United States. Why might a pharmaceutical company do this? If price discrimination were eliminated, would an American who regularly takes the pill pay a lower price? How would the pharmaceutical company react if Africans resold the pill to Americans?

4 What are some costs and benefits of reducing patent lengths from 20 to 10 years?

5 Imagine that the owner of a restaurant in Prague, frequented by foreign tourists, puts up a sign in Czech saying, "locals pay ½ of listed price." What assumptions is this owner making about the relative price elasticities of demand of foreign and Czech diners?

6 Assume that the following chart shows all eight potential customers of a movie theater. It costs the theater nothing to admit additional customers. The theater, therefore, maximizes its profit by maximizing its revenue.

Customer	Most Willing to Pay	Student?
A	$10	No
B	10	No
C	15	No
D	5	Yes
E	9	Yes
F	5	Yes
G	5	Yes
H	1	Yes

If this theater could perfectly price discriminate, what would be its total revenue? If this theater could charge two prices, one for students and the other for nonstudents, what would its total revenue be? If this theater could charge only one price, what would its total revenue be?

7 If a monopolist can perfectly price discriminate then marginal revenue equals price. Why?

8 Do consumers benefit from monopolistic price discrimination? Consider both perfect and imperfect price discrimination. Ignore the fact that many customers work for monopolies and own stock in monopolies.

9 Label the monopolist's profit in Figure 10.10.

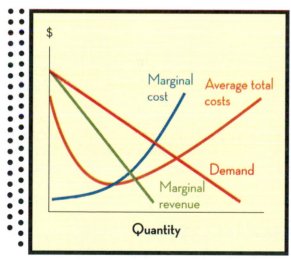

FIGURE **10.10**

> "PEOPLE OF THE SAME TRADE SELDOM MEET TOGETHER, EVEN FOR MERRIMENT AND DIVERSION, BUT THE CONVERSATION ENDS IN A CONSPIRACY AGAINST THE PUBLIC, OR IN SOME CONTRIVANCE TO RAISE PRICES."
>
> —Adam Smith, *The Wealth of Nations*

A MARKET EXAMPLE: OLIGO-RAZOR

You own Oligo-Razor. Oligo-Razor is a manufacturer in a fictionalized U.S. razor market. We'll pretend that there are four firms in this market. Economists would consider our make-believe razor market to be oligopolistic, meaning that it's in between a monopoly (where there is just one firm) and perfect competition (where there are a large number of firms).

Oligo-Razor makes little economic profit since it's in a pricing war with the other three razor firms. Customers consider all razors to be the same and so they buy the cheapest razor. So, all four razor manufacturers compete for customers just on price.

Oligopolistic markets—are in between a monopoly (where there is just one firm) and perfect competition (where there are a large number of firms).

Each firm charges $6 a razor. At this price you and all the other firms make only a small economic profit. Unfortunately, there is no other price you could set that would earn you higher profit. If you charged a lower price, you would initially increase sales (although you would earn less profit from each sale), but then your three rivals would quickly cut their prices to regain lost customers. If you charged a higher price, you would lose most of your customers to the other three firms. You scheme, therefore, to transform the razor market so that it will provide higher profits to Oligo-Razor.

ANTITRUST OBSTACLES

First you consider buying the other three razor manufacturers, but your lawyer laughs at this idea. Because you are such a large company, the U.S. Department of Justice's Antitrust Division would have to consent to your purchase of the other razor firms. Your lawyer explains that since the Antitrust Division tries to prevent monopolies from forming, it would never approve these purchases.

So you can't buy the other firms. But perhaps all four razor companies could come to an agreement to set higher prices. If the four companies charged $10 a razor, you could all make substantial economic profits. You therefore ask your lawyer

CHALLENGE TO MARKET EFFECTIVENESS 2: OLIGOPOLIES

LEARNING OBJECTIVES

AFTER READING THIS CHAPTER, YOU SHOULD BE ABLE TO:

- Explain the Prisoners' Dilemma.
- Discuss how oligopolies use product differentiation to escape the Prisoners' Dilemma.
- Identify oligopolies' incentives to innovate.
- Evaluate how antitrust laws affect oligopolies.

to write a letter to the other firms proposing that the four companies agree to sell razors for no less than $10 each. Your lawyer gags at this idea and says, "You're kidding, right? Please tell me you're just kidding." It seems that agreements among companies to raise prices violate antitrust laws. If your lawyer actually wrote such a letter, both of you would probably go to prison. So you tell your lawyer that of course you were just kidding. But then you ask him how you can legally get the other firms to raise their prices.

AN IMPLICIT AGREEMENT TO RAISE PRICES

Your lawyer explains that although the four razor firms can't legally come to a formal agreement to raise prices, it's perfectly legal for all four firms to just happen to raise prices at the same time. As long as the firms don't discuss or formally coordinate their price increases, no law would be broken if you all near-simultaneously raised prices.

You therefore decide to increase the price of your razors to $10 each. Unfortunately, none of the other firms increases its price, so after a week you lower your price to $4 a razor. You lose money at this low price since the average total cost of making a razor is greater than $4. But the other three firms also lose money when you charge only $4 a razor because they must now either charge a very low price themselves or lose most of their customers to you.

After charging $4 a razor for three weeks, you again increase your price to $10 per razor. This time the other three firms follow your lead and increase their prices to $10. Although you never talked with them, they figured out that if they didn't match your price increase, you would quickly lower your price again. By raising, lowering, and then raising your price, you sent a clear but legal signal to the other firms that you wanted them all to set a price of $10. Each razor firm makes higher profits if they all charge $10 rather than $6 per razor. Consequently, once the other firms figured out what you were asking of them, they eagerly went along with your implicit request for a joint price increase.

THE CHALLENGE OF MAINTAINING HIGH PRICES

Greed, unfortunately, makes it difficult for the four firms to keep charging high prices. When you all charge $6 a razor, each firm makes a low profit. When you all charge $10 per razor, each firm makes a high profit.

But if the other three firms charged $10 while you charged only $9 you would earn an *extremely* high profit. Remember that in this market customers care only about price and so will buy the cheapest razor. So if one firm charges a relatively high price of $9 per razor while the other firms charge even more, the initial firm will get most of the customers while still making a high profit on each razor. Alas, this means that each firm has an incentive to cheat by undercutting the implicit agreement.

Of course, if one firm cheated on the agreement by charging $9 per razor and the other firms found out, they would lower their prices to at least $9 and the cheating firm would lose its low-price advantage. But if one firm could cheat without the other three firms finding out, then the cheating firm would increase its profit. Let's see how such cheating might occur.

THE IMPLICIT-AGREEMENT FRAYS

An assistant manager at Oligo-Razor returns from her Maine vacation with some troubling news. One of your rivals is selling razors in a few small Maine towns for below $10. This rival was no doubt hoping that it could secretly cut prices in a few out-of-the-way areas. By selling razors in these towns for under $10, the rival captured most of the customers in these markets. And if the price cutting had stayed secret, none of the other razor firms would have lowered their prices in retaliation.

The next piece of bad news comes from the Pelham supermarket chain. Pelham had been buying all its razors for $10 each. (Pelham resells the razors to its customers for more than $10.) Pelham used to purchase some razors from each of the four razor firms. But last week Pelham started buying all its razors from just one of your rivals. You call the president of Pelham to ask why he stopped buying your razors. The president at first seems reluctant to answer your question but then confesses that another firm has been giving it a secret $2-per-razor discount. You feel betrayed by your price-cutting rival and so offer Pelham a $2.10 per razor discount. Pelham accepts the discount and resumes stocking its shelves with your razors. (Unknown to you, however, Pelham was never offered a discount by any of your rivals. The president of Pelham lied so you would give him a discount.)

You finally get some good news when your top salesman announces that he has won the exclusive contract to sell razors to the Deerfield supermarket chain. Deerfield will even pay $10 a razor. Your salesmen, however, confesses that he promised to give Deerfield a $3 per item discount on another good that Oligo-Razor sells. So while technically you are keeping to the implicit agreement to charge $10 a razor, you are effectively giving Deerfield a razor discount. Oh, well; as long as your rivals don't find out about this discount, they won't retaliate by lowering their prices.

WAL-MART'S ALWAYS LOW PRICES

The four razor firms sell more to Wal-Mart than to anyone else. Wal-Mart became extremely angry when you all raised the price of razors from $6 to $10. You figured, however, that since Wal-Mart had to sell razors in its stores, it couldn't hurt you if the four manufacturers kept to the implicit agreement of charging $10 per razor. But you made a mistake. Wal-Mart is by far the world's largest retailer. Wal-Mart likes low prices; it has unmatched retail market power, and it uses this power to obtain low prices.

Two months after you raise the price of razors, Wal-Mart summons you and representatives from the other three razor companies to its Arkansas headquarters. Wal-Mart informs you that from now on it will pay only $5.60 per razor. And if you all refuse to sell razors to Wal-Mart for $5.60 then, Wal-Mart says, it will encourage Chinese businesses to start making razors for Wal-Mart. Since Wal-Mart imports a tremendous number of goods from China, all the razor companies believe that Wal-Mart could completely bypass them and buy just Chinese-made razors. Not willing to lose their Wal-Mart sales, all the razor companies agree to sell razors to Wal-Mart for $5.60 each. And once Wal-Mart gets this low price, other retailers demand sub-$6 per razor prices as well.

While flying home you realize how clever and ruthless Wal-Mart is. $5.60 is just slightly above the marginal cost of making a razor. If Wal-Mart had demanded a price a smidgen lower than $5.60 the razor companies would have been better off not selling razors to Wal-Mart. Wal-Mart obviously spent the last two months determining your costs. (Perhaps this is why they hired away your chief accountant 50 days ago.) Wal-Mart used this knowledge to figure out the lowest possible price at which you would still be willing to sell them razors. In your anger you think of Wal-Mart as a parasite that determined exactly how much blood it could regularly suck from its host without killing it. (Of course, Wal-Mart considers the four razor companies to be monopolist wannabees that feebly attempted to use their market power to rip off customers.)

USING TRADE BARRIERS TO COUNTER WAL-MART'S CHINESE STRATEGY

You formulate a long-term plan to beat Wal-Mart. The four razor companies make large contributions to many congressmen and so have considerable political influence. If you could all use this influence to get the United States to impose a large tariff on Chinese razors, you could again force Wal-Mart to pay $10 per razor.

The razor employee unions, furthermore, should be willing to provide political help. Many unions hate Wal-Mart since the retail giant employs little union labor. Furthermore, you will tell your unions that if the government doesn't impose a steep tariff on Chinese razors, you will have to move your razor factories to China. (Just to make this threat believable, you consider starting a small factory in China and firing a few U.S. employees on the pretext that their jobs are now being done by the Chinese.) The unions, therefore, should be willing to use all their political power to try to prevent any future importation of Chinese razors. But it will take several years before you have any chance of getting this tariff implemented. Until then, you seek a way to make substantial economic profits.

WHY YOU DIFFERENTIATE YOUR RAZORS

Wal-Mart has power over you because customers consider all razors to be perfect substitutes for each other. Consequently, Wal-Mart can replace your razors with Chinese-made razors without upsetting shoppers.

Similarly, price competition in the razor business is usually so fierce because customers believe all razors to be alike. If all razors are perceived to be identical, then the customers will buy the cheapest razor. Such customer behavior provides a powerful incentive for each firm to sell the lowest-priced razor. But when all firms seek to offer the cheapest razor, the price of razors gets pushed down to a level where no firm makes much of a profit.

You decide, therefore, to differentiate your razors. You don't want customers going to the store looking for a mere razor. Instead you want them going to the store looking for an *Oligo-Razor*. Then, even if your razors cost a dollar more than your rivals', most of your customers will stick with Oligo-Razors. Similarly, if customers go to Wal-Mart intent on buying Oligo-Razors then Wal-Mart couldn't easily replace your products with cheap Chinese imports.

HOW YOU DIFFERENTIATE YOUR RAZORS

To differentiate your razor, you first get your engineers to change the shape of the blade to offer a sharper cut. Next you hire a design firm to make your razor stylish and elegant. Then you get your marketing people to come up with a snappy brand name. Finally, you fund a big-budget advertising campaign that associates your brand name with your razor's superior performance and chic design. No longer, you hope, will customers think of other razors as strong substitutes for Oligo-Razors.

Your attempts at product differentiation succeed only partially. Modern Americans are so bombarded with advertisements that many are immune to their effects. So while some customers are willing to pay a bit more for your razor than others, most customers still consider all razors to be about the same. Consequently, despite your best efforts, many shavers still just buy the lowest-priced razor.

COMPLICATED PRICING

You decide, therefore, to confuse customers by making it difficult for them to calculate which razor really is the cheapest. Customers need to buy both razors and blades. Normally, customers can use any company's blades in any other company's razor. Consequently, customers seeking low prices buy the cheapest razors and the cheapest blades. But now you deliberately make your razor incompatible with other companies' blades. After today, only Oligo-Razor blades will fit inside of Oligo-Razors. You further decide to sell your razor for a very low price (below its average total cost) while you sell your blades for a much higher price than competitors' blades. Consequently, customers have trouble figuring out which shaving system is really the cheapest. Furthermore, customers who buy razors without checking the price of blades will mistakenly think that your product sells for the lowest price.

INCOMPATIBILITY AND LOCK-IN

By making your razor incompatible with other firms' blades you also lock existing customers into your product line. Once a customer has paid for your razor, he will have to buy another razor if he switches to another firms' blades. Incompatibility, therefore, makes other firms' razor blades poor substitutes for Oligo-Razor blades. Furthermore, after a customer has bought an Oligo-Razor, he would be disappointed if a store, such as Wal-Mart, didn't sell Oligo-Razor blades.

CONCLUSION TO THE OLIGO-RAZOR STORY

Your attempts to get all razor firms to raise their prices failed. You were, however, able to use product differentiation, complicated pricing, and incompatibility to make other shaving systems imperfect substitutes for your own. Consequently, you have reduced the ferocious price competition that used to limit your profits.

CONFESSIONS OF AN ECONOMIST

You have just finished reading a long story about an oligopolistic firm. Unfortunately, when discussing oligopolies, all economic theorists really have are plausible stories.

Economists have excellent theories to explain what happens in perfectly competitive and monopolistic markets. Sadly, we have more difficulty determining what happens in markets that lie between perfect competition and monopoly. This is because we can't be sure when oligopolistic firms will compete and when they will cooperate.

Imagine that if the market for razors were a monopoly, then the monopolist would earn $1 billion a year in profits. If the market were perfectly competitive, as we learned in Chapter 9, intense competition would drive long-run profits to zero. But if the razor market were oligopolistic, then the firms could collectively earn anywhere between $1 billion and zero. If the firms manage to completely cooperate, they will collectively earn the same as a monopolist would have. But to the extent that the oligopolistic firms compete, their profits dissipate, perhaps even going to zero.

Why, you must ask, wouldn't oligopolistic firms figure this all out and decide to cooperate? Well, market forces put tremendous pressure on oligopolies to compete. Sometimes oligopolists can find ways to lesson or resist this pressure. But other times oligopolists capitulate to the pressure and compete away their profits. Unfortunately for economists, we don't have a reliable theory that tells us when oligopolists succeed in cooperating. But economists do understand the forces that often thwart oligopolists' efforts at such cooperation. And the starting point for understanding these forces is the Prisoners' Dilemma.

Industry	Percent of U.S. Market Controlled by Largest Four Firms in the Industry[1]
Breweries	90.5
Cigarette manufacturing	95.3
Electric lamp bulb and part manufacturing	89.6
Light truck and utility vehicle manufacturing	96.7
Guided missile and space vehicle manufacturing	95.3

A Few Oligopolistic Industries

Source: "Concentration Ratios: 2002", U.S. Census Bureau, 2002.

THE PRISONERS' DILEMMA

Although the Prisoners' Dilemma is a "game" that applies to oligopolies, the game, as its name implies, concerns prisoners. Here's how the Prisoners' Dilemma story goes:

The police arrest two criminals guilty of both murder and illegal weapons' possession. The police can easily prove that both men violated weapons laws and could consequently imprison each criminal for one year. If the police could also establish that the criminals committed murder, however, they could send the men to the electric chair. Unfortunately, the police can't establish that either criminal committed murder unless at least one of them confesses.

- ■ If both criminals keep quiet, at worst they'll get one year in jail.
- ■ If either criminal confesses, both men could be sentenced to death.

The captured criminals realize the game they're in, so you might think that neither would ever confess. In the Prisoners' Dilemma story, however, the police create incentives for the men to turn on each other.

The police put the criminals, whom I will name Adam and Ben, in separate rooms. They tell Adam the following:

If Ben confesses, then

- ■ Adam gets the death penalty if he doesn't confess.
- ■ Adam gets life in prison if he does confess.

The police need only one man to confess to convict either criminal of murder. If Adam believes that Ben would confess, then Adam would himself benefit from confessing. If Ben confesses, then by confessing himself, Adam gets life in prison rather than the electric chair. (Assume that both Adam and Ben prefer life in prison to receiving the death penalty.) In their efforts to induce a confession, the police have now made some progress. If Adam believes that Ben will confess, then it will be in Adam's self-interest also to confess.

The police then remind Adam that they already have enough evidence to convict him on weapons charges even if neither confesses. The police tell Adam that

If Ben does not confess, then

- ■ Adam gets one year in prison if he doesn't confess.
- ■ Adam goes free if he does confess.

If Ben does not cooperate with the police, Adam still benefits from confessing. Adam, therefore, should always confess, since regardless of what Ben does, Adam benefits from confessing.

Having been so successful with Adam, the police use the same strategy on Ben. Ben consequently finds it in his self-interest to confess. The police, therefore, have induced both men to confess and put them in jail for life.

Figure 11.1 illustrates the Prisoners' Dilemma. The result is counterintuitive. If both men had kept quiet, they would have gotten only one year in jail. By talking, both criminals get life. Shouldn't the men understand the game they are in and adopt different strategies? No! If Adam thinks that Ben is not going to confess, Adam is still better off talking. Even if Adam could somehow convince Ben to stay silent, Adam would still want to confess.

Wouldn't Adam fear that his confessing would cause Ben to confess? No! The police separate the criminals. When Ben decides whether to cooperate, he has no way of knowing if Adam confessed. The police are certainly not going to tell Ben that he should not confess because his brave partner stayed silent. Ben's confession or lack of confession

Adam \ Ben	Confess	Stay silent
Confess	Adam gets life in prison. Ben gets life in prison. *Adam and Ben will end up here.*	Adam goes free. Ben is executed.
Stay silent	Adam is executed. Ben goes free.	Adam gets one year in prison. Ben gets one year in prison.

FIGURE **11.1**

THE PRISONERS' DILEMMA

Adam and Ben both simultaneously decide whether to confess or stay silent. The two prisoners end up in the box corresponding to their choices. So if Adam stays silent and Ben confesses, the parties are in the box on the lower left where Adam is executed and Ben goes free.

In the Prisoners' Dilemma game, each person is individually better off confessing. So if both Ben and Adam are rational and self-interested, they will both confess and spend their lives in prison.

will have no bearing on whether Adam talks. Consequently, each prisoner benefits from cooperating with the police, even though this causes them to both receive life sentences. The key result in the Prisoners' Dilemma is that even though all the prisoners realize that the outcome is going to be bad, they still confess, guaranteeing that the bad outcome is achieved. Of course, the police are pleased with the results of the Prisoners' Dilemma.

What if the two criminals made an agreement never to confess if caught by the police? If someone is about to commit a murder, he should always make such an agreement. This agreement, of course, shouldn't prevent him from cooperating if caught. Rather, he should make the agreement to keep his naive co-criminal quiet and then confess to escape punishment. True, this means that his partner in crime dies. But so what? She is, after all, a murderer.

DEFINITION OF A PRISONERS' DILEMMA GAME

The Prisoners' Dilemma game applies to far more groups than murderers being interrogated by the police. Generally, those stuck in a Prisoners' Dilemma game can take an action which is either selfish or altruistic. Individually, each player is better off being selfish. Yet the players are all also better off if everyone is altruistic than if everyone is selfish. Figure 11.2 illustrates the general Prisoners' Dilemma game.

FIGURE **11.2**

PRISONERS'
DILEMMA GAME

In this general Prisoners'
Dilemma game, both
players are always
individually better off
being selfish. Yet both
players are also better
off if they are both
altruistic than if they are
both selfish.

Person Two

	Selfish	**Altruistic**
Selfish	Person One does badly. Person Two does badly.	Person One does extremely well. Person Two does very badly.
Altruistic	Person One does very badly. Person Two does extremely well.	Person One does well. Person Two does well.

Person One

STUDENTS' DILEMMA

Let's see how the Prisoners' Dilemma relates to students studying for an exam that will be graded on a curve. Imagine that 35 students are enrolled in a sociology class. The professor announces that he will curve the final exam, and regardless of how the class performs, he will award 10 A's, 10 B's, 10 C's, 3 D's, and 2 F's. None of the students in the class care about sociology and so their goal is to get a good grade without studying too much. Each student's class grade is determined entirely by the final exam.

To keep everything simple, assume that each student can study either zero or 40 hours for the final. Further assume that any given student would get the exact same grade if (1) everyone in the class, including him, doesn't study or if (2) everyone in the class, including that student, studies 40 hours. If, however, everyone else studies zero hours and you study 40 you will get an A, but if everyone else studies 40 hours and you study zero you get an F.

The students in the class would be best off if they could come to a binding agreement not to study for the final. Alas, if no one else studies, each student is better off studying himself. (Assume that a student would prefer to study 40 hours and get an A rather than not study and get an F.) So even if all the students agreed not to study, each student would have an incentive to cheat on the agreement and study for 40 hours.

In classes with curved exams, students are often in a studying Prisoners' Dilemma. When exams are curved, every student harms his classmates by studying. Consequently, the students would often be best off if they could come to some binding agreement not to study. But if no one else studies, you can earn a very high grade by studying yourself. And if everyone else studies, you have to study or you will fail. The Prisoners' Dilemma, therefore, compels students to study and would cause them to cheat on any agreement they made not to study.

Of course students in economics classes are never in a Prisoners' Dilemma. Economics is such an interesting and useful field that students always gain tremendous benefit from studying economics regardless of how such studying affects their grade.

ATHLETES' STEROID DILEMMA

Professional athletes face a Prisoners' Dilemma when deciding whether to use performance-enhancing drugs. Drugs like steroids increase athletic ability. Unfortunately, such drugs have harmful medical side effects. For a top athlete, however, it might be rational to take such drugs. It could be worth suffering the side effects of steroids to win an Olympic medal or get a multimillion-dollar professional football contract. Alas, when all athletes use steroids, none receives a competitive advantage.

Figure 11.3 shows a Prisoners' Dilemma game in which two equally matched runners compete for a prize. They each can take steroids, which would make them faster but would also give them health problems. Since the athletes have equal ability, if only one runner takes steroids, he will win. If it were worth enduring the health problems to win, then either athlete would be willing to take steroids if the other doesn't. Furthermore, if one athlete takes them and the other doesn't, then the abstainer loses. Therefore, it might well be in the interest of either athlete to take the steroids if the other does. Of course, if both runners take steroids then neither is helped in their competition. If, however, they both take the drug, then they both have to suffer the drug's negative side effects. The athletes would be better off if neither took steroids than if both injected them. Unfortunately, the Prisoners' Dilemma might cause them both to use the drugs. To reduce the harm caused by this Prisoners' Dilemma, many sports associations forbid the use of performance-enhancing drugs. Regrettably, as with all attempts to restrict the Prisoners' Dilemma, the players have incentives to cheat and so athletes often find ways around drug restrictions.

If winning is more important than avoiding health problems, then both athletes will individually always be better off using steroids. Yet the athletes are in a Prisoners' Dilemma game because they are both better off if neither uses steroids than if both use steroids.

> "We may, sooner than we think, have to conclude that we can't force Olympic athletes to be drug-free any more than we could force them to remain amateurs. Never forget a survey taken in 1995, when U.S. athletes were asked: If we could give you a drug that would guarantee you a gold medal, would you take it even if you understood it would kill you within five years? More than half of America's swiftest and strongest said, 'Gimme the drug.'"[2]

		Athlete Two	
		Use steroids	Don't use steroids
Athlete One	**Use steroids**	Both athletes have an equal chance of winning. / Both athletes suffer health problems.	Athlete One wins. / Athlete One suffers health problems.
	Don't use steroids	Athlete Two wins. / Athlete Two suffers health problems.	Both athletes have an equal chance of winning.

FIGURE **11.3**

THE PRISONERS' DILEMMA APPLIED TO ATHLETES

281

Most people who take steroids don't do so because they were forced to by the Prisoners' Dilemma. Rather, they take them because they are deluded. It might be worth the risk of taking steroids if they give you a chance at an Olympic gold medal. Even with the aid of steroids, however, the vast majority of people have absolutely no chance of ever entering the Olympics or making a living playing sports. When a college student takes steroids to improve his likelihood of becoming a professional athlete, he is almost certainly risking his long-term health for a trivial chance at fulfilling an unrealistic dream.

ECONOMICS MAJORS AND THE PRISONERS' DILEMMA

Economics majors tend to play the Prisoners' Dilemma game differently than other students do. In a large experiment involving students playing 267 Prisoners' Dilemma games for real money, economics majors chose the selfish action 60.4 percent of the time while noneconomics majors chose the selfish action only 38.8 percent of the time.[3] There are four possible reasons for this:

1. Only the smartest students major in economics.
2. Studying economics increases the intelligence of students more than studying other disciplines does.
3. Only the most self-interested students choose economics as their major.
4. Studying economics increases students' selfishness more than studying other disciplines does.

Question: Which companies do you think are better managed: those run by people who choose the selfish or altruistic actions in oligopolistic Prisoners' Dilemma games?

THE PRICING PRISONERS' DILEMMA

Oligopolists often find themselves in a Prisoners' Dilemma with respect to pricing. Imagine that two firms produce the exact same product and can each set either a high or low price. If both firms set a high price, they earn a high profit. If both firms set a low price, they earn zero profit. So you might think that the two firms would never both set a low price. But let's assume these firms are in a Prisoners' Dilemma.

If one firm sets a low price while the other sets a high price, then the low-pricing firm will win all the customers and make an *extremely* high profit. In contrast, the firm setting a high price (while its rival charges a low price) gets no customers and so loses money. (The firm loses money because it still has to pay its fixed costs.) Figure 11.4 summarizes the game the two firms are in.

If you and another firm play the game just once, then you each have an incentive to charge low prices. If your opponent is charging a high price, then

- You earn an *extremely* high profit if you charge a low price.
- You earn a high profit if you charge a high price.

So you make a greater profit charging a low price. If the other firm is charging a low price, then

- You make zero profit if you charge a low price.
- You make a negative profit if you charge a high price.

So you again make a greater profit charging a low price.

Consequently, regardless of what the other firm does, you are better off charging a low price. Of course, if both firms follow this logic they will both charge a low price and earn zero profit. But firms trapped in a pricing Prisoners' Dilemma might

FIGURE **11.4**

HIGH PRICE/LOW
PRICE DILEMMA

Firm Two

	Set a low price	**Set a high price**
Set a low price	Firm One earns zero profit. Firm Two earns zero profit.	Firm One earns an *extremely* high profit. Firm Two earns a negative profit.
Set a high price	Firm One earns a negative profit. Firm Two earns an *extremely* high profit.	Firm One earns a high profit. Firm Two earns a high profit.

*(Left axis label: **Firm One**)*

still earn zero profit even though they fully understand the nature of their dilemma.

Oligopolists often face a pricing Prisoners' Dilemma. When a few firms sell the same product, they all have incentives to lower their price to capture more customers. When all firms charge a low price, however, none earns a high profit per good sold or captures most of the customers by being the only firm to charge a low price. But if all the other firms are charging a low price, your firm needs to as well or it will have no customers.

USING THE PRISONERS' DILEMMA

You run a company that's being charged "too much" by its suppliers. You should first look for other suppliers. After all, if you're being charged high prices, then your suppliers are making significant economic profits and so other companies should be eager to sell to you. Perhaps firms that make related goods could tweak their manufacturing processes to start making the inputs you need.

If, however, you can't find another supplier, you should plunge your current suppliers into a pricing Prisoners' Dilemma. Pretend that you buy 1,000 wing nuts a week from each of two suppliers. Both suppliers sell wing nuts for $10 each. For simplicity assume that each supplier makes wing nuts at zero cost.

A Prisoners' Dilemma must involve both a reward and a punishment. To create a Prisoners' Dilemma for the wing-nut suppliers, you should reward a firm if it is the only company to lower prices and punish a firm only if it does not offer a discount. Currently, both firms sell you 1,000 wing nuts a week for $10 each, making a profit of $10,000 a week. To create a Prisoners' Dilemma, you should announce that if one firm cuts its price to $6 per wing nut you will buy all your wing nuts from this firm, giving it a profit of $12,000 a week. Consequently, if one firm does not cut its price the other is better off charging you $6. If both firms cut their price to $6, you will continue to buy 1,000 wing nuts from both firms. Figure 11.5 shows the Prisoners' Dilemma game you have created. If the suppliers can't escape your Prisoners' Dilemma, they will both lower their price to $6 per wing nut.

	Firm Two	
	Charge $6	**Charge $10**
Charge $6	You buy 1,000 wing nuts a week from each firm. Firm One earns $6,000 a week in profit. Firm Two earns $6,000 a week in profit.	You buy 2,000 wing nuts a week from Firm One and none from Firm Two. Firm One earns $12,000 a week in profit. Firm Two makes zero profit.
Charge $10	You buy no wing nuts from Firm One and 2,000 a week from Firm Two. Firm One makes zero profit. Firm Two earns $12,000 a week in profit.	You buy 1,000 wing nuts a week from each firm. Firm One earns $10,000 a week in profit. Firm Two earns $10,000 a week in profit.

(Left side label: **Firm One**)

FIGURE 11.5

PRISONERS' DILEMMA FOR SUPPLIERS

ESCAPING THE PRISONERS' DILEMMA THROUGH COLLUSION

Firms trapped in a pricing Prisoners' Dilemma do have a few potential means of escape, the most straightforward being collusion. Consider again the Prisoners' Dilemma games of Figures 11.4 and 11.5. Ideally the firms would come to a binding agreement whereby they both agree to charge high prices. If the Prisoners' Dilemma game is played only once, however, firms should always violate any agreement to charge high prices.

But if a Prisoners' Dilemma is played repeatedly, the participants can sometimes successfully collude. For example, imagine that two firms play a pricing Prisoners' Dilemma game each week: each week they set the price of their product. Both firms could agree always to charge high prices. If one firm cheated by setting a low price, it would suspect that the other firm would punish it in the future by charging a low price itself. When several firms in the same market explicitly agree to charge high prices, they form a cartel.

CARTELS

Cartels are organizations of producers who explicitly collude to charge high prices. The most famous example of a cartel is OPEC, the Organization of Petroleum Exporting Countries. OPEC consists of countries including Iran, Iraq, and Saudi Arabia. OPEC controls about two-thirds of the world's readily accessible oil reserves. OPEC was able to raise the price of oil from $2 per barrel in 1972 to over $12 per barrel in 1974. OPEC, however, was harmed by the elasticity in both the supply and demand of oil. The high price of oil induced firms to look for oil in non-OPEC countries. OPEC went from supplying 50 percent of the world's oil in 1974 to 30 percent by 1985. OPEC was further hurt by consumers responding to high oil prices by purchasing more fuel-efficient products. As OPEC discovered, not even cartels can evade the Laws of Supply and Demand.

Criminal Cartels   Criminal organizations often form cartels to increase the price of illegal products. The Mafia, for example, might control the trade of cocaine and prostitution in a city. Anyone who supplies cocaine or prostitutes would have to pay the Mafia tribute and accept Mafia-dictated prices. The Mafia could increase criminals' profits by reducing price competition among criminals. By the Law of Demand, when the Mafia raises the price of illegal goods, it decreases the quantity demanded of these goods. A successful criminal cartel, therefore, should actually reduce crime.

COLLUDING TO KEEP DOWN WAGES[4]

In both South Africa in the early 20th century and the U.S. South shortly after the Civil War, employers tried to keep down the wages of black workers. South African mines relied on black workers. When one mine wanted to increase its workforce, it would offer black workers from another mine higher wages. To keep its workers from being hired away, therefore, the second mine had to raise its wages as well. Such competition for black labor harmed mine owners. The mine owners pressured the government to solve their problem. The government responded by passing the Native Labour Regulation Act. This act made it illegal for anyone to attract black miners by offering them higher wages than they currently received. The Native Labour Regulation Act succeeded in reducing price competition among miners and so kept down the wages of black workers.

After the freeing of slaves at the end of the U.S. Civil War, white landowners tried to keep down the wages of newly freed blacks. White landowners formed planters' associations whose members pledged not to pay high wages or to lure away black workers from other employers. Fortunately for the blacks, these collusive agreements failed. To attract additional labor, white landowners frequently paid relatively high wages and thus increased the wages paid by most landowners.

Both South African mine owners and Southern landowners tried to collude to lower black wages. The South Africans, however, had much greater success because they got the government to outlaw competition.

A TUTORING CARTEL

Imagine that you and four fellow classmates offer private economics tutoring at your college. Further assume that the opportunity cost of your time is $10 per hour, so each of you is better off tutoring a student as long as you receive more than this amount. Figure 11.6 on page 286 shows the market demand curve for tutoring. If each of you accepts any tutoring job that pays at least $10 per hour, you will work until the price goes down to $10 and so, according to Figure 11.6, you will all work a total of 105 hours. At a rate of $10 per hour, the tutors will collectively earn revenue of $10(105) = $1,050 per month. But now imagine that all five tutors collectively agree to work for $15 an hour. By the Law of Demand this will diminish how many people want your services. According to Figure 11.6 you five will now sell only 100 hours of tutoring per month. But at $15 per hour, the tutors will earn revenues of $15(100) = $1,500 per month. So by colluding to raise prices, the tutors can earn greater revenue while working fewer hours.

ANTITRUST LAWS AND COLLUSION

In many countries including the United States, it's a violation of antitrust laws for firms to come to an agreement to charge high prices. And although the antitrust police probably won't come after you if you start a small tutoring cartel, they do vigorously

FIGURE **11.6**

MARKET DEMAND
CURVE FOR
TUTORING

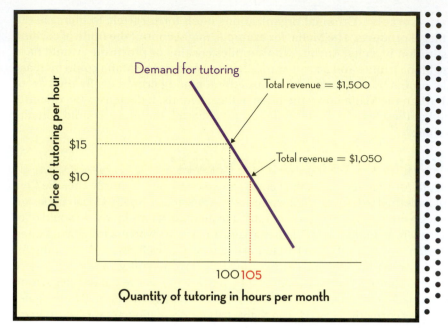

pursue larger cartels. A major purpose of antitrust laws, therefore, is to keep firms in a pricing Prisoners' Dilemma.

But antitrust laws can only prevent firms from making explicit agreements to keep high prices. If two or more firms just happen to charge high prices, they don't violate antitrust laws. Consequently, firms facing a Prisoners' Dilemma can't legally come to a formal agreement to keep high prices. They can both charge high prices in the hope that other firms will follow. Consider firms who set prices each month and so every month are in a pricing Prisoners' Dilemma. Each firm might reason as follows:

> This month I will make a higher profit if I charge a low price because by setting a low price I will steal most of my rival's customers. But if I charge a low price this month, then next month my rival will almost certainly lower its price. I would much rather charge a high price this month than cause my rival to charge a low price in the future. Therefore, I will avoid the Prisoners' Dilemma and so forgo the chance to make an extremely high profit this month. I hope my rival is smart enough to do the same so we will both escape the Prisoners' Dilemma. Unfortunately, I can't mention any of this to my rival without violating antitrust laws.

THE DIFFICULTY OF USING COLLUSION TO ESCAPE THE PRICING PRISONERS' DILEMMA

As the story at the beginning of this chapter shows, firms often have difficulty using implicit collusion to escape a pricing Prisoners' Dilemma. Imagine that several firms have come to an implicit agreement to charge no less than $10 for their product. Since the firms are in a pricing Prisoners' Dilemma, each would benefit if it alone lowered prices. Each firm, therefore, has an incentive to offer secret discounts to customers. Whenever a firm is worried that its rival may be offering secret discounts, it will suspect that any loss of customers is due to its rivals giving illicit discounts. Mistrust and greed, therefore, can easily destroy implicit agreements by firms to maintain high prices. Oligopolists, however, have found a few ways of reducing their own incentives to offer secret discounts to consumers.

USING "PRO-CONSUMER" POLICIES TO PROMOTE COLLUSION

Imagine you are in charge of buying office paper for your firm. Before buying the paper you get a "most favored customer" promise from the supplier. Under the promise, the paper supplier legally promises that the price you are paying for its paper is not higher than the price any other customer is paying. While "most favored customer" promises seem pro-consumer, they actually harm customers.

If all firms in an industry issue "most favored customer agreements," then they can't secretly cut prices for just a few customers. These legally binding promises, therefore, makes it easier for oligopolists to overcome their pricing Prisoners' Dilemma and so maintain high prices.

Price-matching pledges, like "most favored customer" promises, can also harm customers. Imagine that Best Buy promises to match all its rivals' prices. So, if Circuit City sells a certain type of television for $1,209, then Best Buy pledges that it will sell the same television for no more than $1,209. Circuit City has much less incentive to lower its price if it knows that Best Buy must immediately match any price cut. Price matching pledges can, therefore, prevent firms from lowering prices.

THE SOCIAL HARM OF COLLUSION

By the Law of Demand, when oligopolists maintain high prices they reduce sales. In the last chapter, we examined why monopolists sometimes reduce the wealth of society. Oligopolists that collude can cause social harm similar to what occurs when monopolists set high prices. Consider the following simple example:

Customer Type	Value of an Electric Razor
A	$100
B	50

Assume that the marginal cost of making an electric razor is only $40. If the oligopolists were to compete fully, they would sell razors to both Customer Types A and B. But if razor manufacturers were to collude and set the price of razors at $100, then Type B customers won't buy razors. Since it costs only $40 to make an extra razor and since customers in Type B value razors at $50, then each time a razor is sold to a Type B customer, $10 of wealth is created. Consequently, if the razor manufacturers collude to raise the price of razors above $50, they will prevent the creation of an amount of wealth equal to $10 multiplied by the number of Type B customers.

Generally, when oligopolists collude they raise prices above marginal costs. Consequently, customers whose valuation of the good lies between the good's price and the good's marginal cost won't purchase the product. Yet if these customers bought the good at a price they found acceptable, the wealth of society would have been higher. By raising prices above marginal cost, therefore, colluding oligopolists reduce the wealth of society.

OVERCOMING THE WEALTH-DESTROYING EFFECT OF COLLUSION

This chapter has already discussed how greed can destroy collusive agreements. A firm's desire for additional profits will often cause it to violate implicit or explicit agreements to keep high prices. Markets, therefore, reduce (but don't eliminate) the harm caused by oligopolies that collude to increase prices. Later in this chapter we will see how the government sometimes mitigates, but sometimes also magnifies, the wealth-destroying effects of collusion.

MORE ON ESCAPING THE PRISONERS' DILEMMA

PRODUCT DIFFERENTIATION

Competition for Brides Firms often resort to product differentiation when they can't escape a pricing Prisoners' Dilemma through collusion. To understand the value of product differentiation, consider a tale of marriage market competition. Imagine that in ancient times there lived two young and equally desirable maidens named Aphrodite and Venus. Many noble men sought to marry the maidens. Aphrodite considered all of her suitors to be about the same. Consequently, Aphrodite announced that she would marry the man who promised to pay her family the highest bride-price.

Venus, by contrast, recognized many differences among her suitors. Venus chose her husband by considering both her suitors' personal qualities and the size of the bride price these suitors offered.

Since Aphrodite judged her suitors based only on money, each suitor knew that, to win her hand in marriage, he had to offer her family the most money. Aphrodite's suitors, therefore, had a tremendous incentive to promise a high bride-price.

The discriminating Venus received a much lower bride-price than the nondiscerning Aphrodite. Venus compared her suitors across many dimensions. The suitor promising the highest bride-price knew he wouldn't necessarily wed Venus. So the benefit of offering the highest bride-price to Venus was much lower than the benefit of being the highest bidder for Aphrodite.

Differentiation and Competition for Customers Just as our imaginary suitors competed for wives, firms compete for customers. When, like Aphrodite, customers care only about money, firms have a huge incentive to offer customers the best (meaning lowest) price. In contrast, when customers, similar to Venus, base their choice on more than just price, then firms don't have the same pressure to compete exclusively on the basis of price (in this case, by offering to sell for the lowest price). Oligopolists, therefore, often try to convince customers that their product is different from their rivals'.

Let's imagine that there are three makers of plasma televisions in two different types of market competition.

> **Situation One**—All firms sell exactly the same type of plasma televisions and compete just on price.
>
> **Situation Two**—One firm makes 40-inch televisions, the second firm makes 50-inch televisions, and the third manufactures 60-inch sets.

In Situation One all firms face tremendous pressure to charge low prices. Each firm would have few sales if it charged more than a rival, while each firm would have huge sales if it charged a little bit less than everyone else. As a result, competition could easily drive down prices to where each firm made zero profit.

In Situation Two, the three plasma makers compete with each other only indirectly. If one firm cuts prices, it would attract far fewer of its rivals' customers than it would in Situation One. As a result, each firm's price elasticity of demand is lower. The firms, therefore, have a much better chance of escaping their pricing Prisoners' Dilemma in Situation Two than Situation One.

Oligopolists sometimes use style rather than quality to differentiate their wares. For example, many DVD players have essentially the same features. Firms, however, stop customers from buying just the cheapest DVD player by stylistically distinguishing their DVD machines. If customers judge competing products on their looks as well as price, firms have diminished incentives to charge low prices.

Advertising and Brand Names

It's not enough, however, just to differentiate your product. You also have to inform customers about your differentiation. Firms thus spend billions on advertising touting their products' special qualities. They hire celebrity spokespersons and formulate snappy jingles so customers might remember why their products are worth buying even if they cost a bit more than competing goods.

APPLE'S iPOD IS SOLD WITH STYLE.

USING CONFUSING PRICES TO ESCAPE THE PRISONERS' DILEMMA

You're offered a choice between two long-distance services. The first plan charges you five cents a minute and the second charges you six. Obviously, you should go with the first, cheaper, plan. Long-distance providers, however, rarely offer such a stark choice. They present complicated pricing plans that make it difficult to compare long-distance packages.[5]

Complication reduces the damage of price competition. When firms compete directly on price, it's easy for customers to compare. Consequently, there is a massive incentive for every firm to undercut its rivals. When everyone uses complicated pricing schemes, however, the benefits to undercutting your rivals diminish since customers will be challenged to find the low-cost provider.

Airlines achieve complicated pricing through frequent-flyer programs. Frequent-flyer miles effectively change the price of airline tickets. They make it difficult to determine which airline offers the lowest price and consequently reduce the benefit to firms of undercutting their rivals.

Complication reduces the harm of a pricing Prisoners' Dilemma. With complicated pricing, customers can't easily discern which firm is charging the least. Consumers, therefore, won't flock to the low-priced firm. Also, when prices are complicated, firms don't get as significant a benefit from offering the lowest prices. So complicated prices both (a) reduce the incentive for firms to cut prices and (b) reduce the harm to one firm if a rival decreases its price.

Confusing Pricing and Rationality

This textbook has assumed that consumers make rational decisions. Does the above analysis on confusing pricing contradict this? No! Everyone, including rational people, has limited amounts of time. It might take a certain rational person three hours to figure out which of five cell phone plans offers the lowest rate. Rather than spend this time to save a few dollars, a rational person might instead intelligently guess which plan is the best for him. This rational consumer knows he might pick the wrong plan, but it's not worth the three-hour cost to him to eliminate any chance of error.

Confusing Pricing as Price Discrimination[6]   Recall from the last chapter that supermarkets use coupons to price discriminate. Only price-sensitive customers will take the time to use coupons. As a result, coupons allow stores to charge higher prices to price-insensitive customers. Confusing pricing has a similar effect.

Imagine that five cell phone companies each offer five plans. Price-sensitive consumers will take the time to find the plans that are the best for them. In contrast, price-insensitive consumers will guess at which plan is the best. As a result, confusing pricing causes price-insensitive customers to pay, on average, higher prices.

OLIGOPOLIES' INCENTIVE TO INNOVATE

Oligopolies probably have greater incentives to innovate than any other type of firm. Unlike firms in perfect competition, an oligopolist's innovation won't be immediately copied by competitors. Unlike monopolists, oligopolies face direct competition and so must often innovate to survive. But their willingness to engage in disruptive innovation is the primary reason oligopolists usually innovate more than monopolists do.

DISRUPTIVE INNOVATION

Imagine that your firm spent $1 billion developing a drug called Memory-27 that improves the memory of Alzheimer's patients by 27 percent. (Alzheimer's disease gradually destroys the memory of its victims.) One of your scientists, however, comes up with an idea for another drug named Memory-28 that would improve Alzheimer patients' memory by 28 percent. Unfortunately, a patient wouldn't benefit from taking both drugs. So once someone took Memory-28 he would receive no additional memory gain from also taking Memory-27. Developing Memory-28 would cost your pharmaceutical company another $1 billion. Should you develop Memory-28?

Since it's a bit better, Memory-28 would destroy the market for Memory-27. But since it's just a *bit* better, developing Memory-28 wouldn't significantly increase the demand for your firm's memory products. Sure, if you could develop Memory-28 for free, you would do it. But spending $1 billion to develop Memory-28 is probably a bad investment.

Now, however, imagine that the scientist who proposed Memory-28 quits to take a job with another pharmaceutical firm. This second firm currently has no memory drugs. The second firm is therefore vastly more interested in developing Memory-28 than your firm because developing Memory-28 wouldn't reduce the demand for any of its products. If the market for memory-improving drugs were a monopoly, however, there wouldn't exist any other firms with the capacity to make Memory-28, so this slightly better drug would remain undeveloped.

Developing Memory-28 would be an example of disruptive innovation. Disruptive innovation reduces the value of existing products or services. In general, firms are reluctant to develop innovations that reduce the value of their current products by cannibalizing sales. In monopolistic markets, therefore, innovation is limited because disruptive innovation would usually harm the monopolist's product line. In oligopolistic markets, however, firms are usually willing to develop innovations that harm rival firms but not themselves.

Disruptive Innovation Benefits Society   Disruptive innovation is almost always wealth-enhancing. Although it can reduce the value of individual firms, it usually increases the wealth of society by giving it better products.

Innovation is the most important wealth-creating activity firms engage in. But, as we will see in Chapter 13, because of something called *technological spillovers,* firms usually spend less on innovation than would be socially optimal. So oligopolists' relative willingness to conduct disruptive innovation benefits society.

The following are examples of disruptive innovation:

- **Bell Telephone**—Telephone service decimated the market for telegraphs.
- **Black & Decker**—It offered cheap electronic tools for homeowners and disrupted the market for professional tools.
- **Charles Schwab**—This firm offered discount stock brokerage service and so disrupted the traditional full-service (expensive) brokerage market.
- **Dell Inc.**—By selling computers directly to consumers, it was initially able to sell products at a lower price than other computer manufacturers who sold their products through stores. Dell forced other manufacturers to find ways to lower their prices.
- **eBay**—This online auction firm challenged traditional retailing companies.
- **Expedia**—Online travel agencies such as Expedia have disrupted the walk-in travel agencies by offering lower prices.
- **Kodak**—Its simple-to-use camera allowed amateurs to take pictures and so disrupted the market for professional photography.
- **Linux**—This open source, not-for-profit operating system has disrupted the market for operating systems.
- **McDonald's**—By selling fast, inexpensive food, it disrupted the market for mom-and-pop diners.
- **Pixar**—Digital animation produced by firms such as Pixar has almost destroyed the traditional noncomputer-created animation market that had been dominated by Disney.
- **University of Phoenix**—By providing cheap, online college education, it is currently disrupting the college market.
- **Yahoo Email**—E-mail providers such as Yahoo have disrupted the market for traditional mail and have (sadly) facilitated the partial replacement of junk mail by spam.

THE PRISONERS' DILEMMA AND DISRUPTIVE OLIGOPOLISTIC INNOVATION

Oligopolists, however, sometimes collude to avoid disruptive innovation. For example, consider the situation of the big three U.S. car companies (General Motors, Ford, and Chrysler) before they faced significant foreign competition. Each company could have won more customers through innovation. Such innovation might have led to safer, more reliable, and more fuel-efficient cars.

Imagine that you own one of the automobile firms. If none of the other firms innovates, your firm will gain many customers through innovation. Furthermore, if another firm innovates, you will have to innovate or suffer a devastating loss of demand. Consequently, regardless of what the other firms do, your firm receives higher profits from innovating. But since innovation is expensive, you're better off if no one innovates than if everyone innovates. Once the Japanese started selling cars in the

Generally, just as oligopolies benefit from colluding to maintain high prices, they can also benefit from colluding to reduce innovation expenditures. But colluding to suppress innovation is far more dangerous than colluding to set high prices.

Consider three oligopolistic firms in a market. First assume they all collude to charge high prices. If a new firm enters their market and charges low prices, then the old firms could quickly lower their prices to compete successfully with the new firm. But now assume that the three old firms collude to eliminate innovation in their market. A new firm, however, secretly spends a few years innovating and developing better products than the old firms sell. Once the new firm enters the market and starts selling its innovative products, it will take the old firms a few years of innovation to produce products comparable to the new firm's goods. Of course, the old firms might not survive the next few years.

ANTITRUST LAWS

Antitrust laws prohibit firms from colluding or attempting to acquire monopolies. These laws can reduce the deadweight loss caused by monopolies and oligopolies. Antitrust laws, however, are not written and enforced by a benevolent, all-knowing economist wizard. Rather, antitrust laws are enacted and interpreted by imperfect government agents. Sometimes these agents help consumers, but sometimes antitrust law enforcement harms consumers and destroys wealth.

BENEFICIAL ANTITRUST ENFORCEMENT

The 1899 court decision *The United States v. Addyston Pipe and Steel Corporation* presents an ideal example of when antitrust laws should apply. In this case, six manufacturers of cast-iron pipes formed an explicit agreement to jointly set prices. The manufacturers attempted to increase prices by eliminating price competition. Such an agreement would have created a deadweight loss by restricting output below its socially optimal level. The court invalidated the price-setting agreement. In the United States, courts will almost always void agreements among firms that eliminate price competition. Organizations, however, often present consumer-oriented justifications for restricting price competition.

In the 1978 case *National Society of Professional Engineers v. The United States,* the engineering association argued that price competition among engineers harms consumers. The National Engineering Society had a code of ethics forbidding members from competing on price. The Society claimed that if engineers competed on price, they might offer cheap but low-quality services. The Society claimed that consumers should pick the best, not the cheapest, engineer.

Economists, however, believe that consumers are smart enough to understand trade-offs between price and quality. In circumstances in which all engineers could competently complete a task, rational consumers will hire the cheapest engineer. In tasks that require great skill, many consumers will pay more for excellence. In *National Society of Professional Engineers v. The United States,* the U.S. Supreme Court took the position most economists would favor and ruled against the engineering society. The ruling reduced the prices that consumers pay for engineers. The Supreme Court, therefore, forced engineers back into a pricing Prisoners' Dilemma and so reduced their profits.

SHOULD ANTITRUST LAWS BE USED AGAINST THE NCAA?[7]

College athletic programs have been remarkably successful at eliminating price competition for star players. Top college football and basketball players receive free housing, food, and tuition. But the National College Athletic Association (NCAA) rules forbid colleges from giving players cash salaries. Colleges claim that these salary bans actually benefit athletes. Colleges, however, certainly benefit from not having to pay their players salaries.

Some college football and basketball games attract large audiences and generate significant revenue. If colleges competed on the basis of salaries for athletes, some players would undoubtedly make in excess of $100,000 per year.

Any college that paid salaries to athletes would be expelled from the NCAA leagues and would therefore not be able to play games against other college teams. Do you think that antitrust laws should be applied against the NCAA to force colleges to compete on prices for athletes?

Colleges with mediocre teams could benefit from top schools' refusal to pay athletes. If around 10 of these colleges started paying athletes, they could attract the best players. These schools would be kicked out of the NCAA, but they could play against each other. Since these schools would attract the top players, they would have the most interesting games, and their sports revenues would significantly increase. The Prisoners' Dilemma would then force other colleges to pay their athletes. These first schools, however, would probably have a few glory years where only they would get the best amateur athletes money could buy.

Reputation is the most important recruiting tool colleges have. The top athletes want to go to schools with the best programs. Normally, it's nearly impossible for schools with mediocre teams to recruit the best players. Many of the best players hope to eventually play professionally, so they want to get practice playing on teams that also have excellent athletes. If a few schools started paying students, they could attract a large number of top players, and so they could overcome the barriers to recruiting that their mediocre reputations create. Once other schools start paying, however, these schools would still benefit from having a good reputation and so they might be able to continue recruiting top talent. Of course, the colleges that currently have the best players would be devastated if the schools with mediocre teams started paying players.

HARMFUL ANTITRUST RULINGS

The IBM Antitrust Case   In 1969 the U.S. government brought an antitrust case against computer-maker IBM. The government claimed that IBM had an illegal computer monopoly. In 1982 the government dropped the case, admitting that it was without merit. During its 13 years, however, the case generated 66 million pages of documents. Many of these documents were written by lawyers who were paid far more per hour than computer engineers. Imagine how much better computers would be today if IBM had devoted the resources it spent fighting the government to researching and creating computing technology instead.

By the early 1990s IBM utterly lost its dominance of the computer market to Microsoft and Intel. So to recap: the government spent 13 years trying to prove that IBM unfairly monopolized the computer market. Eventually the government itself realized that its antitrust claim was misguided. Shortly after the government dropped its antitrust case, the market terminated IBM's dominance of the computer industry.

Predatory Pricing[8]   Antitrust laws sometimes sacrifice the interests of customers to promote the welfare of firms. For example, antitrust laws occasionally punish firms for charging low prices. Nothing plausible in economic theory says that low prices harm consumers. Many lawyers, however, believe in the theory of predatory pricing. According to predatory pricing theory, firms initially charge low prices to drive other firms out of their market. Then, when the predatory firm becomes a monopolist it raises prices, thereby damaging consumers.

But predatory pricing theory doesn't hold up to scrutiny. Economists have never found any examples of successful predatory pricing, nor do we expect to. If a predatory firm did manage to drive away other businesses by charging low prices, then we would expect these or other firms to return to the market when the predatory firm started charging high prices. Furthermore, economists believe that if predatory pricing were a problem, then the antitrust police should wait for a predatory firm to start charging high prices before seeking to punish it. But predatory pricing litigation always seeks to punish firms when they charge low, not high prices.

In Chapter 7 we saw how governments impose trade tariffs to raise the price of goods. Since firms like high prices, they sometimes induce a government to force consumers to pay these high prices. We should therefore not be surprised that firms sometimes use antitrust laws to increase the prices that consumers must pay. Remember that firms desperately seek to avoid pricing Prisoners' Dilemmas. Antitrust laws are supposed to keep firms stuck in these dilemmas. But firms sometimes use their influence with lawmakers to subvert antitrust laws.

Always Guilty of Something   By aggressively using laws against predatory pricing, price gouging, and collusion, a government can find some way of criminalizing a firm's pricing decisions. Imagine, for example, that a politician sets out to prosecute the owner of a gas station.

If the gas station charges less than its competitors, then the firm can be accused of predatory pricing. The politician could claim that the gas station is setting a low price to drive its competitors out of business so it can obtain an illegal monopoly.

If the gas station charges more than its competitors, then the firm can be charged with price gouging. Recall from Chapter 3, governments sometimes criminalize so-called price gouging. A firm engages in pricing gouging when it sets a price higher than what politicians deem fair.

If the gas station charges the same price as its competitors, then the firm can be prosecuted for engaging in collusion. It's not illegal for two firms just to happen to choose the same price. But governments sometimes use similar pricing as evidence that firms must have illegally colluded. This all means that firms can't afford to make enemies of some powerful politicians, for such politicians have the ability to punish firms.

QUESTIONS YOU SHOULD BE ABLE TO ANSWER
AFTER READING THIS CHAPTER:

1   What is an oligopolistic market? (page 272)

2   What is the Prisoners' Dilemma? (pages 278–279)

3   Why do both criminals confess in the Prisoners' Dilemma? (pages 278–279)

4   How does the Prisoners' Dilemma relate to students studying for a class? (page 280)

STUDY PROBLEMS

1 Which of the following are Prisoners' Dilemma games? (Firm one's profit is the top number while Firm two's profit is the bottom number in each square.)

Firm 2

	High prices	Low prices
Firm 1 — High prices	$1,000 / $1,000	$0 / $1,500
Firm 1 — Low prices	$1,500 / $0	$500 / $500

Firm 2

	High prices	Low prices
Firm 1 — High prices	$1,000 / $1,000	$0 / $1,500
Firm 1 — Low prices	$1,500 / $0	$2,500 / $2,500

Firm 2

	High prices	Low prices
Firm 1 — High prices	$1,000 / $1,000	$0 / $0
Firm 1 — Low prices	$0 / $0	$500 / $500

Firm 2

	High prices	Low prices
Firm 1 — High prices	$5,000 / $5,000	$800 / $6,500
Firm 1 — Low prices	$6,500 / $800	$3,000 / $3,000

2 Imagine that a politician believes oligopolies are cheating customers by colluding to charge high prices. To monitor oligopolies' behavior, this politician forces all oligopolies to publish the prices they charge all their customers. Why might this politician have increased oligopolistic price collusion?

3 Imagine that the only two candidates for a political office agree to limit their campaign spending. Explain how these candidates have just overcome a Prisoners' Dilemma. Do the candidates have an incentive to cheat on their agreement?

4 Plastic surgery is expensive and entails some health risk. Plastic surgery sometimes does, however, improve one's prospects in the dating market. Describe how the existence of plastic surgery might create a Prisoners' Dilemma for single people.

5 Assume that the razors made by two firms used to be exactly the same. If the firms differentiate their razors, what would happen to the razors' cross-elasticity of demand?

6 Your firm has already developed drug Memory-27. Let X equal the fixed cost of developing Memory-28. The marginal cost of producing one more pill of either Memory-27 or Memory-28 is $2. If Memory-28 has not been developed then 10 million people would pay at most $2,000 each for one pill of Memory-27. If Memory-28 is developed then 10 million people would pay $2100 each for one pill of Memory-28. Assume that if Memory-28 is developed the government will ban the sale of Memory-27 because it will be an inferior product. For what values of X should your firm develop Memory-28? For what values of X will some other firm develop Memory-28?

7 Antipolygamy laws make it illegal for a man to have more than one wife. Antipolygamy laws, therefore, reduce competition among men for wives. Do such laws benefit or harm men? Do such laws benefit or harm women? Consider the effect on both high status and low status males and females.

8 Under which situation are lawyers in Cincinnati better off: (a) legal clients perceive all Cincinnati lawyers to be of the same quality or (b) legal clients perceive Cincinnati lawyers to be of differing quality, but the clients disagree over which lawyers are the best and worst?

9 Why do oligopolists often attempt to differentiate their products from rivals? Relate your answer to what happens in the long run in perfect competition.

10 There are three other firms besides yours in a oligopolistic market. Until now all four of you have successfully used confusing pricing. Could you increase your profits by luring customers with a simple pricing plan?

11 A city is considering enacting a law forbidding stores from being open on Sundays. In what ways would such a law help stores? Keep in mind that without the law a store could always choose not to be open on Sundays.

12 Assume that only two firms make Zerons. These two firms decide to divide the market. One firm agrees to sell to only men and the other firm to only women. Why might the firms do this?

"A GOVERNMENT WITH THE POLICY TO ROB PETER TO PAY PAUL CAN BE ASSURED OF THE SUPPORT OF PAUL."

—George Bernard Shaw

PUBLIC CHOICE THEORY

We will now examine government imperfections. This textbook presents many examples of market failures. Many people believe that governments should step in to solve all significant market failures. But governments, like markets, are also subject to failures. So before deciding whether a government should fix a market failure, we must study government imperfections.

The economic study of government is called *public choice theory*. Public choice theory examines how government officials and voters choose. The following fictional story is designed to give you a feel for political decision-making.

A FICTIONAL BUT TRUE-TO-LIFE POLITICAL TALE

You're an ambitious U.S. congressman. Fortunately, you don't have to worry about reelection. Similar to most congressmen, you have a safe district that contains far more voters from your party than from the opposition. You want to run for the U.S. Senate in four years, however, and since this race will be extremely competitive, you desperately need to increase your campaign contribution war chest, political support, and press profile.

SUGAR AND TEXTILE TARIFFS

Congress will soon vote on whether to impose a tariff on sugar. This tariff would raise the price of sugar in the United States and so hurt consumers while helping a few thousand sugar producers. None of these sugar producers lives in your state.

GOVERNMENT IMPERFECTIONS

LEARNING OBJECTIVES

AFTER READING THIS CHAPTER, YOU SHOULD BE ABLE TO:

- Define public choice theory.
- Understand why concentrated interest groups often triumph over diffuse ones.
- Explain the idea of rent-seeking.
- Analyze the implications of politicians spending other peoples' money.
- Identify conditions that can cause governments to become corrupt.
- Demonstrate some of the shortfalls of democracy.

Congress will also soon vote on whether to impose a tariff on textiles, and your district contains many clothing manufacturers. If you vote against the sugar tariff, congressmen from sugar-producing districts will retaliate against you by voting against the clothing tariff. So you will support the sugar tariff. True, the sugar and clothing tariffs will cost the average consumer in your state about $20 a month, but 99.9 percent of them won't notice or blame you. In contrast, if the clothing tariff fails, then a lot of workers will fault you for not protecting their jobs.

THE ELDERLY VERSUS COLLEGE STUDENTS

You're on a congressional education committee that must cut funding from either college financial aid programs or senior citizen art classes. You're obviously going to support the seniors. Elderly Americans are much more likely to vote and make campaign contributions than college students are. Furthermore, the elderly are far better politically organized than college students. If you vote against the elderly, then elderly advocacy groups such as the AARP will broadcast the vote to senior citizens throughout your state. But if you defund some college financial aid programs, few students will ever connect their loss to your vote.

ALLOCATING TELEVISION LICENSES

Besides being on an education committee, you're chairman of the committee that allocates television licenses. These licenses allow stations to transmit their signals through the airways to television sets.

Some economists propose auctioning the licenses. The auctions would raise billions of dollars. Furthermore, the auction winners would presumably be the firms that place the greatest value on the licenses and so would likely make the best use of them.

Yet you strongly oppose such auctions. Instead you intend to give away the licenses to broadcasters. Broadcasters will desperately seek to get the free television licenses as each one will be worth millions to its holder. Broadcasters will therefore make huge campaign contributions to members of your committee in the hopes that the committee will in turn give them licenses. In contrast, if you auctioned the licenses to the highest bidder, you would have no power over broadcasters and so the broadcasters would have no reason to support you.

You realize it would be better for the country to auction the licenses since the money raised through the auctions could be used to cut the budget deficit, reduce taxes, or help the needy. But even if you wanted to auction the television licenses, other members of Congress would never go along. Congressmen care greatly about how their local news stations portray them. Most congressmen would therefore never risk angering broadcasters by selling them something that could instead be given to the broadcasters for free.

MILITARY BASES

The U.S. Air Force has a repair facility in your district. The Air Force has announced that the facility is obsolete and should be shut down. You have mounted a desperate fight to save the facility and protect the jobs it brings to your district. Fortunately, you sit on a committee that must approve anyone in the Air Force who is promoted to the rank of general. You have let it be known that you will delay all such promotions if the Air Force dares shut down its repair facility.

FOOTBALL POLITICS

The star football player for the team in your district was just suspended for five games for using profanity during a television interview. His suspension dominated the local news in your area so you have taken a "brave" public stance against the suspension. You have pledged to remove tax loopholes that benefit the National Football League if they don't remove the suspension. (You have no idea what these loopholes might be, but corporate tax laws are so complicated that every business benefits from some kind of loophole.) You privately lament that voters will pay more attention to your position on this football suspension than to anything else you do. (Of course, this might be a good thing for your political career.)

LOAN GUARANTEE

A major manufacturing plant in your district is in financial trouble and may soon go bankrupt. The plant's owners are lazy idiots, so you fully understand why the plant has been losing money. Still, the plant's closure would eliminate 1,000 jobs and these workers don't deserve to lose their paychecks.

The plant's founder was a manufacturing genius. After the founder died, the plant was taken over by his three sons. These sons, alas, spent all the plant's accounting profits on fast cars, mistresses, and divorce settlements. Because the sons never bought any new equipment, the plant's existing equipment became more and more worn down and obsolete. The sons, however, never seemed to worry about their plant's future. It's almost as if the owners figured that if they got in real trouble some magic fairy would come along to save them. Well, this year the plant *is* in real trouble. Since no magic fairies are around, you have gotten the government to save the plant.

First, you tried to get Congress to give the plant $40 million to buy new equipment. Unfortunately, Congress had too many alternative uses for this money and so your efforts failed.

Instead you got Congress to guarantee a $40 million loan to the plant. Normally, a bank would never lend such a large sum to a horribly run firm for fear that the loan would never be repaid. But under your scheme, a bank lends $40 million to the plant for seven years, and Congress guarantees the loan, meaning that if the plant doesn't repay the money, the U.S. government will. Congress went along with this guarantee because it will cost it nothing for seven years. It's true that in seven years the U.S. government might have to pay $40 million plus interest to the bank. But seven years is forever in politics. Many congressmen won't even be in power seven years from now. Most really don't care if some law today costs the government money in seven years.

OUR FICTIONAL TALE'S CONCLUSION

You try your best to serve your district's interests. Sure, some of the measures you support are harmful to the country as a whole. But every congressman puts his voters' interests above the needs of the country, so if you don't fight for your district, it will suffer a political disadvantage.

Furthermore, you do tend to favor powerful interest groups such as senior citizens and television broadcasters. But if you didn't take into account political realities, you would never have gotten elected. Politicians are pragmatists, not idealists. If you never compromised, you would have no power. Besides, by placating special interests today, you have a better chance of becoming a senator. And as a senator you will have more power to help people. Of course, once you reach the Senate, you might try to become president and so you will continue to support powerful special interest groups.

ECONOMISTS ARE NOT ANARCHISTS, BUT . . .

Governments are necessary. Without a government to provide for the common defense, marauding invaders would ravage a country. Without a government to enforce property rights, economic growth would halt. And without a government to regulate pollution, the air and water of industrial cities would become toxic soups.

But governments can do harm as well as good. By one reasonable estimate, in the 20th century governments worldwide murdered around 262 million people.[1] Besides committing murders, governments can cause harm by taking from the weak and giving to the strong, enforcing silly regulations, demanding tribute, promoting corruption, wasting resources, and restricting trade.

Economists assume that government officials, like normal people, act in their own interests. For example, we believe that congressmen usually enact laws that are the best for themselves, not necessarily the country as a whole. Although this may sound cynical, it really just assumes that government officials are as self-interested as businesspeople.

The key difference between government officials and businesspeople arises from Adam Smith's invisible hand. Recall that Adam Smith's invisible hand often guides self-interested businesspeople to take actions that are in the best interest of society. No such invisible hand guides politicians. A greedy, selfish business owner often best serves her own needs by making low-cost, high-quality products. But, as the quote at the beginning of this chapter illustrates, a greedy, selfish politician often finds it in his best interests to rob Peter to pay Paul because this way Paul will vote for him and contribute to his campaign.

But, you might ask, won't robbing Peter to pay Paul cause the politician to lose the support of Peter? In governments like dictatorships, a troublesome Peter can simply be killed.

TAKING FROM THE WEAK IN DICTATORSHIPS

Until he lost World War II, Adolf Hitler was an extremely popular German leader. A prime source of Hitler's popularity was his practice of killing his enemies, taking their wealth, and giving this wealth to his German supporters.

Or, consider some other dictator who wants to rule over a country of, say, 10 million people. He needs the strong support of at least 2 million fellow countrymen to stay in power. He could randomly pick a group of 2 million people and give these lucky citizens all the important jobs in the army and police. He could then horribly exploit the other 8 million people and give much of their income to the lucky 2 million. The lucky 2 million would benefit from the dictator's rule, and because they run the army and police, their support will keep the dictator in power.

Many dictators use this mechanism to maintain power. Saddam Hussein, the former dictator of Iraq, was a Sunni Muslim. Sunnis make up only about 20 percent of Iraq's population, yet under Saddam's rule they controlled Iraq's military and security forces. Saddam treated the Sunnis far better than the rest of Iraq's population and relied on Sunni support to keep him in power. The Iraqi military killed any non-Sunnis who objected to the power arrangement. They even used poison gas attacks to decimate politically troublesome Iraqi villages.

SADDAM HUSSEIN

TAKING FROM THE WEAK IN DEMOCRACIES

We have seen that dictators can follow a simple three-step formula to maintain power:

1. Take wealth from some disfavored group.
2. Build support among some favored group by giving them the wealth acquired through step (1).
3. Suppress or kill the disfavored group so they can't harm the dictator.

In modern democracies, however, even disfavored groups can vote. A problem for a democratic politician in robbing Peter to pay Paul, therefore, is that Peter may then vote against him and contribute to his opponent's campaign. Yet democratic politicians have found an alternative to the above process. (By democratic politicians I mean politicians living in democratic countries, not necessarily politicians belonging to the U.S. Democratic Party.) Their method for robbing Peter to pay Paul involves

1. Taking wealth from politically inactive groups.
2. Building support among politically active groups by giving them the wealth acquired through step (1).

Take from Those Who Don't Participate in Politics and Give to Those Who Do
Imagine that a country has two groups of people: those who rarely participate in the political process and those who always vote and contribute to campaigns. Politicians will gain money and votes by taking from the first group and giving to the second.

In the United States the elderly vote in much higher percentages than other demographic groups. Consequently, politicians benefit by transferring resources from working people to the retired elderly. And indeed in 2010, U.S. spending on the elderly will likely be around $1 trillion, or 43 percent of the federal budget.[2]

Microsoft's Political Awakening[3]

You open a fancy store in a bad neighborhood but hire no security. You will be robbed by criminals who view you as a rich but weak target.

Microsoft is one of the richest corporations in the world. For a time, Microsoft deliberately avoided participating in politics. Microsoft just wanted to compete in the marketplace and felt that since it didn't need anything from the government, it would ignore politics.

From a political prospective Microsoft was rich but weak. Microsoft didn't make campaign contributions to U.S. politicians while its rivals did. Microsoft's rivals, therefore, had vastly more influence with politicians than Microsoft did. These rivals started using the government to attack Microsoft. As a result, Microsoft became extremely active in politics, spending millions to build political muscle.

Large businesses in the U.S. must be politically active or they will become prey to those who are. Of course, such incentives benefit politicians because they cause businesspeople to pay them tribute.

MICROSOFT FOUNDER BILL GATES

SECRETLY TAKING FROM PETER

Recall that a key problem for democratic politicians is that if they rob from Peter to pay Paul, then Peter might vote against them. But this problem is completely eliminated if Peter never realizes he has been robbed.

Consider two possible laws:

> Law 1: Every American who buys sugar must give $10 to millionaire sugar producers.

> Law 2: The government imposes a high tariff on sugar imported into the U.S.

Let's say that both laws impose the exact same cost on American sugar consumers. Under Law 1 many Americans will realize they are being fleeced to subsidize politically favored millionaires. But most Americans don't understand the economic consequences of tariffs. Consequently, sugar-consuming Americans are far less likely to punish politicians if they pass Law 2 than Law 1. Domestic sugar producers will of course realize that they benefit from sugar tariffs. Thus, by passing Law 2 politicians win the support of sugar producers without incurring the wrath of sugar consumers.

Politicians often use complicated laws to give resources to politically favored groups. For example:

- Televisions stations are not given million dollar checks. Rather, the U.S. government allows them to freely have television licenses worth millions of dollars each.

- Construction unions are not given direct government subsidies. Rather, the U.S. Congress passes laws making it difficult for nonunion laborers to compete against union construction workers.

Economists Are Not Anarchists, but . . .

- The U.S. government doesn't hand ranchers gold coins. Rather, ranchers have the right to use valuable government land for free.
- The U.S. government doesn't send a lawyer-bill to every American forcing them to pay money to trial lawyers. Rather, laws are enacted making it easy for trial lawyers to sue. These laws both enrich trial lawyers and raise the price that Americans pay for many products.

CONCENTRATED INTEREST GROUPS BEAT DIFFUSE ONES

Politicians in democratic countries reward organized, politically active groups. Concentrated interest groups can coordinate their political activities more easily than diffuse groups can.

For example, imagine that Congress is considering enacting a milk price support law. The law will give dairy farmers $30,000 each but will also raise the price of milk by 5 percent. Milk consumers will almost certainly not organize to fight the law. The price of milk is of minor importance to most consumers. Consequently, even if an organization existed to defend the interests of milk consumers, few milk drinkers would ever bother joining it. In contrast, dairy farmers care greatly about the price of milk, and they already belong to organizations that politically support their interests.

Generally, members of concentrated groups such as dairy farmers, truck drivers, lawyers, doctors, trial lawyers, and real estate agents find it relatively easy to organize politically. Members of these groups often socialize and feel a common bond with each other. They typically belong to industrywide organizations that collect dues from most in the profession. These organizations can use these dues easily to contribute to friendly politicians. The organizations can also inform their members about which candidates are most favorable to their interests.

The interests of consumers, however, are almost always diffuse. Consumers buy many goods and so are never affected greatly by the price of just one. Consequently, although the producers of goods often organize to promote their interests, the consumers of goods rarely do. Governments, therefore, are often politically pushed to enact pro-producer, anticonsumer laws.

Interestingly, many people are in both concentrated and diffuse groups. For example, dairy farmers are in a concentrated interest group as milk producers but a diffuse group as sugar buyers. Trial lawyers are in a concentrated interest group as litigators but in diffuse groups for every good they consume.

DESTRUCTION OF WEALTH

Democratic politicians take from some groups to give to others. Most people, however, are in both types of groups. So on average, can politicians still do any harm? Yes!

When politicians transfer resources, they distort the market by raising taxes, enacting tariffs, mandating prices, or restricting entry into professions. These distortions reduce the wealth of society. So if, for example, the government robs $100 from Peter to give to Paul, Paul will get considerably less than $100. The difference between what Peter loses and Paul gets becomes a deadweight loss to society. Transferring money among groups also creates deadweight losses because it encourages rent-seeking.

RENT-SEEKING

Political redistribution of resources also destroys wealth by encouraging rent-seeking. *Rents* are money a person receives beyond what the marketplace would ordinarily give him. So if, for example, a sugar producer would normally make a profit of $10,000 a year but because of tariffs receives a profit of $1,010,000 a year, then the sugar producer has received rents of $1 million a year.

When governments give away resources, they are conferring rents on their recipients. Firms will expend resources to acquire rents. For example, imagine that the government decides to give away a television license worth $10 million. A firm would be willing to spend up to $10 million to acquire this license.

Politicians, of course, benefit from rent-seeking. The more rents they dish out, the more people will attempt to buy their friendship.

> "Asking a politician to come out against rent-seeking is like asking a prostitute to come out against exchanging money for sex." —Arnold Kling (economist)

SPENDING OTHER PEOPLE'S MONEY

I had a great idea for promoting sales of this textbook, but my publisher rejected it for silly ethical reasons. First, I wanted to raise this textbook's price by $50. Second, I wanted to give professors $50 for every student of theirs who bought a new copy of this textbook.

> "Nobody spends somebody else's money as carefully as he spends his own." —Milton Friedman[4]

Students pay for textbooks, but professors choose them. When a professor assigns a textbook, he is essentially spending his students' money. People don't have the same incentives when spending other peoples' money as they do when spending their own.

Economics professors, like nearly everyone else, care mostly about the interests of themselves and their families. A professor with 100 students will choose the textbook for these students that maximizes *his* welfare. Now imagine that my textbook and some other are of equal quality. The other textbook costs students $50 less but if the professor assigns mine he receives $5,000. Surely any rational economics professor would assign my textbook. (Would you even want to take an economics class with a professor who was so irrational as to forgo an easy $5,000?)

Politicians are like textbook-choosing professors. Much of public choice theory concerns the incentives self-interested politicians have to gather and spend other peoples' money.

In 2001, the California government gave the software company Oracle a $95 million software contract. Usually many firms are allowed to bid for California government contracts, and the firm that offers the best deal wins the business. But the California government awarded the $95 million software contract to Oracle without giving other businesses a chance to bid. Two weeks after the contract was signed, Oracle donated $25,000 to the Governor of California's reelection campaign.

California's governor was spending other people's money when he decided how to award the software contract. He rationally awarded this contract in a way that maximized his self-interest.

U.S. Congressman Duke Cunningham was a member of a congressional committee that had considerable power over defense spending. In 2005, Cunningham was forced to resign because he was allegedly caught taking over $2.4 million in gifts from private firms seeking to influence governmental defense expenditures. When Congress decides what type of defense equipment to buy for the U.S. armed forces, they are spending other people's money. Many congressmen naturally spend this money in a way that benefits them.

Lack of subtlety caused Cunningham's collapse. If he just happened to support certain defense contractors and these defense contractors just happened to contribute to his campaign, nothing illegal would have taken place. But by accepting a Rolls-Royce, a yacht, and a 19th-century commode in return for favors, Cunningham's corruption was far too blatant.

IF OTHERS PAY, ORDER THE EXPENSIVE APPETIZER[5]

You go to a restaurant with 99 other people. Everyone agrees to divide the check equally when the meal is over. Consequently, you now have little incentive to care about the cost of the food you eat. If, for example, you were paying the full cost of your own meal, you would never buy a $15 shrimp cocktail. But since the cost of this cocktail will be split by 100 people, your ordering the shrimp increases the amount you pay by only fifteen cents. And fifteen cents for a shrimp cocktail is a very good deal.

True, if everyone else orders expensive appetizers, the check will be huge. But everyone else is likely to order expensive items regardless of what you do. As a result, it's in your self-interest to get tasty but expensive dishes.

Two economists examined how much people eat at a restaurant when they split the check compared to when they each pay individually. They found that diners "consume more when the cost is split."[6]

Pork U.S. Congressmen distributing "pork" are in a similar situation to our check-splitting diners. When a politician brings "pork" to his voters, it means that he gets the government to fund some nonessential project in his district. Real-life examples of pork include:

- $100,000 for Lewis and Clark exhibits in North Dakota.
- $500,000 for a Teapot Museum in North Carolina.
- $550,000 for a Dr. Seuss Memorial in Massachusetts.
- $1 million for the Waterfree Urinal Conservation Initiative in Michigan.
- $1.5 million to refurbish a statue of the Roman god Vulcan in Alabama.
- Billions and billions of dollars to build underground roads in Boston (CAGW).

The people of Alabama likely wouldn't have paid $1.5 million to refurbish their statue of the Roman god Vulcan. But they were grateful to have the federal government pay for the repairs. Alabama has about 1.5 percent of the U.S. population, so let's assume that Alabamians paid 1.5 percent of the cost, or $22,500, to refurbish the statue. At this low price it may well have been worth it for Alabama to have its pagan statue renovated.

Let's assume that Alabamians received only $100,000 in value from having their statue fixed. Because it cost $1.5 million to renovate the statue, the renovation destroyed $1.5 million—$100,000, or $1.4 million, in wealth. But since Alabamians received all of the benefit of the statue but paid only 1.5 percent of the cost, it was rational for them to welcome the refurbishing.

Pork, unfortunately, creates a Prisoners' Dilemma for taxpayers. If the politicians of every other state bring home the pork, you want your state's elected representatives to do so as well. But even if no other politicians engage in pork dealing, you still benefit by having your congressman do so. Consequently, voters from every state want their congressmen to get the federal government to pay for local projects. But when all states get pork, taxes go up. And these taxes have increased to pay for projects that are usually worth less than their cost. Consequently, taxpayers are on average worse off when all politicians seek pork than when no politicians do so.

The pork Prisoners' Dilemma, however, benefits politicians. Pork empowers politicians. If politicians have the ability to get the federal government to pay for local projects, then many local residents will eagerly seek the favor of politicians.

CORRUPTION

ANCIENT CORRUPTION

Corruption is probably as old as government itself. About 2,500 years ago, Solon ruled the city-state of Athens. Solon was concerned about the large debts owed by landholders. So he decided to cancel all these debts. Before pronouncing this law, Solon revealed his plan to a few friends. These friends immediately borrowed money to buy land. When Solon's land law came into force, his friends were able to keep the newly purchased land without having to pay back their debts.

THE MEXICO CITY POLICE

While visiting Mexico City, economist William Easterly did something so incredibly stupid that his Mexican friends "exploded in laughter" upon hearing the tale.[7] What Easterly did was ask a police officer for directions. Many Mexico City policemen view their primary job as extorting bribes. At times, asking the Mexican police for directions can be analogous to asking a mugger to hold your purse while you go to the restroom. To avoid being legally robbed, many Mexicans do their best to avoid contact with these police.

The corruption of the Mexican police may shock some readers. But what really might shock people are honest, not corrupt, police forces. Police have guns and if they rob you, you obviously can't turn to the police for help. So why don't all police forces use their power to extort bribes?

I don't know the answer to that last question. But what I do know is that the more powerful a government official is, the more opportunity he has for corruption.

> Reporting a crime to the [Russian] police is sometimes counter productive, as some of the police themselves are in cahoots with the criminals. In Ozerny, Russia, a robbery victim identified the perpetrator and filed a statement with the police. The victim was understandably distressed later to see 'the policeman drinking with the guy who robbed me.'[8]

MORE GOVERNMENT POWER MEANS MORE CORRUPTION

"When buying and selling are controlled by legislation, the first things to be bought and sold are legislators." —P. J. O'Rourke (Humorist)

The more power politicians have, the more people will pay them for favors. Furthermore, the greater the influence of politicians, the more they can extort money from people in return for not causing them harm. So one means of reducing corruption is to reduce the power of government. When economic decisions are made in markets rather than by the government, politicians have fewer opportunities for corruption.

In the 1970s and 1980s, businesses in India needed government permission to do almost anything. Such government power naturally gave Indian government officials tremendous opportunities for corruption, and many in the Indian government became corrupt. As a result, being a government official was more profitable and even more prestigious than being a businessperson was. These officials resisted pro-market liberalization to protect their power. But in the 1990s, India's slow economic growth rate and a short-term economic crisis finally convinced the Indian government to increase the power of the market at the expense of the government.

CORRUPTION, WEALTH CREATION, AND WEALTH DESTRUCTION

Sometimes corruption helps an economy. Corruption can allow businesspeople to circumvent harmful economic regulations. In the former Soviet Union, much economic activity took place in the illegal underground economy. If government officials had been unwilling to accept bribes from black marketeers, they would have shut down this underground economy, which was one of the most productive parts of the Soviet Union.

Providing corruption opportunities is the only type of salary some cash-poor governments can afford to offer employees. For example, the police in some very poor country might receive no salary but still work because their jobs allow them to extort bribes regularly.

Worldwide, an estimated $1 trillion is spent on bribes each year.[9]

Corruption, however, usually destroys wealth. When corrupt officials are determined to take as much as they can as quickly as they can, economic activity is devastated. Even mild forms of corruption can destroy wealth. Corruption is a tax and so a discouragement of wealth creation. For example, if you must pay off police officers every time you move goods across town, you will be less inclined to make goods.

WHEN GOVERNMENTS ARE EXTREMELY CORRUPT

An old Aesop fable warns against killing the goose that lays the golden egg. But sometimes the best thing you can do with a golden-egg-laying magical goose is to eat it.

Pretend that you have a magical goose but you know that someone else is going to take it away from you in one hour, before it can lay another egg. Well, since the goose will yield *you* no more gold, you might as well kill it and have a hearty meal.

Unstable vs. Stable Dictatorships
Consider some dictator-controlled country that initially has many healthy businesses. To simplify our analysis, assume that each year the dictator can take either 30 percent or 100 percent of each business's revenue.

If the dictator takes 100 percent of the revenues, then the businesses will die. The dictator will have killed the economic goose that lays the golden eggs. In contrast, if the dictator takes only 30 percent of each business's revenue, the businesses will survive and the dictator can continue to take more in the future. Over a period of 10 years, a dictator will get far more loot if he takes only 30 percent a year than if he takes 100 percent one year and gets nothing in the future.

Now consider some dictator contemplating his optimal level of corruption. If the dictator expects to be in power for a long time, he should take only 30 percent this year. But if he expects to soon lose power, he should take all he can today.

Stable dictatorships are vastly better than unstable rotating ones. Imagine that five warlords each periodically gain and lose control of a city. Upon gaining control, each warlord will sack the city, taking everything he can. A warlord who temporarily controls the city will realize that anything he doesn't take will be looted by his successor. Economic development, therefore, will be nearly impossible in this city since the government will quickly confiscate all portable wealth.

DECENTRALIZED VERSUS CENTRALIZED CORRUPTION

Let's assume that some country has a stable dictator who steals only 30 percent of each business's yearly revenue. But there are many other powerful government agencies that also have the opportunity to steal. The police, for example, could steal 5 percent from each business and the army 6 percent. Tax and custom officials could also steal 4 percent from each business. If all government agencies steal from businesses, then the businesses will collapse. A strong dictator, therefore, would stop people other than himself from stealing. But what if the dictator isn't strong enough to stop corruption by others?

Each government agency will find it in its own interest to steal from businesses. The agencies are essentially in a decentralized corruption Prisoners' Dilemma. For example, if everyone else is going to steal, the police should as well, because the economy is going to collapse soon no matter what the police do. If no one but the dictator steals, the police should steal because their theft won't cause the collapse of the economy. Consequently, regardless of what other government agencies do, each agency is better off stealing. As a result, however, the economy will soon collapse. But, knowing that the economy will collapse, everyone is going to take as much as possible today. The only escape from this Prisoners' Dilemma is for the dictator to stop all corruption other than his own. Alas, many dictators are too weak to stop corruption by lesser government officials.

Dictatorships with strong central governments, therefore, tend to have less corruption than ones with decentralized power centers. A prime reason why Africa is so poor is because African dictators frequently can't stop corruption by local government officials. As a result, high African corruption greatly impedes economic development.

ABUNDANT NATURAL RESOURCES INCREASE CORRUPTION

Consider two young adults named Richie Rich and Oliver Twist. Richie Rich has a trust fund that pays him $1 million a month. Oliver Twist comes from a very poor family and has no money but what he earns.

Richie Rich can "afford" to be far more irresponsible than Oliver Twist can. Richie can drink and party all day long and not have to worry about his finances. In contrast, Oliver Twist must be responsible enough to keep a job or else he will starve.

Unfortunately, several oil-rich nations act like irresponsible trust-fund brats. For example, the African nation of Nigeria has large amounts of oil. Regardless of how poorly governed Nigeria is, its government can still use oil revenue to keep itself in power.

The tiny Asian nation of Singapore, in contrast, has no natural resources.[11] When Singapore became independent in 1965, it faced crushing poverty, unfriendly neighbors, and communists trying to take over the country. The government of Singapore could survive only by building a strong economy.

"Nothing is more destructive to a legal order than a rogue government bent on plunder. No property is safe, no agreements can be relied upon, and consequently, no complex division of labor is possible. Economic life remains stunted and impoverished, confined to small-scale, short-term activities that lie low from the rapacious gaze of predatory government.[10]

The Curse of Natural Resources—
Economists have found that "countries with great natural resources tend nevertheless to grow more slowly than resource-poor countries."[12]

Singapore's government was unusually uncorrupt and devoted to economic development. Singapore went from being one of the poorest nations on earth in 1965 to one of the richest today. Singapore was perhaps lucky that it wasn't burdened with natural resources because the lack of natural resources almost forced it to develop an honest government.

COMPETITIVE POLITICS REDUCE CORRUPTION

Jim Wright, former Speaker of the U.S. House of Representatives, was brought down by a corruption scandal in the late 1980s. Congressman Wright had written an uninteresting book. Political organizations seeking influence with Speaker Wright bought multiple copies of the book, earning the Speaker $55,000. The book purchases were widely seen as attempts by political organizations to give Speaker Wright money illegally.

The scandal destroyed Wright because Congressman Newt Gingrich, a member of an opposing political party, relentlessly pursued it. Newt Gingrich hoped to be Speaker of the U.S. House of Representatives himself. It was thus in his self-interest to expose corruption by Speaker Wright. As a result of such exposure, Speaker Wright was forced to resign.

Interestingly, shortly after becoming Speaker, Newt Gingrich negotiated a book deal in which he was supposed to receive a $4.5 million advance from a major media company. Criticism by the opposition party forced Gingrich to give up the advance.

Political competition reduces corruption. Political candidates benefit by exposing wrongdoing committed by their opponents. Fear of exposure surely prevents some politicians from engaging in corruption. Not surprisingly, countries with just one political party tend to have the most corruption.

A Free Press Reduces Corruption

"Sunshine is the best disinfectant." —U.S. Supreme Court Justice Louis Brandeis

Along with political competition, a free press also reduces corruption. News organizations benefit from exposing corruption because doing so attracts customers. Highly corrupt countries usually try to restrict press freedom. The Internet, therefore, could potentially aid people fighting corruption in nations lacking a free press.

A government can control the papers, television, and radio news originating from within its borders. But the Internet is transnational and thus much harder to censor.

The ruling family of Bahrain has huge palaces and private islands which it bans ordinary people from seeing. But these ordinary people used the satellite images on Google Earth to view the restricted lands. Such images illuminated to the people of Bahrain the tremendous income inequality in their kingdom.[13]

Many nations, even dictatorships such as China, believe that Internet access increases economic growth and so they allow their people to use the net. But if Chinese citizens can freely surf the net, then they will come across stories of Chinese political corruption. So China is attempting to get the economic benefits of the Internet without allowing its people to use the Internet to circumvent Chinese press restrictions. Predictably, U.S. technology companies such as Yahoo are helping China filter the Internet.

In 1989, the Chinese government massacred pro-democracy demonstrators in China's Tiananmen Square; many of those killed were college students. In 2004, a Chinese communist party boss gave journalist Shi Tao instructions on how he was supposed to cover the event's 15th anniversary. Shi Tao "secretly" e-mailed a detailed description of these instructions to a pro-Chinese democracy Web site in New York. Unfortunately, Shi Tao had a Yahoo e-mail address, and when the Chinese government asked, Yahoo Inc. complied with its request to hunt him down. He was sentenced to 10 years in prison. When asked about the incident, Yahoo's co-founder Jerry Yang said, "To be doing business in China, or anywhere else in the world, we have to comply with local law."[14]

This Yahoo incident illustrates a paradox of technology and freedom. Driven by a quest for profits, U.S. companies such as Yahoo have unleashed an Internet-based information revolution on the world. By reducing governments' control over information, this revolution could potentially threaten dictatorships. But these same dictatorships offer great profits to U.S. companies that help the dictators censor the Internet. So for the same profit motives, the companies that helped fuel the information revolution are also fighting to contain it.

CORRUPTION BREEDS CORRUPTION

Countries can get into a corruption trap in which past corruption causes future corruption. Consider two police forces, one honest and the other corrupt. Corrupt men will be more inclined to join the corrupt rather than the honest force. Furthermore, a corrupt cop on the honest force will fear being turned in by honest police officers and so might find it in his self-interest to be honest. In contrast, an honest police officer on the corrupt force will fear retaliation if he rats out a bad cop.

Whenever a government organization acquires a reputation for corruption it becomes a magnet for corrupt men. Furthermore, it will be difficult to weed out the corruption since many in the organization will personally benefit from it.

In the 1960s Frank Serpico was one of the few honest police officers in New York City. His attempts to expose police corruption earned him the hatred of almost all of his fellow officers. While in an apartment building with three other police officers, Serpico was shot by a drug dealer. After he was shot, the other officers left the building and didn't call for help. Serpico was only saved because a resident of the apartment building called an ambulance. When testifying about police corruption before a commission, Serpico said "I hope that police officers in the future will not experience the same frustration and anxiety that I was subjected to for the past five years at the hands of my superiors because of my attempt to report corruption. We create an atmosphere in which the honest officer fears the dishonest officer, and not the other way around. The problem is that the atmosphere does not yet exist in which honest police officers can act without fear of ridicule or reprisal from fellow officers."[15]

PROBLEMS WITH DEMOCRACY

This chapter on government imperfections now concludes with problems specific to democratic countries.

VOTING IS IRRATIONAL!

You have a greater chance of being killed in an accident on the way to vote than you do of having your vote making a difference. Consider the U.S. presidential election, in which over 100 million votes are cast. The chance of your one vote deciding who will become president is so small as to be effectively zero. Even the extremely close 2000 U.S. presidential election wasn't decided by one vote. Even if only 10,000 people vote in some local election, the chance of one vote deciding the election is very, very small. So why do people vote? Either they are irrational or they receive some inherent pleasure from voting.

But even if you do vote, you have no incentive to become informed about the candidates before casting your ballot. After all, since your vote isn't going to matter, why should you bother to invest the time necessary to make an intelligent voting decision?

Imagine you're deciding whether to buy Nike or Reebok athletic shoes. You will vote in the marketplace for one of these brands. Since your vote will completely determine which brand of sneakers you get, you have some incentive to investigate the sneakers' quality. Now imagine that two candidates are running for U.S. president. If, as with the sneakers, your vote will decide which president you get, then you would have tremendous incentive to make an informed choice. But since your vote for president will almost certainly have no effect on the outcome, you have almost no incentive to investigate the quality of the candidates.

POLITICIANS HAVE SHORT TIME HORIZONS

Politicians have little incentive to think beyond their political term. Imagine you own a home and plan to sell it in six years. Your home has a roof that, if not repaired, will fall apart seven years from now. Should you bother to repair the roof? Yes. The person who buys your home will pay more if it has a good roof. Thus, even though you don't directly care about what your home's condition will be in seven years, the market forces you to take the long-term future into account.

In contrast, if you are a politician and will leave office in six years you have limited incentives to care about how your actions will affect the world more than six years hence. True, if voters realize that you have done something that will hurt them seven years from now, they might vote against you in the next election. But individual voters have minimal incentives to analyze the long-range consequences of politicians' actions.

GOVERNMENT PROGRAMS DON'T ALWAYS HAVE TO SATISFY CONSUMERS

In 2004 I ran (very unsuccessfully) for the Massachusetts State Senate. I had to file campaign finance reports with my state's Office of Campaign and Political Finance. I was a first-time candidate unfamiliar with the rules. I called the Office of Campaign and Political Finance and was shocked at how helpful they were. They immediately answered my call, were friendly, understood what I needed to do, and were even open on a Sunday before a Monday filing deadline. (Try calling your average government agency on a Sunday and see what kind of service you get.)

Why were they so competent? I suspect it's because the people they help are mostly either politicians or top-staff members of politicians. They could get in serious trouble if they don't satisfy their politically powerful customers.

In contrast, most government agencies lose nothing if they offer poor service. If your state's Department of Motor Vehicles makes you wait in line for a few hours, what can you do? You probably won't vote against a governor because of poor service at a Department of Motor Vehicles.

If a privately run store offers poor service, it will lose customers and eventually go out of business. In contrast, government agencies are supported by taxpayer funds. They can last forever even if they fail to satisfy their customers' desires. The book *Naked Economics* provides an extreme example of this:

> "By 1991, the Hindustan Fertilizer Corporation [of India] had been up and running for twelve years. Every day, twelve hundred employees reported to work with the avowed goal of producing fertilizer. There was just one small complication: The plant had never actually produced any salable fertilizer. None. Government bureaucrats ran the plant using public funds; the machinery that was installed never worked properly. Nevertheless, twelve hundred workers came to work every day and the government continued to pay their salaries. The entire enterprise was an industrial charade. It limped along because there was no mechanism to force it to shut down. When government is bankrolling the business, there is no need to produce something and then sell it for more than it cost to make."

From: *Naked Economics: Undressing The Dismal Science* by Charles Wheelan. © 2002 by Charles Wheelan. Used by permission of W. W. Norton & Company, Inc.

INCUMBENTS RARELY LOSE

In democracies, voters are supposed to choose politicians. But the reverse can occur, with politicians picking their voters. Imagine that a state has 600,000 people and six congressional districts. Each district must have 100,000 people in it. Further assume that the state's voters are equally divided between members of the Democratic and Republican parties. You might think that the equal number of Republican and Democratic voters in the state would mean close congressional elections, but this is not necessarily so.

State legislators usually determine which voters are in which congressional districts. Imagine that our legislator puts 70,000 Republicans and 30,000 Democrats in each of the first three districts and the reverse in districts 4, 5, and 6. The congressional elections in each district will be extremely lopsided. The Republican candidates will easily win the first three districts and the Democratic candidates the second three. Once elected, all six candidates will have very safe seats. But why would the state legislator want to create safe seats for congressional incumbents of both parties?

Incumbent congressmen often have powerful political organizations in their state. They can use these organizations to reward state legislators who give them safe seats. The congressional seniority system also creates incentives for state legislators to give incumbents safe seats.

In the U.S. Congress, the longer a member has been in office the more influence he has. Powerful committee chairmanships usually go to the member of the majority party on the committee who has been in office the longest. And the more powerful a congressman is, the more money he can send to his state. State legislators, therefore, often want powerful incumbent congressmen to get reelected even if they are from an opposition party. Incumbent congressman thus benefit from the seniority system because it creates incentives for their state legislators to give them safe seats.

U.S. incumbent congressmen also receive far more campaign contributions on average than their challengers do. Congressmen have considerable power. This power attracts campaign contributions. And money facilitates election victories.

When politicians arrange voting districts to maximize their own political advantage it's called **gerrymandering.** The term *gerrymander* is a blend of the name *Gerry* and the word *salamander*. Elbridge Gerry (1774–1814) was a governor of Massachusetts who created a salamander-shaped district to harm a political opponent.

Politicians write election rules. Acting in their own self-interests, politicians pick these rules to make it difficult for them to lose reelection. Imagine, for example, that politicians enact campaign finance reform supposedly designed to make elections more honest. Economists would assume that since the reform was written by incumbent congressmen it would benefit incumbent congressmen. The campaign finance law, for example, might make it relatively more difficult for challengers than for incumbents to raise funds.

BUT AT LEAST DEMOCRACIES DON'T HAVE FAMINES

Nobel Prize-winning economist Amartya Sen has pointed out that no functional democracy has ever had a substantial famine. A democratic politician who allowed a famine to occur would lose many, many votes in the next election. So avoiding famines strongly serves the self-interest of democratic politicians.

In contrast, dictators sometimes benefit from famines. Zimbabwe's dictator Robert Mugabe deliberately created famines in parts of his country where he has little support to kill or physically weaken his opposition.[16]

At the end of the 20th century almost all of the rich nations were democratic. Perhaps this is because democracies promote wealth creation or perhaps because rich people want democracies. Either way, this represents a strong endorsement of political freedom. So while democracies have imperfections, it is as Winston Churchill said: "Democracy is the worst form of government except for all those others that have been tried."

QUESTIONS YOU SHOULD BE ABLE TO ANSWER AFTER READING THIS CHAPTER:

1   What is public choice theory? (page 298)

2   What are some reasons why economists believe that government is necessary? (page 301)

3   Whose self-interest do economists believe that politicians serve? (page 301)

4   Why does the key difference between government officials and businesspeople arise from Adam Smith's invisible hand? (pages 301–302)

5   What simple three-step formula can dictators follow to maintain power? (page 302)

6   Why can't democratic politicians follow the above formula? (page 302)

7   What two-step formula can democratic politicians follow to benefit from robbing from Peter to pay Paul? (page 302)

8   Why did Microsoft find it necessary to develop political muscle? (page 303)

9   How can democratic politicians secretly take from Peter? (pages 303–304)

10   Why do concentrated interest groups beat diffuse ones? (page 304)

11   Why do democratic politicians often pass pro-producer, anticonsumer laws? (page 304)

12   What is rent-seeking? (page 305)

STYLE PROBLEMS

STUDY PROBLEMS

1 If you are a citizen of a democratic country, do you intend to vote in your country's next election? If so, why?

2 Should U.S. companies be permitted, under U.S. law, to bribe government officials of foreign countries? How might U.S. companies benefit from a U.S. law prohibiting such bribes?

3 In 2005, the U.S. Congress almost allocated $223 million for an Alaskan bridge that would have connected Ketchikan, Alaska, to an island where only 50 people lived. When interviewed by journalists, these 50 people claimed that they really didn't want the bridge. Why did the Alaskan congressional delegation fight for the U.S. government to fund this bridge?

4 Imagine that some U.S. state has seven congressional districts. To simplify this question, assume that this state has 77 voters, 53 of whom are members of the Democratic Party and 24 of whom are members of the Republican Party. Assume that the state legislator must put 11 voters in each district.

First, assume that the state legislator is controlled by the Democratic Party. How could the legislator allocate voters so Democratic voters form a majority of voters in all seven districts?

Second, assume that the state legislator is controlled by the Republican Party. How could the legislator allocate voters so Republicans form a majority of voters in four of the seven districts?

5   Consider two possible voting laws. The first forces all who don't vote to pay a fine equal to one week's salary. The second law requires that all who do vote must pay a tax equal to one week's salary. If one of the two laws had to be passed, which would you prefer?

6   Which salary for U.S. congressmen would minimize their level of corruption: $0 per year, $150,000 per year, or $10 million per year?

7   Since voters have no incentive to cast informed votes, would a nation benefit if it forced all citizens to pass some test before being eligible to vote?

8   In most parts of the United States, if a police officer stops you for speeding and you offer him a bribe to let you go, the officer will not accept the money but will arrest you. In many other countries, if a police officer stops you and you don't offer him a bribe, you might be taken to jail. Speculate on why some police forces are honest and others corrupt.

9   "The Ten Commandments contain 297 words. The Bill of Rights is stated in 463 words. Lincoln's Gettysburg Address contains 266 words. A recent [U.S.] federal directive to regulate the price of cabbage contains 26,911 words."[17] How could the complexity of federal directives serve the self-interest of government officials?

10 The percentage of elderly in the U.S. population is steadily increasing. What will happen to their political power and their ability to get politicians to transfer resources to them as their relative numbers increase? Is there any factor that could reduce their political influence?

11 The military is often the most effective part of most national governments. Why is this?

12 How does the United States' Electoral College system of choosing a president influence how people run for president? Compare the Electoral College to a system where the candidate who gets the most votes is elected president. (Note: this textbook does not describe the Electoral College.)

13

"THE BAN ON USING DDT IN HOUSES TO FIGHT MALARIA IS AN EXAMPLE OF ENVIRONMENTALISM THAT LOST ALL SENSE OF PROPORTION...AS A RESULT OF THE HYSTERIA AGAINST THE USE OF DDT FOR ANY PURPOSE, MILLIONS OF LIVES WERE LOST UNNECESSARILY DURING THE PAST SEVERAL DECADES TO MALARIA AND SOME OTHER INSECT-BORNE DISEASES."

—Gary Becker[1] (Nobel Prize–winning economist)

THE POLLUTION PROBLEM

Pollution poses a problem for free market admirers. Without government assistance, Adam Smith's invisible hand will do little to reduce pollution. And the pollution that a modern industrial city could produce would choke the life out of most metropolises. So societies need governments to regulate pollution. But as we have seen, sometimes when governments attempt to fix markets, they can also create many problems themselves.

Economists can formulate policies that governments *should* follow to optimally regulate pollution. But economists have absolutely no reason to expect that governments *will* follow these policies. So because pollution is created by imperfect markets and regulated by imperfect governments, there is no ultimate pollution solution.

NEGATIVE EXTERNALITIES

Pollution is an example of a negative externality. A negative externality is a cost paid by people other than the buyer or seller of a good. This cost is incidental or "external" to the production and use of a product. So imagine that I decide to buy something that creates pollution. The cost this pollution imposes on people other than myself and the product's manufacturer is a negative externality. Generally, if other people are harmed by your having a product then that product has negative externalities.

Here are some negative externalities that often afflict college dorm residents:

- Noise—emitted by radios, televisions, and video games.
- Smoke—produced by cigarettes.

CHALLENGE TO MARKET EFFECTIVENESS 3: EXTERNALITIES AND THE ENVIRONMENT

- Stink—radiated by long unwashed clothes and moldy food.
- Vomit—induced by alcohol consumption.
- Roaches—attracted by uneaten food.
- Fire hazards—produced by candles burning under low-hanging curtains.
- Visual pollution—brought forth by tacky posters.
- Police raids—drawn in by illegal drug use.

PRODUCTS WITH NEGATIVE EXTERNALITIES ARE OVERUSED

Absent outside intervention, buyers and sellers don't pay any cost for imposing negative externalities on others. As a result, self-interested consumers and firms usually don't take into account negative externalities in their decision making.

For example, when a student cranks up his radio, he harms people other than himself. This student often pays no cost for inflicting acoustical harm on his dorm mates. Unless his dorm mates find some way to pressure him, a self-interested student will set his radio's volume to maximize his pleasure and so ignore the cost his radio imposes on others.

POSITIVE EXTERNALITIES

Positive externalities are benefits received by people other than the buyer and seller of a good. So, for example, if others can hear your radio and enjoy its sounds, they have received a positive externality from your purchase of the radio. Goods with positive externalities include:

- Vaccines—They reduce the chance of your spreading disease.
- Deodorants, colognes, and perfumes—They improve your smells.
- Shrubberies—They make your lawn look nicer and so improve the appearance of your neighborhood.
- Dogs—They keep watch over your neighborhood and so deter criminals.
- Attractive clothes—They allow strangers to enjoy your appearance.

PRODUCTS WITH POSITIVE EXTERNALITIES ARE UNDERUSED

Self-interested individuals will buy less than the socially optimal number of positive externality goods. To see this, consider an extreme example. Imagine that if you plant a certain type of magical shrubbery, all 1 million houses in your city will be worth $10 more than they were before. This shrubbery, therefore, would add $10 million to the wealth of your city. But assume that the shrubbery sells for $11 while it gives you only $10 worth of benefit. You may not purchase the shrubbery even though doing so would have created enormous wealth.

THE CLUB

EXTERNALITIES AND ANTITHEFT DEVICES[2]

To help you further understand externalities, let's consider anti-car-theft devices that can create either negative or positive externalities. Both LoJack and The Club are anti-car-theft devices. The Club is a metal "club" that locks through a steering wheel, preventing a thief from turning the wheel. LoJack is a tiny electronic locator. When a car with LoJack is stolen, the locator is activated, signaling the car's location to the police. The Club creates negative externalities while LoJack creates positive externalities.

You're a thief looking to steal a car. The first one you come across has The Club installed. So you go on to the next. One car owner's use of The Club, therefore, decreases the chance of his car getting stolen but increases the chance of another car being pilfered. The Club consequently creates negative externalities.

Again imagine that you're a car thief. You have been stealing cars successfully for several years when you suddenly learn about LoJack. You don't know which cars have LoJack, but if you steal a LoJacked car, you will almost certainly get caught by the police. Widespread use of LoJack, consequently, makes it less likely that thieves will steal any car. One car owner's installation of LoJack, therefore, confers a positive externality on other car owners.

Because The Club creates negative externalities, it will be overused from the point of view of what is best for society. Purchasers of The Club don't pay its full cost since some of this cost is incurred by other car owners who are now more likely to have their vehicles stolen. In contrast, LoJack creates positive externalities since it generally deters car thieves. LoJack, therefore, will be underused from the viewpoint of what is best for society since its purchasers don't receive all the benefits of LoJack.

THE NEGATIVE EXTERNALITIES OF LEADED GASOLINE

Imagine that to run your car you must buy either:

Unleaded gasoline at $2.00/gallon.

Leaded gasoline at $1.80/gallon.

Assuming that both would give you the same mileage, a self-interested driver would choose the leaded gas. Leaded gas poisons the atmosphere and lowers the intelligence of children. But other people will suffer almost all of the pollution harm of your using leaded gas. This harm is a negative externality that a self-interested person will ignore.

Even if you have children, you should still buy the leaded gas. To see this let's quantify the harm caused by your use of leaded gasoline. Assume that for every gallon of leaded gas consumed you do $.00001 worth of harm to each child in your city. This means that if parents were fully informed about the harm of lead poisoning and made a deeply considered calculation, they would pay $.00001 per gallon to stop other drivers from using leaded gasoline. This amount is small because the quantity of lead emitted by a gallon of leaded gas is itself extremely small.

If you have a child, then the total cost to you of your using leaded gas is $1.80 + $.00001 = $1.80001. But now assume that your city contains 1 million children. The total cost to your city of the leaded pollution externality is (1,000,000)($.00001)/gallon, or $10 per gallon. So the true cost of leaded gas, which is the cost to you plus the cost to others, is $11.80/gallon. Since the cost of unleaded gasoline is only $2, society is better off if you use unleaded. But absent government intervention, self-interested drivers will buy leaded gas because they don't pay the full cost of its use.

If you have a child, you would prefer that everyone (including you) use unleaded gas than for everyone to use leaded gas. But if just you switched to unleaded, everyone else would still use leaded gas. So your real choice is between (a) having everyone but you using leaded gas, or (b) having everyone including you using leaded gas. You are better off with (b). Parent-drivers are in a leaded Prisoners' Dilemma where everyone is individually better off using leaded gas, but collectively better off if everyone uses unleaded gas. In other words, it's rational for every parent to use leaded gas even though leaded gas makes society far worse off.

So what should the government do to help reduce the harm of leaded gas and other types of pollution? We now consider five possibilities.

FIVE METHODS OF REDUCING THE HARM OF POLLUTION

METHOD 1 OF REDUCING POLLUTION: FORBID ALL POLLUTION

The solution to the leaded gas externality in the last example is easy: The government should ban leaded gasoline. And indeed this is what many governments do.

Other pollution externalities, however, cannot be managed as easily. Leaded gas does a tremendous amount of harm, and unleaded gas is an excellent substitute for leaded gas. Thus, the case for governmental bans on leaded gasoline is strong. The government, however, would cause massive harm to the economy if it similarly banned all pollutants.

Many valuable economic activities create pollution. If the government banned all types of pollution, it would drastically reduce economic production. My guess is that a total ban on pollution would kill over 90 percent of the human population. Many of the tools farmers use cause pollution, so without pollution-causing activities farmers would be unable to feed the world's billions. Furthermore, almost every industry creates pollution. Consequently if all pollution was banned, human civilization would fall to its pretechnological level where life was "nasty, brutish and short."[3] So sane government officials need to consider means other than total bans to handle most types of pollution externalities.

METHOD 2 OF REDUCING POLLUTION: COMMAND AND CONTROL

Under the command and control approach to pollution regulation, the government tells each firm how much it can pollute and what kind of pollution-reducing technologies it must employ. But command and control suffers from two problems: information deficiencies and governmental corruption.

Information Deficiencies

Markets excel at gathering and organizing information, whereas government bureaucrats tend to be informationally challenged. To determine optimally how much each firm should pollute, a bureaucrat would have to learn nearly everything about a company and the people affected by that company's pollution. For example, imagine that a certain type of pollution causes $1 million of harm. Ideally, a company should be allowed to emit this type of pollution only if doing so would create over $1 million of wealth. But how could bureaucrats learn the benefit each firm received from polluting? A company that received only $50,000 of benefit from polluting, for example, would have an incentive to lie and claim that its being able to pollute would create millions in wealth.

Governmental Corruption

Even if the government somehow gathered all the information necessary to make optimal pollution decisions, why would self-interested politicians enact socially optimal pollution regulations? Politicians could instead grant the right to pollute to their supporters. And, as the following example shows, politicians often pass expensive environmental regulations to protect their allies.

Unnecessary Coal Scrubbers[4] In 1970 the U.S. Environmental Protection Agency limited the amount of sulfur dioxide, a cause of acid rain, that coal-burning power plants could release. Power plants could satisfy this limit in basically two ways:

1. They could use "clean" burning coal that contained little sulfur,
2. They could use "dirty" high-sulfur coal and install sulfur-removing scrubbers.

The first option was cheaper for many firms and so the demand for dirty coal plummeted. Most dirty coal was mined in the eastern United States. In 1977 eastern politicians got a law passed through Congress requiring all new coal-burning plants to install scrubbers even though scrubbers weren't needed by plants burning clean coal. But since plants with scrubbers could burn clean or dirty coal, the scrubber requirement eliminated the dirty coal disadvantage and so increased the demand for dirty coal.

In 2007 many advertisements appeared attacking the coal industry as being "filthy." It turns out that the ads were sponsored by a natural-gas-production company. Natural gas is a substitute of coal and so natural gas producers would benefit if the government restricted coal use.[5]

Ironically, this scrubber requirement increased coal pollution. By requiring scrubbers to be installed only in new power plants, the scrubber law increased the cost of building these new plants. As a result, many power companies delayed building modern facilities that would have used superior pollution-reducing technologies.

METHOD 3 OF REDUCING POLLUTION: PIGOVIAN TAXES

Economist Arthur Pigou argued that governments should tax goods that create negative externalities. Such "Pigovian taxes" reduce individual's incentives to use such goods. Pigovian taxes have four advantages over command and control pollution regulation.

ARTHUR PIGOU
(1877–1959)

1. Taxation allows firms to pick their own level of pollution. A firm has greater information about the benefits of its pollution-generating activities than a government does. If the government can correctly assess the harm of pollution and set a tax equal to this level of harm, then a firm will make the socially optimal pollution decision. If, for example, each ton of sulfur dioxide pollution does $100 of harm then the government could impose a $100-per-ton tax on sulfur dioxide emissions. A firm would then emit sulfur dioxide only if the benefit it received from the relevant pollution-generating activities exceeded the externality cost.

2. When firms are taxed based on how much they pollute, they always have an incentive to reduce their pollution since less pollution means lower taxes. In contrast, if the government simply determines the maximum amount a firm can pollute, the firm gains nothing if it pollutes less than this amount.

3. Taxation gives firms flexibility in deciding how to reduce pollution. With Pigovian pollution taxes, for example, firms, and not the government, decide whether to use clean coal, scrubbers, or both. Pollution taxes create incentives for firms to use the most cost-efficient pollution-reducing methods.

4. Finally, taxation creates incentives for antipollution technological innovation. If the government tells each firm what type of pollution control devices it must use, firms lack incentives to innovate and find superior pollution-reducing technologies. In contrast, if the government taxes pollution, then firms gain from discovering new pollution-reducing technologies. Furthermore, pollution taxes create a market for innovators who don't themselves pollute. These innovators can develop, patent, and then sell pollution-reducing technologies to polluting firms.

Supply, Demand, and Pigovian Taxes Supply and demand curves can show the social benefit of Pigovian taxes. First, let's consider the supply and demand curves for a good that gives off pollution. Supply curves show how much producers want to produce at every price. Demand curves show how much consumers want to buy at every price. Externalities, by definition, don't affect consumers or producers directly. As a result, externalities don't have any direct effect on supply and demand curves.

Let's keep everything simple and assume that people in some town can get as much of a good as they want at $10 a unit. The supply curve for this good, therefore, will be horizontal at $10 as shown in Figure 13.1. At the price of $10 people in the town will buy 870 units of the good.

Because the price is $10, people will use the good as long as the benefit they receive from it exceeds $10. But now assume that use of each good imposes a $3 pollution externality on the town. Unless checked, this $3 externality will create a deadweight loss. Consider, for example, Jane. Let's assume that Jane receives $11 of benefit from using

FIGURE **13.1**

SUPPLY CURVE AT
$10 PER UNIT

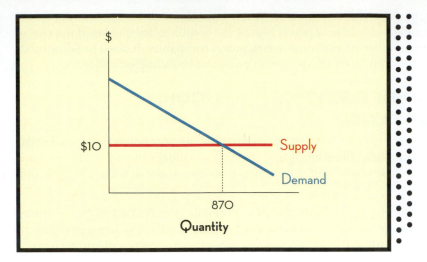

the good. She will buy the good at a price of $10 and so receives a $1 consumer's surplus for her purchase of the good. Jane's use of the good, however, will cause $3 worth of harm to other people. Consequently, Jane's use of the polluting product causes a $2 deadweight loss.

Ideally, we would like people to use the product only as long as they receive more than $13 of benefit from it, because $13 represents the true cost to society of the good's use. A $3 Pigovian tax, fortunately, takes us to this ideal.

After a $3 tax is placed on this good, the supply curve facing the town shifts up by $3. At this price, people will purchase the good only when they get more than $13 of benefit. As Figure 13.2 shows, after the tax is imposed, consumers buy only 491 units of the good—less than before. The Pigovian tax, therefore, has succeeded in reducing the amount of pollution caused by the product.

Internalizing Externalities

Imagine you have two children: Jack, age 8, and Billy, age 5. Jack likes to play "rough" games with Billy. And Billy, who idolizes Jack, always goes along. Unfortunately, sometimes Billy gets hurt. This pain is an externality caused by Jack's playing.

You as a parent don't want to stop your boys from playing. You also understand that boys sometimes get hurt when they play. But you want Jack to take into account the pain that he sometimes causes Billy.

Now imagine that scientists invent a "pain transfer" machine. After you set up this machine in your house, Jack, not Billy, will feel any pain Billy would normally experience as a result of the two's rough play. This pain transfer machine forces Jack to "internalize" any negative externality he would have otherwise inflicted on his brother. After the machine is installed, Jack will take far more care when roughhousing with Billy.

Pigovian taxes, ideally, force people and firms to internalize any externalities they cause. Imagine that your use of a product inflicts $3 worth of harm on others. If the government imposes a $3 tax on you and gives this money to those you hurt, then the government has forced you to fully pay the cost of your externality. Such a Pigovian tax transfers the pain of your externality from others onto you. This pain transfer won't necessarily stop you from causing externalities, but it certainly will force you to fully take into account the harm your externalities cause when deciding how much of the product to use.

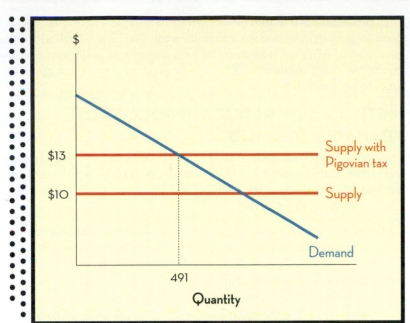

FIGURE **13.2**

SUPPLY CURVE
WITH PIGOVIAN TAX

$

$13 — Supply with Pigovian tax

$10 — Supply

Demand

491

Quantity

In real life, Pigovian tax revenue is rarely given to those harmed by externalities. Rather, the money is often kept by the government and spent however politicians wish. Still, by forcing the creators of externalities to pay a tax equal to the harm caused to others by their activity, Pigovian taxes cause consumers and firms to engage in externality-causing activities only when the benefit of the activity exceeds the total social cost of the activity.

Price Signposts   Prices are signposts that guide consumers and firms. When Adam Smith's invisible hand operates well, the signposts guide market participants to take the socially optimal path. Externalities, however, cause market prices to give "bad directions" that result in market participants deviating from the optimal path. The greater the externality, the bigger the deviation. When the government uses socially optimal Pigovian taxes, it corrects the marketplace's price signposts.

For example, again assume that leaded gas costs $1.80 while unleaded gas costs $2. In this instance, the marketplace is signaling to consumers that leaded gas is cheaper and should be preferred to unleaded gas. As a result of this price sign, consumers will indeed prefer leaded to unleaded gas. But if a $10 Pigovian tax was imposed on leaded gas, then the marketplace would be signaling loudly that it's better to use *unleaded*.

The Disadvantage of Pollution Taxes   Pigovian taxation works best when the harm of pollution is always proportional to the amount of pollution. For example, taxes would work well if every ton of emitted sulfur dioxide does $100 of harm because then the government could simply impose a $100-per-ton tax. But what if after a certain amount of pollution has been released, extra pollution causes an environmental catastrophe?

Consider a simple example where each ton of sulfur dioxide does $100 of harm as long as the total amount emitted is less than 40 million tons. But if much more than 40 million tons are emitted, then something horrible happens to the environment, causing trillions of dollars of harm.

In this example it would be dangerous to impose a $100-per-ton tax because then firms might pollute more than 40 million tons. In general, with Pigovian taxation the government can't set limits on the total amount of pollution. Fortunately, governments can enact another market-friendly method of pollution control that does allow them to set a total pollution limit.

METHOD 4 OF REDUCING POLLUTION: TRADABLE PERMITS

Imagine that each student in my economics class is supposed to turn in a paper by December 15th. I don't mind if a few students are late, but if more than five students are late, it will greatly inconvenience me because I want to grade all the papers by Christmas. What should I do?

Grant no extensions (analogous to no pollution)—This approach is inefficient. I don't suffer if the number of students turning in late papers is fewer than six. But some students might receive tremendous benefit from receiving extensions.

I pick the five students who can be late (analogous to command and control)— How would I know which students would receive the greatest value from an extension? Do I give the extensions to the students who: (a) have just been dumped by their boyfriends/girlfriends, (b) have some illness, (c) have an important upcoming sporting event, (d) have multiple papers due on the 15th, (e) are struggling with the class, (f) are doing a fantastic job in the class, (g) have a series of upcoming job interviews, (h) must work 40 hours a week at some job, (i) have had a relative die recently, (j) have trouble writing in English, or (k) continually tell me what a great professor I am? Regardless of how I make my decision, students will suspect that I used (k) as my criterion and this could hurt my student evaluations.

I tax late papers—Students who turn in a late paper must donate $50 to the charity of my choice. The advantage of this taxation approach is that only students who place a relatively high monetary value on being late will turn in a late paper. Also, unlike the last approach, I won't have to evaluate each student's individual reason for wanting an extension. The disadvantage of using taxation, however, is that far more than five students might choose to pay the tax.

Tradable permits—I create five lateness permits. The holder of each permit can turn in his paper late. I auction off the certificates and give the money to charity. The five students who bid the most each get a permit. But students can buy and sell these permits among themselves. If, therefore, one student buys a permit but then unexpectedly finishes the paper on time, he could sell his permit to another student. Similarly, if a student without a permit faces some unexpected crisis, she could buy a permit from another student.

Under the tradable permit plan, the students who place the highest monetary value on being late will buy the permits. Furthermore, tradable permits in this example are superior to taxation because they ensure that five and only five students will turn in late papers. Finally, the price that the permits trade for will provide me with information on how much students value being late. If a lateness permit sells for $700, for example, I will know that some students desperately need extensions.

Since 1990 the United States has used a tradable permit system for sulfur dioxide. Under this system companies are given permits to pollute. A firm can use its permits, buy permits from other firms, or sell its permits to other firms. But a firm can pollute only up to the amount covered by its permits.

Most of the advantages of tradable permits are identical to the benefits of Pigovian taxes. Both pollution-reducing methods (a) give tremendous flexibility to firms in deciding how to combat pollution, (b) ensure that only firms that place a relatively high value on pollution end up polluting, and (c) create a market for pollution-reduction innovations. But there are some key differences between tradable permits and Pigovian taxes.

Tradable Permits versus Pigovian Taxation

Only tradable permits allow the government to set the total amount of pollution that will be generated. So if the government can somehow determine the optimal level of pollution, then tradable permits are socially superior to Pigovian taxes. But if the government doesn't know the optimal level of pollution but does know how much harm each unit of pollution causes, then the government should use Pigovian taxes to allow the market to set the optimal level of pollution.

Environmentalists Buying Tradable Permits

A tradable permit system allows environmentalists to buy and then not use pollution permits. Assume, for example, that the government issues permits for emitting 40 million tons of sulfur dioxide. An environmental group could buy, say, permits for 1 million tons and industry could then pollute only 39 million tons. This approach is analogous to environmental groups buying land and then not allowing any development on the land.

METHOD 5 OF REDUCING POLLUTION: THE COASE THEOREM

RONALD COASE (1910–)

The final method of reducing pollution is for the government to do nothing and allow the Coase Theorem to work. To understand the Coase Theorem, let's revisit the problem of dorm negative externalities.

Assume some dorm resident named Jack receives $3 of benefit from playing his radio at a high volume. But this noise pollution inflicts $1 of harm on each of the other 20 people living on Jack's hall. If the 20 other residents do nothing Jack will play his radio at a high volume.

But what if Jack and his dorm mates could negotiate? Jack should be willing to accept, say, $4 to stop playing his radio at a high volume. And collectively his dorm mates would be better off paying this amount than being subjected to the noise pollution. So if all the parties concerned can negotiate, Jack could be bribed not to blast his radio.

The Coase Theorem, named after is originator Ronald Coase, holds that if there are no barriers to negotiations, then all wealth-destroying negative externalities should be eliminated through negotiations. Let's consider the Coase Theorem in the abstract. Some activity gives Jack a gain of G but imposes negative externalities totaling N. If the activity is wealth destroying, then N>G. But if N>G, then the people damaged by the externality should be able to bribe Jack, paying him something between G and N, to get him to stop. Because the bribe is greater than G, Jack is better off accepting the bribe than engaging in the activity. Because the bribe is less than N, everyone else is better off paying the bribe than suffering the harm of the externality.

According to the Coase Theorem, if parties can negotiate they will always be able to eliminate wealth-destroying negative externalities. But, as Ronald Coase recognized, there are often many barriers to negotiation. In our dorm situation perhaps it would be too difficult for all 20 people harmed by the externality to come together and bribe Jack. Or perhaps Jack is untrustworthy and if he accepted $4 to turn off his radio, he would pocket the money and keep playing the radio.

Generally, we would expect the Coase Theorem to solve problems involving relatively few people. If, for example, sulfur dioxide pollution harmed 100 million people, it would be nearly impossible for them, absent governmental help, to come together and bribe the negative externality's creator. But when a small group of people are harmed by an externality, the Coase Theorem indicates that they might be able to remedy the situation through negotiations.

ARE POOR COUNTRIES UNDERPOLLUTED?[6]

Imagine that the United States is considering building a "dirty" petroleum refinery that produces high-quality fuel. Unfortunately, the refinery will create a significant negative pollution externality afflicting everyone living near it. Should the refinery be built in the United States?

Let's assume that the refinery will be built in either the United States or Africa. If the dirty refinery were built in the United States, it would inflict $100 million in pollution harm. This means that if you built the refinery in the United States, you would have to pay local residents a total of $100 million to compensate them fully for exposure to the negative pollution externality. If the refinery were built in Africa, it would pollute the air breathed by 10,000 people. But these 10,000 people make around $1 a day. They would gladly accept the refinery in return for each receiving five years income, or $5 × 365 = $1,825. Indeed, if you build the factory in Africa and give each of the affected residents $1,825, then you would make each resident far better off than if you left them alone. The cost of giving $1,825 to 10,000 people is only $18.25 million.

So the United States must either (1) build the refinery in the United States and impose $100 million of pollution costs each year on Americans or (2) build the refinery in Africa and pay local residents a total of $18.25 million and ship the refined fuel to the United States. Both the United States and Africa are far better off with option (2).

A clean environment is a normal good, meaning that the richer someone is, the greater monetary value they place on it. Polluting the air of a poor country, therefore, causes less harm (measured in dollars) than polluting the air of a rich country. As a result, everyone could benefit if rich countries exported their polluting industries to poor nations and compensated these poor countries for the pollution externalities.

Of course, poor people benefit from taking in dirty industries in return for compensation only if they actually receive the compensation. If the United States builds the refinery in Africa, gives African politicians $18.25 million, but these politicians keep the money, then the poor Africans harmed by the pollution will have been made worse off.

GLOBAL WARMING

Burning fuels such as oil and coal gives off greenhouse gases. Most, but not all, climate scientists believe that these greenhouse gases are causing the temperature of the earth to rise.[7] And most, but not all, scientists believe that if global warming occurs, it will harm humanity.

If global warming is a threat, then burning fuels creates a global negative externality. Whenever people in one country burn coal, they increase the severity of global warming for everyone. The best way to reduce greenhouse gas emissions is to tax them or set up a system of tradable greenhouse gas emission permits.

A TECHNOLOGICAL ARGUMENT FOR DOING NOTHING ABOUT GLOBAL WARMING

Even if global warming is a real danger, however, we still might want to ignore it for the next 20 years. If global warming is occurring, it's happening slowly. Furthermore, there is a huge lag between greenhouse gas emissions and the earth's temperature. So any efforts we take today to reduce greenhouse gases won't have much effect on the earth's temperature for a few decades.

But in a few decades' time, humanity will have vastly better technology that will probably make it cheaper to end global warming. For example, imagine that in 20 years humans build the space elevator described in Chapter 8. We could use this elevator to put in orbit a cheap space shield that blocks a small percentage of the sunlight that normally hits the earth. It would cost trillions of dollars today to significantly reduce greenhouse gas emissions. But in 20 years time, new technologies might make it possible to solve the global warming problem for a fraction of this amount.

A TECHNOLOGICAL ARGUMENT FOR TAKING IMMEDIATE ACTION AGAINST GLOBAL WARMING

Technological innovation can be a long and costly process. If we imposed, say, a $100-billion-a-year tax on global warming emissions, innovators would greatly increase their efforts at finding greenhouse gas-reducing technologies. So to find a long-term technological solution to global warming, perhaps we should start taxing greenhouse gases today.

WEALTH CREATION—THE BEST DEFENSE AGAINST GLOBAL WARMING

Within a span of two weeks in 2003, similarly sized earthquakes struck both California and Iran. Although the Iranian earthquake killed over 28,000 people, the quake in California killed fewer than 10. Economist Thomas Sowell[8] explained that this difference in death tolls was due to the difference in wealth between California and Iran. Wealth is the best defense against environmental catastrophe. We don't know if in 30 years the earth will be too hot or too cold. But we do know that the richer we are, the better we will be able to handle any temperature-related problems. The best long-term environmental strategy to protect us from global warming, therefore, is to keep increasing the wealth of humanity.

TRAFFIC JAMS

We now turn from pollution externalities to traffic externalities. Each vehicle on a crowded road increases the time it takes other cars to reach their destination. Traffic delay, consequently, is a negative externality of driving. And this delay imposes monstrous economic costs on society. In 2005, for example, traffic jams cost the U.S. economy about $65 billion.[9]

An altruistic motorist would take into account the delay his being on the road creates for other drivers. Assume that his going to the movies would cause 500 other drivers to take an extra 10 seconds to reach their destinations. Consequently, our altruistic

CARACAS, VENEZUELA

motorist would go to the movies only if the benefit exceeded this 5,000-second delay cost.

Very few motorists are altruistic enough to take into account their negative traffic externalities, so we must rely on the government to reduce traffic jams. Let's evaluate four methods governments use to reduce traffic congestion.

METHOD 1 OF REDUCING TRAFFIC JAMS: GAS TAXES

Gas taxes raise the cost of driving and so reduce traffic jams. But gas taxes are a blunt traffic-fighting tool because they don't distinguish between drivers on crowded and nearly empty roads. For example, imagine a motorist must choose between driving to work at 7 a.m. or 8 a.m. At 7 a.m. the roads are empty, so an additional driver won't contribute to traffic jams. In contrast, at 8 a.m. the roads are crowded, so each driver creates a significant traffic externality. Ideally, we would want to tax the worker only if he drove at 8 a.m. But the gas tax hits the worker regardless of when he drives.

Gas taxes reduce the total amount of driving. But they fail to induce motorists to switch to driving at times or on roads where there is little traffic. And under some circumstances, gas taxes can even increase traffic congestion. For example, imagine that a driver can take one of two paths to work:

- Path 1—Distance: 20 miles. Drivers on this path must cross a crowded bridge. There is a significant traffic externality for each driver who takes this path.
- Path 2—Distance: 40 miles. This path has minimal traffic. There are no traffic externalities for drivers who take this path.

Drivers who take the longer Path 2 will use more gas. A high gas tax, therefore, will induce drivers to take Path 1. But only drivers on Path 1 impose a traffic externality on other drivers. So in this example a gas tax increases traffic congestion.

METHOD 2 OF REDUCING TRAFFIC JAMS: TOLL ROADS

Tolls are economists' favorite method of reducing traffic jams. Tolls can force drivers to internalize their negative traffic externalities. And unlike gas taxes, governments can impose tolls just on motorists driving over busy roads.

For example, imagine that a road gets crowded only around 8 a.m. A city could impose a toll on only 8 a.m. driving. Such tolls would cause some former 8 a.m. drivers to leave for work a little earlier or later.

Unfortunately, most U.S. states use toll roads as a source of revenue, not for traffic management. States often impose tolls on big highways that are almost never congested. In contrast, states rarely impose tolls where they are most needed: on busy city streets.

In 2003 the city of London started charging a £5 toll on drivers entering the city. The tolls decreased traffic by about 20 percent. The city-state of Singapore has also successfully used tolls to reduce traffic.

There is one extremely crowded bridge near the college where I teach. I have long thought it would make an interesting civil disobedience project to get my students to stand on the bridge and demand that drivers who wish to cross pay them a toll.

METHOD 3 OF REDUCING TRAFFIC JAMS: SUBSIDIZE MASS TRANSPORTATION

Governments often attempt to reduce traffic by subsidizing mass transportation such as buses, subways, and commuter trains. By the Law of Demand, such subsidies increase use of mass transport. Furthermore, since mass transport and driving are substitutes, you might think that reducing the cost of mass transport reduces the demand for driving. But such mass transportation subsidies can have a fatal flaw.

As some motorists switch to mass transport, traffic delays initially decline. But this decline in traffic reduces the opportunity cost of driving and so increases the number of drivers. In extreme situations, mass transport has no long-run effect on traffic jams.

An Example Where Mass Transit Doesn't Decrease Traffic Jams

Assume that 10,000 people consider driving to work at 8 a.m. Each motorist will drive at 8 a.m. so long as the traffic delay at this time is 20 minutes or less. If the delay exceeds 20 minutes, drivers will go some other time, such as 6:00 a.m., when there is almost no traffic.

If the 8 a.m. traffic delay were less than 20 minutes, new drivers would take to the road at 8 a.m., thereby increasing the delay. If the 8 a.m. traffic delay were greater than 20 minutes, then some 8 a.m. drivers would leave the road and so decrease the delay. Consequently, the only equilibrium is when there is exactly a 20-minute delay. Assume that it takes 7,000 drivers for there to be exactly a 20-minute delay. Therefore, 7,000 drivers go to work at 8 a.m. and 3,000 drivers leave for work at some other time.

Now assume that the government subsidizes some type of mass transport that causes 1,000 people to stop driving to work. What happens to the 8 a.m. traffic delay? Motorists will still drive at 8 a.m. if the delay is 20 minutes or less. Consequently, the only equilibrium will again be when the delay is exactly 20 minutes. So with mass transport, 7,000 workers drive to work at 8 a.m., 2,000 workers drive at some other time, and 1,000 people use mass transport. In this example a mass transport subsidy has done nothing to reduce traffic jams! (Question: If there were only 7,100 rather than 10,000 initial drivers, then the mass transport subsidy would reduce the 8 a.m. delay. Why is this?)

Why Mass Transportation Doesn't Necessarily Reduce Traffic Jams

Drivers will use a road as long as they get some benefit from doing so. But as more people use a road, the congestion on that road increases and so the benefit from using the road decreases. In equilibrium on crowded roads, drivers essentially receive zero economic profit. If they receive a positive profit, new drivers will enter the road, decreasing their profit. If they receive negative profit, some drivers will leave the road, raising their profit. So on crowded roads in equilibrium drivers receive zero profit.

When the government initially subsidizes mass transportation, the number of drivers on a busy road decreases. But this creates a disequilibrium because drivers on this slightly less-busy road now receive positive profits. These profits attract new drivers and so increase the delay. In equilibrium drivers must again receive zero profit and face the exact same delay they did before the mass transport system was built.

METHOD 4 OF REDUCING TRAFFIC JAMS: BUILD MORE ROADS

"If you build it, they will come." That's what happens when the government builds more roads. Building additional roads attracts new drivers. Road construction, therefore, often doesn't reduce traffic congestion.

Many people work in cities but live in suburbs. Housing prices are usually cheaper the farther you live from a city. But the farther away you live, the longer the commute. When a government builds new roads, it initially reduces this commute time and so subsidizes people living farther from their city jobs. And as workers move farther from their jobs, they drive more miles, creating more negative traffic externalities.

POLITICS AND EXTERNALITIES

Governments play a huge role in regulating externalities. We will now consider four additional automobile-related externalities and see how the U.S. state and federal governments have either reduced, increased, or ignored the respective negative externality.

ACCIDENTS AND CAR WEIGHT

Two cars collide. One is a giant sports utility vehicle (SUV) and the other a small subcompact. Which would you rather be in?

The bigger the car, the greater the crash damage it potentially causes other vehicles. The heavier the car, therefore, the greater the car's crash negative externality. Because self-interested individuals ignore negative externalities when making decisions, consumers tend to buy cars that are too large from the point of view of what is best for society.

Since heavy cars create significant negative externalities, many economists would prefer that governments discourage consumers from buying SUVs. Perhaps the government could tax SUVs or subsidize small cars. But for a period the U.S. government provided massive subsidies for SUVs. Under this subsidy, many people who purchased SUVs could count them as a business deduction on their taxes. Buying an SUV, therefore, significantly reduced many Americans' taxes. As a result, many Americans who would have bought small or medium-sized cars were induced by the government to buy an SUV instead.

DRIVING WHILE ELDERLY

"Weller was 86 on July 16, 2003, when he turned his 1992 Buick LeSabre into the Santa Monica Farmers' Market and kept pressing on the accelerator even as his car smashed into a crowd of shoppers. In addition to those killed—nine adults and a 2-year-old—more than 70 people were injured. [At his trial] Weller's lawyers said he had confused the brake with the accelerator." Weller was found guilty, but because of his ill health, Weller was sentenced to probation rather than prison.[10]

Imagine that you are a U.S. state senator who has somehow angered a powerful demon. In retaliation this demon forces you to propose a law that either:

1. Advocates the torture of cute baby pandas.
2. Requires elderly drivers to take a yearly test to see if they should still be permitted to drive.

For the sake of your political career, you should go with the panda torture. As we get older, we often lose some of our driving skills. Impaired elderly drivers, therefore, create greater negative externalities for every mile they drive than younger drivers do because the elderly are more likely to get into a crash. A rational driving policy would require all drivers over 80 to pass a new driver's test every year or so. But the elderly have tremendous political power in the United States. Politicians, therefore, fear restricting the driving rights of the elderly.

DRIVING WHILE DRUNK

Drunk driving significantly increases the risk of car crashes. Drinking alcohol before driving, therefore, creates negative externalities. The group Mothers Against Drunk Driving (MADD) has led a successful long-term U.S. political campaign to increase penalties for drunk drivers. MADD was founded in 1980 by the mother of a 13-year-old girl who was killed by a repeat drunk-driving offender. This driver had "three prior

CHAPTER 13 • Challenge to Market Effectiveness 3: Externalities and the Environment

drunk driving convictions and was out on bail from a hit-and-run arrest two days earlier."[11]

Readers eager to get the government to correct negative externalities should learn from MADD. MADD teaches that it's never enough just to point out to government officials that people are creating harmful externalities. To get the government to take action against such externalities, you must organize politically so that it becomes in the self-interest of politicians to regulate the externality.

DRIVING WHILE CELL-PHONING

Several studies have concluded that talking on a cell phone while driving is about as dangerous as driving while drunk.[12] So why don't U.S. states treat driving while cell-phoning similarly to drunk driving? Because there has been no MADD-like campaign against cell-phone driving. Consequently, politicians have been under less political pressure to punish cell-phone driving than drunk driving.

Some states allow telephoning drivers to use only hands-free cell phones. Unfortunately, studies indicate that hands-free car phones create just as many accidents as traditional cell phones do.[13] (Apparently drivers are impaired by the mental, not physical, distractions of cell phone use.) Of course, most voters are unaware of these studies. So by requiring drivers to use hands-free cell phones, politicians can, without significantly angering cell-phone users, claim to have increased traffic safety.

In summary: Drivers who are impaired because they are (a) enfeebled by old age, (b) using a cell phone, or (c) driving while drunk, create tremendous negative externalities for other motorists. The elderly have significant political power, so politicians dare not restrict their driving rights. Politicians often try to satisfy both cell-phone users and motorists concerned about cell phone drivers by imposing hands-free phone restrictions that are superficially appealing but do nothing to improve traffic safety. But since MADD has successfully demonized drunk driving, politicians feel compelled to impose significant criminal punishments on drunk drivers' negative externalities.

GOVERNMENT-CAUSED ENVIRONMENTAL PROBLEMS

Many of the worst environmental problems of the 20th century were caused by governments. Here are a few examples:

- **Subsidizing Pollution**—Governments spend hundreds of billions of dollars each year subsidizing activities such as logging, fishing, and mining that create negative environmental externalities. By ending these subsidies, governments could both help the environment and cut taxes. So who could possibly object to terminating these subsidies? Loggers, fisherman, and miners could and most certainly would object.[14]

- **Banning DDT**—Mosquito-born diseases are one of the greatest killers of humans. The mosquito-killing insecticide DDT, therefore, is a candidate for being the greatest innovation of all time. "In 1970 the National Academy of Sciences estimated that the chemical had prevented 500 million deaths." DDT is cheap, effective and almost certainly safe.[15]

  Rachel Carson's influential 1962 book *Silent Spring*, however, argued that DDT harms the environment. Although the book lacked serious scientific evidence, it had huge popular appeal and resulted in many governments banning DDT. The U.S. and the Western European nations not only banned DDT in their own borders but also used their foreign aid budgets to bully poorer nations to ban DDT.

But after DDT was banned, the population of disease-carrying mosquitoes increased in many poor countries. Each year an estimated 1 to 3 million people die because of malaria.[16] Many of these malaria deaths are due to restrictions on DDT.

Recent scientific evidence indicates that people with malaria are more susceptible to being infected with the AIDS virus.[17] One of the reasons, therefore, why AIDS is so widespread in Africa may be because malaria infects many Africans. Banning DDT will undoubtedly go down as one of the greatest blunders or perhaps even crimes of the 20th century.

HOORAY FOR DDT'S LIFE-SAVING COMEBACK

Who says there's never any good news? After more than 30 years and tens of millions dead—mostly children—the World Health Organization (WHO) has ended its ban on DDT. DDT is the most effective anti-mosquito, anti-malaria pesticide known. But thanks to the worldwide environmental movement and politically correct bureaucrats in the United States and at the United Nations, the use of this benign chemical has been discouraged in Africa and elsewhere, permitting killer mosquitoes to spread death.

DDT was banned by President Richard Nixon's Environmental Protection Agency in the early 1970s, after Rachel Carson's book *Silent Spring* claimed to show that DDT threatened human health as well as bird populations. But some scientists found no evidence for her claims. Even if there was danger to bird eggs, the problem was the amount of DDT used, not the chemical itself.

Huge amounts of the chemical were sprayed in America. I've watched old videos of people at picnics who just kept eating while trucks sprayed thick white clouds of DDT on top of them. Some people even ran toward the truck—as if it was an ice-cream truck—they were so happy to have mosquitoes repelled. Tons of DDT were sprayed on food and people. Despite this overuse, there was no surge in cancer or any other human injury.

Nevertheless, the environmental hysteria led to DDT's suppression in Africa, where its use had been dramatically reducing deaths. American foreign aid could be used to finance ineffective alternative anti-malaria methods, but not DDT. Within a short time, the mosquitoes and malaria reappeared, and deaths skyrocketed. Tens of millions of people have died in that time.

DDT advocates pointed out that the ban amounted to mass murder. But they could not move the rich white environmental dogmatists who reflexively condemn all kinds of chemicals, and presumably lost no sleep when millions of poor African children died.

But now this has changed. Last month, the WHO announced that it supports indoor spraying of DDT and other insecticides "not only in epidemic areas but also in areas with constant and high malaria transmission, including throughout Africa."

"The scientific and programmatic evidence clearly supports this reassessment," said Dr. Anarfi Asamoa-Baah, WHO assistant director-general for HIV/AIDS, TB, and malaria. "DDT presents no health risk when used properly."

WHO now calls DDT the "most effective" pesticide for indoor use. Some environmental groups have also changed their anti-DDT tune, including Greenpeace, Environmental Defense, and the Sierra Club. Last year, Greenpeace spokesman Rick Hind told *The New York Times,* "If there's nothing else and it's going to save lives, we're all for it. Nobody's dogmatic about it."

Junk-science debunker Steven Milloy, an adjunct scholar with the Competitive Enterprise Institute, wonders why the environmentalists took so long to change their minds. "There are no new facts on DDT—all the relevant science about DDT safety has been available since the 1960s," Milloy says.

John Stossel, "Hooray for DDT's Life-Saving Comeback," October 4, 2006, Creators Syndicate. By permission of John Stossel and Creaters Syndicate, Inc.

- **Banning Supposed Frankenfoods[18]**—Without the slightest bit of scientific evidence, the European Union believes that genetically modified foods, what some call "Frankenfoods" after Frankenstein's monster, are dangerous to humans. Americans eat this kind of food all the time because genetically modified crops are more resistant to pests, require less fertilizer, and grow faster.

  The European Union has prevented many African nations from using genetically modified crops. These nations both fear that the Europeans might be right about the crop's dangers and know that if they use the crops, Europe won't buy their food exports.

  Tragically, in 2002 Zambia and Zimbabwe refused to accept U.S. food aid because it was genetically modified. At the time starvation was rampant in Zambia and Zimbabwe, so these nations' rejection of food aid killed people. In sum, starving Africans refused to accept food that Americans regularly ate because of unscientific beliefs held by a few rich European governments.

- **Drying of the Aral Sea[19]**—Among the environmental disasters caused by the former Soviet Union was the drying out of the Aral Sea to obtain water to grow cotton. As a United Nations publication said: "The 3.5 million people who live in the region have seen their health, jobs and living conditions literally go down the drain. The once thriving fishing and canning industry has evaporated, replaced by anemia, high infant and maternal mortality, and debilitating respiratory and intestinal ailments."

THE DRYING OF THE ARAL SEA

- **Killing Sparrows[20]**—Former Chinese dictator Mao Zedong decided to kill all of China's sparrows. Mao believed that since sparrows eat grain, wiping out the sparrow population would increase China's grain harvest. By forcing hundreds of millions of Chinese to attack sparrows, Mao succeeded in greatly reducing the bird's population. But while sparrows do eat grain, they also eat grain-eating pests. As a result, Mao created an environmental catastrophe. To restore its ecological balance, China had to ask the Soviet Union, in the name of "socialist internationalism," to send it 200,000 sparrows.

- **Destroying Trees to Make Useless Steel[21]**—Mao Zedong also wanted to rapidly increase China's production of steel. He forced Chinese peasants to set up small steel furnaces all over China. To feed these furnaces, peasants cut down all the trees on many mountains and hillsides. This mass denuding of forests caused flooding for several decades afterwards. The small steel furnaces created extremely poor quality steel that was completely useless to the Chinese economy.

Government-Caused Environmental Problems

FORESTS PAYING THE PRICE FOR BIOFUELS

The drive for "green energy" in the developed world is having the perverse effect of encouraging the destruction of tropical rainforests. From the orangutan reserves of Borneo to the Brazilian Amazon, virgin forest is being razed to grow palm oil and soybeans to fuel cars and power stations in Europe and North America. And surging prices are likely to accelerate the destruction.

The rush to make energy from vegetable oils is being driven in part by European Union laws requiring conventional fuels to be blended with biofuels, and by subsidies equivalent to 20 pence a liter. Last week, the British government announced a target for biofuels to make up 5 percent of transport fuels by 2010.

Rising demand for green energy has led to a surge in the international price of palm oil, with potentially damaging consequences. "The expansion of palm oil production is one of the leading causes of rainforest destruction in south-east Asia. It is one of the most environmentally damaging commodities on the planet," says Simon Counsell, director of the UK-based Rainforest Foundation. "Once again it appears we are trying to solve our environmental problems by dumping them in developing countries, where they have devastating effects on local people."

The main alternative to palm oil is soybean oil. But [harvesting] soya is the largest single cause of rainforest destruction in the Brazilian Amazon.

Fred Pearce, "Forests Paying the Price for Biofuels," *The New Scientist*, 25 October 02. Used with permission.

TECHNOLOGICAL SPILLOVERS

We will conclude this chapter by discussing the most important of all externalities: technological spillovers. Innovation is the primary cause of economic growth. Yet on average around 80 percent of the gain from innovations goes to people other than the innovators.[22]

This 80 percent spillover means that if an innovator creates $1 billion of wealth, on average the innovator receives only 20 percent or $200 million of it. The rest goes to everyone else in society as positive externality or spillover. Most of the wealth that people in rich countries have is due to these technological spillovers.

One famous spillover occurred at Xerox's Palo Alto Research Center. The center created the modern personal computer graphical user interface. Xerox, not realizing how important personal computers would soon become, did a very poor job of profiting from their key innovation. As a result, almost all of the profits from this innovation went to others.

But even when firms succeed in profiting greatly from their innovations, they still create enormous spillovers. For example, Wal-Mart was an innovator in using computers to manage its inventory. But other retailers quickly copied Wal-Mart's success.

The benefits we receive from televisions, radios, refrigerators, air-conditioners, automobiles, planes, aspirin, and anything else developed a relatively long time ago come to us through technological spillovers. When innovators develop a new product, they often receive a patent. Once this patent expires, however, anyone can legally make and sell the product. As a result, innovators can substantially capture the benefit of their innovation only during the life of their patents. Most of the benefits of an innovation that arise after the patent expires are, therefore, technological spillovers.

Spillovers occur even while an innovation is protected by a patent. To get a patent, an innovator must fully disclose how he developed his product. Others can use this information to help figure out how to produce innovations.

Although technological spillovers create tremendous benefits for society, they have a downside. Because innovation creates such enormous positive externalities, firms engage in less than the socially optimal level of innovation.

QUESTIONS YOU SHOULD BE ABLE TO ANSWER AFTER READING THIS CHAPTER:

1   Why are products with negative externalities overused? (page 319)

2   What are negative externalities? List some examples. (pages 318–319)

3   What are positive externalities? List some examples. (page 320)

4   Why are products with positive externalities underused? (page 320)

5   Why, from the viewpoint of what is best for society, is The Club overused and LoJack underused? (page 320)

6   What would happen if the government banned all pollution? (pages 321–322)

7   What are the two major problems of using command and control methods to reduce pollution? (page 322)

8   What are Pigovian taxes? (page 323)

9   Why do Pigovian taxes give firms more flexibility than command and control pollution regulations do? (page 323)

10 Why do Pigovian taxes create incentives for pollution-reducing innovations? (page 323)

11 How are prices like signposts and why do externalities cause these signposts to point in wrong directions? (page 325)

12 What is the main disadvantage of Pigovian taxes? (pages 325–326)

13 What are tradable pollution permits? (page 326)

14 When are tradable permits socially superior to pollution taxes? (page 327)

15 How can environmentalists use tradable permits to reduce pollution? (page 327)

16 What is the Coase Theorem? (page 327)

17 Are poor countries underpolluted? (pages 328)

18 What is a technological argument for doing nothing about global warming? (page 329)

19 What is a technological argument for taking immediate action against global warming? (page 329)

20 Why is wealth creation the best defense against global warming? (page 329)

21 Why are gas taxes a blunt traffic-jam-fighting tool? (page 330)

22 Why are toll roads economists' favorite method of reducing traffic jams? (page 330)

23 What is the major problem with using mass transport subsidies to reduce traffic jams? (page 331)

24 What are the problems of combating traffic jams by building new roads? (page 331)

STYLE PROBLEMS

1 What are some negative and positive externalities caused by gun ownership?

2 Examine the externalities caused by: air bags, antilock breaks, car radios, and automobile headlights.

3 The U.S. government forces automobile manufactures to make their cars more fuel efficient. Does this requirement correct or worsen negative automobile externalities?

More trouble brewing

THE FAR SIDE® BY GARY LARSON

© 1994 FarWorks, Inc. All Rights Reserved/Dist. by Creators Syndicate

CRUTCHFIELD'S CROCODILE FARM

ANDERSON'S SKY DIVING SCHOOL

The Far Side® by Gary Larson © 1994 FarWorks, Inc. All Rights Reserved. The Far Side® and the Larson® signature are registered trademarks of FarWorks, Inc. Used with permission.

4 Describe how the Coase Theorem relates to the cartoon on the left.

5 Describe negative and positive externalities created by a couple choosing to have another child.

6 A candy bar costs $1 to produce and sells for $1. Eating the candy bar does $1.17 of health damage to you. What is the size of the externality created by this candy bar?

7 "Behind every Prisoners' Dilemma lies an externality." Justify this statement.

8 Assume you're a state senator greatly concerned about impaired elderly drivers. You won't do anything to restrict or tax elderly drivers and can enact only measures that the elderly approve of. What laws could you still propose that would reduce elderly driving?

9 Does government-mandated recycling correct any negative externalities?

10 "The trouble with cars these days is that they're too safe. Of course, I don't write as a driver; I write as a cyclist."[23] What could the author mean by this?

11 In 2006 the city of Madrid banned extremely skinny women from appearing in fashion model shows. What negative externalities might this ban address?

12 We learned in Chapter 6 that taxes create deadweight losses. Can Pigovian taxes create deadweight losses? Does the normal deadweight loss of taxation strengthen or weaken the desirability of imposing Pigovian taxes?

13 Assume that every home alarm system automatically calls the police when a burglar breaks into a protected home. Examine the externalities created by the following:

    A. Homes that have alarm systems and have prominent signs indicating that the homes are protected by alarms,

    B. Homes that have alarm systems but don't have any signs indicating that the homes are protected by alarms,

    C. Homes that don't have alarm systems but have prominent signs falsely indicating that the homes are protected by alarms,

    D. Homes that have neither alarm systems nor signs indicating that the homes have alarm systems.

14 Assume that 38,000 people want to drive from Point A to Point B at 8 a.m. Each person will undertake the drive as long as the drive takes 40 minutes or less. Assume that the following graph shows how long it takes to drive from Point A to Point B if there are either one or two roads going from the two points. How long will it take drivers if there is only one road? How long will it take drivers if there are two roads? How many 8 a.m. drivers would benefit from the building of the second road? Explain your answers.

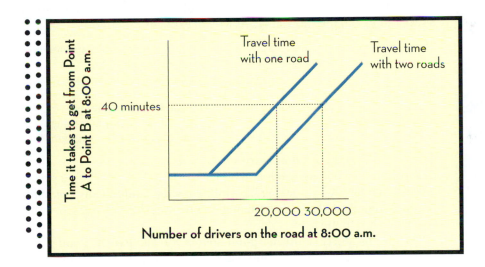

15 One economist jokingly wrote "My suggestion would be to make purchasing a product from a spammer a crime, punishable by a fine or imprisonment. I'd even advocate making it a capital offense."[24] How does this suggestion relate to externalities?

WHY CAMBODIAN GIRLS NEED PROPERTY RIGHTS

Srey Neth was a Cambodian teenage prostitute/sex-slave. *The New York Times* columnist Nicholas Kristof purchased her freedom for $150. After Srey Neth returned to the village she grew up in, Kristof gave her $100 so she could start a small shop. But the shop failed. As Kristof explains:

"The problem was her family. Srey Neth's parents and older brothers and sisters had a hard time understanding why they should go hungry when their sister had a store full of food. And her little nephews and nieces, running around the yard, helped themselves when she wasn't looking.

'Srey Neth got mad,' her mother recalled. 'She said we had to stay away, or everything would be gone. She said she had to have money to buy new things.'

But in a Cambodian village, nobody listens to an uneducated teenage girl."*

Srey Neth's shop failed because she lacked property rights. Like any business person, she bought goods and hoped to resell them at a higher price. But because her family kept taking her stuff, the shop couldn't survive. Without property rights, neither Cambodian girls nor American businesspeople can easily succeed in the marketplace.

To have property rights in a good means you can use the good yourself, sell it to others, or prevent others from using the good. This chapter explores the importance of property rights. Almost one-half of the world's population lives on less than $2 a day. This chapter argues that a prime reason for such widespread devastating poverty is that the majority of the world's poor live in countries that lack adequate property rights. The chapter also shows how, when property rights aren't secure in rich countries, markets have difficulty creating wealth.

Nikolas Kristof. "Leaving the Brothol Behind."

CHALLENGE TO MARKET EFFECTIVENESS 4: INADEQUATE PROPERTY RIGHTS

LEARNING OBJECTIVES

AFTER READING THIS CHAPTER, YOU SHOULD BE ABLE TO:

- Understand the importance of property rights.
- Define the tragedy of the commons.
- Identify public goods and intellectual property.
- Define dead capital.

PAIN BEFORE PLEASURE

Investments bring pain before pleasure. A peasant must plant, cultivate, and harvest his crops before eating them. Businesspeople must invest their time and resources before earning a profit.

But without property rights, the initial pain of investment often leads to disappointment rather than to pleasurable profits. A peasant without property rights might tirelessly work his land only to have his harvest appropriated by a greedy aristocrat. A businessperson who invests millions but lacks meaningful property rights might have her profits confiscated before she can enjoy spending them.

People without property rights, therefore, often have no incentive to suffer the initial pain that investment requires. The girls in Srey Neth's village, for example, have surely learned they shouldn't start a small business. This village won't benefit from the wealth-creating ventures that these girls would have started if they had property rights.

Most of this textbook's readers live in societies with secure property rights. But such security is a historical anomaly. Throughout most of history, everything that a common person had was subject to being taken by a king or local lord. In Chapter 6 we learned that in the 1,500 years before the early 19th century's industrial revolution, the average economic growth rate was approximately *zero*. A key reason for the lack of economic growth during these times was that property rights in these societies were poorly defined or insecure, often subject to arbitrary confiscation by governments. Consequently, people had limited incentives to invest in wealth-creating ventures. The tremendous economic growth that began during the early 19th century's industrial revolution was fueled in part by property rights.

RUSSIAN INVESTMENTS

After the fall of the Soviet Union, Russia tried to become a capitalist society. It initially attracted many foreign investors. But these investors quickly found that they had no real property rights. For example, an American who invested $10 million in a factory might have found it taken over by the Russian Mafia. Or, an investor might have bought 25 percent of a Russian company for $10 million. The Russian company, however, might then simply ignore the foreign investor and never give him any of the firm's profits.

Many predicted that Russia would experience rapid economic growth after it separated from the Soviet Union in 1991 because Russia intended to build a market-oriented economy. But Russia, especially in its early years, experienced disappointing growth. Russia lacked secure property rights. As a result, after the initial economic euphoria over its supposed pro-market policies, few people invested in Russia. Even rich Russians invested their money abroad.

Why, you might ask, didn't the Russian government create secure property rights to attract investors? Unfortunately, creating secure property rights is difficult. It took centuries for Western Europe to develop them. For property rights to be secure, they must be respected at many levels of society. Not only must the central government refrain from arbitrary confiscation, but local governments also must avoid taking property. In addition, secure property rights require honest courts that can adjudicate disputes among businesspeople, and honest police who prevent criminal gangs from seizing property. And as we saw with Srey Neth's shop, secure property rights require families to respect the individually owned property of their members.

GRADE STEALERS

To further understand the importance of property rights, consider how insecure property rights in grades would affect study habits. Imagine that a gang of computer hackers at your school learns how to steal grades. This gang identifies high-performing students and then breaks into the campus computer system to exchange grades with them. So, if you get an A in microeconomics while a hacker receives an F, this hacker might take your A and give you his F.

This gang would greatly reduce studying at your school. Fewer students would bother suffering the pain of studying if it didn't lead to the reward of receiving high grades. Furthermore, since the gang targets students with good grades, students would avoid earning As. Smart students might deliberately miss a few questions on exams to avoid receiving an A. In a world without property rights, people often try not to appear successful so they don't become targets.

HIDING WEALTH

While plowing his fields in the 12th century, a peasant found a buried treasure consisting of a gold statue and some coins. The peasant's feudal lord heard about the discovery. As you would expect, the lord took the treasure for himself. The lord, however, foolishly allowed his king, Richard the Lionhearted of England, to learn of the treasure. King Richard naturally demanded that he be given the treasure.

The peasant made a stupid mistake. Since the peasant lacked property rights, he should have known that if his lord learned about the treasure he would confiscate it. The peasant should have hidden the treasure until he could sell it or pass it along to his children.

When you don't have property rights, you avoid creating wealth because that wealth can be easily stolen. But if somehow you happen upon wealth and you don't have property rights to it, you should hide it.

In poor countries, prosperous peasants and small business people often avoid looking rich so they don't become targets of the strong. They might want their houses and businesses to look shabby so others think they are poor. Unfortunately, when people hide their wealth, they can't easily use their wealth to create more wealth. A prosperous peasant, for example, might avoid buying a tractor because having a tractor would cause the local police force to think he could be shaken down for a bribe. The prosperous peasant might deliberately use an inefficient method of farming just so other people will think he is poor.

COLLECTIVE OWNERSHIP

For property rights to create wealth, they must belong to individuals, not groups. Imagine that rather than giving each individual student a grade, your microeconomics professor assigns a single grade to the entire class based on the class's total test average. In a large class, each student would have a very small incentive to study. For example, in a class of 100 students, if one student studied to raise her grade from an 80 percent to a 100 percent, this would increase the overall class average by only .2 percent, a tiny amount. As a result of collective grading, most of the students would spend little time studying and the entire class would likely earn a bad grade.

Soviet Agriculture   The wealth-creating superiority of individual over collective property rights was well shown by Soviet agriculture. Ninety-nine percent of all farm land in the Soviet Union was collectively owned, meaning that the government owned it in the supposed name of the people. Peasants had to farm this land, but they didn't have the right to keep what was grown on it. Consequently, peasants often did a shoddy job of farming the collectively owned land.

The Soviet Union, however, allowed most peasants individually to own a small plot of land. A peasant could keep all the food grown on this land. As economist Milton Friedman pointed out, although these small privately owned plots accounted for only 1 percent of the farm land in the Soviet Union, they produced nearly one-third of all the food grown in the country.

These private plots must have been a horrible embarrassment to the Communists who ran the Soviet Union. The Communists were opposed to individual property rights. Communist ideology claimed that the government could make far better use of resources, such as land, than private individuals could. Yet the greater agricultural yields on privately owned land provided strong evidence that Communism was a failure. Perhaps the success of private plots was a key reason why, shortly before the Soviet Union's fall, its Communist leaders tried to create a market-oriented economy.

> "When everybody owns something, nobody owns it, and nobody has a direct interest in maintaining or improving its condition. That is why buildings in the Soviet Union—like public housing in the United States—look decrepit within a year or two of their construction . . ."
> —Milton Friedman[2]

DR. SEUSS'S *THE LORAX*[3]

Dr. Seuss's environmentally-based story, *The Lorax,* illuminates another problem of inadequate property rights. Here's a brief summary of the story:

A creature called the Once-ler came to town and saw "mile after mile" of Truffula trees. The Once-ler discovered that he could use the soft tuft of a Truffula tree to make Thneeds. And the demand for Thneeds would be extraordinarily high because:

"A Thneed's a Fine-Something-That-All-People-Need!
It's a shirt. It's a sock. It's a glove. It's a hat.
But it has *other* uses. Yes, far beyond that.
You can use it for carpets. For pillows! For sheets!
Or curtains! Or covers for bicycle seats!"*

The Once-ler soon made a high profit selling Thneeds. And to increase his profit, he accelerated the production of Thneeds. So the Once-ler needed to cut down more and more Truffula trees.

Another creature, called the Lorax, who claimed to "speak for the trees," strongly objected to the Once-ler's felling of Truffula trees. The Once-ler ignored the Lorax's protestations and continued to make Thneed creations. But the Once-ler's business quickly went under as the very last Truffula tree was soon knocked asunder. And so the Once-ler's Thneed firm shut down as no more beautiful Truffula trees could be found.

A PROPERTY RIGHTS INTERPRETATION OF *THE LORAX*

Did a shortsighted craving for material goods cause the extinction of the Truffula tree woods? No. What really "did in" the Truffula trees was lack of property rights.

The Once-ler discovered that Truffula trees were extremely valuable because they could be used to make Thneeds. No one owned the Truffula trees, so the Once-ler, along with everyone else, had the legal right to cut them down.

In a few weeks businesspeople from other towns would have undoubtedly seen the profitability of the Thneed business and come to cut down Truffula trees. The Once-ler, therefore, had a very short time period in which he was the only person around town who had the necessary equipment to cut down the Truffula trees. Any trees that the Once-ler didn't quickly take would soon be cut down by others. The Once-ler, therefore, rationally cut down Truffula trees as fast as possible. Even if the Once-ler had listened to the Lorax and stopped making Thneeds, the Truffula trees would still be doomed as other businesspeople would have cut them all down.

Now imagine what would have happened if the Once-ler owned all the Truffula trees. As the owner, the Once-ler would not have had to rush to cut down all the trees before other people did. Furthermore, the Once-ler would never have cut down all the trees. He would have managed his Truffula forest so that it would continually renew itself. (Timber companies that own forests and sell wood products carefully manage their forests so they can be continually harvested over the long term.) Without property rights, the Once-ler cared only about the short term, because he knew that the Truffula trees would never survive in the long run. But if he had property rights, the Once-ler would have known that he could let a tree grow for a few years and still retain ownership. So property rights would have caused the Once-ler to take a long-term view of the Truffula trees.

The Lorax said he spoke for the trees, but this was wrong. Only the owner of a tree can speak for it, because only the owner can stop other people from cutting it down. No one—not the Lorax or the Once-ler—spoke for the trees, and this is why they perished. In general, when a resource such as Truffula trees is not owned by anyone, it will be overused. Economists call this phenomenon *the tragedy of the commons*.

---

*From *The Lorax* by Dr. Seuss, TM and © Dr. Seuss Enterprises, L.P. 1971, renewed 1999. All Rights Reserved. Used by permission of Random House Children's Books , a division of Random House, Inc., and Dr. Seuss Enterprises, L.P.

TRAGEDY OF THE COMMONS

Consider a village in which many people own cattle. The cattle graze on a grass commons. This commons is owned by no one; anyone from the village can use it.

The villagers will overuse the common land. Each villager will realize that any grass his cattle don't eat will likely be eaten by other villagers' cattle. As a result, each villager will allow his cattle to gorge themselves on grass. Such mass gorging will kill the grass. Next year, therefore, tragedy will strike as the cattle will not have any grass to dine on.

A tragedy of the commons arises when a resource, such as grassland, is rival but nonexcludable. A resource is rival if one person's use of it reduces the amount left for other people to consume. If your cows eat grass then there is less grass for everyone else, so grass is a rival good. In contrast, a song is nonrival. After you listen to a song, that song can still be heard by other people.

A resource is excludable if people can be prevented, or excluded, from using it. Since everyone had the legal right to cut Truffula trees or set their cattle to graze on the common grassland, these two resources were nonexcludable.

Rival resource—One person's use of the resource reduces the amount of this resource available to others.

Excludable resource—People can be prevented from using this resource.

The tragedy of the commons arises when a resource is rival but nonexcludable.

A nonexcludable resource will continue to be used as long as some people benefit from it. But if the resource is rival, then each person's use harms other people. So resources that are rival but nonexcludable will (tragically) tend to be used until they are depleted or destroyed.

THE BUFFALO TRAGEDY

In 19th century America, buffalo hides were worth good money. Weapon technology made it very easy for hunters to kill buffalo. Any American, furthermore, had the right to kill buffalo. Buffalos consequently were killed in great number and American buffalos were almost hunted to extinction.

LAKE COMMONS

Imagine that many people live near a lake that initially contains many tasty fish. Fish are a rival resource because you can't eat a fish that another person has already consumed. Let's assume that the fish in this lake are nonexcludable, so anyone has the right to fish in the lake.

People will continue to fish this lake until all the yummy fish have been caught. Alas, this means that the fish won't survive to spawn new fish. Next year the lake will be barren of fish.

Fishermen would be better off if, say, only 25 percent of the fish could be caught each year. This would ensure that enough fish survive to repopulate the lake. But if the fish are a nonexcludable resource, then this 25 percent limit is nonenforceable as each fisherman will always be better off individually catching a few more fish.

When a common resource is owned by no one, each user can benefit from using the resource. But because the resource is rival, each person's use of the resource creates negative externalities on everyone else. These negative externalities arise because each man's use of the resource reduces the amount and quality of the

BIKE COMMONS

In 2004, Purdue University tried to make 25 bikes available to all students. The bikes "were painted bright gold and placed all over campus. All students could ride the bikes."[5] Within one month, 20 of the 25 bikes were unusable because of vandalism, evidence that people often treat their own property far better than they treat commonly owned goods.

resource available to others. As we said in the last chapter, people tend to overuse goods that have negative externalities. It's no surprise, therefore, that the tragedy of the commons problem arises because, absent some corrective measure, common resources are frequently used until depletion.

PROPERTY RIGHTS TO THE RESCUE

Property rights solve the tragedy of the commons problem. Secure property rights, by definition, make a resource excludable. If the Truffula trees, grassland, or lake were owned by someone, then the owner would have an incentive to manage the resource for the long term. The lake's owner, for example, might charge for fishing. He would make a higher long-term profit if he limited fishing each year so as not to wipe out the fish population.

PROPERTY RIGHTS PROTECT NIGER TREES

"From colonial times, all trees in Niger had been regarded as the property of the state, which gave farmers little incentive to protect them. Trees were chopped for firewood or construction without regard to the environmental costs. Government foresters were supposed to make sure the trees were properly managed, but there were not enough of them to police a country nearly twice the size of Texas.

But over time, farmers began to regard the trees in their fields as their property, and in recent years the government has recognized the benefits of that outlook by allowing individuals to own trees. Farmers make money from the trees by selling branches, pods, fruit and bark. Because those sales are more lucrative over time than simply chopping down the tree for firewood, the farmers preserve them."

Lydia Polgreen. "In Niger, Trees and Crops Turn Back the Desert," From The New York Times, 2/11/2007 © 2007 The New York Times. All Rights Reserved. Used by permission and protected by the copyright laws of the Unites States. The printing, copying, or redistribution of the material without express written permission is prohibited.

WHEN ECONOMICS MAJORS FALL IN LOVE

Vedran Vuk, while an undergraduate economics major at Loyola University, explained the relationship between property rights and love:

"An ex-girlfriend once told me, 'You treat me like a piece of property.' As an economics major, my first reaction was: How great that the center of my affection truly understands the way I feel! Butterflies in my stomach, rainbows, unicorns, big red hearts shot through my enamored mind. When someone truly understands you, what can you feel but joy?

If I treated her as if she were my property, after all, it means that I would take care of her, protect her, and treat her well above all things not in my possession. Suddenly, I realized the look on her face did not reflect the combusting happiness within me. . . .

'Do you mean [individually or collectively owned] property?' Well, she never answered verbally, but she did proceed to administer a big red slap mark across my face. I'll never truly know what I did wrong, but such is the life of a lonesome economics student. I never saw that girl again . . .

And a final word of advice for lovers: If your beloved is not treating you at least a little bit like a piece of private property, it's time to rethink this romance."[5]

PUBLIC GOODS

Sixty-five million years ago, an asteroid probably crashed into the earth, wiping out the dinosaurs. Humankind could suffer a similar fate. In fact, some scientists estimate that the chances of the average American being killed by an asteroid strike is about the same as dying in a plane crash.

Most asteroids that pass near the earth currently go undetected. To deflect a human-extinguishing asteroid from hitting the earth, we would need at least 20 years advance notice. So the first step in asteroid defense is for astronomers to locate all the asteroids that might hit us. Unfortunately, Adam Smith's invisible hand won't guide self-interested humans to protect the earth from asteroids.

Imagine that somewhere in space looms Asteroid-X. There is a 1 in 1,000 chance that Asteroid-X will crash into the earth and destroy mankind. If we assess the value of a human life at $1 million, then the average harm that Asteroid-X will cause is:

$$(\$1 \text{ million}) \times (\text{Human population of 6.7 billion}) \times \left(\frac{1}{1,000}\right) = \$6.7 \text{ trillion.}$$

So, from a cost-benefit analysis, it's worth spending up to $6.7 trillion to eliminate the chance of Asteroid-X hitting earth. But any one person would receive only a tiny fraction of this benefit. Consequently, it's in no one's self-interest to spend anywhere near $6.7 trillion to deflect or destroy Asteroid-X.

Asteroid defense is a public good. A public good is any product or service that is nonrival and nonexcludable. Because it's nonrival, one person's use of a public good doesn't harm other people. Because it's nonexcludable, anyone can benefit from a public good regardless of whether they have contributed to creating it.

> **Public good:** Any product or service which is nonrival and nonexcludable.

If an asteroid is going to hit, we won't be able to tell beforehand where it will strike the earth. And if the asteroid is big enough, it really won't matter where it hits since it will kill us all. Anyone who spends resources on asteroid defense necessarily helps all humans.

If you, but not I, spend $10 on a pizza, then you get a pizza while I get nothing. But if you, but not I, contribute $10 million toward asteroid defense, then we both get an equal amount of protection. Consequently, people have an incentive to free-ride off of others' asteroid defense expenditures.

FREE-RIDING MICE

The fable *Who Will Bell the Cat?* perfectly illustrates the free-rider problem:

> "A family of mice could get no food because of its fear of a cat. The mice decided that the best thing to do would be to tie a bell around the cat's neck. That would tell them where the cat was. All agreed that it was a splendid idea until one wise old mouse stepped up and asked, 'Who will bell the cat?'"

Once the cat is belled, all the mice benefit equally. But whichever mouse attempts to bell the cat might get eaten. Each mouse, therefore, rationally hopes to avoid danger by free-riding off the belling exploits of others. But if all the rodents free-ride, the cat remains a silent, looming menace.

PROPERTY RIGHTS *NOT* TO THE RESCUE

Because public goods are nonexcludable, their creators can't acquire property rights in them. For example, imagine that if some firm spent $1 billion on asteroid defense it would create a $6.7 trillion benefit for humanity. If a firm had a property right to the benefit of asteroid defense, it would spend the $1 billion and then collect the $6.7 trillion. But since asteroid defense is a public good, it's impossible for a firm to have such a property right. Consequently, the free market won't induce self-interested people to engage in asteroid defense because they would receive only a tiny fraction of the benefits of their efforts.

If (absurdly) one person owned the earth, then she would have an incentive to provide for the optimal level of asteroid defense to protect her nice blue planet from a small chance of destruction. But because the earth belongs to no one (or equivalently because the earth belongs to everyone), it's in no one's strong self-interest to spend a huge amount of money to slightly reduce the chance of an asteroid destroying the earth. We all rationally hope that someone else will undertake the task. But if all humans try to free-ride off of other people's asteroid defense efforts, then asteroids will remain a silent-looming menace.

Exclusion represents the essence of property rights. If you can't exclude people from some good or service you provide, you lack property rights. And without property rights, markets don't easily allow you to profit from your efforts, so Adam Smith's invisible hand of the marketplace won't push you to take socially beneficial actions.

NATIONAL DEFENSE

Asteroid defense is a **global** public good, meaning that everyone in the world benefits from it. National defense, by contrast, is a **national** public good that benefits everyone in a country. If the U.S. military deters terrorists from attacking the U.S., then all Americans—even those who don't like the military—benefit. Consequently, national defense is nonexcludable. National defense is also nonrival since, for example, the benefit I receive by being defended by the U.S. Marines doesn't reduce the benefit any other American receives from this protection.

GOVERNMENTS TO THE RESCUE

Because national defense is a public good, and therefore nonexcludable, we can't rely on markets to protect us from armed invaders. To solve this problem, most societies have their government tax citizens to fund a military. Through compulsory taxes, the government can prevent people from free-riding off others.

Unfortunately, since asteroid defense is a global and not a national public good, no one government can compel all the people who benefit from it to contribute to asteroid defense. Each nation, therefore can hope to free-ride off of the asteroid defense efforts of others.

BUT SOMETIMES MARKETS *CAN* SOLVE THE PUBLIC GOODS PROBLEM

Radio programs are public goods. They are nonrival since your listening to a program doesn't reduce the amount of programming available to others. And, before satellite radio, programs were nonexcludable since anyone in range who had a radio could pick up a program. In the early days of radio, some people thought that the government would have to pay for programming since there was no way to charge listeners.[6]

Fortunately, the market was creative enough to solve the radio program public good problem. In 1922 the firm AT&T discovered that it could sell advertising time on the radio. Radio stations learned that advertising could pay for the costs of programming. Radio stations, thereafter, gave up trying to sell programs to listeners and instead started selling listeners to advertisers.

INTELLECTUAL PROPERTY

CHARLIE AND THE CHOCOLATE FACTORY

We now turn from public goods to intellectual property and will use Roald Dahl's novel, *Charlie and the Chocolate Factory*, to discuss intellectual property theft.

Willy Wonka owned a chocolate factory. It produced the most scrumptious chocolate creations the world had ever known. But spies infested Wonka's factory. Using the information gathered by their spies, other chocolate firms started selling the exact same products that Willy Wonka produced.

One bitter day Willy Wonka shut down his factory. Willy Wonka had thrived in the cutthroat chocolate marketplace through innovation. He spent considerable time and money developing superior sweets. Due to high innovation costs, Wonka's average total costs were higher than his rivals. As long as Wonka could sell better products, however, he could charge a higher price than his rivals and still make a profit. But if other chocolate firms could cheaply copy his candy creations, he could no longer successfully compete. So, because of the widespread theft of his chocolate innovations, Willy Wonka had to shut down his factory. Insufficient property rights, therefore, caused Wonka to stop making candy.

Although *Charlie and the Chocolate Factory* is fiction, the candy spies it describes are real. As an article in Slate.com describes, during Roald Dahl's childhood, "the two largest British candy firms, Cadbury and Rowntree, sent so many moles to work in competitors' factories that their spying became legendary."[7]

> "The real-life espionage became so pervasive that candy makers in Europe . . . began routinely employing detectives to keep track of workers. Sensitive manufacturing processes were off-limits to all but the most loyal workers."
>
> "When Nestlé first figured out how to successfully blend milk and chocolate, only a handful of Nestlé executives knew how the complete milk chocolate-making process worked. The company also conducted employee background checks and put 'suspicious' workers under surveillance. At Hershey's, an elite few are privy to the proper mix of cocoa beans required to produce Hershey's distinct chocolate flavor. And Mars blindfolds outside contractors when it's necessary to escort them through its factories."

To protect their innovations, chocolate makers had to impose draconian security on their factories.

Willy Wonka eventually reopens his factory after determining how to keep out spies. Wonka stopped his employees from spying on him by hiring only the tiny creatures called Oompa-Loompas. Mr. Wonka rescued the Oompa-Loompas from Loompaland where they were starving and constantly hunted by Snozzwangers. The Oompa-Loompas are so grateful to Mr. Wonka that they would never betray his candy secrets to another confection maker.

Willy Wonka's chocolate innovations were a form of intellectual property. Intellectual property is information rather than physical goods. Intellectual property can consist of the formula for making Everlasting Gobstoppers, the code behind a software program, or the composition of notes making up a song. To have secure property rights in intellectual property means that no one can use the proprietary information without your permission.

Reprinted by permission of SLL/Sterling Lord Literistic, Inc. Copyright by Joel Brenner.

INTERNET PIRACY

Intellectual property theft caused Willy Wonka to close his factory. Internet piracy might soon cause the closure of music and movie producing firms. And unfortunately these entertainment businesses won't be able to solve their property theft problems with Oompa-Loompas.

Internet piracy has eroded intellectual property rights in music and movies. As many college students know, it's relatively easy for the electronically well connected to steal music and movies off the Internet. The Internet, therefore, has made music and movies far less excludable. Such theft of property poses a significant threat to the for-profit production of movies and music.

Many people consider intellectual property theft far less immoral than the theft of physical goods. I suspect that many who believe that thieves generally belong in prison have few moral qualms about downloading pirated intellectual property from the Internet. This attitude is illustrated by a store in Singapore that sold illegally pirated products but had a sign reading "Shoplifters will be prosecuted."[8] This store's owner undoubtedly thought it was perfectly appropriate for him to cheaply sell illegally copied CDs. But if someone dared to steal a CD from his store, then he would have called the police.

Perhaps many people don't morally object to stealing intellectual property because it is nonrival. If you illegally download pirated music, you haven't prevented other people from hearing the song. In contrast, if you steal a candy bar, that particular candy bar can't be eaten by others. Of course, if piracy causes you to spend less money on music than you otherwise would have, your theft has economically damaged intellectual property owners.

But if you don't morally object to intellectual property theft, pirated copies of music and movies are perfect substitutes for legal copies. And why pay for a product you can get for free?

Movies and music have high fixed costs. As the demand for legal copies of movies and music falls, firms will be less willing to pay these high fixed costs. As a result, Internet piracy might significantly reduce the quantity and quality of movies and music.

As of this writing, authors are safe from Internet piracy because most book readers still prefer printed words to electronic text. We may soon, however, see electronic paper that is as easy to read as printed pulp. Electronic paper combined with intellectual property theft could decimate the demand for books. How much money, for example, would you pay for this textbook if you could download an exact copy in under a minute for free?

Although Internet piracy is illegal in most countries, these laws mean nothing if they are not seriously enforced. As of this writing, the average college student has little to fear from illegally downloading a few movies or songs.

The difficulty of stopping Internet piracy is similar to the challenge of halting illegal drug use. When a car is stolen, the victim contacts the police. But when illegal drugs are sold or a song illegally copied, the police have no easy way even to find out about the crime. As a result, the police have difficulty stopping intellectual property theft.

Solutions to the Internet Piracy Problem
- **Increase the moral cost of theft**—Hollywood is trying to use advertising to convince people that theft of intellectual property is wrong. If they succeed,

then pirated copies will become imperfect substitutes for legal versions of movies.

- **Action figures/concerts**—Creators of intellectual property could still profit even if everyone freely took their property. Movie producers, for example, could profit from selling action figures based on film characters and musicians could profit from selling tickets to their concerts.

- **Advertising**—Movies, music, and books could incorporate commercials into their plots. Perhaps the next Star Wars movie will focus on a Jedi's quest to satisfy the Pepsi Challenge.

- **Tips**—Intellectual property creators could ask for tips from consumers. Many Internet bloggers rely on tips to finance their writings and shareware software programmers often ask users to contribute if they like the product.

- **Self-enforcement**—Many shop owners keep guns behind their counters to protect their physical property. Likewise, intellectual property holders could use virtual weapons to protect their stuff. For example, a music company could create an "infectious" version of a song and place it on a Web site frequented by pirates. If you download the song, a computer virus will erase all the data on your computer. Or perhaps after playing the song nothing bad will happen to your computer for six months. During this time you might allow some friends to copy your illegal version of the song. But after six months, a destructive virus will strike everyone who has downloaded the infectious song. If customers fear that illegal copies of intellectual property might contain viruses, they will pay a higher price for legal copies.[9]

- **Not-for-profit production**—Even with rampant intellectual property theft, amateurs will still produce movies, music, and books for pleasure and fame. Of course, without the hope of profits, few will spend large sums of money creating intellectual property. Although rampant piracy won't destroy garage-band music production, it will stop anyone from making a $100 million special-effects laden movie.

THE INTELLECTUAL PROPERTY OF FRENCH CHEFS[10]

French chefs have done a far better job protecting their intellectual property than music and movie producers have. Recipes are an important source of intellectual property for top French chefs. To maintain their reputations these chefs must continually come up with new recipes. They consequently have tremendous incentives to steal menu ideas from each other. The French legal system offers almost no protection for recipes. Yet French chefs mostly respect each others' intellectual property. Usually, they copy another chef's recipe only if given permission and then they fully credit the recipe's originator.

French chefs protect their intellectual property by ostracizing those who steal. As one chef said, "If another chef copies a recipe exactly we are very furious; we will not talk to this chef anymore, and we won't communicate information to him in the future." Fear of ostracism deters would-be thieves. This recipe self-protection shows that intellectual property can sometimes be defended without governmental help.

A Four-Part Classification of Goods
Figure 14.1 puts what we now know about goods into a chart.

	Rival	Nonrival
Excludable	**Most "normal" goods** such as food, clothing, and housing are excludable and rival. The free market does an excellent job of supplying these kinds of goods. Most of the analysis presented in this textbook is of excludable and rival goods.	Goods which are excludable but nonrival can be **produced at zero marginal cost.** There are usually high fixed costs to make these types of goods, but once one copy of the good has been made, an unlimited number of additional copies can be produced almost costlessly. Internet-supplied music, movies, and software are examples of excludable but nonrival goods. (This assumes that the goods can not be illegally downloaded.) Firms will produce these types of goods since they can charge for their use.
Nonexcludable	Goods which are rival but nonexcludable are called **common resources**. Common resources will tend to be overused. The two possible solutions to the common resource overuse problem are (1) to assign property rights to common resources and thus make them excludable or (2) to have the government forcibly limit individual use of the common resource.	Goods that are nonexcludable and nonrival are **public goods**. Examples include asteriod defense, national defense, and fireworks displays. Markets tend to underproduce public goods.

FIGURE **14.1**

A FOUR-PART CLASSIFICATION OF GOODS

REAL ESTATE PROPERTY RIGHTS

We now leave the world of intellectual property to study real estate. Real estate consists of land and buildings. Markets perform wonders when combining banks with secure real estate property rights. First, we will examine how this magic operates in rich countries. Then we will study why insecure real estate property rights deprive poor countries of wealth-creating opportunities.

REAL ESTATE IN RICH COUNTRIES

Imagine that after college you want to buy a $200,000 home. It would probably take you many years to save $200,000. But in the United States, a bank might easily lend you $180,000 for a $200,000 home purchase. Why, you might ask, would a bank ever trust you with $180,000? Because you will use the home as collateral. Collateral is what a bank can take if you fail to repay a loan. So the bank will trust you with $180,000 because they will have the legal right to seize your $200,000 home if you don't repay them. Collateralized property loans allow many Americans to buy homes.

Many Americans also use collateral-backed loans to start small businesses. Imagine that after working for a few years you begin to hate your job. You want to quit to start your own restaurant. Building a restaurant, however, will cost $1 million. Fortunately, you can use the land the restaurant is on, the proposed restaurant itself, and even the furniture that will be in the restaurant as collateral for a loan to build the restaurant. In addition, you can take out a second loan on your home, using this home as collateral, to get additional funds. As a result, you could access $1 million.

Without collateral-backed loans, only the rich could start most types of small businesses. But such loans allow members of the American middle class to become independent businesspeople. Without collateral-backed loans there would be far fewer homes and businesses in rich countries such as the United States.

MYSTERY-ACRES

The ownership of every home, building, and piece of land in most rich countries is diligently recorded by the government. Banks readily make collateral-backed loans because of such careful records.

Imagine, however, that the ownership of a hypothetical piece of property called Mystery-Acres was not recorded. A bank would be reluctant to lend you money to buy Mystery-Acres because it couldn't be sure you would give the money to the land's rightful owners. If the bank lent you, say, $600,000 and you gave this money to someone only pretending to own Mystery-Acres, the bank couldn't take the property if you failed to repay its loan.

Careful records also allow people to see which property is currently being used as collateral. For example, imagine that someone uses Mystery-Acres as collateral for a $600,000 loan. This person then sells you Mystery-Acres without telling you about the loan. After the crooked seller leaves the country with your cash, the bank announces that if someone doesn't repay the loan it will take Mystery-Acres.

Fortunately, however, property laws in rich countries require banks to create a public record whenever a property is used as collateral. Before you buy a home, therefore, you can check to see if any bank has the legal right to seize it for nonrepayment of a loan.

But without careful public property records, banks wouldn't make collateral-backed loans. Unfortunately, most of the real estate owned by poor people in poor nations is not publicly recorded. Consequently, the world's poor are denied the benefits of collateral-backed loans that so benefit citizens of rich nations.

PROPERTY IN POOR COUNTRIES

Most of the property possessed by poor people in poor countries is only informally owned. For example, a family in Peru might have lived on a property for generations. Everyone living nearby may accept that the family owns the property. Yet the government has no official record of the family owning the land. Because no one officially owns the land, the property legally belongs to the government.

Economist Hernando de Soto refers to informally owned property as *dead capital*. Capital is another word for assets. Dead capital refers to assets that can't be used to create new wealth. An American who legally owns his home can use his dwelling as collateral for a loan to start a business. A Peruvian who only informally owns his home can't, because a bank won't be able to legally seize a home which officially resides on state land.

Banks, furthermore, are extremely reluctant to give loans to people who want to build homes on dead capital. This is because, if the loan is not repaid, the dead capital, which officially belongs to the government, can't be seized by the bank.

Utilities, such as power, water, and telephone companies, are reluctant to provide service to informally owned homes. In the United States, a utility company can seize a home if the owners don't pay their bills. But a utility in a poor country can't seize an informally owned home. As a result, utility companies face far greater risk in offering service to informally owned homes.

TRIBAL LAND OF AMERICAN INDIANS[11]

In the United States, many Native Americans live on tribally-owned land. Individuals on this land can't sell their own homes to someone outside of the tribe since the land the home is on belongs to the entire tribe. This tribal land, therefore, is dead capital. An individual Native American can't use his home as collateral for a loan because a bank can't legally seize tribal land. As a result, many Native Americans can't use their homes as collateral to start small businesses.

Native American reservations are often pockets of poverty in an otherwise mostly wealthy America. Lack of individual property rights, which creates dead capital, is a prime reason for Native American poverty.

INFORMAL BUSINESS OWNERSHIP

Many business "owners" in poor countries lack official property rights in their businesses. To start a business in the United States, or most other countries, you have to register officially with the government. If I started and registered a business called, say, "Adventures in Economics," I would legally and securely own the business and all its assets.

Unfortunately, in many poor countries it takes a tremendous amount of time and money to register a business officially. As an experiment, Hernando de Soto sent a team to Peru to legally register a small garment workshop. The team had to work six hours a day for 289 days to accomplish the task.[13] Because of such huge administrative hurdles, most businesses in poor countries are not officially registered and so operate outside of the law.

Informally owned businesses suffer tremendous disadvantages. They must continually pay bribes to officials who can shut them down for operating illegally. They can't borrow money, buy insurance, or rely on courts to enforce contracts. Their illegal status prevents them from enjoying many of the wealth-creating benefits of markets.

PROPERTY RIGHTS OF THE DEAD

Dead people can't own property. You might not think this is a big problem as the dead usually have little need for worldly possessions. But not all the legally dead have stopped living.

The Indian government has mistakenly classified many living people as dead. These legally dead people can't engage in many wealth-creating activities such as buying property. Fortunately, dead Indians have started a lobbying group called the Association of the Dead to pressure government officials to bring the breathing dead back to legal life. The group was founded by Lal Bihari (1961–). Lal Bihari found out he was dead when he unsuccessfully sought a bank loan. It took him 19 years to convince the Indian bureaucracy to give him back his legal life.

WHAT HAPPENED TO SREY NETH?

Let's return to Srey Neth, the poor Cambodian teenager. Recall that after she was freed from sexual servitude, her store failed. Many poor girls in Srey Neth's situation would have returned to prostitution. But she was lucky. Using money donated by some *New York Times* readers, Srey Neth attended school to become a beautician.

But why did Srey Neth need charity to afford school? In the United States, families often borrow money, using their homes as collateral, to pay for their kids' educations. Poor people in poor countries have trillions of dollars of informally owned real estate assets that they could potentially use to finance education. But Srey Neth's family likely possessed only dead capital that couldn't be used as collateral for a loan. So without charitable assistance, Srey Neth would not have been able to pay for her beauty school education.

Poor countries are filled with teenagers like Srey Neth. They have the skills to run small businesses, but their lack of property rights often makes this impossible. If they could borrow a little money, they could attend school and learn a marketable trade. But again their lack of property rights stymies them because their family's dwellings are usually dead capital that can't be used as collateral for a loan. Deprived of the ability to sell goods or learn a trade, they often turn to the one profession that thrives even in the absence of property rights: prostitution.

WHERE PROPERTY RIGHTS ARE *NOT* NEEDED

This chapter has argued that secure property rights are necessary to spur wealth creation. But we now consider a counterexample: Free Software Projects.

The free software movement purposefully rejects property rights to deliberately create public goods. Free software products include the computer operating system Linux and the online encyclopedia Wikipedia. Both are built by volunteers and are freely and legally accessible to everyone.

Normally, if a good were given away for free, its supplier would quickly run out of product. But Linux and Wikipedia are nonrival and so one person's use of them doesn't reduce the amount available for other people.

Almost anyone can contribute to the Wikipedia encyclopedia by adding or editing entries. Wikipedia is constantly being updated. I have found Wikipedia to be extremely reliable and have often consulted it to get background information for writing this textbook.

Interestingly, however, Wikipedia has had trouble with one type of contributor: staff members of U.S. Congressmen. Most U.S. Congressmen have entries in Wikipedia. In 2006 Wikipedia discovered that the employees of many congressmen were editing their bosses' entries to remove true but damaging information.[14] Wikipedia temporarily forbade people using computers located in some congressmen's offices from editing entries.

The operating system Linux is managed, but not owned, by Linus Torvalds. Linus Torvalds coordinates the efforts of volunteers to continually improve the free computer operating system Linux. As of this writing, Linux poses the greatest threat to Microsoft's near-monopoly on operating systems.

Since Wikipedia and Linux deliberately forsake property rights, their tremendous success poses a challenge to the worldview of those, including myself, who believe in the importance of property rights for wealth creation. Wikipedia was founded by Jimmy Wales and Larry Sanger in 2001. I confess that if they talked to me in early 2001 and asked whether I thought Wikipedia would succeed, I would have answered no. I would have told the two men that since contributors wouldn't have any property rights in Wikipedia, they wouldn't profit from its success. As a result, I would have mistakenly said that Wikipedia will almost certainly fail.

QUESTIONS YOU SHOULD BE ABLE TO ANSWER AFTER READING THIS CHAPTER:

1 Why did Srey Neth's store fail? (page 340)

2 What does it mean to have property rights in a good? (page 340)

3 Why does investment bring pain before pleasure? (pages 340–341)

4 Why does lack of property rights discourage people from making investments? (page 341)

5 Why did lack of property rights reduce investment in Russia? (page 342)

6 Why would insecure property rights in grades cause students to study less? (page 342)

7 Why does lack of property rights cause people to hide wealth? (pages 342–343)

8 Why does collective ownership discourage wealth creation? (page 343)

9 What happened on private plots of farm land in the former Soviet Union? (page 343)

10 Why did lack of property rights doom the Truffula trees in Dr. Seuss's *The Lorax?* (page 344)

11 What is the "tragedy of the commons"? (page 345)

12 What are rival goods? (page 345)

13 What are excludable goods? (page 345)

14 What happens to resources afflicted by the tragedy of the commons? (page 345)

15 Why would making a lake excludable help preserve a fish population? (page 346)

16 How do secure property rights solve the tragedy of the commons problem? (page 346)

17 What are public goods? (page 347)

18 Why doesn't Adam Smith's invisible hand cause self-interested people to provide public goods? (page 347)

19 What are free-riders? (page 347)

20 What is the difference between a national and global public good? (page 348)

21 Why are governments usually needed to provide public goods? (page 348)

22 In *Charlie and the Chocolate Factory* why did Willy Wonka initially shut down his factory? (page 349)

23 What is intellectual property? (page 349)

24 Is intellectual property rival or nonrival? (page 350)

25 Has the Internet made music and movies more or less excludable? (page 350)

26 How could movie, music, and book producers profit even if people freely take their property? (page 351)

27 How could intellectual property holders use self-enforcement to reduce Internet piracy? (page 351)

28 What is real estate? (page 352)

29 What is collateral? (page 352)

30 Why do collateral-backed loans make it much easier for people in rich countries to buy homes? (pages 352–353)

31 Why are banks reluctant to make collateral-backed loans on property whose ownership isn't diligently recorded? (page 353)

32 What is informal ownership? (page 353)

33 What is dead capital? (page 353)

34 What is the problem with dead capital? (pages 353–354)

35 Why is Native-American land in the U.S. dead capital? (page 354)

36 Why are so many businesses in poor countries only informally owned? (page 354)

37 What problems plague informally owned businesses? (page 354)

38 What are Linux and Wikipedia? (page 355)

39 Who owns Linux and Wikipedia? (page 355)

40 Why does the success of Linux and Wikipedia challenge the worldview of those who believe in the importance of property rights for wealth creation? (page 355)

STUDY PROBLEMS

1 Why do people volunteer to work on Wikipedia or Linux?

2 Do you steal intellectual property? If yes, do you consider your behavior immoral? Why or why not?

3 Property rights in grades are limited because you can't sell your grades to other students or buy other students' grades. Would you be better off if this wasn't true? Why or why not?

4 Elephants are often killed in Africa for their ivory tusks. Why might elephants in Africa be safer if it were legal to sell elephants' tusks?

5 Does stealing intellectual property cause more or less harm to property holders than stealing physical property does? Consider marginal costs, fixed costs, and what the thief would have done had he not stolen.

6 List some examples of public goods not mentioned in this chapter.

7 List some examples of tragedy of the commons not mentioned in this chapter.

8 Discuss whether police protection is a public good.

9 How do Wikipedia and Linux create wealth? Who gets this wealth?

10 I have a great idea for a fiction book. I want to retell the *Lord of the Rings* from the viewpoint of Sauron. In the original book Sauron was evil, but in my book he will be good. I would retell the original story showing how Sauron's actions were all justified by the oppression of elves and wizards. In my book the hobbit "heroes" of the original novels will be seen as dupes of the cowardly elf elite. Unfortunately, under current copyright laws I couldn't write the book without getting the permission of the original author's family. I can't imagine this family would give me permission unless I gave them many millions of dollars, and I can't imagine anyone giving me several million dollars to write this book. Copyright laws, therefore, effectively prevent me from writing my book. Is this economically efficient?

11 If French chefs regularly stole each others' recipes there would probably be less innovation in French cooking. Why is this?

12 In *The Lorax* story, should the government have forbidden the cutting down of any Truffula trees?

13 Imagine that 20 freshmen in a dorm share a bathroom. Is this bathroom a rival resource? Is it an excludable resource? Imagine that the college makes no provisions for cleaning the bathroom. What is likely to happen?

14 Look up an entry on www.Wikipedia.org that you know a lot about. Improve the entry by adding additional, useful information. If you were assigned this question by your professor, print out the entry before and after your addition. Clearly indicate the changes you made.

15 What's wrong with this picture? Relate your answer to the relevant concept covered in this chapter.

CHAPTER 15

GROUCHO MARX

In December 2006, some Taco Bell customers didn't quite get what they paid for. Seventy-one of them got sick after ingesting *E. coli* bacteria at the restaurant chain.

When you buy food at a restaurant, you can't be sure that your meal will be safe. When you purchase a car, you don't know if it will soon break down. And even when you see your doctor, you can't be certain that he will give you good advice. Life is full of uncertainty, and this uncertainty permeates markets.

Ideally, product markets would work like this: customers determine what they want and then they trade their money for some known product. Unfortunately, because customers usually have incomplete information about products' qualities, customers don't always get what they want. This chapter examines how markets function in the presence of uncertainty. We analyze some effects of uncertainty concerning (1) products, (2) employees' activities, (3) potential employees, (4) insurance customers, (5) romantic dates, and (6) politicians.

1. INCOMPLETE INFORMATION ABOUT PRODUCTS

Businesses sometimes use uncertainty to cheat customers. Other times firms, such as Taco Bell, mistakenly sell defective products. Because consumers have incomplete information about most products, they sometimes get less than they pay for.

Product uncertainty harms firms as well as consumers. Consumers pay less for a product the less sure they are of the product's safety and reliability. Thus, firms that can somehow earn consumers' trust increase the demand for their products. Brand names can help firms earn this trust.

BRAND NAMES

You're visiting an impoverished country that has questionable water quality. You're desperately thirsty but want to avoid waterborne parasites. Fortunately, you see Coke for sale and know you have found something safe to drink. For people in underdeveloped

CHALLENGE TO MARKET EFFECTIVENESS 5: INCOMPLETE INFORMATION

. . . .

LEARNING OBJECTIVES

AFTER READING THIS CHAPTER, YOU SHOULD BE ABLE TO:

- Explain the logic behind the quote at the beginning of this chapter.
- Identify the purpose of brand names.
- Understand the consequences of having incomplete information about employees' activities.
- Describe adverse selection.

. . . .

countries, the Coke brand name essentially means, "Drinking this won't cause diarrhea." In poor countries, Coke costs more than locally made beverages. But consumers are willing to pay a premium price for Coke because the Coke brand name reduces uncertainty over the safety and taste of their drink.

McDonald's, too, has a very valuable brand. Restaurants in general vary greatly in quality. Before going into a restaurant for the first time, a consumer usually doesn't know what kind of food he will get or how clean the bathrooms might be. But all McDonald's restaurants are pretty much alike, so when you go to any McDonald's, even in a city you have never visited before, you do know exactly what kind of dining experience you will have. The McDonald's brand name, therefore, greatly reduces the uncertainty facing consumers.

Imagine that you are going to start a company that will cut costs by having poor quality control. You estimate that 10 percent of your products will have defects. Should you spend millions promoting a brand name? No! An expensive brand name is a hostage to honesty—a hostage that dies if customer trust is lost. A well-known brand name is an asset only if customers have positive experiences with your products. A company that disappoints customers is harmed by a brand name because a brand makes it easy for customers to associate their negative experiences with the branded company.

Taco Bell's *E. coli* outbreak greatly harmed the company. Because of its well known brand name, it was easy for consumers to remember that the outbreak occurred at Taco Bell. Taco Bell, therefore, has a strong profit incentive to prevent a repeat of the incident. The invisible hand pushes Taco Bell along with all other branded restaurant chains to maintain high sanitary conditions.

Here are just a few ways that sellers can use the cloak of uncertainty to cheat customers:

- A college that gives generous financial aid packages to attract new students could take away much of this aid from students after they have completed their first year of college.
- A firm could offer a mail-in rebate but then make the rebate so difficult to obtain (because you have to send letters to several places and include multiple copies of receipts) that only a small number of customers ever actually get the rebate.
- A college's promotional brochures could show many pictures of students frolicking outdoors in wonderful weather. But the college might be located in a town that has nice weather only during the summer when the school is closed.
- A beer advertisement could imply that its male drinkers always attract beautiful women. Yet consuming this beer might negatively impact the sex lives of men.
- A movie advertised as a sexy thriller could actually be an existential examination of ennui.

The Value of Brands   The following chart is a 2005 estimate of the value of fifteen different brands:

Company	Value of Brand
Coca-Cola	$67.5 billion
Microsoft	59.9 billion
IBM	53.4 billion
GE	47.0 billion
Intel	35.6 billion
Nokia	26.5 billion
Disney	26.4 billion
McDonald's	26.0 billion
Toyota	24.8 billion
Marlboro	21.2 billion
Mercedes-Benz	20.0 billion
Citi	20.0 billion
Hewlett-Packard	18.9 billion
American Express	18.6 billion
Gillette	17.5 billion

Source: Robert Berney and David Kiley, "Interbrand, Global Brands," *Business Week,* July 2005.

The value of a brand is basically how much extra profit over the long term a company receives because of the brand. So if Pepsi employed a demon to magically erase all knowledge of Coca-Cola's brand from human brains, the Coca-Cola company would be worth $67.5 billion less.

Certified Humane   Not-for-profit groups can sometimes use brand names to promote their causes. For example, the Humane Farm Animal Care organization seeks to improve the treatment of farm animals. Some consumers are willing to pay more for meat that comes from humanely treated animals. It is ordinarily difficult for a consumer buying pork, for example, to know how the pig was treated before it died. To combat this uncertainty, Humane Farm Animal Care created a brand name called "Certified Humane." Sellers of meat can only use this brand name if the meat they sell comes from humanely treated animals. If enough consumers are willing to pay premium prices for Certified Humane meat, then farmers will have a financial incentive to treat their animals more kindly.

MONEY-BACK GUARANTEES

Besides promoting brand names, firms also use money-back guarantees as a means of winning customers' trust. Money-back guarantees allow consumers to recover most of the cost of buying a product if the product proves defective. Customers rationally assume that a store would not offer such a guarantee and then knowingly sell a defective product.

Consumers should be somewhat wary of buying nonreturnable products. Imagine, for example, that an electronics store sells two types of computer monitors. They look identical, but one has a 90-day money-back guarantee, whereas the second is nonreturnable. A consumer should wonder why the second monitor can't be returned. Perhaps it's because customers often find defects in this type of monitor and so offering a money-back guarantee would be extremely costly to the store.

EBAY RATINGS

Uncertainty might have doomed eBay. eBay is an online auction Web site that allows anyone to buy and sell goods. If, for example, you don't find this textbook worthy of a permanent place in your personal library, you can sell it on eBay.

On eBay, potential buyers bid for sale items. The buyer who bids the most wins the good. The winning buyer is supposed to send payment to the seller, and the seller is supposed to send the item to the buyer. Both the buyer and seller have the ability to harm each other. The seller could refuse to send the good, or send a good inferior to what he advertised on eBay. The buyer could not send payment, or send a fake check. eBay has succeeded only because it has created a system under which buyers and sellers mostly trust each other.

To increase trust, eBay has a buyer and seller rating system. After completing a trade, the buyer and seller can comment on each other. Buyers and sellers often read these comments before engaging in a trade. Here are some of the comments I have proudly received as an eBay buyer:

- Great e-bayer fast payment a real pleasure A++++++.
- great e-mails quick to pay pleasure to do business with highly recommend thanks.
- Very Professional, Super E-Bayer, Will do business with ANYTIME! 5-STARS*****.

- Excellent communication, fast payment. Thanks again! A+++++.
- Fast Payment! Great Ebay buyer! Recommend to all Ebay Users! AAA+++.
- Super transaction! Fast payment! Would do business again in a flash. A+++ Thanks.
- Fast pay, easy to do business with!

After checking out my ratings, a seller would, I hope, trust me. eBay's rating system not only provides buyers and sellers with information about each other but also gives eBay users an incentive to behave honestly.

eBay represents a triumph of markets over uncertainty. On eBay, complete strangers trade with each other. Sometimes fraud does strike eBay users. But enough people are willing to trade on eBay so that, as of this writing, the company is worth about $42 billion.

HIDING INFORMATION[1]

Firms sometimes attempt to deliberately increase consumer uncertainty by hiding information. These firms are essentially given the chance to speak about their products but remain silent. Unfortunately for the firms, however, consumers can easily hear the sound of their silence. Consider the following kissing story.

Imagine that you have a friend who is a 20-year-old female undergraduate. You see her kissing a high school boy. You determine that the boy must be 14, 15, or 16. It would be very embarrassing for a college girl to be caught kissing a boy that young.

Assume that your friend's honesty prevents her from lying to you—if she told you the boy was 16, you would believe her. Although she won't lie, she is willing to tell you to mind your own business. So if you ask the boy's age, your friend will either tell you his true age or say, "Mind your own business." When you ask your friend how old the boy is, what should your friend say?

Obviously, the older he is, the less embarrassed she will be. She knows that you would never think him over 16. Thus, if he is 16, she will tell you. If he is 16, she wouldn't, by assumption, lie. If she says, "Mind your own business," at best you will think he is 16, but you will probably deduce that he is younger. Consequently, if he is 16, she will always make herself look better by revealing it.

Now let's assume that the boy is only 15. What should she do? Her choice is either to say he's 15 or to tell you to mind your own business. If she says "Mind your own business," however, you will know the boy could not possibly be 16 because if he is 16, she would reveal it. Thus, if she uses her "none of your business" strategy, you will believe that the boy is 15 or 14. Since she would rather you think him 15 than 14, she will reveal his age if he is indeed 15.

We have established that your friend will tell you the boy's age whenever he is 15 or 16. Consequently, if she says, "None of your business," you know the boy is 14. This is a stable equilibrium, for if you assume that "none of your business" means 14, it will be in your friend's interest to tell you his age, unless he is indeed 14. Since your friend can't lie, she must reveal the truth. Your friend, therefore, can't really stay silent, since silence tells you the boy is only 14.

The key result from this story is that when someone can't lie, she also can't stay silent, for silence communicates information. Silence signals that the situation is very bad because if it wasn't, she would have an incentive to say something. This "sound of silence" result has strong applications to consumer product markets.

Imagine that chocolates are either high or low calorie. You're in the grocery store and see some chocolates labeled as low calorie and some with no calorie labels.

Assume that consumer antifraud laws prevent chocolate makers from falsely labeling their products. What should you assume about the unlabeled chocolates? Since most consumers prefer low-calorie foods, manufactures of low-calorie products will label their goods as such. Thus, no label means high in calories. In a deep sense, therefore, all the chocolates are labeled. When a product is not labeled for some characteristic, you should assume that either most people don't care about the trait, or that the product's hidden trait is "bad."

Mandatory Disclosure Laws   Governments frequently force disclosure on firms. For example, purveyors of packaged foods in the United States must list their goods' nutritional ingredients. But as the above analysis shows, consumers don't obviously benefit from mandatory disclosure laws because firms will find it in their self-interest to disclose beneficial ingredients, and consumers can rationally assume that lack of disclosure suggests that a product contains "bad" ingredients.

Mandatory disclosure laws frequently force firms to reveal information that consumers don't care about. As a result, labels on products sometimes become so cluttered that few bother reading them. Mandatory disclosure laws can, therefore, actually reduce the amount of information consumers acquire about products.

ADVERSE SELECTION[2]

Uncertainty creates distrust. Unfortunately, this distrust is sometimes magnified by the phenomenon known as *adverse selection*. Adverse selection is an extremely powerful force in economics that we will encounter many times in this chapter. Before discussing how it relates to product markets, let's study it in educational markets.

Imagine that a few years after graduation you apply to 10 Masters in Business Administration (MBA) programs. You get into nine but are rejected by one. Tragically, you most wanted to attend the one school that rejected you. Bad karma? No, adverse selection.

Adverse selection manifests when you attract those with whom you least wish to interact. You probably want to attend the most exclusive MBA program that will have you. An exclusive school, by definition, is difficult to get into. Therefore, the lower a school's admissions standards, the less you should want to attend.

What would it signal if an MBA program really wanted you? It might show that the school believed you were a good match for its program. More likely, however, the school believed that admitting you would significantly increase the quality of its student body. Of course, if you were far better than the program's average students, you should probably look elsewhere. This means that if you were a bad enough student, you would not want to attend any school that would admit you, for by admitting you, the school signals its exceptionally low quality.

This chapter begins with the Groucho Marx quote: "I refuse to join any club that would have me for a member." Groucho knows something about a club that accepts him: the club has low enough standards that it's willing to accept him as a member. If you desire to join only an exclusive club, but you are not the type of person that an exclusive club should accept, then you should indeed decline to join any club that would have you as a member.

I attended a graduate school that admitted me from its waiting list, long after it had made most of its admission decisions. Of all the schools that accepted me, it considered me the least worthy. This school therefore was obviously the best that

> **Adverse selection** occurs when you attract those with whom you least want to interact.

I could get into, and naturally the one that I decided to attend. When adverse selection applies, you should want most those who least want you.

Used Cars and Adverse Selection
Adverse selection haunts the used car market. When buying a used car, you most want to attract sellers of high-quality automobiles. Alas, sellers would most want to part with vehicles of low quality.

To simplify matters, assume that you are considering buying a used Honda Civic that will be of either high or low quality. The car's quality determines its value to you.

Car's Quality	Car's Value to Buyer
High	$10,000
Low	3,000

If you know everything about the quality of the car, then you need not worry about adverse selection. But let's assume that you don't know the car's quality. You should be reluctant to pay more than $3,000 for the car because sellers are far more likely to sell low- than high-quality cars.

Assume that 90 percent of all used Honda Civics are of high quality. Further assume that current owners know their car's quality, but prospective buyers don't. If all buyers are aware of adverse selection, then the price of used cars will be far below $10,000. This low price for used cars will mean that owners of excellent cars will be even less willing to sell them. Adverse selection thus creates a vicious circle.

As adverse selection lowers the price of used cars, fewer used cars of high quality are sold, which by definition increases the strength of adverse selection, which further lowers the price of used cars, which causes even fewer used cars of high quality to be sold, which . . . . As a result, if buyers can't determine car quality then even though 90 percent of used Honda Civics are of high quality, almost all of the used cars on the market will be of poor quality.

Countering Adverse Selection in the Used Car Market[3]
The cure for adverse selection is additional information. Imagine that you want to sell a high-quality used car. Because of adverse selection, buyers will initially disbelieve that your car is indeed of high quality. But if an independent mechanic verifies your car's quality, then a buyer should be willing to pay around $10,000.

If for some reason the buyer can't hire a mechanic, you could offer him a warranty on the car obligating you to pay all necessary car repairs for the next few years. The warranty signals to the buyer that you think the car is of high quality because if you thought the car was likely to need expensive future repairs the warranty would be too expensive for you to offer. The warranty also reduces the harm of hidden information because if the car was not of excellent quality and broke down, the buyer would receive compensation.

Some firms use brands to reduce adverse selection in the used auto market. BMW, for example, offers its own "certified pre-owned vehicles." Since BMW is willing to associate its valuable brand name with its used cars, buyers can perhaps trust that its used cars are of high quality.

2. INCOMPLETE INFORMATION ABOUT EMPLOYEES' ACTIVITIES

We will now shift from discussing incomplete information in product markets to considering how firms can be harmed by having incomplete information about their employees. Imagine you sell office supplies. You have a meeting with the manager of a big company. This manager makes the office supply purchasing decisions for his employer. You should, therefore, probably treat this manager very well, perhaps buying him a nice meal, taking him to a sporting event, or maybe even giving him an expensive gift.

Many workers have the power to spend their employers' money. These workers have a strong incentive to spend the money in ways that help themselves, not their employers. Consequently, a manager who buys vast amounts of office supplies for his company benefits from purchasing these supplies from the salesman who offers him the best gifts.

When employees make decisions for their employers, they act as agents. These agents have an interest in maximizing their own welfare, not the welfare of their employer. Economists have a special term for the problems caused by agents who work to their own benefit to the detriment of their employers: *agency costs*.

> **Agency costs**—The harm suffered by employers when employees make decisions that help themselves but harm their employers.

Agency costs arise because firms have incomplete information about their employees' activities. Pretend, for example, that you own a law firm. You don't have time, however, to make all the decisions yourself, so you delegate authority to an office manager. One decision the office manager makes is determining which company the law firm buys paper from. Assume that the office manager buys $20,000 of paper from the Wunder-Pifflin paper company. You can't be sure if the manager did this because Wunder-Pifflin offered the best paper deal or because a Wunder-Pifflin salesman gave your manager an expensive gift.

Companies, of course, are aware of agency costs and take steps to reduce them. Wal-Mart, for example, has a policy of forbidding employees from accepting any type of gift from those who sell goods to the company. But sometimes, however, the bribes get through, and agency costs strike at firms' profits.

FREQUENT FLYER MILES[4]

Frequent flyer miles exploit business travelers' willingness to spend other peoples' money. Airlines give their passengers frequent flyer miles that they can exchange for free flights. Frequent flyer miles are a great deal for business travelers because while the business pays for the ticket, the traveler often can use the miles for personal travel.

Imagine that you have a choice between two flights. The first is cheaper, but the second gives you more frequent flyer miles. If you're paying, you would probably take the less expensive ticket. If, however, your company pays for the ticket but you get to keep the frequent flyer miles, wouldn't it be tempting to pick the flight that gives you the most miles? After all, if you're spending other people's money, what do you care about the ticket price? Frequent flyer miles can be a bribe for employees to waste their company's money.

It's very cost effective to bribe those who spend other people's money. If I'm spending $1,000 of my own money, then to get me to spend it on your product, you would actually have to give me something worth at least $1,000. If I'm buying for my company, with my company's money, however, I should be willing to give you $1,000 in return for you giving *me* only, say, $100.

BRIBING PILOTS WITH MEAT[5]

Several years ago *The Wall Street Journal* ran an interesting article on how airline refuelers bribe pilots of corporate jets.[6] Since corporate jets can be refueled at multiple airports along their routes, refuelers intensely compete for their business. Normally, you might think that these refuelers would compete on price. These refuelers, however, realized that the pilots decide where to refuel, but the jet's owner pays for the gas. The refuelers take advantage of the pilots' spending other people's money by bribing the pilots to refuel at their base. One company "hands out one 8-ounce steak for every 100 gallons of fuel purchased." The steaks are given to the pilots by attractive, scantily-clad women. The pilots are usually given their freebies only if they "forgo discounts on fuel." The refuelers are careful to give the pilots their freebies secretly, thus proving that the pilots and refuelers fully understand the game being played.

Why don't the refuelers simply give direct cash bribes to pilots? These bribes would probably be illegal, so pilots, fearing criminal prosecution, would be reluctant to accept them. Bribing pilots with meat is more effective because it's legal.

AGENCY COSTS ARE EVERYWHERE

Agency costs are everywhere and don't just affect firms. Consumers should be especially wary of anyone who (a) gives them advice and (b) takes their money. For example, stockbrokers often get paid based on the number of stocks their customers buy and sell. As a result, stockbrokers have an incentive to recommend that their customers engage in an excess amount of stock trading.

Home buyers often hire real estate agents. These agents give advice to home buyers. Real estate agents get paid by receiving a percentage of the purchased home's sales price. These agents, therefore, benefit when buyers pay a large amount for a home because this increases their sales commission.

Real estate agents get paid the same amount regardless of how much time they spend helping their clients find a home. Real estate agents usually go with clients to look at every home the buyer is considering purchasing. Sometimes clients buy the first or second house they look at. Other times clients look at 20 or 30 homes before making a decision. Real estate agents, therefore, save tremendous amounts of time when their clients buy one of the first few houses they look at. These agents, consequently, serve their own self-interests by pushing their clients to make quick purchasing decisions. Imagine, for example, that a client is looking at his second home. The agent might be aware that the asking price for this home is too high. But the agent would be better off herself if the client bought this home and didn't spend the agent's time looking at dozens more houses. The agent, therefore, might find it in her self-interest to lie to her client and tell him that the home is really a tremendous bargain.

Of course, just because a real estate agent can benefit from lying doesn't mean that she actually will lie. To protect themselves from deception, however, clients of real estate agents must understand the conflict between their own and their real estate agent's self-interests.

Doctors and Cheerleaders
Doctors work for their patients; therefore, they are their patients' agents. These doctor-agents make many decisions for patients, including determining what types of prescription drugs their patients take.

The pharmaceutical companies that make these drugs are certainly aware that doctors, not patients, make most drug-buying decisions. As a result, pharmaceutical companies hire drug representatives who try to convince doctors to prescribe their firm's pills.

Let's consider a typical 50-year-old male doctor. He is an extremely busy man. He doesn't have time to listen to every sales pitch the pharmaceutical industry would like to subject him to. Pretend that representatives from two rival pharmaceutical companies show up at this doctor's office. The doctor has time to see only one of them. The first representative is a 40-year-old scientist who is an expert in pharmaceutical chemistry. He wants the doctor to watch a one-hour statistical presentation on the benefits of his firm's drugs. The second drug representative is a gorgeous 25-year-old woman. She wants to take the doctor to lunch, flirt with him, and ask him pretty please to use her company's products. If the doctor cared about what was best for his patients, he would listen to the first representative. But if the doctor did what was most enjoyable for himself, he would (almost certainly) go to lunch with the beautiful 25-year-old.

Pharmaceutical companies, at least, seem to believe that doctors would rather listen to sales pitches from beautiful young women than average-looking middle age men. As *The New York Times* reported, pharmaceutical companies frequently hire young ex-cheerleaders as drug representatives.[7] So the next time your doctor suggests you take some drug, it might be because a pretty young woman smiled and seductively asked him to prescribe the drug to his patients.

FDA to the Rescue?

Because of agency costs, patients can't have complete trust that their doctors will prescribe them the best medicines. The U.S. government tries to help patients by preventing its citizens from using unsafe or ineffective medicine. Before a drug can be sold in the United States, it must be approved by the Food and Drug Administration (FDA), a powerful governmental agency.

In the late 1950s, pregnant women in many countries took the drug thalidomide to combat morning sickness. The FDA, however, had doubts about the safety of thalidomide and so blocked its sale in the United States.

The FDA's fears proved tragically true. Thousands of children outside of the United States developed birth defects because their moms used thalidomide while pregnant. The FDA's blocking of thalidomide was a great triumph for the FDA and its regulation of the pharmaceutical market.

Despite its thalidomide success, however, some critics of the FDA believe this government agency has done more harm than good. To understand why critics have this view, let's consider two types of errors the FDA can make:

1. The FDA could mistakenly allow a "bad" drug to be sold.
2. The FDA could mistakenly prevent a "good" drug from being sold.

Political pressures, unfortunately, cause the FDA to worry too much about the first type of error relative to the second. If the FDA allows a "bad" drug to be sold then those damaged by the mistake will be identifiable. These people, if still alive, will know they have been harmed and their harm will be recognizable to others. If the FDA makes the first type of mistake, consequently, people will know that the agency erred.

But when the FDA is too cautious and prevents a "good" drug from being sold, the victims are usually invisible. For example, imagine that the FDA mistakenly blocks the sale of a drug that would have reduced cancer deaths by 5 percent. Cancer patients would never encounter the drug and so most would be unaware that the FDA prevented them from using it. And even if a patient knew about the drug, he could never be sure that taking the drug would have helped. Consequently, the FDA doesn't look bad if it prevents Americans from buying a "good" drug. Some economists believe that because of these incentives, the FDA is far too cautious and blocks many drugs that would have been helpful to consumers.

The FDA forces all pharmaceutical companies to test drugs extensively before the companies are permitted to sell their drugs to consumers. This testing increases drug safety, but this increased safety comes at a huge cost. Because of FDA testing requirements, a new drug does not become available to consumers for 12 to 15 years after its discovery. This delay greatly harms some patients. Indeed, many patients who could benefit from newly discovered drugs die before their needed drugs obtain FDA approval.

3. INCOMPLETE INFORMATION ABOUT POTENTIAL EMPLOYEES
HIRING AND ADVERSE SELECTION[8]

One of the most important decisions firms make is deciding whom to hire. Adverse selection complicates this decision.

Imagine that a company advertises to hire a computer programmer for $80,000 a year. Many apply for the position. Which applicant would most want the job? The answer is someone whose lack of talent would ordinarily bar him from making anywhere near $80,000. Adverse selection would manifest because the least-qualified person would have the greatest desire to get hired. The person the company would most want to hire would probably not even bother applying because she would be such a talented programmer that she could easily make more than $80,000.

When you consider hiring someone, you don't have complete information about her qualities, so you must guess based upon signals. A candidate's desire to work for you provides a powerful signal about her quality. On average, job candidates who would be the happiest with the offered salary are the candidates of the lowest quality since the marketplace values them the least.

To combat the appearance of adverse selection, a job candidate should avoid appearing overeager. Rather, a candidate should consider playing hard to get and let her prospective employer believe that she has many attractive offers. If a job candidate really is hard to get, then she is not desperate, and an employer doesn't have to worry about adverse selection.

Adverse Selection and Children[9]
Recall that adverse selection occurs when you attract those with whom you least wish to interact. The types of people whom daycare centers, elementary schools, and summer kid's camps least want to attract as employees are pedophiles. Unfortunately, child molesters are especially attracted to jobs that allow them to work with children. Organizations that work with children, therefore, need to be especially concerned about adverse selection. These organizations can combat adverse selection by gathering information about potential employees and screening out undesirables. Fortunately for these organizations, the vast majority of people who want to work with kids are not motivated by deviant desires.

RESUME OMISSION

We learned earlier in this chapter how the "sound of silence" can harm firms that wish to keep quiet about characteristics of their products. The same sound of silence can damage job applicants.

Imagine, for example, that after graduation you send in your resume to apply for a job. Your resume, however doesn't list your overall college grade point average (GPA). If everyone knows that this employer doesn't care about college grades, then you don't suffer from omitting your GPA. But let's assume that the employer does put at least some weight on grades. To keep everything simple, assume that your overall average is either an A, B, C, or D. If you have an F average you would not have graduated.

If you have an A average, you would surely list it on your resume. Consequently, not revealing your grades signals loudly that your grades aren't spectacular. If your GPA is a B, you would also have revealed it. Not revealing your GPA means that you don't have an A average. Consequently, if you have a B GPA and don't list it, your employer will at best think you have either a B, C, or D average. You would prefer that he be sure you have a B to thinking you might have a B, C, or D. If, therefore, you have a B average, you will indicate this on your resume.

But since you would list your grades if you had an A or B, you should also reveal them if your GPA is a C. Not revealing your grades means you don't have an A or B. You would prefer that the employer think you had a C average than think you had either a C or a D. Consequently, if you do have a C average, you will reveal this. The employer, therefore, will assume that if you don't list your grades, you have a D average.

If employers reason that only applicants with D averages don't list their grades, then job-seekers will reveal their grades whenever they are above a D. Consequently, the only people who don't list their grades will indeed have D averages.

STATISTICAL DISCRIMINATION

Firms have incomplete knowledge concerning potential employees' qualities, and so often need to estimate which applicant would be best for any given job. This estimating can lead to firms engaging in statistical discrimination. Statistical discrimination occurs when someone is discriminated against for being in a group whose members have, on average, some undesirable quality. For example, women in their late 20s are sometimes discriminated against in hiring because many women this age soon leave their jobs to raise children.

Imagine: A company wants to hire an employee who will stay at the job for at least seven years. The company is considering two candidates:

Zachary, a 29-year-old man

Tessa, a 29-year-old woman

Let's assume that both Zachary and Tessa seem equally qualified. Because of statistical discrimination, however, the firm might prefer to hire Zachary.

Remember, the firm wants to hire someone who will stay around for at least seven years. Many women in their late 20s to mid-30s leave the workforce to raise children. There is no biological reason why women rather than men should be the ones who quit their jobs to raise young children. But employers know that women are far more likely than men to quit their jobs after they have one or two children. Thus, if an employer wants to hire someone who will stick around for many years it might rationally avoid hiring a 29-year-old woman and instead hire Zachary.

Of course, in our hypothetical example it's entirely possible that, if hired, Tessa would stay at the job for far longer than Zachary would. Perhaps Tessa has no intention of having children or intends to continue working full time after having children. In contrast, Zachary might be planning to have children at age 33 and then leave his job to care for his offspring. The employer, however, can't know for certain whether Zachary or Tessa will, if hired, leave the workforce in the next seven years. The employer does know, however, that on average because Tessa is a woman and Zachary a man Tessa is less likely than Zachary to stay in the workforce. Thus the employer might rationally decide to hire Zachary.

In the United States it is illegal for a company to favor one job applicant over another for reasons of sex. But if our hypothetical company hires Zachary because he is a man, it will not stupidly tell Tessa that she was rejected because of her sex. Rather the company will likely make up some non-sex-based reason as to why it preferred to hire Zachary. (Question: Do you think it would be unethical for the company to hire Zachary just because he is a man?)

4. INCOMPLETE INFORMATION ABOUT INSURANCE CUSTOMERS

We will now change focus to consider how incomplete information challenges the insurance industry.

HEALTH INSURANCE AND ADVERSE SELECTION

People buy health insurance due to uncertainty over their future health care needs. Next year, for example, you may need no medical care or a $100,000 operation.

When you buy health insurance, you pay a fixed sum of money. In return, the health insurance company basically promises to pay your future health care costs. So if you end up needing no medical treatment, the insurance company makes a profit off of you, whereas if you require expensive medical care, the insurance company loses money.

Adverse selection creates potential problems for health insurance companies. Insurance companies least want to sell insurance to people with the greatest medical needs. But people most want to buy insurance when they predict they will need costly medical care.

Imagine that health insurance costs $5,000 per year. Sickly Sally knows she faces a 50 percent chance of needing a $100,000 operation next month while Healthy Henry is almost certain he will need no medical treatment over the next year. An insurance company would profit from selling insurance to Healthy Henry but may well lose considerable money by doing business with Sickly Sally. Sickly Sally, however, would very much want to buy health insurance while Healthy Henry might rationally forgo paying $5,000 for something that he will probably not need. Consistent with adverse selection, the people who most want to buy health insurance are the people whom the health insurance companies least want to insure.

Countering Adverse Selection in the Health Insurance Market   Health insurance companies counter adverse selection by gathering information about potential customers. If, for example, they can determine which of their customers are like Sickly Sally, they can refuse to sell them insurance or charge them extremely high prices.

Health insurance companies also escape adverse selection by not providing coverage for preexisting conditions. Consequently, if Sickly Sally buys insurance after finding out she needs a $100,000 operation, her insurance won't cover the operation's cost.

Government Interference in Health Insurance Markets

Governments sometimes prevent insurance companies from fighting adverse selection. Imagine, for example, that a health insurance company currently charges Healthy Henry-like customers $1,000 a year and Sickly Sally-like customers $50,000 a year. The government, however, deems it *unfair* that Sickly Sally types must pay more than Healthy Henry types. The government, therefore, enacts a nondiscrimination law forcing insurance companies to charge all customers the same rate.

If the insurance company charges a low rate, then both types of customers will buy insurance. Unfortunately, the insurance company will soon go bankrupt paying Sickly Sally-type customers' medical expenses. If, however, the insurance company charges a high price, then Healthy Henry-like customers won't buy insurance. The insurance companies will then have to charge very high rates because all of their customers will be sickly.

We previously saw that in the used car market, unfettered adverse selection results in mostly low-quality cars being sold. Similarly, in the health insurance market, unchecked adverse selection will drive healthy customers out of the market, resulting in only sickly people buying insurance.

If the government forces insurance companies to charge all customers the same rate, then sickly people will always be more willing to buy health insurance than healthy people. Consequently, health insurance companies would have to charge a high enough price to provide treatment for all their sickly customers. But by charging a high price, insurance companies will cause healthy people to stop buying insurance. As a result, only the sickly will buy health insurance.

GENETIC TESTING AND ADVERSE SELECTION[10]

Genetic testing poses perhaps the greatest threat to the health insurance market. Genetic testing holds the promise of determining which diseases people will get. The health insurance industry, however, depends upon blissful ignorance and will be imperiled by genetic testing.

Imagine there was some magical test that could determine who would win the next Buffalo Bills football game. The mere existence of this test would probably prevent people from betting on the Bills. Everyone who didn't use this test would fear making a bet because they would suspect that the person on the other side of their bet did use the test.

People buy health insurance because they don't know whether they will get sick. For example, assume that 1 percent of 25-year-olds will incur significant health care expenses over the next year. It's currently worthwhile for most every 25-year-old to get health insurance.

Now imagine that there was some genetic test that could determine whether you would get sick next year. If you took this test, you would only buy insurance if the test indicated that you would get sick. Of course, if the only people who bought insurance were those who will get sick, then the insurance companies would go bankrupt.

If there were genetic tests that could determine when someone would get, say, cancer or heart disease, then the insurance companies would be reluctant to sell coverage to anyone they had not tested. These companies would fear that the people who wanted coverage had been tested themselves and knew they would get sick.

The genetic tests would create tremendous adverse selection problems for the health insurance industry. Remember that when adverse selection strikes, those you least want to interact with are the people who most want to do business with you. Health insurance companies take money from insurance buyers who remain healthy and give money to insurance buyers who become sick. Consequently, they least want customers who are likely to become sick in the future. But with genetic testing, people with "healthy" genes may think they don't need to buy insurance, while those who determine they have "bad" genes will purchase large amounts of health insurance to cover their future medical costs.

If the insurance companies tested potential customers, it would still not solve this genetic testing problem. The insurance companies would be unwilling to sell insurance to someone whose genetic test reveals he will get cancer next year unless this person pays the full cost of cancer treatment. This person would thus not buy insurance; he would be paying for cancer treatment.

True, with genetic testing one could still insure against accidents. Also, a genetic condition might mean one has, say, only a 50 percent chance of getting some disease. You could still insure against this 50 percent risk. To the extent that genetics determine your future health expense needs, however, genetic testing poses a tremendous problem for the health insurance industry. I personally don't know how insurance companies will overcome this problem. But I'm certain that insurance companies have given this problem much more thought than I have and that markets will greatly reward companies that solve the problem.

5. INCOMPLETE INFORMATION ABOUT ROMANTIC DATES

DATING AND ADVERSE SELECTION

Imagine you're interested in dating Pat. You find out from a friend that Pat is *extremely* interested in dating you. Pat's tremendous desire for you should diminish your interest in Pat.

You want to date someone of high qualities. Unfortunately, the higher someone's qualities, the better they will do in the dating market and the less interest they will have in you. Pat's extreme interest in you probably signals that Pat has low qualities.

You should be the most interested in pursuing Pat if Pat would barely consider dating you. Under this circumstance Pat is likely the highest-quality person you have the potential of dating.

All of this means that if you *are* desperate to date someone, you should hide your true feelings. If the object of your desires asks you out on a date, you should suppress your joy and pretend to consider whether you can fit him/her into your busy social schedule.

ONLINE DATING

Uncertainty makes dating markets difficult to navigate. Does he want a serious relationship? Will she understand my three divorces? Does he want children? Will she dump me after learning about my criminal record? Does she share my faith? Will he respect that I won't go past first base until I'm in love? You traditionally don't know the answers to many important questions before going on a first date. As a result, fundamental incompatibilities doom most first dates to failure.

Dating market participants are willing to pay money to reduce uncertainty. This desire, combined with online technology, has spawned Internet dating services.

Internet dating services allow users to post pictures and provide detailed information about themselves. True, users can use the remoteness of the Internet to lie to potential dates by, for example, posting altered or 10-year-old pictures. But the popularity of online dating services proves that many people benefit from using them.

What if someone chooses not to post a picture of himself? Should you assume that the person is of average appearance? Actually, the fact that someone decides not to post a picture tells you something: the individual believes he will do better in the dating market if people don't initially know what he looks like. Not posting a picture of yourself, therefore, provides a great deal of information about what you look like.

Online daters respond negatively to those who hide their appearance. One study showed that men who fail to post a photo of themselves received on average only one-fourth of the responses of those who did reveal their appearance, while women who didn't post photos received only one-sixth of the responses.[11] (Question: Does this show that compared to women men are (a) more careful or (b) more superficial?)

From *The Wall Street Journal*. Permission, Cartoon Features Syndicats.

I LIKE YOU, EDDIE, BUT ON THE INTERNET, YOU CAME ACROSS AS SOMEWHAT OLDER.

My Old Dating Troubles   When I was a single college professor, I used an online dating service. Nothing ever came of it. I didn't post my picture or use my full name because I was afraid that my students would find my profile and make fun of me. I now realize that people who examined my profile likely concluded that I was hiding information because I was a total loser.

6. INCOMPLETE INFORMATION ABOUT POLITICIANS[12]

The Russian, Chinese, Cuban, and French revolutions all produced narcissistic, brutal governments. In each country, many people bravely fought to replace old, corrupt leaders with men they hoped would do a better job running their nation. Yet the revolutions were betrayed by leaders who cared far more about personal power than the good of their people. Were these nations just unlucky? No, they were victims of adverse selection.

Imagine you are a poor peasant revolutionary. You have incomplete information about your revolutionary leaders. Sure, they talk about liberty, freedom, and equality, but do they really mean it? Unfortunately, adverse selection means the answer is probably no.

Adverse selection contaminates most revolutions because the only types of people capable of acquiring power in revolutionary environments are those skilled at murder and betrayal. Many revolutionary leaders such as Stalin and Mao only achieved near absolute power after betraying and killing many of their comrades. In a volatile revolutionary environment, it's the men who are willing to do anything to succeed, including killing their friends, that are most likely to end up on top. Those who are most likely to become successful revolutionary leaders, therefore, are those who you would least like to run your country.

> "Nearly all men can stand adversity, but if you want to test a man's character, give him power." —Abraham Lincoln

GEORGE WASHINGTON[13]

Americans consider George Washington to have been one of the greatest leaders the world has ever known. Adverse selection justifies this assessment. President Washington was a skilled general who used force of arms to expel the British. He had the strength and ruthlessness necessary to lead a colonial insurrection against Britain,

then the world's greatest power. George Washington, however, did not lust for power himself. Yes, he became president, but he respected the limitations on presidential power inscribed in the U.S. Constitution. Furthermore, he voluntarily chose not to seek a third term as president even though he would almost certainly have won reelection. George Washington, therefore, had the personality that allowed him to both take and abdicate power. This combination has seldom been seen in world history. Usually the only men strong enough to take power through blood are men like Lenin, Mao, Castro, and Napoleon; men who do not give up spilling blood once they seize control. The unique success of the American Revolution is due to its escaping adverse selection.

CINCINNATUS, CAESAR, AND THE U.S. CONSTITUTION

Lucius Quintus Cincinnatus was a fifth-century B.C. Roman farmer. Twice the Roman Republic gave Cincinnatus near absolute military power so he could defend the Republic. Twice Cincinnatus successfully protected the Republic but then voluntarily gave up his power and returned to the life of a simple farmer.

Cincinnatus's virtue allowed the early Roman Republic to survive. Later the Roman Republic would fall as military commanders such as Julius Caesar used their command of Roman armies to acquire dictatorial powers.

> "In order to get power and retain it, it is necessary to love power; but love of power is not connected with goodness but with qualities that are the opposite of goodness, such as pride, cunning, and cruelty." —Leo Tolstoy

The framers of the U.S. Constitution knew that power more often attracts men like Caesar than Cincinnatus. Just as day-care centers sometimes attract pedophiles, political offices often attract would-be dictators. The framers no doubt believed that American voters would never knowingly elect as president a man who intended to make himself a dictator. But voters always have incomplete information about presidential candidates. The framers believed it impossible to prevent "bad" men from winning office. So instead they set up a system that made it very difficult for any such "bad" men to make themselves a dictator.

The framers of the U.S. Constitution set up a governmental system of checks and balances so that no man would ever have the institutional capacity to make himself a dictator. For example, although the U.S. president is the commander–in–chief of the military, he must rely on Congress to provide funds for the armed forces. Under the U.S. Constitution, the power of both Congress and the presidency is partially checked by an independent court system in which judges are appointed for life to insulate them from political pressure. The power of the U.S. federal government is further limited by the strength of state governments that have independent authority from the federal government. The ultimate check on U.S. governmental power, however, comes from private citizens who have the right under the U.S. Constitution to vote, bear arms, and publicly criticize their government.

QUESTIONS YOU SHOULD BE ABLE TO ANSWER AFTER READING THIS CHAPTER:

1 How do brand names reduce uncertainty? (pages 360–361)

2. Why might customers have increased trust in branded products? (page 361)

3 Why are brand names hostages to honesty? (page 361)

4 Was the value of Coca-Cola's brand name in 2005: (a) $677.5 billion, (b) $67.5 billion, (c) $6.75 billion, (d) $675 million, or (e) $67.5 million? (page 362)

5 Why do money-back guarantees help fight uncertainty over product quality? (page 363)

6 Why does eBay represent a triumph of markets over uncertainty? (pages 363–364)

7 Why is it difficult for firms to hide information if they are forbidden to lie but have the option of not releasing information? (pages 364–365)

8 Why can mandatory disclosure laws reduce the amount of information that customers acquire about products? (page 365)

9 Why would you probably want to attend the graduate school that least wants to accept you? (page 365)

10 What is adverse selection? (page 365)

11 Why would unfettered adverse selection cause almost all used cars for sale to be of low quality? (page 366)

12 How can adverse selection in the used car market be countered? (page 366)

13 What are agency costs? (page 367)

14 How do agency costs harm firms? (page 367)

15 Why does Wal-Mart forbid employees from accepting any type of gift from those who sell goods to the company? (page 367)

16 How can agency costs harm home buyers? (page 368)

17 How can agency costs harm doctors' patients? (pages 368–369)

18 What does the FDA do? (page 369)

19 How does adverse selection complicate firms' hiring decisions? (page 370)

20 Why must organizations that work with children be especially concerned about adverse selection? (page 370)

21 What should an employer assume if you don't list your GPA on your resume? (page 371)

22 What is statistical discrimination? (page 371)

23 Why do people buy health insurance? (page 372)

24 Why does adverse selection pose a challenge to health insurance companies? (pages 372–373)

25 How do health insurance companies fight adverse selection? (pages 372–373)

26 What can happen when the government requires health insurance companies to charge the same price to all customers? (page 373)

27 Why does genetic testing pose a tremendous future challenge to health insurance companies? (pages 373–374)

28 Why should you probably avoid dating people who are extremely interested in dating you? (page 374)

29 What does it signal if a customer on an online dating site chooses not to post his or her own picture? (page 375)

30 How does adverse selection explain why many revolutions produced narcissistic, brutal governments? (page 375)

STUDY PROBLEMS

1. Essay question. How much freedom do you believe consumers should have to buy pharmaceutical products? Let's just consider drugs that are not addictive or pleasure causing and are used to treat diseases. Keep in mind that it is often very difficult to determine which drugs a sick person should take, and a sick person can greatly worsen his condition by taking the wrong combination of drugs. Also keep in mind that, just as with every other type of professional, some doctors are incompetent. Which of the following governmental policies do you think is the best?
   A. Adults can buy any drugs they want.
   B. Adults with sufficiently high education and intelligence can buy any drugs they want. The rest of the population is limited to option (C).
   C. Adults can buy any drugs they want if they get their doctor's approval.
   D. Adults can only buy drugs that their doctor approves of and that the FDA rules are safe and effective.

2. Provide some examples of adverse selection not mentioned in this chapter.

3. Would suppliers of illegal products such as drugs, prostitutes, and stolen merchandise benefit from using brand names? (Please don't conduct any first-hand research on this question.)

4. Why don't colleges offer money-back guarantees? On which products or services should firms fear offering money-back guarantees?

5. When a customer buys life insurance, he pays the insurance company a fixed amount each year. If the customer dies, his relatives receive a large sum from the life insurance company. Why do many life insurance policies not pay off if the customer commits suicide? Could a firm ever make a profit selling suicide life insurance?

6. Imagine that someone living in California advertises his used car for sale. The advertisement contains the words "Must sell because moving to Europe." How might this advertisement relate to adverse selection?

7. How could a man desperately want to get married but rationally refuse to marry anyone who would agree to marry him?

8. Indicate whether each of the following would, for health insurance companies, (1) increase adverse selection, (2) decrease adverse selection, or (3) have no effect on adverse selection:
   A. Smokers become especially willing to buy health insurance because they rationally fear their habit may cause cancer.
   B. Cell phone users become especially willing to buy health insurance because they irrationally fear that cell phone radiation causes cancer.
   C. People who are very careless about their health decide not to buy health insurance because they irrationally assume they will never get sick.
   D. Rich people become especially willing to buy health insurance.

E. For some inexplicable reason, blonds become very reluctant to buy health insurance.

F. Massachusetts forces all its citizens to buy health insurance.

G. California forces health insurance companies to pay the full cost of sex change operations for all insurance company customers who get this procedure.

H. North Carolina forbids health insurance companies from charging higher prices to smokers.

I. Florida forces health insurance companies to charge their lowest rates to senior citizens.

J. Nevada forces health insurance companies to offer discounts to heavy gamblers.

A top computer programmer is worth "300 times" more than an average one, according to a Google vice president.[1] What does this 300X factor mean for income inequality?

300X—WHY ARE SOME WORKERS WORTH SO MUCH MORE THAN OTHERS?

Consider three students, Literary Laura, Average Arnie, and Top Tony, who all major in computer science at your college. After graduation, Average Arnie and Top Tony both get programming jobs with Google for the same initial salary. Literary Laura, however, decides she likes words more than machines and so becomes an author.

Like most fiction writers, Literary Laura doesn't earn a high income. Seven years after graduation Literary Laura earns about $30,000 a year. Average Arnie turns out to be an average programmer and, after working for seven years, receives $100,000 a year from Google.

Top Tony, however, becomes a programming superstar. Tony was born with extremely strong mathematical reasoning skills. Tony also works 20 hours a week more than other programmers. And in his spare time Top Tony studies new programming techniques. Because of his tremendous effort and natural ability, after seven years of working for Google, Top Tony becomes what's known as a magician.

"There are two kinds of geniuses: the 'ordinary' and the 'magicians.' An ordinary genius is a fellow whom you and I would be just as good as, if we were only many times better. There is no mystery as to how his mind works. Once we understand what they've done, we feel certain that we, too, could have done it. It is different with the magicians. Even after we understand what they have done it is completely dark."*

*Adapted from Mark Kac, *Enigmas of Chance: An Autobiography.* Published by Basic Books, a Member of the Perseus Book Group.

CHALLENGE TO MARKET EFFECTIVENESS 6?: INEQUALITY

LEARNING OBJECTIVES

AFTER READING THIS CHAPTER, YOU SHOULD BE ABLE TO:

- Explain why some companies will pay one employee far more than another.
- Recognize problems with giving to the poor and taking from the rich.
- Identify ways to accumulate great wealth.
- Understand how markets can subvert racial discrimination.
- Define educational premiums.

Top Tony will write some computer code and give it to his co-workers. These co-workers will understand how the code works and realize its tremendous usefulness. But these fellow programmers will also realize that even in 100 lifetimes they couldn't duplicate the quality of Tony's work.

If it merely took the efforts of 10 average computer programmers to match the work of Top Tony, then Tony would never be worth more than 10 times what an average employee was. But since Tony can accomplish tasks that no amount of "submagician" labor could do, he is well worth hundreds of times as much as an average employee.

Because of his "magical" programming abilities Tony becomes, let's say, 300 times more valuable to Google than Average Arnie. Recognizing his talent, and terrified they will lose him to a rival firm, Google pays Top Tony 300 times more than it does Average Arnie.

Employee	Salary per Year
Literary Laura	$30,000
Average Arnie	100,000
Top Tony	30 million

We may all be equal before God, but we certainly aren't before markets. Some people, such as Literary Laura, deliberately choose low-paying careers. Others, such as Top Tony, are extremely skilled at their already high-paying professions and so make much more than others.

What, if anything, should we do about Top Tony? Some people believe that the government should impose very high taxes on Top Tony to reduce income inequality. This chapter will explore why markets pay Top Tony-like people so much and will consider some implications of having the government reduce income inequality.

This textbook has so far looked at five challenges to market effectiveness. Each one, unless overcome, reduces the wealth of society. Inequality, however, is different because it doesn't lower a nation's wealth. Indeed, government efforts at reducing inequality often lower a country's wealth. So why do many people object to income inequality? One reason is fairness.

Population Group	Average Family Income
Poorest fifth	$ 10,665
Second fifth	27,357
Middle fifth	46,301
Fourth fifth	72,825
Richest fifth	159,583

U.S. Income 2005

Population Group	Share of Income
Poorest fifth	3.4%
Second fifth	8.6
Middle fifth	14.6
Fourth fifth	23.0
Richest fifth	50.4

U.S. Income 2005[2]

Country	Average Income in $ per Person in 2007*
Albania	6,137
Argentina	17,062
Austria	34,359
Bolivia	3,017
Brazil	9,531
China	8,486
Egypt	5,109
Ethiopia	1,094
France	31,873
Greece	27,360
Haiti	1,906
India	4,031
Ireland	46,786
Israel	31,768
Italy	31,694
Japan	34,011
Mexico	11,761
Nigeria	1,285
Norway	45,453
Pakistan	2,917
Philippines	5,604
Poland	15,894
Russia	13,210
Singapore	34,435
Spain	28,445
Sweden	35,729
Turkey	9,629
United Kingdom	36,567
United States	45,176
Zimbabwe	2,370

World Income[3]

*IMF, Gross domestic product based on purchasing-power-parity per capita GDP current international dollar.

FAIRNESS

But is it necessarily unfair that Top Tony has a much higher income than Average Arnie? True, Top Tony makes 300 times more than Average Arnie does. But Top Tony labors many more hours than his average co-worker. Perhaps because of the long hours he puts into the job, Top Tony has no life outside of the office. In contrast, Average Arnie might be happily married with two children. And even if both Tony and Arnie have children, only Arnie's work schedule has allowed him to spend large amounts of time with his family.

Imagine that when Top Tony graduated from college he decided to devote himself to becoming one of the best computer programmers in the world. Average Arnie, in contrast, decided to have a more balanced life. Arnie realized that he would never spend enough time at his job to be a programming superstar. But Arnie was willing to be average at his job in return for having plenty of time to spend with his wife and children.

Seven years after college, both Average Arnie and Top Tony have achieved their objectives. Average Arnie is probably envious of Top Tony's income. But Top Tony might be envious of Average Arnie's family life. Can we really say that by the fairness criteria Top Tony, compared with Average Arnie, has too much?

Literary Laura has far less income even than Average Arnie. But she deliberately chose a low-paying field. Laura presumably did this because she would rather make a small income as a fiction writer than a larger salary as a computer programmer. Maybe Literary Laura wanted to be a full-time stay-at-home mom. As a writer she is free to pick her own hours. Perhaps Literary Laura, along with Average Arnie and Top Tony, has accomplished exactly what she wanted to. So from her viewpoint, Literary Laura is not worse off than Top Tony. Consequently, we can't necessarily claim that it's *unfair* that Top Tony earns one thousand times more than Literary Laura.

CHOICE AND INEQUALITY

A key lesson of economics is that trade-offs are everywhere. One trade-off many of you will soon make is choosing between free time and income. Some professionals such as doctors, investment bankers, and corporate lawyers receive high salaries but must put in long work hours. Other jobs pay less but also require less time. And as our example with Top Tony and Average Arnie illustrates, even within a profession, people have considerable choice over how much time they work. So when considering the fairness of inequality, you shouldn't just look at inequality of income because people who choose low-paying jobs might receive compensating benefits such as having large amounts of free time and less job stress.

BUT NOT EVERYONE HAS COMPARABLE CHOICES

Examining issues of fairness by solely looking at Top Tony, Average Arnie, and Literary Laura is misleading because these three people all had roughly equal opportunities. So to further explore fairness concerns, let's bring two additional characters into our inequality drama: Richie Rich and Oliver Twist. Richie Rich has a trust fund that pays him $1 million a month. He did nothing to earn his income other than being born lucky. Oliver Twist, by contrast, was born an orphan and has had to struggle just to get enough to eat.

By most definitions, it *is* unfair that Richie Rich has so much more than Oliver Twist. But does this mean that the government should take money from Richie Rich and give it to Oliver Twist? Just because an outcome is unfair doesn't mean it should be changed. Whether fairness is important is a moral issue lying outside the boundaries of economics. But let's assume that fairness is an important goal. This still doesn't necessarily mean that the government should adopt Robin Hood-like tactics and take from the rich to give to the poor. When the government transfers wealth to the poor, it actually encourages more people to become poor.

Job	Hourly Wage
Dishwashers	$ 7.45
Parking lot attendants	8.14
Preschool teachers	10.57
Actors	13.60
Farmers and ranchers	16.41
Carpenters	17.11
Clergy	18.53
Insurance sales agents	20.36
Loan officers	23.77
Sociologists	25.37
Registered nurses	26.28
Chemists	27.83
Computer programmers	30.49
Civil engineers	31.82
Electrical engineers	35.34
Economists	35.43
Lawyers	47.56
Dentists	60.24
Family doctors	67.50
Chief executives	68.48

Some Median Hourly Wages in the U.S. (2005)[4]

PROBLEMS WITH GIVING MONEY TO THE POOR

When the government gives money to the poor, it reduces poor people's incentives to work. Oliver Twist, however, is a hard-working chap, and even if the government transfers wealth to him, he will still keep a job and try to better himself. But not all people have Oliver Twist's work ethic.

Dropout Dropsy was born to a nice middle-class American family. At age 16 she dropped out of high school to devote herself full-time to sex and drugs. Dropout Dropsy's parents stopped supporting her in the hope that financial desperation would force their daughter to mend her ways. But Dropout Dropsy's drug dealer informed her that the government gives money to poor moms with children. So Dropout Dropsy deliberately decided to have three babies before she was 20. As a result, the government now gives her enough money to survive (and pay for a microwave, refrigerator, cable television, and other staples of American life).

When the government gives money to people in a category, some individuals will strive to be in that rewarded category. The South African government, for example, gives $130 a month to citizens disabled by AIDS. Some South African AIDS patients deliberately don't take free antiretroviral AIDS drugs so they will be sick enough to get the $130 payments. (The drugs don't cure AIDS but do greatly improve the health of AIDS victims.) "Two AIDS counselors at one of Durban's [South Africa] biggest hospitals estimate 30 percent of their clients say they don't follow their antiretroviral regimens because they hope to become sick enough to qualify for a disability grant."[5]

When the government taxes smoking, fewer people smoke. Similarly, if the government were to subsidize smoking, more individuals would smoke. When the government gives money to people for being poor, it subsidizes poverty and can cause more people to take actions that result in their being poor. Imagine, for example, that someone initially has two choices:

1. Work 40 hours a week for $7 an hour.
2. Not work and not have money for food or rent.

Most people would prefer option 1. But now assume that the government offers its citizens another option:

3. Not work but receive welfare payments that cover food and rent.

Some, but not all, citizens who before picked option 1 will now choose option 3. Those who pick option 3 deliberately throw themselves into poverty to receive government assistance.

> "The ultimate result of shielding men from the effects of folly is to fill the world with fools." —Herbert Spencer (19th century political theorist)

Sometimes, as with Dropout Dropsy, poverty is a choice. Other times, as with Oliver Twist, poverty is involuntary. But it's almost impossible for the government to give money only to the involuntarily poor. After all, Dropout Dropsy's children are themselves involuntarily poor. If the government helps Dropout Dropsy's children by improving their living conditions, then it will necessarily help Dropout Dropsy and will encourage more people to drop out. And the more the government tries to help Dropout Dropsy-like people by giving them money, the more Dropout Dropsies will arise.

Some readers might conclude that the government should never give welfare to people who can work. But then what do you do about the children of poor people who reject work? Do you let these children starve? Do you forcibly take these children away from their parents just because their parents are poor? If you are unwilling to let poor children starve or forcibly remove them from their parents, then you must support giving welfare to parents who decline to work.

PROBLEMS WITH TAKING AWAY MONEY FROM THE RICH

When the government gives money to the poor, it creates incentives for people to become poor. Similarly, when the government takes wealth from the rich, it reduces people's willingness to work hard to become rich.

Top Tony, recall, achieved his programming superstar status in part through hard work. Tony's reward is an extremely high salary. If, however, the government takes away much of this salary, Top Tony-like people will have fewer incentives to work hard. As a result, reducing inequality might turn Top Tony into another Average Arnie.

Top Tony, remember, is 300 times more valuable to Google than Average Arnie. Top Tony, therefore, creates tremendous wealth. Top Tonies do much to power an economy. Without them, we would all be much poorer. So if the government, through reducing inequality, discourages the creation of Top Tonies, it reduces the income of everyone.

But, you might argue, couldn't the government take money from the undeserving rich like Richie Rich and leave the Top Tonies of the world alone? Unfortunately, it would be difficult to impose high taxes on Richie Rich without harming Top Tony. Top Tony might be working very hard so he can give wealth to his kids. So if we prevent people such as Richie Rich from inheriting wealth, we reduce incentives for Top Tony to labor long hours to financially enrich his children.

"But of the vast increase in the well-being of hundreds of millions of people that has occurred in the 200-year course of the industrial revolution to date, virtually none of it can be attributed to the direct redistribution of resources from rich to poor. The potential for improving the lives of poor people by finding different ways of distributing current production is *nothing* compared to the apparently limitless potential of increasing production." —Robert Lucas, Nobel Prize-winning economist.[6]

GRADE REDISTRIBUTION

Imagine that a college decided to redistribute test points to increase *grade equality*. Students who get high test scores will be forced to give some of their points to students who do poorly on exams. Such redistribution would decrease the benefit of doing well on exams and so diminish high test-scoring students' incentives to study. The redistribution would also mitigate the harm of doing poorly on exams and so would reduce the incentives for low test-scoring students to study.

PUBLIC CHOICE THEORY AND INEQUALITY

Another problem with transferring wealth from the rich to the poor is that the transferring won't be done by benevolent magic fairies. Rather, the transferring will probably be implemented by self-interested politicians. These politicians may see reducing income inequality as a means of enriching themselves.

Politicians who take money from one group of people and give it to another become extremely important politicians. Both those likely to lose and gain wealth will spend resources trying to influence the politicians.

There is no reason to expect that most politicians will even try to take money from just the undeserving rich and give it only to the deserving poor. Perhaps people like Richie Rich have more free time to lobby the government than Top Tony-like people do. As a result, politicians bent on reducing inequality may focus on taking income from Top Tonies. Furthermore, if the elderly have more political influence than impoverished children such as Oliver Twist, then politicians will become far more interested in transferring resources to senior citizens than to poor children.

SO SHOULD THE GOVERNMENT REDUCE INCOME INEQUALITY?

We have considered four problems with reducing income inequality:

1. Reducing income inequality could be unfair because some people with relatively low incomes might, overall, be no less happy than those with high incomes.

2. Reducing income inequality creates incentives for people to stop working and become poor so they can receive welfare from the government.

3. Reducing income inequality punishes the rich, reducing incentives for people to work hard to become rich.

4. Reducing income inequality empowers politicians and so increases the amount of resources citizens spend lobbying politicians.

These four reasons, however, don't necessarily imply that we shouldn't significantly reduce income inequality. If you are morally committed to notions of fairness and equality, you could rationally decide that even though significantly reducing income inequality causes some problems, the government should still do it.

The above analysis assumes that people acquire wealth in ways that benefit society. Many people, however, believe that excessive wealth acquisition is socially destructive. For them, the case for wealth redistribution is very strong.

THE RICH: HEROES OR VILLAINS?

Peter Singer, a Princeton professor of bioethics, wrote in *The New York Times:* "The rich must—or so some of us with less money like to assume—suffer sleepless nights because of their ruthlessness in squeezing out competitors, firing workers, shutting down plants or whatever else they have to do to acquire their wealth."[7] This influential professor thinks of the rich as villains who won their wealth by harming others.

> "How can I be overpaid? The boss wouldn't pay me that amount if I wasn't worth it." —Jackie Gleason (Entertainer)

If the rich really are villains, then there is a strong case for taking wealth from them and giving it to the poor. Villainous rich don't deserve their wealth. Furthermore, giving their wealth to the poor, under this scenario, merely returns to the poor what the rich have stolen or exploited from them. Finally, since the rich acquired their wealth through destructive means, taking money from them reduces their incentives to engage in destructive wealth-acquiring tactics.

Another view of the rich, however, holds that they mostly earned their wealth by creating wealth for others. Under this view, for example, although Microsoft founder Bill Gates has $50 billion himself, he earned many times this amount for other people. Proponents of the rich-as-heroes view believe that many poor people have more wealth because of Bill Gates. If you believe that the rich are heroes, you probably don't believe that they deserve to have wealth taken from them. Furthermore, you would fear that if their wealth was taken, then they would reduce their beneficial wealth-acquiring activities.

In the real world, some rich people are heroes while others are villains. Most (but not all) academic economists believe that in free market economies the rich have primarily acquired their wealth in ways that have helped non-wealthy people. In contrast, many social science and humanities professors who are not economists believe that the rich are mostly villains and so society would be far better off if governments took more from the rich so they could give more to the poor.

THREE PATHS TO GREAT WEALTH

To make an extremely high income while working for other people, you first need to be one of the best in your field. But excellence isn't enough. The best maids, nurses, high school teachers, or 14th-century historians will never become millionaires. To become really rich you need not only to excel but to find a way of getting customers to pay huge amounts for your services. There are three general ways to accomplish this:

1. **Get very wealthy people to value your work highly.** Sick millionaires, for example, will pay huge sums to the surgeon who offers them the best chance of survival. Rich criminal defendants will likewise pay millions to the defense lawyer who provides them with the best chance of escaping prison.

2. **Excel at running a large organization.** A manager who can slightly improve the performance of a large organization has tremendous value. If, for example, a company has costs of a billion dollars a year and you can reduce these costs by a mere 5 percent, then you are worth $50 million a year to the firm.

3. **Get millions of people to value your work.** You will have a bountiful income if millions of people are each willing to pay a few dollars for your labors. A Hollywood studio, for example, will pay tens of millions to a movie star who can draw in an extra few million people to see a film. Similarly, a sports star who can slightly increase game attendance and television viewership is worth millions to his team. Employees such as Top Tony who can improve the quality of a product used by tens of millions also have tremendous value in the marketplace. If, for example, Top Tony makes Google's Internet search engine better each year, then he has well earned his $30 million-per-year salary.

TOURNAMENTS

To become one of the best, you must essentially win a tournament. Many extremely attractive young men and women compete to become movie stars. Only a few succeed. Those that do earn millions of dollars each year, whereas those who fail move on to other professions. Each year thousands of extremely bright young lawyers join large corporate law firms. A few will be judged the best and allowed to become partners. The rest will be let go and have to subsist on sub-multimillionaire wages.

To win a labor market tournament, you must be willing to risk failure because only a few can ever win such tournaments. You also must toil long hours at your craft. Alas, a parent who devotes 40+ hours a week to her child will be at a significant, although overcomeable, disadvantage in any labor market tournament.

SEX AND INCOME INEQUALITY

In the U.S. full-time working women make about 76 percent as much, on average, as full-time working men.[8] There are many possible reasons for this. Many people, including numerous economists, believe that discrimination against women explains some of the income gap. Another explanation is that women more often than men prefer lower-paying professions such as elementary school teaching. I won't attempt in this chapter to explore all the possible reasons for the income gap.

This section, however, considers how child-rearing decisions made by women significantly contribute to the male/female income disparity.

Working parents face a trade-off between spending time with their children and at their jobs. The more time you devote to your career, the more productive an employee you will be. Consequently, any parent who devotes 40+ hours a week to child care is not going to be as valuable an employee as a similarly skilled person without significant child care responsibilities.

Economics doesn't dictate that women should devote more time to child care than men do, but this is what happens in every society I have ever heard of. Given that women choose to spend more time taking care of children than men do, it's not surprising that women usually make less money than men.

Consider two equally intelligent lawyers, both of whom graduate from law school at age 26. Both get similar jobs. At age 32 they both start having children. One of the lawyers quits to become a full-time mom while the other continues to work and relies on his wife to be the primary child caregiver. After seven years the female lawyer returns to the legal marketplace. Unfortunately, during these seven years she has lost contact with clients. In contrast, her male counterpart has been honing his legal skills. As a result, the male lawyer is likely to have a higher income for the rest of both lawyers' working lives.

When people leave the labor force for a few years, their skills atrophy. Women are far more likely than men to stop working for a few years to become stay-at-home parents. It's understandable, therefore, that in the United States, full-time working women make significantly less, on average, than full-time working men.

THE MOMMY WARS

SIMONE DE
BEAUVOIR

Many feminists strongly object to men making on average more than women do. Simone de Beauvoir, one of the 20th century's leading feminists, made a radical proposal for reducing this sexual income inequality. She said:[9]

> "No woman should be authorized to stay at home to raise her children. Women should not have that choice, precisely because if there is such a choice, too many women will make that one."

Forbidding women from being stay-at-home moms would indeed reduce income inequality between men and women. Most economists, however, would strongly object to Simone de Beauvoir's proposal.

Child rearing is an extraordinarily important economic activity. A woman who leaves her job for seven years to raise young children contributes to the wealth of society. True, because of the time she took off from work she will not be as productive an employee. But her children are likely to be more productive members of society because of the time their mom devoted to them. So even though parents don't get paid for taking care of their children, economists consider parenting a wealth-creating activity.

ASSORTATIVE MATING

> "Once, it was commonplace for doctors to marry nurses and executives to marry secretaries. Now the wedding pages are stocked with matched sets, men and women who share a tax bracket and even an alma mater."[10]

Barbara Bush, wife of one U.S. President and mother of another, attended Smith College, the place where I teach. But in 1944 she dropped out right before marrying George Bush. This was very normal behavior for the time. In 1944, married women rarely pursued high-income careers. This actually reduced household income inequality.

It used to be extraordinarily rare for a woman to be a doctor, lawyer, investment banker, or corporate executive. So in past times, a high-income male lawyer would often marry a woman who had a nonexistent or low income. But now, with women making up a significant part of all high-paying professions, it's common for high-income men to marry high-income women whom they meet in the workplace.

Men and women are engaging in assortative mating, meaning they marry people like themselves. By teaming up high-income individuals, assortative mating has increased household income inequality.

RACIAL DISCRIMINATION

In 1922, South Africa was an extremely racist country. White workers were paid much more than equally skilled black workers. Mine owners decided that they could save money by replacing some of their white employees with cheaper black workers. The white employees rebelled. The local communist party supported the white workers and used the slogan "Workers of the World Unite for a White South Africa!" Eventually the South African government supported the white mine workers, protecting them from black competition.[11]

Discriminatory wages made it profitable for the mine owners to hire black workers. Black and white miners were substitutes for each other. Had the owners been allowed to hire blacks, then the demand for black miners would have increased while the demand for white miners would have decreased. This would have raised black wages while lowering white wages.

Often when one group is discriminated against in employment, a firm can increase profits by hiring members of this group. This leads to the fat bald guy rule (FBGR) of hiring:

> "The FBGR posits that, when considering otherwise roughly equivalent candidates for any job whose formal requirements don't include being good-looking, hire the fat bald guy. The reason is simple: Society gives all sorts of unearned preferences to good-looking people, so when a fat bald guy manages to assemble a résumé that at first glance resembles that possessed by his good-looking competition, the FBGR assumes that the former record is actually far more impressive than the latter, all things considered."[12]

The FBGR works if fat bald guys are discriminated against irrationally. If employers pay fat bald guys less than people equally qualified for jobs, then you could profit by hiring fat bald guys. Of course, the FBGR doesn't apply to jobs where looks matter. For example, Hollywood blatantly discriminates against fat bald guys. This means that if a handsome actor and a fat bald guy actor make the same salary, then the fat bald guy is almost certainly a much better actor. But the FBGR doesn't imply that a movie studio could profit by hiring fat bald guys to play romantic leads, because moviegoers prefer handsome lead actors. Similar reasoning shows when markets don't correct racial discrimination.

. . . .

ROSA PARKS AND HISTORY

"The death of Rosa Parks has reminded us of her place in history, as the black woman whose refusal to give up her seat on a bus to a white man, in accordance with the Jim Crow laws of Alabama, became the spark that ignited the civil rights movement of the 1950s and 1960s.

Most people do not know the rest of the story, however. Why was there racially segregated seating on public transportation in the first place? "Racism" some will say—and there was certainly plenty of racism in the South, going back for centuries. But racially segregated seating on streetcars and buses in the South did not go back for centuries.

Far from existing from time immemorial, as many have assumed, racially segregated seating in public transportation began in the South in the late 19th and early 20th centuries.

Those who see government as the solution to social problems may be surprised to learn that it was government which created this problem. Many, if not most, municipal transit systems were privately owned in the 19th century and the private owners of these systems had no incentive to segregate the races.

These owners may have been racists themselves but they were in business to make a profit—and you don't make a profit by alienating a lot of your customers. There was not enough market demand for Jim Crow seating on municipal transit to bring it about.

It was politics that segregated the races because the incentives of the political process are different from the incentives of the economic process. Both blacks and whites spent money to ride the buses but, after the disenfranchisement of black voters in the late 19th and early 20th century, only whites counted in the political process.

It was not necessary for an overwhelming majority of the white voters to demand racial segregation. If some did and the others didn't care, that was sufficient politically, because what blacks wanted did not count politically after they lost the vote.

The incentives of the economic system and the incentives of the political system were not only different, they clashed. Private owners of streetcar, bus, and railroad companies in the South lobbied against the Jim Crow laws while these laws were being written, challenged them in the courts after the laws were passed, and then dragged their feet in enforcing those laws after they were upheld by the courts.

These tactics delayed the enforcement of Jim Crow seating laws for years in some places. Then company employees began to be arrested for not enforcing such laws and at least one president of a streetcar company was threatened with jail if he didn't comply.

None of this resistance was based on a desire for civil rights for blacks. It was based on a fear of losing money if racial segregation caused black customers to use public transportation less often than they would have in the absence of this affront . . .

People who decry the fact that businesses are in business 'just to make money' seldom understand the implications of what they are saying. You make money by doing what other people want, not what you want.

Black people's money was just as good as white people's money, even though that was not the case when it came to votes."

Thomas Sowell, "Rosa Parks and History." *Jewish World Review,* October 27, 2005. By permission of Thomas Sowell and Creators Syndicate, Inc.

· ·
· · · · · · · · · ·

WHEN MARKETS DON'T FIGHT RACISM

Imagine that restaurant owners in some town discriminate against black waiters. Assume that this discrimination occurs because owners, but not customers, dislike blacks. The owners would rather hire white waiters at $8 an hour than pay $6 an hour for equally qualified black waiters. As a result, black waiters in this town will receive lower salaries than white waiters. But markets will punish the racist restaurateurs. A nonracist could start a restaurant and hire only black waiters, paying them less than $8 an hour. This nonracist owner's lower cost would give him a significant competitive advantage. Over the long run, nonracists would eventually drive racist restaurateurs from the market.

CHAPTER 16 • Challenge to Market Effectiveness 6?: Inequality

But now imagine that it's the customers who are racists. Assume that customers prefer restaurants that don't have black waiters. Under this assumption, a nonracist restaurant owner couldn't earn a higher profit by hiring blacks. As a result, black waiters will earn persistently lower wages (if they are hired at all) than white waiters.

(Question: What would happen to the relative wages of black waiters if "only" 20 percent of restaurant customers were racists?)

BASEBALL IN BLACK AND WHITE

Baseball's willingness to hire black players in the 1940s shows when markets can and can't counteract racism. Before 1947 all major league baseball (MLB) players were white. Because they excluded blacks, some of the best baseball players were in the Negro League and not MLB.

MLB teams surely knew that there were players in the Negro League who were superior to many of their own players. MLB also understood that because they paid higher salaries than the Negro League, they could potentially recruit almost any Negro League players to their teams. Each MLB team, therefore, must have realized that it could improve its team's baseball playing quality if it hired a few black players.

So why didn't MLB teams hire black players before 1947? The primary goal of a baseball team is not to win games, but to earn profits. Teams in the 1940s made most of their revenue from ticket sales. Teams generally sell more tickets the more games they win. But some of MLB's fans were racists. These racist fans were more likely to buy tickets to see an all-white team that won 40 percent of its games than to see an integrated team that won 60 percent of its games. MLB team owners who refused to hire black players were, therefore, probably maximizing their profits.

If a restaurant, law firm, or athletic team refuses to hire people from a given racial group, then that firm's quality will suffer. If customers care only about quality, therefore, then profit-maximizing firms won't discriminate. But if customers care about both quality and the racial makeup of employees, then racial discrimination may be profit maximizing.

In 1947, the MLB team the Brooklyn Dodgers hired black player Jackie Robinson. In his first season Jackie Robinson won the Rookie of the Year award, meaning that of all the players who began playing major league baseball in 1947, Jackie Robinson was considered the best. In 1949 he won the Most Valuable Player award, indicating that in 1949, he was the best player in all of major league baseball. Robinson's outstanding performance was not surprising. In 1947, the Brooklyn Dodgers were the only MLB team willing to hire a black player, and they wanted to hire only one. Given that they probably could have hired any black player in the world, they were obviously going to hire the best. Furthermore, the Dodgers wouldn't have paid the cost of upsetting the subset of their fans who were racists unless hiring Robinson would significantly improve the team's performance.

Economists often try to figure out why some groups of people earn much more than others. Racism, as we have seen, can sometimes explain such income discrepancies. In the U.S. economy today, however, educational differences are probably the most important factor influencing income inequality.

JACKIE ROBINSON (1919–1972)

EDUCATIONAL PREMIUMS

In the United States, college graduates make around $1 million more over their lifetimes than non-college graduates do.[13] There are two possible reasons for this. First, colleges probably teach people useful stuff and so likely make them more productive workers. Second, many highly intelligent people go to college and so naturally earn more when they graduate than other workers do.

Education Level	Average Income In 2005
Advanced degree	$74,602
Bachelor's degree	51,206
High school diploma only	27,915
No high school diploma	18,734

Average Yearly Income for Different Education Levels (U.S.)[14]

What would happen if politicians decreased the educational income advantage? Fewer people would go to college. College is expensive and for some students (those not studying economics) even boring. Fewer people would go to college if attending college did not significantly boost their incomes.

GENERATIONAL MOBILITY

We should expect that the children of rich parents grow up to earn higher average incomes than the children of poor parents do. The richer the parents, the more money they can give their children and the more resources they can contribute to their children's education.

In the United States, college educated, left-handed men earn on average 15 percent more than college educated, right-handed men.[15] It's not clear why this is so.

Financially successful parents may also pass down attitudes that promote wealth accumulation. For example, parents who have attended college are likely to have higher incomes than those who haven't. And parents who have gone to college will probably stress the importance of college to their children and so are more likely to convince their kids to attend college.

Some of my students have gotten summer internships or jobs through parental connections. Wealthy parents tend to have better business connections than poor parents do. The kids of wealthy parents, therefore, have networking advantages over other children.

Parents who engage in destructive behavior are likely to harm both their own immediate incomes and the future incomes of their children. For example, a parent who abuses drugs may both lose his job and do a poor job of imparting skills to his child. Furthermore, the child of a drug addict might come to see excessive drug use as "normal and acceptable" and so be more likely to become a drug addict herself.

Having a child outside of marriage significantly harms the earning opportunities of single women. And unfortunately, being born out of wedlock reduces the average child's lifetime income. So it's not surprising that many poor adults grew up in poor, fatherless families.

Many kids born to poor parents, however, overcome their background and earn high lifetime incomes. And many children born to rich parents end up earning much less than their parents do.

Economists use statistics to measure generational wealth mobility. One study, for example, examined kids who grew up in households that were among the 20 percent poorest of the U.S. population.[16] The study determined how many of these kids grew up to be affluent adults who were among the richest 40 percent of the U.S. population.

If there were no generational mobility in the United States, then you would expect that 0 percent of these adults born to poor parents would end up in the top 40 percent. If having poor parents in no way influenced a child's lifetime income then you would expect that 40 percent of these adults would end up in the top 40 percent. It turns out that the United States is exactly in the middle of these two mobility extremes because 20 percent of these adults ended up in the richest 40 percent of the U.S. population. This shows that being born to a poor parent is a significant, but surmountable, obstacle to earning a high income as an adult.

HIGH FIXED-COST GOODS AND INEQUALITY

If you morally object to inequality, you should do so only to the extent that having extra money can buy you better stuff. But the increasing importance of high fixed-cost goods actually lowers the "stuff benefit" of being rich.

If Microsoft billionaire Bill Gates and I caught the same disease, he could afford better doctors than I. We would both, however, probably use the same pharmaceuticals to treat our condition. Although Gates has a much nicer house than I do, I can afford to watch the same movies as he sees.

As Chapter 8 showed, when a firm faces high fixed costs but low marginal costs, it profits most by selling the same good to many customers. Consequently, the world's rich and middle class generally buy the exact same high-fixed cost/low-marginal costs good. As a result, the world's rich and middle classes watch the same movies, listen to the same music, read the same books, use the same pharmaceuticals, play the same video games, and run the same computer operating systems. The cost structure of many goods, therefore, has created a significant level of consumption equality between the rich and middle class. But the prevalence of high-fixed cost goods has still not given us total consumption equality, so it's understandable why so many people envy Bill Gates.

ENVY AND MENTAL EXTERNALITIES

The 10th Commandment instructs believers in the Bible not to covet their neighbors' goods. Many of us, however, do envy the rich. Imagine I am rich and getting richer. But the richer I get, the unhappier my envious neighbors become. My acquiring wealth, therefore, creates a negative "mental" externality for my neighbors.

But should economists "count" mere mental externalities? Imagine I make widgets in my house. If my production of widgets creates pollution that harms my neighbors, then economic analysis suggests that the government should tax or limit my widget production. But now assume that my widget production creates no physical negative externalities. Producing widgets, however, makes me rich, and seeing me have great wealth makes my neighbors unhappy. Does this negative envy externality create a justification for the government to tax or limit my widget production?

DATING MARKET INEQUITIES

There are many inequalities in life besides inequality of income. Let's now examine inequality in dating, and consider one final character: Gorgeous George. Gorgeous George was born with genetics that make him extremely attractive to women. Genes have given Gorgeous George tremendous dating market success. In college the men who knew both Gorgeous George and Richie Rich were far, far more jealous of George.

Gorgeous George no more deserves his good looks than Richie Rich does his inherited wealth. Many of you, I suspect, believe that the government should take away income from Richie Rich and give it to poor people. But do you also believe that the government should forcibly spread around the benefits of Gorgeous George's handsomeness?

Obviously, the government can't redistribute George's handsomeness to other men. But the government could impose a beauty tax on George and give the tax revenue to unattractive people. The tax would lower George's happiness while raising the happiness of unattractive people. The beauty tax, therefore, would make the world more equal.

Rank	Name	Citizenship	Source of Wealth	Net Worth in $ Billions (U.S.)
1	William Gates III	U.S.	Microsoft	50.0
2	Warren Buffett	U.S.	Extremely skilled investor	42.0
3	Carlos Slim Helu	Mexico	Telecommunications	30.0
4	Ingvar Kamprad	Sweden	Ikea	28.0
5	Lakshmi Mittal	India	Steel	23.5
6	Paul Allen	U.S.	Microsoft	22.0
7	Bernard Arnault	France	Luxury Goods	21.5
8	Prince Alwaleed Bin Talal Alsaud	Saudi Arabia	Oil/Banking	20.0
9	Kenneth Thomson & Family	Canada	Publishing	19.6
10	Li Ka-shing	Hong Kong	Diversified	18.8
11	Roman Abramovich	Russia	Oil/Gas	18.2
12	Michael Dell	U.S.	Dell Computers	17.0
13	Karl Albrecht	Germany	Supermarkets	17.1
14	Sheldon Adelson	U.S.	Casinos/Hotels	16.1
15	Liliane Bettencourt	France	Manufacturing	16.0
15	Lawrence Ellison	U.S.	Oracle Computers	16.0
17	Christy Walton	U.S.	Wal-Mart	15.9
17	Jim Walton	U.S.	Wal-Mart	15.9
19	S. Robson Walton	U.S.	Wal-Mart	15.8
20	Alice Walton	U.S.	Wal-Mart	15.7
21	Helen Walton	U.S.	Wal-Mart	15.6
22	Theo Albrecht	Germany	Supermarkets	15.2
23	Amancio Ortega	Spain	Fashion	14.8
24	Steven Ballmer	U.S.	Microsoft	13.6
25	Azim Premji	India	Software	13.3

Forbes List of the 25 Richest Real People in the World (Feb. 2006)[17]

- Will your name ever be on this list?
- Would you be willing to work 90 hours a week for 20 years for a slight chance of making it?
- Are these 25 people extremely happy?

Rank	Name	Fictional Appearance Place	Source of Wealth	Net Worth in $ Billions (U.S.)
1	Santa Claus	He is real!	Toys/candy	Infinite
2	Daddy Warbucks	Annie comic strip	Defense Industries	27.3
3	Richie Rich	Comic strip	Inheritance	17
4	Lex Luthor	Superman comic strip	Defense, Technology, Evil Doings	10.1
5	Charles Montgomery Burns	*The Simpsons* TV series	Energy	8.4
6	Scrooge McDuck	Cartoon	Mining	8.2
7	Jed Clampett	*Beverly Hillbillies* TV series	Oil & gas	6.6
8	Bruce Wayne	Batman comic strip	Inheritance	6.5
9	Thurston Howell III	*Gilligan's Island* TV series	Howell Industries	5.7
10	Willy Wonka	*Charlie and the Chocolate Factory*	Candy	2.3
11	Arthur Bach	*Arthur* movies	Inheritance	2
12	Ebenezer Scrooge	*A Christmas Carol* novel	Banking, investments	1.7
13	Lara Croft	Video game/movie	Inheritance, antiques	1
14	Cruella De Vil	*101 Dalmatians* movie	Inheritance	1
15	Lucius Malfoy	*Harry Potter* books	Inheritance	.9

Forbes List of the 15 Richest Fictional People

Reprinted by permission of Forbes Magazine. © 2007 Forbes, LLC.

Should we confiscate Santa Claus's wealth and give it to the world's poor?

EXTREME METHODS OF REDUCING INEQUALITY

Kurt Vonnegut's science fiction short story "Harrison Bergeron" presents a radical method of eliminating inequality. The story takes place in 2081 when:

"Everybody was finally equal. They weren't only equal before God and the law. They were equal every which way. Nobody was smarter than anybody else. Nobody was better looking than anybody else. Nobody was stronger or quicker than anybody else."

And how was this total equality achieved? The government nullified all individual advantages. The government put a radio receiver in the ear of every smart person. Every twenty seconds the radio gave off a loud noise to keep the smart people from "taking unfair advantage of their brains." The government forced graceful people to wear heavy bags to hinder their movements. Strong people were forced to carry around scrap metal. And good-looking people had to wear hideous masks or put red rubber balls on their noses.

Sadly, history provides us with a method of reducing equality far more radical than that used in "Harrison Bergeron." In the 1970s a communist gang known as the Khmer Rouge shot their way to power in Cambodia. The Khmer Rouge were determined to create a classless society. They killed everyone who had more than a basic education. They forced all city dwellers to leave their homes and live in rural communes. Everyone was made to work long hours as a peasant farmer. All who opposed their attempts at creating a classless society were eliminated. The Khmer Rouge murdered about 1.7 million Cambodians out of a population of 7.1 million.

CREDITS: THE FICTIONAL CAST OF CHAPTER 16

Average Arnie: Google employee. He makes $100,000 a year.

Dropout Dropsy: Born to a middle-class family. Now a drug addict mom on welfare.

Gorgeous George: Very good looking man. He does extremely well in the dating market.

Literary Laura: Fiction author. She makes $30,000 a year. She gave up a programming career.

Richie Rich: Has a trust fund that pays him $1 million a month.

Top Tony: Google employee and programming magician. He earns $30 million a year.

Oliver Twist: Hardworking, poor orphan.

QUESTIONS YOU SHOULD BE ABLE TO ANSWER AFTER READING THIS CHAPTER:

1   In 2005 in the United States, was the richest fifth of the population's share of the national income (a) 20.21%, (b) 50.4%, (c) 85.6%, or (d) 98.1%? (page 382)

2   Many people have a choice of how much to work. How does this affect the fairness of income inequality? (page 384)

3   What problem can occur when the government gives money to the poor? (pages 385–386)

4   What problem can occur when the government takes money from the rich? (pages 386–387)

5   Why does reducing inequality empower politicians? (page 387)

6   List three paths to achieving a tremendously high income. (pages 388–389)

7 Why must you essentially win a tournament to be a labor market superstar? (page 389)

8 What is a significant reason that full-time working women in the United States make about 76 percent as much, on average, as full-time working men? (pages 389–390)

9 How does assortative mating contribute to income inequality? (pages 390–391)

10 When do markets punish racists who refuse to hire members of some racial groups? (pages 391–392)

11 When do markets not correct racial discrimination? (pages 392–393)

12 What would happen if the government tried to reduce the educational income advantage? (pages 393–394)

13 Why does the existence of high-fixed cost/low-marginal cost goods reduce consumption equality among the world's rich and middle class? (page 395)

STUDY PROBLEMS

1 Which of the following would do more to reduce income inequality?
  A. The government pays for 50 percent of the cost of college for everyone who attends college.
  B. The government imposes a large tax on all college graduates.

2 Would a wealthy college reduce income inequality more if it (a) spent $10 million giving financial aid to its poor students or (b) gave $10 million to poor people who will never attend college?

3 Consider three possible welfare programs. Under the first, the government gives everyone $10,000. Under the second, the government gives everyone with an income under $10,000 a payment of $10,000−$I$, where I is the recipient's income. Under the third program the government gives everyone with an income under $20,000 a payment equal to $10,000−(.5)I$. Compare how each program (a) helps the poor, (b) affects income inequality, and (c) influences poor people's incentives to work.

4 How do low-skilled immigrants in a rich country affect income inequality in that country? Consider the supply and demand for low-skilled labor.

5 How would increasing the minimum wage affect income inequality?

6 A high school principal announces that over the last year his school has greatly reduced the inequality of mathematical ability among its students. How might the school have accomplished this without improving the mathematical ability of any student?

7 Assume that jobs X and Y require equal skill. Any worker who could do job X could also do job Y. If job X requires workers to labor several more hours a week than job Y, then the salary of job X will be higher than that of job Y. What other working conditions might cause the market wage of job X to be higher than that of job Y?

8 An effective way to stop people from smoking is for the government to impose a heavy tax on people who smoke. Would an effective means of reducing poverty

be for the government to impose a heavy tax on people who are poor? Is there any way in which such a "poor tax" could reduce poverty?

9 Economist Milton Friedman said, "A society that puts equality before freedom will achieve neither equality nor freedom." What could he have meant by this? Do you agree with the quote? (Many economists don't.)

10 The Americans with Disabilities Act, which went into effect in 1992, requires firms to provide reasonable accommodations to employees with disabilities. Firms, for example, must make their workplaces accessible to employees with physical disabilities. The act also makes it unlawful for firms to discriminate in the hiring or firing of people with disabilities. A firm, for example, can't fire a secretary who lost his hearing; rather the firm would either have to find the secretary a comparable job or make reasonable accommodations so the now deaf secretary could still perform his job. The purpose of the act is to help people with disabilities, and many Americans with disabilities have benefited from the act. But how might the act harm some disabled Americans?

11 Imagine that in 10 years, geneticists and economists conclusively determine (a) a person's intelligence is mostly genetically inherited from his or her parents and (b) a person's income is tremendously influenced by his or her intelligence. How would such a finding influence your beliefs about the desirability of redistributing wealth from the rich to the poor? How would it influence your beliefs about the desirability of implementing the type of grade redistribution that was discussed in this chapter?

12 Imagine that in 10 years, economists and brain scientists conclusively determine that for most people (a) if your income is less than $100,000 a year, then having additional income makes you much happier, but (b) if your income is greater than $100,000 a year, then having additional income won't make you much happier. How would such a finding influence your beliefs about the desirability of redistributing wealth from the rich to the poor?

13 Moral Question: The poor in the United States have much greater wealth than the average person does in many other nations such as Ethiopia and India. Imagine that for fairness reasons the U.S. government decides to take money from the rich in the United States to help the poor. Should this money go to the poor in the United States or to the poor in poor nations?

14 J.K. Rowling, author of the Harry Potter books, is one of the world's richest people. Because of technology, she has made far more money than Shakespeare ever did.[18] What types of technologies have enabled Rowling to so profit from her writings? How might this technology be harming other modern-day authors?

part four

ECONOMICS IS EVERYWHERE

401

"IMPROVE A MECHANICAL DEVICE AND YOU MAY DOUBLE PRODUCTIVITY. BUT IMPROVE MAN, YOU GAIN A THOUSAND FOLD."

—Khan Noonien Singh (*Star Trek*, the original series, episode "Space Seed")

PART A: USING ADAM SMITH'S INVISIBLE HAND

We learned in Chapter 6 that Chinese peasants worked much harder after the government dissolved its agricultural communes. Before this dissolution, each peasant received almost no personal benefit from working. As a result, it was in each peasant's self-interest to work as little as possible. After the communes' destruction, however, each peasant could keep most of what he grew. Consequently, Adam Smith's invisible hand now pushed self-interested peasants to labor long hours.

Adam Smith's invisible hand has massive motivational powers. But, as this textbook has shown, it operates only under certain circumstances. The next six short essays expand on these circumstances.

Think of the invisible hand as a tremendous power source. By dissolving the communes, the Chinese government "hooked up" peasants to this power source, thereby motivating them to produce vastly more food. The following examples show how to "hook up" other types of people to the invisible hand.

A1: STRENGTHENING AIRPORT SECURITY[1]

Imagine you're an airport security worker in the United States and therefore a government employee. Regardless of how well you do your job, you probably would not be fired because it's difficult to fire government workers. Furthermore, your salary is based mostly on how many years you have worked. Consequently, you can assume that doing an outstanding job won't increase your paycheck.

And even if you do an excellent job, how would anyone ever find out? Terrorists strike infrequently. So regardless of your performance, you will almost certainly never catch a real terrorist.

As with all employees, you have the ability to slack off or work diligently. Perhaps out of altruism you will work as hard as you can. But you don't personally benefit from diligence. The invisible hand, therefore, won't motivate you to excellence.

ECONOMICS IS EVERYWHERE

LEARNING OBJECTIVES

AFTER READING THIS CHAPTER, YOU SHOULD BE ABLE TO:

- Identify the economic elements of airport security, school choice, and gift giving.
- Describe the effects of prizes for innovation.
- Understand the economic workings of the stock market.
- Explain education and signaling in economic terms.
- Understand the economic implications of Moore's Law.

We have seen that competition strengthens firms. When firms compete they must continually improve to survive. Airport security providers, however, rarely compete. They potentially compete against terrorists. But because terrorists rarely attack, airport security workers are like football players on the bench who almost never get to play.

But the invisible hand could actually strengthen airport security. I believe that ordinary citizens should be given the opportunity to try to smuggle fake–but–realistic-looking bombs or weapons past security. If they succeed, they should be rewarded. This will give airline security a regular foe to battle.

If the rewards were great enough, professional smuggling firms would arise that regularly try to smuggle fake contraband aboard planes. The firms would use the latest technology to try to evade airport security. Any airport security service that could defeat these firms would be well-equipped to stop terrorists.

The salaries of airport security workers should be tied to how well they do against the fake terrorists. Markets work in large part because they reward success and punish failure. Promoting fake terrorism would provide airport security with

Do not try this at home! Attempting to smuggle weapons (real or fake) through airports is a felony that is punishable by fines and prison time.

feedback. If customers frequently return a certain product, then the manufacturer knows something is wrong with it. Similarly, if airport security guards consistently fail to stop a certain type of fake smuggling, they would gain valuable information about their deficiencies.

We could publish each airport's success rate against fake terrorists. Publication would allow passengers to distinguish between safe and dangerous airports. Many passengers would avoid airports that had poor security. The profits of these unsafe airports would fall, giving them an incentive to improve security. (Question: What problems might arise from publishing data on airport security effectiveness?)

A2: REHABILITATING EX-CONS[2]

Crime imposes enormous costs on society. Governments are lousy at rehabilitating criminals. Much crime is perpetrated by career criminals who have already served jail time for previous offenses. We could unleash the power of markets on criminal rehabilitation.

Imagine that career criminal Carl has been sentenced to 20 years in prison for his latest armed robbery. Because of prison overcrowding Carl gets out in eight years. For the remaining 12 years he is free on parole. (In the U.S., prisoners are commonly released on parole before completing their sentences.) While on parole Carl reports to his government parole officer who is in charge of his rehabilitation. This parole officer has the power to send Carl back to prison to serve the rest of his sentence.

Like most government officials, parole officers are rarely fired. So the parole officer pays no personal cost if he fails to rehabilitate Carl. Rather, the cost of nonrehabilitation is paid by the people that Carl murders, rapes, or robs. The invisible hand, therefore, does not motivate parole officers.

Private firms rather than government parole officers should be in charge of Carl's rehabilitation. These private firms should be rewarded if they succeed in rehabilitating Carl, but punished if they fail to reform him. Let's examine how this could work:

A rehabilitation firm could agree to reform Carl. If Carl doesn't get caught committing any crimes for the next 12 years, the government will pay the private firm, say, $100,000. If however, Carl does get caught committing some crime over the next 12 years, then the firm must pay the government $100,000.

The rehabilitation firm, therefore, has a financial incentive to prevent Carl from committing new crimes. It could, for example, offer him job training, drug treatment, spiritual guidance, or whatever else it thinks might work.

We will need to give the rehabilitation firm some power over Carl so that he follows the firm's directives. While Carl is on parole, therefore, this firm will have the ability to send him back to prison to serve the remainder of his term. If the firm does send Carl back to jail, then let's say the firm must give the government $20,000. It's better to lose $20,000 than $100,000. So if the firm believes that Carl will commit another crime, it will send him back to jail. The firm, however, would be better off rehabilitating Carl than returning him to prison.

A3: A BILLION FOR BIN LADEN[3]

As of this writing the United States is offering a $25 million reward for terrorist Osama Bin Laden. This just isn't enough. Sure, $25 million would induce some poor peasant to turn in Bin Laden. But it's not enough to attract professional firms to the hunt. The United States should instead offer a $1 billion bounty for Bin Laden. With the possibility of earning this large sum, professional Bin Laden hunting firms would form, allowing the United States to enlist the efficiency and creativity of the free market in the fight against Osama.

With a $1 billion reward in place, an international group of intelligence, military, and terrorist experts that could credibly claim to have, say, at least a 10 percent chance of finding Bin Laden could say, raise, $30 million from investors to finance their search.

Bin Laden, hopefully, will be apprehended by the time you read this, but unfortunately other international terrorist leaders will no doubt be at large. With significant rewards on international villains, firms would come into existence that specialized in capturing different types of criminals. Some, for example, would go after South American drug barons while others might concentrate on Middle Eastern terrorists.

A4: SCHOOL CHOICE

Pretend that you run a gym. Consider your incentives to serve customers under two different payment schemes:

1. Customers pay you directly. You operate as a normal business. Customers that want to use your gym must pay the price you set. If you make your gym very valuable to customers, you will prosper. If you fail to attract and then retain many customers, you will be forced to exit the industry.
2. Customers pay you indirectly. The local government gives you, say, $1 million a year. The government gets this money by imposing a gym tax on local residents. All residents must pay this gym tax regardless of whether they use your gym. You must freely admit to your gym anyone who lives in your town.

Under (1), Adam Smith's invisible hand fully incentivizes you to serve customers. You, however, have much more limited incentives under (2) to take care of your gym's users. True, if you do an extremely horrible job, people will complain to government officials and they might penalize you. Also, if no one visits your gym, the local government might cut your funding.

But the marginal cost to a citizen of using your gym under scheme (2) is zero. Local residents' taxes finance your gym. These taxes, however, must be paid regardless of gym usage. If a resident uses a gym other than yours, however, let's assume that they must pay the full price. Consequently, local residents are likely to use your gym even if they would greatly prefer another.

Perhaps for reasons of pride or altruism you would want to run a high-quality gym even if doing so didn't benefit you financially. Consequently, you might take great care in running the gym under scheme (2). But your altruism and pride will also motivate you to excellence under scheme (1), plus under scheme (1) you have a financial incentive to do an excellent job. Consequently, under any reasonable circumstances, you will put more time and effort into operating your gym under scheme (1).

U.S. Public Schools
Public schools in the United States are financed similarly to scheme (2) and consequently have much lower incentives than private companies do to serve their customers. If private companies do well, their owners earn profits.

But if a public school does an exceptional job, its teachers and principal rarely get a merit-based raise.

Failing businesses shut down. Failure both motivates firms and clears the marketplace of incompetence. Public schools, however, keep operating no matter how little their students learn.

Public schools are often run more for the benefit of teachers than students. Teachers' unions are among the most powerful political forces in many states. They induce politicians to make it almost impossible for principals to fire teachers. In some cases, the New York City public school system, for example, doesn't even fire teachers who are so horrible that they pose a danger to students. Rather, New York City keeps these teachers in "rubber rooms" where they are kept away from students but still paid. In 2006 New York City spent $20 million paying teachers in these rubber rooms.[4]

A private firm that paid employees who didn't work would suffer in the marketplace. But because public schools face limited competition, they can afford to keep paying unproductive employees.

School Choice

Many economists support using school choice to inject competition into the public school system. To understand school choice, consider a hypothetical student named Heidi. In Heidi's state, the government spends $10,000 per student per year on public schools. Normally, if Heidi attended a private school, this school would get nothing from the state. Rather, Heidi's parents would have to pay for their daughter to attend private school.

Under school choice, however, whatever qualified school Heidi attends receives $10,000 from the government. With choice, therefore, Heidi could freely attend any qualified private school that cost no more than $10,000. So, school choice makes Heidi much more likely to attend a private school.

School choice forces public schools to compete for students. The fewer students a school attracts, the less money it has. A public school that draws too few students would have to shut down. And perhaps this failed school's facilities would be taken over by a successful school. School choice, therefore, makes it in the self-interest of public schools to satisfy their customers.

School choice allows excellent public school teachers to start their own school. Imagine a group of 20 teachers at some public high school who believe that students would learn far more if these 20 teachers were in charge. Under school choice these teachers could quit their jobs and open their own school. They could persuade their old students to join them at their new school. And if they attracted enough students, their school would succeed and the teachers would profit personally.

A5: PRIZES

Perfect Numbers The number 28 can be divided evenly only by the numbers 1, 2, 4, 7, and 14. Interestingly $1 + 2 + 4 + 7 + 14 = 28$. Twenty-eight, therefore is defined as a *perfect number*. Six is also a perfect number because it can be divided evenly only by 1, 2, and 3 and $1 + 2 + 3 = 6$. Other perfect numbers include 496; 8128; and 33550336. As of this writing humans know of only 44 perfect numbers.

Now imagine you were fairly good at math and became obsessed with perfect numbers. How could you find more? One good way would be to study finance and make a fortune as an investment banker. You could then offer a $1 million prize for the discovery of every additional perfect number.

Perfect numbers may be interesting, but there is currently no profit to finding them. Adam Smith's invisible hand, therefore, does not push people to locate perfect numbers. But through offering a prize, you could cause the invisible hand to motivate perfect number finders.

Actual Prizes   Several organizations have offered real prizes for innovations. For example:

- **The Methuselah Foundation**—Currently offers a prize for anyone who greatly extends the lifespan of mice. Mice and humans are both mammals. If scientists could significantly extend the lifespan of mice, they would learn much about how mammals age. The Methuselah Foundation hopes this knowledge could then be used to expand the lifespan of humans.

- **The X-Prize Foundation**—Offered "$10 million for the first team to build a ship with private funds and fly three people (or one pilot with equivalent deadweight) to an altitude of 100 kilometers—and to do it twice within a two-week period." This prize was actually won in October 2004. The X-Prize Foundation continues to offer other prizes to promote space development.

- **The Longitude Prize**—In 1714 the British government offered a substantial prize to anyone who could figure out a way for ships to determine their longitude. Ships need to know their longitude to know their location. It turns out that if a ship has a very accurate clock it can determine its longitude. The Longitude Prize was eventually won by John Harrison for developing an extremely precise timepiece.

Other Prizes   Prizes could be used to motivate people to accomplish nearly anything. You could, for example, offer a prize to whomever finds you a mate, develops a testable theory of quantum gravity, predicts earthquakes, or determines a practical means of providing clean drinking water to a remote village in Bangladesh.

Prizes vs. Grants   Imagine you run a charity that is trying to cure breast cancer. Your charity has $200 million. Normally, your charity would give grants to scientists. Scientists who have ideas for how to cure breast cancer would write proposals describing their research plans. You would then review each proposal to decide which receive funding. Rather then giving out grants, however, you could offer a $200 million prize to whomever found a cure for breast cancer.

One major disadvantage of offering a prize is that scientists wouldn't get any money from you until they found the cure. With a prize, therefore, scientists would have to look elsewhere for their initial funding.

An advantage of the prize approach, however, is that anyone can compete for it. In contrast, only established scientists receive grants. So if there is a significant chance that some unknown innovator could find a cure for breast cancer, then offering a prize is superior to giving grants.

With the prize, your charity has to pay money only if a cure is actually found. In contrast, you could easily allocate $200 million in grants to scientists who never find a cure.

Your charity would have fewer administrative costs with a prize than with grants. When a charity offers grants, it must carefully review each proposal. Such reviews are expensive and time-consuming. In contrast, with the prize you have only the cost of verifying a winner's claim.

Unfortunately, if you use a prize, your job as a charity director becomes relatively unimportant. If your charity gives grants, you will allocate millions of dollars to scientists. You will have considerable power over who gets these millions. Scientists and the organizations they work for will consequently have a tremendous incentive to win your favor. They will flatter you and invite you to all their parties. In contrast, when you offer a prize you have no choice as to who wins the $200 million. As a result, no one will have any incentive to kiss up to you. So it may well be in your self-interest as a charity director to give grants rather than to offer a prize.

A6: CURING CANCER WITH AUCTIONS

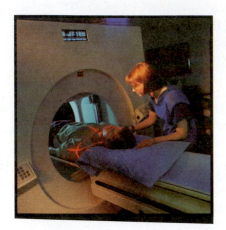

I know what I would do if I were a billionaire who developed terminal cancer. I would promise my medical team $30 million for every year it kept me alive.

And I would use an auction to choose my medical team. The team that offered to pay me the most would gain the right to treat me. So imagine that three teams bid $27 million, $60 million, and $70 million. The team that bid $70 million would: (1) immediately pay me $70 million, (2) provide me with medical care, and (3) receive $30 million for every year I lived.

The medical team that bid the most would be the one most confident in its ability to keep me alive. It would, therefore, likely be the best. Furthermore, this team would have a tremendous financial incentive to provide me with effective treatment.

PART B: AN ECONOMIC ANALYSIS OF SOME DIVERSE TOPICS

The next four essays provide an economic analysis of some diverse topics.

B1: THE ECONOMICS OF CRIME

Crime is often a career choice. A criminal chooses crime because the benefits to him of criminality exceed the cost. For society, however, crime differs from most other professions because it destroys rather than creates wealth.

Let's consider how theft reduces the wealth of society. Superficially, it seems that theft just transfers wealth from victims to criminals. After all, if someone steals an object from you, you lose the object while the criminal gains it.

Crime, however, imposes costs on everyone. To deter crime, homeowners buy locks, guns, and alarm systems. Many of you readers, no doubt, have lost some of your freedom due to crime. If you avoid walking alone at night because of the possibility of being mugged, then you are indeed paying a high cost for crime even if you never become a direct victim. All taxpayers are harmed by crime as taxes fund police forces. Many firms hire private security guards to stop crime. The cost of these guards increases prices and reduces profits.

In 2005 in the United States there were 18.0 million property crimes and 5.2 million crimes of violence.[5]

Why Not Kill All Criminals? Criminals, like everyone else, respond to incentives. A man considering mugging you will weigh the costs and benefits. The greater the punishment if caught, the less likely he will engage in crime. So to minimize crime, should society kill all captured criminals?

Pretend that the penalty for theft is death. How would this death penalty affect your behavior? You would obviously be much less likely to steal. But you might also fear entering a store. People sometimes accidentally take stuff not belonging to them. Imagine that you go into a store and pick up a candy bar intending to buy it. But while holding the candy bar you see a friend outside of the store and walk out to talk with her. If such absentmindedness could cost you your life, you might avoid shops.

Also imagine that the penalties for speeding and plagiarism were death. In these circumstances you might drive 30 miles an hour under the speed limit and avoid taking classes with papers. If the government imposed extremely high penalties for crimes, people would avoid coming near the crime. This avoidance would impose huge costs on society.

In 2003 in the United States, 16,503 people were murdered but only 65 prisoners were executed.[6] U.S. murderers, therefore, should not much fear the death penalty.

Marginal Deterrence   Marginal deterrence provides another reason why we shouldn't kill all criminals. Consider the laws of two hypothetical countries:

	Penalty for Mugging	Penalty for Murder
Country A	Death	Death
Country B	1 year	Death

The penalty for mugging is higher in Country A than Country B. Consequently, you are less likely to be mugged in Country A. But if you do get mugged, you are better off being in Country B.

A mugger has a greater chance of getting caught if he lets you live. Let's assume that a mugger who lets his victim live has a 5 percent chance of being caught. In contrast, a mugger who kills his victims faces only a 2 percent chance of apprehension.

Muggers in Country A face the same penalty if caught regardless of whether they kill their victims. To reduce their chance of capture, therefore, muggers in Country A should kill all witnesses.

Muggers in Country B, however, might be better off not killing their victims. If these muggers prefer having a 5 percent chance of receiving one year in prison to a 2 percent chance of receiving the death penalty, then they will let their victims survive. Country B, but not Country A, therefore, provides marginal deterrence against muggers committing additional crimes.

A criminal who has already committed a crime is marginally deterred if he has strong incentives not to commit a second crime. If, for example, a government imposes the death penalty on all murderers, then a criminal who has killed once has no incentive not to kill again. In contrast, a government that imposes life in prison for one murder and the death penalty for multiple murders provides for marginal deterrence against those who have already killed once.

In 2004 there were 2,135,901 prisoners in the United States.[7]

Why Do the Poor Commit So Many Crimes?   Most property and violent crimes such as burglary and mugging are committed by poor people. Opportunity costs partly explain why. To keep everything simple imagine there are only six possible careers one could engage in. Assume that the following is how you would rank these careers:

1. Economist (first choice)
2. Investment banker
3. Writer
4. Criminal
5. Minimum wage worker
6. College administrator (least desired career)

If you have the opportunity to pursue any of these six careers you will become an economist, not a criminal. In contrast, if your lack of skills and education prevents you from being anything other than a criminal or a minimum wage worker, you will embark on a life of crime.

Another reason that the poor commit more crimes than the rich and middle class is that the poor face lower penalties if sent to prison. Part of the cost of going to prison is the difference in happiness you receive between living in your current residence and living in jail. So the better your current residence, the more harm being sent to prison causes you.

The poor also engage in more crime than the rich and middle class because they face lower career costs if convicted of a serious crime. You don't earn income while in jail. The poor, by definition, don't have high-paying jobs. As a result, they lose much less income than most others if sent to prison.

Going to prison often destroys the careers of professional people. If, for example, an economics professor was sent to jail for mugging an old lady, he would lose his job. He would furthermore find it nearly impossible to get another teaching job. As a result, he would have to give up being an economist and work at some lesser profession. In general, going to prison significantly reduces the future income of rich and middle class workers.

People who have already been convicted of a serious crime have the least to lose from going to jail. Morality alone hopefully prevents your economics instructor from mugging old ladies. But if your economics instructor is morally unconstrained, then fear of losing his teaching career would almost certainly prevent him from mugging. But imagine that some old lady falsely accuses your instructor of mugging her. As a result your economics instructor gets fired and spends one month in jail. Upon getting out of prison your instructor might rationally turn to crime. After all, getting convicted of mugging a second time can't further destroy his already terminated teaching career.

B2: GIFT GIVING[8]

Economists believe that people seek to maximize their own pleasure, but this self-interested assumption doesn't present an obstacle to our understanding of gift giving. Most humans seem to receive pleasure from giving to those they care about.

But why do people predominately give material gifts rather than money during Christmas? If you wanted to give $1,000 to, say, the American Cancer Society, you would never go out and buy $1,000 worth of stuff that you thought they could use and then donate the stuff rather than the money.

Yet on Christmas we usually give nonmonetary gifts. Most people have a better understanding of their own needs than you do and so would presumably rather have, for example, $50 in cash than a $50 gift. So why do rational individuals give nonmonetary presents to their friends and family?

Some economists believe that when you give a gift someone wants, you signal your understanding and empathy for your recipient.[9] Most people get pleasure from knowing that others care about us, and this is one of the reasons we like to receive gifts. But when someone buys us something we like, we know not only that they are willing to give up resources for us, but also that they have taken enough time to learn about us and understand our needs. Consequently, to make someone really happy, you should spend a lot of money on an unusual gift that she will love but that few other people would enjoy.

There appears to be a negative undertone to giving money as a gift to adults, for it's often taken to mean that the gift giver doesn't greatly care about his recipient. Assume that, for whatever reason, a long time ago people inferred that those who gave money rather than things didn't care very much about their gift's recipient. If everyone believed this then they would take the time to buy nonmonetary gifts for all those they cared about. Consequently our nonmonetary gift-giving equilibrium is probably self-perpetuating.

Some economists believe that a stigma associated with buying certain luxury items for oneself explains some nonmonetary gifting behavior.[10] By giving luxury items people don't feel comfortable buying for themselves, donors can allow their recipients to have the luxury without paying the social stigma cost.

Other economists think that people might not give cash gifts precisely because cash is so valuable.[11] You don't want people to be your friend just to get your money, yet you want to show them that you care, so you give less valuable nonmonetary gifts. Some people might give things rather than money because they enjoy shopping. Many Americans like to shop but have run out of relatively inexpensive goods to buy for themselves so they use Christmas as an excuse to shop for others.

Of course, if we all gave each other money on Christmas, much of our gift giving would cancel out. Perhaps the only way we can experience the joys of giving and receiving Christmas gifts is if people don't give each other cash for the holidays.

PEOPLE WILL SPEND BILLIONS ON GIFTS THIS CHRISTMAS. INQUIRING ECONOMISTS WANT TO KNOW WHY.

B3: THE STOCK MARKET

This section gives you some basic facts about investing in the stock market. Companies issue stock to raise money. When you buy stock in a company, you own part of that company. You are entitled to some of its future profits. The value of a company's stock is determined by estimates of these profits. Here are some stock prices as of this writing:

	Value of Each Share	Total Value of All Shares
Microsoft	$22.08	$230 billion
Intel	18.40	106 billion
Coke	43.01	101 billion
Pepsi	59.61	98 billion

The total value of all a firm's stock, also known as a company's market capitalization, is how much the company is worth.

Many people believe they can predict which companies' stock prices will rise. Many other people believe in Bigfoot, astrology, alien abductions, and the healing power of crystals. Stock prices are random. (Take a course in finance to find out why.) Most everyone other than Warren Buffet (do an Internet search to find out about him) seems unable to consistently determine which stocks will rise. Picking which stock will increase is essentially like guessing what number will win the lottery. You might get it right, but if you do you were just lucky.

If stock prices are random, why should you ever buy stocks? Because on average stocks go up. Buying stock is like gambling where the odds favor you. So, for example, there might be a 60 percent chance that a certain stock will go up by $10 and a 40 percent chance that it will go down by $10. Although you don't know if this stock will do well or poorly, on average you will make money investing in it.

Many people invest in stocks through mutual funds. When you buy a mutual fund, you hire a firm to pick stocks for you. Economists believe that stock investors should hold diversified portfolios. Having a diversified portfolio means investing in many types of stocks. Diversifying lowers your risk without lowering your average gains. One easy way to diversify is to buy a type of mutual fund called an *index fund.*

Index funds buy all the stocks in their index. The most popular type of index funds in the United States are S&P 500 index funds. These funds invest in the 500 largest U.S. companies that issue stock. When you invest in index funds, you are not trying to beat the market by guessing which stocks will increase. Rather, you are buying a highly diversified portfolio and betting that on average the values of all the stocks in the index will go up. I put most of my investments in S&P 500 index funds.

Index funds usually charge lower fees than other types of mutual funds. Over the long run, it's extremely important for investors to keep down their investment fees. When deciding which mutual fund to invest in, pay very careful attention to the different funds' fees. Some mutual funds charge ridiculously high fees that are completely unjustified by any services the funds provide.

To fully diversify, investors should buy stocks in foreign companies. Generally, the larger the economy of a nation, the more of the country's stocks you should buy to properly diversify your portfolio. Many mutual funds sell index funds that invest in foreign stocks.

The Little Book of Common Sense Investing by John Bogle, the originator of the S&P 500 index funds, provides an excellent introduction to the benefits of indexing.

Many U.S. workers invest in 401(k) retirement plans. You invest in 401(k) plans through your employer. You gain a tremendous tax benefit by investing in 401(k) plans. Minimizing taxes is extremely important to rational investors. The government limits how much money you can put in these plans each year. A very wise investment strategy for U.S. taxpayers is to put money in their 401(k) plans every single month of their working life.

Because of the power of compounded interest, you can best save for retirement if you start saving in your 20s. Assume, for example, you buy $1,000 of stock at age 25. Further assume that the stock's price goes up 8 percent a year. By the time you are 75 years old, the stock will be worth $46,902. In contrast, if you bought $1,000 of this stock when you were 55 it would be worth only $4,661 when you were 75.

Stock investments are risky. But you can't avoid risk. And if you don't invest in stocks, you risk losing out if the stock market does extremely well.

B4: EDUCATION AND SIGNALING

As we learned in Chapter 16, college graduates have much higher incomes than non-graduates. But why? The standard answer is that college teaches people useful things. A signaling theory about college, however, shows that college could increase a student's earning capacity even if it teaches him nothing of value. Signaling occurs when someone tries to show others that he has some desirable hidden trait such as intelligence.

Consider a very simple model consistent with the signaling theory of college. Assume people are born either smart or stupid. Employers, unfortunately, have difficulty determining at job interviews whether someone is smart or stupid. But they suspect that stupid people rarely graduate from college. Graduating from college, therefore, signals to a firm that a potential employee is smart. Even if college teaches you absolutely nothing, therefore, firms would still want to hire college graduates under this signaling model. As a result, college graduates would make more than nongraduates even if the graduates learned nothing in college.

The U.S. Marines vs. The Ford Modeling Agency

I once read an interesting comparison between the U.S. Marines and the prestigious Ford Modeling Agency. You know a lot about someone if they are either a Marine or a Ford Model. Marines are strong, brave, and deadly. Ford Models are tall, thin, and beautiful.

The Marines will accept an average healthy 18-year-old and turn him or her into a Marine. In contrast, less than 1 percent of all 18-year-olds could ever qualify to be a Ford Model. The Ford Modeling Agency doesn't create models. Rather, it finds them. The Marines will take someone and give him skills. The Ford Modeling Agency will find someone and certify that he or she has the characteristics of a model.

The key question before us is whether colleges are closer to the Marines or to the Ford Modeling Agency. If colleges are like the Marines, they would take an average 18-year-old and give him skills. When the student graduated, he or she would be transformed into someone much smarter than a person who never went to college.

If colleges are like the Ford Agency they would find smart people. Colleges would then put these people through a few years of tests to make sure they really were smart. When the students graduated, people would know they were smarter than most non-college graduates. College would not have made them smarter, but rather college would have tested and proved the student's intelligence. If the signaling theory of colleges is correct, then colleges are more like the Ford Agency than the Marines. Economists disagree over the validity of the signaling theory. Students at Shengda College in China, however, certainly believe in it.

Rioting in China

In 2006 students at China's Shengda College rioted after reading their diplomas. When the students enrolled at Shengda College, the school promised them that their degrees would be from Zhengzhou University. Zhengzhou University is a far more prestigious school than Shengda College. To attract students, Shengda worked out a deal that had allowed it to put Zhengzhou's name on its diplomas. (It would be analogous to graduates from a community college in Massachusetts getting diplomas from Harvard.)

Unfortunately for the students, a recent Chinese law forced Shengda College to put its own name on its diplomas. Students from Shengda feared that having a diploma from Shengda would hurt their chances of getting a good job. The students were so upset that they rioted:

> "Groups of students marauded around the campus, smashing cars, offices or any piece of property they felt belonged to someone in power. The front gate and a statue of the college's founder were toppled. The local police arrived to break up the protest, but they retreated after they were barraged by bottles and rocks."*

The name on the diploma obviously didn't affect what the students had learned. The students must have rioted, therefore, because they were strong believers in the signaling theory of higher education.

PART C: THE FUTURE

In the next two essays I take a guess at what will be the most important economic phenomena over the next 50 years.

C1: INTELLIGENCE ENHANCEMENTS

This textbook has stressed the importance of innovation to wealth creation. Intelligence drives innovation. In the near future we humans may artificially boost our intelligence.

As of this writing pharmaceutical companies are developing around 40 intelligence-enhancing drugs "designed to improve wakefulness, attention, memory, decision making and planning."[12] Widespread use of these drugs could add trillions to the world economy.

Consider the implications of a pill that gave you a perfect memory. Imagine how much study time this pill would save you. Imagine how much more you would know now if you took such a pill.

Don't imagine, however, that your schooling would be much easier if such memory pills were widely used. If your teachers knew you could quickly memorize anything, they would assign you considerably more homework.

Although I have no empirical evidence, I strongly believe that the widespread use of antidepressant drugs like Prozac has already increased the effectiveness of many workers. Prozac, by reducing depression and anxiety, makes it easier for many to concentrate on productive activities.

Comparisons to Steroids It's tempting to compare intelligence-enhancing drugs to steroids. Athletes take steroids to boost their physical prowess. But society doesn't benefit when all athletes take steroids. Sports fans care about the relative performance of athletes. If steroid use added 20 percent to the muscle mass of all football players, games wouldn't be more interesting.

But outside of sports, it's absolute, not relative, performance that counts. If, for example, intelligence enhancers improved the skills of all cancer researchers, software engineers, and teachers by 20 percent, then society would indeed benefit greatly.

Negative Side Effects Intelligence enhancers, like steroids, may have negative side effects. Some people might worry that if they don't use the enhancers but everyone else does, then they won't be able to compete. But if they do use the drugs they will suffer ill health effects, so the drugs offer a lose-lose proposition. But labor markets would compensate users for the negative effects of the drugs. Workers who took intelligence enhancers would do better at their jobs and so get paid more. Furthermore, they would take the drugs only if the extra pay was worth the increased health risks.

No One Country Can Stop Them Countries will find it extremely costly to ban the use of intelligence enhancers. If, for example, the United States banned them while China didn't, then China would gain a tremendous advantage over the United States. Furthermore, the U.S. economy currently benefits from an international brain gain because the best and the brightest desire America's freedom. But if the U.S. government prevents American brains from reaching their admittedly unnatural maximum, then the world's intellectual elite would seek friendlier shores. After all, if your dream in life is to cure cancer and only in China can you use a drug that raises your IQ by 15 points, wouldn't you move there?

A Virtuous Circle   It takes quite a bit of human intelligence to design effective intelligence-enhancing drugs. Consider what would happen if these drugs' designers used their own product. Unenhanced humans are currently creating the first generation of these drugs. The second generation of intelligence enhancers will be better in part because their human designers will be on the first generation of the drugs. For analogous reasons the third generation of the drugs will be even better than the second. Where will this cycle take humanity? I'm not (currently) smart enough to know. But I do enjoy speculating.

C2: A TECHNOLOGICAL UTOPIA BY 2050?

Gordon Moore co-founded computer chip maker Intel. In 1965 he predicted that the number of transistors on a computer chip would double about every two years. His prediction, now known as Moore's Law, has held true (see Figure 17.1).

Because of Moore's law, "A musical birthday card costing a few U.S. dollars today [2006] has more computing power than the fastest [computers] of a few decades ago."[13]

You don't have to grasp the technological complexities of transistors to understand their importance. Basically, more transistors mean faster and cheaper computers. An implication of Moore's Law is that the computing power you can buy for $1,000 doubles every year.[14] Let's assume that Moore's Law will continue to hold until 2050.

Moore's Law might, and I repeat *might*, lead to a technological utopia by 2050. In this utopia humans would achieve immortality. Here's how it could happen:

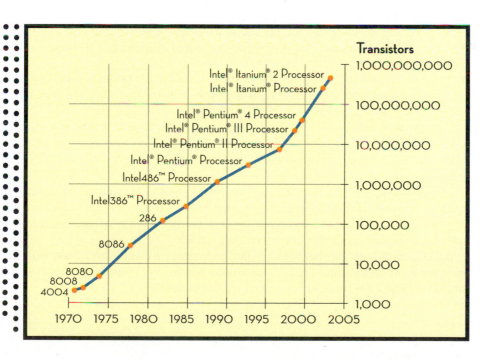

FIGURE 17.1
MOORE'S LAW

Source: http://www.intel.com/technology/silicon/mooreslaw/

Computers are machines that perform computations. A computation, for example, might consist of adding two numbers together. As of this writing, personal computers can perform about 3 billion computations per second.

Your brain is also a computer that performs computations. Most of you would probably guess that the human brain is fairly slow compared to mechanical computers. Your brain, however, is actually an astoundingly fast computer.

True, human brains are much slower than computers at doing repetitive tasks such as adding numbers. But the human brain far exceeds computers in accomplishing more complex undertakings such as seeing, hearing, and understanding language.

Scientists have estimated how many calculations per second the human brain performs. To do this, scientists add up all the computations a computer would have to accomplish if it performed the same task as a brain. Although these estimates vary, it's not unreasonable to assume that as of this writing in the year 2007 a human brain is around 1 million times faster than a $1,000 personal computer.*

But because of Moore's Law, computers are quickly catching up in speed to brains. Recall that so long as Moore's Law holds, the amount of computing power you can buy for $1,000 doubles every year.

The Power of Doubling
To understand the doubling power of Moore's Law, imagine you start with $1. Every year your wealth doubles. So after one year you have $2, after two you have $4, and after three you have $8. After 20 years you will have slightly over $1 million. When you double something 20 times you increase its size by about a million.

1, 2, 4, 8, 16, 32, 64, 128, 256, 512, 1024, 2048, 4096, 8192, 16384, 32768, 65536, 131072, 262144, 524288, 1048576

20 Years to Catch Up
So let's assume that a human brain is about 1 million times faster than a $1,000 personal computer. It will take only 20 Moore's Law doublings for computers to catch up. Let's be conservative and assume that it takes until 2030 for a $1,000 personal computer to become equal in speed to a human brain.

Software
Speed, of course, isn't everything. To match the performance of a human brain, a fast computer needs the right software. Software tells a computer how to operate.

Over the next several decades, computer programmers might be able to create software that allows fast computers to act with the same intelligence as human brains. But if we can't create the software ourselves, we could always copy it from the human brain.

Our ability to scan the human brain is growing at an exponential pace. Both designing computer chips and scanning human brains require technologies that allow us to work on microscopic levels. So as we get better at creating computers, we will almost automatically get better at understanding brains.

By 2050 there is an excellent chance that technology will allow us to take extremely accurate three-dimensional images of human brains. We could then use these pictures to simulate the running of a brain on a computer.[14]

---

*This is a very rough estimate. See Ray Kurzweil, *The Singularity Is Near: When Humans Transcend Biology*. New York: Viking., p. 124.

Think of the human brain as a book that could tell us how an intelligent being thinks. Currently the writing on such a book is too small for us to read. But our ability to read small "brain print" is increasing rapidly. By 2050 we will probably be able to read "brain books." We could then simply use the information in these books to program intelligent computers.

Let's assume that by 2050 scientists will be able to write or copy software that allows a computer to think at least as well as a human.

Three Assumptions to Utopia

Let's restate the three key assumptions we have made in this section:

1. Moore's Law will continue to hold at least until 2050.
2. In 2030, a $1,000 personal computer will be as fast as a human brain.
3. In 2050, we will have computer software that simulates human intelligence.

If these three assumptions hold, then humankind will be able to accomplish almost anything (by today's standards) in the year 2050.

Imagine that in 2050 we buy 1 billion $1,000 computers. On each computer we simulate the intelligence of a human scientist. By assumption, in 2030 a $1,000 computer will run as fast as a human brain. This means that in 2050 these $1,000 computers will run 1 million times faster than a human brain does.

So in 2050 we will have 1 billion computer-scientists that think a million times faster than human scientists. These scientists, therefore, will likely accomplish in one year what human scientists would have needed a million years to accomplish.

A million years is a huge amount of time. Human civilization is only around 10,000 years old. In a million years, human scientists will probably be able to solve any problem we can think of today. They would almost certainly figure out how to cure death and give us wealth beyond our imagining. If the three assumptions hold, therefore, we will probably live in a technological utopia by 2050.

Are the Three Assumptions Reasonable?

The three assumptions might, in fact, be too conservative. Perhaps we will be able to simulate human intelligence on computers in 2035 and by 2040 these computers will have conquered human death and solved most of the universe's mysteries.

The last section considered the benefits of drugs that enhance human intelligence. These drugs will no doubt help humans design faster and smarter computers. Faster and smarter computers, furthermore, will help pharmaceutical companies develop more potent intelligence-enhancing drugs. Some time in the next few decades humanity might therefore experience an "intelligence explosion," because as our minds and machines improved, we would get better and better at improving our minds and machines. Such an "intelligence explosion" would quickly lead to a technological utopia, at least if we didn't use our new intelligence to destroy or enslave ourselves.

In my opinion, the assumption most likely to fail is the first, that Moore's Law will continue until 2050. It's hard to predict exactly what will happen with technologies. Maybe Moore's Law will stall. But technologies that go by the names of massive parallel processing, quantum computing, self-assembly nano-manufacturing, and three-dimensional chip architecture all hold the potential to continue Moore's Law until 2050.

FURTHER READING

The technological utopia described in this section is often called "The Singularity." If you are interested in doing further reading on this topic, you should read Vernor Vinge's essay "The Coming Technological Singularity" (do an Internet search to find it) and the book by Ray Kurzweil titled *The Singularity Is Near.* Both Vinge and Kurzweil believe that a technological utopia will occur before 2050.

417

Perhaps none of these technologies will prove strong enough to continue Moore's Law. But they might.

What Happens To Economics?

If this utopia comes to pass, what will happen to economics? Economics is essentially about decision making when resources are limited and individuals are forced to make *trade-offs*. A technological utopia might push us past all the limits humanity currently faces. It might, therefore, make economics as we know it today obsolete.

Why Did I End My Textbook with This Stuff?

You probably didn't expect your microeconomics textbook to end with a discussion of super-smart computers and immortality. I concluded the textbook with this to show the unlimited potential of markets.

Markets drive Moore's Law. Hundreds of millions of people contribute to the continual improvement of computers. The small number of people who design computers obviously helps keep Moore's Law going. But these designers rely on the skills of millions of others, from the farmers who grow their food to the miners who extract the minerals needed to make computer chips. And it's markets that coordinate these huge numbers of people, causing them to create products of continually improving value.

The fantastic progress represented by Moore's Law manifests only because of Adam Smith's invisible hand. This invisible hand constantly pushes companies to find better ways of satisfying customers. And when one company comes up with a better product, the invisible hand pushes other companies to top it. The result: constant improvement!

Firms, in the selfish quest for profits, keep pushing the technological frontier forward. What's so exciting is that this frontier might lead us to something truly fantastic in the 21st century.

QUESTIONS YOU SHOULD BE ABLE TO ANSWER AFTER READING THIS CHAPTER:

1   Why does the invisible hand not motivate airport security workers? (page 402)

2   Why does the invisible hand not motivate probation officers? (page 404)

3   How could we get the invisible hand to motivate private rehabilitation firms? (page 404)

4   What would happen if we offered a large amount of money to anyone who caught an international super-outlaw? (pages 404–405)

5   Why does the invisible hand not motivate public schools? (pages 405–406)

6   What is school choice? (page 406)

7   How would school choice inject competition into public school systems? (page 406)

8   How could prizes motivate perfect number pickers? (pages 406–407)

9   What are the advantages and disadvantages of offering prizes as opposed to giving research grants? (pages 407–408)

10 What would this author do if he were a billionaire who developed terminal cancer? (page 408)

11 Why shouldn't we kill all criminals? (pages 408–409)

STUDY PROBLEMS

1 (Essay Question) For question one you must evaluate a market solution so radical that you may initially react to it with disgust. The proposal is:

Babies unwanted by their relatives should be sold at auction.

In the U.S., state agencies determine which couples adopt which babies. Employees of these agencies are usually paid low salaries. These agencies handle many children and so don't have the resources to investigate each couple thoroughly. Rather, the agencies generally do a superficial background check on couples and put those who pass on a wait list. Each baby is allocated to the couple who has been on the list the longest. There is a shortage of healthy babies in the U.S., so couples sometimes have to wait years to adopt. To avoid this wait, couples often quickly adopt children from poor countries.

Under the baby-selling proposal anyone wishing to adopt a baby would first submit themselves to the above-described superficial background check. Those who pass can participate in baby auctions. Each baby unwanted by his or her relatives would be put on a "baby eBay." Bidders could visit the baby and view the baby's medical records. The couple who bids the most for any given baby would adopt the child. If this couple abused the baby it would be subject to the same child-abuse laws that govern all parents.

Write an essay describing the benefits and costs of this proposal. Your essay must contain a supply and demand curve diagram. It must list at least one positive and one negative aspect about the proposed auction. You must also come to a final conclusion about whether you support or oppose baby auctions. If baby auctions were to occur explain whether you would prefer each winner's money to go to the government or to the baby's biological mother.

2 (Essay Question) Evaluate the following proposal:

Exclusive colleges should auction off some of their admission spots to the highest bidders.

Imagine that 1,000 students enroll as freshman at Adam Smith University each year. Adam Smith University is very exclusive and normally accepts 10 percent of its applicants. Under the proposal Adam Smith University might choose 900 students by merit and the other 100 by auction. Write an essay describing the benefits and costs of this proposal.

3 (Essay Question) Evaluate the following proposal:

The U.S. should auction off immigration spaces to the highest bidders.[15]

Wages in rich countries are far higher than in poor ones. As a result, a tremendous number of people would love to immigrate to rich nations. I suspect, for example, that the U.S. would more than double its population over the next five years if it let in everyone who wanted to reside in the U.S. Currently, government officials decide who gets to immigrate legally to the U.S. Instead, the U.S. should auction off spaces and so let the market determine who becomes an American.

Assume that the U.S. decides to admit 100,000 new legal immigrants next year. Under the proposal the U.S. would hold an auction and let in the 100,000 people willing to pay the most for entry. All the high bidders, of course, would have to pass a background check showing they were not terrorists or criminals. Write an essay describing the benefits and costs of this proposal.

4 Would the children of poor or rich parents benefit more from school choice?

5 Could school choice harm children who choose to stay in public schools? Could it help these children?

6 In Chapter 10 we learned how patents can encourage innovation. In this chapter we studied how prizes can promote innovation. But when do prizes work better than patents? Consider four possible innovations:
   A.   A cure for a disease that afflicts only extremely poor people.
   B.   A cure for a disease that afflicts poor and rich people.
   C.   A computer program that aids perfect number finders.
   D.   A computer program that improves video game graphics.

Which of the above innovations would patents not help promote? Prizes, of course, could be used to promote all of the above innovations. Explain generally when prizes do a much better job of promoting innovation than patents. Bonus: Relate your answer to public goods, which were described in Chapter 14.

7 Imagine that a pharmaceutical company develops a drug that significantly increases human intelligence. The drug works for 80% of people and all 80% take the drug. The drug has no negative side effects. Unfortunately, you are in the 20%

of the population for whom the drug is ineffective and no drug will ever raise your intelligence. Will you be better off or worse off because of the drug's existence?

8 It's a crime to attempt to kill someone even if the attempt fails. Consider two failed attempts at murder:

   A. Lisa shoots at her intended victim. Unknown to Lisa, her gun is broken. The gun doesn't fire and the victim is unharmed.

   B. Paul tries to kill his victim by placing a magic curse on her. The victim survives.

   Most people would probably believe that Lisa but not Paul should be sent to prison. Provide an economic justification or counterargument for this.

9 Imagine you were forced to choose between the following:[18]

   A. You attend classes at your college for the length of time it normally takes to graduate. But you will be forbidden from ever telling an employer you have been to college.

   B. You are forbidden from going to classes. But after a length of time equal to how long it normally takes to graduate you will be given a diploma from your college. You will also be given a transcript saying you earned an A average at college.

   Which option would someone believing in the signaling theory of college prefer? Under which option would you likely have a higher lifetime income?

10 Most 17-year-old girls would prefer to receive $200 in cash from their parents than a $200 nonreturnable gift that their parents picked out. Most 17-year-old girls would also, however, prefer to receive a $200 nonreturnable gift that their boyfriend picked out than $200 in cash from their boyfriends. Why is this?

11 Imagine that in some crime-ridden neighborhood, police arrest 100 people a week. What would happen to the number of arrests made if the police double the number of officers who patrol this neighborhood?

GLOSSARY

ABSOLUTE ADVANTAGE when a producer can make a good using fewer resources than its trading partners can.

ACCOUNTING PROFIT total revenue minus total cost. Here, cost does NOT include all opportunity costs.

ADVERSE SELECTION in this book, a situation in which an individual attracts those with whom she least wishes to interact.

AGENCY COSTS the harm suffered by employers when employees make decisions that help themselves but harm their employers. Agency costs also apply when an individual hires an agent, such as a doctor or stockbroker, and the agent makes decisions to help himself at the expense of the individual.

ANTITRUST LAWS government regulations that are intended to increase competition by reducing the prevalence and strength of monopolies.

ASSORTATIVE MATING when people marry others like themselves.

AVERAGE FIXED COSTS = $\dfrac{\text{fixed costs}}{\text{output}}$

AVERAGE TOTAL COSTS total cost divided by output, or $\dfrac{\text{fixed costs}}{\text{output}} + \dfrac{\text{variable costs}}{\text{output}}$

AVERAGE VARIABLE COSTS = $\dfrac{\text{variable costs}}{\text{output}}$

BARRIERS TO ENTRY anything which prevents firms from entering a market.

BLACK MARKETS markets in which goods are unlawfully traded.

CARTEL a group of firms that collude to raise prices.

CETERIS PARIBUS Latin for "other things being equal."

CHANGE IN DEMAND occurs when a change in something other than the price of the good causes you to move to another demand curve.

CHANGE IN QUANTITY DEMANDED occurs when a change in the price of the good causes you to move along a demand curve.

CHANGE IN QUANTITY SUPPLIED occurs when a change in the price of the good causes you to move along a supply curve.

CHANGE IN SUPPLY occurs when a change in something other than the price of the good causes you to move to another supply curve.

COLLECTIVE OWNERSHIP a situation where several people own a singular good.

COLLUSION when firms cooperate, implicitly or explicitly, to raise prices.

COMMAND AND CONTROL a method of pollution control in which the government tells firms how much they can pollute and what types of pollution-reducing technologies they must use.

COMPARATIVE ADVANTAGE when a nation, individual, or company can produce a good at a lower opportunity cost than its trading partners can.

COMPETITIVE MARKETS when individual buyers and sellers in a market cannot set prices. A competitive market has many buyers and sellers.

COMPLEMENTS two goods (such as cars and gas) where an increase in the price of one good decreases the demand for the other.

COMPLICATED PRICING when firms' pricing plans are made deliberately confusing so customers cannot easily compare prices.

CONSTANT RETURNS TO SCALE when long run average total costs stay the same as output increases.

CONSUMER'S SURPLUS the highest amount an owner would have paid for a good minus the amount the owner actually paid

COPYRIGHT HOLDERS an individual or company that has the exclusive right to sell a copyrighted product. Software, books, movies, and music can be copyrighted.

CROSS ELASTICITY OF DEMAND =

$$\frac{\text{Percentage change in quantity demanded of good A}}{\text{Percentage change in the price of good B}}$$

Cross elasticities of demand are positive for substitutes and negative for complements.

DDT (Dichloro–Diphenyl–Trichloroethane) an inexpensive pesticide.

DEAD CAPITAL real estate which cannot be used as collateral for a loan.

DEADWEIGHT LOSS a loss one party suffers that does not benefit another party or, restated, a loss that reduces society's net wealth.

DEMAND the entire relationship between price and quantity demanded over a given time period. Demand is never just a single number.

DEMAND CURVE a graph of demand.

DIMINISHING MARGINAL RETURNS when an individual receives lower and lower benefits from increasing the amount of input used.

DISECONOMIES OF SCALE when long run average total costs increase as output increases.

DISRUPTIVE INNOVATION when innovation on one product lowers the value of other products.

ECONOMICS the study of human behavior.

ECONOMIC PROFIT total revenue minus total cost. Costs include all opportunity costs.

ECONOMIES OF SCALE when long run average total costs decrease as output increases.

EDUCATIONAL PREMIUMS when workers' average earnings increase as their level of education increases.

ELASTICITY a measure of market responsiveness.

EMINENT DOMAIN the power of a government to take private property.

EQUILIBRIUM point of stability in a market.

EXCLUDABLE RESOURCE people can be prevented from using this resource.

EXITS THE INDUSTRY when a firm leaves its former industry, produces zero output in this industry, and pays no fixed costs for this industry. Occurs only in the long run.

EXPORTS goods people in one nation sell to those living in other nations.

EXTERNALITIES a cost or benefit that is incidental (or external) to the production and use of a product.

FIRMS business organizations that seek to maximize their profits.

FIXED COSTS costs that are the same regardless of output. These costs must be paid even if a firm produces zero output.

FIXED INPUTS inputs that can be changed in the long run but not the short run.

GERRYMANDERING when politicians draw electoral districts to serve their own self-interests.

IMPERFECT PRICE DISCRIMINATION when customers pay different prices but are not subject to perfect price discrimination.

IMPORTS goods people in one nation buy from those living in other nations.

INCOME ELASTICITY OF DEMAND

$$= \frac{\text{Percentage change in quantity demanded}}{\text{Precentage change in income}}$$

Income elasticities of demand are positive for normal goods and negative for inferior goods.

INCREASING MARGINAL COST when marginal costs increase as output increases.

INDEX FUNDS mutual funds that invest in all stocks in a relevant index in proportion to each stock's relative market capitalization.

INFANT INDUSTRIES industries that have recently been created.

INFERIOR GOODS goods consumed in larger quantities as a consumer becomes poorer, and in lesser quantities as a consumer becomes richer.

INFORMALLY OWNED BUSINESSES businesses that are not legally registered with the government.

INNOVATION finding new and improved ways of producing goods and services.

INPUTS what firms use to make goods.

INTELLECTUAL PROPERTY nonphysical property such as patents and copyrights.

INVISIBLE HAND, THE A theory proposed by eighteenth-century economist Adam Smith. When markets function well, Adam Smith's invisible hand pushes self-interested people to take actions which are in the best interests of society.

JOINT PRODUCTION two or more goods are jointly produced if the process that produces one of the goods necessarily produces the others.

LAW OF DEMAND consumers buy less of a good as its price increases and more of a good as its price decreases.

LAW OF SUPPLY firms produce less of a good as its price falls and more of a good as its price increases.

LINUX a computer operating system that is free to users. Linux was created and is continually improved by volunteers.

LONG RUN a period of time over which firms can innovate and/or change their fixed inputs.

LUDDITES people opposed to technological change.

MACROECONOMICS a subfield of economics that focuses on the performance of entire economies and looks at issues such as unemployment, inflation, and monetary policy.

MALARIA an infectious disease often spread by mosquitoes that kills between one and three million people each year worldwide.

MARGINAL COST the extra cost of increasing output by one unit.

MARGINAL DETERRENCE when a criminal who has committed a crime but has not yet been caught has an incentive to not commit another crime.

MARGINAL REVENUE the increase in total revenue a firm receives by selling one more good.

MARGINAL VALUE how much value a consumer received from the last unit of the good she consumed.

MARKET CAPITALIZATION a firm's stock price times the total number of shares of the firm's stock held by the public.

MARKET DEMAND the sum of all individual demand curves for a good.

MARKETS places where individuals and businesses voluntarily exchange money, goods, services, and labor.

MICROECONOMICS a subfield of economics that focuses on individuals and businesses.

MINIMUM WAGE a price floor set on wages by government. Firms cannot legally pay workers less than the minimum wage.

MONEY TRANSFER money paid from one person to another.

MONOPOLY a firm that does not have significant competition in a market.

MOORE'S LAW a prediction that the number of transistors on a computer chip will double about every two years.

MUTUAL FUND an investment service that picks stocks for its investors.

NATURAL MONOPOLIES monopolies based on economies of scale.

NEGATIVE EXTERNALITIES costs that are incidental (or external) to the production and use of a product.

NEO-MALTHUSIANS individuals who believe that lack of natural resources will soon cause an economic catastrophe.

NORMAL GOODS goods consumed in larger quantities as a consumer becomes richer, and in lesser quantities as a consumer becomes poorer.

OLIGOPOLIES markets that fall between perfect competition and monopoly.

OPPORTUNITY COSTS the value of the next best alternative that must be given up in order to engage in any economic activity. Opportunity cost equals best opportunity lost.

OUTPUT the number of goods produced.

PATENT an authorization that gives an individual or company the exclusive right to sell a specific good. Goods made with some new and innovative design can be patented by the good's inventor.

PERFECT COMPETITION when the market forces firms to intensively compete for customers. Perfectly competitive markets have many buyers and sellers who are all price takers.

PERFECT PRICE DISCRIMINATION when the price charged to each customer equals the most that the customer is willing to pay. Extreme price discrimination.

PIGOVIAN TAXES taxes on goods with negative externalities.

PORK wasteful government spending that benefits a politician.

POSITIVE EXTERNALITIES benefits that are incidental (or external) to the production and use of a product.

POTENTIAL COMPETITION firms that are not yet in a market but might enter in the future.

PREDATORY PRICING when a firm charges a very low price to drive its competition out of the market.

PRICE the amount of money needed to purchase a good, or the amount of money a seller is willing to accept for a good.

PRICE CEILING a maximum price for a good set by the government.

PRICE DISCRIMINATION charging different customers different prices for the same good.

PRICE ELASTICITY OF DEMAND
$$= \frac{\text{Percentage change in quantity demanded}}{\text{Precentage change in price}}$$

PRICE ELASTICITY OF SUPPLY
$$= \frac{\text{Percentage change in quantity supplied}}{\text{Precentage change in price}}$$

PRICE FLOOR a minimum price set by the government for a good.

PRICE GOUGING when politicians believe that firms charge "excessively" high prices.

PRICE TAKERS firms and consumers who cannot influence prices.

PRISONERS' DILEMMA when each individual in a situation is better off acting selfishly but everyone would be better off if all people acted altruistically.

PRODUCER'S SURPLUS a good's price minus the cost to the seller of making the good.

PRODUCT DIFFERENTIATION when firms change their products slightly to make their products weaker substitutes for a competitor's. Product differentiation reduces competition among firms.

PRODUCTION POSSIBILITY FRONTIERS a graphic representation of all the points where society efficiently uses all its resources.

PROFIT Total revenue minus total cost.

PROPERTY RIGHTS the ability to own a good, use a good, sell it to others, or prevent others from using the good.

PUBLIC CHOICE THEORY examines how government officials and voters make political decisions.

PUBLIC GOOD any nonrival and nonexcludable good.

QUANTITY DEMANDED the amount of a good consumers want to purchase at a specified price over a specified time period.

QUANTITY SUPPLIED the amount of a good suppliers want to produce at a given price over a specified time period.

QUOTAS government-imposed limits on imports.

RATIONAL INDIVIDUALS people who consider all the significant consequences of their actions and make decisions that further their self-interests.

RATIONING when goods are allocated other than through price.

REAL ESTATE land and buildings.

RENTS money a person receives beyond what the marketplace would ordinarily give him. Rents occur when politicians intervene in the market to help favored individuals.

RENT CONTROL a price ceiling set on the housing market.

RENT-SEEKING spending resources to capture rents. These resources are usually spent trying to influence politicians.

RIVAL RESOURCE one person's use of a rival resource reduces the amount of this resource available to others.

ROUNDABOUT PRODUCTION a situation where, instead of making a good directly, an individual makes another good and then trades this second good for the original good desired.

SCABS derogatory name for those who fulfill the employment tasks of striking employees.

SELF-INTERESTED INDIVIDUALS people who maximize their own welfare, however they define it.

SELF-SELECTION when members of more than one group take actions that reveals which group each person is in.

SHORT RUN a period of time over which firms cannot innovate or change their fixed inputs.

SHORTAGE when quantity supplied is less than quantity demanded.

SHUTDOWN when a firm produces zero output but still must pay some fixed costs. Occurs only in the short run.

SPECIALIZATION when people produce what they are best at making and trade for what they do not produce.

STATISTICAL DISCRIMINATION when a member of a group is discriminated against because of negative traits that many members of his group have.

STRIKE when employees of a firm refuse to work until the firm improves wages, benefits, or working conditions.

STRONG COMPLEMENTS two goods that almost always go together.

SUBSTITUTES two goods are substitutes when an increase in the price of one good causes an increase in demand for another.

SUNK COSTS costs that cannot be recovered regardless of what you do.

SUPPLY the entire relationship between price and quantity supplied over a specified time period.

SUPPLY CURVE a graphical representation of supply.

SURPLUS when quantity supplied is greater than quantity demanded.

TARIFFS taxes on imports.

TECHNOLOGICAL SPILLOVERS gains from innovation that go to people other than the innovator or those that helped pay for the innovation.

TOTAL COSTS fixed costs plus variable costs.

TOTAL REVENUE price multiplied by sales.

TOTAL SURPLUS the sum of consumers' and producers' surplus.

TRADABLE PERMITS permits giving firms the right to emit certain amounts of pollution. Firms can buy tradable permits and sell those permits they do not use.

TRAGEDY OF THE COMMONS arises when a resource which is rival but nonexcludable is used until depletion.

UNION an organization of workers.

VALUE the most a good's owner would pay for the good.

VARIABLE COSTS costs that vary with output. Variable costs are always zero if output is zero.

VARIABLE INPUTS inputs that can be changed in both the short and long run.

WEALTH an individual's wealth is the value of all his possessions. The total wealth of society is the sum of each individual's wealth.

WIKIPEDIA a free online encyclopedia written by volunteers.

ENDNOTES

Chapter 1

1. Derived from Adam Smith, *The Theory of the Moral Sentiments*, 1759.
2. Arthur Allen, "Flag on the Field." *Slate.com*, May 16, 2006.
3. Agence France Presse, "Twin Births Boom in China as More Women Take Fertility Drugs," February 13, 2006, http://asia.news.yahoo.com/060213/afp/060213050951asiapacificnews.html.
4. Reuters, "Sailors Took Sham Brides to Boost Pay, US Says," April 11, 2006.
5. Joshua S. Gans and Andrew Leigh, "Born on the First of July: An (Un)natural Experiment in Birth Timing." (Working paper) June 2006.
6. *Salary Survey,* National Association of Colleges and Employers, Spring 2007.
7. James Felton, research reported in " 'Hotness' and Quality," *Inside Higher Ed*, May 8, 2006, http://www.insidehighered.com/.
8. Barry Nalebuff and Ian Ayres, *Why Not* (Boston: Harvard Business School Press, 2004).

Chapter 2

1. Inspired by Frank Herbert's *Dune* (New York: G.P. Putnam's Sons, 1965).
2. Marina Murphy, "Viagra Gives Wildlife a Boost," *New Scientist,* October 25, 2002. Used with permission.
3. William Easterly, *The Elusive Quest for Growth* (Cambridge, MA: The MIT Press, 2002).
4. Alex Tabarrok, Blog, *Marginal Revolution*, April 1, 2005, http://www.marginalrevolution.com/marginalrevolution/2005/04/invitro_meat_an.html.
5. Glenn Reynolds, *Instapundit.Com*, March 5, 2005, http://instapundit.com.
6. Theodore Dalrymple, "Torn Jeans," *City Journal*, Autumn 2004.
7. Tim Appenzeller, "The End of Cheap Oil," *National Geographic*, June 2004.
8. *The Simpsons,* "Lisa the Vegetarian," original airdate October 15, 1995.

9. Robert H. Frank, *The Economic Naturalist* (New York: Basic Books, 2007).

Chapter 3

1. Thomas Sowell, *Basic Economics* (New York: Basic Books, 2004).
2. Alex Tabarrok, "Giving Thanks," *Marginal Revolution*, November 24, 2005, http://www.marginalrevolution.com/.
3. Derived from Thomas Sowell, *Basic Economics* (New York: Basic Books, 2004).
4. Derived from John Stossell and Gena Binkley, "Price Gouging is Bad," *ABC News 20/20*, May 12, 2006.
5. Douglas Adams, *The Ultimate Hitchhiker's Guide to the Galaxy* (New York: Ballantine Books, 2002).
6. Carl Mortished, "World 'Cannot Meet Oil Demand,'" *Times Online*, UK, April 8, 2006.

Chapter 4

1. "17 cents for a grocery bag? We must be in California." http://the-econoclast.blogspot.com/2004/12/17-cents-for-grocery-bagwe-must-be-in.html, December 28, 2004.
2. Badi H. Baltagi and Rajeev K. Goel, "Quasi-Experimental Price Elasticity of Liquor Demand in the United States: 1960-83," *American Journal of Agricultural Economics*, 1990; George C. Davis and Michael K. Wohlgenant, "Demand Elasticities from a Discrete Choice Model: The Natural Christmas Tree Market," *American Journal of Agricultural Economics*, 1993; Hans Van Driel, Venuta Nadall, and Kees Zeelenberg, "The Demand for Food in the United States and the Netherlands: A Systems Approach with the CBS Model," *Journal of Applied Econometrics,* 1997; Steven E. Landsburg, *Price Theory and Application*, 5th ed. (Stamford, CT: South-Western, 2002).
3. Author's note, Philip K. Dick, *A Scanner Darkly* (New York: Doubleday & Co., 1977).
4. Adam Hochschild, *Bury the Chains* (New York: Houghton Mifflin Books, 2005).

5. Charles Wheelan, *Naked Economics* (New York: W.W. Norton & Company, Inc., 2003).

Chapter 5

1. James D. Miller, "French-ifying Retail America," *TCS Daily*, January 9, 2005, http://www.tcsdaily.com/article.aspx?id=060905D.

2. William W. Lewis, *The Power of Productivity* (Chicago: The University of Chicago Press, 2004).

3. D. Mark Wilson, "Who Is Paid the Minimum Wage and Who Would Be Affected by a $1.50 per Hour Increase," *WebMemo #19*, The Heritage Foundation, June 28, 2001.

4. *ACORN vs. Dept. of Industrial Relations* 41 Cal App 4th 298 (1995).

5. Ralph E. Smith and Bruce Vavrichek, "The Wage Mobility of Minimum Wage Workers," *Industrial and Labor Relations Review,* October 1992.

6. Andrew Dickson White, *Fiat Money Inflation in France* (San Francisco: The CATO Institute, 1980)

7. "Porn Square," *The Wall Street Journal*, March 18, 2005.

8. For more information, see David L. Kaserman, "Market for Organs: Myths and Misconceptions," *Journal of Contemporary Health Law and Policy*, 18, 2002.

9. United Network for Organ Sharing, www.unos.org.

10. Sally Pipes, "The Best Medicine the 1970s Can Provide," *TechCentralStation* (now *TCS Daily*), October 15, 2003.

11. Virginia Postrel, "More Cosmetics, Fewer Cures?" *Dynamist.com,* December 16, 2003, http://www.dynamist.com/weblog/archives/000756.html.

12. John Norberg, *In Defense of Global Capitalism* (Washington D.C., The CATO Institute, 2003).

13. Brian M. Riedl and John E. Frydenlund, "At the Federal Trough: Farm Subsidies for the Rich and Famous," *The Heritage Foundation Backgrounder #1505,* November 26, 2001.

14. Facts taken from Jeffrey A. Miron, "Drug War Crimes," The Independent Institute, 2004; Michael J. McGinnis and William H. Foege, "Actual Causes of Death in the United States," *The Journal of the American Medical Association,* November 1993; Jeffrey G. Wiese, Michael G. Shlipak, Warren S. Browner, "The Alcohol Hangover," *Annals of Internal Medicine*, June 2000.

Chapter 6

1. William Baumol, *The Free-Market Innovation Machine: Analyzing the Growth Miracle of Capitalism* (Princeton, NJ: Princeton University Press, 2002).

2. John R. Lott, *Freedomnomics* (Washington D.C.: Regnery Publishing, Inc., 2007).

3. National Resources Defense Council, "Alfalfa: The Thirstiest Crop," June 7, 2001, http://www.nrdc.org/water/conservation/fcawater.asp.

4. Jung Chang and Jon Halliday, *Mao* (New York: Alfred A. Knopf, 2005).

5. John McMillan, *Reinventing the Bazaar* (New York: W.W. Norton & Company, Inc., 2002).

6. Caroline Baum, "Thanksgiving Is Incentive Success Tale," Bloomberg News, November 24, 2004.

7. Ed Mecka, "N.Y. Eminent Domain Fight Appealed to the U.S. Supreme Court," November 13, 2006, http://www.edmecka.com/.

8. See the U.S. Supreme Court decision *Kelo v. City of New London* 545 US 469 (2005); see also John Tierney, "Supreme Home Makeover," *The New York Times*, March 14, 2006.

9. Joseph A. Schumpeter, *Capitalism, Socialism, and Democracy*, (3ed. ©1942, 1947 by Joseph A. Schumpeter Reprinted by permissions of Harper Collins and Taylor & Francis, Ltd. 1976).

10. Tyler Cowen, *In Praise of Commercial Culture* (Cambridge MA: Harvard University Press, 1998).

11. Quoted from Bill Beaty, *Weird Science,* http://amasci.com/freeorg/laughed.html.

12. Orson Scott Card, *Magic Street* (New York: Ballantine Books, 2005).

13. Douglas Adams, *The Ultimate Hitchhiker's Guide to the Galaxy* (New York: Ballantine Books, 2002).

14. Will Woodward, "Sellers Should Pay Stamp Duty to Help First-Time Buyers, Says Hain," *The Guardian*, June 7, 2007, http://politics.guardian.co.uk/homeaffairs/story/0,,2097261,00.html.

Chapter 7

1. Richard D. Horan, Erwin Bulte, and Jason F. Shogren, "How Trade Saved Humanity from Biological Exclusion: An Economic Theory of Neanderthal Extinction," *Journal of Economic Behavior and Organization* 58, no. 1, September 2005; see also Jackson Kuhl, "Trade and Troglodytes," *TCS Daily*, April 4, 2005, http://www.tcsdaily.com/.

2. GAO, "Sugar Program: Supporting Sugar Prices Has Increased Users' Costs While Benefiting Producers," *United States General Accounting Office Report to Congressional Requesters,* June 2000.

3. Bjorn Lomborg, ed., *How to Spend $50 Billion to Make the World a Better Place* (New York: Cambridge University Press, 2006).

4. Bryan Ward-Perkins, *The Fall of Rome: And the End of Civilization* (New York: Oxford University Press, 2005).

5. Johan Norberg, *In Defense of Global Capitalism* (The Cato Institute: Washington DC, 2003).

6. Nicholas D. Kristof, "Inviting All Democrats," *The New York Times*, January 14, 2004.

7. Martin Wolf, *Why Globalization Works* (New Haven: Yale University Press, 2004).

8. Nicholas D. Kristof, "In Praise of the Maligned Sweatshop," *The New York Times*, June 6, 2006.

9. Johan Norberg, *In Defense of Global Capitalism* (The Cato Institute: Washington DC, 2003).

10. Thomas L. Friedman, *The World Is Flat* (New York: Farrar, Straus and Giroux, 2005).

11. Randall Parker, "Brazil Gets 40 Percent of Gas Vehicle Fuel from Ethanol," *FuturePundit,* August 20, 2006, http://www.futurepundit.com.

12. Todd G. Buchholz, *New Ideas from Dead Economists* (New York: Plume, 1990).

13. Frederic Bastiat, *A Petition from the Manufacturers of Candles, Tapers, Lanterns, Sticks, Street Lamps, Snuffers, and Extinguishers, and from Producers of Tallow, Oil, Resin, Alcohol, and Generally of Everything Connected with Lighting*, 1845, http://bastiat.org/en/petition.html.

14. See "I, Pencil" by Leonard F. Read, 1958, http://www.econlib.org/LIBRARY/Essays/rdPncl1.html

15. Robert Heinlein, *Time Enough for Love* (New York: G. P. Putnam's Sons, 1973).

Chapter 8

1. Paul R. Ehrlich, *The Population Bomb* (New York: Ballantine Books Inc., 1968).

2. Tina Rosenberg, "The Scandal of 'Poor People's Diseases,'" *The New York Times*, March 29, 2006.

3. Nick Gillespie, ed., *Choice: The Best of Reason* (Dallas, TX: Benbella Books, 2004).

4. Thomas Sowell, "Drugs and Politics," *Capitalism Magazine,* November 26, 2001, http://www.capmag.com.

Chapter 9

1. As quoted in www.quotationspage.com, September 14, 2007.

2. Parts of this section derived from James D. Miller, *Game Theory at Work* (New York: McGraw-Hill, 2003).

3. Don Coursey, "Vernon Smith, Economic Experiments, and the Visible Hand," *The Library of Economics and Liberty,* October 28, 2002, http://www.econlib.org/.

4. As quoted in "Why We Should Say No to the IMF" CATO Policy Report, May/June 1998.

5. Mark Kramer, *Three Farms* (Toronto: Bantam Books, 1981).

6. Johan Norberg, *In Defense of Global Capitalism*, (The Cato Institute: Washington DC, 2003).

Chapter 10

1. John Stossel, *Myths, Lies, and Downright Stupidity: Get Out the Shovel—Why Everything You Know Is Wrong* (New York: Hyperion, 2006).

2. Morris M. Kleiner, "Our Guild-Ridden Economy," *The Wall Street Journal*, October 15, 2005.

3. See Sidney L. Carroll and Robert J. Gaston, "Occupational Restrictions and the Quality of Service Received: Some Evidence," *Southern Economic Journal*, Vol. 47, No. 4, April 1981.

4. U.S. Department of Labor, "Median Salaries of Lawyers 6 Months after Graduation, 2001," March 21, 2004.

5. Alex Tabarrok, "Indian Forecast Error," *Marginal Revolution*, July 18, 2005, http://www.marginal-revolution.com/.

6. John Micklethwait and Adriun Wooldridge, *The Right Nation: Conservative Power in America* (New York: The Penguin Press, 2004); Bureau of Labor Statistics, "Union Member Summary," 2006.

7. "Seriously Silky," *Dallas Observer,* September 29, 2005.

8. Jone Johnson Lewis, "Chinese Empress Discovers Silk-Making," *About.com: Women's History*, http://womenshistory.about.com/od/inventors/a/discovery_silk.htm. Accessed August 1, 2007.

9. Tim Parks, *Medici Money: Banking, Metaphysics and Art in Fifteenth Century Florence* (New York: Atlas Books, 2005).

10. "A Survey of Patents and Technology," *The Economist*, October 22, 2005.

11. Charles Wheelan, *Naked Economics* (New York: W.W. Norton & Company, 2002).

12. Tyler Cowen, *In Praise of Commercial Culture* (Cambridge, MA: Harvard University Press, 1998).

13. D. Felton and James D. Miller, "Truth Inducement in Greek Myth," *Syllecta Classica* (13, 2002:104-125).

Chapter 11

1. "Concentration Ratios: 2002," U.S. Census Bureau, 2002.

2. Frank Deford, "A Culture of 'sis.'" *SI.com,* September 13, 2000, http://sportsillustrated.cnn.com/.

3. Robert H. Frank, Thomas Gilovich, and Dennis T. Regan, "Does Studying Economics Inhibit Cooperation?" *The Journal of Economic Perspectives* 7, no. 2. Spring 1993.

4. Walter E. Williams, *South Africa's War against Capitalism* (New York: Praeger, 1989).

5. Adam Brandenburger and Barry Nalebuff, *Co-opetition* (New York: Doubleday, 1997).

6. Tim Harford, "Confusing Pricing," *Slate.com,* April 15, 2006.

7. See James D. Miller, *Game Theory at Work*, (New York: McGraw-Hill, 2003).

Chapter 12

1. R.J. Rummel, July 31, 2007, http://www.hawaii.edu/powerkills/.

2. Jonathan Weisman, "Aging Population Poses Global Challenges," *Washington Post*, February 2, 2005.

3. Michael Kinsley, "Special K Street," *Slate.com*, September 17, 2003.

4. Milton Friedman, "The Real Free Lunch: Markets and Private Property," quoted in David Boaz, *Toward Liberty* (Washington, DC: CATO Institute, 2002).

5. Russell Roberts, "If You're Paying, I'll Have Top Sirloin," *The Wall Street Journal*, May 18, 1995.

6. Uri Gneezy, Ernan Haruvy, and Hadas Yafe, "The Inefficiency of Splitting the Bill," *Economic Journal* 114, no. 495, April 2004.

7. William Easterly, *The Elusive Quest for Growth* (Cambridge, MA: The MIT Press, 2002).

8. William Easterly, *The White Man's Burden: Why the West's Efforts to Aid the Rest Have Done So Much Ill and So Little Good* (New York: The Penguin Press, 2006).

9. How to Spend $50 Billion to Make the World a Better Place, Ed. Bjørn Lomborg (Cambridge University Press, Cambridge, 2006).

10. Brink Lindsey, *Against the Dead Hand: The Uncertain Struggle for Global Capitalism* (New York: John Wiley & Sons, Inc., 2002).

11. I thank Lewis Davis for giving me this Nigeria/Singapore example.

12. J. D. Sachs and A.M. Warner, "The Curse of Natural Resources," *European Economic Review*, May 2001.

13. William Wallis "Google's Gaze over Palace Walls Spurs Equality Drive in Bahrain," *The Financial Times,* November 25, 2006.

14. "Obeying Orders," editorial, *The Washington Post,* September 18, 2005.

15. From Frank Serpico's testimony before the Knapp Commission, New York City, 1970.

16. "Mugabe Is Starving His Own People," Telegraph.co.uk, September 8, 2002.

17. Richard Thompson, "Ruling on R-E-S-P-E-C-T," *Homeowners Associations*, August 26, 2000, http://realtytimes.com.

Chapter 13

1. "DDT and Deaths from Malaria," *The Becker-Posner Blog*, September 24, 2006, http://www.becker-posner-blog.com/archives/2006/09/ddt_and_deaths.html. Used with permission.

2. Barry Nalebuff and Ian Ayres, *Why Not* (Boston: Harvard Business School Press, 2003).

3. Thomas Hobbes, *The Leviathan*, 1651.

4. See George I. Sitgler, *Memoirs of an Unregulated Economist* (Chicago: University of Chicago Press, 2003).

5. John J. Fialka, "Coalition Ends Ad Campaign Bashing Coal," *The Wall Street Journal,* April 27, 2007.

6. See Larry Summer's 1991 World Bank memo.

7. Gary Becker and Richard Posner, "Global Warming," *The Becker-Posner Blog,* December 19, 2004, http://www.becker-posner-blog.com/.

8. Thomas Sowell, "Two Earthquakes and Their Results under Two Different Social Systems," *Capitalism Magazine,* December 30, 2003, http://www.capmag.com/.

9. TTI (Texas Transportation Institute), 2005 Annual Urban Mobility Report, May 2005.

10. Cindy Chang, "Elderly Driver Who Killed 10 Gets Probation," *New York Times,* November 21, 2006.

11. Mothers Against Drunk Driving (MADD) website, http://www.madd.org/aboutus/1194, (accessed July 29, 2007).

12. Donald A. Redelmeier and Robert J. Tibshirani, "Is Using a Car Phone Like Driving Drunk?" *New England Journal of Medicine*, vol. 10, no. 2, 1997.

13. Donald A. Redelmeier, and Robert J. Tibshirani, "Association between Cellular-Telephone Calls and Motor Vehicle Collisions," *New England Journal of Medicine*, Vol. 336, February 13, 1997;

"Is Hands-Free Actually Safer?" *CNN/Money*, June 9, 2005, http://money.cnn.com/2005/06/09/technology/personaltech/car_cell_phones/index.htm.

14. Johan Norberg, *In Defense of Global Capitalism*, (Washington DC: The Cato Institute, 2003).

15. Sebastian Mallaby. "Look Who's Ignoring Science Now," *The Washington Post,* October 10, 2005.

16. *How to Spend $50 Billion to Make the World a Better Place*, Bjørn Lomborg, Ed. (Cambridge University Press, Cambridge, 2006).

17. "A Vicious Circle," *The Economist.* December 8, 2006.

18. Duane D. Freese, "Un-Happy Halloween! Eco-Scare Tactics Are Designed to Poison Minds," October 31, 2007, *TCS Daily.*

19. Beatrice Grabish, "Dry Tears of the Aral," *United Nations Chronicle Online Edition*, November 1, 1999, http://www.un.org/Pubs/chronicle/1999/issue1/0199p38.htm

20. Jung Chang and Jon Halliday Mao (Alferd A. Knopf: New York, 2005).

21. Jung Chang and Jon Halliday Mao (Alferd A. Knopf: New York, 2005).

22. William J. Baumol, The Free Market Innovation Machine (The Princeton University Press: Princeton, 2002).

23. Tim Hartford, "The Undercover Economist," *FT Magazine*, February 4, 2006.

24. Arnold Kling, "Shoot the Stupid Consumer," *TCS Daily,* February 10, 2005, http://www.tcsdaily.com/.

Chapter 14

1. Tod Lindberg, "All Washed Up," *The Weekly Standard*, September 17, 2007.

2. Milton Friedman and Rose Friedman, *Free to Choose* (San Diego, CA: A Harvest Book, 1990).

3. Jonathan Adler, "The Lorax Revisited," July 28, 2005. http://commonsblog.org/archives/000498.php.

4. Liz Bower, "Police Cancel Bike Lending on Campus," *The Exponent Online,* 2004, http://www.purdueexponent.org/.

5. Vedran Vik, "You Treat Me Like Property," *Mises.org*, February 14, 2006, http://www.mises.org/story/2058. Reprinted with permission.

6. John Lott, *Freedomnomics* (Washington DC: Regnery Publishers, Inc, 2007).

7. Joel Glenn Brenner, "Chocolate Wars," *Slate.com*, July 15, 2005.

8. "BSA: Singapore Piracy Is Rampant," Reuters, May 7, 1998.

9. James D. Miller, *Game Theory at Work* (New York: McGraw-Hill, 2003).

10. Emmanuelle Fauchart and Eric von Hippel, "Norms-Based Intellectual Property Systems: The Case of French Chefs," *Working Paper*, January 2006.

11. Charles Wheelan, *Naked Economies* (New York: W.W. Norton & Company, 2003).

12. Hernando de Soto, *The Mystery of Capital: Why Capitalism Triumphs in the West and Fails Everywhere Else* (New York: Basic Books, 2000).

13. Yuki Noguchi, "On Capitol Hill, Playing Wikipolitics," *Washingtonpost.com*, February 4, 2006.

Chapter 15

1. Some material in this chapter taken from James D. Miller, *Game Theory at Work* (New York: McGraw-Hill, 2003).

2. From James D. Miller, *Game Theory at Work* (New York: McGraw-Hill, 2003).

3. From James D. Miller, *Game Theory at Work* (New York: McGraw-Hill, 2003).

4. From James D. Miller, *Game Theory at Work* (New York: McGraw-Hill, 2003).

5. From James D. Miller, *Game Theory at Work* (New York: McGraw-Hill, 2003).

6. Scott M. McCartney, "Jet Refuelers Offer Wine, Women, and Beef to Lure Pilots to Fill Up," *The Wall Street Journal*, September 8, 1998.

7. "Gimme an Rx! Cheerleaders Pep Up Drug Sales," *The New York Times,* November 28, 2005.

8. From James D. Miller, *Game Theory at Work* (New York: McGraw-Hill, 2003).

9. From James D. Miller, *Game Theory at Work* (New York: McGraw-Hill, 2003).

10. From James D. Miller, *Game Theory at Work* (New York: McGraw-Hill, 2003).

11. Steven D. Levitt and Steonen J. Dubner, *Freakonomics: A Rogue Economist Explores the Hidden Side of Everything* (New York: HarperCollins Publishers, 2005).

12. From James D. Miller, *Game Theory at Work* (New York: McGraw-Hill, 2003).

13. From James D. Miller, *Game Theory at Work* (New York: McGraw-Hill, 2003).

Chapter 16

1. Pui-Wing Tam, and Kevin J. Delaney, "Talent Search Google's Growth Helps Ignite Silicon Valley Hiring Frenzy," *The Wall Street Journal Online*, November 23, 2005.

2. From Table A-3, Selected Measures of Household Income Dispersion: 1967-2005, U.S. Census Bureau

3. International Monetary Fund World Economic Database, April 2007, http://www.imf.org/external/data.htm

4. From U.S. Dept. of Labor, Bureau of Labor Statistics, Occupational Employment Statistics, May 2006.

5. Michael M. Phillips, "In South Africa, Poor AIDS Patients Adopt Risky Ploy," *Wall Street Journal Online*, April 7, 2006, http://online.wsj.com/public/us.

6. Robert Lucas, 2003 Annual Report, *The Industrial Revolution* (Federal Reserve Bank of Minneapolis, 2003).

7. Peter Singer, "What Should a Billionaire Give—and What Should You?" *The New York Times Magazine,* December 17, 2006.

8. "Income Stable, Poverty Up, Number of Americans without Health Insurance Rise, Census Bureau Reports," *U.S. Census Bureau News*, August 26, 2004.

9. Simone de Beauvoir, from an interview with Betty Friedan published in "Sex, Society, and the Female Dilemma," *Saturday Review*, June 14, 1975.

10. Annie Murphy Paul, "The Real Marriage Penalty," *The New York Times Magazine*, November 19, 2006.

11. Marian L. Tupy, "South Africa's Potential," *Cato Institute*, June 6, 2004.

12. Paul C. Campos, "America wants beauty, not fat bald men," Deseret News (Salt Lake City), March 12, 2006, Scripps-Howard News Service. Reprinted with permission.

13. David Epstein, "Sticker Shock," *Inside Higher Ed,* March 21, 2006, http://insidehighered.com/news/2006/03/21/cost.

14. "College Degree Nearly Doubles Annual Earnings," *U.S. Census Bureau*, March 28, 2005.

15. Christopher S. Ruebeck, Joseph E. Harrington, Jr., and Robert Moffitt, "Handedness and Earnings," *Working paper*, 2006.

16. Kerwin Kofi Charles and Erik Hurst, "The Correlation of Wealth Across Generations," *Journal of Political Economy,* December 2003.

17. Source: "The World's Billionaires," *Forbes.com*, March 8, 2007.

18. Alex Tabarrok, "Harry Potter and the Mystery of Inequality," Marginal Revolution, April 23, 2007, http://www.marginalrevolution.com/marginalrevolution/2007/04/harry_potter_an.html

Chapter 17

1. James D. Miller, "Security, Smith's Way," *The National Review Online*, October 30, 2001, http://www.nationalreview.com/

2. James D. Miller, "Compassionate Conservatism for the Ex-Prisoner's Dilemma," *TCS Daily*, February 25, 2004.

3. James D. Miller, "A Billion for Bin Laden," *TCS Daily*, August 9, 2004, http://www.tcsdaily.com/article.aspx?id=080904D.

4. John Stossel, "Stupid in America," *Reason Online*, January 13, 2006, http://www.reason.com.

5. U.S. Department of Justice, Bureau of Justice Statistics, Criminal Victimization Summary Findings, http://www.ojp.usdoj.gov/bjs/cvictgen.htm, (accessed August 5, 2007).

6. U.S. Department of Justice, Bureau of Justice Statistics, "Federal Bureau of Investigation Press Release: Criminal Victimization," *Key Facts at a Glance*, October 25, 2004.

7. U.S. Department of Justice, Bureau of Justice Statistics, *Key Facts at a Glance*, http://www.ojp.usdoj.gov/bjs/glance/tables/corr2tab.htm.

8. James D. Miller, "The Economics of Gift Giving," *TCS Daily*, December 23, 2004, http://www.tcsdaily.com/article.aspx?id=122304H; I'm grateful to Ardith Spence for help with this section.

9. Canice Prendergast and Lars Stole, "The Nonmonetary Nature of Gifts," *European Economic Review,* December 2001.

10. Gertrud Fremling and Richard Posner, "Market Signaling of Personal Characteristics," Working paper, 1999.

11. H. Lorne Carmichael and W. Bentley MacLeod, "Gift Giving and the Evolution of Cooperation," *International Economic Review*, August 1997.

12. Graham Lawton, "The New Incredible," *The New Scientist*, May 13, 2006.

13. Ray Kurzweil, *The Singularity Is Near: When Humans Transcend Biology* (New York: Viking, 2005).

14. http://www.intel.com/cd/corporate/techtrends/emea/eng/209729.htm. 11/20/07.

15. Ray Kurzweil, *The Singularity Is Near: When Humans Transcend Biology* (New York: Viking, 2005).

16. Gary S. Becker, and Guity Nashat Becker, *The Economics of Life: From Baseball to Affirmative Action to Immigration, How Real-World Issues Affect Our Everyday Life* (New York: McGraw-Hill, 1997).

17. Bryan Caplan, "Mixed Signals: Why Becker, Cowen, and Kling Should Reconsider the Signaling Model of Education," *EconLog*, The Library of Economics and Liberty, February 5, 2006, http://econlog.econlib.org/archives/2006/02/mixed_signals.html.

PHOTO CREDITS

Chapter 1

Page 2 © Images.com/Corbis.

Page 7 © Royalty-Free/CORBIS./dal

Page 9 Andy Alberitton/Getty Images./dal

Page 11 Public domain image from the Department of Defense.

Page 16 (left) © Mario Anzuoni/Reuters/Corbis.

Page 16 (right) © Neal Preston/CORBIS.

Page 17 © istockphoto.com/Lori Alden, Econoclass. com, 2005. All rights reserved.

Chapter 2

Page 20 © Digital Vision/PunchStock./dal

Page 29 © James Leynse/CORBIS

Page 38 © Lara Solt/Dallas Morning News/ Corbis.

Chapter 3

Page 46 © Brand X Pictures/PunchStock./dal

Page 54 © Eyewire (Photodisc)/PunchStock./dal

Page 58 NASA/Jeff Schmaltz, MODIS Land Rapid Response Team./dal

Page 67 Brand X/Fotosearch./dal

Page 72 © istockphoto.com/Lori Alden, Econoclass. com, 2005. All rights reserved.

Chapter 4

Page 74 © Brand X Pictures/PunchStock./dal

Page 79 © Royalty-Free/CORBIS./dal

Page 80 © Brand X Pictures/PunchStock./dal

Page 89 © Colin Garratt; Milepost 92½/CORBIS.

Chapter 5

Page 104 Photo courtesy of Walter E. Williams.

Page 115 © Barry Lewis/Corbis.

Page 117 Library of Congress./dal

Page 118 © Olivier Matthys/epa/Corbis.

Page 123 © Beathan/Corbis./dal

Chapter 6

Page 134 © Brand X Pictures./dal

Page 137 © Digital Vision/PunchStock./dal

Page 159 Time & Life Pictures/Getty Images.

Chapter 7

Page 166 The Bridgeman Art Library/Prehistoric/ Getty Images.

Page 169 PhotoLink/Getty Images./dal

Page 174 © Bettmann/CORBIS.

Page 188 © Royalty-Free/CORBIS./dal

Chapter 8

Page 194 © Brand X Pictures/PunchStock./dal

Page 201 © Royalty-Free/CORBIS./dal

Page 202 © Royalty-Free/CORBIS./dal

Page 209 Pixtal/age Fotostock./dal

Chapter 9

Page 220 © Royalty-Free/CORBIS./dal

Page 225 © Royalty-Free/CORBIS./dal

Page 229 © Royalty-Free/CORBIS./dal

Page 239 B. Drake/PhotoLink/Getty Images/dal

Chapter 10

Page 244 © Goodshoot/PunchStock./dal

Page 248 Getty Images.

Page 249 © Jose Luis Pelaez, Inc./CORBIS.

Page 264 © The Gallery Collection/Corbis.

Page 266 © Thinkstock/Corbis.

Chapter 11

Page 272 © Royalty-Free/CORBIS./dal

Page 275 The McGraw-Hill Companies, Inc./John Flournoy, photographer.

Page 278 © Royalty-Free/CORBIS./dal

Page 289 © Roberts Publishing Services.

Page 293 © Royalty-Free/CORBIS./dal

Chapter 12

Page 298 © Comstock/Corbis./dal

Page 302 © Reuters/CORBIS.

Page 303 © Reuters/CORBIS.

Page 309 © Royalty-Free/CORBIS./dal

Chapter 13

Page 318 U.S. Fish & Wildlife Service./dal

Page 320 © Roberts Publishing Services.

INDEX